CLINICAL PSYCHOLOGY

A MODERN HEALTH PROFESSION

Wolfgang Linden

University of British Columbia

Paul L. Hewitt

University of British Columbia

Prentice Hall

Boston   Columbus   Indianapolis   New York   San Francisco   Upper Saddle River
Amsterdam   Cape Town   Dubai   London   Madrid   Milan   Munich   Paris   Montreal   Toronto
Delhi   Mexico City   São Paulo   Sydney   Hong Kong   Seoul   Singapore   Taipei   Tokyo

Executive Editor: Susan Hartman
Editorial Assistant: Kerri Hart-Morris
Marketing Manager: Nicole Kunzmann
Marketing Assistant: Shauna Fishweicher
Production Manager: Meghan DeMaio
Creative Director: Jayne Conte
Cover Designer: Suzanne Duda
Cover Design: © Henrik Weis/Digital Vision/Getty Images
Photo Researcher: Martha Shethar
Editorial Production and Composition Service: Jerusha Govindakrishnan/PreMediaGlobal

Library of Congress Cataloging-in-Publication Data

Linden, Wolfgang, Dr.
  Clinical psychology / Wolfgang Linden, Paul Hewitt.—1st ed.
    p. ; cm.
  Includes bibliographical references and index.
  ISBN-13: 978-0-13-239727-8
  ISBN-10: 0-13-239727-7
  1. Clinical psychology. 2. Psychotherapy. I. Hewitt, Paul L. (Paul Louis) II. Title.
[DNLM: 1. Psychology, Clinical. 2. Career Choice. WM 21]
  RC467.L56 2012
  616.89'14—dc22
                                                            2010054084
              Printed in Canada

Prentice Hall
is an imprint of

www.pearsonhighered.com

ISBN-10:   0-132-39727-7
ISBN-13: 978-0-132-39727-8

Dedication

This book is dedicated to my family, near and far, but especially to my late brother Heiner who never got to enjoy the gift of a healthy life.

W.L.

To my family, who are always encouraging and supportive. Thank you Barbara, Harris, JC, Jack, and Mac.

P.L.H.

CONTENTS

PREFACE   XVII

◇**CHAPTER ONE**
BEING A CLINICAL PSYCHOLOGIST   1

Chapter objectives   1

Describing the profession   1

The challenges and responsibilities of four different psychologists   2
  A clinical psychology student   2
  Clinical psychologist A—Working in a general hospital setting   5
  Clinical psychologist B—Working in a private practice setting   7
  Clinical psychologist C—Working in an academic setting   9

Practice realities in clinical psychology   11

Conclusion   15

Ongoing considerations   15

Key terms learned   15

Thinking questions   16

References   16

◇**CHAPTER TWO**
BECOMING A CLINICAL PSYCHOLOGIST   17

Chapter objective   17

Considerations for career planning   17

Concrete planning steps   18

Maximizing your academic preparation and building the best possible
  application package   21
  Application forms   21
  Grade-point averages   21

Graduate record examination   23
  The statement of interest   25
  Letters of reference   26
  Research or clinical experience?   27
  Timing issues   27
  Getting the most out of graduate school   28
  Postdoctoral training   29
  Getting licensed   30

Conclusion   31

Ongoing considerations   31

Key terms learned   31

Thinking questions   32

References   32

⬦**CHAPTER THREE**
METHODS FOR RESEARCH AND EVALUATION   33

Chapter objective   33

Chapter organization   33

Properties of psychological tests   34

    Reliability   35

    Validity   39

    How should tests be described with respect to their reliability
        and validity?   41

Measuring change in therapy   42

Methods used to learn about therapy outcome   43

    Case studies   43

    Therapy outcome research   45

    Qualitative research   50

    Program evaluation   51

Conclusion   53

Ongoing considerations   53

Key terms learned   53

Thinking questions   54

References   54

⬦**CHAPTER FOUR**
ETHICAL DECISION-MAKING   56

Chapter objective   56

Setting the tone   56

Defining what ethical behavior is   57

Our profession's commitment to ethical standards of practice   59

    Legal facts and ethics   60

    Practice guidelines/codes of conduct   61

    Custody and access reports: Necessary and contentious   64

    Codes of ethics   64

Conclusion   73

Ongoing considerations   73

Key terms learned   73

Thinking questions   73

References   74

Excellent websites   75

◇ CHAPTER FIVE
THE NATURE OF PSYCHOPATHOLOGY   76

Chapter objective   76

Psychological problems that clinical psychologists focus on   78

Defining psychological problems   79
Statistical or normative approach   79
Subjective interpretation (psychological pain)   79
Judgments of maladaptive functioning   79

Issues in defining psychological problems   80

Some important concepts in defining psychological problems   82
Sign   82
Symptom   82
Syndrome   83
Mental disorder   83

Psychological problems: What processes are affected?   83
Emotions and emotional regulation   84
Thoughts/cognitions, intellectual functioning, information processing   84
Perceptions   85
Interpersonal processes   85
Regulatory or coping behavior   85
Development   85
Environment   86

Conceptualizations of psychological problems   86
Philosophical underpinnings of orientations to psychopathology   87
Symptom as focus   89
Underlying cause as focus   89
Current conceptualizations of psychopathology   89
Diagnostic classification systems   90

Specific current classification systems   91
International classification of diseases   92
THE DIAGNOSTIC AND STATISTICAL MANUAL OF MENTAL DISORDERS, 4TH EDITION,
TEXT REVISION (DSM-IV-TR)   92
THE PSYCHODYNAMIC DIAGNOSTIC MANUAL   94

Conclusion   96

Ongoing considerations   96

Key terms learned   96

Thinking questions   97

References   97

◇ **CHAPTER SIX**
OVERVIEW OF ASSESSMENT   99

Chapter objective   99

Overview   99

What is psychological assessment?   102

Psychological testing versus psychological assessment   102

Psychological assessment in practice and training   103

Purpose of assessment   104

The tools of psychological assessment   104

Types of psychological assessment   106

Goals of psychological assessment   107

   Problem explication   107

   Formulation   109

   Prognosis and treatment outcome   111

   Treatment recommendations   112

   Provision of a therapeutic context   112

   Communication of findings to referral source and to the patient(s)   113

Research   122

Importance of context   122

Interpretation, decision-making, and prediction   122

   Quantitative or actuarial approach   123

   Clinical judgment or subjective approach   123

   Clinical decision-making and errors in judgment   124

Conclusion   126

Ongoing considerations   126

Key terms learned   126

Thinking questions   126

References   127

◇ **CHAPTER SEVEN**
PSYCHODIAGNOSTIC ASSESSMENT   130

Chapter objective   130

Psychodiagnostic assessment   130

What are the tests and tools used in psychodiagnostic assessment?   131

Clinical interviews   132

   Unstructured interviews   136

      PROS OF UNSTRUCTURED INTERVIEWS   137

      CONS OF UNSTRUCTURED INTERVIEWS   137

   Structured interviews   137

      PROS OF STRUCTURED INTERVIEWS   138

      CONS OF UNSTRUCTURED INTERVIEWS   138

Objective tests   138

Minnesota multiphasic personality Inventory (MMPI-2), MMPI-2
   Restructured Form (MMPI-2-RF), and MMPI-Adolescent (MMPI-A)   139
     Validity scales   141
     Clinical scales   141
     Interpretation   142
     Reliability and validity   142
     Pros of the MMPI-2   144
     Cons of the MMPI-2   145
     MMPI-2 reconstructed form   145
     MMPI-A   145

Other omnibus self-report measures   146
     Millon clinical multiaxial inventories   146
          Pros of the MCMI-III   146
          Cons of the MCMI-III   146
     Personality assessment inventory   147
          Rating Scales   147

Projective techniques   147
     Rorschach inkblot technique   148
          Reliability and Validity   150
          Pros of the RIT   151
          Cons of the RIT   151
     Thematic apperception test   151
          Reliability and Validity   153
          Pros of the TAT   153
          Cons of the TAT   153
     Drawing tasks   154
          Reliability and Validity   154
          Pros of the Drawing Tasks   155
          Cons of the Drawing Tasks   155

Conclusion   155

Ongoing considerations   155

Key terms learned   156

Thinking questions   156

References   156

◇CHAPTER EIGHT
COGNITIVE AND NEUROPSYCHOLOGICAL
ASSESSMENT   159

Chapter objective   159

Intellectual assessment   159
     Purpose of intellectual assessment   160
     Domains assessed in intellectual assessment   160

What is intelligence?   161

What is IQ?   162

Intelligence tests   163

Stanford-Binet scale   164
      STANFORD-BINET-5   164
   Wechsler scales of intelligence   165
      WECHSLER ADULT INTELLIGENCE SCALE-IV (WAIS-IV)   166
      WECHSLER INTELLIGENCE SCALE FOR CHILDREN-IV (WISC-IV)   166
      WECHSLER PRESCHOOL AND PRIMARY SCALE OF INTELLIGENCE-III
      (WPPSII-III)   168
   Interpreting and using intelligence test scores   168

Clinical neuropsychology and neuropsychological evaluations   168
   Purposes of neuropsychological assessment   169
   Assumptions underlying neuropsychological assessment   171
   Domains important to assess   172

How is a neuropsychological evaluation done?   176

Neuropsychological tests: Fixed batteries   178
   Halstead reitan   178
   Luria nebraska   178

Neuropsychological assessment: Flexible or process approach   179

Conclusion   180

Ongoing considerations   180

Key terms learned   181

Thinking questions   181

References   182

◇ CHAPTER NINE
BEHAVIORAL AND BIOLOGICAL ASSESSMENT   184

Chapter objective   184

Behavioral assessment   184
   Rationale and basic principles   184
   Validity and ethics in implementation and interpretation   185
   Maximizing the usefulness of observations   188
   Self-monitoring   188
   Conclusion   190

Biological assessments   190
   Physiological systems   191
   Measurement of physiological activity   194
      RELIABILITY AND VALIDITY   196
   Applications   196

Conclusion   198

Ongoing considerations   198

Key terms learned   198

Thinking questions   199

References   199

◇ **CHAPTER TEN**
THE PROCESS OF PSYCHOTHERAPY   201

Chapter objective   201

Defining psychotherapy   202

The therapy environment   202

Homework assignments   204

Therapy length   205

Multiclient therapy   206

Elements in the process of therapy   208

The client   208

  Who goes into therapy?   208

  Client readiness   208

  Characteristics of the therapist and outcome   211

Techniques   215

  Typical presenting problems   215

  The therapeutic relationship   217

Cultural competence in clinical psychology   219

Conclusion   222

Ongoing considerations   223

Key terms learned   223

Thinking questions   223

References   224

◇ **CHAPTER ELEVEN**
PSYCHOTHERAPIES I   227

Chapter objective   227

Psychoanalysis   227

  Terminology   227

How common is psychoanalysis and psychodynamic treatment?   229

Primary assumptions and principles of psychoanalytic treatment   230

Evolution of psychoanalytic theory   233

Phases of classical psychoanalysis   235

Ego psychology   237

Object relations theory   240

Self psychology theory   243

Short-term dynamic psychotherapies   243

Goals of psychoanalysis and psychoanalytic psychotherapy   244

Psychoanalytic treatment   246

    Vehicles for behavior change in psychoanalytic treatment   247

New issues in the field   249

Person-centered therapy   249

    Theory   250

    Person-centered psychotherapy   251

    Empathy   252

    Unconditional positive regard   252

    Genuineness   253

Systems therapies   256

    Systems theory   256

    Specific systems therapy approaches   264

Conclusion   267

Ongoing considerations   267

Key terms learned   268

Thinking questions   269

References   269

◇ CHAPTER TWELVE
PSYCHOTHERAPIES II   273

Chapter objective   273

Behavior therapy   273

    Roots and underlying theory   273

    Ethical considerations   276

    Punishment   277

    Reinforcement   278

    Concluding observations   283

Cognitive therapy   288

    Two major proponents: Ellis and Beck   290

Cognitive-behavioral therapy   295

Biofeedback, relaxation, and stress management   296

    Biofeedback   298

        THE TRAINING PROCESS   300

    Relaxation or self-regulation methods   300

    Summary   301

    Stress management   302

    A model of the stress process: Major components and moderating variables   303

    Summary   305

Emotion-focused therapy   307

Motivational interviewing   308

Dialectical behavior therapy   311

Rationale   311
Method   311
Conclusion   313
Ongoing considerations   313
Key terms learned   313
Thinking questions   314
References   314

◇ **CHAPTER THIRTEEN**
PSYCHOTHERAPY OUTCOME   317
Chapter objective   317
Methods   317
A brief history of therapy outcome research   322
What questions are meta-analytic reviews trying to answer?   323
What has been learned from existing meta-analyses?   329
Cost-effectiveness of psychological therapies   333
Controversies around knowledge translation from therapy outcome research   334
Conclusion   338
Ongoing considerations   338
Key terms learned   339
Thinking questions   339
References   339

◇ **CHAPTER FOURTEEN**
INNOVATIVE/MYSTICAL THERAPIES   343
Chapter objective   343
Defining treatment specificity and uniqueness   343
Hypnosis   346
    Description and rationale   346
    Hypnotic susceptibility   348
    Understanding and measuring hypnotic trance   349
    The method   349
    Treatment outcome   350
        EVIDENCE FOR POSITIVE TREATMENT OUTCOME   350
        IS IT POSSIBLE TO TEST FOR THE SPECIFICITY OF THE RATIONALE?   350
        IS THERE EVIDENCE FOR SPECIFICITY?   350
    Summary of hypnosis   350
Eye movement desensitization and reprocessing   351
    Description, rationale, and method   351
    Treatment outcome   352
        EVIDENCE FOR POSITIVE OUTCOME   352

IS SPECIFICITY TESTING POSSIBLE?   352

IS THERE EVIDENCE FOR SPECIFICITY?   352

Summary of EMDR   353

Acceptance and commitment therapy   353

Description, rationale, and method   353

Treatment outcome   354

TREATMENT EFFECTIVENESS   354

IS SPECIFICITY TESTING POSSIBLE?   354

IS THERE EVIDENCE FOR SPECIFICITY?   354

Summary of ACT   354

Mindfulness meditation   354

Roots, rationale, and procedure   354

The method   355

Treatment outcome   355

IS SPECIFICITY TESTING POSSIBLE?   357

HAS SPECIFICITY BEEN DEMONSTRATED?   357

Summary of MM   357

Revisiting claims of uniqueness and specificity for all four treatments described   357

Conclusion   360

Ongoing considerations   360

Key terms learned   361

Thinking questions   361

References   361

◇CHAPTER FIFTEEN
CHILD CLINICAL PSYCHOLOGY   365

Chapter objectives   365

Developmental stages and childhood psychopathology   367

Ethical challenges   368

Impact of development on assessment   370

Intervention   373

Behavior therapy   373

Play therapy   373

Systems therapy   374

Overview of treatment outcome   374

The example of attention deficit and hyperactivity disorder   376

Conclusion   377

Ongoing considerations   377

Key terms learned   378

Thinking questions   378

References   378

◇**CHAPTER SIXTEEN**
FORENSIC PSYCHOLOGY   381

Chapter objective   381

What is forensic psychology?   381

Forensic psychology today   383

The clinical forensic psychologist   383
    Police psychology   384
    Crime and delinquency   384
    Victimology   385
    Correctional psychology   385
    Psychology and law or legal psychology   385

Differences between traditional clinical psychology and forensic psychology
    practice   386

Tasks of the clinical forensic psychologist   387
    Assessment   387
    Forensic assessment tools   388
    Forensically relevant assessment tools   388
    Clinical measures and assessment techniques   389

Treatment   389
    Treatment of perpetrators of crime   390
    Treatment of victims of crime   391
    Treatment of workers in the field   392

Consultation and opinions   393

Lie detection   393

Conclusion   399

Ongoing considerations   399

Key terms learned   400

Thinking questions   400

References   400

◇**CHAPTER SEVENTEEN**
**HEALTH PSYCHOLOGY AND BEHAVIORAL
MEDICINE   403**

Chapter objective   403

Understanding health and the causation of disease   405

Early-life influences on health   408

Prevention and management of chronic diseases   409

Adherence   412

Pain   415
    Understanding pain   415
    Acute pain   415
    Chronic pain   416

Working with cardiovascular disease patients   418

Hypertension   420

Chronic heart failure   421

Heart transplantation   422

Restenosis   423

Working with cancer patients   423

Conclusion   426

Ongoing considerations   427

Key terms learned   427

Thinking questions   427

References   428

◇ CHAPTER EIGHTEEN
PSYCHOPHARMACOLOGY   433

Chapter objectives   433

A clinical case scenario   434

The language of pharmacology: important concepts   435

Frequently used terms and abbreviations   436

Types of psychopharmacological medication and areas of application   436

How the arrival of the internet has changed clinical practice   440

Should psychologists have drug prescription privileges?   440

Conclusion   442

Some (sobering) additional considerations   442

Key terms learned   443

Thinking questions   443

References   443

◇ CHAPTER NINETEEN
CURRENT TRENDS AND THE FUTURE OF CLINICAL
PSYCHOLOGY   445

Chapter objective   445

Changes in health care   446

Clinical training   448

Prescription privileges   450

Clinical psychology, computers, and the web   450

Research in clinical psychology   452

Positive psychology and spirituality   454

Conclusion   455

Key terms learned   455

References   455

NAME INDEX   457

SUBJECT INDEX   462

PREFACE

The decision to write this textbook stems from Wolfgang Linden's experience of more than 2 decades of teaching a fourth-year undergraduate introductory clinical psychology course and from many conversations with representatives from college textbook publishers who just could not provide the kind of text he was seeking for his class. Of course, the textbook publishers' representatives who came to the university campus routinely said "Why don't you write a textbook yourself that suits your needs?" As the existence of this book in your hands proves, the dam finally broke, and two authors with complementary areas of expertise in clinical psychology joined forces to do just that. Paul Hewitt also believed that many of the existing clinical psychology textbooks missed critically important aspects of contemporary clinical and research work and revealed a sometimes not-so-subtle bias against particular domains of clinical inquiry. Hence, the authors decided to try to create a textbook that addresses the missing components. Moreover, the authors wished to provide an international flavor to the textbook so as to teach students about the larger field of clinical psychology, not the field of clinical psychology as it is narrowly practiced in any one country or jurisdiction. In the end, this was not particularly difficult because the similarities of the field between countries greatly outweigh the differences. However, at times there are emphases on certain aspects of the field that different countries promote, and practitioners in different countries can inspire each other by sharing their knowledge. The fact that clinical psychology is embedded in country-specific systems of health care delivery also allows comparisons and identification of innovative strategies that may invite application elsewhere for the benefit of better patient care.

Why could we not find another book that satisfied our needs? There are many reasons. First of all, both Wolfgang and Paul considered existing texts too narrow in their coverage and at times presenting somewhat antiquated views of the field. Also, a predominant habit of existing texts in clinical psychology is to start at the beginning with a lengthy chapter on history. While we agree that it is important to understand the roots and the context for developments in clinical psychology, we think that more curiosity is raised in students by starting *today*, by appreciating what kinds of problems clinical psychologists solve every day, and by delineating the satisfactions they derive from their work. This presentation of day-to-day realities sets the stage for appreciating the tools needed to complete daily tasks and solve problems. To make this approach come alive, we present these tools, work our way through ethical considerations, assessment, and treatment issues, deal with what works in therapy and what does not, and raise questions about where the future may take us. The objective of this book is not just to teach facts about clinical psychology but to encourage the student to think like a clinical psychologist and to develop an integrated sense of how science, experience, ethical behavior, and intuition get woven into our professional identity.

By attempting to make clinical psychology real and timely, we are seeking to arouse curiosity in readers so that they truly want to move through the text and find the answers, just like in a good thriller where you want to find out who did it and why and "how the gardener almost got away with murder"!

What else makes this book different?

■ We portray clinical psychology as a modern *health care profession* that bridges physical and mental health, that is psychosomatic, and that takes a holistic stance; this book does not see clinical psychology as just a branch of mental health care.

■ We recognize the importance of biological/physiological assessments because no existing text covers physiological measures beyond offering a mere mention (if that!).

■ This book takes an international perspective, trying to describe similarities but also differences between countries and how clinical psychology is practiced in different contexts.

■ This book recognizes how clinical psychology changes as health care systems change and stresses that training models and practice patterns need to match these changes.

■ We try to breathe life into the dynamic nature of change in the therapy process and how different approaches weave into one another, cross-fertilize, and grow.

■ We tried to create excitement by building the text around fairly typical psychologists and the problems they need to solve, stressing how assessment is much more than testing and how treatment rationales are tailored to individual problems, their histories, and the client's current environment.

■ We show that psychoanalysis and psychoanalytic psychotherapies have not stalled and are not disappearing; instead, they continue to develop and draw interest.

We know that clinical psychology is offered as a one-semester course in some colleges and universities but also as a full-year course elsewhere. Given that this book is meant to support one-semester and two-semester courses alike, it is not likely that instructors can cover all chapters of this book in full detail if their course spans only a single semester. Therefore, we planned the book such that a number of chapters and their corresponding topics could be left out altogether or left as assigned reading to students. This is most likely applicable to chapter 2 (how to get into graduate school and psychologists' career paths); the chapters or sections on subspecialties like innovative therapies, health, forensic psychology, child clinical psychology, psychopharmacology; and chapter 19 (outlook to the future). The sequence of the chapter presentation is mapped onto the sequence of topics covered in Wolfgang Linden's course, which is based on over 2 decades of teaching experience; student feedback had indicated that this order represented a good flow.

We want to alert the reader to certain issues of style and use of terminology that are germane to this book. Throughout the field of mental health, the individuals who receive services are called *patients*, *clients*, or *consumers*. The term "patients" is most likely used in hospitals or other medically dominated environments, whereas the term "clients" is typically used in private practice environments. The notion of "patient" embeds the idea that the individual is in pain or distress and that a professional "healer" is involved, whereas "client" also harbors the recognition that there is usually a two-sided contract between the therapist and the client. "Client" also implies more client control over the therapy (or assessment) process than is typically true for patients in hospital environments. Philosophically, we hope that in the long run nobody is seen as a passive recipient of care and that instead we treat patients as partners in care. Given that this book provides numerous examples of clinical practice in widely different environments, we are using the terms "patients" and "clients" interchangeably and do not want the reader to look for some profound rationale for choosing one term over another at different times.

The term "consumer" is most often used by individuals who work in volunteer mental health organizations or receive services by these organizations. The philosophy of these not-for-profit helping organizations is one of empowerment; they tend to reject the terminology of a more hierarchically organized medical world and its pathologizing labels. While we recognize and appreciate the reasoning and suitability of the term "consumer" in this environment, it is not routinely adopted for this textbook.

The world of clinical psychology consists of men and women, in provider and client roles, as well as people of different cultures, skin colors, religions, and sexual orientations. In order to recognize the full representation of both genders in all roles and to avoid the stilted (over-) use of the awkward term "they," we randomly alternate between "she" and "he" when we refer to either patients or psychologists or other individuals. In no case should the reader think that a gender-specific bias is implied if a police officer was referred to as "he" or a nurse was referred to as "she." In fact, we made efforts to occasionally use gender labels that go against such stereotypes.

When clinical psychologists enter the world of health care, they enter a world that is strongly dominated by two health care professionals, namely nurses and physicians. In fact, many people portray the health care system as consisting only of physicians and nurses, and unfortunately this is equally prevalent in the media who use this descriptor ad nauseam. We want to encourage all clinical psychologists to actively contribute to raising awareness in the general public that there are many different health care professions. In the university where we teach, there are no less than 11 (!!) different professions being trained to become health care professionals. Of course, there are more nurses and physicians in the health care system than other health professions, but that simply means that these other health care professionals need to make more noise to raise their individual visibility and market themselves. Along these lines we strongly discourage clinical psychologists from participating in the confusing and self-handicapping habit of referring to physicians as doctors. For unclear reasons of tradition, medical professionals in North America are often referred to as doctors although the roots of the term "doctor" have no connection with medicine whatsoever. "Doctor" stems from the Latin verb "docere," which means to teach. Hence, a doctor is a teacher or scholar, and, in fact, universities have a thousand-year old tradition of awarding the title "Dr." to the most extensively trained scholar. Interestingly, a British-trained physician is awarded a bachelor of medicine degree (MB) and not a doctorate title. Also, the title confusion does not exist in other languages as well such that Spanish-speaking people have a "Medico," the French their "Medicin," and the Germans their "Arzt." In order to take the place that psychologists deserve in the health care system, we encourage doctoral-level trained psychologists to actively use their hard-earned Dr. title and to avoid insidiously eviscerating the power of their own profession by referring to physicians as doctors.

◇ SUPPLEMENTS

Pearson Education is pleased to offer the following supplements to qualified adopters.

Instructor's Manual and Test Bank (ISBN 0132397633). The instructor's manual is a wonderful tool for classroom preparation and management. Each chapter in the teaching aids section includes a chapter overview, detailed outline, lecture suggestions, discussion questions, class activities, and media resources. The test bank contains a set of questions for each chapter, including multiple choice, true/false, short-answer, and essay questions. The tests are also available in the MyTest (0132397641) computerized version for ease in creating tests for the classroom.

PowerPoint Presentation (0132397668). The PowerPoint Presentation is an exciting interactive tool for use in the classroom. Each chapter pairs key concepts with images from the textbook to reinforce student learning.

◇ ACKNOWLEDGEMENTS

Writing an undergraduate textbook is a rather gargantuan undertaking that takes committed authors who put much of their lives on hold "until the textbook is done"; they need families that support them; colleagues who suggest, criticize, and occasionally praise; and an editor who fully stands behind them.

On our home turf, there were the diligent and hard-working editorial assistants Alena Talbot Ellis, MA (who had actually taken Wolfgang Linden's course 2 years before working on this book); Roanne Millman, BA; the tireless Victoria Bae, BA; Jonathan Blasberg, BA; Jacqueline Hewitt; Melanie J. Phillips, BSc; Heather Roxborough, MA; and Christopher Siu, BA; who read sections of this book and provided feedback. Friends and colleagues graciously read and commented on some chapters, and we thank Charlotte Johnston, PhD, Roy O'Shaughnessy, MD, and Mark Gelfer, MD, for their critical reading of our material on child clinical psychology and psychopharmacology, respectively. As well, many conversations with colleagues and students over the years have contributed ideas, critiques, and opposing points of view that have influenced the ideas presented in this work. The first major group to thank is the more than 1000 students who have taken Wolfgang Linden's clinical psychology course and Paul Hewitt's various clinical courses over the years and who participated in, or triggered, lively in-class discussions on a myriad of topics. We thank them for their willingness to keep us on our toes but whose curiosity also kept us excited about our field. We greatly appreciate this and especially thank Samuel Mikail, Gordon Flett, Simon Sherry, Dayna Sherry, Brandy McGee, Carol Flynn, and Lindsey Thomas, who through many years of discussion helped shape how we think about the field and how the course is taught. We would also like to thank the many patients and clients that we have seen over the years, all of whom have also been instrumental in shaping and guiding our thoughts, ideas, and understandings of clinical psychology.

We are greatly in debt of those colleagues who have critically reviewed our manuscript: Sheryl Reminger, University of Illinois, Springfield; Karen Mottarella, UCF Palm Bay Campus; Jim Sullivan, Florida State University; Daniel Niederjohn, Kennesaw State University; Augustine Osman, The University of Texas at San Antonio; Cole Barton, Davidson College; David Gard, San Francisco State University; Hal Arkowitz, University of Arizona; Denise Sloane, Temple University; Wesley Allan, University of North Carolina at Greensboro; Steven L. Berman, University of Central Florida; Kimberly Wilson, Stanford University; Amanda Schurle Bruce, Penn State University; and Barb J. Heine, University of California, Irvine. Their input was pivotal in identifying the weak spots and achieving balanced coverage.

Jeff Marshall has been our acquisition editor at Prentice-Hall, and we are sincerely grateful for his enthusiasm and support in the start-up phase. When he first responded to our book prospectus, we knew that he was excited too. We thank the production staff Kara Kikel, Laura Barry, Kerri Hart-Morris and senior editor Susan Hartman in nudging and supporting us through the final stages. Jerusha Govindakrishnan served as our diligent text editor assuring homogeneous use of language, completeness, and consistency in style. We are grateful for your fine eye and patience.

Textbook authors also have the good fortune to receive input from (at least initially anonymous) colleagues who provide reviews and feedback through the publisher; their job is not to bolster the egos of the authors with flattering feedback but to take critical stances and comment on all aspects of the product, style, appeal, comprehensiveness, depth, and so forth. We are profoundly grateful to these colleagues (named earlier) for their critical feedback that gave us a chance to make changes that hopefully maximize the attractiveness of the book for textbook adoption. Where things were done right we owe all the individuals above; where things got messed up, it was our own doing. Last but not least, we truly welcome student and faculty feedback; feel free to write to us, or comment on needed improvements for future editions.

CHAPTER ONE

BEING A CLINICAL PSYCHOLOGIST

CHAPTER OBJECTIVES

The authors of this textbook strongly identify with the profession of clinical psychology and have been ardent defenders of the idea that it is a distinct profession. The objective of this chapter is to circumscribe the profession, make it come alive, and get you as excited as we are about our profession even after decades of practice. The learning objectives for this chapter are:

- An appreciation of diverse problems that clinical psychologists face, the actual work that is being done, and the expertise needed to do this work competently.

- An understanding of some of the training that is involved in the development of a clinical psychologist.

- An appreciation for the diverse tasks as well as some difficult ethical challenges that these psychologists tackle.

◇ DESCRIBING THE PROFESSION

Clinical psychologists see patients for formal assessments, conduct psychotherapy, do research, consult, and educate. The claim for "distinctness" of their profession, however, takes some explaining. Specialty areas within psychology are defined by certain subsets of questions or fields of inquiry that they focus on. Developmental psychology, for example, is interested in growth and change, and biological psychology is interested in the relationship of biology, physiology, and behavior. Of course, both domains inform other research domains and areas of application. Clinical psychology, on the other hand, denotes a profession that applies knowledge from many subspecialties within psychology to solve everyday problems in health care. Also, given their scientific training, clinical psychologists actively research the questions that they deal with in clinical practice, and, vice versa, use their clinical experience to feed new insights and ideas back to researchers. The most frequently used term to describe this two-way flow of ideas is **"scientist-practitioner."** To some degree, clinical psychology can be defined by how it is different from related disciplines like **psychiatry** and **social work** or **counseling psychology** (see Box 1.1 that describes the difference between clinical psychologist, psychiatrist, and social worker).

Without going into much detail, the student of clinical psychology should be aware that the field really began to exist as a distinct specialty only after World War II. At that time, clinical psychologists made concerted efforts to define how the topic should be taught and what knowledge practitioners should have. Consistent with the scientist-practitioner model, it was decided that the knowledge base of clinical psychology was so thin and underdeveloped that all students were to be trained in skills needed to continue building the knowledge base while also practicing and applying it. This decision was made at the so-called Boulder (Colorado) Conference, and the scientist-practitioner model is therefore also sometimes called the Boulder model. Today, clinical psychology is typically taught via well-structured, **accredited training programs**; these programs provide its graduates with an identity, and clinical psychologists now have an established place in health care (Linden, Moseley, & Erskine, 2005). Rather than first exposing the reader to a detailed history of the field, we will start by describing three different kinds of clinical psychologists and one clinical psychology graduate student. Typical work days and challenges will be illustrated.

The detailed descriptions of a graduate student's and the three psychologists' daily lives are amalgamations of the work that psychologists known to us really do, and they also cover tasks that we ourselves are involved in. None of the descriptions of specific work environments are intended to reflect critically upon any existing facility; they should be treated as fictional.

Our clinical graduate student is roughly at the midpoint of his academic training. The three clinical psychologists to be described work in a hospital setting, in full-time private practice, and as a university professor.

◇ THE CHALLENGES AND RESPONSIBILITIES OF FOUR DIFFERENT PSYCHOLOGISTS

A Clinical Psychology Student

Description of a Typical Day

Vincent S is a fourth-year clinical psychology graduate student who entered a clinical psychology graduate program because of his strong desire to help others, his marked curiosity in understanding the way people function, and his desire to do both clinical work and research. A reasonably typical day in his life involves a busy schedule of training activities that involve both research and clinical work.

The 3-hour seminar on psychopathology (i.e., abnormal behavior) involves a detailed analysis and discussion of models and treatment options for somatoform disorders. Based on assigned readings and on a critical analysis of those readings it was expected

BOX 1.1

WHAT IS A CLINICAL PSYCHOLOGIST?

Brace yourself. If you are a clinical psychologist, graduate or even undergraduate student in psychology, you are prone to be asked at various family gatherings or other social events what the difference is between a psychiatrist and a psychologist. Aside from referring to both as "headshrinkers" and to get that pesky questioner out of your hair, here are some standard definitions that you can supply.

A **psychologist** is a scientist and/or clinician who studies psychology—the systematic investigation of the human mind, including behavior and cognition. Psychologists are usually categorized by their area of specialty. The most well-recognized subgroup in the community is that of the "clinical psychologist," who provides health care, conducts assessments, and provides psychological therapy.

In North America, the typical **clinical psychologist** holds a Doctor of Psychology (PsyD) degree if he or she was trained in a professional school, or a Doctor of Philosophy (PhD) if he or she was trained in university-based psychology departments. It typically takes 6–7 years above and beyond a bachelor's degree to become a clinical psychologist. What makes clinical psychologists stand apart from other mental health experts is the balance in their training requiring expertise in both science and practice (see Linden et al., 2005, for a review). In much of Europe and Australia, clinical training is offered at the level of master's degrees and may require additional supervised training before graduates can become independent practitioners and/or are allowed to do third-party billing.

Counseling psychologists are in many ways similar to clinical psychologists but are more likely to become service providers at the master's degree level (implying a total of 2–3 years of graduate training), have less training and expertise in formal psychodiagnostic assessments, and are less likely to work with populations that have psychoses or severe personality disorders.

Psychiatrists are physicians (and in North America usually doctors of medicine [MD]) who are certified in treating mental illness using a biologically based approach to mental disorders. Psychiatrists first complete regular medical school and then acquire specialty training through a 4-year residency during which they may also go through training to conduct psychotherapy. But it is their medical, biology-based training that allows them to prescribe medication and that differentiates them from other mental health professionals. In North America, it typically takes 8–9 years above and beyond a bachelor's degree to become a licensed psychiatrist.

The main tasks of **professional social workers** are case management (linking clients with agencies and programs that will meet their financial and psychosocial needs), medical social work, counseling (psychotherapy), human services management, social welfare policy analysis, community organizing, advocacy, teaching (in schools of social work), and social science research. Some social workers, usually those with a graduate degree (MSW), also provide one-on-one clinical services, often in the area of child and family. The training background of social workers who function as psychotherapists can be quite heterogeneous.

BOX 1.2

A TYPICAL DAY OF VINCENT S

Time	Activity
9 a.m.–12 p.m.	Participates in a 3-hour advanced seminar on psychopathology
12 p.m.	Clinical supervision session
1 p.m.–4 p.m.	Eats a quick lunch and then researches articles pertaining to his dissertation topic and makes notes
4 p.m.	Meets the lab team; an advanced graduate student gives a dry-run of her presentation for the upcoming thesis defense; deals with logistical issues for setting up a study protocol for a new study in the laboratory
5 p.m.	Workout in the university gym
6 p.m.	Dinner break
7 p.m.–9 p.m.	Sees patients in the psychology clinic

that Vincent, along with his other five classmates, evaluates the support, or lack of support, for various theoretical models. Following the clinical seminar, Vincent was scheduled to have supervision with his clinical supervisor who was overseeing Vincent's treatment of a patient who exhibited both marked depression and anxiety in response to upcoming applications to several very prestigious law schools. The issues of a strong desire for achievement and real concern over one's ability to perform at a high level were also concerns that Vincent, personally, had experienced and, at times, continues to experience. Vincent believed, correctly, that his own personal concerns with the same issues might interfere with the treatment he was providing or, at least, might cloud his judgment somewhat. The clinical supervision involved first discussing Vincent's personal issues over performance as well as a discussion of how his own views/feelings might influence the treatment process in order to help Vincent become better at the treatment. Following supervision, Vincent felt better able to deal with the patient's issues next session. Next, Vincent spent several hours reading research articles pertaining to his dissertation topic. The dissertation is to be a major original research project designed to have the student conduct an independent (although supervised by a faculty member), and relatively large-scale, research work that produces new knowledge within a particular field in psychology. Vincent was at the stage of formulating a research question within the area he had chosen, namely, personality factors and their link to suicide behavior, and was working on a review of the relevant literature to determine areas that required further investigation. He would be meeting with his research supervisor in several days and would go over a written document that detailed the rationale for several potential research questions.

Following a break for dinner, Vincent was slated to see patients in the departmental teaching clinic. The psychology clinic is kept open one evening every week to accommodate clients with full-time jobs. The first appointment was with the client described earlier, and, as a result of reviewing his notes and the supervision he received earlier, Vincent felt prepared. The second appointment was a couple who were having marital difficulties, and this was a first session. Although Vincent had not previously seen any couples for treatment, he was simultaneously anxious and keen to see them. He had read extensively about marital therapy, taken a marital/family treatment clinical course last year, and had met with his clinical supervisor regarding this particular couple and discussed approaches for dealing with the first session. At the conclusion of the last treatment session, he completed case notes and made preparations for the next day.

Specific Concerns

- How does Vincent critique, analyze, and synthesize both theoretical models and clinical research pertaining to those models and discuss these in a coherent fashion? (Chapters relevant: 4–13)

- How does Vincent suspect that his personal issues may be influencing his treatment of a patient, and how does he know what to do about it? (Chapters relevant: 4 and 10)

- Where does Vincent look for relevant literature for his dissertation and produce a clinically relevant research project? (Chapters relevant: 3–9)

- How does Vincent know that he has commenced marital therapy in an ethically appropriate fashion that will maximize helping the couple? (Chapters relevant: 4 and 10–12)

Clinical Psychologist A—Working in a General Hospital Setting

Dr. Marisa A is trained in clinical psychology with a subspecialty in **behavioral medicine**. She is employed full-time by a large general hospital and spends her time doing about equal portions of (a) direct service provision (providing individual and group treatments) for distressed patients who have been diagnosed with cancer or heart disease and (b) consultation with various in-house services that might need her help on an ad hoc basis (e.g., the eating disorders program or the organ transplant team).

She has completed 2 years of specialty training after she had completed her PhD in this type of hospital setting and has had multiple interesting job offers given the breadth of her skills. She has been at this hospital for 15 years and feels respected by her medical and nursing colleagues.

A particularly exciting and challenging request presented to Dr. A was to develop a distress screening program for the cancer clinic. The cancer clinic had been told by an accreditation committee that it failed to have systematic procedures for identifying

BOX 1.3

A TYPICAL DAY OF MARISA A

Time	Activity
9 a.m.	Visits two patients on the surgical recovery ward who had a heart transplant and coronary bypass surgery, respectively. Discusses plans for their release and the need to make life-style changes
10 a.m.	Conducts an assessment of the suitability of a patient with alcohol problems for a possible liver transplant
11 a.m.	Meets the multidisciplinary transplant team to determine who of three new referrals is suitable to go on to the wait-list for an organ transplant
12 p.m.	Attends grand rounds to learn about the latest in sequelae of head injuries
1 p.m.	Eats lunch with a colleague who plans to set up a specialty clinic for borderline personality disorder and needs some collegial feedback on how to go about it
2 p.m.	Supervision session with three interns who go through various rotations while on internship in her hospital
3 p.m.	Catches up on e-mails and prepares for the 4 p.m. group she leads
4 p.m.	Runs a 90-minute psychoeducational group for patients in curative cancer treatment
5:30 p.m.	Writes up notes from psychoeducational group
6 p.m.	Goes home

cancer patients in greatest need of professional psychological support. Although a family support and counseling service was available to patients, there was the suspicion that only those patients who were particularly vocal in asking for help ended up receiving it. There was a good chance that uneducated and unassertive patients were left out.

Dr. Marisa A decided to develop a **distress screening** tool that was brief, easy to read even for patients with poor reading skills, and that would have the ability to quickly and precisely identify the patients most in need.

Specific Concerns

Dr. A made a list of questions she knew she had to tackle:

- What psychological characteristics will be the most important ones to measure?
- Even if distress was readily measurable with this new tool, how will she know how much distress or anxiety is too much and requires professional support?

- Will there be enough resources in the hospital or the community to handle the problems that screening will identify?

- Should screening actually go ahead if one knows ahead of time that identified needs cannot be met?

- How does one actually develop a test, write test items, and evaluate their usefulness? How can she establish that the test is measuring what it is supposed to and that it does so reliably?

- Once the test is developed, will the clinic staff readily accept and use it? How can it be applied most efficiently?

The kind of information that Dr. A will need to meet these challenges covers issues of ethics (see chapter 4)—an understanding of the sometimes complicated administration and internal politics of medical clinics and the health care system in general (see chapters 17 and 19) as well as the more theoretical and practical questions of test development and test application itself (see chapters 3 and 6–8).

Clinical Psychologist B—Working in a Private Practice Setting

Description of a Typical Day

Dr. Ramin B is a clinical psychologist in general private practice in a small community; his work entails mainly clinical assessments and treatment of adults with various psychological problems, although he also sees children and adolescents for assessment and treatment of specific disorders including depression and anxiety.

Dr. B has, what he would term, an eclectic orientation, meaning that he pulls from a variety of clinical perspectives in assessing and treating individuals. He also endorses that his main theoretical perspective would be consistent with a psychodynamic perspective. He has been trained in both psychodynamic and cognitive-behavioral techniques, and he carefully chooses the one approach most suitable to the client's presenting problem.

A typical day might begin with an assessment of an individual who reported marked dissatisfaction with life including intimate relationships, work, and family and described long-standing dysthymia and a recent significant depressive episode. Dr. B was evaluating data from an initial assessment he had completed on this patient, and it was clear that the patient, on objective measures and during the interview, was quite defensive in his responding. Information from projective testing was consistent with a defensive and constrictive approach to processing information, and Dr. B was attempting to determine recommendations for the referring agency in order to facilitate optimal treatment for this individual. Although he wanted to respect the patient's desire not to be forthcoming, it appeared to Dr. B that this particular issue of not being entirely open and

BOX 1.4

A TYPICAL DAY OF RAMIN B

Time	Activity
9 a.m.	Reads a medical chart to prepare for an assessment to begin at 10 a.m.
10 a.m.–12 p.m.	Conducts a formal clinical assessment on a depressed client currently on medical leave. This involves a structured interview and standardized personality tests to help prepare a report to the client's insurance company
12 p.m.	Scores the tests and dictates case notes while the memory is fresh
1 p.m.	Eats lunch and returns phone calls
2 p.m.	Attends a lengthy conference with a community care team regarding a care plan for an elderly, widowed patient with dementia
3 p.m.	Interpersonal psychotherapy for depression
4 p.m.	Psychotherapy with a client who presents with perfectionism and obsessive-compulsive cleaning habits
5 p.m.	Marital therapy with a couple considering divorce
6 p.m.	Writes up case notes and returns more phone calls
6:30+	Goes home

forthcoming in certain situations may be one of the contributing factors to his dysthymia and current depression. Moreover, this style of behaving could be problematic for the patient's relationships, including being able to establish a good working relationship with a therapist. He decided that these issues would be at the forefront of the feedback session he was going to provide the patient and would form the cornerstone of the core issues to address in treatment.

In addition to working on the assessment for the patient described earlier, Dr. B was also preparing to see a long-term patient later that day. In the last session, this patient had begun to discuss suicidal tendencies that Dr. B immediately assessed using a sequence of questions designed to gauge the degree of risk. Dr. B had determined that there was little actual suicide risk for the patient, although he was reviewing his notes and attempting to determine what may have precipitated the suicidal tendencies. He planned on evaluating the suicidal tendencies when he saw the patient later that day and reviewed his options for responding, including escorting the patient to an emergency room if suicide was deemed imminent, having the person sign a suicide contract which stipulated that if the patient was feeling suicidal, she would contact Dr. B, who in turn would then consider appropriate next steps of action. If he found that suicidality was low or nonexistent, he would continue the treatment as is. Lastly, Dr. B was considering a consultation with the parents and, potentially, school officials, of a depressed 13-year-old boy whose depression was characterized by sadness, self-reproach, angry outbursts, and, at times, violent behavior. Based on an assessment of the boy, his family situation and support, and support from the school, Dr. B wanted to help build a supportive environment for the patient and locate an appropriate child psychologist to treat the child and the family.

Specific Concerns

Although Dr. B was confident that the results from the projective testing he had conducted were valid, he is aware that there is a controversy in the field as to the utility of projective testing.

- How does he reconcile both the validity of his assessment findings and the potential response of the referring agency to his conclusions based on the projective testing? (Chapters relevant: 3 and 5–7)
- What are the ethical concerns with respect to ensuring the safety of the patient who is exhibiting some suicidal tendencies? What are the appropriate ways to assess risk, and what are the appropriate responses the clinician needs to make? (Chapters relevant: 4–7)
- Is Dr. B appropriately trained for consultation with the adolescent, school officials, and parents? What is his responsibility in getting an appropriate clinician to aid in treatment? (Chapters relevant: 4 and 9)

Clinical Psychologist C—Working in an Academic Setting

Dr. Ann C is a tenured Associate Professor working in a major university where she is one of nine faculty members in their accredited Clinical Training Program. She supervises five graduate students and runs a research program that focuses on cognitive-behavioral approaches for treating anxiety, depression, and pain. She teaches abnormal psychology at the undergraduate level and provides clinical supervision for graduate students working in the department's teaching clinic.

Her recent research focuses on interpersonal factors in understanding pain and its management, and she is actively involved in a professional association where she is organizing a program for an upcoming international conference. She holds two large research grants, employs two full-time research coordinators, four part-time staff, and one postdoctoral fellow, and she has eight undergraduate student volunteers work in her laboratory. On any given day, this laboratory is a beehive of activity, and Dr. C

BOX 1.5

A TYPICAL DAY OF ANN C

Time	Activity
9 a.m.–12 p.m.	A 3-hour block of time when she closes her office door to focus on scientific writing
12 p.m.–2 p.m.	Eats lunch with her research team, and over tuna sandwiches and orange juice, the team does "journal club" in which all team members discuss a controversial recent article. Then provides individual feedback for 30 minutes on a student thesis proposal
2 p.m.–4 p.m.	Teaches a graduate seminar in empirically based treatments
4 p.m.	Sees a private practice patient
5 p.m.	Answers e-mails and phone messages
6 p.m.–9 p.m.	Goes home, has dinner with family, helps children with homework
9 p.m.–10 p.m.	Cursory reading of latest issue of a psychology journal

occasionally complains about how much administrative work is involved in keeping such a large laboratory going.

A typical day begins with a 3-hour block of time when she closes her office door to focus on writing. On one day this involves finishing an invited review paper for a major journal (which she thinks will be another step toward promotion to Full Professor). From 12 noon to 2 p.m. she may have lunch with her research team, and over tuna sandwiches and orange juice the team does "journal club" where all team members discuss a recent controversial article. She then spends a half hour with one of her graduate students providing feedback on a thesis proposal. Almost 60% of her time is taken up with research-related activities and writing. Although she is very busy, she is adamant about protecting family time (she has two teenage children) and does not stay in the office beyond 6 p.m.

Specific Concerns Regarding a Current Clinical Problem

Dr. C maintains a small private practice outside of her academic responsibilities. A family physician has referred a patient with depression, anger, and chronic back pain. This physician has often sent her patients, and Dr. C has helped a great many of them with pain management. Furthermore, this physician has been a collaborator with her on a clinical trial for an innovative pain treatment, and he has found himself impressed with Dr. C's knowledge and professionalism. Pain medication had initially worked but does not seem to help this patient any more. The patient has an unresolved claim with the Workers Compensation Board, and he is hoping for a disability pension, given that his pain has remained steady for over a year and he seems unable to return to work. He is fortunate to have an employer-provided psychological assistance plan that will pay for a psychologist to help him cope with his back pain. Dr. C knows from the literature and her experience that clients with unresolved claims are often angry with the compensation process and sometimes unable to fully concentrate on helping themselves. Given that there is no medical evidence of a specific injury in his case, the Compensation Board is slow to make a decision, and Dr. C has to figure out whether the patient may have ongoing soft-tissue injury and/or is now suffering from generalized pain worsened by the depression and physical inactivity that is typical with chronic pain clients.

- Which tests will help her decide on the nature and origin of the pain, and to what degree is the patient's self-report of pain colored by the unresolved compensation claim? (Chapters relevant: 6–8)
- Will she be able to provide relief? Maybe even to the point of allowing return-to-work?
- If she explained to her patient that treatment might not work unless he settled with the Workers Compensation Board first, would he be able to trust her judgment rather than feeling rejected?
- Given that her client does not directly pay for her services, who is her client? What are her responsibilities?

For Dr. C to make the right decisions, she will need to be well versed in ethical principles (chapter 4), understand the options and limitations of various assessment methods for chronic pain and its psychological correlates (chapters 5–9), and possess the skills and experience to help this pain patient in therapy (chapters 10, 12–14, and 17).

◇ PRACTICE REALITIES IN CLINICAL PSYCHOLOGY

The learning objective of this chapter was to stimulate thinking by describing realistic problems and by highlighting the skills needed to be a competent professional, but we intentionally did not provide any answers at this stage. This is meant to create a positive tension that the reader can relieve by working through the rest of the book (and the accompanying course).

In order to move from the work of these four individuals to a broader perspective on the profession, here is a snapshot of where clinical psychologists typically work, how practice patterns have changed over time, how clinical psychologists divide up their time, and what kind of compensation they can expect (Robiner, 2006).

As you can see in Table 1.1, more clinical psychologists work in private practice than in any other environment; in fact almost half of practicing psychologists are in private practice, part- or full-time. We posit that most readers would have expected more psychologists

TABLE 1.1 Primary Employment Sites

Employment site	1960 [a]%	1973%	1981%	1986%	1995%	2003%
Psychiatric hospital	15	8	8	9	5	4
General hospital	15	6	8	5	4	3
Outpatient clinic	15	5	5	4	4	4
Community mental health center	NR	8	6	5	4	2
Medical school	7	8	7	7	9	8
Private practice	17	23	31	35	40	39
University psychology	20	22	17	17	15	18
University, other department	NR	7	5	4	4	4
VA medical center	NR	—	—	—	3	3
None	NR	1	1	4	1	0
Other	20	11	12	10	11	15

[a] The percentage figures given for the Kelly (1961) study are approximate since exact figures were not reported.

Source: Norcross, Karpiak, & Santoro (2005). Clinical psychologists across the years: The division of clinical psychology from 1960 to 2003. *Journal of Clinical Psychology, 61,* 1467–1483.

TABLE 1.2   Professional Activities of Clinical Psychologists

Activity	% INVOLVED IN			MEAN % OF TIME				
	1986	*1985*	*2003*	*1973*	*1981*	*1986*	*1995*	*2003*
Psychotherapy	87	84	80	31	35	35	37	34
Diagnosis/assessment	75	74	64	10	13	16	15	15
Teaching	55	50	49	14	12	14	9	10
Clinical supervision	67	62	50	8	8	11	7	6
Research/writing	54	47	51	7	8	15	10	14
Consultation	63	54	47	5	7	11	7	7
Administration	55	52	53	13	13	16	11	13

Source: Norcross, Karpiak, & Santoro (2005). Clinical psychologists across the years: The division of clinical psychology from 1960 to 2003. *Journal of Clinical Psychology, 61,* 1467–1483.

to be working in hospitals and clinics. Over the last three to four decades, the single most pronounced change in the field has been a major shift away from salaried employee positions in hospitals and clinics to private practice where services are either delivered by individual practitioners who run their own business or by privately organized provider groups like Employee Assistance Programs (EAP) or Health Maintenance Organizations (HMO). Otherwise, the distribution of work settings for clinical psychologists has not changed very much over time. These figures clearly spell out a need for academic training programs to prepare clinical psychologists for a business model that requires knowledge in administration and self-promotion so that they are better able to educate the public about access to services as well as the benefit of clinical psychology.

In Table 1.2 you will find information on the typical activities of clinical psychologists and how much time they spend in each activity.

The numbers in Table 1.2 reflect averaged percentages describing the mix of daily activities of psychologists as a function of work setting. A private practitioner on the one hand spends more time on assessment and therapy than the average clinical psychologist, and an academic psychologist spends more time on research and teaching. Anecdotally, the least pleasant change over time reported by psychologists has been the greatly increased need for administration and paperwork given that we are living in an increasingly more litigious world where every action needs to be documented.

While this may all be very interesting, a back-to-basics question is, "how much can I earn as a clinical psychologist?" Organizations like the American Psychological Association make ongoing efforts to learn actual salaries of psychologists (see http://www.apa.org/workforce/publications/09-salaries/index.aspx or similar websites). These figures are likely to be somewhat out-of-date by the time they are accumulated and published. Nevertheless, they are the relatively best source available, and they reveal many pertinent differences between employment settings, location, and salary differences between master's level and doctoral level providers. This knowledge is bound to have a major influence on future clinical psychologists' specific career decisions.

The most transparent sector of practice is that of psychologists who are employees of government or other service agencies. There is not too much variation here in income, and adding years of seniority is associated with only modest gains in income. Limited knowledge is available about earnings in private practice. Even if this information was available, it would be difficult to figure out how many hours these practitioners actually had worked to obtain the incomes. Those billing at top rates may want to downplay their earnings in public to avoid professional jealousy.

Academic careers are somewhat unique because they have a wide range of incomes as a function of seniority and prestige of the institution. A beginning level Assistant Professor typically earns only about half of what a Senior Full Professor can take home; in some universities that spread can be as wide as 3:1. The difference is largely performance-driven because only productive academics get promotions and reach the associated higher pay levels, and it is equally typical that the top performers get annual merit increases. "Productivity" is usually defined as bringing in grant money and publishing articles in scientific journals. Especially in the United States, there is a very wide margin between the pay scales of prestigious, Ivy League-type universities and the smaller, less well-known universities or colleges that may not have graduate programs. In part, this derives from the fact that well-funded research professors can draw part of their salary from research grants, a phenomenon that does not exist in other countries, like Canada or Germany.

Not surprisingly, the earnings of clinical psychologists in private practice are exceedingly variable because they work highly different numbers of hours, with a portion only maintaining a small private practice. Some psychologists work part-time because they are in partial retirement or they may be parents carrying a full load of childcare and home responsibilities at the same time. Also, there is no such thing as a guaranteed 35-hour/week schedule with job security and a benefits package for private practitioners. In many jurisdictions, the billing rates for third-party payer services are fixed by edict or negotiation and can be as far ranging as $50/hour to $200/hour. Otherwise, there is negotiation between psychologist and client. Many use a sliding scale to adjust their fees to the client's ability to pay. Senior psychologists willing to engage in potentially litigious, forensic work involving assessment and court appearances can (and do) occasionally bill in excess of $200/hour. If they are also willing to work long hours and take few holidays, they can generate annual revenues in the range of $300,000–$400,000 from which, however, they have to deduct overhead for office rental and secretarial services, as well as health insurance and pension plan deductions for themselves.

While private practice can be lucrative for those with specialty skills, good business sense, and a willingness to work long hours, it is also more risky than employment (for tips on how to set up and run a private practice see the websites of state/provincial or national psychology associations). One such example with information equally relevant for practice in different countries is found on the website of the Canadian Psychological Association (http://www.cpa.ca/cpasite/userfiles/Documents/publications/PAA%20Guidebook.pdf).

Based on many conversations and observations about the career path of our graduates and colleagues, we strongly suggest not to jump both feet first into private practice immediately upon graduation. A private practice can thrive when the practitioners have long-standing roots in the community, have built up their referral sources, and are known for their particular skills. None of this can happen overnight, and the most effective referrals are via word-of-mouth. For those aspiring to private practice, it is still advised to spend a substantial number of years in employee roles to hone clinical skills and build the necessary connections for referrals to a strong private practice.

Overall, the compensation for a clinical psychologist reflects what is happening elsewhere in our society; safety and protected hours pay less well than long hours and risk-taking. How do psychologists feel about their career choice? A survey of more than 27,000 people in the United States revealed that fewer than half were satisfied with their jobs or careers (http://www.livescience.com/health/070417_job_satisfaction.html). Particularly unhappy were laborers (21%), clothing sales people (24%), food preparers (24%), and cashiers (25%). At the other end of the scale, psychologists were pleased with their choice (67%), and find themselves in a similar neighborhood to special education teachers (70%) and writers (74%) but not quite as high as clergy (87%) or firefighters (80%).

◇ CONCLUSION

This chapter was not so much about facts that students can commit to rote memory than it was a chance to take an inside look into the profession. The vignettes of four different psychologists offered a glimpse into the diversity of activities that clinical psychologists work on. Furthermore, it provided information to help interested students uncover which subfields they might be interested in and figure out what the right balance is (for them as individuals) between direct clinical work, administration, research, and teaching.

◇ ONGOING CONSIDERATIONS

We anticipate that clinical psychologists will continue to differ in their opinions about striking the right balance between clinical skill training and research training (i.e., living up to the scientist-practitioner model). The fact that there is a high demand but limited supply of training spots will not change, and, unfortunately, the gap between the demand for internship training spots relative to training opportunities has recently widened, making it difficult for students to secure a training spot (Robiner, 2006). Academic training programs and service-based clinical psychologists need to work hard to convince other decision-makers in the health care system to sustain this critical training environment.

◇ KEY TERMS LEARNED

Accredited training programs	Professional social workers
Behavioral medicine	Psychiatrists
Clinical psychologist	Psychiatry
Counseling psychologists	Psychologist
Counseling psychology	"Scientist-practitioner"
Distress screening	Social work

◇ THINKING QUESTIONS

1. Which profession is best suited to train psychotherapists?

2. How much research training do clinical psychologists need? More specifically, do they need to be trained to be knowledgeable consumers of research publications or should all clinical psychologists have the skills and drive to expand this literature?

3. Should we have distinct subspecialties of counseling psychology versus clinical psychology?

◇ REFERENCES

Linden, W., Moseley, J. V., & Erskine, Y. (2005). Psychology as a health care profession: Implications for training. *Canadian Psychology, 46*, 179–188.

Norcross, J. C., Karpiak, C. P., & Santoro, S. O. (2005). Clinical psychologists across the years: The division of clinical psychology from 1960 to 2003. *Journal of Clinical Psychology, 61*, 1467–1483.

Robiner, W. N. (2006). The mental health professions: Workforce supply and demand, issues, and challenges. *Clinical Psychology Review, 26*, 600–625.

CHAPTER TWO

BECOMING A CLINICAL PSYCHOLOGIST

CHAPTER OBJECTIVE

This chapter raises issues of immediate and personal concern for many students who work with this textbook in their clinical psychology course. Given that there is more demand for clinical training than there are a supply of training spots, we can at least try to bridge this gap with useful, practical information. When thinking about graduate school as a possible next career step, it requires diligent preparation (Kuther, 2006). First of all, it is important to learn about the type of work that different psychologists do and how these activities suit the student's personality, aspirations, and personal style. In chapter 1, we tried to give "a flavor" of the profession, and you may by now have identified aspects of practice you can really get excited about.

◇ CONSIDERATIONS FOR CAREER PLANNING

When you are planning for a career in the mental health professions, you need to learn about degree options and the job market. Here are key questions to answer:

- In what profession and in what specialty field is there most work?
- How strong is your own academic background? Or, asked differently, how competitive is your application package?
- Will you go for a master's degree (usually 2–3 years of graduate work) or a combined master's and doctoral degree (6–7 years of graduate training)?
- Are you leaning more toward clinical work and less toward research? Then a professional degree (**PsyD**, psychology doctorate) may be your choice. The more you enjoy research, the more you may want to seek out a **PhD** (doctor of philosophy) in a traditional university. As you will see later in this chapter, there are major financial reasons for choosing a traditional, university-based program.

These decisions are very much affected whether or not you possess the academic record needed to gain admission to the type of program you may seek. Also, there is the question of how to pay for needed education and where you may want to, or need to, go to receive this training. In the United States, for example, there are huge differences in tuition costs depending on where the student enrolls. In public institutions, tuition is usually 2× or even 3× higher if you are not a state resident. In the year 2000, the corresponding average rates were US$3,178 versus US$8,416. Count on a steady increase in these fees every year to match inflation. Prestigious private research universities and free-standing PsyD programs may charge over US$20,000 annually for tuition alone. If you are a strong applicant, a well-endowed research university often waives tuition fees but a free-standing PsyD program is usually unable to do that. Tuition fees in Canadian and some other foreign universities by comparison are quite a bargain; tuition fees for Canadian citizens rarely exceed Can $5,000/annually, and in some schools they are completely waived for graduate students. For foreign nationals, rates may be higher but are still unlikely to exceed Can$10,000/annually.

These differential fees, of course, affect the success rates of applicants. The usual formula is the lower the fees, the more students apply; it follows basic rules of supply and demand. Mayne, Norcross, and Sayette (1994) report an overall 10% acceptance rate for APA-accredited clinical psychology programs, but this mean number hides great variability ranging from a low of 6% acceptance in research-oriented PhD programs to a high of 23% acceptance in PsyD programs. Consistent with the rules of supply and demand, 95% of research-oriented PhD programs offered financial assistance but only 37% of PsyD programs did (Sayette, Mayne, & Norcross, 2004).

Mayne and her collaborators provided a densely packed summary table (Table 2.1) of some key distinguishing variables between various types of programs.

Don't be discouraged, the individual probability of admission success is a lot higher than the one for just one specific program because students apply to multiple programs, and those lucky students who receive multiple offers can accept only one, of course. This clears the way for other applicants with slightly weaker records.

◇ CONCRETE PLANNING STEPS

There are many ways one can prepare for the decision on what program to apply to. Here is a little exercise, or a self-test, to get you started. Rather than being preoccupied by what title is given to your intended profession (like "I want to be a **Psychoanalyst**"), it may be better to ask yourself more basic questions about who you are and what you like doing. By thinking forward to where you might want to be 20 years from now, consider the type of work you would want to do to make you happy. Here are some questions to guide this search process:

- Are you the kind of person who enjoys working alone, or are you more in need of a group of people to work with? If you enjoy working alone, then maybe private practice is suitable for you.

TABLE 2.1 Comparisons among APA-Accredited PsyD, Practice-Oriented PhD, and Research-Oriented PhD Programs in Clinical Psychology

Variable	APA-ACCREDITED PsyD PROGRAMS		PRACTICE-ORIENTED AND EQUAL-EMPHASIS PhD PROGRAMS		RESEARCH-ORIENTED PhD PROGRAMS		
	M	SD	M	SD	M	SD	F
Admission statistics							
No. of applications	149.7	81.1	133.7	83.5	168.5	87.4	3.2*
No. of acceptances	57.4^a	39.1	18.5	19.6	14.1	10.8	54.1**
% accepted	41.3^n	19.8	16.8^a	13.9	11.3^a	10.3	66.2**
No. enrolled	33.1^a	20.8	9.9	702	8.6	9.3	64.2**
% enrolled	59.3	13.5	62.7	19.3	60.0	17.2	0.7
Theoretical orientation							
Psychodynamic/ psychoanalytic (%)	29.4	17.7	29.6	23.1	12.0^a	12.5	23.0**
Radical behavioral (%)	7.6	8.4	8.1	11.5	11.1	15.7	1.4
Systems (%)	18.9	10.2	20.6	17.8	14.5	15.9	3.1
Humanistic/ phenomenological (%)	11.2	8.4	11.7	49.0^a	25.0	64.4^a	20.7
Cognitive–behavioral (%)	32.8^a	17.9	49.0^n	25.0	64.4^a	20.7	30.2**
Financial aid							
Tuition waiver only (%)	7.9	16.6	5.2	15.3	2.2	11.8	2.4
Assistantship only (%)	19.5	22.6	25.7	37.4	8.5^a	24.8	6.7**
Both tuition waiver and assistantship	17.5^a	22.6	57.2^a	41.7	84.2^a	31.6	48.0**
Student characteristics							
Women (%)	69.9	8.6	71.6	8.1	70.8	11.1	0.5
Ethnic minority (%)	20.8	16.0	19.7	13.5	18.7	10.1	0.4
Possessed master's (%)	35.2^a	24.8	23.8^a	17.1	17.2^a	11.7	18.5**
Students entering APA internships (%)	74.4^a	25.6	90.8	16.7	95.5	10.0	22.4**
Years to complete degree	5.1^a	0.7	6.1	0.8	6.2	0.9	27.7**

Note: Sample sizes were 40–41 for APA-accredited PsyD programs, 71–74 for practice-oriented and equal-emphasis PhD programs, and 80–85 for research-oriented PhD programs.
[a]This group differs significantly from all other groups (p < .05 by Newman–Keuls procedure).
*p < .05, **p < .01.

- Are you prepared for the rewards and challenges of a leadership position, or are you happy to share your work with a group of like-minded people? If you seek leadership, you may want to accept administrative responsibilities, engage in advocacy for the profession, seek grant finding, and build a research laboratory.

- Are you comfortable with routines, or do you thrive on novelty, risk, and innovation? The routine seeker may like a government and agency job with clear expectations best.

- Are you willing to work long hours and take chances to gain a large income, or do you prefer to have a job that pays reasonably well and offers benefits and stability; are you willing to accept limitations of opportunity for growth by trading it for security? The psychologists willing to work long hours may be the ones geared for a busy private practice.

- Do you plan to have a family, and if so, how much time do you want to devote to work versus family? This decision may require a discussion and agreement between the psychologist and her life-partner. It could consist of an agreement that one partner puts his ambitions on hold and deals more with family issues until his partner has obtained a tenured position in a university; then they reverse the roles and balance of responsibilities for the sake of fairness.

The answers to these kinds of questions may partly derive from having experiences in various part-time jobs even if they are not directly related to psychology. You can also learn from conversations with family and friends. Or, if you were planning a career in a field that sounds good from a distance, but that you have little direct knowledge of, it is an excellent idea to job-shadow for a day. You may be surprised how many people, including total strangers, will agree to let you do that simply because they are proud of their own profession. Once you figure out what type of work and kind of work environment you like best, it is time to think about what academic qualifications you will need to gain admission to the training program that maximizes your own strengths and preferences.

Another very pragmatic issue is whether or not you are geographically mobile. Given that admission to graduate school is usually quite competitive, you should apply to multiple programs (we usually recommend at least 10) including some that are not in your hometown or even your home state or province. However, with applications fees probably averaging $100 each, this becomes quite an investment. If you are in a committed relationship, you need to think about, and discuss with your partner, what is possible and reasonable for you and your partner. If you had an initial knee-jerk attitude about a particular program (like "I could never live there because the winter is too cold"), applicants often see such a program when it has actually offered them admission in a new, appealing light. For a detailed listing of available programs and entry requirements, see the APA Guide to Graduate Study (APA, 2010).

Once you are clear for yourself in which direction you want to go and where you might want to apply, you can focus on building your application package. Having ample lead time is pivotal; a strong application package is the result of years of careful forward-directed planning.

◇ MAXIMIZING YOUR ACADEMIC PREPARATION AND BUILDING THE BEST POSSIBLE APPLICATION PACKAGE

Even if you apply to many different universities, you will be expected to assemble a similar-looking application package, typically requiring you to provide the following information:

1. An application form that is unique to the university to which the student applies

2. Official transcripts from all secondary institutions you have attended

3. Official documentation from the Educational Testing Service that you have completed the graduate record examination (GRE) with both the general test (and its verbal, quantitative, and analytical subsections) and the psychology subject test

4. Three letters of recommendation

5. A statement of interest

Let us discuss each component and what you can do to make it as strong as possible.

Application Forms

Not much needs to be said other than that neatness and completeness are important. There is usually little opportunity to market yourself here. Provide as much contact information as possible. Try not to leave boxes or fields in your form empty. For example, if you are asked for awards you have received you may be too modest to mention the $100 travel award to present your honor's thesis at a conference or the book prize for the best essay in the history of psychology class you took last year. Our tip: Do mention them. If you are asked for publications in peer-reviewed journals and you do not have any, this field needs to be left blank, of course. Another tip: If you have a paper under review, do list it, but make sure that it does not appear in the section under "publications" if it has not yet survived peer review. This kind of boasting is inappropriate and may reduce your credibility.

Grade-Point Averages

The most likely formats for reporting academic grades are letter grades (particularly true in the United States) and percentage grades. We will comment on both separately because there is no agreed-upon formula how one of these can be converted into the other. Just to clarify this point, a student who has consistently obtained grades between 75% and 78% will of course end up with a 76.5% or a grade-point average (GPA) of 3.0. The exact same percentage could also lead to a better GPA of 3.5 if this student had a good number of courses in which she obtained a letter grade of A and a similar number of courses where she obtained grades of B− or C. Not surprisingly, a GPA of 3.5 looks noticeably stronger than one of 3.0. Thus letter grades can be a bit deceiving. Percentage grades are less ambiguous because they employ no drastic cutoff values even though getting a 79% in a course is a rather frustrating experience when 80% would have meant an "A" equivalent in the letter grade system.

As a rule of thumb, it is unlikely that a student will be successful with an application to a prestigious clinical or counseling psychology program if he or she does not have a GPA of at least 3.5 (but even here there are exceptions). The corresponding percentage number would be around 80%. It is considerably easier to obtain offers of admission from professional schools typically offering master's or PsyD degrees where the success rate of applications may be as high as 40%. To some degree, students can make up for weak GPAs by strong performance on the GRE. Also, knowledge of performance on the GRE (which is fully standardized for all test writers) helps the program admissions committees judge to what degree some universities engage in grade inflation or are very conservative in their grading practices. Students graduating from universities that are known to be conservative graders often fear that they are disadvantaged relative to graduates from universities with liberal grading patterns. The obtained scores on the GRE are very helpful in revealing such patterns and allow corresponding adjustments to be made. Professors (like us) who have participated in many admission decisions have found that students with a mediocre performances on the GRE but strong academic performances (as reflected by high GPAs) may actually be less promising than applicants from University X with only moderately strong grade-point averages but routinely strong performances on the GRE. In the latter case, the faculty will know that a lower grade from University X is still descriptive of a very strong student. The take-home message regarding grades is, of course, obvious: It is important to do well throughout one's entire undergraduate career. It is fairly typical that students do much better in years three and four than they did in year one when they needed to take lots of required courses and were struggling to adjust to university life.

Students often ask: "Will the admissions committee look at my overall GPA or that of only the last two years?" The answer is that anybody reading a student's application will see the entire academic transcript at once and is likely to form a first impression of the student. In addition, of course, the admission secretaries may formally compute GPAs based on the transcripts provided; often the GPA is computed and printed right onto the transcripts. Strategically, this means that students should withdraw early from a course in which they fear failure (either for reasons of personal emergencies or lack of giftedness in a particular domain). A letter grade of "F" does not look well in such a transcript. Sometimes, programs compute two sets of GPAs for consideration, one for the entire undergraduate years, and another one for the last two years in which students typically focused on their majors.

One question, often asked, is whether taking additional courses as an unclassified student is recommended to boost a GPA. Our personal view is that this rarely pays off. First of all, it would be naive to presume that in a fifth year, a student will perform dramatically different from he has in the four years prior. Also, the mathematical averaging process is not to his advantage. If a student had a 75% GPA resulting from 40 different one-semester courses taken in years 1–4 and now added another 8 one-semester courses where he succeeded in obtaining an average grade of 85%, he would still have increased his overall GPA by only 2%, and it would have taken an entire year to achieve this relatively small gain.

Having said that, students may have never taken a course in the biological basis of psychology and this is a notable gap in their academic record. In this case, it would make good sense to take such a course later. Or, a student may have done poorly in an undergraduate statistics course and feels that this is a blemish on his record that may impact graduate school admission chances (rightly so). He also knows that he could perform much better when he is not bogged down with having to juggle two part-time jobs and five other courses at the same time. In this case, it may indeed be wise to take this course over.

Another related question is whether one needs to have an undergraduate degree with a psychology major to be able to apply to a clinical psychology graduate program. While it is undoubtedly recommended to have a psychology undergraduate degree, and some programs are sticky about it, it is not absolutely necessary. In our own program, we have taken on students who were majors in computer science, in music, in social work, or in sociology. When that was the case, it did make sense for the students to have taken additional courses in psychology to make sure that they are on the same level of knowledge in their chosen field when competing with others for graduate school, and also to prevent finding themselves at a grave disadvantage if indeed they are accepted to graduate school and are sharing seminars with other graduate students who had taken five times as many undergraduate psychology courses.

◇ GRADUATE RECORD EXAMINATION

The **GRE** is understandably unpopular in the eyes of many students because it is effectively a one-shot test of considerable importance where student performances are directly compared with those of many others. It is also quite expensive. There are some programs that do not place great emphasis on GRE scores; however, most programs do. Because it is a single test occasion, one needs to seriously prepare for it to assure maximal performance on the test day.

One part of the GRE is referred to as the *subject test*, and if you are applying to psychology, you may be writing the psychology subject test. Note, however, that there is general trend to move away from requiring subject tests because they are seen as redundant with grades in psychology courses. The psychology subject test is a multiple-choice test much like what you are familiar with from your undergraduate program; students who have obtained good grades in their psychology courses also tend to do well in this subject test. If students' grades in psychology courses are stronger than their performance on the GRE psychology subject test, then readers of the student's application are more likely to judge student's potential by their grades rather than by the GRE subtest. If, however, you apply to graduate school and did not major in psychology as an undergraduate, then the subject test performance allows the admissions committee to compare the readiness of the applicant with that of students who have taken many more psychology courses. In this case, it is particularly useful to prepare for the subject test. To assist with preparation, there are thick, reasonably priced, and very useful softcover texts sold in university bookstores. In larger cities, there may be useful courses offered by commercial test preparation agencies. At a minimum, we recommend that prior to actually writing the GRE, students complete the practice tests in the preparation books to familiarize themselves with the material and to obtain feedback on their performance. Having realistic performance feedback allows you to judge how much preparation may be needed prior to writing the actual test.

Strong performance on the general GRE test tends to be of greater importance than the actual subject test performance. The GRE has three sections, each rated on a 0–800-point scale and also expressed as percentile performance relative to how well other test takers performed. The **verbal section** assesses the candidate's vocabulary, comprehension, and overall grasp of the language. The **quantitative section** taps mathematical ability and comprises test questions on mathematical materials that were likely taught in early- to mid-high school. The format of the **analytical section** has undergone a lot of changes and was at some point based on multiple-choice tests similar to what students might find in admissions tests to law school. In the early 2000s, the multiple-choice format was replaced by an essay, which is graded on a 0–6 scale. Given the many changes that the analytical subtest has undergone in past years, it is difficult to advise people on how to prepare for it. The nature of the verbal and quantitative test sections has changed very little over the years; these sections use multiple-choice formats. Many universities will require a minimal achievement on the combined verbal/quantitative subtests; the cutoffs can range from 1000 to 1200. Each student's performance is not only expressed in absolute scores on this 800-point scale but is compared with the performance of others who have written the same test and is then expressed as a percentile score. Because the difficulty levels of the various forms of the GRE can vary, admissions committees rely mostly on these percentile scores to make judgments about a student's potential.

One question frequently asked by students who have written the GRE is "what absolute number or percentile rank is a safe bet for admission?" This is tough to answer because each program has its own standards and the degree of competition for the limited number of training spots fluctuates somewhat from year to year. A suggestion based on many years of reading graduate school applications is that students who scored on average in the 80th percentile or better should not consider rewriting the test in the hope to improve their score; they probably won't. A performance of over 80th percentile is considered excellent and promising. Students averaging less than 50th percentile are unlikely to get admitted, and performance on any subtest of less than the 50th percentile may also be problematic.

A few observations are offered to help interpret the test scores and assist with test preparation efforts. The verbal test scores tend to be very stable over a lifetime and are a reflection of the test taker's literacy and erudition. Students who have done a fair bit of reading as a hobby do noticeably better than those who spent much of their childhood in front of the television. Parts of the test evaluate knowledge of sophisticated vocabulary that often has Greek or Latin roots (think of words like "paramount," "expedient," "punctilious," or "obstreperous"). To some degree this knowledge can be improved by compiling word lists and learning them like vocabulary in a foreign language. The Reader's Digest, for example, offers 20 such terms in a quiz form at the beginning of each edition; also there are websites that offer assistance (try http://www.wordsmith.org or http://www.bestvocab.com). Other parts of the verbal subtest are more difficult to prepare for, and there is a limited amount of gain to be expected from preparing for the GRE verbal subtest.

Unlike the verbal subtest, the quantitative subtest is much more easily influenced by preparation, and performance is greatly predictable by (a) how long ago the test taker has covered this material in high school and (b) how well he or she did in math at that time. In preparation for this test, it is relatively easy to review math formulas and principles by pulling out old high school math books or GRE preparation books. A test taker who did poorly on the quantitative section first time around has an excellent chance of improving this score when he or she takes the test again after relearning this material. At times, students do not do well in this subtest despite the fact that they had obtained good grades in undergraduate statistics courses. The admissions committees may still look favorably at such candidates because the committees tend to believe that having obtained an "A" twice in a semester-long course is a more meaningful indicator of a student's statistics learning potential than is performance on a single, one-shot test like the GRE.

Many students writing the GRE will have scores falling between the problematic cutoff of 50th percentile and the relative safety of a >80% score, and they need to make a decision for themselves whether they want to spend the time and money to prepare better and then rewrite the test. This decision should be based on a realistic assessment of what happened when they took the GRE the first time. If a student had been foggy-headed because of the party the night before or recovering from a nasty flu, then her performance may have underestimated her true ability. If, however, she has the perception that she did as well as she could, then she might decide to just let it be.

Students are strongly advised to plan the timing of writing the GRE so that they can send test scores to the universities in time (namely, prior to the application deadline). And it is even better to take the test so early that students can take it again if they are unhappy with their first test scores, and still get the results from their repeated test to the universities on time.

One additional note of caution is that the GRE is of questionable validity for applicants for whom English is a second language. This is particularly true for the verbal subscale. If a student with English as a second language applies from outside the country, the universities usually expect these applicants to also have written the test of English as a foreign language (TOEFL), and a performance of 550–600 (the best possible score is 800) is expected. When second language applicants do show a predictable weak performance on the verbal subtest, it may be especially necessary that the writers of reference letters qualitatively assess and comment on the student's ability to perform in English, to make up for the seemingly flawed standard test performance on the GRE.

The Statement of Interest

Applicants are expected to write a personalized essay with each application, and we urge you to invest a fair bit of time in preparing this essay. A good length is usually about two pages in which applicants will want to strike a good balance between pointing out how they have developed their career interests, how they have systematically prepared for graduate school, what they want to do for the rest of their career, and which topics within clinical psychology they find particularly exciting (Forsyth & Wolfert, 1999). It is a good idea to stress how a particular school that students are applying to will help meet those needs. The statement of interest is also an opportunity to demonstrate how applicants have met the specific requirements and represent a strong match with the mission statements of the universities they are applying to. It is not wise to talk about very narrow interests that few, if any, of the faculty may share with the applicant. For example, applicants will predictably run into trouble finding a mentor when they tell all the universities that they are interested in studying only cognitive distortions in bald, middle-aged men who had parents with alcohol problems. Nor should applicants claim that they are willing to work on any topic as long as the university only admits them. It is more opportune to tell the story about how you've been fascinated by the problem of, for example, substance abuse, that you have taken courses to help understand the social and biological causes of substance abuse, and that you have done volunteer work in a local shelter for substance abusers. There is no need to point out that you learned about the disastrous effects of chronic substance abuse in your own family. Such a topic may be of interest to a number of faculty in a reasonably sized department, and they may clamor to work with the student who has been so thoughtful in preparing the application. While it is recommended to make this a clearly personal statement, it is not advisable to elaborate on great personal catastrophes like having been hospitalized six times for anorexia or having survived abusive parenting. Make sure that your statement of interest is proofread by a professor you work with or maybe a graduate student.

Many universities follow a mentor model where the entire admissions process is characterized by a gradual matching of student interests to those of a particular faculty member who will then agree to be a mentor to this incoming student. When programs follow this model, it is very useful to write early (like 3 to 6 months prior to the application deadline) to all the individuals whom students are considering as mentors and ask them whether or not they are prepared to take on a new student in the following year. On this occasion, potential applicants can also point out their overlapping interests and may even include a copy of their résumé. It may very well be that this faculty member is going on sabbatical next year, or has just taken on a new student, and has no intention of taking you on, irrespective of how brilliant you are. If there's no other mentor of interest in this particular department, the applicant might otherwise have wasted quite a bit of time and money to apply to this program. The great majority of faculty members we know are likely to give you a swift answer to this question although they will not comment on your chances of admission at this time.

Recall that we said earlier to carefully read the mission statements for clinical training programs. If a mission statement reads, for example, that a program in your hometown has a strong research component, and you happen to not care much about research but would still like to get a degree from this program simply because you do not want to move, you are about to deceive yourself and the faculty. This kind of self-deception sets you up for a miserable experience. It is strongly discouraged to apply to programs whose mission and philosophy are mismatched to your own.

Letters of Reference

Letters of reference are considered important because they provide an opportunity for readers to learn something about applicants that is not apparent in standardized GPAs and GRE scores. Especially for clinical programs, the faculty are concerned about social skills and interpersonal sensitivity of applicants given that this information does not come through in academic transcripts. The very fact that at some point senior psychologists will be needed to write reference letters for you also means that you need to make an effort to get to know individuals who would be good as authors for your reference letters in the future. This is one of many reasons why students volunteer or do paid work as a research assistant or volunteer in their community. If you approach a professor with whom you and 399 other students have taken a course, this person cannot write a meaningful reference letter. Only professors for whom you have worked as a research assistant or who have been involved in your honor's program will be able to provide meaningful commentary. References from friends of the family or the neighbors whose children you have babysat are totally unsuitable. They cannot speak to the probability of your professional success. Try to get as many letters of reference from university professors because (a) some of the people reading your reference letters may actually know the letter writer and trust his or her judgment and (b) professors are very familiar with the admissions process and tend to write particularly strong letters on your behalf. When you do ask for letters of reference, ask the specific question: "Would you be willing to write me a *good* reference letter for admission to a clinical program?" Then listen carefully to the answer; if this professor is reluctant and provides all kinds of qualifiers and conditions, he or she may be telling you that that the resulting letter may not be a strong one although he or she is principally willing to write one. In this case, choosing an alternative letter writer is better. Give people at least 2 to 3 weeks notice because you cannot expect that they drop everything for you and create such a letter from one day to the next. This would be unreasonable and will create a bad ambience that can affect the praise you might have otherwise received in the letter itself. Because professors are likely to have to write letters for many different people, each of whom applies to 12 or more programs, it is important to make it very easy for them by carefully preparing application packages, prestamping envelopes, providing all addresses, giving detailed instructions, pointing out deadlines, and providing clear information about which letters are to be sent directly to the universities and which should be sealed and returned to the applicant.

Research or Clinical Experience?

The most important response to this question is that any experience is highly appreciated because it teaches useful skills and demonstrates that someone has initiative. Having experience in both domains is of course preferable to having experience in only one. An important aspect to consider is the nature of the program that the student is applying to, and it will come as no surprise that a strongly research-oriented program will favor the research experience or that the more practitioner-oriented programs are likely to favor the practical experience. If one had to choose one over the other, our suggestion is to seek research experience because it brings potential graduate school applicants into closer contact with faculty who could write reference letters and ensures that students will spend at least some of their time interacting with graduate students who can provide them with tips and advice on how to get into graduate school and how to survive once you are there.

Timing Issues

In North America, there is a widely accepted agreement that application deadlines are mostly in December or January and that programs must make their first round of offers of admission no later than April 1. This means that the months of February and March are critical. Programs interested in particular students need to be able to quickly get hold of applicants to either invite them to come for interviews or conduct interviews over the telephone. Although it is unfortunately often a financial and logistical burden for students to fly, on short notice, to a different state or province for an interview, the applicants are strongly advised to attend if they are serious about this particular program. Whenever applicants are interacting with individual faculty who may serve as mentors or members of admissions committees, they should have some familiarity with the university and this person's work. For many students, this time period from application to actual admission decisions represents an emotional roller coaster because letters of rejection will arrive in the mail and, even if some programs make an effort to word these letters kindly, a rejection still means a painful "no." On the other hand, this situation may remind one of the old saying: "You cannot win in the lottery if you don't buy a ticket," and this means that students will also receive indications of interest, in some fortunate cases, from more than one of the universities to which they have applied. When students actually feel that they are being pursued by prestigious academic programs rather than being the beggars themselves, it can be quite an emotional high and a moment of justified personal pride. Students with multiple offers have the opportunity to do a bit of diplomatic bargaining about the financial packages offered by various universities.

At this time, it is strongly suggested that students who have applied to multiple programs also have established a clear hierarchy of the programs which they consider most attractive. If a student has applied to 12 programs, and was fortunate to receive offers from the ones ranked 11th, 4th, and 3rd, then it makes sense to focus on the top two choices and let the other program quickly know that he or she will not come. This will make other applicants with slightly weaker records very happy because they can now be considered without further delay. It is then recommended to visit those top two choices in person if that has not already happened, and to learn as much as possible about the program regarding features that are not described in the program brochures. For example, we think it is extremely smart to contact one or more graduate students in each of these programs and ask them questions about the inside scoop, like who are the most popular supervisors, how many students end up leaving the program without getting a degree, how much intellectual, financial, and emotional support programs provide, and what the quality of life is on a day-to-day basis. Once you know all these things, you are ready to make your decision.

Getting the Most Out of Graduate School

There are a number of good books and articles written about how to thrive and survive in graduate school, and they can be easily located using various web search engines. The experience of graduate school can vary greatly from one student to the next as a function of whether the student is well matched to the program and to his or her particular supervisor. Many students experience graduate school as demanding but also exciting because they enjoy the interaction with their classmates and the faculty and the intellectual stimulation and prestige of a major university. Of course, successful students will tell you that they have worked at least 60, if not 80, hours a week, but they also report the thrill of finally doing something practical, that is interesting, to actually seeing patients (rather than reading about them), and working on ideas and projects that they can clearly identify as their own.

Among many tips for doing well in graduate school are as follows:

1. Do not let unresolved situations drag on.
2. Communicate clearly and early with supervisors about problems and solicit their help.
3. Fully use supervisors and other students as supports and make plans together.
4. Get input from other students and friends to resolve problematic issues that can arise.

The big shift from undergraduate to graduate school is that no one can hide. In a graduate course with six students, everybody knows if you're not there or show up late on a regular basis. If you felt that it was difficult to juggle many balls as an undergraduate student, you better get used to it in graduate school, and later on as a professional. You need to learn to prioritize and produce high-quality products in limited time and not perfect products in unlimited time. The single biggest potential stumbling block is your own research, as programs typically require a master's and a PhD thesis. This is new territory, and the typical graduate student underestimates how long this process can take and how many time-consuming logistical hurdles have to be jumped over (e.g., getting ethics approval on a controversial study or recruiting 200 participants who are left-handed, depressed, and between 20 and 40 years old). Really good supervisors are very assertive about not letting students take on projects that cannot be completed with a good level of quality in a reasonable amount of time.

The good news about most graduate programs is that the faculty sees you as an investment; they have carefully chosen you from a very large pool of applicants because they believe you are bright and promising. Even if they do not tell you this very often, they think highly of you and want to see you succeed. Having graduated a first-class PhD is a source of great pride for academic supervisors. Also, program faculty often work hard to find financial support for students because they want to see them make swift progress and not get sidetracked with having to earn a living by working part-time in a coffee shop or burger joint.

Graduates of scientist-practitioner programs have the great advantage that at this stage: All kinds of career options are open to them. They can go for some more specialty training at the postdoctoral level, set up a private practice (although not recommended at this level), apply for academic or hospital jobs, teach, or seek out consultancies.

Postdoctoral Training

In nonclinical domains of psychology, there are few well-developed career tracks, and most graduates target academic careers. It has become standard practice to prepare for these careers by completing additional training at the postdoctoral level because it offers additional time and opportunity to boost one's publishing record and acquire specialty skills. For people with degrees in clinical psychology, this is less typical because not all licensing bodies require postdoctoral training although it is more often the norm than not. The degree to which supervised postdoctoral training is necessary for licensure varies from one state or province to another, and candidates need to carefully study and compare these differences in requirements. There is a lot of ambivalence in the profession about the practical aspects and the need for postdoctoral training because it takes a significant amount of time, during which students earn little or no money.

So, should you do a postdoc after all? If you have broad-based clinical training but have identified a particular specialty area that you would like to practice in for the rest of your life, you might want to seek out postdoctoral training to make yourself look particularly competitive in this specialty area. A student from a generalist training program in clinical psychology might have discovered that he or she is really keen on neuropsychology and needs more training via a postdoc. If you are heading for an academic career, a postdoc can be a great opportunity to learn new techniques, develop a specialty, boost the publication record and be seen as a hot commodity when applying for tenure-track jobs. For others, the main interest is to simply get out of school and into the labor market. If the state where you want to live and practice requires postdoctoral training, you will need to do it, of course.

Getting Licensed

In North America and many other jurisdictions, clinical psychologists are expected to be licensed (also referred to as registered or chartered) to practice. Governments have put such licensing requirements in place to protect the public from harm that may arise from incompetent or unethical practice. This also means that insurance carriers are unlikely to make payments for psychological services to anybody who is not licensed. Therefore, getting registered or licensed is vital to the financial well-being of psychologists in the marketplace. Unfortunately, this is neither a simple, quick, or cheap process. Applicants need to carefully document all their practical experience, provide transcripts, letters supporting their good character, have a criminal record check, write a standardized licensing exam (the examination for the professional practice in professional psychology [EPPP]), and reach a passing score (usually 70%). Some jurisdictions also require a jurisprudence exam for licensing. On the web, one readily finds information about how well graduates from various programs are doing on the EPPP (http://www.socialpsychology.org/clinrank1997.htm), and it is well established that the highest average performance is seen in graduates from research-oriented PhD programs and noticeable weaker scores are seen in graduates from free-standing PsyD programs (Yu et al., 1997). A website released in 2008 (http://web.uvic.ca/psyc/clinical/epppresults.html) informs readers that the average performance of all doctoral level test takers in all jurisdictions of the Association of State Professional Psychology Boards was 67.4%, whereas the top performing program reached as high as an 84% correct rate. The overall averaged success rate for all Canadian doctoral graduates in clinical psychology programs was 80%.

Once registered or licensed, practitioners are expected to engage in ongoing continuing education and avoid getting into problematic situations that may tempt patients to forward complaints about incompetent or unethical behavior on the part of the psychologist. Even if such a complaint does not lead to disbarment (it rarely does), the process is lengthy, expensive, and beset with uncertainty and fear. Paying good attention to chapter 4 on ethics in this book can assist you in avoiding such trouble and save you much money.

Going through a complaints process can be draining, and nothing is smarter than trying to practice in such a fashion that complaints are not forthcoming at all. Many complaints are around issues of confidentiality, perceived competence, and recordkeeping. A therapist found guilty of sexual misconduct cannot easily claim ignorance given the intense and unequivocal teaching on this topic: No, you cannot have sex with your clients! (see chapter 4 on ethics). Sexual impropriety complaints are those most likely to result in loss of license.

Once you have been in practice (as an employee or self-employed), avoiding the risk for *burnout* requires preparation and planning. Burnout is especially likely if you are a solo practitioner and are highly specialized working with the same type of problems and clients for a long time. Anecdotal evidence clearly suggests that engaging in a variety of professional tasks, participating in regular upgrades of skills, interacting regularly with a network of your peers, volunteering for your profession as an examiner or as a board or committee member of a state association, and maybe participating in supervision and training of younger colleagues are all activities that help to prevent burnout and maximize the enjoyment of the career choice of clinical psychologist.

◇ CONCLUSION

This chapter provided details and tips on the process of applying for graduate school, and we hope that some of the tips may also help improve the student's chances. Furthermore, steps were described how to start a career after completion of graduate school and how to enjoy a lifelong career in clinical psychology.

◇ ONGOING CONSIDERATIONS

There is much disagreement among the faculty of varying academic training programs about how much emphasis to place on GRE scores. At the level of personal opinion, the authors of this textbook find it very difficult to make good use of the analytical test portion of the GRE in making decision about applicants. The debate over the usefulness of the GRE will continue, and some subtests may see further changes in their format. For future psychologists there will be a continuing need to plan their career well ahead of time. It is surprising how much time is involved in getting the most out of this planning process and in maximizing opportunities. Candidates have to make difficult, very personal choices regarding PsyD or PhD in clinical psychology or counseling psychology as well as where to apply.

◇ KEY TERMS LEARNED

Analytical section
Graduate record examination (GRE)
PhD
Psychoanalyst

PsyD
Quantitative section
Verbal section

◇ THINKING QUESTIONS

This chapter is not well suited as the basis for thinking or exam questions because there is so much opinion offered here that is based on experience rather than "facts to be learned."

◇ REFERENCES

American Psychological Association (Corporate Author) (2010). *Graduate Study in Psychology*, Washington, D.C.

Forsyth, J. P., & Wulfert, E. (1999). Applying to doctoral training programs in clinical psychology: Writing an effective personal statement. *The Behavior Therapist, 22*, 113–115.

Kuther, T. L. (2006). *Your career in psychology: Clinical and counseling psychology*. Belmont, CA: Thompson Wadsworth.

Mayne, T. J., Norcross, J. C., & Sayette, M. A. (1994). Admission requirements, acceptance rates, and financial assistance in clinical psychology programs: Diversity across the practice research continuum. *American Psychologist, 49*, 605–611.

Sayette, M. A., Mayne, T. J., & Norcross, J. C. (2004). *Insider's guide to graduate programs in clinical and counseling psychology*. New York: Guilford Press.

Yu, L. M., Rinaldi, S. A., Templer, D. I., Colbert, L. A., Siscoe, K., & Van Patten, K. (1997). Score on the examination for professional practice in psychology as a function of attributes of clinical psychology graduate programs. *Psychological Science, 8*, 347–350.

CHAPTER THREE

METHODS FOR RESEARCH AND EVALUATION

CHAPTER OBJECTIVE

The reader will have likely received basic training in research methodology prior to taking course work in clinical psychology. Clinical psychology pulls together a number of different knowledge domains from psychology at large and applies them to real-world problems and populations. Therefore, there is inevitable overlap in the methods used in the practice of clinical psychology and those used to acquire core knowledge in psychology. General principles of experimentation in the laboratory are least relevant in this context and will not receive much attention here (for a review we recommend Howitt, 2005; Rosnow & Rosenthal, 2001). This chapter will therefore focus on research methods and introduce the relevant concepts that clinical psychologists should be familiar with. A clinical psychologist should be particularly familiar with:

- Test development and test validation
- Evaluations of the effects of treatments and innovative clinical practices
- Methods of research on psychopathological mechanisms

✧ CHAPTER ORGANIZATION

Clinical psychology is a vibrant field that continuously renews itself and becomes involved in many knowledge applications, including being called on to add to validation work on existing tests and also to develop new tests. Recall that in chapter 1 you read about psychologist A, who was supposed to develop a screening tool for distress in cancer patients. In addition, researchers are concerned with documenting the process of change in psychotherapy, helping us to better understand who gets better and by what process, as well as figuring out to what degree therapy success has made individuals fully functional again. This information, in turn, is then taught to the next generation of clinical psychologists.

Making research directly serve the improvement of clinical practice sets clinical psychology apart from other branches of psychology. On the one hand clinicians want to know when and how their clients are getting better, and from a larger perspective, psychologists need to make a case for the cost-effectiveness of their work to health care administrators and policymakers. Those psychologists involved in health care will have learned over the last few decades that professions that can demonstrate their cost-effectiveness are somewhat protected against cutbacks and sudden policy changes.

The following methods that will be elaborated on in this chapter are quite relevant for clinical practitioners and researchers:

Observational methods become the basic skills for conducting structured clinical interviews to learn from patients by carefully observing them in session or in their natural environments.

Surveys and **questionnaires** are frequently used in research and clinical assessment as self-report tools of personality and psychopathology. When psychologists work with standardized assessment tools (and they should), it is critical that they are aware of a tool's potential and limitations. It is unethical to use measurement tools that are not suitable for a given client or for presenting a problem, and in some circumstances, especially in court cases, psychologists are queried in great detail about the psychometric properties of tests they have used to aid in their decision-making.

Single case study methodologies are especially suitable when therapists work with new methods or new types of clients and want to evaluate how clients respond to innovative or experimental interventions. Knowledge thus acquired can then guide their future work with similar patients or problems and lead to the development of more formal clinical trial protocols and treatment manuals.

Therapy outcome studies are pivotal to document the value of existing or novel clinical interventions and help understand why and how interventions work. Therapy outcome can be studied with varying degrees of sophistication where randomized, controlled clinical trials are considered the gold standard for creating knowledge that can be trusted to drive clinical practice.

This chapter will therefore begin with a section on psychometrics and test development, then focus on research designs that help to document the outcome of therapy, and lastly, pay attention to research designs that can convince outsiders that clinical psychologists have been doing valuable work.

◇ PROPERTIES OF PSYCHOLOGICAL TESTS

When well-trained clinical psychologists read a manuscript in which the authors bluntly state that, "in this study we used the *xyz* test of depression that is reliable and valid" they see red, and so they should. Such a glib glossing over a very complex process of determining test reliability and validity is a disservice to the profession and is also considered sloppy. How can reliability and validity be established, and when it does exist, how should it be described?

Reliability

Reliability refers to a test's ability to produce the same results over its repeated administrations. There are many subforms of reliability but not all of them are applicable to every test. The degree of reliability a test possesses is described by the "reliability coefficient" or coefficient r, for which scores range from 0 to 1.00, with high scores indicating high reliability. Interpretation of reliability coefficients is not as simple as it may appear at the outset.

Especially when it comes to observation of behavior, it needs to be recognized that human observers themselves have been shaped through their values, personal experiences, and habits. When we try to use human observers and maximize their reliability, the possibility of observer disagreement needs to be considered from the beginning.

A good example for illustrating inter-rater reliability is that of a behavioral coding system for aggressive behaviors in children. Researchers may want to observe and videotape children in their natural environment; this can actually be done without the children paying much attention, which in turn increases the trustworthiness of results. When the children don't know that they are being observed, they're not likely trying to show their best behavior but are typically just themselves. In order to have a meaningful test, researchers need to define in behavioral terms what observers are expected to watch out for; this is the foundation of a reliable, structured coding system. Asking a coder whether or not a child behaved "aggressively" is problematic because "aggressive" can mean different things to different observers, which can lead to low inter-rater reliability (the degree of agreement between two or more parallel observers). Concrete behavior descriptions like "pushed other children," "didn't listen," and "interrupted when others were talking" are more useful because they are distinct, overt behaviors that different observers are still likely to perceive the same way. To illustrate how this works, Table 3.1 shows items from the direct observation form (DOF) of the child behavior coding system developed by Achenbach (1986).

It is critical to the usefulness of a coding system that the observers notice the same behaviors and have similar views of the frequency or intensity. Because each observer brings to the task his or her own learning history and values, it is not safe to see even diligent observers as absolutely objective. They need to be trained to have the same understanding of what to look for and to push aside their personalized interpretations; observers need to agree on how often a distinct behavior like "hitting" may have happened during a given time. If researchers have trained their observers to extract the same information, then **inter-rater reliability** has been established. It is usually described on a scale from 0 to 1.0, using the correlation coefficient r or the methodologically more sophisticated coefficient "kappa" (Cohen, 1960). The kappa coefficient takes into account that raters can agree on the presence or absence of the same behavior, but also have one observer claim that the behavior was present while the other failed to see it. This translates into four possibilities: both observers agree the behavior was present, both agree it was absent, observer A thinks the behavior was seen but B disagrees, and vice versa. The kappa coefficient is computed using the following formula:

The value of kappa is defined as:

$$\kappa = \frac{p_o - p_e}{1 - p_e}$$

TABLE 3.1 Achenbach Child Behavior Checklist

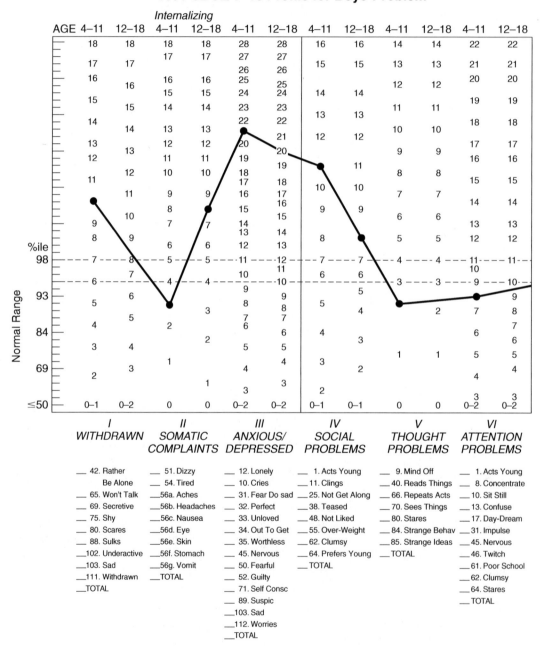

where p_o is the observed frequency of a behavior and p_e the expected or predicted probability by chance. The observer ratings should be independent of each other, and independence implies that pairs of raters agree about as often as two pairs of people who have flipped coins to make their ratings would. The maximum value for kappa occurs when the observed level of agreement is 1.0, which makes the numerator as large as the denominator. As the observed probability of agreement declines, the numerator declines. It is possible for kappa to be negative, but this rarely happens. In such a case, the value of kappa implies that there is no agreement between the two rates. Rater training usually proceeds until inter-rater reliability is at least 0.8. Experienced researchers know that it takes quite a bit of time and effort to train observers to achieve this level of reliability. When new coding systems are used, it is sometimes necessary to stop rater training when it takes too long to achieve a good level of agreement. In this case, researchers need better operational definitions of the behaviors to be coded, and coder training will need to restart.

When applying a behavioral coding system in clinical practice or research, it is ideal to have two or more observers present at all times to record the target behaviors. However, this practice is very expensive and not always realistic. Alternatively, the behaviors are recorded on videotape for rating later in a quiet environment. This process assures that critical behaviors are not missed because they happened too quickly or were subtle. Even in professional sports it is now common practice to record a game or performance so that the referees can replay critical moments. A generally accepted compromise is that one well-trained observer does all the ratings based on videotapes (if necessary, replaying the tape multiple times), and a second rater later extracts at random 10 or 20% of these videotapes and rates them again so as to assure that the primary rater had accurately used the coding system.

While inter-rater reliability may take time and money to reach acceptable levels, this is less of a problem in self-evaluations of behavior where people provide information about themselves via a standardized test or score sheet. This might be a test anxiety evaluation on a scale from 1 to 5, using items like this: "During the night before an exam I often sleep poorly because I worry about my performance." If the respondent then circles the number four on this 1–5 scale, there is little reason to fear that somebody scoring the test will misread this rating. It does, however, require that the respondent understands the meaning of a 1–5 scale that presumes interval-scale principles, such that the distance from 1 to 2 is the same as the distance from 3 to 4. For research purposes, it is still a good idea to have self-reported responses double-checked; minimal training, if any, is needed for scoring such self-report tests. Some researchers have begun to use tablet computers or palm pilots where the test taker just needs to mark the right answer with a stylus on a touch-sensitive screen. When the test taker is finished answering questions, a built-in software program does the scoring and stores the data. Thus, much time and expense for hand scoring (with its in-built error proneness) can be saved.

Self-report tests of typical behaviors or preferences usually have many items; in the case of one of the most often-used psychopathology tools (see chapter 7), it may indeed be more than 500 items. Tests with such a large number of items are not designed to assess a single phenomenon like test anxiety but are actually composite tests that try to tap as many as 10 or 12 different psychological constructs. If one took, for example, a self-report test of irritability, this test may consist of only 10 or 20 items that assess various aspects of irritability, so that together these 10 items capture the phenomenon of irritability well. One concern test developers should always have is to make the test as short as possible but also as comprehensive as necessary. This can be a difficult balance to achieve and takes effort in test development, involving multiple loops of test item writing, first evaluation of a pilot sample, revisions, application to a large first sample, and later factor analytic strategies to make sure that all the test items make a useful contribution to the measurement and decision-making process (Clark & Watson, 1995; Floyd & Widaman, 1995; Reise, Waller, & Comrey, 2000). To determine how useful each item is for measuring the overall construct, the test statistic to be computed is **internal consistency**, also referred to as Cronbach's alpha. Alpha coefficients, by definition, have to be between 0 and 1.0. It is not surprising that coefficients approaching 1.0 are considered to be more desirable than low scores are. A test where items average an internal consistency score of greater than .8 is considered very good. On the other hand, internal consistency of less than .6 typically means that a test is considered "noisy" and problematic. While it is desirable to have high internal consistency, achieving a perfect internal consistency of 1.0 (i.e., what looks like a perfect score) is actually a problem. Why is that? Well, if, for example, somebody composes a test of irritability and used the hypothetical test item "I get easily ticked off" 10 times in a row, then it is probable that the internal consistency will be perfect. However, in this case not much good has been achieved; quite the reverse is true. You wasted a lot of the test takers' time because you made them answer redundant test items. The ideal test has a very high, but not perfect, internal consistency.

If the test has many similar items measuring, for example, short-term memory, then one can split this group of test items into two equal-sized halves and compare the reliabilities of one half of the items with the other. If the scores are very similar, then the researcher would have demonstrated **split-half reliability**.

Last but not least, psychological testing typically involves measurement of individual differences, and the resulting knowledge can aid in decisions like which child should be offered placement in an advanced math course. Any test that aids with decisions that have a long-term impact on a person's life presumes that the phenomenon we are trying to measure is actually stable. Imagine a test of communication skills to determine which of two boyfriends would make a good future husband. If communication skills are presumed to predict marital stability, but the responses on your test items change from one day to the next, then it wouldn't be of much use to develop a test and use a test score to make a prediction about who makes a better husband. Therefore, as much as the construct itself should be reasonably stable, it needs to be shown that the tool that measures a construct such as communication skills also produces similar results when repeated at a later time. When a test has been taken twice, within, for example, a 6-month interval and still leads to similar test scores, we have a high **test-retest reliability**. As a rule, it is predictable and not problematic that test-retest reliability scores gradually weaken as the time interval between repeat tests grows because individuals make many new life experiences that may affect their moods or self-perceptions.

This section on the properties of good psychological tests began with a presentation on the different types of reliability that one can and needs to show in justifying the use of particular test. Reliability was discussed first because it can be considered the foundation for the establishment of good test properties.

Validity

In addition to being reliable, tests need to demonstrate that they actually measure what they purport to measure; a so-called intelligence test should really capture what intelligence is all about, and the test of depression should clearly identify those individuals who are gloomy and negativistic. When the test measures what it is supposed to measure, this is referred to as **validity**. The literature on test development and validity describes many different types of validity that to some degree overlap, and there is considerable potential to get confused by all the terminology used in the validity research literature. Given that this is not a textbook of just psychological testing, only a few types of validity will be discussed, namely, the ones specifically relevant to the practice of clinical psychology.

When clients take a test, they have at least some idea why they take the test and they form their own hypotheses about the implications of what they say and try to guess what the psychologist might want. The psychologist Norbert Schwarz (see Schwarz, 1999; Sudman, Bradburn, & Schwarz, 1996) has written extensively about this phenomenon, which is quite a threat to interpretability and ultimately the usefulness of the answers. When it is very obvious what a test is trying to measure, it is described as having high **face validity**. Test takers who know right away what a test is trying to tap into likely have that knowledge color their responses. This can be good or bad, depending on the circumstances. Let us presume that a questionnaire is asking questions about a person's gregariousness and social skills in a personnel selection environment where job applicants are screened for their suitability as sales managers. Here, the test taker will readily make the connection between what the test tries to measure and what one is supposed to say in order to be successful in this hiring process. Respondents likely know that the interviewer expects sales managers to have good social skills and be outgoing. Therefore, it is a problem to work with tests that have high face validity when important decisions of benefit (or disadvantage) to test takers are at stake. Of course, you want to look gregarious to get the sales manager job. And, yes, you want to look like a responsible parent in a custody and access evaluation that is completed as part of divorce proceedings. And you do not want to appear to be a high risk for re-offending when assessed as part of a parole hearing in prison.

Similarly, a bright but unfortunately depressed and suicidal person readily understands that she may end up being hospitalized against her will when she answers the question about suicidal ideation in a positive way and may therefore deny that she has thought about killing herself. On the other hand, if there is no reason to believe that an individual will be negatively affected by knowing what the test is about (like telling a therapist about one's ambitiousness at work), then it may simplify the situation if the psychologist uses a face valid test that directly targets what is to be learned. For example, one can ask a client who sought help with smoking cessation: "On a scale from 1 to 10, how keen are you to stop smoking tomorrow?" This test item has high face validity, but the answer is still likely to be very meaningful because in this context there is no reason to believe that the test taker wants to fool the therapist or himself.

When a new test is being developed, it is not necessarily obvious what the right test items will be, and test item writers need to know what they should target with their questions. To assist with the task of developing a questionnaire on delusional thoughts, for example, a test developer may talk to a number of experts (let's say psychiatrists and psychologists who have worked for decades with delusional patients) and ask them what types of delusions are frequent, how they know that it really is a delusion, and so forth. When this information obtained from experts in the field is used for test item writing, a test is considered to have **content validity**, which is defined as a test quality that taps into what experts think the construct is all about.

Another desirable feature of a newly developed test is that resulting test scores should be very similar to those obtained with other tests that measure similar psychological constructs. A test of generalized anxiety would be expected to correlate with other tests of anxiety. When that is the case, a test is described as possessing good **concurrent validity**. It is tempting to think of very high concurrent validity as a good thing when a newly developed test produces test scores that perfectly overlap with those of another test, but this is not much of an achievement because all we now have is two tools that do the same job; in fact, the entire effort of test development may reveal itself as having been redundant. Very high concurrent validity, on the other hand, might be a desirable feature if a new test helps to identify the same people but with only 30% of the length of another test. The bottom line is that test developers should not glibly refer to certain test characteristics as ideal when the context is actually critical to decide on the question of usefulness.

A test of generalized anxiety was referred to earlier. Seasoned clinical psychologists know that measures of negative affect intercorrelate with each other because all of them reflect emotional distress, and that is especially true for various measures of anxiety. The phenomenon of emotional distress is composed of many features, and the person with generalized anxiety is also more likely to be worrisome, pessimistic, or depressed. Therefore, a newly developed test in the area of anxiety would have to show the predicted linkages with other aspects of anxiety; it needs to reveal natural and meaningful connections with other psychological constructs around the theme of distress. When that applies, a test is described as possessing **construct validity**.

Lastly, all tests are of course developed and used to have practical applications and help us in our decision making. A good test may help to answer questions like: (a) Is this patient well-adjusted and functioning, or is he suicidal and such a risk to himself that he needs the protection of a hospital? or (b) Is this prison inmate who is considered for release on parole likely to re-offend and represents a risk to the public? Let us presume that a previous study had shown that high scores on such a test can differentiate who is at risk for harming himself or which offender has in the past re-offended; in this case the test has **criterion validity**. The test scores represent criteria to help us with real-world decision-making.

Being able to make true and useful predictions about the future is particularly desirable as shown by the example of a formerly dangerous offender now being released to the community. It is extremely desirable for parole boards to be able to rely on test results for a sense of comfort about their decision to release an offender into the community. Therefore, a particularly useful form of validity is that of **predictive validity**. Predictive validity is generally considered the most desirable type of criterion validity.

How Should Tests Be Described with Respect to Their Reliability and Validity?

As discussed at the beginning of this chapter, the following statement is unacceptable to professional psychologists: "We used test X to measure intelligence; *test X is reliable and valid.*" Having seen a more detailed description of how many ways there are to establish reliability and validity, the reader now has a clearer sense about why such a simplistic description of test properties is inappropriate, or even misleading. Consider a test that has excellent test-retest reliability over 12 months (r = .88), but has low internal consistency (alpha = .54); how could any one descriptive adjective capture this discrepancy? Well, it cannot. Simplistic statements like "the test is valid" also ignore the fact that tests are developed and normed for particular groups of people and specific purposes. Intelligence tests used frequently in North America have usually been developed using middle and upper-middle class respondents who grew up in an English-speaking environment (Neisser et al., 1996). It is rare that norms are available for subcultures like African-Americans or immigrants whose mother tongue is not English. This is not trivial because a 2001 census by Statistics Canada showed that in metropolitan areas like Vancouver, approximately 38% of the people do not have English as their mother tongue. In the United States there is a sizeable proportion of the population who speak only Spanish (especially in U.S. states bordering Mexico), and a test may not be validated for this particular population. Doing poorly on an IQ test because the test taker was not educated in the language of the test and does not understand the instruction means only that the test is invalid, not that the test taker is dumb.

Sticking with the example of intelligence tests, validation research strongly suggests that IQ scores are quite good in predicting school performance from elementary school levels to high school levels but do not have much predictive validity for later life job performance and career success (Hunter & Hunter, 1984; Neisser et al., 1996); hence, it does not even make sense to glibly state that IQ tests have high predictive validity; for some age groups they do, but not for others. Therefore, a psychologist using IQ tests is expected to know what the test has predictive validity for and limit its use to those applications.

Instead of using the categorical (and inadequate) phrase: "Test X is reliable and valid," a more informative description would read as follows:

> . . . to determine the prevalence of depression in our sample, we used the ABC test of depression developed by Down and In-the-Dumps (1986). The ABC is a 25-item self-report scale of depressed mood, each using a 1–5 scale where a larger number indicates higher depression. Scores obtained with the ABC have been shown to have a test-retest reliability of r = .91 for a 2-week test–retest and r = .74 for a 6-month interval, determined in an Australian college student population. ABC also has been shown to have an internal consistency coefficient of .86 which is generally considered to be very

TABLE 3.2 Types of Reliability and Validity
Earlier in this chapter we have introduced and defined each of these new terms. To maximize learning, these new terms are listed here again in a summary format. Instead of providing the reader with pregiven answers, we believe more effective learning will happen when the students themselves complete the empty space with definitions in their own words.

	DEFINITION (TO BE FILLED IN BY STUDENT)
Reliability	
Internal consistency	
Test–retest reliability	
Inter-rater reliability	
Split-half reliability	
Validity	
Face validity	
Content validity	
Construct validity	
Criterion validity	
Predictive validity	
Concurrent validity	

good. Test items were written by the researchers and were then validated using college students and adults living in the community. To avoid unnecessary length, the original 96-item list was reduced to parsimonious 24 items via factor analytic approaches which confirmed that ABC measures a single factor, named depression. Test scores derived with the ABC have been shown to have criterion validity in that they are sensitive to change in individuals undergoing psychological therapy, and they are able to differentiate recently diagnosed from not recovered depressive individuals.

Table 3.2 summarizes the newly introduced terms for the types of reliability and validity.

◇ MEASURING CHANGE IN THERAPY

A very important question raised in the profession of psychology is whether or not our interventions are effective. Chapters 13 and 14 in this book provide extensive discussion on this issue, and this chapter refreshes the concepts that need to be clearly understood to get the most out of these later chapters. Even psychologists in private practice working with individual patients have an interest in knowing how much their patients improve and which of their interventions is particularly critical for this improvement. A hospital administrator wants to see that patients seen by the hospital psychology service are improving to such a degree that the existence of the psychology department and the associated budget are justifiable to the taxpayer, insurance companies, or government officials involved in health care. Researchers continue to carefully test which therapies are best suited for which kind of patient and seek to create a knowledge foundation to assist practitioners and answer questions such as:

■ How many therapy hours are needed before patients start to make substantial improvements?

■ How much therapist training is needed to create a pool of skilled therapists that can do the job in the most cost-efficient manner?

■ Is the outcome of all therapies likely the same, or are some therapies superior to other treatments?

■ Is therapy X better than Y for anxiety but Y better than X for marital problems?

■ Is there one type of treatment approach best suited to preventing relapse from alcohol abstinence?

■ What percentage of patients is likely to show meaningful improvement?

■ Which specific trainable therapist skills are critical for maximizing good outcomes?

◇ METHODS USED TO LEARN ABOUT THERAPY OUTCOME

Case Studies

In clinical psychology, a great deal of learning is achieved by carefully studying individual cases. Practicing psychologists discuss complex cases with each other, seek occasional help, or may even brag a little bit about particularly great success they achieved with a difficult client. Case conferences are one vehicle where ongoing cases are discussed, and supervisors and students engage in case conferences as part of the training process. Particularly interesting cases may be presented in hospital Grand Rounds, or even get published in professional journals to assist others in developing protocols for similar types of clients. Essentially, the study of individual cases can follow one of two formats. Probably the most frequently used format is that of using a structured narrative where therapists present an interesting case like telling a story. There is no rigid format for such exchanges, but these presentations are likely structured the same way the therapist would structure a written intake report that the reader will learn about in chapter 8.

Another way of studying individual cases is to see a single patient as an opportunity to conduct an experiment. This is particularly likely to happen in behavioral therapies (see chapter 11), because they have the strongest roots in experimental methodology. Furthermore, because the target for change is usually overt behavior, the effect of various manipulations can be studied directly. Parents, for example, can conduct their own experimental case study by systematically studying the effect of screaming at their kids when they are fighting with each other, hoping that that stops the fighting. If it fails to work (which is rather likely, and you will find out the reason in chapter 12), then they could threaten withdrawal of the kids' weekly allowances (which might work if they are very consistent and the children are old enough to remember) or ignore the fighting (which incidentally has the most promise of success). As long as the strategies are tested in a structured format and the subsequent responses are carefully studied, this can be seen as an n = 1 experiment (where n denotes the number of subjects that have participated), and the results are informative about which strategies to use in the future. Similarly, a psychotherapist may work with a new presenting problem and try a creative approach that has not yet been described in the literature. This was exactly what Freud and other innovative therapists had to do because there was no literature on psychotherapy they could have consulted. When such treatments work, predictably the therapist will apply the same method to the next patient presenting with a similar problem and may ultimately treat a number of similar cases the same way. If the treatments and subsequent changes are carefully recorded, the therapist may even want to present this systematic study of multiple cases at an annual conference to other psychotherapists or write it up for publication in a professional journal. The *Journal of Behavior Therapy and Experimental Psychiatry*, for example, has a long history of publishing original and informative case studies that have helped many budding clinicians find tips for therapeutic work with their own clients. Observation of individual patients and the conduct of a systematic case study is often the cornerstone of innovation in psychotherapy research and is a systematic tool for teaching psychotherapy. The early methods of psychotherapy were taught via case studies, and the corresponding psychotherapy textbooks are usually a blend of theory and descriptions of applications for individual cases (for examples see Frankl, 1963; Freud, 1949).

More detailed descriptions of how behavioral experiment within behavior therapy can be done and additional case descriptions will be provided in chapter 12. Nevertheless, the basic methods are best explained in this chapter to provide the reader with the tools to get the most out of the subsequent chapters.

A particularly sophisticated way of testing the effect of a treatment with a single case design is via a four-phase protocol where baseline recordings and treatment phases alternate twice. The baseline data collection and treatment phases are referred to as the A phase and B phase, respectively; thereby an **ABAB design** gets created. It is pivotal that a baseline recording of the "normal" frequency of the behavior is obtained against which treatment effects can be contrasted (e.g., how much time does patient x spend on nail-biting in a given week?). Then a treatment stage follows with additional recordings to see whether the treatment works. Next the treatment is halted to create another phase without intervention, and finally a second treatment stage is reintroduced to see whether the success of the first phase can be repeated. If this approach shows that a treatment works for the active phase and ceases to work during the passive phase, and this phenomenon can be replicated, then a strong case has been made about the reliability of the intervention.

In addition to providing a convincing demonstration of the effectiveness of the intervention, the record of the changes also provides reinforcement for the client and even the therapist himself, as seeing these steady and seemingly predictable changes as a line in a chart is very satisfying.

Therapy Outcome Research

The trustworthiness of evidence regarding the effectiveness of psychological therapy is usually gauged by the quality and quantity of the studies that have been conducted using similar treatments for comparable problems. Not surprisingly, high-quality studies of treatment effects can be expensive and laborious to conduct. The simplest form of learning about treatment-induced change is via the so-called single-group, pre-post treatment design, where patients are assessed prior to treatment and then reassessed when treatment is completed. It is tempting to interpret any change that has occurred in-between these two measurement points and to attribute improvements to the therapy that patients have received. Unfortunately, this is not a safe assumption at all because this type of design cannot rule out many alternative explanations. It is possible that a group of depressed patients who had been assessed in January, then received 4 months of treatment, and were reassessed in May, improved because their depression was affected by the lack of light that is typical in Northern winters, and the arrival of spring lifted their spirits; hence, the improvement would likely have happened without any psychological therapy in between. Or, a drug company may have released a new over-the-counter medication that seemed very promising and many patients participating in a psychotherapy study saw the ads and decided to try this new medication. This would be considered a **confounding treatment**, and any observed pre-post test changes could then be due to this medication, the psychotherapy, or a combination of the two, and unfortunately we would not know which component is effective.

Also, there is the well-known **placebo effect**, which indicates that people are likely to get somewhat better simply by believing that they are in active treatment. As will be described in chapter 13, this belief is a very potent component of successful therapies that may account for as much as half of observed effects. These kinds of threats to the interpretability of observed changes are clustered together as the **history effect**, and this problem is remedied using a study design referred to as **"randomized, controlled trial"** where patients are randomly assigned to at least two groups, namely, an active treatment group and a control group that receives either no treatment or a control treatment. The randomization helps to assure that two groups are being created who start therapy at a similar level of distress or anxiety and who are also similar on other possible moderator variables like gender, age, or travel distance to the clinic, for example.

What exactly is done to the control group will determine what conclusions can be drawn from a particular type of experimental design, and this will be elaborated on here. A comparison of the results of an active treatment group with that of a no-treatment control group permits the determination of whether or not treatment success would have happened anyway because of any outside influence that could not have been anticipated or controlled (like the drug company releasing the new over-the-counter antidepressant medication). A so-called **wait-list control group** means that the patients expect to be treated later, after the first treatment is completed and post-treatment measures have been taken. In this type of design, the effects of expectancy are controlled for. Also, wait-list control designs are popular because they motivate patients to enroll in studies given that they are guaranteed to get the desired treatment at least at some point, and it is ethically appealing to the researcher who would likely feel guilty for leaving a complete group of needy people untreated. In fact, many Ethical Review Committees require such designs because they reflect fairness, in that patients should be offered comparable treatments or services; this requirement of equitable treatment is also referred to as the **equipoise** principle (Freedman, 1987).

Another possibility, in principle, is to use a placebo control treatment, however, this is problematic in psychotherapy research because the placebo concept was initially developed and is routinely used in drug treatment studies where researchers have a very clear idea about which active chemical ingredient in a drug is meant to produce the hoped-for benefits. In the case of a drug study, the definition of placebo is to give an empty pill to the patient, who does not know whether it contains active ingredients because the pill looks, tastes, and feels the same as the new drug to be tested that does have active ingredients. This type of study is described as a **single-blind study** because the patient is "blind" in that that the patient doesn't know which of the two types of pills he or she is getting. In this case it is possible that the physician prescribing the medication and looking after the patient in a drug study could be influenced by the knowledge of which patient is receiving the active medication and which one the placebo pill. If the treating physician knew that the patient was taking the sugar pill, he or she might unintentionally pay more attention to the patient and thus bias the results. The most conservative approach is to also assure that the researchers prepare the drugs in such fashion that the treating physicians themselves do not know whether the patient is on the active medication or a placebo pill. This is referred to as a **double-blind study** because both physician and patient do not know which condition they are actually in. Double-blind studies are considered the gold standard in this type of research. Applying these concepts to psychotherapy research is a dual problem because, first of all, it is inherently impossible to keep the therapists blind to the very treatment they are supposed to be administering. A psychoanalyst providing psychoanalytic therapy knows what he or she is offering to his or her patients, and a behavior therapist is no different. Similarly, patients themselves have some understanding of what psychological therapy is; it is normal and ethical to explain to them what is about to be done and why, and how it works, and therefore it is not really possible or ethical for the patients not to know that they are in a placebo condition. Hence, double-blinding in psychotherapy cannot exist.

To some degree, it is possible for psychotherapy researchers to get around part of this problem by assigning patients to a treatment which they know from experience has a weak effect, let's say an unstructured discussion group where patients can talk about their feelings. It is also possible in biofeedback research to provide visual or auditory signals to clients that look like genuine biological signals (like heart rate), but that is actually false or non-contingent. This would provide some degree of blinding for the patient. Nevertheless, there is always an ethical concern when patients are actively deceived like this, and knowingly offering a treatment that the researcher knows is minimally effective is rarely acceptable.

While this may sound complicated enough, unfortunately there are more concerns. Usually, psychotherapy researchers want to know not only whether treatment produces desirable effects (relative to a no-treatment control group), which is also referred to as **efficacy**, but also whether the experimental treatment may be better than an already existing active treatment, and they may want to learn whether or not the treatment actually works for the reason that it is presumed to work. Seeking the answer to this question is a test of **treatment effect specificity** (see also chapter 14). In the first case, it is a waste of time and money to develop and test a new therapy that produces the same results for the same amount of money as an already existing treatment. Whereas this is not a problem if the new treatment has been developed to help with a problem that was previously untreatable; in this case the new treatment would be called efficacious. It is, however, more likely that treatments that have been shown to benefit at least some patients are already available, and showing that a new treatment is clearly superior is a significant challenge for therapy researchers. The second issue is important for those who are testing particular theories or models of psychotherapy in the hope of showing that this innovative intervention works for the reasons that the therapy researcher hypothesizes. In cognitive therapy, for example, it is presumed that depression is the result of irrational, negatively toned thought patterns that the cognitive therapist tries to identify and change. If cognitive therapy is to be demonstrated as having specific effects, then the researcher needs to show that the treatment affected these cognitions, and that the change in these cognitions toward a more optimistic outlook can be statistically shown to account for the mood improvement of the study patients (Table 3.3).

When data have been collected about change in psychotherapy, researchers will then conduct statistical tests to determine whether change was very small and likely due to chance or, hopefully, it was of much benefit to patients' quality-of-life. The typical statistical approach would be a significance test (typically an F- or a-test) with a repeated measure (namely, before and after therapy). If the probability of an accidental difference between the pre- and post-treatment measures can be ruled out using a threshold of $p < .05$, by tradition this is called a **statistically significant effect** and usually makes researchers happy. However, what does all this mean in the real world, and is statistically significant effect always important? Let's say that government invested \$5,000,000 in an educational program to help 1,000 unemployed individuals with a history of schizophrenia to acquire job hunting skills. Even 6 months after the end of the program, only 2 of the 1,000 participants had found work (and this difference is not statistically different from zero), but their scores on a self-report test of friendliness improved from 5.7 on a 10-point scale to 6.1, and this change is statistically significant with $p = .04$. From the perspective of government who funded the program, these results are not **clinically significant** because the main variable the program was to have influenced was unemployment. No politician will dare to go back to taxpayers and tell them that for \$5,000,000 the unemployed now feel slightly friendlier. The take-home message is that success is usually defined by a blend of statistical significance and change in something of value to society.

This section revealed that to answer the many relevant questions that psychotherapy research tries to address, fairly complicated treatment designs may be needed; and more likely than not, multiple studies will have to be conducted (LaVaque et al., 2002). A comprehensive trial usually involves one group receiving a new experimental treatment, another group not receiving any treatment at all, maybe a third group receiving a treatment that controls for expectancies, and a fourth one receiving an active therapy that is considered the industry standard. Provided that the samples for these studies are large enough to actually allow for sufficient statistical power in the analyses (Cohen, 1977), careful analysis and interpretation of the changes observed in all these treatment groups then permits determination of to what degree the observed outcome is unique to the novel treatment, or

TABLE 3.3 Types of Therapy Outcome Study Design and Question Answered by Each

TYPE OF DESIGN	ADVANTAGE	DISADVANTAGE
Pre-post evaluation	Simple, inexpensive, and allows computation of a statistic that describes amount of change; no problem with ethics because all patients received the treatment	Cannot rule out any alternative explanations or explain specificity
Two-group design: Experimental treatment versus no-treatment control	Controls for history effects	Cannot reveal specificity or untease treatment effect from expectancy effect; problem with ethics because typically half of the patients go untreated; patients are not very motivated to participate
Two-group design: Experimental treatment versus wait-list control	Controls for history effects, ethically acceptable because ultimately all patients do receive the treatment; patients are motivated to participate in this type of study	Cannot reveal specificity or untease treatment effect from expectancy effect; does not allow for long-term follow-up of the wait-list group because they have now been treated as well
Two-group design: Experimental treatment versus placebo or minimal treatment control	Controls for history effects and can clarify what part of the observed treatment effect was expectancy; this helps explain specificity	Problem with ethics because patients received treatment of unequal value; cannot reveal whether new treatment is superior to existing active treatments
Three-group design: Experimental treatment versus no-treatment or wait-list control versus competing active treatment control	Controls for history effects and can clarify what part of the observed treatment effect was expectancy; this helps explain specificity; also shows whether a new treatment is superior or just equivalent to other available active treatments ; if active treatments were equivalent in benefit, principally, it allows for long-term follow-up without confounding	Complicated and expensive; somewhat unpopular with patients who have a low probability to be assigned to the treatment they were originally interested in

due to nonspecific but still beneficial effects of psychological therapy (to be discussed in detail in chapter 8), or simply a random effect.

In the last two or three decades, researchers have engaged in thousands of therapy outcome studies, and the standards for a high-quality study has grown substantially (much to the chagrin of researchers learning this craft). Today, a really good study is one that meets all the requirements listed in Table 3.4.

TABLE 3.4 Quality Criteria for Therapy Outcome Research Protocols

1 Random assignment to conditions

2 Adequate control conditions (balance of ethics and scientific rigor), controlling for passage of time, nonspecific effects, patient expectations

3 Avoidance of treatment confounds

4 Specific, reliable measures valid for the purpose of the study

5 Therapists who are well-trained, adhere to a protocol, and are bias-free

6 Samples with adequate power

7 Follow-up

8 Intent-to-treat principle in analysis

9 Checks on therapist adherence to treatment protocol and techniques

10 Client credibility ratings of therapy

Once a number of therapy outcome studies have been published, they are likely to get reviewed by individual writers or consensus committees, and the evidence is judged via the use of a rating system regarding its quality and trustworthiness. There are multiple such systems around, but the good news is that are quite similar. The one described here has been used by the Association for Biofeedback and Applied Psychophysiology (LaVaque et al., 2003) and overlaps with the one used by the American Psychological Association. Here are the levels of quality of evidence (low score = weak evidence) and their definitions:

Level 1: Not empirically supported: Supported only by anecdotal reports and/or case studies in nonpeer reviewed venues.

Level 2: Possibly efficacious: At least one study of sufficient statistical power with well-identified outcome measures, but lacking randomized assignment to a control condition internal to the study.

Level 3: Probably efficacious: Multiple observational studies, clinical studies, wait-list controlled studies, and within-subject and intrasubject replication studies that demonstrate efficacy.

Level 4: Efficacious:

a. In a comparison with a no-treatment control group, alternative treatment group, or sham (placebo) control utilizing randomized assignment, the investigational treatment is shown to be statistically significantly superior to the control condition, or it is equivalent to a treatment with established efficacy in a study with sufficient power to detect moderate differences.

b. The studies have been conducted with a population treated for a specific problem for whom inclusion criteria are delineated in a reliable, operationally defined manner.

c. The study used valid and clearly specified outcome measures related to the problem being treated.

d. The data are subjected to appropriate analysis.

e. The diagnostic and treatment variables and procedures are clearly defined in a manner that permits replication of the study by independent researchers.

f. The superiority or equivalence of the investigational treatment has been shown in at least two independent research settings.

Level 5: Efficacious and specific: The investigational treatment has been shown to be statistically superior to credible sham therapy, placebo control treatment, or alternative bona fide treatment in at least two independent research settings.

Consistent with this category system, the greatest value is usually placed on randomized controlled studies and aggregations of such studies via **meta-analysis**. In essence, meta-analysis is a quantitative review method that selects similar studies from the literature (e.g., all studies using psychological treatments for "fear of flying") and then extracts the same information about mean change and variability of change from each study. It treats many possible small studies, as if they had actually been one large study; and each patient in these trials is treated as contributing the same valuable information to the conclusion. More detail about meta-analysis procedures and findings is found in chapter 13. Meta-analysis has the advantage that it goes beyond the evidentiary possibilities inherent in narrative reviews. However, it also has a variety of limitations, which need to be carefully considered in order to arrive at meaningful conclusions. Meta-analysis has the unique advantage of allowing aggregation of nonsignificant singular results, which when pooled may show clinically meaningful and statistically significant effects after all. We will not provide a detailed criticism of all potential flaws of meta-analysis here, but refer the reader to Rosenthal's (1987) excellent review. Note that the most critical features to be considered are the following:

- Publication bias (given that studies with positive results are more likely to get published than those with null findings)
- Retrieval bias (referring to the tendency of researchers to ignore or find flaw with studies that do not fit with their hypotheses)
- Extraction of truly comparable studies
- Clear definitions of target populations
- Randomization and blinding
- Drop-out analysis
- Presence or absence of follow-up
- Description and statistical handling of confounds
- Treatment integrity (referring to therapists actually following a form of manualized or somewhat standardized treatment)

Qualitative Research

Clinical psychology research has greatly benefited from the rigors of experimental methodologies, and the acceptance of clinical psychology in health care systems is in good part due to this research tradition. Nevertheless, there has been well-argued criticism that hypothesis formulation and testing via strictly quantified approaches has inherent limitations, in that one cannot learn anything beyond what has been specifically targeted for inquiry. It is easy to miss important information when a search is overly focused. The kind of thinking that leads from casual observation to experimentation has become a process of intense study itself, and a certain amount of rigorous questioning and systematic analysis has also been applied to this stage. The methods used in this arena are clustered together under the label **qualitative research**.

Qualitative research is not hypothesis-driven, does not block knowledge acquisition outside the hypotheses to be tested, and therefore allows for discovery of new insights. In order to be meaningful, qualitative research needs to extract observations and categorize them into themes or patterns. For example, we may have no idea what it is like for a depressed, middle-aged man to convince others in his social network that he cannot motivate himself to get going in the morning. A qualitative researcher may conduct partially structured interviews with open-ended answer options to provide a forum where depressed male patients try to describe their experiences. The patients' statements will be videotaped or audiotaped and transcribed so that a permanent record exists that can be subjected to look for commonalities between these patients' experiences. Some statistics packages are currently available to assist with the search for underlying themes, improve replicability of findings, and save time for the researcher analyzing the data. Determining which themes are the most important is nevertheless partially subjective, and there is opportunity for researcher bias to slip into this analytical process. One, now widely accepted, criterion for a stronger methodology in qualitative research is that the researcher does not undertake all the research steps himself or herself. Interview questions should be clearly defined a priori, and either the interview or the analysis part (or both) should be conducted by an unbiased individual, not by the researcher (Mays & Pope, 2000).

Qualitative research does not have much of a foothold in clinical psychology although it has gained considerable popularity in education, anthropology, sociology, counseling psychology, and nursing. It is debatable whether it is the typical embedding of clinical psychology training programs in quantitatively oriented, experimental psychology departments or the nature of the typical questions asked in clinical psychology research that accounts for its lack of enthusiasm for qualitative research methods. Following are the criticisms leveled against qualitative methods:

- Problems with reliability in the data acquisition process
- Reliability of extraction methods
- Subjectivity of interpretation processes

The publication of guidelines for high-quality qualitative research (see Mays & Pope, 2000) has helped proffer against this criticism.

Program Evaluation

The typical training program in clinical psychology follows the scientist-practitioner model that endeavors to provide sufficient training so that clinical psychologists can function in research as well as clinical settings with the implicit expectation that this type of training allows their clinical work to be guided by empirical evidence and to ensure that research is relevant for clinical practice. As Linden, Moseley, and Erskine (2005) have shown, this dual-target approach to professional training is unusual in the health care field and provides clinical psychologists who work in applied settings with a stronger research base and more methodological skills than is seen with the other health care providers (Linden et al., 2005). It is therefore likely that clinical psychologists will initiate or be drawn on to assist with evaluating new programs that are being developed in clinical settings. Typically, such programs are meant to reflect and guide clinical practice without suffering from the stringent requirements of clinical trials that often limit recruitment of patients to groups with very clean diagnoses and few comorbidities, thereby limiting their ultimate generalizability. The goals and methods of **program evaluation** are therefore distinct from the methods of randomized clinical trials. Program evaluation seeks to find whether a particular service is useful and needed, and if so whether it would be taken up if offered, and by whom, and whether it would produce the desirable effects. A typical approach in program evaluation follows a four-step sequence (Posavac & Carey, 2003):

1. **Assessment of Needs** Simple economics dictates that no new program should be offered to a community or a hospital without an awareness of whether indeed there is a need for such a program. A very simple example would be to ask residents in a senior's home whether they are interested in participating in a set of evenings where somebody teaches them the card game Bridge. The implicit hope is that a card game will get people together, help build social support networks, and keep seniors mentally alert. There would be no point in scheduling such an evening and hire a trainer if none of the residents indicated an interest.

2. **Program Planning** Once it has been established that a reasonable number of residents are interested, it makes sense to find out how many evenings a course should last, what time the class should begin and how long it should last, and whether there is a particularly good or bad time of year to begin such a program. Also, one can tackle questions like whether to charge a fee, either to recuperate expenses or to get people to make a salient commitment to their enrolment. Clearly, if the proposed service was a more complex program of activity, and maybe even politically loaded, like a safe-injection site for drug users, this planning process needs to be broader and politically astute; locations are critical, neighbors need to be consulted, risks need to be assessed and minimized, funding needs to made stable, and so on (Linden, 2007).

3. **Formative Evaluation** This particular phase follows along with the actual implementation of the program to make sure that the original plan is indeed being executed. It would be silly to evaluate a program that exists only on paper but that has never actually been implemented.

4. **Summative Evaluation** This fourth step is similar to a post-test in treatment research, but researchers are not so much interested in whether people have actually changed, but this step seeks to answer the question of whether the program should be continued, modified, or abandoned. Do benefits outweigh disadvantages? In addition, this would also allow for some parallel quantitative evaluation where a researcher might track whether implementing a regular Bridge night in the seniors' home also makes participants happier and results in fewer visits to the nurse's station with vague health complaints.

As is apparent from the earlier example, how program evaluation is conducted will depend very much on the environment, the nature of the program, and the type of people involved.

◇ CONCLUSION

This chapter did not attempt to provide an overly broad review of research methods in psychology but focused on research methods of particular interests to clinical psychologists. As such, we reviewed the concepts of reliability and validity for the kinds of standardized tests and observational methods that are often used in the field. We have illustrated how multi-faceted reliability and validity is and why a statement like "test x is reliable and valid" is much too coarse and "primitive" as a descriptor of a test. The second major domain of interest was the measurement of change in therapy. This information is helpful in better understanding our coverage of therapy outcome research discussed in chapter 13, and it assists the presentation of innovative therapies in chapter 14.

◇ ONGOING CONSIDERATIONS

The basic logic and most of the concepts used for dealing with test reliability and validity have been essentially unchanged for decades and are not controversial. They represent, however, standards that require a huge amount of work to meet. Many psychologists, including the authors, deplore explosive growth of research on standardized tests that often duplicate previous efforts and may be published and used before a reasonable level of reliability and validity research has been conducted. We advocate for higher standards in test development and support detailed descriptions of test psychometrics in publications.

◇ KEY TERMS LEARNED

ABAB design
clinically significant effect
Concurrent validity
Confounding treatment
Construct validity
Content validity
Criterion validity
Double-blind study
Efficacy
Equipoise
Face validity
History effect
Inter-rater reliability
Internal consistency
Meta-analysis
Observational methods
Placebo effect

Predictive validity
Program evaluation
Qualitative research
Questionnaires
Randomized, controlled trial
Reliability
Single-blind study
Single case study
Split-half reliability
statistically significant effect
Surveys
Test-retest reliability
Therapy outcome studies
Treatment effect specificity
Validity
Wait-list control group

◇ THINKING QUESTIONS

1. Can a test be valid when it is not reliable?

2. What does it mean when a self-report test has a perfect internal consistency score of 1.0?

3. Is high face validity of a test good or bad?

4. How can qualitative and quantitative research methods complement each other?

◇ REFERENCES

Achenbach, T. (1986). *Direct observation form of the child behavior checklist.* Burlington: University of Vermont, Department of Psychiatry.

Clark, L., & Watson, D. (1995). Constructing validity: Basic issues in objective scale development. *Psychological Assessment, 7,* 309–319.

Cohen, J. (1960). A coefficient of agreement for nominal scales. *Educational and Psychological Measurements, 20,* 37–46.

Cohen, J. (1977). *Statistical power analysis for the behavioral sciences* (Rev. ed.). New York: Academic Press.

Floyd, F., & Widaman, K. (1995). Factor analysis in the development and refinement of clinical assessment instruments. *Psychological Assessment, 7,* 286–299.

Frankl, V. (1963). *Man's search for meaning.* New York: Washington Square Press.

Freedman, B. (1987). Equipoise and the ethics of clinical research. *The New England Journal of Medicine, 317,* 141–145.

Freud, S. (1932). *Vier psychiatrische krankengeschichten.* Wien: IPV.

Freud, S. (1949). *An outline of psychoanalysis.* (J. Strachey trans.). New York: W. W. Norton.

Howitt, D. (2005). *Introduction to research methods in psychology* (1st ed.). Upper Saddle River, NJ: Prentice Hall.

Hunter, J., & Hunter, R. (1984). Validity and utility of alternative predictors of job performance. *Psychological Bulletin, 96,* 72–98.

LaVaque, T., Hammond, D., Trudeau, D., Monastra, V., & Perry, L. P. (2002). Template for designing guidelines for the evaluation of the clinical efficacy of psychophysiological evaluations. *Applied Psychophysiology and Biofeedback, 27,* 283–281.

Linden, I. (2007). Unpublished Honor's Thesis in Sociology. University of Waterloo, Ontario, Canada.

Linden, W., Moseley, J. V., & Erskine, Y. (2005). Psychology as a health care profession: Implications for training. *Canadian Psychology, 46,* 179–188.

Mays, N., & Pope, C. (2000). Assessing quality in qualitative research. *BMJ, 320,* 50–52.

Neisser, U., Boodoo, G., Bouchard, T., Jr., Boykin, A., Brody, N., & Ceci, S., et al. (1996). Intelligence: Knowns and unknowns. *American Psychologist, 51,* 77–101.

Posavac, E., & Carey, R. (2003). *Program evaluation: Methods & case studies* (6th ed.). Englewood Cliffs, NJ: Prentice Hall.

Reise, S., Waller, N., & Comrey, A. (2000). Factor analysis and scale revision. *Psychological Assessment, 12*, 287–297.

Rosenthal, R. (1987). *Judgment studies: Design, analysis, and meta-analysis.* Cambridge, MA: Cambridge University Press.

Rosnow, R., & Rosenthal, R. (2001). *Beginning behavioral research: A conceptual primer* (4th ed.). Upper Saddle River, NJ: Prentice Hall.

Schwarz, N. (1999). Self-reports: How the questions shape the answers. *American Psychologist, 54*, 93–105.

Sudman, S., Bradburn, N., & Schwarz, N. (1996). *Thinking about answers: The application of cognitive processes to survey methodology.* San Francisco, CA: Jossey-Bass.

CHAPTER FOUR

ETHICAL DECISION-MAKING

CHAPTER OBJECTIVE

Ethics can be a difficult-to-grasp content area of clinical psychology because it comes with few facts, some principles, and a lot of ambiguity (Keith-Spiegel & Koocher, 1985; Mills, 1984). Still, for clinical psychologists concern about behaving ethically needs to be ever present, like a critical virus-detection program that is always running in the background of the computer. This chapter begins with an attempt to ease you into the spirit of what ethical behavior is all about and to alert you to the many traps out there. A description of the facts and rules that can help you to make sound decisions follows next. Finally, we walk through an example, using a principle-guided decision-making process.

◇ SETTING THE TONE

In chapter 1, we described the typical work activities of clinical psychologists; overall, these activities involve many clinical judgments that can have both constructive and harmful effects on the clients they work with. All judgments made by clinical psychologists are governed by expectations for high professional competence and moral standards. Unlike most of what students learn in their undergraduate training, ethical behavior and decision-making is rarely black or white, right or wrong, because the context and circumstances are everchanging and ethical dilemmas are not absolutely preventable, even by the most skilled and seasoned psychologist. The first thing we teach students when discussing ethics is that beginning clinical psychologists need to learn the **process of ethical decision-making** and need to be familiar with the **ethical principles** that guide this process. These are the critical tools clinical psychologists need to have at their fingertips; we cannot afford to become complacent and just trust our gut. Even equipped with these tools, ethics is one area of clinical psychology practice where necessity requires that we learn to live with some degree of uncertainty. Students new to the topic of ethics usually want to jump right ahead and find out from the professor what the right answer is. Our response to such requests is highly unsatisfying to these keen students because we stress that, yes, there are ethical guidelines for practice but the best answer for each scenario lies in reflection and the use of a systematic process. We discourage any belief that a perfect and obvious solution lies right around the corner or that we as experienced psychologists have them at our fingertips either.

◇ DEFINING WHAT ETHICAL BEHAVIOR IS

The core of ethical decision-making is derived from principles of religion and philosophy that are thousands of years old, focusing on respect and dignity toward others. The same thinking has shaped early views of medical practice, which has been summarized as, "above all, do no harm" (the Roman physician Galen, quoted on: http://www.medscape.com/viewarticle/543882), and this is no different in psychology.

But how do we know that we are doing the right thing, or at least following the right process? It helps to think of moral, professional behavior as happening on a continuum where one extreme end is criminal behavior, well-defined by laws and subject to punishment by the authorities. At the other end of the spectrum is selfless giving for the benefit of others, exemplified in the behavior of famous people awarded sainthood or Nobel Prizes for Peace. The one extreme end is, of course, illegal behavior governed by criminal codes that are quite easy to understand because they are long lists of do-not-do behaviors: "Do not kill another human being" or "do not steal." Unfortunately such prescription of "do nots" is not sufficient to define the right way to behave in everyday clinical practice and to tell us what represents a high standard of moral behavior. Nevertheless, the two extremes on this spectrum embrace a middle ground where psychologists struggle to make ethical decisions. Mandated behaviors are easiest to understand for practicing psychologists whose nonobservance may not be outright criminal but still borders on felonious behavior such as "do not double-bill for your services." An imperative like "treat your clients with respect and dignity" is much, much harder to define. How exactly does one show respect? Another way of looking at this spectrum of right and wrong is to think of one end as a threshold or minimal level (as in "do no harm") and the other end as **aspirational**, meaning that the behavior is a long-term goal that we should continuously strive for even if we are not likely to fully reach it. The major principles defining ethical behavior are not particularly difficult to understand because they arose out of religious and philosophical teachings readers have been exposed to before in their families, churches, and schools. We are expected to be honest, be caring, try hard to do a complete and competent job, and protect and look out for our clients and others around us. Similarly, most violations of these principles are obvious violations as in the case of the therapist who has sex with his teenaged clients, the marital therapist who immediately sides with one partner in a troubled relationship (instead of listening to both), or the psychologist who (mis-) uses a complex test that she was never been trained to use and interpret (Housman & Stake, 1999). A more subtle set of skills to acquire are those that prevent future problems, like good record-keeping, clear contracts, maximizing practice setups for confidentiality, and considering the consequences of one's own actions. We will provide overarching principles that assist with these types of decision-making later in this chapter.

The real difficulties arise when two or more principles, each one a good, moral principle on its own, are in conflict with one another.

To flesh out the idea of ethical decision-making and ethical conflicts, we begin with three vignettes of ethical dilemmas from everyday practice that are reality based but have been modified to prevent recognition of any particular individuals. The first vignette describes what was actually a straightforward situation with an easy solution but where the psychologist created unnecessary problems because he did not follow guidelines.

How the dilemmas represented in vignettes 2 and 3 can be solved is discussed later in this chapter. On the other hand, we believe that the presentation of rationales and the history of the development of ethical codes will be a lot more meaningful and stimulating when the reader knows what these codes and problem-solving steps can be used for. The chapter will then finish with a demonstration of how ethical principles and problem-solving steps can actually be applied to resolve one of the dilemmas presented in Box 4.1.

BOX 4.1

Vignette 1: Dr. Marisa A has completed a neuropsychological assessment on a patient (with a major personality disorder) who is seeking compensation in a car accident case. The patient (Suzy Q) senses that Marisa A's report is probably not going to help her court case and complains bitterly about Dr. A to her long-term therapist John D, who has been working with Suzy Q in his private practice helping with her adjustment. Suzy Q claims that A was mean (forgetting that a building of a therapeutic alliance is not part of formal assessment for court) and suggests incompetence. John D is inexperienced and does not really know that this pattern of complaining is typical of some personality disorders; he asks some leading questions to Suzy Q and concludes that Marisa A was unprofessional and incompetent in her assessment. Rather than informing Suzy Q that she is free to complain to the College of Psychologists, he takes it upon himself to make a complaint about Marisa A who purportedly conducted an unprofessional assessment. The complaint was fully processed; Marisa A had to provide reams of documents to the investigation committee and waited 6 months for a decision. The complaint was categorically dismissed because there was no evidence of wrongdoing on Marisa A's part.

Author comment: This is a disguised but true event. Why describe it here? It is offered as an example here because one of the decision-making guidelines is that the first attempted solution to a potential problem is to minimize the number of people involved and the damage that may arise from rash decision-making. In this case, the guideline specifically state that it was John D's responsibility to first contact Marisa A and get her side of this story. Had he done that Marisa A could have described her role in this case, provide the context, and point out to John D how the personality disorder that Marisa had diagnosed in Suzy Q had likely aggravated Suzy Q's dissatisfaction. Had John D followed the guidelines and talked to Marisa first, colleague to colleague, he would have likely realized that there was no substance to Suzy Q's complaining. This was not a difficult situation, and it was clear what the right thing to do was. If the conversation with Marisa A had been highly unsatisfying and possibly making him believe even more that Suzy Q was right, he was still free to make a formal

BOX 4.1 CONTINUED

complaint about Marisa A. Instead, however, his rash response cost Marisa A a lot of time and stress for nothing.

Vignette 2: Clinical psychologist Dr. Ramin B (who we introduced to you in chapter 1) has received specialized training in marital therapy and follows the recommended routine of meeting each partner separately when first beginning joint marital therapy. A couple came for therapy because they agree that their marriage is "on the rocks." The husband convinced his wife that therapy might be the answer and made the appointment. Both partners provide similar descriptions of the sad state of the marriage. The husband does not understand how things got this bad and wants to work things out. The wife on the other hand, in the one-on-one session, tells the psychologist that she has been having an affair with a distant mutual acquaintance for the last year, and she does not want to end this affair. She absolutely forbids the therapist to tell the husband who seems to have no clue; yet, the wife still wants to engage in therapy because she thinks that the husband is basically a good man, and the economic stability that the marriage currently offers is good for the children and herself. Can the psychologist still conduct meaningful conjoint marital therapy when he has important information about one partner that the other one is not allowed to know about? Common wisdom among marital therapy experts is that such therapy cannot work because the partners are not on the same level of willingness to repair the relationship, and the therapist runs a high probability of "slipping up" by accidentally revealing something about the wife's affair although he is strictly forbidden to do so. What can the psychologist do?

Vignette 3: Dr. Anne C (who you met in chapter 1) is a faculty member in a clinical psychology program. She lives in the same neighborhood as an undergraduate student who is taking a small seminar class with her ("S"). She accidentally overhears a conversation her teenage children are having revealing that "S" is a frequent marijuana user and a small-scale dealer, supplying the neighborhood with marijuana. Her children don't know that "S" is taking a class with their mother. "S" uses the proceeds of his marijuana sales to fund his education. What, if anything, is Dr. Anne C expected to do?

◇ OUR PROFESSION'S COMMITMENT TO ETHICAL STANDARDS OF PRACTICE

Currently, any academic program that seeks accreditation for its clinical psychology training is required to have an organized and systematic way of teaching ethical decision-making. Furthermore, in order to become licensed or registered as a psychologist, applicants will have to write the professional practice exam described in chapter 2, which has a section on ethical behavior. The applicants for licensure will also need to complete either written or oral exams (often both) on ethical behavior and local legislation before they are given the right to practice independently.

What can be learned from the problems that are known to arise? In determining what features of ethics are most in need of teaching, let's look at the most frequent reasons why psychologists receive complaints against them (Hall & Hare-Mustin, 1983). In the year 2006, the College of Psychologists of British Columbia listed the following three types as the most frequent complaints (http://www.collegeofpsychologists.bc.ca/documents/Summary% 20of%20Discipline%20Information%20-%202006.pdf):

1. Inappropriate assessment procedures (37.3% of all complaints)
2. Lack of professional competence (13.5%)
3. Client relationships—key problems here are confidentiality and boundary violations (13%)

In order to learn from this listing of frequent trouble spots, researchers have investigated the attitudes, beliefs, and context variables that can lead to these ethical violations. An important predictor for complaints received is area of practice. As the above-mentioned data on the frequency of complaints suggest, assessment results may have a major impact on people's lives: Children may not qualify for certain remedial treatments, or adults may not receive the disability pension they think they have a right to if a psychologist drew faulty conclusions from an assessment. Another relatively frequent problem is a **boundary violation**; examples might be that a psychologist asks a police officer who received help for depression to "fix" a parking ticket as a favor to the psychologist. Another example of a boundary violation is to sexually exploit a client who is enthralled by the therapist. Boundary violations have received much attention over the last two decades. For example, clinical psychologists' and nonpsychiatric physicians' attitudes and behaviors in sexual and confidentiality boundary violations were examined and compared (Rubin & Dror, 1996). The 171 participants' responses were analyzed by profession, sex, and status (student, resident, professional) and on their interpretation of boundary violation vignettes. Psychologists rated sexual boundary violation as more unethical than did physicians. Both professional groups agreed that there were times in a therapist-client relationship when a client is particularly vulnerable. Actual violators (based on self-report) rated vignette violators more leniently than did nonviolators.

Lack of professional competence may indeed harm a patient and is therefore taken very seriously; however, it is also difficult to quantify and requires expensive and laborious inquiry. Typically, this type of complaint, if found to be substantive, leads to a reprimand rather than loss of license. Violations of confidentiality are unfortunate insofar as they are usually irreversible. For example, if a psychologist revealed at a party (after a few drinks too many) that he had a famous local person as a patient (with an embarrassing personal problem), leakage of this information to the public means that the damage cannot be reversed. Even sincere apologies may not suffice here.

Legal Facts and Ethics

It is very important for psychologists to be familiar with the laws of their country (or state or province). What may look like a difficult ethical decision can be easy to solve when there is a pertinent law or legal precedent. Unfortunately, there are not many examples of potential ethical dilemmas that laws have resolved for us, but the ones that do exist are clear in their implications. In order to be licensed, clinical psychologists need to be familiar with local legislation, which usually includes laws specific to the state or province in which they work or specific to their country. Often, the most critical legislation to know about is provincial or state legislation. For example, in all provincial and state jurisdictions that we know of, there is a mandatory reporting requirement for *neglect and physical and sexual abuse of children*. A clinical psychologist and other health care providers have no choice under these laws but to report suspected abuse even if that means violating client confidentiality. The reporting usually involves contacting child welfare agencies, ministries of child development, or similar government bodies.

The psychologist also needs to be familiar with legislated **limitations on confidentiality**. A judge can order a psychologist to provide his or her case files if the client is involved in a trial; this includes absolutely every document that a psychologist has on this particular client. In consequence, it is also good practice to ask the client at the beginning of an assessment or therapy process whether or not the client is involved in an ongoing or pending court procedure. This knowledge can and should shape how the psychologist keeps the client's records, guided by the question: "Is this written material factually correct and complete, and is it expressed in a constructive, nonoffending language?"

Another widespread requirement is the duty to inform the Department of Motor Vehicles when the psychologist learning that a client is operating a motor vehicle although the client's competence is impaired due to senility or brain injury, for example. While this makes sense for the protection of others, the psychologist needs to anticipate that a patient who is about to lose his or her driving license (and associated mobility) may be very unhappy with this decision, and this will likely impact the relationship between the psychologist and the client.

The issue of limits to confidentiality has received much publicity in a famous California court case (typically referred to as "The Tarasoff decision") that is summarized in Box 4.2 (extracted from: http://www.adoctorm.com/docs/tarasoff.htm).

The Tarasoff decision reveals two important things for psychologists. On the one hand, it reveals how far they are expected to go to protect their clients. Furthermore, this case represents a strong precedent for guiding future decisions regarding their duty of care.

Practice Guidelines/Codes of Conduct

In addition to outright legal requirements for specific situations, licensing bodies in psychology have spent much effort accumulating information about areas of frequent psychology practice and have provided concrete **practice guidelines** on how to handle certain predictable professional responsibilities. Having these guidelines is tremendously helpful for psychologists because, if followed, the psychologists will indeed know what to do and be difficult to challenge in court by a disgruntled client who may not like the recommendation made by the clinical psychologist when this recommendation was logically derived from a well-defined, competent assessment process. Given that many situations in professional training, research, assessment, and treatment are similar, one can indeed spell out how to

BOX 4.2

A LANDMARK COURT RULING: *TARASOFF V. THE REGENTS OF THE UNIVERSITY OF CALIFORNIA*, SUPREME COURT OF CALIFORNIA, 1976

Facts: Prosenjit Poddar, an Indian graduate student studying naval architecture at the University of California, Berkeley, started to date a fellow student named Tatiana Tarasoff. He kissed her a few times and felt he had a special relationship with her. He was totally unfamiliar with American mores and had never had a date before. He felt betrayed when Tatiana flaunted her relationships with other men. Because of his depression he went to a psychologist, Dr. Moore, at the University Health Service. He revealed his intention to get a gun and shoot Tatiana Tarasoff. Dr. Moore sent a letter to the campus police requesting them to take Poddar to a psychiatric hospital. The campus police interviewed Mr. Poddar but he convinced them that he was not dangerous. They released him on the promise that he would stay away from Ms. Tarasoff. When the Health Service psychiatrist in charge returned from vacation, he directed that the letter to the police be destroyed and no further action taken. Mr. Poddar moved in with Tatiana's brother over the summer while Tatiana was visiting her aunt in Brazil. When Tatiana returned, Mr. Poddar stalked her and stabbed her to death.

The parents of Tatiana sued the campus police, Health Service employees, and Regents of the University of California for failing to warn them that their daughter was in danger.

Decision: In 1974, the California Supreme Court held that a therapist bears a duty to use reasonable care to give threatened persons such warnings as are essential to avert foreseeable danger arising from a patient's condition. This is known as the Tarasoff decision which is based on the following court conclusion:

"When a therapist determines, or pursuant to the standards of his profession should determine, that his patient presents a serious danger of violence to another, he incurs an obligation to use reasonable care to protect the intended victim against such danger. The discharge of this duty may require the therapist to take one or more of various steps. Thus, it may call for him to warn the intended victim, to notify the police, or to take whatever steps are reasonably necessary under the circumstances."

The defendants contended through amici briefs, including an APA brief, that psychiatrists were unable to accurately predict violence. The Court replied that they did not require therapists to render a perfect performance, "but only to exercise that reasonable degree of skilled care ordinarily possessed by members of their profession under similar circumstances." Proof, aided by hindsight, is insufficient to establish negligence. In the Tarasoff case itself, the therapist did accurately predict Poddar's danger of violence.

Authors' note: This text is a slightly shortened version of the website reprint; we removed procedural legal details of limited interest for psychologists' ethics.

behave in many such situations. This is made explicit in publications of licensing bodies that are called **codes of conduct** or practice guidelines, and practicing psychologists should be thoroughly familiar with or at least have ready access to these guidelines.

We will also talk about **basic principles of ethics** because the same organizations that wrote practice guidelines discovered quickly that the individual circumstances and context variables do not always fit these generic guidelines. The specific circumstances need to be diligently considered in the decision-making process. But first, let's look at the use of practice guidelines. Here, the reader will find a number of examples from practice guidelines that offer concrete help in making decisions. These examples are just samples from many existing lists of guidelines that are easily accessed on websites of national and state licensing bodies. Next, for demonstration purposes, we discuss one specific set of practice guidelines, namely, those used in **custody and access assessments**, which can be very controversial and litigious (Mnookin, 1975; Weithorn, 1987).

Here are four examples of guidelines from various domains of practice (http://www.apa.org/ethics):

Example 1

2.01 Boundaries of Competence

(a) Psychologists provide services, teach, and conduct research with populations and in areas only within the boundaries of their competence, based on their education, training, supervised experience, consultation, study, or professional experience.

Example 2

3.10 Informed Consent

(a) When psychologists conduct research or provide assessment, therapy, counseling, or consulting services in person or via electronic transmission or other forms of communication, they obtain the informed consent of the individual or individuals using language that is reasonably understandable to that person or persons except when conducting such activities without consent is mandated by law or governmental regulation or as otherwise provided in this Ethics Code.

Example 3

5.05 Testimonials

Psychologists do not solicit testimonials from current therapy clients/patients or other persons who, because of their particular circumstances, are vulnerable to undue influence.

Example 4

6.03 Withholding Records for Nonpayment

Psychologists may not withhold records under their control that are requested and needed for a client's/patient's emergency treatment solely because payment has not been received.

Custody and Access Reports: Necessary and Contentious

Guidelines for custody and access reports are a particular good example of useful guidelines, and their description illustrates how good guidelines can help you. Given their training and experience, clinical psychologists can provide valuable services when it comes to assisting parents with respect to child custody and access decisions in a divorce process. In the overwhelming portion (90%) of divorce custody cases, parents agree on custody arrangements without the help of courts (and save themselves extensive legal fees in the process) (Melton, Petrila, Poythress, & Slobogin, 1987). However, the cases that do go to court tend to be complex, bitter, and vexatious. One potential explanation for such complicated and litigious approaches is that a disproportionate number of custody cases that do go to court (rather than quickly settle) have at least one parent with a major personality disorder (Johnston, 1992, 1995). Individuals with personality disorder greatly aggravate legal proceedings (Eddy, 2006) and are much more likely to be unhappy with decisions and lash out at psychologists for their dissatisfaction by charging them with incompetence or bias. Given that such complaints are unfortunately frequent, psychologists are keen to ascertain that a competent assessment is to protect the children, satisfy the parent (as much as that is possible), and protect themselves from vexatious ethical complaints. To assure competent handling and minimize complaints from disgruntled parents, such specific guidelines assist the psychologist; they are given in Box 4.3.

Codes of Ethics

Having access to detailed codes of conduct greatly simplifies the life of clinical psychologists, and many situations that could become problematic are avoidable by simply following these codes. However, even if the psychologist has followed this code of conduct to the letter, dilemmas are sometimes forced upon them, just like in the two problem vignettes described at the beginning of the chapter. By definition, being in such a dilemma means that no answer is readily available, and we hope that in the end the psychologist will minimize damage while realizing that one or the other principle has to suffer.

Given that the details of such dilemmas and context variables are highly situation-specific and a conflict of principles cannot always be avoided, the psychologist needs tools to resolve the situation while doing the least harm. Furthermore, the construction of a specific code of conduct requires a foundation of basic, shared underlying values. This kind of foundation is reflected in what we call **codes of ethics**, which are very general listings of prescriptions for professional behavior with a high moral standard. Beginning with the release of the first codes of ethics in the United States in 1953 (American Psychological Association, 1953), psychologists in essentially all state and national jurisdictions have spent endless hours

BOX 4.3

GUIDELINES FOR CHILD CUSTODY EVALUATIONS IN DIVORCE PROCEEDINGS

I. Orienting Guidelines: Purpose of a Child Custody Evaluation
    1. The primary purpose of the evaluation is to assess the best psychological interests of the child.
    2. The child's interests and well-being are paramount.
    3. The focus of the evaluation is on parenting capacity, the psychological and developmental needs of the child, and the resulting fit.

II. General Guidelines: Preparing for a Child Custody Evaluation
    4. The role of the psychologist is that of a professional expert who strives to maintain an objective, impartial stance.
    5. The psychologist gains specialized competence.
    6. The psychologist is aware of personal and societal biases and engages in nondiscriminatory practice.
    7. The psychologist avoids multiple relationships.

III. Procedural Guidelines: Conducting a Child Custody Evaluation
    8. The scope of the evaluation is determined by the evaluator, based on the nature of the referral question.
    9. The psychologist obtains informed consent from all adult participants and, as appropriate, informs child participants.
    10. The psychologist informs participants about the limits of confidentiality and the disclosure of information.
    11. The psychologist uses multiple methods of data gathering.
    12. The psychologist neither overinterprets nor inappropriately interprets clinical or assessment data.
    13. The psychologist does not give any opinion regarding the psychological functioning of any individual who has not been personally evaluated.
    14. Recommendations, if any, are based on what is in the best psychological interests of the child.
    15. The psychologist clarifies financial arrangements.
    16. The psychologist maintains written records.

assembling and discussing codes of ethics that reflect their values and advertise that psychology professionals are of high moral virtue. These codes of ethics are revised and expanded on a regular basis (American Psychological Association, 1985, 1992, 1993). Comparing codes of conduct across different countries gives you an overwhelming impression that psychologists do care about the same things and that as a profession we have shown impressive maturation and growth. Box 4.4 lists the general principles underlying the codes of ethics of the American Psychological Association (http://www.apa.org/ethics:)

BOX 4.4

GENERAL PRINCIPLES OF THE APA CODE OF ETHICS (QUOTED DIRECTLY FROM THE APA WEBSITE)

This section consists of General Principles. General Principles are aspirational in nature. Their intent is to guide and inspire psychologists toward the very highest ethical ideals of the profession. General Principles, in contrast to Ethical Standards, do not represent obligations and should not form the basis for imposing sanctions.

Principle A: Beneficence and Nonmaleficence

Psychologists strive to benefit those with whom they work and take care to do no harm. In their professional actions, psychologists seek to safeguard the welfare and rights of those with whom they interact professionally and other affected persons, and the welfare of animal subjects of research. When conflicts occur among psychologists' obligations or concerns, they attempt to resolve these conflicts in a responsible fashion that avoids or minimizes harm. Because psychologists' scientific and professional judgments and actions may affect the lives of others, they are alert to and guard against personal, financial, social, organizational, or political factors that might lead to misuse of their influence. Psychologists strive to be aware of the possible effect of their own physical and mental health on their ability to help those with whom they work.

Principle B: Fidelity and Responsibility

Psychologists establish relationships of trust with those with whom they work. They are aware of their professional and scientific responsibilities to society and to the specific communities in which they work. Psychologists uphold professional standards of conduct, clarify their professional roles and obligations, accept appropriate responsibility for their behavior, and seek to manage conflicts of interest that could lead to exploitation or harm. Psychologists consult with, refer to, or cooperate with other professionals and institutions to the extent needed to serve the best interests of those with whom they work. They are concerned about the ethical compliance of their colleagues' scientific and professional conduct. Psychologists strive to contribute a portion of their professional time for little or no compensation or personal advantage.

Principle C: Integrity

Psychologists seek to promote accuracy, honesty, and truthfulness in the science, teaching, and practice of psychology. In these activities psychologists do not steal, cheat, or engage in fraud, subterfuge, or intentional misrepresentation of fact. Psychologists strive to keep their promises and to avoid unwise or unclear commitments. In situations in which deception may be ethically justifiable to maximize benefits and minimize harm, psychologists have a serious obligation to consider the need for, the possible consequences of, and their responsibility to correct any resulting mistrust or other harmful effects that arise from the use of such techniques.

BOX 4.4 CONTINUED

Principle D: Justice

Psychologists recognize that fairness and justice entitle all persons to access to and benefit from the contributions of psychology and to equal quality in the processes, procedures, and services being conducted by psychologists. Psychologists exercise reasonable judgment and take precautions to ensure that their potential biases, the boundaries of their competence, and the limitations of their expertise do not lead to or condone unjust practices.

Principle E: Respect for People's Rights and Dignity

Psychologists respect the dignity and worth of all people and the rights of individuals to privacy, confidentiality, and self-determination. Psychologists are aware that special safeguards may be necessary to protect the rights and welfare of persons or communities whose vulnerabilities impair autonomous decision making. Psychologists are aware of and respect cultural, individual, and role differences, including those based on age, gender, gender identity, race, ethnicity, culture, national origin, religion, sexual orientation, disability, language, and socioeconomic status and consider these factors when working with members of such groups. Psychologists try to eliminate the effect on their work of biases based on those factors, and they do not knowingly participate in or condone activities of others based upon such prejudices.

These general principles are then applied to the following specific areas of practice, also referred to as 10 ethical standards:

1. Resolving ethical issues
2. Competence
3. Human relations
4. Privacy and confidentiality
5. Advertising and other public statements
6. Record-keeping and fees
7. Education and training
8. Research and publication
9. Assessment
10. Therapy

(The full ethics code took effect on June 1, 2003; information regarding the code can be found on the APA website, http://www.apa.org/ethics.)

While being in accord with the principles of the APA code, the Canadian Psychological Association devised its own code of ethics that takes a number of important concepts a step further (Canadian Psychological Association, 1998; Pettifor & Sinclair, 1992). There are nine unique features that set the Canadian code of ethics apart from others, and they are designed to maximize the usefulness of the code for ethical decision-making. Note that the practical features of this code are useful in any jurisdiction.

The nine core features of the Canadian code of ethics are:

1. In order to write this code the authors began with a critical analysis of many other existing codes.

2. Particularly innovative in this code is the inclusion of what is called a **social contract** that calls for respect for one's own profession, which in turn is embedded in a similar contract with other professionals and the population at large.

3. The code was developed using a series of vignettes that were tested on practicing psychologists, and their feedback was used to revise the listing of ethical principles.

4. The principles underlying this code are organized around four major ethical principles (a list of the major and minor principles is provided in Box 4.5).

5. Given that an ethical dilemma involves not being able to honor all principles of ethics alike, the Canadian Psychological Association decided that to assist decision-makers it would be helpful to assign differential weights to the importance of the four major principles. Principles on the left of the tabular display are considered the most important, and those further to the right are of lesser importance.

6. Another important feature is that not only are principles offered with differential weighing, but the code comes with an explicit set of 10 steps of ethical decision-making, which are listed in Box 4.6.

7. As the fourth major principle indicates, Canadian psychologists see themselves as having a professional conscience that goes beyond mere ethical behavior toward their individual clients, and they also consider the larger societal good.

8. This code embraces the idea of minimal standards (like "do not harm," "do not deceive") as well as more idealistic and aspirational standards like expectations to "acquire knowledge about culture" or "contribute to the knowledge base of the profession."

9. The APA and CPA codes of ethics are considered to be umbrella documents, which means that the authors perceive them as a good foundation for the development of specific practice guidelines (like the ones on child custody evaluations we described earlier) and that this document will require regular review and potential revision.

These three items, namely, an understanding of the unique features of the Canadian code of ethics, the four basic ethical principles (and general, more detailed principles listed within each), as well as the 10 steps to ethical decision-making, can serve as the major toolbox in helping psychologists to resolve dilemmas such that they can defend their ultimate decisions. To illustrate this claim, we now consider the first vignette (depicting a dilemma that the psychologist did not initiate or otherwise cause but unfortunately still has to solve) and demonstrate how following the 10 steps can assist with decision-making (Box 4.7). We explicitly don't repeat this exercise for the second vignette because there now is an excellent opportunity for the student to apply what he or she has learned to resolve the dilemma described in the second vignette.

BOX 4.5

THE FOUR ETHICAL PRINCIPLES OF THE CPA CODE OF ETHICS WITH THEIR RESPECTIVE VALUES AND STANDARDS

I. Respect for the Dignity of Persons	II. Responsible Caring	III. Integrity in Relationships	IV. Responsibility to Society
1. *General respect*: respect others and abstain from degrading others	1. *General caring*: protect welfare, avoid harm, and accept responsibility	1. *Accuracy/honesty*: fraud, credentials, competency, and research findings	1. *Development of knowledge*: contribute to knowledge base
2. *General rights*: respect human rights	2. *Competence/self-knowledge*: training, self-development, know own biases, self-care	2. *Objectivity/lack of bias*: self-reflection and distortion of facts	2. *Beneficial activities*: participated and contributed to continuing education, contribute to the profession (e.g. accreditation), volunteer or pro bono work
3. *Nondiscrimination*: do not practice discrimination, seek to correct it, and develop research to address	3. *Risk/benefit analysis*: know who is affected, pilot work, carry out work only if benefit is greater than harm	3. *Straightforwardness/openness:* results of assessment, honor contracts, and role clarity	3. *Respect for society*: acquire knowledge about culture and know laws
4. *Informed consent*: seek full and active participation in consent process, ensure that purpose and nature of activity, confidentiality, and risks and benefits are understood	4. *Maximize benefit*: coordinate services, keep good records, monitor own work, teach, and research	4. *Avoidance of deception*: use only if there is no other alternative, debrief fully, re-establish trust, and give option to remove data	4. *Development of society*: research, advocacy, and reporting of data
5. *Freedom of consent*: ensure that consent is not given under coercion, pressure, or undue reward	5. *Minimize harm*: power differential, record keeping, termination of services	5. *Avoidance of conflict of interest*: dual relationships	5. *Extended responsibility*: encourage others to exercise responsibility
6. *Fair treatment/due process*: for research, fees, compensation	6. *Offset/correct harm*: termination, physical harm, debriefing	6. *Reliance on discipline*: know and follow rules and regulations and seek consultation	
		7. *Extended responsibility:* Encourage others to relate with integrity and assume responsibility of supervises	

BOX 4.6

TEN STEPS TO ETHICAL DECISION-MAKING

1. Identify all people (individuals and/or groups) who may be affected.

2. Clarify which ethical issues and principles apply to the situation.

3. Consider whether or not you may have personal biases, conflicts of interest, or may be experiencing personal stress that may unduly affect your decision-making in this situation.

4. Outline multiple possible plans of action without immediately judging them as "good" or "bad."

5. Weigh the risks and benefits of each possible action, and consider possible short- and long-term effects of each.

6. Make a relatively best choice after careful weighing of the relevant existing ethical principles.

7. Act on your first-choice decision, and accept responsibility for your action.

8. Carefully evaluate whether or not your action was a constructive one once you see the results of your action.

9. Continue to accept responsibility such that a second course of action may be needed to correct unforeseeable consequences or that another action is needed to resolve the situation.

10. Review the events with a view toward prevention of similar problems for the future.

Adapted from the Canadian Code of Ethics (1991), Ottawa, Ontario, Canada.

BOX 4.7

USING THE STEPS OF ETHICAL DECISION-MAKING

Step 1: Identify people and groups affected The key individuals to be considered are the psychologist Dr. B (henceforth B), the wife (W), the husband (H), and the wife's lover (L).

Step 2: Identify relevant issues On the surface, the decision to be made is whether or not to continue with therapy. Principles that the psychologist needs to consider (moving from left to right, from major principles 1 to 4) is that patients have the right to make their own decisions, that psychologists cannot act without informed patient consent, that they have an obligation to care for the well-being of their patients, to avoid or minimize harm, and that the therapist needs to be honest and open, avoiding deception. In this case, there does not appear to be an imminent threat to major principle 4, namely, Responsibility to Society. In this particular case, the problem largely arises from the fact that the psychologist

BOX 4.7 CONTINUED

has a couple as a client but also two individuals who make up this couple. If he respects the wife's wish to keep a secret, then the husband remains uninformed of a critical issue for therapy, and there is very high likelihood that the therapist does not have an honest shot at successfully responding to the husband's request for joint marital therapy.

Step 3: Consideration of personal biases   Dr. B., as an experienced marital therapist, will have heard of marital infidelities and marital problems before and is not likely shocked by this scenario. Nevertheless, Dr. B needs to ask himself whether he might have a particular moral stance on the topic of marital infidelity that could be different from those of his two clients and that his personal values may interfere with the wife's request of not revealing the critical information.

Step 4: Alternative courses of action   Dr. B sees two possible courses of action: (a) the first course would be to attempt to continue with therapy, and (b) the second would be to stop therapy after the wife's revelation because Dr. B is convinced that he cannot offer effective treatment to this couple; he does not want to take their money for a process that cannot work.

Step 5: Analysis of risks and benefits of available courses of action   If the psychologist continues with the therapy, he would indeed respond to the original quest of both individuals to conduct marital therapy. He may see a chance that the wife would at some point either stop the extramarital affair or inform her husband about it, or both. If that was the case, there would be no secret anymore, and he would be able to continue therapy in an equitable fashion for both partners. However, he is also painfully aware that it is extremely difficult to treat both parties fairly when he holds back on critical information that one of the two parties is not allowed to know about. Furthermore, he has reason to be afraid that he may somehow, somewhere, slip up and inadvertently reveal something to the husband that would open his eyes, thereby violating the instruction of the wife to maintain confidentiality that he had effectively promised by continuing with the therapy. He has to gauge the probability that he may be able to persuade the wife over the next few sessions to be honest with her husband. Should that not be the case, he has reason to believe that the treatment cannot succeed because the wife's stated objective of wanting to collaborate in the marital therapy endeavor is clearly undermined by her continuing involvement with her lover.

The second course of action is to stop therapy after the wife's revelation because Dr. B. believes that the therapy cannot succeed and that the husband has a right to openness; due care is unacceptably violated, and it makes a mockery out of conjoint therapy. If, however, the therapist refuses at this stage to continue with therapy, it is also quite likely that the husband will want to know why, and it will be exceedingly difficult to come up with a credible reason that would not somehow draw attention to the wife's ambivalence and dishonesty.

Step 6: Choose course of action   Once the wife reveals the affair to the therapist, the therapist has some time to work with her and explain the bind that he finds himself in. As described earlier, both courses of action on part of the therapist are very problematic, and it is not immediately obvious which one is superior (or at least less harmful). It makes sense

(continued)

BOX 4.7 CONTINUED

for the therapist to try to convince the wife to be honest with her husband and thereby set the stage for a possible constructive continuation of marital therapy, given that now both would be at a similar level of honesty with each other. The therapist can also point out that it is likely going to be difficult, if not impossible, for the wife to continue the illicit affair and pretend goodwill in therapy and that this alone may be a good reason to come forward and find the courage to be honest now. Should the wife at this point agree to openly discuss the affair with her husband, a solution with the least harm in the long run would be achieved. The price of course will be a very distressing revelation for her and her husband.

Another alternative might be to work with the wife to come up with an explanation about why the couple should not engage in marital therapy and she could tell the husband about her intention not to continue. At a minimum, the advantage is that the therapist does not need to violate confidentiality. However, it would also mean that the therapist is incapable of being honest with the husband and is not able to act on the husband's wish to engage the therapist in trying to improve the marriage.

A third possibility is to try to balance the wife's desire for keeping her husband in the dark and the husband's wish to improve the marriage, by attempting at least a brief period of therapy while keeping a close eye on possible progress. Should it come clear within a few sessions, but it is simply not possible to maintain the secrecy about the wife's ongoing affair, he would still have an obligation to terminate the therapy because he knows he cannot succeed.

Step 7: Action The most promising action appears to be to put considerable pressure on the wife to be open with her husband and not continue with the therapy unless she's willing to do so on a "level playing field." It may be necessary for the therapist to be blunt and declare this being the fairest solution. Continuing therapy with a secret in the closet, or sudden declarations of not wanting to continue, is very problematic and not fair to the husband. Either of these actions is inferior to the first suggestion of getting the wife to reveal her affair to her husband.

Step 8: Evaluating the results of the course of the action If the wife makes a revelation to her husband and both continue with the therapy hoping to rebuild trust, the therapist would be able to witness the result of this difficult choice and hopefully be able to play a constructive role in rebuilding the relationship. If therapy would cease, Dr. B is unlikely to hear about the long-term effects of his decision.

Step 9: Taking responsibility for the consequences of action The wife's desire to keep a secret is clearly putting the therapist into an impossible situation that will probably force his hand, one way or another. Having reasoned through the possible courses of action and attempted the least harmful option first, the therapist ought to be able to comfort himself that the right thing has been done.

Step 10: Prevention of future occurrences Given that the problem was not initiated by the therapist and may be endemic to marital therapies, there does not appear to be a guarantee that such a situation can be avoided in the future by a change in the therapist's behavior. The therapist could of course choose to abandon the practice of marital therapy or never have individual sessions again with each of two partners; however, people need quality of care and would not benefit from such evasive action.

◇ CONCLUSION

The topic of ethical behavior is fascinating, critical to the survival of our profession and its public image, and often very frustrating. It is easy to understand and empathize with the desire to do the right thing, but when it comes to ethics, there is often no perfect solution. Contexts change frequently and are important to consider, and many of our decisions are imperfect even though they represent the best that we can do. This raises the question of how we can comfort ourselves to accept this perpetual ambiguity. At one extreme, laws tell us clearly what not to do and what the punishment is when we violate such laws. Practice guidelines are meant to help with more routine practice decisions although they cannot tell you what happens when you violate these guidelines. The overarching ethical principles are very general and have to be fitted to each individual situation and circumstance.

◇ ONGOING CONSIDERATIONS

We cannot encourage psychologists to ever feel totally safe. Using the earlier analogy of the virus-check on your computer, you don't turn off your virus-check even if you have not had a virus in all of the last year. Just the opposite, you want to upgrade your virus program on a regular basis just as much as you want to remain sensitized to ethical challenges. Aside from the fact that licensing bodies expect psychologists to regularly update their knowledge on ethical decision-making, we urge all psychologists and psychology students to build and nurture a network of psychologist friends with whom they can discuss ethical dilemmas, who under-stand the frustrations, and who can assist by being the second conscience that is sometimes required to make sound, reasoned decisions. Complaints investigation committees of licens-ing bodies tend to provide regular feedback to registrants about the nature of complaints that have been brought forward; these make interesting reading, and it is comforting to read that the majority of complaints were avoidable if only the clinical psychologists had been familiar with the content of this chapter and had followed the instructions provided.

◇ KEY TERMS LEARNED

Aspirational	Custody and access assessments
Basic principles of ethics	Ethical principles
Boundary violation	Limitations on confidentiality
Codes of conduct	Practice guidelines
Codes of ethics	Process of ethical decision-making
Confidentiality	Social contract

◇ THINKING QUESTIONS

1. How does an aspirational principle differ from practice guidelines?
2. Practice guidelines are useful but what are their limits?
3. How different (or not) are the codes of ethics in different countries?
4. What specific practices and habits should clinical psychologists develop to protect themselves from complaints being brought forward against them?

◇ REFERENCES

American Psychological Association. (1953). *Ethical standards of psychologists*. Washington, DC: Author.

American Psychological Association. (1985). *Standards for educational and psychological testing*. Washington, DC: Author.

American Psychological Association. (1992). Ethical principles of psychologists and code of conduct. *American Psychologist, 47*, 1597–1611.

American Psychological Association. (1993). *Record keeping guidelines*. Washington, DC: Author.

Canadian Psychological Association. (August 1998). Special issue on the Canadian code of ethics. Pettifor, J. L. & C. Sinclair (Eds.), *Canadian Psychology, 39*, 1–245.

Eddy, W. A. (2006). *High conflict people in legal disputes*. Calgary: Janis Publications.

Hall, J. E., & Hare-Mustin, R. T. (1983). Sanctions and the diversity of ethical complaints against psychologists. *American Psychologist, 38*, 714–729.

Housman, L. M., & Stake, J. E. (1999). The current state of sexual ethics training in clinical psychology: Issues of quantity, quality, and effectiveness. *Professional Psychology: Research and Practice, 30*, 302–331.

Johnston, J. R. (1992). High-conflict and violent parents in family court: Findings on children's adjustment, and proposed guidelines for the resolution of custody and visitation disputes. *Section III: Proposed guidelines for custody and visitation for cases with domestic violence*. Corta Madera, CA: Center for the Family in Transition.

Johnston, J. R. (1995). Research update: Children's adjustment in sole custody compared to joint custody families and principles for custody decision making. *Family and Conciliation Courts Review, 33*, 415–425.

Keith-Spiegel, P., & Koocher, G. P. (1985). *Ethics in psychology*. New York: Random House.

Melton, G. B., Petrila, J., Poythress, N. G., & Slobogin, C. (1987). *Psychological evaluations for the courts: A handbook for mental health professionals and lawyers*. New York: Guilford Press.

Mills, D. H. (1984). Ethics education and adjudication within psychology. *American Psychologist, 39*, 669–675.

Mnookin, R. H. (1975). Child-custody adjudication: Judicial functions in the face of indeterminacy. *Law and Contemporary Problems, 39*, 226–293.

Pettifor, J. L., & Sinclair, C. (Eds.). (1992). *Companion manual to the Canadian Code of Ethics for Psychologists*. Ottawa: CPA.

Rubin, S. S., & Dror, O. (1996). Professional ethics of psychologists and physicians: Morality, confidentiality, and sexuality in Israel. *Ethics & Behavior, 6*, 213–238.

Weithorn, L. A. (1987). *Psychology and child custody determinations: Knowledge, roles, and expertise*. Lincoln: University of Nebraska Press.

◇ EXCELLENT WEBSITES

http://www.kspope.com/consent/index.php

http://www.apa.org/ethics/code2002.html

Web-based course:

http://webclientsit.captus.com/cpa/courses.html

CHAPTER FIVE

THE NATURE OF PSYCHOPATHOLOGY

CHAPTER OBJECTIVE

In this chapter we will not be describing the types and kinds of abnormal behavior, as is done in most psychology texts. Rather, we will try to address several important and overarching issues pertaining to psychological problems that are of importance to research and practice in clinical psychology. These issues reflect the processes by which behavior is considered to be maladaptive or abnormal. In other words, we address the question as to how clinical psychologists determine whether certain behaviors or constellations of behavior are in need of assessment and treatment and should, thus, be the focus of research. Second, we will discuss issues involving the kinds of behaviors that constitute abnormal behavior (also known as **psychopathology**). Third, we will discuss issues involving the current classification systems that are in use that help the clinical psychologist make determinations about people's psychological problems and provide a snapshot of the kinds of disorders that exist today.

We will begin with case vignettes that illustrate day-to-day issues with psychopathology that clinical psychologists are involved with. Students will recognize that some of these issues involve questions about the specific nature of psychological problems, the importance of defining problems in different contexts, and how best to characterize the psychological problems that people experience. Some of the topics discussed in the chapter follow.

VIGNETTE 5.1

In order to determine appropriate treatment, Vincent, the clinical psychology graduate student, is completing a project for a course that describes different ways of understanding psychological problems that people have. The paper he is writing deals with the issues regarding whether a person's psychological problems stem from long-standing issues, such as interpersonal relationship problems, that underlie the symptoms or whether the symptoms themselves constitute the disorder and the focus of treatment. He has been reading several different literatures in the field and has gained important knowledge from these different sources. Vincent discusses the issues such that in the former model, where the underlying causes produce the symptoms, treatment should focus on changing those underlying causes whereas in the second model, changing the symptoms themselves becomes the focus of treatment.

VIGNETTE 5.2

Dr. A is assessing the psychological status of a father whose 4-year old daughter has been diagnosed with cancer. Dr. C is attempting to determine whether the father has an adjustment, depressive, or anxiety disorder or some other form of psychological difficulty, how the symptoms and characteristics of the disorder(s) might affect the daughter and other family members, and how to best deal with these overwhelming affective responses. The psychologist is particularly interested in determining whether the reactions and behaviors of the father are normal (but very distressing) responses to a devastating life event or whether the responses and behaviors would constitute a diagnosable disorder. In other words, she was interested in determining whether the distress the patient was experiencing was abnormal or not. Knowing the answer to this question will influence the interventions the psychologist would recommend for the patient. For example, if the responses are expected or normal responses to a major stressful event, then a supportive treatment that helps the father cope with the diagnosis of his daughter would be appropriate. On the other hand, if the responses and behaviors represent a formal psychological disorder, then a more in-depth treatment would be appropriate that aims at both reducing symptoms and helping the father acquire new behaviors to reduce the likelihood of relapse.

VIGNETTE 5.3

During a multidisciplinary case conference, psychologist Dr. B was asked for an opinion on a patient who had been provisionally diagnosed with borderline personality disorder (BPD). He decided to present a description of the kinds of signs and symptoms found in the kind of psychopathology the patient exhibited and also a description of some of the underlying potential causes of the disorder. Dr. A began to discuss the symptoms (frequent depressive episodes, an overwhelming fear of rejection, and pervasive difficulties with emotional regulation) the patient exhibited and commensurate with the descriptions in the *Diagnostic and Statistical Manual of Mental Disorder, IV, Text Revision (DSM-IV-TR)*, one of the more frequently used diagnostic system available. In addition to indicating how the patient's symptom picture met the diagnostic criteria of the *DSM-IV-TR*,

Dr. A discussed how there are different personality constellations that can underlie a BPD and have a significant influence on the symptom picture, prognosis, and treatment options. He discussed how one personality constellation focuses on self-definitional and autonomy features; whereas another constellation focuses on interpersonal relatedness and relationships with others. These were presented to provide a point of discussion to understand the nature of the patient's difficulties, determine the best treatment options, and inform other clinicians regarding potentially difficult issues that may arise in the treatment, prognosis, and, finally, potential causal factors for the BPD.

VIGNETTE 5.4

Psychologist Dr. C has a particular interest in attempting to understand the underlying causes of psychological difficulties. Although there have been many descriptions of the nature of both depression and pain in the literature, she had noticed in her practice that chronic pain (her specialty area) is often associated with depression. However, it has remained unclear whether the depression causes additional pain or influences the experience of pain, or whether the depression is a consequence of the pain. She therefore engaged in designing a research project looking at some of the psychological variables that may be predictive of the onset of depression. From several different perspectives, vulnerability to depression is seen as including dysfunctional attitudes and thoughts that engender harsh self-criticism, interpersonal styles of relating to others based on early attachment styles developed in childhood interactions, and the experience of a loss of an important relationship in childhood. Each of these factors has been espoused to predispose an individual to depression, and Dr. B wants to establish, empirically, whether these experiences are relevant in depression and which ones might be most important. She is engaged in designing a grant proposal with several studies addressing these issues.

◇ PSYCHOLOGICAL PROBLEMS THAT CLINICAL PSYCHOLOGISTS FOCUS ON

When an individual, couple, or family enters a clinical psychologist's care, how does that clinical psychologist determine what behavior is normal (and by definition should not be altered or changed) or what behavior is abnormal or maladaptive? The answer to this question is rather complex and not necessarily easy to answer. The question can be broached broadly in two ways. The first deals with the processes of determining how a person's behavior is defined as abnormal or maladaptive. The second deals with the processes clinical psychologists pay attention to when they try to determine whether some behavior is abnormal or maladaptive.

◇ DEFINING PSYCHOLOGICAL PROBLEMS

In defining abnormality, there are at least three major approaches used in research and clinical work. Each of these approaches has strengths and limitations and can be used, in some cases, simultaneously or in combination by clinical psychologists.

Statistical or Normative Approach

In this approach to defining abnormality, a judgment is made whether a person's behavior conforms, generally, to the standards, expectations, or norms of a particular society or social group. Although different cultures and societies may have different standards or expectations, all cultures and societies have standards for appropriate behavior (Gorenstein, 1992). If a person's behavior falls outside the norm, that person's behavior is considered to be abnormal, problematic, and in need of amelioration. Thus, behaviors that are unusual, occur rarely, or otherwise are not engaged in by most people can be considered to be abnormal. For example, viewing an individual having an animated and emotional conversation with a telephone pole would likely result in an interpretation that the individual's behavior is abnormal because the majority of people do not have conversations with telephone poles.

Although this statistical approach captures or defines many individuals who do exhibit psychological problems and who can likely benefit from treatment, it has several difficulties or shortcomings. For example, there are many cultural differences in terms of behavior that falls within norms. What is seen as normal in one culture may be viewed as abnormal in another. Likewise, there are many individuals with behaviors that fall well outside the norm (e.g., Mozart, Rembrandt, Einstein are all examples of individuals whose creativity is far outside normative standards) but would neither be considered problematic nor in need of changing. In fact, typically we revel in these kinds of individuals' deviations from the normative standards.

Subjective Interpretation (Psychological Pain)

In this approach, individuals themselves make judgments as to whether their own behaviors are abnormal, maladjusted, or otherwise in need of changing. Thus, rather than using standards or norms from a particular society or culture, the person himself or herself makes a judgment of the adaptiveness or abnormality of his or her own behavior. An individual may view himself or herself as exhibiting behavior that is technically not a disorder but is nevertheless bothersome or distressing. For example, a couple may notice an increase in arguments that is not statistically different from couples within the culture, but the couple may want to work to decrease the number of arguments nonetheless. Thus, the couple (or individual) defines their own behavior as abnormal and in need of attention. This kind of defining of abnormality is what likely brings the majority of patients to the therapist's office.

Judgments of Maladaptive Functioning

In this approach, typically an expert makes a judgment as to whether a person's behavior is abnormal or maladaptive. Clinicians would normally make this judgment, based, generally, on whether the person's behavior interferes with his or her ability to work and/or to develop and maintain relationships (APA, 2000). This approach does not rely on statistical norms nor does it rely on an individual's own level of discomfort to make a decision about abnormality or maladaptiveness. Rather, a judgment of whether the person's behavior is maladaptive is made based on his or her functioning in two broad domains: work and interpersonal relationships. For example, a clinician may conclude that a man has a drinking problem, even though the frequency and amount he consumes is within statistical norms. The man in question may not view his own drinking behavior as distressing or problematic, but because he cannot hold down a job and/or has lost significant long-term relationships, he is deemed as having a psychological problem. Individual patients may not agree with these experts' opinions and choose not to seek help; alternatively if they are forced into therapy by a judge or a spouse threatening divorce, they are likely unmotivated and very difficult to work with.

◇ ISSUES IN DEFINING PSYCHOLOGICAL PROBLEMS

Although these approaches represent ways in which individuals are defined as exhibiting abnormal behavior, the astute reader may note that what is defined as abnormal behavior may or may not represent formal psychological disorders. In fact, many problems that come to the attention of clinical psychologists might be better labeled as **problems in living** (Szasz, 1961) rather than diagnoses. For example, it is often assumed that clinical psychologists research, assess, and treat only formal psychological disorders. Although the majority of problems that clinical psychologists study, assess, and treat will likely meet diagnostic criteria for some disorder (i.e., disorders listed in one of the current diagnostic manuals in use), many problems that clinical psychologists deal with do not necessarily constitute formal diagnostic entities. For example, some of the issues that people will seek assessment of and/or treatment for (and clinical psychologists will conduct research on) are the following:

Relationship problems (e.g., intimate relationship difficulties, relationship breakdown, problematic work-related relationships, family problems)

Personal difficulties (e.g., self-esteem problems, identity-related problems, lack of general satisfaction in life)

Achievement problems (e.g., feelings of stagnation and dissatisfaction with work, test anxiety, job or life transition)

Physical problems (e.g., weight control, reduction of blood pressure, sleep problems)

Problems that reflect normal but distressing processes (e.g., grieving losses arising from death or divorce)

These problems in living can produce significant distress and disruptions for individuals, couples, or families suffering from these issues. Moreover, it can often be the case that when treating individuals with psychological disorders, problems in living often accompany many formal disorders and can become the focus of treatment (Bergin & Lambert, 1978).

BOX 5.1

WHAT IS NORMAL BEHAVIOR?

Clinical psychologists struggle with this issue as they often need to make judgments about whether or not a person's behavior is abnormal or in need of treatment, how abnormal a person's behavior is, and when a person returns to a state of normality. Although there has been extensive research and theorizing on abnormal behavior, less attention has been directed at normal or healthy personality. Early attempts to describe healthy personality include work by Sydney Jourard (1958) who grounded his conceptualization of normal personality in terms of expression of values. He stated that a healthy personality involves the ability to meet and satisfy needs with behavior that conforms to both the norms of a society and the requirements of the person's conscience. More recently, there have been attempts to describe normality in terms of psychological well-being. For example, Carol Ryff (1989) described six dimensions of psychological well-being including the presence of positive relationships, autonomy, personal growth, self-acceptance, purpose in life, and environmental mastery. The *Psychodynamic Diagnostic Manual* (to be discussed later) is the only formal diagnostic manual that attempts to describe normal behavior. It details seven characteristics or capacities that healthy personalities have and that individuals with abnormal behavior lack or have difficulties with. These include the capacities to: (1) see both the self and others in complex, stable, and accurate ways, (2) maintain intimate and satisfying relationships, (3) experience the full range of emotions, (4) regulate emotions and impulses adaptively and flexibly, (5) function in a fashion consistent with morals, (6) appreciate conventional notions of what is realistic, and (7) respond to stress resourcefully. Each of these capabilities can provide benchmarks for contrasting a person's behavior in order to help determine whether that person's behavior is abnormal.

It may seem that in determining some behavior as abnormal that the behavior is viewed as entirely negative or pathological and in need of elimination. It is also tempting to view the abnormal behavior as similar to a pathogen, like a virus, that is foreign and invasive, and needs to be eradicated. However, it is important to understand that abnormal behavior is often a part of an individual's total behavioral repertoire and is often tightly intertwined with the individual's personality, interpersonal relationships, and his or her general environment. It can be the case that what is determined as abnormal or pathological at one point in time could have been very adaptive at another time. For example, if a woman has severe social anxiety that interferes with her ability to find satisfying work and to develop an intimate relationship because she cannot present herself as someone who "stands out from the rest," everyone would likely agree that she has a significant psychological disorder or problem. However, this exact behavior may have been extremely adaptive if, for example, this woman grew up in an abusive family where she observed an older sibling experience severe physical abuse by parents. This woman, as a young girl, may have learned that if she stands out or is noticed by others, it is dangerous, and she learns not to stand out in any way.

In other words, she "blended into the woodwork" so as not to be noticed or focused upon and, by doing so, avoided the same abuse her sister experienced. Thus, her behavior that involves not being noticed or standing out is maladaptive in one context or at one point in time and extremely adaptive in another context or time. Moreover, some pathological states, such as some forms of depression, have been described not as negative and maladaptive, but as necessary and positive processes of disengaging from goals that are not met or are inappropriate to pursue (e.g., Klinger, 1975). Likewise, the processes involved in grieving losses are seen as both necessary and, at times, indistinguishable from symptoms of major depression, which is viewed as psychopathology. This suggests that the mere presence of certain behaviors or constellations of behavior that can be defined as pathological are not necessarily always pathological. Thus, it is extremely important to take the context of the person into account when defining abnormal behavior.

Lastly, in terms of defining abnormal behavior, it must be remembered that the judgments of abnormality tend to be subjective and are reflective of the culture and society (see Box 5.2 on homosexuality as a disorder). Moreover, what is defined as abnormal and in need of treatment depends greatly on the cultural context and the prevailing norms, standards, and mores.

◇ SOME IMPORTANT CONCEPTS IN DEFINING PSYCHOLOGICAL PROBLEMS

Before we discuss the specific processes and focuses of abnormal behavior, we need to define and discuss the features of a person's behavior that are informative to the clinician, namely, **sign**, **symptom**, and **syndrome**. In addition, we will discuss the concept of **mental disorder**.

Sign

A sign is thought to be a problem or abnormality that can be observed by a clinician but that is not necessarily perceived by the patient. It is considered to be an "objective manifestation of a pathological condition" (APA, 2000, p. 827). For example, the use of neologisms (words that do not exist in language) can be seen as a sign of schizophrenia.

Symptom

A symptom is thought to be an abnormality or complaint that is perceived by a patient, although the term is often used to refer to any indications of a patient's experience or behavior that reflects a particular disorder. Thus, symptoms are considered to be "subjective manifestations of a pathological condition" (APA, 2000, p. 828). Some characteristic of a patient can be both a sign and a symptom if both the patient and the clinician observe that characteristic. For example, some newly acquired speech difficulties, such as inability to articulate words, can be both a sign and symptom. Some characteristics, such as particular thoughts, pain, or emotions can only be symptoms, as they cannot be directly observed by the clinician.

Syndrome

A syndrome represents a group or set of signs and/or symptoms that, in combination, reflect a specific health-related condition. The co-occurrence of the signs and/or symptoms is often thought to reflect underlying pathology.

Mental Disorder

The definition of mental disorder is tricky. Although there is very good agreement on the definitions of "sign," "symptom," and "syndrome," there is no generally agreed upon definition of mental disorder. In fact, the concept of psychological or mental disorder has various definitions depending on the society, theoretical orientation, or the purpose for the need to define mental disorder (WHO, 2005). According to the International Classification of Diseases (WHO, 2005), a disorder is normally thought of as a term used to imply the existence of a clinically recognizable set of signs, symptoms, or behaviors that often produce distress and interference with personal functions. The authors of the *Diagnostic and Statistic Manual of Mental Disorders–IV–TR* likewise state that "no definition adequately specifies precise boundaries of the concept of mental disorder (APA, 2000)," although they suggest that a disorder constitutes a manifestation of a behavioral, psychological, or biological dysfunction in an individual. Thus, we can think of a mental disorder as a recognized amalgamation of signs, symptoms, and behaviors that likely causes distress for the person or others and interferes with the person's ability to behave in a healthy and adaptive fashion.

It is tempting to think of the diagnostic process as a process of discovering an underlying fact (i.e., the presence of a distinct disease); this makes sense for the assessment of a stomach pain as a sign of an infected appendix or a blood test for the presence of the AIDS virus. We cannot just adopt this model to psychological problems because we often deal with complex presentations that may have arisen from an interaction of genetic, early learning, and current contextual factors.

◇ PSYCHOLOGICAL PROBLEMS: WHAT PROCESSES ARE AFFECTED?

When people experience psychopathology (which can be mild, moderate, or severe, and can be slightly or significantly debilitating), what behaviors or processes do clinical psychologists pay attention to? Psychopathology can be thought of as problems or difficulties that affect numerous processes in people's functioning. In many cases the amalgamation of the behaviors can reflect problems in the person's personality, whereas in others the problems may be seen as outside of or separate from the person's personality. For example, an individual may have anger/hostility problems that are long-standing and evident in almost all of his or her interactions. Another person may develop debilitating anxiety related to a discrete entity, such as presence of snakes. In the former, the difficulties are seen as part of the person's personality and makeup, whereas the latter may be seen as situation-specific and distinct from the person's personality. Although not all clinical psychologists will place a great emphasis on personality per se, for most, personality variables are the key features for assessment, treatment, and research. For example, various personality traits (e.g., dependency or conscientiousness) are considered pathological when they are extreme and there are numerous personality processes (e.g., the interpersonal expression of traits; Hewitt et al., 2003) that have also been shown to be relevant in psychopathology.

Some processes or characteristics we will discuss can be directly observed; whereas others can only be inferred. Likewise, some can be thought of as causes or manifestations of psychopathology. A discussion of some of the major processes and characteristics follows. Depending on the theoretical perspective, these processes can be viewed as descriptors, maintenance factors, or causes of the problem(s).

Emotions and Emotional Regulation

Emotion or affect is a major domain that is affected in psychopathology and is a focus on much research and clinical work. In fact, there are at least two sets of disorders, depressive disorders and anxiety disorders, that have marked emotional disturbance as the primary symptom, and by far the majority of other disorders and psychological problems have negative emotional components (Clark & Watson, 1991). Although any emotion can be viewed as pathological in extreme cases, we typically see anxiety, depression, and anger as the most predominant emotions reflective of psychological disorders. The ability to control the experience and expression of negative emotions, known as **emotional regulation**, is also seen as a significant contributing factor in psychological problems. Lastly, both reduced emotional expression, known as blunted or flat affect, and an absence of certain emotions, such as empathy, remorse, or guilt, are considered indicators of some psychological problem.

Thoughts/Cognitions, Intellectual Functioning, Information Processing

Another domain of importance, and one that clinical psychologists pay close attention to, involves thoughts and thought processes as well as intellectual functioning. With many forms of distress, psychological problems, and mental disorders, whether mild, moderate, or severe, individuals have compromised cognitive features. For example, with serious psychopathology, such as with disorders reflecting schizophrenia, individuals can have unusual or bizarre beliefs not shared by most people (i.e., delusions) and very odd, eccentric ways of thinking. Likewise, with several disorders, individuals can have significant information processing difficulties whereby they interpret and focus only on the negative aspects of the world, the self, and the future (e.g., Beck, Rush, Shaw, & Emery, 1979) or on the potential sources of threat. Moreover, rumination, seen in numerous disorders, reflects a lack of ability to control thoughts and in extreme cases can be debilitating to people (e.g., obsessive-compulsive disorders). Lastly, cognitive processing and intellectual functioning problems are seen in many neuropsychological issues involving brain damage in addition to other disorders.

Perceptions

Perceptual processes involve cognitive processes that give rise to perceptual experiences. Again, in the severe range of psychopathology, perceptual difficulties, such as hallucinations (e.g., hearing voices, seeing images), are important indicators of psychopathology such as schizophrenia. At less extreme levels, there are various forms of person perception whereby the individuals respond to others based on inaccurate perceptions, or they perceive the world as inordinately hostile, dangerous, or depressing. For example, individuals with social anxiety will respond as if others are consistently critical and judgmental (Taylor & Alden, 2008).

Interpersonal Processes

Another important domain that clinical psychologists focus upon involves interpersonal processes. Clinical psychologists pay a great deal of attention to issues such as a person's capacity, history, and stylistic aspects of relationships with others. This includes not only intimate relationships but also friendships, networks of social support, and relationships with family and coworkers. In addition, the relationship schemas or representations of others (i.e., **object relations**) that individuals develop (St. Clair, 2004) and the relationship a person has with himself or herself are also of interest (Sullivan, 1953). By this we mean that self-esteem and self-regard, which are issues in numerous kinds of psychopathology, whereby the individual's view of the self, are unrealistically low, unrealistically high, or too reactive.

Regulatory or Coping Behavior

Everyone experiences demands, stressors, and anxiety that require adaptation and coping. An important domain that clinical psychologists focus on deals with not only whether a person can cope with life's demands, but also the manner in which the individual does attempt to cope and whether it is effective. For example, it is assumed that there are adaptive and maladaptive ways of coping (Lazarus & Folkman, 1984) and both mature and immature defenses (Vaillant, 1977) that can help or hinder an individual in dealing with the internal and external world. It is believed, generally, that coping inappropriately can produce or increase psychological and physical problems (Anna Freud, 1937). Furthermore, several theorists have suggested that inflexible coping or defending (i.e., using only one or two strategies irrespective of the situation) can have a decided effect on psychopathology (Sullivan, 1953).

Development

Developmental issues are always important to consider in determining abnormality, but these issues are most commonly focused on with children or adolescents. In this regard, the clinical psychologist pays attention to whether the individual has met developmental milestones and presents expectations of normal development, whether it is normal child cognitive development or adult social development. One domain of child clinical psychology, known as **descriptive psychopathology**, views psychopathology from a developmental perspective (see also chapter 15). In other words, what is normal for a child at one age may be indicative of a psychological problem for a child at another age. Moreover, most clinical psychologists are interested in understanding parts of the past in a person's life, whether it is to understand previous level of functioning, onset of the problem, or concern; determine learning histories; explore early relationships; or identify difficulties with establishment of identity. Lastly, based on experiences over the course of a lifetime, various existential issues (e.g., dealing with one's own death, death of loved ones, meaningfulness in one's life) can also become a focus. Thus, developmental issues are often an important component in the work clinical psychologists do.

Environment

It is safe to say that all clinical psychologists will pay careful attention to environmental issues for people they are working with. As discussed in Issues in Defining Psychological Problems section, in terms of defining abnormality, the clinical psychologist needs to take into account the environmental context and issues that can influence the psychological problems. Moreover, the environment can play a key role in causing and maintaining psychological difficulties, and helping the individual, couple, or family alter the environment can be a focus of treatment. In chapter 12, the importance of the environment in either maintaining or reducing a behavior will be apparent.

Although the list of focuses of clinical psychologists in dealing with abnormality is not exhaustive, the domains discussed represent some of the major ones. Psychologists from particular orientations will emphasize or focus upon certain problematic behaviors over others, both in terms of the research they conduct and the clinical work they are engaged in. In addition, there are aspects of these domains that exist in individuals experiencing all manner of physical ill health (see also chapter 17). Whether it is depression or anxiety that exists in just about any major physical health problem (e.g., osteoarthritis or heart disease) or existential processes and the emotional and cognitive upheaval in being diagnosed with a serious or terminal illness, it is important to understand that these behaviors can become important focuses for research, assessment, and treatment.

◇ CONCEPTUALIZATIONS OF PSYCHOLOGICAL PROBLEMS

Historically, definitions and conceptualizations of psychopathology shifted and changed over time. As knowledge accumulates, theoretical perspectives accommodate to new information, new perspectives appear or often reappear, and, as values of society shift, definitions of psychopathology likewise shift. Just as views of the nature, causes, and treatments of psychological difficulties shifted between demonological models and more "scientific" or natural perspectives over the past centuries (Ellenberger, 1970), current conceptualizations of psychopathology used in clinical psychology are not necessarily uniform or static, nor are components necessarily generally agreed upon. What is seen as a disturbance or problem today may not be seen as psychological disturbance tomorrow. There can be many causes of this phenomenon. For example, some disorders appear to be decreasing in frequency due to either an actual decrease in the incidence (i.e., the development of new cases) of the disorder

BOX 5.2

HOMOSEXUALITY AS A DISORDER?

Until the 1980s, homosexuality was considered to be a psychological disorder, but in 1980, with the American Psychiatric Association's publication of *DSM-III*, homosexuality was removed from the list of disorders and was not considered a form of psychopathology. Based, in large part, on political pressure from various groups in the United States (Spitzer, 1981) and from a more accepting view of homosexuality during the 1970s and 1980s, homosexuality was no longer viewed as a disorder. The dropping of homosexuality from the diagnostic system is an example of how societal values can influence what is defined as abnormal behavior and demonstrates that what is defined as abnormal is not necessarily static.

due to treatment and prevention (e.g., conversion disorders; American Psychiatric Association, 2000) or a refinement in diagnosis so that other disorders or problems that are similar to the disorder in question are no longer lumped together (e.g., schizophrenia and bipolar affective disorder; attention deficit disorder and hyperactivity). This can result in true decreases in a diagnostic entity or in decreases due to a redefinition of the behaviors as not indicative of a psychological disorder (e.g., see Box 5.2).

Philosophical Underpinnings of Orientations to Psychopathology

As outlined throughout this book, the work that clinical psychologists do is strongly influenced by their theoretical orientation, and the field of clinical psychology is not necessarily a unified whole with only one or two theoretical orientations. Instead, working from one of various theoretical orientations provides the clinical psychologist with a philosophical stance, tools, techniques, and skills in order to deal with particular clinical or research issues. One of the fundamental underpinnings of the theoretical orientation involves the clinical psychologist's views of the nature of psychopathology and how people function normally and abnormally. The adherence to a particular paradigm influences the actual work that will be done by a particular clinical psychologist. For example, psychologists working from a behavioral or cognitive-behavioral perspective will not only conduct psychological interventions in a different manner from that of psychodynamic psychologists, but will also have fundamental beliefs in the nature of the person's problems that differ substantially from psychodynamic psychologists. The perspective determines what information is viewed as relevant to clinical or research questions, what kind of information is sought and focused upon, the particular assessment procedures and protocols used to obtain information, the kind of information not emphasized, and the focus of treatment (e.g., symptom reduction, re-educative goals, supportive treatment, exploratory psychotherapy, and so forth). What are these philosophical underpinnings?

A historical review is beyond the scope of this chapter; however, a brief description of past conceptualizations of psychopathology can aid in understanding the basic orientations toward views of people, the problems they have, and, ultimately, the manner in which the problems are treated. Zuckerman (1999) has described an approach that Emil Kraepelin used in the late 19th and early 20th centuries to attempt to understand psychopathology and categorize disorders into a classification scheme. Kraepelin believed that the best way to establish diagnoses and diagnostic entities was to use observable behaviors and symptoms. Followers of Kraepelin's approach (known as the neo-Kraepelinians) developed classification systems listing psychological disorders based solely on descriptors or observable signs and behaviors. This approach results in a **descriptive classification system** as exemplified today in the ***Diagnostic and Statistical Manual of Mental Disorders, 4th Edition, Text Revision*** (*DSM-IV-TR*; American Psychiatric Association, 2000). The *DSM-IV-TR* is purported to be an atheoretical (i.e., not based on any one theory) descriptive classification scheme that focuses on observable behaviors in defining various disorders.

In contrast, a contemporary of Kraepelin, Sigmund Freud, and his followers proposed diagnostic entities that, rather than being simply descriptive, were based on presumed theoretically derived causes of the signs, symptoms, and syndromes (Zuckerman, 1999). In other words, based on various aspects of his theories of psychoneuroses and character disorders, Freud and his followers developed diagnostic entities that were based upon or incorporated presumed causes of the disorders rather than descriptors of the behaviors constituting the disorder. The presumed causes were reflected in the personality, developmental patterns, and history of individuals, and, although the causes have shifted and evolved as the psychodynamic approaches have shifted and evolved, there is still an emphasis on theoretically derived causes in classifying psychopathology. This approach is reflected in several classification schemes including those in the ***Psychodynamic Diagnostic Manual*** (PDM Task Force, 2006) used mainly in the United States and the **Operationalized Psychodynamic Diagnostics System** (OPD Task Force, 2008) used mainly in Europe.

These approaches have developed and evolved as better and more accurate descriptions of disorders have been developed and as theoretical models of underlying causes have evolved and can be viewed as being reflected in the field of clinical psychology. One trend focuses on overt behavior or signs and symptoms in defining disorders, and the other focuses on underlying processes that produce the symptoms. Both approaches have very different fundamental views of psychological issues, problems, disorders, and treatments, and each has evolved in quite significant ways over the decades. One fundamental difference between these two broad domains is reflected in how the characteristics of psychopathology or maladjustment are viewed. The former tends to view symptoms as the essence of the disorder, hence, the focus on treatment is on the manifestation or the symptom level, and the latter tends to view psychopathology or symptoms as the result of some underlying process, typically involving the interplay of psychological and biological variables, in nature and origin. The underlying process is thought to cause the existence of the signs, symptoms, and syndromes, which are viewed as markers or manifestations of the underlying process, hence, the focus of treatment is on the underlying process. Following is a depiction of these two approaches:

Symptom as Focus

1. This approach conceptualizes psychological problems as a group of symptoms or observable behaviors and the cause of the difficulty with the psychological problem as the presence of the symptoms and behavior.

2. Focus of assessment and treatment is to delineate the symptom picture and eradicate the symptoms. The assessment instruments and techniques are designed to ferret out the symptoms, and elicitors of the symptoms and treatment would focus on symptom or behavior reduction.

3. It can be argued that this is the orientation of the behavioral school as well as the *International Classification of Diseases, Chapter V* (*ICD-10*) and *DSM* nomenclatures.

4. It can also be argued that this has been embraced by managed care and insurance companies that are unlikely to pay for treatment unless it is treatment for a diagnosable disorder.

Underlying Cause as Focus

1. This approach conceptualizes psychological problems as caused by some underlying process that may or may not be inherently pathological but that at the current time creates difficulties for the person, the manifestation of which are the symptoms.

2. Focus of assessment is to determine what causal and contributing factors produce the psychological problem (i.e., personality, interpersonal styles, defensive or coping styles, and so forth). The instruments and techniques for assessment would have the focus of determining the underlying cause of the psychological problem, and the focus of treatment would be on the cause rather than on the symptoms.

3. This is the orientation of the psychodynamic schools, interpersonal schools, cognitive schools, and the *PDM*.

Current Conceptualizations of Psychopathology

Generally, a good indication of the current views of psychopathology can be seen in the diagnostic schemes that are in use. These diagnostic schemes have historically derived from the field of medicine, psychiatry in particular, and set the standard for the definitions of mental disorders used by clinical psychologists as well as other mental health professionals. These classification systems define what constitutes psychological disorders and provide details as to what specific criteria are necessary in diagnosing those disorders. Two of the most commonly used systems are the *ICD-10* and the *DSM-IV-TR*. Recently, the *PDM* (PDM Task Force, 2006) has also been published as a supplementary classification in diagnosis of psychopathology that is used to complement the *DSM-IV-TR* or *ICD-10*, which will be described next. The *DSM-IV-TR* and the *ICD-10* reflect descriptive classifications by observable signs and symptoms; whereas the *PDM* reflects a classification scheme that incorporates proposed etiological or causal components. They are not the only classification schemes that have been developed for psychopathology, but they do represent the most commonly used (see Box 5.3).

BOX 5.3

CLASSIFICATION SYSTEMS AROUND THE WORLD

Although the *ICD* and *DSM* are used broadly, numerous other classification schemes exist in other countries. For example, there is a Chinese Society of Psychiatry's Chinese Classification of Mental Disorders (CCMD-3; Chinese Society of Psychiatry, 2001), which in some ways is similar to the *ICD* and *DSM* although there are many disorders that are more culturally distinctive. Similarly, the Latin American Guide for Psychiatric Diagnosis and the Cuban Glossary of Psychiatry also incorporate more culturally appropriate diagnoses that the *ICD* and *DSM* do not list (Berganza, Mezzich, & Jorge, 2002; Otero-Ojeda, 2002). Also, there are other systems that have been discussed as alternative to the diagnostic approaches, an example of which is termed interpersonal diagnosis (Benjamin, 1996). In this approach, because the essence of being human involves interpersonal connectedness, it is argued that the causes, diagnosis, formulation, and treatment of psychological disorders are also inherently interpersonal. Thus, Lorna Benjamin has developed an elaborate approach to categorizing psychological problems based on interpersonal behaviors. Finally, the Operationalized Psychodynamic Diagnostics (OPD) is a multiaxial system that is used in psychodynamic classification and diagnosis that is widely used in Germany and other European countries (OPD Task Force, 2001). It represents a theoretical approach to classification and uses four axes to make diagnoses:

1. Illness experience and treatment assumptions, which reflect the patient's motivation and markers to evaluate appropriateness of psychodynamic treatment.
2. Interpersonal relationships, which focus on the relationship schemas that a patient has developed and how this can translate into transference and countertransference issues.
3. Mental conflicts, which include seven basic conflicts (such as dependence versus autonomy, submission versus control, and so forth).
4. Structure, which reflects the degree of integration (i.e., disintegrated, low, moderate, or high integration). Integration refers essentially to the development of an autonomous self that exhibits psychological strength to tolerate conflict or stress.

Diagnostic Classification Systems

Diagnostic classification systems represent current conceptualizations of psychopathology and provide a means by which clinical psychologists can define and identify psychological disorders. **Classification systems**, in general, are a basic part of scientific attempts to understand the nature of areas of inquiry, and these classification systems (also known as **nosologies**) attempt to make information more meaningful, more accessible, and less cumbersome than long descriptions of the entities of interest. Although these classification systems can be used for any domain of science, for our purposes, they provide a listing and a means of identifying mental disorders that constitute a compendium or list of psychological disorders as defined at this point in time. Classification systems are always under revision as new scientific knowledge accumulates and as societal values, judgments, and standards change.

Not only do classification systems represent our current conceptualization of psychological disorders; there are also several other purposes that classification systems serve, such as:

Descriptions: They provide good descriptions of disorders such that the disorders and problems can be identified reliably and validly. We need to know what does or does not constitute a particular disorder in order to do meaningful research and clinical work.

Communication: In order for clinicians and researchers to communicate effectively about people with particular psychological problems or about psychopathology, there needs to be a common language and definitions of concepts and terms.

Research: This is similar to the previous point and refers to the notion that in order for appropriate research to be done, it is imperative that good definitions and operationalizations of the constructs (i.e., disorders) exist. For example, in attempting to advance our knowledge of schizophrenia, different researchers need to be studying the same disorder and there must be agreement for what constitutes that disorder. If researchers use different definitions for schizophrenia, it is impossible to truly advance our knowledge of schizophrenia.

Theory development: With the research of well-defined disorders, models and theories of those disorders and psychopathology more generally can be revised or abandoned, or new theories and models can be espoused.

Treatment: It is often assumed and hoped that appropriate and careful diagnosis can lead to appropriate and differential treatment choices. Certainly knowledge of the diagnosis is one important component in making treatment choices.

Education: The diagnostic systems, as indicators of current knowledge and conceptions of psychopathology, are useful in the training and education of clinical psychologists and other health professionals.

Insurance and reimbursement: The classification systems are used by governments and insurance agencies to provide resources and to pay for assessment and treatment of disorders. There may be differences in rates of reimbursement for the treatment of certain disorders, and treatment for some disorders may not be reimbursable at all. A classification system can be used for the purpose of guiding these decisions.

Epidemiological information: Classification schemes can be vital in assessing increases and decreases in disorders in a population. This is important to keep track of changes in incidence and prevalence of different kinds of disorders.

Overall, classification systems give us a snapshot of what behaviors are viewed as abnormal and what constitutes psychopathology and also serve a variety of purposes.

◇ SPECIFIC CURRENT CLASSIFICATION SYSTEMS

Although numerous classification systems exist with respect to psychopathology, we will discuss two widely used systems, the *ICD-10* and the *DSM-IV-TR*, and one newer system, namely, the *PDM*.

International Classification of Diseases

One of the first formal classification systems that included psychological disorders was the International Classification of Diseases. This system (actually a family of classification systems) was originally developed to classify causes of death and represented a combination of German, French, and Swiss systems. Although earlier versions had different names (e.g., the first version was known as the List of Causes of Death), the *ICD-10* is thought to be the most commonly used system for clinical work internationally (Sorensen, Mors, & Thomsen, 2005).

The *ICD-10* was developed by the World Health Organization (WHO) and provides diagnostic information on diseases and causes of death. One chapter (albeit a 267-page chapter) the *ICD-10* **Classification of Mental and Behavioural Disorders** is included in this nosology. This chapter presents both a description of the clinical features of disorders and associated features of the disorders. There is an indication of the number of symptoms required for a "confident" diagnosis as well as provisions for tentative diagnoses when the clinician is less sure of an accurate diagnosis. The *ICD* is used worldwide and has been translated into at least 42 languages.

The *ICD* is a descriptive classification scheme. There are 10 major categories of disorders, and within each category there are numerous disorders with specific diagnostic criteria. These categories include:

1. Organic mental disorders (e.g., various dementias, delirium)
2. Mental and behavioral disorders due to psychoactive substance use (e.g., acute intoxication, dependence syndrome)
3. Schizophrenia, schizotypal, and delusional disorders
4. Mood disorders (e.g., mania, depressive episode)
5. Neurotic, stress-related, and somatoform disorders (e.g., anxiety, dissociative disorders)
6. Behavioral syndromes associated with physiological disturbances and physical factors (e.g., eating disorders, sleep disorders)
7. Disorders of adult personality and behavior (personality disorders, sexual disorders)
8. Mental retardation
9. Disorders of psychological development (e.g., speech and language disorders, autism)
10. Behavioral and emotional disorders with onset usually occurring in childhood and adolescence (e.g., conduct disorders, emotional disorders).

The Diagnostic and Statistical Manual of Mental Disorders, 4th Edition, Text Revision (DSM-IV-TR)

The *DSM-IV-TR*, developed by the American Psychiatric Association (2000), is a detailed and comprehensive manual that provides specific criteria for the diagnosis of psychological disorders and other information relevant to understanding the nature of various mental disorders. It has been developed, especially in later editions, paying close attention to the *ICD* criteria, and it often provides more specific detail regarding diagnostic entities. It has become one of the most commonly used diagnostic systems in the field for conducting research, and it is likely most commonly used in the United States. Like the *ICD-10*, the *DSM-IV-TR* attempts to take a descriptive approach with respect to mental disorders. The clinician determines whether the symptoms are present and, if so, makes a diagnosis.

Whereas the *ICD-10* and the *DSM-IV-TR* emphasize the specific signs, symptoms, and behaviors that reflect the diagnostic criteria for clinical diagnoses, the *DSM-IV-TR* also takes into account other features of the disorder and of the individuals experiencing the disorder. For example, a particular mental disorder will include:

Diagnostic features: The type and number of diagnostic criteria necessary in order for a diagnosis to be assigned

Associated features and disorders: Behaviors or characteristics that often accompany the mental disorder

Associated laboratory findings: Findings from a variety of tests that aid in definitive diagnosis

Age-, culture-, and gender-related features: Information that can be helpful in understanding the characteristics that may or may not be present depending on age, culture, or gender.

In addition, the *DSM* uses five separate axes to conduct a complete diagnosis. These axes are presented here and represent an attempt to take into account a variety of variables that are important in understanding, diagnosing, and treating the disorders. The five axes are:

Axis I: Clinical disorders or other conditions that may be a focus of clinical attention (e.g., bipolar disorder, schizophrenia, depression)

Axis II: Personality disorders and mental retardation (e.g., avoidant personality disorder, borderline personality disorder)

Axis III: General medical conditions (e.g., any physical ailment present such as cerebral palsy and hypothyroidism)

Axis IV: Psychosocial and environmental problems (e.g., recent stressful events and occurrences)

Axis V: Global assessment of functioning (e.g., highest level of functioning over the recent past)

The *DSM-IV-TR* lists over 400 mental disorders or problems that are being considered to be disorders for future editions of the DSM. The *DSM* has existed in one form or another for over 50 years and has been translated into over 20 languages indicating its wide usage.

The *Psychodynamic Diagnostic Manual*

Recently, a diagnostic manual has been published that takes a different view of disorders from either of the *ICD* or *DSM*. According to Greenspan, McWilliams, and Wallerstein (PDM Task Force, 2006) the *PDM* is "diagnostic framework that describes the whole person—both the deeper and surface levels of an individual's personality and that person's emotional and social functioning" (p. 4). Rather than attempting to be atheoretical and solely descriptive, the *PDM* was written from a psychodynamic perspective by numerous psychodynamic and psychoanalytic organizations and attempts to incorporate knowledge based on "current neuroscience and treatment outcome studies" as well as contemporary psychodynamic theory based on object relations theory, attachment theory, and psychoanalysis (PDM Task Force, 2006). The *PDM* is suggested to be used as a complement to the *DSM* or *ICD* rather than supplanting either of them. In essence, rather than focusing solely on observable signs and symptoms, the *PDM* attempts to focus on a person's ". . . full range of feelings and thoughts (personal experience) in the context of his or her unique history" (PDM Task Force, p. 6). In other words, the *PDM* offers a system that attempts to provide an understanding of the whole person and his or her psychological difficulties.

The proponents of the *PDM* suggest that there is more to people than what is contained in the *DSM-IV-TR* and that it attempts to describe and categorize elements in individuals not found in the *DSM-IV-TR* such as both surface and deeper ingrained elements of mental and interpersonal functioning. The system focuses and describes on three major components of a person's functioning:

1. Healthy and disordered personality functioning
2. Individual profiles of mental functioning involving relationships, expression and understanding of emotions, coping and defenses, self-awareness, and forming moral judgments
3. Symptom patterns that involve the idiosyncratic and subjective experience of symptoms

In order to address these three major components, the *PDM* uses a multidimensional approach with three axes for adults.

Personality patterns and disorders (P-axis): This axis, which focuses on the personality of the individual as the starting point for diagnostic work, includes two components; the first is the person's location on a continuum of healthy to disordered personality functioning, and the second is the characteristic or idiosyncratic mental functioning and how the person interacts with the world.

Mental functioning (M-axis): This axis involves a more detailed description of emotional functioning including information processing, forming and maintaining relationships, expression and understanding emotion, and characteristic coping and defense strategies.

Manifest symptoms and concerns (S-axis): The third axis describes most of the clinical syndromes found in the *DSM-IV-TR* or *ICD-10* (as well as others) and extends the descriptions to include the person's subjective experience of the difficulties and behavioral patterns found to be associated with each of the syndromes. This allows viewing the syndromes in the context of the person's unique personality and context.

Although the *DSM-IV-TR*, *ICD-10*, and the *PDM* all attempt to provide good descriptions of psychopathology and aid in the research and treatment of psychological problems, there are many differences among them. For example, although both the *ICD-10* and the *DSM-IV-TR* represent descriptive classification systems and there are many similarities between them, they differ in terms of the kinds of disorders that are included and how personality disorders are categorized. The *PDM*, as an **etiological classification system**, attempts to classify and focus on the underlying and contextual components of psychopathology. It also includes disorders that the *DSM* and *ICD* do not.

A major difference between the *DSM* and *ICD* on the one hand and the *PDM* on the other is that the *PDM* starts with personality as the beginning point of thinking about psychopathology. The *DSM* and *ICD* start with the clinical syndrome as the beginning point and incorporate personality (only disordered personality) and other components of the person's context only secondarily.

BOX 5.4

DIAGNOSIS OF DISORDERS IN CHILDREN

Although the *DSM* and the *ICD* include childhood disorders to a degree, the focus with these two systems has clearly been on adult disorders. For example, with the *DSM*, many of the diagnostic criteria for various disorders were used for children and adolescents although there is "Disorders first evident in childhood" section. The *PDM* has emphasized diagnostic issues with children and adolescents, and there is a strong emphasis on the developmental context of psychological problems. Also, there have been several newer classification systems and approaches to aid specifically in the diagnosis of the psychological difficulties of childhood disorders. The Diagnostic Classification of Mental Health and Developmental Disorders of Infancy and Early Childhood (DC:03) is used to help in the identification of mental health needs for infants and toddlers. Finally, Achenbach (Verhulst & Achenbach, 1995) developed an empirically based assessment and taxonomy for psychopathology in children and adolescents. Using ratings from a number of domains of specific behaviors, they obtain empirically derived syndromes of psychological problems that are used to identify specific types of psychological problems.

◇ CONCLUSION

Overall, this chapter has attempted to provide an overview of some of the relevant issues in defining, conceptualizing, and understanding psychopathology. We presented information regarding the means by which clinical psychologists determine abnormality and discussed issues regarding the kinds of behaviors that constitute domains of importance in making judgments of abnormality. Finally, we described several of the current classification systems that are in use that help clinical psychologists make determinations about people's psychological problems.

The student should have an understanding of the processes involved in defining abnormality and some of the issues, processes, and procedures that are used in determining what is considered abnormal behavior. Moreover, it should be apparent that there are numerous different conceptualizations of psychopathology and there is a dynamic nature to defining, categorizing, and understanding psychopathology.

◇ ONGOING CONSIDERATIONS

It should be clear to the student that diagnostic systems and even disorders themselves can shift and change. All the diagnostic systems discussed in this chapter are either under revision or being considered for revisions. This underscores the dynamic nature of our understanding of psychopathology, and, as research findings accumulate and our understanding of psychopathology broadens and deepens, there will be further changes.

Except the *PDM*, because it is relatively new, the existing diagnostic systems have been criticized over the years and are seemingly always being revised. For example, preparations for the next version of the *DSM* have been under way for some time, and many of the issues and the progress can be found at the *DSM-V* Prelude Project: http://www.dsm5.org/. Similarly, the *ICD* is updated frequently, and a revision of the *ICD-10* (the *ICD-11*), is scheduled for implementation in 2014; some major changes are being proposed (Masten & Curtis, 2000). With respect to the *PDM*, it is too early to evaluate both its impact and the possible changes for the future.

◇ KEY TERMS LEARNED

Classification systems
Descriptive classification system
Descriptive psychopathology
Diagnostic and Statistical Manual of Mental Disorders, 4th Edition, Test Revision (DSM-IV-TR)
Emotional regulation
Etiological classification system
ICD-10 Classification of Mental and Behavioural Disorders
International Classification of Diseases, Chapter V (*ICD-10*)

Mental disorder
Nosologies
Object relations
Operationalized psychodynamic diagnostics system (OPD)
Problems in living
Psychodynamic Diagnostic Manual (PDM)
Psychopathology
Sign
Symptom
Syndrome

✧ THINKING QUESTIONS

1. What are the two philosophical issues underlying clinical psychologists' views of psychopathology. How do they influence decisions that clinical psychologists make?

2. Compare and contrast the *DSM-IV-TR* and the *PDM* in terms of philosophical stance. How do they define psychological disorders?

3. What are some arguments as to why psychological disorders should not be considered like pathogens or alien entities in people?

4. We described two general types of diagnostic systems, one based on descriptive and the other based on theoretical characteristics. Which kind of diagnostic system do you believe is most appropriate? Why?

5. Describe the types of behaviors that clinical psychologists tend to be aware of when making judgments about psychopathology. Are there any others you believe might be relevant?

✧ REFERENCES

American Psychiatric Association. (2000). *Diagnostic and statistical manual of mental disorders* (4th ed., text revision). Washington, DC: Author.

Beck, A. T., Rush, A. J., Shaw, B. F., & Emery, G. (1979). *Cognitive therapy of depression.* New York: Guilford Press.

Benjamin, L. S. (1996). *Interpersonal diagnosis and treatment of personality disorders.* New York: Guilford Press.

Berganza, C. E., Mezzich, J. E., & Jorge, M. R. (2002). The Latin American guide for psychiatric diagnosis: A cultural overview. *Psychopathology, 35,* 185–190.

Bergin, A. E., & Lambert, M. J. (1978). The evaluation of therapeutic outcomes. In S. L. Garfield & A. F. Bergin (Eds.), *Handbook of psychotherapy and behavior change: An empirical analysis* (2nd ed., pp. 139–190). New York: John Wiley.

Chinese Society of Psychiatry. (2001). *International classification and diagnosis.* Author.

Clark, L. A., & Watson, D. (1991). Tripartite model of anxiety and depression: Psychometric evidence and taxonomic implications. *Journal of Abnormal Psychology, 100,* 316–336.

Ellenberger, H. F. (1970). *The discovery of the unconscious.* New York: Basic Books.

Freud, A. (1946). *The ego and mechanisms of defense.* New York: International Universities Press.

Gorenstein, E. E. (1992). *The science of mental illness.* San Diego: Academic Press.

Hewitt, P. L., Flett, G. L., Sherry, S. B., Habke, M., Parkin, M., & Lam, R. W., et al. (2003). The interpersonal expression of perfectionism: Perfectionistic self-presentation and psychological distress. *Journal of Personality and Social Psychology, 84,* 1303–1325.

Jourard, S. M. (1958). *Personal adjustment: An approach through the study of healthy personality.* New York: MacMillan Co.

Klinger, E. (1975). Consequences of commitment to and disengagement from incentives. *Psychological Review, 82,* 1–25.

Lazarus, R. S., & Folkman, S. (1984). *Stress, appraisal, and coping*. New York/USA: Springer Publishing Company.

Masten, A. S., & Curtis, J. W. (2000). Integrating competence and psychopathology. Pathways toward a comprehensive science of adaptation in development. *Development and Psychopathology, 12,* 529–550.

OPD Task Force. (2008). *Operationalized psychodynamic diagnostics* (2nd ed.). New York: Hogrefe & Huber.

Otero-Ojeda, A. A. (2002). Third Cuban glossary of psychiatry (GC-3): Key features and contributions. *Psychopathology, 35,* 181–184.

PDM Task Force. (2006). *Psychodynamic diagnostic manual.* Silver Spring, MD: Alliance of Psychoanalytic Organizations.

Ryff, C. D. (1989). Happiness is everything, or is it? Explorations on the meaning of psychological well-being. *Journal of Personality and Social Psychology, 57,* 1069–1081.

Sorenson, M. J., Mors, O., & Thomsen, P. H. (2005). *DSM-IV* or *ICD-10-DCR* diagnoses in child and adolescent psychiatry: Does it matter? *European Child & Adolescent Psychiatry, 14,* 335–340.

Spitzer (1981). The diagnostic status of homosexuality in the *DSM III*: A reformulation of the issues. *American Journal of Psychiatry, 138,* 210–215.

St. Clair, M. (2004). *Object relations and self psychology.* New York: Brooks Cole.

Sullivan, H. S. (1953). *The interpersonal theory of psychiatry.* New York: W. W. Norton.

Szasz, T. (1961). *The myth of mental illness: Foundations of a theory of personal conduct.* Harper & Row.

Taylor, C. T., & Alden, L. E. (2008). Self and interpersonal judgment biases in social anxiety disorder: Changes during treatment and relationship to outcome. *International Journal of Cognitive Therapy, 1,* 125–137.

Vaillant, G. E. (1977). *Adaptation to life.* Boston, MA: Little, Brown.

Verhulst, F. C., & Achenbach, T. M. (1995). Empirically based assessment and taxonomy of psychopathology: Cross-cultural applications. A review. *European Child & Adolescent Psychiatry, 4,* 61–76.

World Health Organization (2005). *WHO resource book on mental health, human rights, and legislation.*

Zuckerman, M. (1999). Diagnosis. *Vulnerability to psychopathology: A biosocial model* (pp. 25–83). Washington, DC: American Psychological Association.

CHAPTER SIX

OVERVIEW OF ASSESSMENT

CHAPTER OBJECTIVE

This chapter provides an overview of some of the principles, aims, and procedures involved in conducting various kinds of psychological assessments. We will be discussing the commonality and importance of psychological assessment in clinical psychologists' work in addition to issues regarding the training of graduate students in assessment practices. Moreover, the chapter will cover issues relating to what constitutes psychological assessment broadly as well as the specific aims and purposes of assessment and different types of psychological assessments used in research and clinical practice. Lastly, we will be addressing the kinds of issues related to clinical decision-making that arise from psychological assessment and how the decisions can have an impact on people's lives.

◇ OVERVIEW

Generally, psychological assessment has been and continues to be an important component in the training and the work of clinical psychologists as well as other kinds of psychologists. Psychological testing began in the early 1900s with attempts by Alfred Binet in Paris, France, to determine appropriate classroom placement for school children based on test scores and with attempts in the United States to separate out those military personnel with emotional or cognitive problems (Gregory, 2004). Psychological testing was viewed as an effective way to quickly understand multiple aspects of people's functioning and was used to predict success in a variety of domains. It was embraced by the psychological community, especially in the United States; it became an important tool for psychologists and provided the impetus for further development of psychological assessment as an important clinical activity.

Psychological assessment has been seen as one of the defining and unique roles that clinical psychologists play in health-related activities. Certain types of assessments, in particular, neuropsychological, psychophysiological, and multidimensional personality assessments, are almost exclusively aligned with the field of clinical psychology, and for these domains we have essentially no competition in the marketplace. Although other health

VIGNETTE 6.1

Vincent, the clinical psychology graduate student, was in the process of learning clinical interviewing skills and was trying to determine the differences between a structured clinical interview that focuses on carefully determining a *DSM-IV-TR* diagnosis for research purposes and a semistructured clinical interview that emphasizes understanding the symptom picture, the context the person exists in, and process-related variables such as motivation of the patient and how the problems are likely caused and maintained. He was going to be completing his first clinical assessment on a young woman who was having difficulties in university due to problems such as inability to focus, emotional reactivity, initiating projects, and maintaining personal relationships for any significant period of time. Vincent was attempting to provide a rationale for the interview and other assessment tools that would be presented to his clinical supervisor for approval to use with the patient. The interview was going to form the basis of a clinical assessment that would include other assessment techniques and tests.

professional groups can provide treatments for, and in some cases, diagnoses of, individual patients, couples, and families, this does not really apply to psychological assessment. The assessment practices have also extended from the more traditional mental health– and education-related work to other domains such as neuropsychology and medical, industrial, and forensic psychological practices, and many clinical psychologists earn a very good living specializing in this work. Psychological assessment is used not only for clinical decision-making in mental health but also for assessing variables by health psychologists, functional status and rehabilitation potential in injuries by rehabilitation psychologists, brain-related problems and strengths in brain-injured persons by neuropsychologists, and various crime-related behavior and treatment by forensic psychologists.

This chapter begins with a few vignettes of psychologists working on assessment-related issues in the field.

VIGNETTE 6.2

Dr. A is presenting some psychological assessment data to a case conference group regarding contributing factors to a patient's anxiety and hypertension. The focus of the presentation is on the signs and symptoms the patient was exhibiting as well as personality features, including interpersonal and relationship variables that may have contributed to coronary artery disease. Specifically she was focusing the presentation on the levels and types of hostile interpersonal relationships the patient exhibited and how this interpersonal style may also interfere with treatment of the patient. The data presented involved information from self-report instruments and from psychophysiological monitoring of heart rate and blood pressure in a variety of simulated interactional situations. The information was presented to the case conference group in order to contribute to the clinical picture of the patient.

VIGNETTE 6.3

Dr. B was conducting a complete psychodiagnostic assessment on a patient who had been referred from a psychiatrist to his private practice. The patient presented a very complicated diagnostic picture, and it was not clear to the psychiatrist whether the patient exhibited a schizophrenia-like disorder, a bipolar affective disorder, or some organically based disorder and what sorts of treatments might be most appropriate. Dr. B had completed a clinical interview with the patient and an interview with the patient's parents. As well, the patient completed several psychological tools including the Minnesota Multiphasic Personality Inventory 2, an objective measure of psychopathology and personality, several specific rating scales, and the Rorschach Inkblot Technique and Thematic Apperception Test, two projective measures of cognitive and perceptual processing and interpersonal relatedness variables, respectively. Dr. A was in the process of attempting to synthesize and integrate the clinical interview and testing material to aid in determining the diagnostic picture of the patient. In addition, he was attempting to establish factors that may have contributed to the development of the psychological problems and factors that might be maintaining or exacerbating those problems. He will be creating a report for the psychiatrist, who referred the patient, and also preparing feedback on the assessment that he will be providing to the patient.

VIGNETTE 6.4

Dr. C has been interested in studying the effects of pain on children and attempting to develop strategies to help young children deal with pain that accompanies some medical procedures and some medical problems. The challenge she faced was developing not only cognitive strategies for young children that might help them cope with their discomfort but also appropriate, reliable, and valid measures of pain and changes in pain for young children who may have rather limited verbal abilities. The measure was especially important so that the strategies could be evaluated in terms of how effective they might be. She was starting at "square one" as she believed there were no appropriate measures available. Although there has been a great deal of research and writing on measurement of pain and change in pain for adults that she was familiar with, there was relatively little work done on appropriate and effective means of measuring pain behaviors in young children. She had started accessing and carefully perusing the literatures on nonverbal expressions of emotion, coping strategies for children as well as the cognitive development literature, and psychological assessment in children. Moreover, she was planning a meeting with several other child clinical psychologists, graduate students, and staff from a pediatric department to brainstorm potential strategies that might be effective. She was hoping to develop several different measures that could be evaluated in several research projects.

◇ WHAT IS PSYCHOLOGICAL ASSESSMENT?

There have been numerous and broad characterizations of assessment offered by psychologists over the years. Groth-Marnat (1999) suggests that psychological assessment involves the evaluation of an individual who is experiencing some difficulty so that the information gleaned can be useful in dealing with the problem. Cohen, Swerdlik, and Phillips (1996) define psychological assessment as:

> . . . the gathering and integration of psychology-related data for the purpose of making a psychological evaluation, accomplished through the use of tools such as tests, interviews, case studies, behavioral observation, and specially designed apparatuses and measurement procedures. (p. 6)

Building upon these definitions, we can state that psychological assessment involves a clinical psychologist who has expertise in human behavior, psychological problems and strengths, assessment tests and techniques, and the genesis and treatment of psychological problems. The clinical psychologist gathers, synthesizes, and integrates the psychological, historical, contextual, and collateral (i.e., from other sources) data to generate and test hypotheses regarding behavior. This is done in an effort to develop descriptions, explanations, predictions, and recommendations regarding the psychological difficulties a person experiences. The ultimate goal is to provide quality information that can aid in the treatment of the patients' difficulties.

When undertaking an assessment, the clinical psychologist needs not only to collect and analyze data from multiple sources in order to describe problems and characteristics, but also, and perhaps most important, to integrate the information so as to understand the problems and the person who exhibits the problems in order to aid that person. The clinical psychologist is attempting to answer fairly specific questions and to engage the individual, couple, or family in a collaborative and supportive process that, in and of itself, can initiate the therapeutic process.

◇ PSYCHOLOGICAL TESTING VERSUS PSYCHOLOGICAL ASSESSMENT

Although sometimes the terms psychological assessment and psychological testing are used synonymously, there is a difference between the two. **Psychological testing** is thought of as the process of administering, scoring, and interpreting psychological tests (Maloney & Ward, 1976). Test scores provide the information that the clinical conclusions, decisions, and recommendations are based upon (Cohen et al., 1996). **Psychological assessment**, on the other hand, goes beyond test scores and uses many sources of data (including tests) to arrive at conclusions regarding psychological problems that an individual(s) is seeking help for. Moreover, according to Maloney and Ward (1976), whereas psychological testing measures the issues, problems, concerns, strengths, and limitations a person has, psychological assessment extends this to include how and why the person developed the problems and how the problems are maintained. Thus, psychological assessment is seen as broader and more encompassing than psychological testing.

A psychological assessment is usually thought of as very formal, with extensive coverage of behavior, and is used in the treatment or remediation planning for a patient (Butcher, 1995). However, psychological assessment can be more specific and can address a limited number of components of behavior or functioning for use in selecting appropriate placements or monitoring symptom levels over treatment (see Beck, Rush, Shaw, & Emery, 1979). Although traditionally assessment has been thought of as an activity relevant only for individual patients, assessment practices and protocols have been extended to couples and families (Krishnamurthy et al., 2004; Sperry, 2004).

◇ PSYCHOLOGICAL ASSESSMENT IN PRACTICE AND TRAINING

How much of a clinical psychologist's work is dedicated to assessment activities? There has been some variation over the years in the time clinical psychologists spend in conducting clinical assessments; however, assessment remains a focus of clinical work and research for clinical psychologists. After provision of treatment, clinical assessment has been found to be the second most frequent activity for clinical psychologists (Meyer et al., 1998). For example, in several surveys of clinical psychologists from Britain and North America (e.g., Lucock, Hall, & Noble, 2006; Norcross, Karpiak, & Santoro, 2005), it was estimated that clinical psychologists spend about 13–15% of their time in assessment-related activities and approximately 90% of clinical psychologists engage in some kind of assessment-related activities. Moreover, assessment is seen as an important activity in training clinical psychology graduate students, and in a recent conference dedicated to establishing training goals and directions for clinical psychology (The Competencies Conference: Future Directions in Education and Credentialing in Professional Psychology) there was widespread consensus that every practicing psychologist should continue to have exposure to and training in psychological assessment (Krishnamurthy et al., 2004).

In the Competencies Conference, it was determined that there are specific **core competencies** (i.e., areas of expertise) related to psychological assessment that were deemed "essential to all health-service practices in psychology, transcending specialties" (p. 732). These competencies not only provide an example of the extensive coverage and training necessary to develop assessment skills in clinical psychology but also point out the knowledge and skills that would likely be focused on in graduate school.

The majority of clinical psychology graduate curricula cover psychological assessment, and graduate students are trained not only in diagnosis based on current classification systems but also in test construction, administration, scoring, interpretation of assessment material based on knowledge of psychopathology, normal behavior, and treatment. Moreover, there are training emphases on the synthesis of relevant data in coming to an understanding of the nature of a person's difficulties (Krishnamurthy et al., 2004). Although the specific focuses or emphases of assessment may depend on the theoretical orientation of the program, the curricula of most schools and internships indicate that interviewing, behavioral observation, and objective and projective testing form a basis for clinical assessment (Childs & Eyde, 2002).

◇ PURPOSE OF ASSESSMENT

Psychological assessment has one of two overarching purposes. The first purpose is to understand an individual, couple, or family and the psychological issues that pertain to that individual, couple, or family. This is known as an **idiographic** approach to assessment that provides specific, detailed, and idiosyncratic information about a particular patient, couple, or family's difficulties and any other information related to the difficulty or the treatment of the difficulty. Idiographic approaches are typically done in a clinical context and can be used mostly for psychodiagnostic and treatment-planning purposes. For example, the assessment of a person with depression would be done in order to determine, for the specific individual, the severity and type of depression (e.g., unipolar versus bipolar depression; mild, moderate, or severe symptom severity; and so forth); the specific nature of the symptoms and potential causes of depression (e.g., mainly biological symptoms, family history of depression, lots of stressful life events, personality features that might create vulnerability to depression); maintenance factors of depression (e.g., presence of chronic stressors, poor social network), and so forth.

A second approach to assessment is known as the **nomothetic** approach whereby, rather than focusing on an individual, couple, or family, assessments are done on groups of individuals in order to understand broader issues or constructs pertaining to the types of problems or treatments. Whereas an idiographic approach is used in direct clinical work, a nomothetic approach tends to be used in research in order to understand how certain variables that exist in people, couples, or families are related to other relevant clinical variables such as treatment outcomes, efficacy, or process. For example, in order to determine whether certain family environments contribute to the maintenance or worsening of symptoms of schizophrenia generally, psychological instruments measuring various family environments and schizophrenia symptom severity, duration, and intensity might be administered.

◇ THE TOOLS OF PSYCHOLOGICAL ASSESSMENT

Clinical psychologists use a variety of tools in their assessments of individuals' problems. Two major types of tools can be seen in psychological assessment: tests and techniques. **Tests** can be thought of as highly reliable and valid instruments that have been developed to measure specific aspects of a person's functioning. Typically, patients are asked to report on their own behavior (e.g., make ratings of how sad they feel), and the tests produce scores in one or more domains. Those scores can be compared to normative information in order to determine whether an individual scores the same as or different from a normative sample. In developing the tests, careful attention is paid to issues of both validity and reliability of the measures. Examples of tests, some of which are described in detail in chapter 7, are listed here:

1. Wechsler Intelligence Tests, including multifaceted tests of intelligence or memory functioning (e.g., Wechsler, 1997)
2. Minnesota Multiphasic Personality Inventory 2, which is a broad self-report measure of personality features and psychopathology (Butcher, 1990)
3. Child Behavior Checklist, which is a broad measure of psychological difficulties for children (Achenbach & Edelbrock, 1992)
4. Behavioral Anger Response Questionnaire, a multidimensional measure of anger coping styles used in cardiac health-related research and treatment (Linden, 2006)

Techniques in psychological assessment can be thought of as tools that provide relevant clinical information that does not necessarily involve the patient reporting on his own behavior and that are often, but not always, compared to norms. The approach is thought to provide important information for the clinician either in the form of hypothesis generation, hypothesis confirmation or disconfirmation, or information germane to a variety of treatment issues. These tools are seen as going beyond simple test scores and measuring information that is not so easily accessed by the patient himself. Examples of a few clinical techniques that are used are:

1. Semi- or unstructured clinical interviews
2. Projective techniques such as the Thematic Apperception Test or drawing tasks
3. Collateral reports
4. History taking
5. Behavioral observations

There is a great deal of concern that both tests and techniques provide useful and high-quality information and that both of them are valid and reliable. If necessary, the reader can refresh knowledge on reliability and validity concepts in chapter 3. Both tests and techniques have strengths and weaknesses. For example, tests have to have demonstrated levels of reliability and validity to be used in clinical work; however, sometimes, in efforts to have very good reliability and validity, the depth of information gleaned from tests is quite restricted. For example, some symptom-rating scales that measure simply the presence of a list of symptoms give only information regarding the level of severity of symptomatology. Techniques can often provide a good deal of depth and breadth of information, but some are viewed as having less than ideal levels of reliability and validity. For example, semi- or unstructured clinical interviews are thought to have quite poor reliability and validity (e.g., Dougherty, Ebert, & Callender, 1986) yet are used very commonly. Lastly, it should also be added that some assessment tools have been considered to be both tests and techniques (e.g., Rorschach Inkblot Technique; Rose, Kaser-Boyd, & Maloney, 2001).

⋄ TYPES OF PSYCHOLOGICAL ASSESSMENT

One of the most comprehensive approaches to clinical assessment in mental health was based on work initially developed at the Menninger Foundation (Rappaport, Gill, & Schafer, 1968) that was referred to as **psychodiagnosis**. Psychodiagnosis is not simply a procedure of determining a diagnosis or symptom picture. It is a process that uses both psychological tests and psychological tools to gather data in order to provide comprehensive information about a unique individual and her assets, liabilities, strengths, defenses, conflicts, symptoms, vulnerabilities, and so forth, in order to provide important information regarding the nature and origins of problems for treatment planning. This approach has provided a template that most clinical assessments have followed.

There are different types of and numerous purposes for psychological assessments. We outline here numerous types of assessments that clinical psychologists perform. Several of these are described in detail in subsequent chapters. It should be noted that these assessments are often combined and most of these assessments will often use the same tests and techniques. Moreover, the assessments can be done for idiographic purposes in order to understand clinical issues for an individual or for nomothetic purposes in order to understand more general principles. These assessments are used in both children and adults.

1. Psychodiagnostic assessment: This type of assessment focuses on issues such as personality variables, symptom picture, environmental influences, personality structure including underlying dynamics and conflicts, and other issues that contribute to the psychological problems the patient is struggling with. This often involves either assigning a formal diagnosis or describing diagnostic impressions and the nature and potential causes of the problem as well as suggestions for treatment of the difficulties (Wolber & Carne, 2002). The assessment described in the first vignette is an example of a psychodiagnostic assessment.

2. Intellectual/cognitive: This assessment approach deals with the determination of intellectual and cognitive functioning. It focuses on both the strengths and the liabilities of functioning. One particular type of cognitive assessment is known as neuropsychological assessment that assesses intellectual, cognitive, and behavioral strengths and liabilities of brain functioning in brain-injured individuals.

3. Behavioral: In behavioral assessment, there is an attempt to determine antecedents, reinforcement histories, and maintenance issues for psychological or behavioral problems. The focus tends to be on environmental determinants of the patient's behavior. For example, the clinical psychologist might focus on the assessment of specific drinking behavior, cues or contexts that influence drinking behavior, and situations or stressors that impact on desire for drinking.

4. Health: With respect to health-related assessments, the clinical psychologist attempts to determine behaviors, personality structures, and environmental features that influence a patient's physical health status. For example, when assessing contributions to hypertension, there may be a focus on assessing anger styles and levels of hostility, ability and strengths in managing stress reactions, and cognitions related to interpersonal problems.

5. Psychophysiological: In this type of assessment, the focus is on assessment of physiological processes, such as heart rate, skin temperature, or muscle control that are factors in physical and psychological health problems. For example, in the assessment and treatment of sex offenders, there may be assessments of sexual arousal in response to specific types of stimuli.

6. Rehabilitative: In rehabilitation assessment, clinical psychologists attempt to determine the functional capacity of individuals following psychological or physical injury. This can take the form of cognitive assessments following head injuries or more broad assessments of functioning following a traumatic experience.

7. Forensic: In forensic assessments, clinical psychologists assess factors that may have contributed to criminal behavior, likelihood of reoffending, and treatment of issues pertaining to criminal behavior.

In each of these types of assessment, the clinical psychologist is attempting to gather information in a reliable and valid fashion, develop and test hypotheses, develop an understanding of the nature of the problems including the development and maintenance of the problems or difficulties, and offer suggestions for remediation or treatment.

◇ GOALS OF PSYCHOLOGICAL ASSESSMENT

Although there will be some differences in emphases depending on the theoretical orientation of the clinical psychologist and based on the type of assessment, there are several major goals of a clinical assessment, which are listed here:

Problem explication

Formulation

Prognosis

Treatment issues and recommendations

Provision of therapeutic context

Communication of findings

Problem Explication

A major concern of the clinical psychologist is, of course, to have detailed information about the problem for which the person is seeking help. This entails establishing detailed descriptive features and information regarding the nature of the problem(s). Often, this takes the form of establishing a formal diagnosis based on one of the classification systems that exist or a description of the diagnostic picture without providing a formal diagnosis. For example, an individual may exhibit behaviors (i.e., signs, symptoms, and/or syndromes) that are consistent with one or more of the DSM-IV-TR or ICD-10 diagnostic categories. The types of assessments that could involve actually assigning a diagnosis (or diagnoses) are psychodiagnostic, intellectual, neuropsychological, and forensic assessments; whereas the other types of assessments, for the most part, may be concerned more with detailed descriptions of the problems rather than providing a diagnostic label, for example, behavioral (for more detail see chapter 9).

Although diagnosis is an important component in clinical assessment, it is often thought to be the only relevant component. This not only is incorrect but also represents missing out on additional opportunities for acquiring knowledge and critical clinical information. The diagnostic label is seen as critical and sufficient for the determination of treatment by some clinicians/researchers, and it is seen as almost irrelevant by others who see other purported causal issues of the psychological problems to be of more importance in treatment rather than the diagnosis. For example, much research on the empirical validation of certain treatments views an Axis 1 diagnosis as a sufficient defining feature for the determination of appropriate treatment. A basic assumption in this process of diagnosis is that there is uniformity of the psychological disorder. In other words, even though there are numerous diagnostic criteria for the various disorders and individuals have to have a certain number of criterion items in order to be diagnosed, the assumption is that depression is still depression even if individuals have different constellations of the symptoms. It is this assumption that allows clinicians and researchers to discuss various diagnostic entities based on the current nomenclature. On the other hand, other clinical psychologists view the diagnosis as important but not sufficient to determine treatment. Instead they focus on variables such as personality, interpersonal and family relationships, cognitive/intellectual abilities, environmental variables, and so forth, in determining appropriate treatment rather than focusing on the diagnostic label (see Hewitt et al., 2008). The assumption here is that diagnosis, by itself, does not inform the clinician about the person, but rather provides information about the presence or absence of a diagnostic entity. Information about the person and his characteristics and dynamics are often seen as more germane to appropriate treatment choices (Blatt, Auerbach, Zuroff, & Shahar, 2006).

Irrespective of whether diagnosis is seen as the most important goal of assessment or not, diagnosis based on nosology is one general purpose of the assessment. For example, one using the *DSM-IV-TR* would gather information pertinent to the different axes of the DSM. This could take the form of using a structured clinical interview or, more likely, using a semi- or unstructured clinical interview and, possibly, using objective testing and projective techniques as well as behavioral and physiological techniques (Box 6.1).

One of the difficulties with diagnosis in clinical assessment is that individuals seeking treatment or assessment may not fully meet the diagnostic criteria for any particular psychological disorder. Numerous individuals will endorse psychological problems and distress and seek psychotherapy or treatment for some difficulties that do not meet the criteria for current definitions of a disorder (American Psychiatric Association, 2000). This does not mean that these individuals are not in psychological pain or are inappropriate for treatment. Another potential difficulty with diagnosis, as stated earlier, is that establishing the diagnosis does not necessarily provide the most relevant information as to the appropriate treatment. Often factors other than the diagnosis will play a greater role in determining appropriate treatment. For example, issues such as how currently distressed the person is, the chronicity of the disorder, availability of resources, and strengths and resources the patient has can all be determinants of appropriate treatment recommendations.

Not all assessments will establish diagnoses. Many may emphasize detailed descriptions of the nature of the difficulties. This can take the form of narrative descriptions or can be indicators of the presence of a variety of symptoms or signs of psychological difficulties.

BOX 6.1

EXAMPLE OF DSM-IV DIAGNOSIS

The following example would constitute the multiaxial diagnosis of a patient who experienced significant depressive features for a period of time following an unanticipated job loss. Moreover, he experienced delusional thinking characterized by a belief that he was "rotting from the inside." As well, this patient was suspected of having "a thyroid condition" that might influence depression symptoms. The diagnosis would have been presented as follows:

Axis I	296.23	Major depressive episode, severe with mood congruent psychotic features
Axis II		No diagnosis, dependent personality features
Axis III	244.9	Acquired hypothyroidism
Axis IV		Recent unemployment
Axis V	GAF = 40 (on admission)	
	GAF = 90 (highest level past year)	

For example, behavioral assessment involves assessment techniques that provide detailed descriptions of various components of behavior that will inform the treatment (Ciminero, Calhoun, & Adams, 1986).

Formulation

Problem explication does not necessarily inform the clinical psychologist about some important information that is directly germane to understanding potential causes, maintenance factors, or treatment-related issues (Blatt et al., 2006). Thus, an additional concern of clinical psychologists when conducting assessment is the **formulation**. A formulation involves attempts to determine the causes, maintenance factors, and interplay of issues that influence the genesis and continuation of problems or difficulties. It can be seen as an idiographic model of how psychological, environmental, interpersonal, and other factors interact with one another to produce and maintain the problems for a particular individual, couple, or family, and it provides information and guides to appropriate treatment. The formulation differs in the different types of assessments, but, essentially, almost all forms of assessment attempt to determine how and why the person(s) developed the difficulties experienced and what variables or conditions might maintain or exacerbate the difficulties. This can involve assessing personal characteristics, attributes, and behaviors as well as assessing interpersonal relationships, historical information, and environmental issues.

Formulations are usually done based on the theoretical orientation of the clinical psychologist who may focus on some components of functioning and exclude others.

For example, a clinical psychologist from a behavioral orientation would likely attempt to understand reinforcement histories and current reinforcement contingencies, whereas a psychologist from a cognitive-behavioral orientation would likely want to understand dysfunctional cognitions, self-statements, and underlying dysfunctional attitudes (Beck et al., 1979). Finally, a clinical psychologist from a psychodynamic orientation would likely emphasize past histories of interpersonal relationships, the establishment and development of interpersonal styles, and current relationship patterns (e.g., McWilliams, 1999).

Case formulation has always been emphasized by psychodynamic therapists as a cornerstone of psychodynamic treatment, and in behavior therapy, a functional analysis serves a similar purpose. For example, the purpose of a psychodynamic case formulation is "to increase the probability that psychotherapy for a particular person will be helpful" (McWilliams, 1999, p. 11). It is an attempt to understand the idiosyncratic way a person organizes knowledge, cognitions, emotions, and behavior so that the therapist can have an understanding of the dynamic or holistic nature of the individual's difficulties. Recently there has been an interest in the cognitive-behavioral literature for more comprehensive case formulations in order to facilitate treatment, especially for complex cases that may not be amenable to manual-driven treatments (e.g., Persons, 2006). Although case formulation can be a complex component of the assessment in attempting to establish hypothesized causal judgments about the genesis and maintenance of a disorder (Garb, 1998), it does provide highly relevant information, especially with respect to treatment (Box 6.2).

As discussed previously, diagnosis assumes that the diagnostic entities are uniform, whereas formulation assumes that the symptom patterns, causal or developmental pathways for the symptoms, personality of the individual(s), coping and defenses, and context are all idiosyncratic or demonstrate individual differences. Thus, formulation involves the person; diagnosis involves the diagnostic construct. Some potential difficulties or problems that can influence formulations involve the fact that they can be based on different theoretical orientations and, therefore, may emphasize different behaviors, maintenance factors, and potential causal factors. Moreover, they can be difficult to complete due to the complexity of human behavior and the need to incorporate often disparate and contradictory findings.

What sorts of information are used in formulation?

1. *Intraindividual issues* (e.g., motivation, dynamics, learning history, cognitive styles, interpersonal styles, reinforcement history).

2. *Interpersonal issues* (e.g., ability to establish relationships, social network, intimate relationships)

3. *Environmental issues* (e.g., types of traumatic or other events, current situation the person is living in, presence of relationships, past and current family environment, events that can reinforce maladaptive behaviors)

4. *Process-related issues* (i.e., variables related to the person in a clinical context, including behaviors exhibited in the interview such as openness, motivation and willingness to participate in treatment, level of anxiety in interacting with the psychotherapist).

BOX 6.2

EXAMPLE OF A PSYCHODYNAMIC FORMULATION

The following is an excerpt from the treatment by one of the authors (PLH) of a patient experiencing profound depression and suicidal tendencies following the death of her mother. The formulation is being given to the patient:

> It sounds as if the period of time you were separated from your mother when you were five years old not only was extremely distressing to you but also initiated a way of being in the world. It resulted in you being driven never to be separated from her again once you were reunited which became almost an obsession or way of life for you. In fact, it appears that, in order to ensure you are not separated from her again, you attempted to become the perfect daughter to her in any and all ways, and, as you grew up, you needed always to be in close proximity to her. That is likely why you were driven for perfection in everything you attempted, chose the same career as she had, chose the same place of employment as her, and how you and your husband chose to live in a house immediately next door to her. It seems that being perfect and having her close by was one of the major motivating factors in your life and a driving force in your perfectionism. Now that your mother has passed away, you are experiencing the profound grief, hopelessness, helplessness, sense of failure, and depression of your inability to never be separated from her. You were not able to stop her from leaving. Does that make sense to you?

Prognosis and Treatment Outcome

The term **prognosis** refers to the expected course of a disorder and the expected degree and speed of recovery from the disorder. This component entails determining what can be expected in terms of the problems worsening or getting better either with or without treatment. An important component of an assessment is to provide information on the likely outcome of the difficulties in terms of the expectations regarding improvement or worsening of difficulties and potential effectiveness of available treatment options. The current research on empirical validation of treatments provides valuable information on the treatment of *DSM-IV-TR* Axis 1 disorders and is helpful in determining potential outcomes. On the other hand, because the groups typically chosen in this kind of research are carefully diagnosed and they exhibit little if any comorbidity and there is an attempt to control coping strategies (e.g., not abusing drugs, alcohol, etc.), it is not necessarily clear what the prognosis may be based solely on diagnosis information. Based on the clinical psychologist's knowledge of psychopathology, the obtained formulation, the nature of the individual's psychopathology and other psychological problems and issues, results of the assessment, rapport established, available resources, and so forth, the clinical psychologist makes professional judgments regarding the prognosis and appropriate treatment options. Obviously, a large number of variables need to be considered when making judgments regarding prognosis.

In addition to the disorder itself, other issues can affect prognosis. For example, motivation to get better, ability to form a therapeutic alliance, availability of treatment, social and family support, and finances can all have an influence on prognosis.

Treatment Recommendations

Although one of the major purposes of clinical assessment is to determine the difficulty and why the difficulty exists, the ultimate purpose is to try to facilitate appropriate treatment for the difficulties the person is experiencing. The assessment, of course, provides invaluable information for appropriate treatment and for determining issues that might interfere with or be particularly helpful with therapy. Based on the clinical psychologist's knowledge of efficacious treatments, the diagnosis and formulation inform the assessing clinical psychologist about potentially appropriate treatments. Moreover, various aspects of the person's functioning can be informative with respect to not only what treatment options are appropriate, but what sorts of issues might be particularly challenging for the treating clinician or what issues may have a negative impact on the treatment. For example, information as to whether the person has a history or the capacity to form relationships can strongly influence whether a therapeutic alliance will be established. Because a therapeutic alliance is seen as the basis from which good treatment outcomes arise (Rogers, 1961), this is crucial information. As well, interpersonal styles such as difficulty with authority figures, dependency, excessive hostility, passive aggressive interpersonal behavior, or desire to get better can all have an impact on treatment (see Bergin & Lambert, 1978). An important component of treatment recommendations is availability of treatment options in the geographic area. It makes no sense to recommend treatment that is impossible for the patient to access.

Also, treatment recommendations can be influenced by factors such as intelligence, tolerance of anxiety, and psychological mindedness. **Psychological mindedness** refers to an individual's ability to observe her own internal life, see patterns in her own behavior, and develop insight. Some people are more fragile and cannot tolerate anxiety or other emotions as effectively as others. This concept is referred to as **ego-strength**, and it derives from psychoanalytic theory. Most often treatment of psychological issues involves emotional experiences and a degree of anxiety. Whether the treatment involves a behavioral exposure to a feared object (e.g., exposure treatment for a spider phobia) or long-term treatment of a personality disorder, the treatment process involves many anxious moments for the patient. Thus, patients need to be able to tolerate certain levels of anxiety or other emotional states in order to participate in and benefit from the treatment. Also, the context of the patients is highly relevant. For example, if a clinical psychologist is going to recommend a behavioral program to treat some behavioral difficulties a child is experiencing, the clinical psychologist needs to have the cooperation, agreement, and a commitment from the parents to follow through. Thus, the environmental context of the person is crucial for appropriate treatment of problems.

Provision of a Therapeutic Context

In an assessment, it is important to establish a collaborative, positive, and therapeutic experience for the person(s) being assessed (Groth-Marnat, 1990). Although psychological assessment is often seen as an activity separate from treatment or therapy, it is important to understand that the assessment itself can be therapeutic for patients (Hilsenroth & Cromer, 2007). For example, the assessment can often be the first exposure the patient has to the clinical enterprise, and the clinical psychologist conducting the assessment may be the first clinician the person will have contact with. This provides an important opportunity for the clinical psychologist to create an atmosphere that is conducive to a good clinical outcome for the person. Certainly the clinical psychologist must exhibit the same clinical stance as in conducting psychotherapy, namely, warm, open, nonjudgmental, and professional demeanor, in conducting the interview and testing. This kind of clinical stance has been seen as very helpful to people. Moreover, it can be pivotal in helping to establish a positive or optimistic attitude toward the clinical enterprise and provide both hope and optimism for obtaining help with the problem that has also been implicated in good clinical outcomes (Frank, 1973).

Communication of Findings to Referral Source and to the Patient(s)

A psychological assessment typically begins with either the patient or a referring professional who requests answers to specific questions regarding the patient's difficulties. The clinical psychologist communicates his findings to the referral source. This typically takes the form a psychological report (see Box 6.3 for a description of a psychological report) that outlines the problem, formulation, prognosis, and treatment recommendations.

BOX 6.3

EXAMPLE OF A PSYCHOLOGICAL REPORT

The following is an example of a psychological report presented in Wolber and Carne (2002). The student can see that although a formal *DSM-IV-TR* or ICD-10 diagnosis is not given, the diagnostic impressions of the psychologist are described in detail.

CONFIDENTIAL PSYCHOLOGICAL EVALUATION

NAME: Jane Q. Patient
DATE OF BIRTH: 8/26/73
AGE: 28

SEX: Female

OCCUPATION: Unemployed
MARITAL STATUS: Single
REFERRAL SOURCE: H. E. Goode, PhD, Clinical Psychologist
DATE OF EVALUATION: 9/21/01

Reason for Referral

Ms. Jane Q. Patient was referred for psychological evaluation by H. E. Goode, PhD, Clinical Psychologist and the subject's therapist. Dr. Goode stated that Ms. Patient has been experiencing problems with sleep and appetite and has been complaining of problems with concentration. He stated that she has been having crying spells and reports feeling sad much of the time. Dr. Goode also

(continued)

BOX 6.3 CONTINUED

reported that Ms. Patient has reported hearing "voices." Dr. Goode requested evaluation to differentiate between psychosis and major depression as well as to assist with clarification of psychodynamic factors.

Notification of Purpose and Limits of Confidentiality

The purpose of the report was explained to Ms. Patient as well as the limits of confidentiality. She was told that the report would be sent to Dr. Goode, her therapist, and possibly used to assist with her treatment. She indicated that she understood and agreed to continue with the assessment.

Evaluation Instruments and Sources of Information

Wechsler Adult Intelligence Scale-Third Edition (WAIS-111); Wide Range Achievement Test, Third Revision (WRAT-3); Bender-Gestalt; Minnesota Multiphasic Personality Inventory, Second Edition (MM P1-2); Rorschach Inkblot Technique; Thematic Apperception Test (TAT); Incomplete Sentences; Kinetic Family Drawing; interviews with subject, Jane Q. Patient, and subject's mother and father, Mary and George Patient; consultation with H. E. Goode, Clinical Psychologist (subject's therapist), review of subject's medical records from Central County Hospital; review Social History (MSW, 4/24/00).

Background Information

Subject Demographics and Developmental History: Jane Q. Patient is a 28-year-old, single, Caucasian female who lives in Anytown, USA with her parents, Mary and George Patient. According to Mrs. Patient (mother),

the subject's birth was uncomplicated and she met developmental milestones at age-appropriate times. Mrs. Patient also reported that her daughter "was a rather shy child" who had few friends and would "prefer to be alone." She went on to report that Ms. Patient dated one male peer in high school and this relationship lasted for about 6 months. Mrs. Patient stated that she does not believe that her daughter has ever been the victim of physical or sexual abuse. Ms. Patient reported the same. The subject's mother also stated that Ms. Patient has an older brother, age 37, who is currently married and, reportedly, doing well. Mrs. Patient is a housewife and her husband is retired from the military.

Familial History and Significant Relationships

Ms. Patient has not been married nor does she have children. She reported that since high school, she has been in two relationships, both of short duration. She described these relationships as "unsatisfactory" and that the males with whom she was involved had "many problems." She described her relationship with her parents as "OK" but "distant." She reported that she currently has one "friend" with whom she "has dinner or goes to a movie once in a while."

Education and Employment History

Ms. Patient reported that she is a high school graduate. She also stated she did not participate in special education classes nor was she diagnosed as learning disabled. She reported that her grades were "good—mostly A's and B's." Her mother indicated that Ms. Patient was not a behavioral problem in school but "stayed mostly to

BOX 6.3 CONTINUED

herself." She further stated the subject played an instrument in the band for I year but stopped in order "to concentrate on her grades." Ms. Patient enrolled in college but left school after 2 years citing "emotional problems" as her reason for not continuing. She is currently unemployed but has held a variety of jobs including secretary, sales clerk, and legal assistant. Her longest period of employment was 6 months; however, her mother indicated that when she did work, she was a reliable and conscientious employee. She does not receive any form of benefits nor was she in the military.

Medical and Psychiatric History

Ms. Patient reported, and her mother confirmed, that she has no known major medical problems. Both the subject and her mother denied that Ms. Patient has ever experienced seizures, significant head trauma, diabetes, hypertension, or thyroid problems. Her mother reported that she had "asthma as a child" but "outgrew it." Ms. Patient did report that "Sometimes, I have bad headaches and feel light-headed." Ms. Patient has a documented history of psychiatric problems for approximately the last 10 years. Her medical records indicate that she first experienced emotional problems in 1991 concurrent with self-destructive ideation. At that time, she was hospitalized at Central County Hospital for 30 days and was given a discharge diagnosis of Major Depression, Single Episode. She was placed on Zoloft, an antidepressant, with follow-up care with the Anywhere Community Mental Health Center. Her compliance with medication and attendance for therapy was described as "poor." Ms. Patient was again

hospitalized on 7/3/97 for a period of 2 weeks. She had cut her wrist in an apparent suicide attempt. This attempt was described as "serious," requiring several sutures. Ms. Patient has been in outpatient therapy with H. E. Goode, PhD, for the past 3 months and is currently hospitalized following another suicide attempt (i.e., again cutting her wrist).

Alcohol and Drug History

Ms. Patient, according to her medical records and her mother, has used alcohol excessively during "binge drinking." Ms. Patient admitted to use but indicated that she only "has a few beers on the weekend at the most." She also reported that she has tried marijuana in the past. She denied any other drug/alcohol involvement.

Factors Prompting Referral

As indicated above, Ms. Patient is currently hospitalized following a suicide attempt. Her therapist, Dr. Goode, reported that she had been missing her therapy appointments and not taking her medication. He also reported that when he did see her, she appeared to be experiencing problems with concentration, sleep, and appetite and reported that she felt sad much of the time. He further stated that she had again been hearing voices of a self-deprecating nature (e.g., "You don't deserve to live"). Dr. Goode referred Ms. Patient for psychological evaluation to aid in clarification of diagnosis and to assist in determining psychological dynamics.

Behavioral Observations

Ms. Patient arrived to the evaluation session on time. She was brought by a mental health technician on the staff of the hospital

(continued)

BOX 6.3 CONTINUED

in which the evaluation took place. She was neatly dressed and hygiene good. She stands approximately 5 ft. 6 in. tall and she reported that she weighs about 150 lbs. The purpose of the evaluation was explained to Ms. Patient. She was told a report would be developed concerning her psychological functioning and the results shared with her therapist, Dr. Goode, and possibly other staff of the hospital involved in her treatment. She indicated that she understood and agreed to continue with the assessment. Ms. Patient completed all test tasks asked of her and she was cooperative throughout the assessment. She gave poor eye contact, spoke in a soft, hesitant voice, and offered little verbally beyond that which was asked of her. She seemed to easily comprehend instructions but did not initiate tasks or conversation on her own. Periodically, Ms. Patient had to be refocused on the task and tended to stare off into space. When she did offer spontaneous comment, she spoke in a self-deprecating manner about herself and her life. During the clinical interview, Ms. Patient answered questions but seemed reluctant to offer information about her feelings and thoughts. Ms. Patient did not exhibit grossly inappropriate behavior, such as delusions or hallucinations, during the entire evaluation.

Intellectual and Cognitive Functioning
Ms. Patient was oriented to time, person, and place. She also was aware of the circumstances under which she was evaluated. Ms. Patient's sensory-perceptual functioning seemed intact, although she reported that she sometimes wears glasses; however, she also reported that she did not need them most of the time and did not

appear to have any difficulty seeing items related to the testing. Her concentration and attention appeared impaired, probably as the result of emotional problems.

On the test of intelligence, Ms. Patient scored a Verbal IQ of 118, a Performance IQ of 102, and a Full Scale IQ of 109. This places her at the upper end of the Average Range of intelligence. Subtest Scale Scores are as follows:

Verbal		Performance	
Information	14	Picture Completion	12
Similarities	12	Picture Arrangement	11
Vocabulary	15	Block Design	9
Arithmetic	11	Digit Symbol	11
Comprehension	12	Matrix Reasoning	9
Digit Span	14		

A disparity of 16 points between Verbal and Performance Subtests was evident, likely due, at least in part, to psychomotor retardation related to motor slowness and possibly the effects of medication. Given this, it is estimated that Ms. Patient's potential level of intellect likely falls within the High Average Range. Ms. Patient scored highest on subtests of the test of intelligence which have been found to measure one's vocabulary and fund of general information as well as the ability to recall material immediately after it has been presented. She scored significantly above average on these subtests. She scored somewhat above average on subtests measuring the performance of verbal abstractions, the ability to evaluate a situation and respond appropriately, and the capacity to discern the important details from a total situation. Her next highest scores, which were slightly above average, were on subtests that measure

BOX 6.3 CONTINUED

the ability to perform mental math, employ eye-hand motor coordination and speed, and arrange events in an appropriate sequence. She scored just below average on subtests of the test of intelligence that assess visual organization and visuomotor organization.

Ms. Patient's immediate, recent, and remote memories appeared intact, although she reported that she has difficulty remembering recent events. This seems likely to be related to some difficulty with concentration as the result of emotional factors. Ms. Patient, at times, exhibited some difficulties with attention but was quite capable of remaining focused on task. Her capacity to express herself and understand what was said also seemed intact. On a screening test of academic achievement, she scored on a college level for both reading and spelling. On a separate test of visuomotor integration, Ms. Patient exhibited mild deficits, likely the result of observable tremulousness. Overall, in terms of intellectual and cognitive functioning, Ms. Patient scored within the Average Range of intelligence which likely is an underestimate of her potential, given emotional factors and the effects of medication. Her verbal abilities, including vocabulary, were well above average, and she exhibited some motor slowness, likely the result of psychomotor retardation and/or problems with concentration. On a screening test of academic performance, she scored on a college level for both reading and spelling. Screening for possible central nervous system impairment was negative.

Personality Functioning

Ms. Patient was well oriented. During the evaluation, she exhibited flat affect, or emotional level, for the most part. Her speech was hesitant and slow and, as indicated above, she exhibited some psychomotor retardation, some of which may be due to the effects of medication. She exhibited periods of tearfulness when discussing her life circumstance, especially relationship issues. Ms. Patient's speech was logical and coherent and she did not exhibit indications of looseness of associations, tangential thinking, or pressured speech. She experienced problems with concentration. Assessment did not reveal indications of psychosis, underlying or overt. She denied current hallucinations both visual and auditory; however, she did report that she has heard a voice in the past of a degrading nature, telling her "You don't deserve to live." She stated that the voice is that of a female and that it comes from inside her head. Ms. Patient did not exhibit delusional thinking during the assessment, and collateral information does not support the existence of past delusional thought. She reported that she has been feeling depressed and sleeping much of the time. She also reported that her appetite is "too good" and she has little interest in activity of any type. Ms. Patient denied current suicidal and homicidal ideation, although she reported that she has had self-destructive thinking as recent as the day prior to this examination.

On an intrapsychic level, assessment revealed that Ms. Patient experiences problems integrating emotional experience; that is, she is sometimes overwhelmed by her emotions to the extent that she is unable to think clearly. She reported significant feelings of depression and on projective assessment Ms. Patient produced themes of sadness. She admits to problems with

(continued)

BOX 6.3 CONTINUED

emotional control (i.e., periods of crying and anger). On exploration, Ms. Patient reported that she sometimes wakes up in the morning and "I feel like breaking something." Ms. Patient tends to deny and minimize the extent of her problems and resulting emotional unrest. These feelings build and are discharged in a sometimes uncontrolled manner. Ms. Patient tends to take a passive stance to her anger, internalizing her feelings, which results in depression. She often feels remorseful and guilty about her behaviors in an intropunitive manner. This results in feelings of self-rejection and self-destructive ideation. Ms. Patient has a strong need to be seen in a positive light by others. This not only serves to compensate for feelings of inadequacy but also serves as a defense mechanism (reaction formation) to protect against the expression of hostile impulses which she would consider unacceptable. Her auditory hallucinations, which are of a self-condemning nature, act as a form of self-punishment. Although Ms. Patient has a strong need to be seen in a positive light by others, she also has a need to be viewed as having severe emotional problems. This allows her to rationalize to herself and others the lack of meeting her own internal standards and her passive stance. Assessment revealed that Ms. Patient is pessimistic about the future with little hope of her life improving. Her thoughts about herself are of a negative nature and maintain her passive and self-deprecating posture. All of this contributes to frustration, confusion, and an extremely poor self-image. Although Ms. Patient denies current self-destructive intent, the above psychological symptoms and dynamics are indicative of significant risk for self-destructive behavior in the future. While Ms. Patient does exhibit some insight into her problems, recognizing she experiences significant difficulty with depression, she does not realize that she contributes to her own problems via her negative thought patterns and passivity.

On an interpersonal level, Ms. Patient relates in a passive-dependent fashion. She resents her dependency upon her parents but feels inadequate to separate from them. Although she desires to please her parents, she believes that she has not met their expectations for her and projects feelings of rejection onto them. Personality assessment indicated that Ms. Patient feels alienated from her family and from society in general. She does not feel that she is part of any social group and believes she is viewed as inferior by others. Ms. Patient feels uncomfortable in social settings and tends to withdraw and isolate. She experiences considerable anxiety about relating to the opposite sex. Her hostility and inappropriate behaviors (e.g., self-destruction and social avoidance) result in rejection by others. This rejection serves to reinforce her underlying hypothesis about herself that she is inferior, and adds to feelings of lack of self-worth.

Impressions

Overall, Ms. Patient appears to be experiencing significant feelings of depression with periodic psychotic symptoms which seem to be consistent with her depressed mood. Assessment did not support the existence of severe personality disorganization or a major psychosis. She also exhibits dependent personality characteristics and

BOX 6.3 CONTINUED

has experienced problems with substance abuse/dependence.

Summary

Ms. Patient is a 28-year-old, Caucasian, single female who has been referred for psychological evaluation to assist in differentiating between major depression and psychosis. She is currently hospitalized following an attempted suicide. Ms. Patient was well oriented to time, person, and place. She also was well aware of the circumstances under which she was evaluated. On the test of intelligence, she scored within the Average Range although it is estimated that her potential level of intellect is within the High Average Range. On a screening test of academic achievement, she scored at a college level for both reading and spelling. Assessment revealed indications of psychomotor retardation, probably due to emotional factors and/or the effects of medication. This likely had a negative impact on her performance on the test of intelligence; it is estimated that Ms. Patient's potential level of intellect falls within the High Average Range. Screening measures for neuropsychological dysfunction did not indicate impairment. Assessment did not reveal that Ms. Patient was experiencing a psychosis, and her perception of reality appeared generally intact. However, there were indications that, when stressed, she may exhibit psychotic symptoms (auditory hallucinations) consistent with her depressed mood. When overwhelmed with emotion, her thinking becomes confused. Ms. Patient appears to be experiencing depression of major proportion. This depression also seems to be relatively longstanding. Assessment

also revealed underlying hostility and feelings of a lack of self-worth. Interpersonally, she relates in a hostile-dependent manner. She tends to repress unwanted emotions and project feelings of rejection onto others. Ms. Patient also tends to isolate and withdraw from social contact. Although she denies current suicidal and homicidal ideation, she has tried to harm herself in the recent past and assessment reveals self-destructive tendencies.

Recommendations

Ms. Patient was cooperative during the evaluation session and completed all tasks asked of her. Although she did not appear to be experiencing a major mental illness that would significantly distort her perception of reality, there were indications of considerable emotional conflict. Problem areas, along with strengths, are discussed below with recommendations.

1. *General Psychological Functioning:* At the time of this assessment, Ms. Patient did not appear to be experiencing psychosis with significant personality disorganization. However, assessment did reveal that she has been experiencing a major mental illness for some time which appears to be a recurrent Major Depression with psychotic features. Given the degree of her depression and self-destructive behavior, continued hospitalization and stabilization of her mood is recommended at this time. Ongoing evaluation and monitoring of her medication is imperative. Continued individual

(continued)

BOX 6.3 CONTINUED

psychotherapy is also recommended to address her depression, social withdrawal, and lack of activity in her life. A cognitive-behavioral approach to this may prove beneficial. It is also recommended that she be supported in the constructive expression of anger and that her destructive hostile behaviors be addressed through anger management.

2. *Educational/Vocational Issues:* Ms. Patient was, reportedly, a good student while she was attending school. She completed 2 years of college but left school for "emotional" reasons. On the test of intelligence, she scored within the Average Range, although psychological factors, as well as the effects of medication, likely lowered her score. It is estimated that her potential level of intelligence is within the High Average Range. On a screening test of academic achievement, she scored at a college level for both reading and spelling. Given these scores, Ms. Patient appears to have the potential to perform well in educational/training pursuits. Also, when she was employed, she had been described as a reliable employee who performed well. It is recommended that these strengths be integrated into her treatment as a means of increasing her sense of positive self-esteem. Assisting Ms. Patient in developing vocational/educational goals is recommended. *Lack of Treatment Compliance:* Ms. Patient has not been compliant with treatment in the past,

both in terms of taking prescribed medication and attendance to therapy. It is recommended that this lack of compliance be explored with her in therapy, as it relates to possible resistance/passive aggressive behavior. It is imperative that she remain medication compliant and develop an emotional investment in therapy.

3. *Substance Abuse:* Ms. Patient appears to have a history of substance abuse/ dependence. Her substance of choice has been alcohol. She likely has used substances as a means of self-medicating her depression. Alcohol consumption can have a negative impact on medication effectiveness and retard psychological growth. Alcohol use can also negatively affect judgment, disinhibit emotional controls, and contribute to central nervous system damage. It is recommended that Ms. Patient participate in services to address her substance involvement and to monitor closely for use/abuse, especially alcohol. If use is suspected, random drug screens may be appropriate to monitor for use and to assist with determining level of denial.

4. *Suicidal Ideation/Behavior:* Ms. Patient has exhibited suicidal behavior on at least three known occasions. Her last suicide attempt appeared serious and was relatively recent. She cut her wrist deeply requiring several sutures. Although she currently denies any self-destructive intent, her depression and history of attempts to harm

BOX 6.3 CONTINUED

herself places her at risk for future self-destructive behavior. It is recommended that she be monitored closely for suicidal ideation and that she remain compliant with her medication. It is also recommended that self-destructive tendencies be explored with her in therapy as well as developing means to identify when she begins to experience self-destructive thoughts. Alternative behaviors to self-harm and cognitive intervention may prove beneficial. Given her recent suicidal attempt and level of current depression, continued hospitalization is recommended at this time.

5. *Social Withdrawal and Lack of Activity:* Ms. Patient, as stated above and prior to her suicide attempt, was reportedly withdrawn and isolated. In addition, she had not been involved in any known positive activity. It is recommended that behavior shaping be employed to address this issue.

Given that she reportedly functioned well when she was working, vocational pursuits may also help with socialization. Reports revealed that Ms. Patient has had an interest in music, which could be another possible avenue for activity. Exploration of relationship issues is also recommended along with assessment of her social skills and thinking about herself concerning social withdrawal as well as lack of positive activity.

6. *Dependency Issues:* Psychological assessment indicated that Ms. Patient is dependent on her parents but that she resents this dependency. This contributes to her hostility. Exploration of issues of autonomy versus dependency in therapy is recommended with the goal of Ms. Patient achieving independent functioning to the extent appropriate.

Reprinted from Wolber and Carne (2002) with permission.

In addition to providing feedback to the referral source, the clinical psychologist must provide clear and detailed feedback to the patient regarding the findings, recommendations, and suggestions based on the assessment, and this provides an additional opportunity where the therapeutic benefits of the assessment can be enhanced. Several studies (e.g., Newman & Greenway, 1996) have found that providing patients with specific and detailed feedback from the assessment can increase patients' self-esteem and reduce indicators of distress, both of which are seen as therapeutic. Newman and Greenway suggest that the therapeutic benefit comes from patients not only being able to name and explain some of their distressing experiences but also from understanding the nature of their difficulties and feeling more optimistic about dealing with them.

◇ RESEARCH

Assessment can play a very important role in various forms of research, for example, establishing effectiveness of various treatment regimens for specific disorders. Normally, a great deal of attention is paid to clearly diagnosing potential participants in the research project, and detailed assessments are often done on the participants (e.g., Imber et al., 1990). The assessments are done in order to be certain that the experimental group clearly has the disorder of interest and that the control groups do not have the disorder of interest or any similar disorder. In addition, the assessments provide information regarding the nature of the disorder (e.g., severity and chronicity of symptoms, comorbidity or co-occurrence of other symptoms, and so forth). Assessments would be completed prior to and following treatment in order to determine whether the treatment had an effect on the signs or symptoms of the disorder.

This research is done in order to determine the efficacy of treatments for specific disorders and to, of course, contribute to research knowledge regarding psychological interventions. It is also the case that, in individual clinical practices, clinical psychologists are encouraged to gather data in a similar fashion so that they can assess their own clinical work and evaluate the effectiveness of their own treatments. The ethical principles and standards of practice from numerous countries indicate that this should be done. Moreover, clinical psychologists are encouraged to publish their own work, including case reports, because information on assessment data can contribute to the quality of assessments in the future.

◇ IMPORTANCE OF CONTEXT

Gender, race, socioeconomic status, family history, history of the symptom picture, history of interpersonal relationships, history of functioning, current symptoms, relationships, functioning, and culture are all important factors to take into account to understand and help a patient(s) who is seeking treatment. For example, knowing that a person who meets the diagnostic criteria for major depressive disorder in the *DSM-IV-TR* has received the diagnosis following the death of his children, who has worked diligently and successfully in a competitive building construction environment, and desires strongly to be rid of the depression may be dealt with clinically in a very different manner from an individual who has the same diagnosis but has had it for 20 years, has never worked for more than a few months or established or maintained any relationships, and has adapted to the level of depression.

Thus, interview information, scores on psychometric instruments, and other information collected during a clinical assessment must be interpreted given the context of the person's life, gender, history, living circumstances, and culture.

◇ INTERPRETATION, DECISION-MAKING, AND PREDICTION

In the work of clinical psychology, clinical psychologists are seemingly always weighing alternatives, interpreting responses and scores, making decisions, and drawing conclusions. Whether the decisions reflect clinical issues such as diagnosis or formulation, prediction of specific behavior such as suicide potential, or research issues such as selection of appropriate measures to be included in a study or which statistical test to use, appropriate choices and conclusions need to be made.

There is often an enormous amount of information the clinical psychologist has when conducting assessments, and, at times, judgments and decisions need to be made based on information that may or may not have good reliability or validity. Information from the referral source, initial interviews, reports from family, psychological testing data from several different psychological instruments, as well as clinical impressions, all provide data relevant to the assessment. It is normally expected that some information gleaned from the data collection in assessments will be complex, and, at times, contradictory, ambiguous, and inconsistent. It is the job of the clinical psychologist to reconcile or understand the complexities and inconsistencies, to integrate this information and make appropriate clinical decisions. How does the clinician come to conclusions and make appropriate decisions? Generally, there are two approaches, both of which can be used in clinical assessments: the quantitative or **actuarial approach** whereby scores on measures are used in statistical formulae in making decisions and the **clinical judgment approach** whereby clinical experience and clinical intuition are used in making judgments.

Quantitative or Actuarial Approach

The nature of some of the data in a clinical assessment lends itself to fairly straight-forward interpretation. With psychological tests, scores that a person or people obtain on the tests can be compared to normative data in order to determine whether the person scores, generally, low, average, or high on the measure and then a clinical judgment can be made. Thus, there is little interpretation or subjective judgment needed in understanding the level of the score. When the process of making decisions or predictions involves the clinical psychologist assigning a score to some characteristic of a person and the use of statistical formulas or cutoff scores it is known as a **quantitative approach**. In other words, rather than using clinical impressions or basing decisions on clinical experience, the clinical psychologist uses the scores from tests or other information in a statistical fashion in order to make decisions or come to conclusions.

Clinical Judgment or Subjective Approach

In assessment there are many decisions that are made based on clinical experience, intuition, subjective impressions, and idiosyncratic information relevant to the individual patient. When the process of making decisions is based on these kinds of processes, it is known as **clinical judgment**. This is often based on information that can be quantitative, qualitative, or impressionistic in nature. At times, the information used can be somewhat unclear and ambiguous on the one hand, but can provide information that is broader and deeper due to the exploration of issues, psychological processes, and symptoms. For example, interpretation of interview and historical information can often be ambiguous and potentially inaccurate, not because people are trying to create inaccurate pictures of themselves, but because people are not very good personal historians (Kerns, 1986). The clinical psychologist will need to integrate this information and determine first if the information is reliable or accurate, and second, the best way to integrate the information.

Although it is possible to use both actuarial approaches and clinical judgment in some assessments, there has been a great deal of attention paid to how accurate each approach is in making clinical predictions. Paul Meehl (1954) published a landmark paper that suggested that when attempting to make specific clinical decisions using data from assessments, actuarial methods of decision-making in clinical work were better than decisions based on clinical judgment. These findings created quite a controversy within clinical psychology, and a great deal of research has been done on this issue since the original article. The findings of this research, in general, provide evidence that statistical models are better than or equal to clinical judgment (Grove, Zald, Lebow, Snitz, & Nelson, 2000) in some, but not all, clinical decisions. It is important to note, however, that both approaches are utilized in clinical assessment and other aspects of a clinical psychologist's work. Each type of decision-making process has shortcomings and a place in making clinical judgments.

Clinical Decision-Making and Errors in Judgment

Although there is always concern for good decision-making, clinical psychologists are human and susceptible to some of the cognitive and decision-making errors or biases that everyone is prone to. This stems from the fact that clinical psychologists use the same processes in making decisions and judgments that others use and can be susceptible to the same errors that others make in decision-making. This can be the case in both clinical work and in research of clinical psychologists (Tversky & Kahneman, 1974). Of course, the decisions can often have a major impact on people's lives, and the quality of their lives can be, sometimes, profoundly affected.

In fact, there seems to be consensus within the field of clinical psychology that making clinical decisions can be compromised because of cognitive errors that clinicians can make. For this reason, a good deal of attention has been paid to the possible sources of error in the clinical decision-making process. What are some of the major sources of error that may be particularly relevant to clinical psychologists?

1. Base rate issue: In making judgments or predictions, clinicians can make errors by not taking account of the rate that particular behaviors, traits, symptoms, or disorders occur in the general population (i.e., **base rates**). For example, in making judgments about low-frequency events, it is easy to view these events as more common than they actually are due to not taking base rates into account.

2. Barnum effect: A variation on the base rate issue is the notion of Barnum statements or the **Barnum effect**, named after PT Barnum, the American showman and circus owner who was known for creating hoaxes and for his famous quote: "There's a sucker born every minute." The idea with the Barnum effect is that statements can be made of an individual that sound idiosyncratic and uniquely descriptive, but are actually so commonplace among people that the statements become meaningless for the particular person. For example, read the following description:

This is a person who can handle stress reasonably well, but, at times, that person can feel somewhat burdened and overwhelmed by demands. At these times she may feel less than self-confident and exhibit low self-esteem, especially if the stress involves some type of event that has resulted or may result in a failure of some sort. She may also feel somewhat depressed or anxious at times and, in times of significant distress, feel somewhat helpless. This is especially the case if the person experiences a personal loss of some sort.

Although this paragraph may sound like it pertains to a particular person, it describes many, many individuals. Reread the paragraph and see if it describes you.

3. Illusory correlation: Based on steadfast beliefs in the relationship between certain clinical variables, clinicians may make judgments based on these nonveridical relationships known as **illusory correlations**. For example, many people believe that the full moon will produce untoward and chaotic responses in individuals. Even though there is no data supporting the supposed correlation between phase of moon and erratic behavior, many people maintain this belief. This is known as an illusory correlation and can be seen with clinicians who believe that certain signs or behaviors may be indicative of some meaningful clinical entity when, in reality, there is no relationship.

4. Preconceived ideas and confirmatory bias: This source of error is similar to the illusory correlation in the sense that, based on preconceived ideas or on a theoretical perspective, clinicians will look for evidence to confirm their prejudged or preconceived notions and, importantly, ignore disconfirming information. In continuing with our example of the moon and erratic behavior, one way that the myth is maintained is that people will notice and pay attention to times and situations where there is a full moon and evidence of erratic behavior, but not notice or pay attention to times and situations where there is a full moon and no evidence of erratic behavior or when there is no full moon and lots of erratic behavior. In effect, the model, that full moon produces erratic behavior, does not get evaluated or modified based on the disconfirming evidence.

5. Inappropriate use of heuristics: Heuristics are cognitive shortcuts that normally serve us well in making quick judgments and decisions (Elstein, 1988). Errors can occur when the heuristics are used inappropriately or in inappropriate situations. Two heuristics, in particular, can come into play in clinical work, the **representativeness heuristic**, which leads to the erroneous belief in the reliability and validity of small numbers, and the **availability heuristic**, which leads to putting too much weight on vividly recalled information (Grove et al., 2000). For example, the availability heuristic involves the belief that the more easily we can bring an event to mind, the more frequently that event must occur. The availability heuristic is at play when we believe we are in danger of crashing when flying because we can easily recall horrific airline crashes or when buying a lottery ticket we may believe we have a good chance of winning the lottery because we can recall photos of winners in the newspapers or on television. In terms of clinical judgment, because some low-frequency event may have occurred in a dramatic fashion (e.g., suicide) the clinician may have the belief that that event occurs more frequently than it actually does.

Fortunately, clinical psychologists are taught strategies to combat these and other sources of bias and error in their work (Turk & Salovey, 1988).

◇ CONCLUSION

Overall, the student should have an overview and a general understanding of the domain of clinical assessment for clinical psychologists. It is an important component of a clinical psychologist's work and can provide extremely important information regarding the difficulties a person, couple, or family experiences as well as options regarding attempting to treat the difficulties. Moreover, assessment is one of the unique abilities that clinical psychologists utilize that other mental health professionals do not have the training or expertise to perform.

◇ ONGOING CONSIDERATIONS

Assessment has a long history in clinical psychology, and it remains one of the truly unique aspects of the identity of clinical psychologists. There has been some concern that assessments were becoming less relevant to clinical psychology; however, it is clear that this type of activity remains one of the important tasks that clinical psychologists perform. Recently there has been concern that psychological assessments procedures, like psychotherapy, have to have empirical support in order for these procedures, be they tests or techniques, to be used. There certainly has been a long-standing tradition of demonstrating the reliability and validity of assessment procedures; however, there are even higher expectations of the efficacy and utility of psychological assessments. Furthermore, clinical psychologists need to remain sensitive to the fact that every assessment modality has unique strengths and weaknesses and that the hallmark of competence in assessment is knowing how to aggregate an assessment package where the various modalities balance each other's strengths and weaknesses.

◇ KEY TERMS LEARNED

Actuarial approach
Availability heuristic
Barnum effect
Base rates
Clinical judgment
Clinical judgment approach
Core competencies
Ego-strength
Formulation
Heuristics
Idiographic

Illusory correlation
Nomothetic
Prognosis
Psychodiagnosis
Psychological assessment
Psychological mindedness
Psychological testing
Quantitative approach
Representativeness heuristic
Techniques
Tests

◇ THINKING QUESTIONS

1. What are the differences between diagnosis and formulation? What role does each play in an assessment?

2. Explain the major goals of psychological assessment.

3. What are the similarities and differences between tests and techniques in assessment?

4. Describe the different types of psychological assessments, and give examples of each.

5. Clinicians, like other people, can make cognitive errors when making judgments or decisions. Describe the kinds of errors. What sorts of effects do you believe these errors can have? Give examples.

6. Why do you think it is important to provide feedback to patients following an assessment?

◇ REFERENCES

Achenbach, T. M., & Edelbrock, C. E. (1992). *Manual for the child behavior checklist*. Department of Psychiatry, University of Vermont.

American Psychiatric Association. (2000). *Diagnostic and statistical manual of mental disorders* (4th ed., text revision). Washington, DC: Author.

Beck, A. T., Rush, A. J., Shaw, B. F., & Emery, G. (1979). *Cognitive therapy of depression*. New York: Guilford Press.

Bergin, A. E., & Lambert, M. J. (1978). The evaluation of therapeutic outcomes. In S. L. Garfield & A. F. Bergin (Eds.), *Handbook of psychotherapy and behavior change: An empirical analysis* (2nd ed., pp. 139–190). New York: John Wiley.

Blatt, S. J., Auerbach, J. S., Zuroff, D. C., & Shahar, G. (2006). Evaluating efficacy, effectiveness, and mutative factors in psychodynamic psychotherapies. *PDM task force. Psychodynamic diagnostic manual*. Silver Spring, MD: Alliance of Psychoanalytic Organizations.

Butcher, J. (1990). *MMPI-2 in psychological treatment*. New York: Oxford University Press.

Butcher, J. (1995). *Clinical personality assessment*. New York: Oxford.

Childs, R. A., & Eyde, L. D. (2002). Assessment training in clinical psychology doctoral programs: What should we teach? What do we teach? *Journal of Personality Assessment, 78*, 130–144.

Ciminero, A. R., Calhoun, K. S., & Adams, H. E. (Eds.). 1986. *Handbook of behavioral assessment* (2nd ed.). New York: Wiley.

Cohen, R. J., Swerdlik, M. E., & Phillips, S. M. (1996). *Psychological testing and assessment: An introduction to tests and measurements* (3rd ed.). Mountain View, California: Mayfield.

Dougherty, T. W., Ebert, R. J., & Callender, J. C. (1986). Policy capturing in the employment interview. *Journal of Applied Psychology, 71*, 9–15.

Elstein, A. S. (1988). Cognitive processes in clinical inference and decision making. In D. C. Turk & P. Salovey (Eds.). *Reasoning, inference, and judgement in clinical psychology*. London: Collier Macmillan Publishers.

Frank, J. D. (1973). *Persuasion and healing*. Baltimore: Johns Hopkins University Press.

Garb, H. N. (1998). *Studying the clinician: Judgment research and psychological assessment*. Washington, DC: American Psychological Association.

Gregory, R. J. (2004). *Psychological testing: History, principles, and applications* (4th ed.). Boston: Pearson/Allyn & Bacon.

Groth-Marnat, G. (1990). *Handbook of psychological assessment*. New York: John Wiley & Sons.

Groth-Marnat, G. (1999). *Handbook of psychological assessment*. New York: John Wiley & Sons.

Grove, W. M., Zald, D. H., Lebow, B. S., Snitz, B. F., & Nelson, C. (2000). Clinical versus mechanical prediction: A meta-analysis. *Psychological Assessment, 12,* 19–30.

Hewitt, P. L., Habke, A. M., Lee-Baggley, D. L., Sherry, S. B., & Flett, G. L. (2008). The impact of perfectionistic self-presentation on the cognitive, affective, and physiological experience of a clinical interview. *Psychiatry: Interpersonal and Biological Processes, 71,* 93–122.

Hilsenroth, M. J., & Cromer, T. D. (2007). Clinician interventions related to alliance during the initial interview and psychological assessment. *Psychotherapy, 44,* 205–218.

Imber, S., Pilkonis, P. A., Sotsky, S. M., Elkin, I., Watkins, J. T., Collins, J. F., Shea, M. T., Leber, W. R., & Glass, D. R. (1990). Mode-specific effects among three treatments for depression. *Journal of Consulting and Clinical Psychology, 58,* 352–359.

Kerns, L. L. (1986). Falsifications in the psychiatric history: A differential diagnosis. *Psychiatry, 49,* 13–17.

Krishnamurthy, R., VandeCreek, L., & Kaslow, N. J., et al. (2004). Achieving competency in psychological assessment: Directions for education and training. *Journal of Clinical Psychology, 60,* 725–739.

Linden, W. (2006). Psychological treatment of hypertension. In A. V. Nikcevic, A. R. Kuczmierczyk, & M. Bruch (Eds.). *Formulation and treatment in clinical health psychology.* London: Routledge.

Lucock, M. P., Hall, P., & Noble, R. (2006). A survey of influences on the practice of psychotherapists and clinical psychologists in training in the UK. *Clinical Psychology and Psychotherapy, 13,* 123–130.

Maloney, M. P., & Ward, M. P. (1976). *Psychological assessment: A conceptual approach.* New York: Oxford University Press.

McWilliams, N. (1999). *Psychoanalytic case formulation.* New York: Guildford.

Meehl, P. E. (1954). *Clinical versus statistical prediction.* Minneapolis: University of Minnesota Press.

Meyer, G. J., Finn, S. W., Eyde, I. D., Day, G. G., Kobiszyn, T., Moreland, K., Eisman, E., & Dies, R. (1998). *Benefits and costs of psychological assessment in healthcare delivery: Report of Board of Professional Affairs Psychological Assessment Working Group, Part II.* Washington, DC: American Psychological Association.

Morrison, J. R. (1995). *DSM–IV made easy: The clinician's guide to diagnosis.* New York: Guildford.

Newman, M., & Greenway, P. (1997). Therapeutic effects of providing MMPI-2 test feedback to clients at a university counseling service: A collaborative approach. *Psychological Assessment, 9,* 122–131.

Norcross, J. C., Karpiak, C. P., & Santoro, S. O. (2005). Clinical psychologists across the years: The division of clinical psychology from 1960 to 2003. *Journal of Clinical Psychology, 61,* 1467–1483.

Persons, J. (2006). Case-formulation driven psychotherapy. *Clinical Psychology: Science and Practice, 13,* 167–170.

Rappaport, D., Gill, M. M., & Schafer, R. (1968). *Diagnostic psychological testing* (Vol. 1). Chicago: Yearbook.

Rogers, C. R. (1961). *On becoming a person.* Boston: Houghton Mifflin.

Rose, T., Kaser-Boyd, N., & Maloney, M. P. (2001). *Essentials of Rorschach assessment.* New York: Wiley.

Sperry, L. (2004). *Assessment of couples and families: Contemporary and cutting-edge strategies*. New York: Brunner-Routledge.

Turk, D. C., & Salovey, P. (1988). *Reasoning, inference, and judgement in clinical psychology*. London: Collier Macmillan Publishers.

Tversky, A., & Kahneman, D. (1974). Judgments under uncertainty: Heuristics and biases, *Science, 185,* 1124–1131.

Wechsler, D. (1997). *WAIS-III administration and scoring manual*. San Antonio, TX: Psychological Corporation.

Wolber, & Carne (2002). *Writing Psychological Reports: A guide for clinicians* (2nd ed.). Sarasota, FL: Professional Resources Press.

CHAPTER SEVEN

PSYCHODIAGNOSTIC ASSESSMENT

CHAPTER OBJECTIVE

In the previous chapter, we discussed the role of the clinical psychologist in psychological assessment as well as the purposes of assessment in practice and research. Chapters 7 and 8 will provide descriptions and critical evaluations of the many tools available to the clinical psychologist for assessing individual differences: making diagnoses, formulations, and treatment recommendations and tracking progress in therapy. This chapter will discuss one particular type of clinical assessment, namely, the psychodiagnostic assessment and the techniques and tools used to conduct this kind of assessment.

◇ PSYCHODIAGNOSTIC ASSESSMENT

One of the more common kinds of assessments done by clinical psychologists is the psychodiagnostic assessment. These kinds of assessments are also referred to as personality assessments, diagnostic assessments, pretreatment assessments, or just plain psychological assessments. In these assessments, patients' problems and concerns are delineated and diagnostic status is determined, as are issues pertaining to the formulation of the problem, contextual features of the individual and situation, and issues regarding appropriate treatment for the particular patient. Although the choice of particular tools used in these assessments and the inferences made from these tools can vary somewhat from clinician to clinician, based on the theoretical orientation of the clinical psychologist, the most comprehensive assessments usually include a clinical interview and psychological testing. The tests include both objective (e.g., self-report questionnaires) and projective techniques (e.g., responses to ambiguous stimuli). The assessment can also involve information from collateral sources (i.e., reports from other mental health clinicians, referral information, and information from family members) and will also include a feedback session that clarifies issues in the assessment, describes the relevant findings, and presents the treatment options to the patient. Finally, the assessment is formalized into a report to the referral source. An example of a comprehensive psychodiagnostic assessment is presented in Box 6.3. The students a strongly encouraged to return to that example as they work through this chapter.

Although there are large numbers of possible psychodiagnostic assessment tests and techniques available, for the most part, only relatively few are used commonly and most have been refined and revised over the years. The following sections present some of these tests and techniques. It should be noted that the well-trained clinical psychologist uses a **multimethod approach** in assessment to balance out the relative strengths and weaknesses of any one single instrument and no one instrument is used solely. All information needs to be considered, and both confirming and, as discussed in chapter 6, disconfirming evidence and contradictory evidence need to be taken into account.

◇ WHAT ARE THE TESTS AND TOOLS USED IN PSYCHODIAGNOSTIC ASSESSMENT?

Several surveys have been done over the years to determine which psychological tools are used most frequently by clinical psychologists. Typically, these studies survey clinical psychologists to determine what instruments they use in their assessments and, essentially, tally up the numbers and present a percentage of the sample using a particular instrument. Not all psychological tests used in assessments will necessarily show up in these surveys; however, the major instruments certainly do.

The majority of the surveys have focused on American samples and have found a surprising consistency over the years. Two of them (Camara, Nathan, & Puente, 2000; Watkins, Campbell, Nieberding, & Hallmark, 1995) assessed samples of American Psychological Association members who indicated that clinical psychology was their specialty, and asked numerous questions about their assessment practices. The most frequently used tests for these two studies are included in Table 7.1. The top 10 instruments are similar in both studies, suggesting a surprising consistency in instruments used over the years. In fact, many of these same instruments or revisions of the instruments show up in similar surveys from decades before (e.g., Lubin, Wallace, & Paine, 1971). Both objective (MMPI-2) and projective techniques (RIT and TAT) were in the top 10, suggesting that these assessment instruments are consistently and frequently used.

One study on assessment practices outside North America (Bekhit, Thomas, Lalonde, & Jolley, 2002) assessed 158 supervisors from a British university regarding assessment practices and instruments used. Approximately 13% of the clinical psychologist's time was spent in clinical assessment. Most commonly, clinical interviews were mentioned, and there seemed to be less use of formal objective and projective assessment instruments than in North America.

TABLE 7.1 Frequency of Test Use

TEST	WATKINS ET AL. (1995) RANKING	CAMARA ET AL. (2000) RANKING
Clinical Interview	1	Not included in study
Wechsler Adult Intelligence Scale	2	1
MMPI-2	3	2
Sentence Completion	4	
Thematic Apperception Test	5	6
Rorschach Inkblot Technique	6	4
Bender-Gestalt	7	5
Drawing Tests	8	8
Beck Depression Inventory	9	10
Wechsler Intelligence Scale for Children	10	3
Wide Range Achievement Test	—	7
Wechsler Memory Scale	—	9

◇ CLINICAL INTERVIEWS

As the information in the Watkins et al. (1995) study suggest, the clinical interview is likely the mainstay of clinical assessment and used in essentially all clinical endeavors. Irrespective of the clinical orientation of the clinical psychologist, the clinical interview (also known as the initial interview) serves numerous purposes:

1. Is a means of gathering clinical data and provides information on the difficulties the individual has as he perceives them.

2. Provides information about **process-related variables** such as how comfortable the patient is with the clinical enterprise, whether the person is forthcoming with information, whether the person is likely to engage in the therapeutic process, or whether the patient is aloof and hostile, to name a few.

3. Provides, for many people, their first clinical exposure (in their first clinical encounters, many patients have some inaccurate preconceived notions of what the process might entail. For example, the only information people may have about psychotherapy might be from television sitcoms or B-horror movies) and an opportunity to have a positive clinical experience.

4. Provides an opportunity to initiate and develop a good therapeutic alliance, which is crucial for proper assessment and to facilitate effective treatment.

5. Provides a context for understanding the nature of the difficulties and the important contextual variables that can contribute to treatment.

An interview can be thought of as a one-sided social conversation with an agenda of attempting to understand the patient from a clinical perspective. In other words, the clinical psychologist engages the patient in a dialogue that focuses on the personal issues the patient is requesting help with. The dialogue is not a two-way dialogue, as in social situations where both participants discuss and disclose personal aspects of their lives, but rather it focuses solely on the patient's issues. The clinical psychologist gathers information by observing and questioning, discussing, and commenting upon the patient's behavior. Importantly, the clinical psychologist learns about the patient not only from what the patient says about herself, but also by how the patient says it and how she presents herself in the interview. A somewhat hidden, second objective of this clinical interview, especially when it marks the likely beginning of psychotherapy, is the initial building of a therapeutic alliance. The psychologist will want to encourage the patient's belief that this clinical psychologist is worth returning to.

The clinical psychologist has to create an environment that is safe, secure, private, and free from interruptions so that the patient feels free to talk about issues that are often deeply personal and that may have never been revealed to others. The clinical psychologist needs to create an atmosphere of acceptance, warmth, and professionalism so that the patient can feel as comfortable as possible in revealing personal information. A clinician conducting interviews must have the following skills:

1. Ability to listen closely and in a nonjudgmental fashion to the content of the patient's utterances
2. Ability to observe how the person says things
3. Awareness of nonverbal behavior and subtle changes (e.g., tone of voice, facial expressions) in the behavior of the patient during the interview
4. Ability to connect disparate kinds of information
5. Knowledge of probing questions to ask in order to uncover relevant information

Typically the interview is the first task the clinical psychologist engages in with a patient, and rather than simply passively sitting and nodding his head in a rather bored fashion, the clinical psychologist is very busy gathering data from multiple sources and processing and connecting that information, formulating and testing hypotheses about the patient, looking for confirming and disconfirming evidence, keeping track of time, remembering what aspects of personality and psychopathology to tap, and so forth. The clinical psychologist does this so that he can derive some tentative conclusions regarding the diagnostic picture and the clinical formulation. The clinical psychologist derives these hypotheses and conclusions not only from what information the patient provides or what she says, known as the **content information**, but also from the manner in which the person behaves and provides information, known as the **process information**. For example, a patient may provide information regarding feelings of disconnection and unreality (known as **derealization**) but does so in a vague, nonforthcoming manner. Both aspects of the information, the presence of derealization and the vague presentation of the information, will be processed by the clinical psychologist and help her to derive conclusions regarding the assessment of difficulties and treatment possibilities.

A very useful general approach to assessment derives from a concept that Sigmund Freud described known as **psychic determinism**. Essentially the idea with psychic determinism is that everything (i.e., every overt and covert behavior) has some goal, meaning, purpose, and cause. Thus, the clinician needs to be aware of and pay attention to all (or as many as he possibly can) behaviors the patient exhibits. It is important to understand that paying attention to all behaviors does not mean that the clinical psychologist will necessarily know the meaning or cause of every behavior of a patient, but orients the clinician to pay attention to as much of the patient's behavior as he can. Much of this information may be particularly useful in the assessment. Thus, the clinical psychologist starts gathering information about a person during the person's initial contact on the telephone, when meeting the person in the waiting room, by paying attention to the person's dress and how the person interacts with receptionist, and so forth. The clinical psychologist must always have his clinician's hat on when interacting with a patient.

The areas usually covered in a clinical interview include:

1. **Demographic information:** Name, age, sex, marital status, people in family, religion, race, occupation, marital status, contact information, and so forth.

2. **Presenting problem and reason for referral:** What are the major complaints that the patient is seeking help with, and what are the specifics of the problem (e.g., signs, symptoms, duration and severity of signs and symptoms)?

3. **History of problem and psychological history:** How long have difficulties been present, and what are the events or situations that may have triggered the initiation of the symptoms or difficulties? What significant or traumatic events has the person experienced? What other disorders, syndromes, or symptoms have bothered the patient in the past?

4. **Medical history and present medical conditions:** What are the significant events in the patient's medical history, and what medical conditions are currently present?

5. **Current and past social situation:** What is the nature and quality of the current living situation, intimate relationships, friendships, social network, and sources of support? What were past relationships like? What are current relationships like?

6. **Family history:** Are there psychological difficulties among family members? What family stressors exist?

7. **Childhood, adolescence, and early adulthood history:** What was the family environment when the patient was growing up? Was the family or parents supportive and available? What were significant events during this time, and how well did the patient perform academically and socially?

8. **Previous treatment sought:** Has the patient ever sought treatment for current problem(s) or for other issues in the past? Was the assistance provided helpful, and did the patient connect well with the therapist?

Although we have presented these areas as discrete sections of the interview, in reality, the clinical psychologist will cover these areas not necessarily in a stepwise fashion but in a more flowing interaction with the patient. **Open-ended questions** (i.e., questions that are not typically answered with a one-word, yes-no answer, such as "What was it like growing up in a logging camp?") are typically utilized in the interview. In order to get specific information, at times, the clinical psychologist will follow up open-ended questions with more specific **closed-ended questions** (i.e., questions that ask for very specific information such as "Did you feel isolated in the camp?"). The clinical psychologist will attempt to conduct the interview as if it were a warm social interaction rather than a stilted automated gathering of information.

An additional interview component, known as the **Mental Status Exam** (MSE), is used and, typically, is incorporated throughout the clinical interview. The MSE is thought of as the equivalent of a physical examination in medicine; it attempts to cover most areas of functioning that reveal signs and symptoms of psychological problems. The domains that are either focused on explicitly (i.e., directly questioned) or observed include:

1. **Appearance:** Patient's appearance and dress.

2. **Behavior:** Patient's oddities of speech, behavior, involuntary movements, and so forth.

3. **Orientation:** Patient's **orientation to time** (i.e., knows year, month, date), **orientation to place** (i.e., knows where he is), and **orientation to person** (i.e., knows who he is).

4. **Memory:** Patient's memory for recent and distant past events.

5. **Sensorium:** Problems with any of the five senses.

6. **Psychomotor activity:** Patient's behavior, such as exhibiting slowness of behavior (psychomotor retardation) or agitation/accelerated behavior (psychomotor agitation).

7. **States of consciousness:** Patient's level of awareness ranging from confusion and bewilderment to alertness and awareness.

8. **Affect:** Patient's emotional expression as well as the level and appropriateness of affect (e.g., laughing while disclosing sad events).

9. **Mood:** Patient's general mood in the interview (e.g., angry, sad, apprehensive).

10. **Personality:** General terms used to describe the patient (e.g., extroverted, manipulative, stubborn).

11. **Thought content:** The presence of **hallucinations** (seeing, hearing, smelling, or otherwise experiencing perceptions of things that are nonexistent) or **delusions** (i.e., untrue, unfounded beliefs, such as belief being followed by government agents, aliens communicating with him).

12. **Thought processes:** Patient's speech in terms of whether it is logical or rambling or whether the patient has disconnected thoughts, loosening of associations (i.e., jumping very quickly from topic to topic and idea to idea), tangential speech, and so forth.

13. **Intellect:** The judged level of intelligence of the patient, often based on the vocabulary of the patient.

14. **Judgment and insight:** The quality of the patient's decision-making and the patient's own understanding of his problems.

In addition to the MSE, the clinical psychologist may have specific clinical concerns that are addressed in the interview. For example, if there is reason to believe the patient may be suicidal or homicidal, the clinical psychologist will do a suicide or homicide risk assessment. A procedure used to assess suicide or homicide risk is presented in Box 7.1.

Unstructured Interviews

Initial interviews can vary in terms of structure. For example, the previous description of a clinical interview is based largely on an unstructured or semistructured interview that is likely by far the most common type of clinical interview (Mohr & Beutler, 2003). Some interviews will be almost completely unstructured where there is no standardized format.

BOX 7.1

ASSESSMENT OF SUICIDE RISK

Although completed suicide is a rare event, it is a real concern for individuals with a variety of disorders and psychological problems. Because suicide tends not to be an impulsive act but rather an act that has been thought about, considered, and sometimes even talked about with others (Yufit & Lester, 2005), the risk for attempting suicide can be evaluated. In the assessment of suicide or homicide risk, the patient is asked a series of questions that reflect the degree to which the patient has considered suicide. A positive response to each question increases the risk. The questions are:

1. Are you thinking of suicide?
2. Do you have a plan, and, if so, what is the plan? (The more detailed the plan, the greater the risk.)
3. Do you have the means to execute the plan (e.g., do you know which bridge you are going to jump from, do you have a gun at home with bullets)?
4. Are you going to attempt suicide? Have you ever attempted it in the past?
5. If not, what is keeping you from making the attempt, that is, what are some reasons you are not making the attempt? The clinical psychologist is interested in determining if there are any significant reasons for living—such as religious beliefs or protection of the person's family from the devastation suicide would cause.

Moreover, these interviews can be very flexible in that the clinician allows the patient to talk about whatever issues come up and the clinician may probe further into some aspects of the patient's functioning based on her clinical judgment. These sorts of interviews are often used by psychodynamically trained clinicians and by those who work from a client-centered perspective. Because of the lack of structure and the clinical judgment that is inherent in these unstructured interviews, they have been viewed by some as lacking in reliability and in some forms of validity. Some of the benefits and drawbacks of the unstructured and semistructured interviews are mentioned here:

Pros of Unstructured Interviews

1. The unstructured interviews facilitate rapport with the patient.
2. The flexibility of interview can be shifted and altered based on the patient's responses.
3. The interviews can be modified both before the interview and "on the fly."
4. The interviews are not limited by certain tools or norms.

Cons of Unstructured Interviews

1. It is difficult to know the reliability and validity of the interviews given the variation from clinician to clinician.
2. The unstructured interviews lack reliability.
3. The interviews may be susceptible to clinical biases.

Structured Interviews

Other interviews, especially those used in research, are highly structured and are used specifically for establishing diagnostic or symptom information. These types of interviews are known usually as **structured diagnostic interviews** and are typically based on the diagnostic criteria of the *DSM-IV-TR* or some other diagnostic system. The major purpose of the structured diagnostic interview is to provide a clear diagnosis, and it does not necessarily provide information on other domains of clinical interest. In these interviews, the clinical psychologist follows a specific regimen of questions and covers very specific topics. A finite list of signs and symptoms associated with various disorders is spelled out, and all the questions are prepared beforehand with specific phrasing and specific decision trees to follow based on the responses of the patient. Also, typically, choices for responses are also given. According to Mohr and Beutler (2003) the Structured Clinical Interview for Diagnosis (SCID; First, Spitzer, Gibbon, & Williams, 1997) is the gold standard for establishing *DSM-IV-TR* diagnoses.

Structured diagnostic interviews are used mainly in research contexts because the structured nature of the interview enhances the reliability of the diagnosis. These kinds of interviews are not typically used in clinical contexts due, likely, to the length of time it takes to complete the interview, and the clinician is often interested in more information than simply the presence or absence of signs and symptoms.

Pros of Structured Interviews

1. Structured interviews have high levels of reliability of diagnoses.
2. They provide good tools for research settings.
3. They can have modules for specific disorders.

Cons of Structured Interviews

1. The interview's content is constrained only to diagnosis.
2. It is time consuming to conduct the interview.
3. The interview does not give information pertinent to treatment other than diagnosis.
4. The interview is not as conducive to establishing rapport.
5. Process information is not seen as relevant.

◇ OBJECTIVE TESTS

Most times, clinical psychologists want to quickly and efficiently assess a variety of factors related to psychopathology such as symptom levels, personality factors related to the development and maintenance of psychopathology, and factors related to the treatment of the psychological difficulties. The clinical psychologist can use what are termed **objective tests** or tests that have carefully worded self-report questions to be answered or items to be rated. Objective tests are structured tests that usually take the form of presentation of a series of items (e.g., "I am sad" or "I am afraid of people") assessing some facet of personality or psychopathology and a rating of the items with a limited range of responses (e.g., True or False, Agree or Disagree, or ratings of agreement on a scale from 1 to 7). The tests are objective in the sense that the items and possible responses are predetermined, measure aspects of functioning that the patient is aware of and can rate, and are amenable to scoring in an objective fashion (i.e., often by just summing the ratings).

Objective tests, also referred to as **self-report inventories**, have been used historically, frequently, and in a variety of settings and represent an important tool for clinical psychologists. The tests, very generally, assess conscious aspects of a person's functioning. In other words, the patients rate their behavior based on their own knowledge and awareness of their own behavior. Thus, information that is not necessarily accessible to the individual (e.g., process-related issues, unconscious processes, defenses) is not tapped.

Although objective tests have many advantages including ease of administration, economy in terms of time and cost (e.g., self-report inventories can be administered to large groups of individuals at one time and can be completed without a clinician present), ease of scoring, and, frequently, ease of interpretation, they can be problematic for the patient because there are no opportunities to qualify answers or expand upon and explain what each response means. As well, due to the ease of scoring and seeming ease of interpretation, self-report measures can be used inappropriately.

One particular difficulty that exists due to the fact that the objective tests assess behaviors the patient is aware of is that patients can answer in ways that present a false picture of themselves to the clinician. For example, some individuals may want to present themselves in the best possible light (e.g., if being assessed for custody or if being assessed for early parole from jail) or in the worst possible light (e.g., if being assessed for psychological trauma from car accident for insurance purposes or if trying to get quicker access to services). These are known as **response sets** or **test-taking attitudes**, and they can influence the accuracy of the assessment data being gathered. There are numerous types of response sets including:

1. **Underreporting of psychopathology:** The patient attempts to present himself in an overly positive or favorable light.

2. **Overreporting of psychopathology:** The patient attempts to present himself in an overly negative or unfavorable light.

3. **Acquiescence:** The patient agrees with whatever the item states.

4. **Nonacquiescence:** The patient disagrees with whatever the item states.

5. **Carelessness or inconsistency:** The patient is not being consistent in responding or not paying attention or responding randomly to items.

6. **Self-deception:** Patients may chronically underestimate problems or may be overly optimistic and positive.

Thus, when conducting an assessment, it is important to assess and control these response sets to determine whether a particular patient's responses are valid or not. Test developers have developed some very creative ways to tackle these issues. It should be noted that although the measurement of response sets is used to determine whether the test results are accurate and valid and whether the instrument itself should be interpreted, the measures themselves can also provide important information regarding how the patient is approaching the clinical experience and, potentially, the aspects of the person's personality (e.g., Butcher, 1990). For example, it is very useful to know that the person tends to be, for example, dishonest in her participation in the clinical process. How the response biases are dealt with varies from test to test and will be described in the context of a number of very popular psychodiagnostic tests that require extensive training to ensure proper interpretation.

◇ MINNESOTA MULTIPHASIC PERSONALITY INVENTORY (MMPI-2), MMPI-2 RESTRUCTURED FORM (MMPI-2-RF), AND MMPI-ADOLESCENT (MMPI-A)

The Minnesota Multiphasic Personality Inventory (MMPI; Hathaway & McKinley, 1940), and its revision, the MMPI-2 (Butcher, Dahlstrom, Graham, Tellegen, & Kaemmer, 1989), is one of the most frequently used and most researched self-report clinical personality instruments (Nichols, 2001). It has a long history of usage in clinical psychology and has been used in assessments since its development in the 1940s. Initially developed by the psychologist Starke Hathaway and the psychiatrist John McKinley to aid in the quick diagnosis of psychiatric patients in Minnesota, the MMPI quickly developed into one of the most accepted and frequently used self-report psychological assessment instruments used in the world. It also has an incredible amount of empirical attention with thousands of research articles published on the MMPI itself or using the MMPI in a research protocol (Nichols, 2001). Although the MMPI was seen as an extremely useful measure, over the years, numerous shortcomings of the instrument were identified (e.g., poor normative sample and inappropriate wording and word usage). It was revised in August 1989 and named MMPI-2. The revision attempted both to retain the strengths of the original MMPI and to correct some of the more problematic issues by using a more appropriate normative sample, correcting grammatical errors, updating the language, and incorporating new items and subscales of clinical significance.

The MMPI/MMPI-2 is appropriate for adults 18 years old and above, and in addition to psychodiagnostic assessments it has been used for a variety of purposes such as initial screening for psychopathology, personnel selection, marital therapy and marital suitability, and treatment-outcome studies (Greene, 2000). It has a total of 15 scales, including 5 validity scales used to assess test-taking attitudes and 10 clinical and personality-related scales. Table 7.2 presents the names and brief descriptions of the scales. In addition, the MMPI-2 has incorporated numerous additional clinically relevant scales.

TABLE 7.2 Minnesota Multiphasic Personality Inventory-2 Scales

SCALE NAME	DESCRIPTION
Validity Scales	
L (Lie)	Defensiveness
F (Infrequency)	Over-reporting of symptoms
K	Subtle defensiveness
TRIN (True Response Inconsistency)	
VRIN (Variable Response Inconsistency)	
Clinical Scales	
1 Hypochondriasis	Body complaints
2 Depression	Depression
3 Hysteria	Histrionic defenses
4 Psychopathic Deviation	Psychopathy
5 Masculinity/Femininity	Gender role identity
6 Paranoia	Paranoid thoughts and ideas
7 Psychasthenia	Obsessive rumination and anxiety
8 Schizophrenia	Psychotic and social withdrawal
9 Hypomania	Mania or submanic behavior
10 Social Introversion	Social introversion

Validity Scales

Hathaway and McKinley identified early on that response sets of patients were going to be an issue, and in order to control these response biases, three subscales were developed and are referred to as the validity scales. Validity, in this case, refers to how valid the test results are for a particular patient. A high score on one or more of the validity scales can invalidate the entire test results, and with more moderate scores the response set must be taken into account when interpreting the findings.

There are two measures of defensiveness or under-reporting of psychopathology. The **L Scale**, originally called the Lie Scale, was designed to measure defensiveness; it contains items that reflect behaviors that are somewhat negative but are also quite common, such as, "I do not always tell the truth" or "I get angry sometimes." If a person is not prepared to reveal anything negative or unfavorable about himself, then that person will score highly on this measure. The **K Scale**, which was also developed as a means of assessing frankness and desire to present an overly positive image of the self. The items of the K Scale are more subtle than those of the L Scale (e.g., "People often disappoint me" and "I like to let people know where I stand on things") and, hence, are less susceptible to overt conscious attempts to overreport or under-report psychopathology. Finally the **F Scale**, also known as the Infrequency Scale, is a measure of unusual attitudes and behaviors seen in severe psychopathology or in individuals seeking to present themselves in a negative and unfavorable light. Items that reflect the unusual content of the F Scale such as "When I am with people, I am bothered by hearing strange things" and "No one cares much what happens to you." The scores on these scales and particular patterns among the three scales can provide information on test-taking attitudes and the aspects of the person's personality styles (Graham, 2000).

In the MMPI-2, the three validity measures were retained, and several other measures assessing test-taking attitudes and the consistency of responding (i.e., assessing whether the person was consistent in her responding throughout the test) were added to facilitate the assessment of response sets.

Clinical Scales

With respect to subscales assessing clinical syndromes and personality features more specifically, both the MMPI and the MMPI-2 have 10 major clinical scales with labels that are, in some cases, somewhat antiquated but indicate the nomenclature of the time of the development of the MMPI. Nowadays, rather than using these old terms, the subscales are referred by numbers, as indicated in Table 7.2. There are four clinical scales that assess disorders within the neurotic spectrum: Hypochondriasis, Depression, Hysterical Neuroses, and Psychasthenia (Scales 1, 2, 3, and 7); one that measures behaviors consistent with psychopathy, called Psychopathic Deviation (Scale 4); and three that measure disorders in the psychotic spectrum: Paranoia, Schizophrenia, and Hypomania (Scales 6, 8, and 9). Finally, the last two clinical scales measure clinically relevant personality characteristics relating to social inhibition and introversion, known as the Social Introversion Scale (Scale 10), and traditional gender role identity, known as the Masculinity/Femininity Scale (Scale 5).

Although the clinical scales mostly bear the names of various disorders, they actually measure behaviors and characteristics that are evident in individuals with those disorders rather than behaviors that are uniquely diagnostic of the disorder. For example, according to Groth-Marnat (1990), Scale 1 (the Hypochondriasis Scale) indicates "a variety of personality characteristics that are often consistent with but not necessarily diagnostic of hypochondriasis" (p. 200). Thus, elevations on this clinical scale *may be* suggestive of a diagnosis of hypochondriasis but are more indicative of personality characteristics and behaviors that reflect high concern with illnesses: tend to be dissatisfied, immature, pessimistic, and controlling of others. Other clinical scales are understood as measuring characteristics of the disorder rather than the disorder per se.

Interpretation

The MMPI was originally designed to aid in the quick diagnosis of patients with one or more of the commonly occurring disorders of the time. It was thought that one or two of the clinical scales would be elevated in a patient and that the elevations could aid in quickly diagnosing the individual. Instead, it became clear that patients' profiles did not conform to such a simple notion and that, often, numerous clinical scales were elevated (Graham, 2000). The initial purpose of the MMPI was not met in terms of quick diagnosis, but the interpretation of patterns and configurations of elevations was found to be very useful and is, essentially, the procedure that is used today. Many of the relevant clinical correlates and combinations of the scales, through the extensive research that has been done over many years, form the basis for the interpretation of the MMPI and MMPI-2. So, for example, in addition to providing diagnostic and symptom information, the MMPI-2 provides other kinds of information relating to interpersonal issues, personality characteristics, coping and defenses, issues related to personality disorders, and so forth.

The actual process of interpretation involves a multistage process that is pretty consistent with the interpretation of any measure used in clinical assessment. First, the clinical psychologist must ensure that the proper conditions for testing were established. Second, the clinical psychologist needs to determine the validity of the test responses and ensure that the protocol is valid. Third, the clinical psychologist interprets the clinical scales and patterns of scores. Fourth, the clinical psychologist interprets the other scales in the MMPI or MMPI-2 (e.g., supplementary scales and other content scales) to facilitate and fine-tune the overall interpretation.

An example of the interpretation of the MMPI-2 profile of "Greg" is given in Box 7.2.

Reliability and Validity

It is incumbent on clinical psychologists to ensure that the tools used in assessments have both reliability and validity for the particular client's culture and the testing objective. These concepts should be familiar to the student from previous course work and chapter 3 of this book. The MMPI and the MMPI-2 have had extensive attention to assessing their reliability and validity, and there are many studies attesting to the psychometric strengths of the instruments. In terms of reliability, the MMPI-2 has been shown to have reasonable levels

BOX 7.2

MMPI SCORES AND INTERPRETATION OF "GREG"

Scale	Raw Score	T Score
Validity Scales		
Frequency	17	90*
Back Frequency	11	87*
Lie Scale	5	55
K Scale	10	39
VRIN	8	60
TRIN	10	63
Clinical Scales		
Scale 1 Hypochondriasis	10	42
Scale 2 Depression	18	50
Scale 3 Hysteria	12	33
Scale 4 Psychopathic Deviate	24	52
Scale 5 Masculinity/Femininity	27	52
Scale 6 Paranoia	18	79*
Scale 7 Psychasthenia	30	56
Scale 8 Schizophrenia	44	81*
Scale 9 Mania	25	62
Scale 10 Social Isolation	25	50

Note: *Score is above the clinical cutoff of 65.

The validity scales (L, F, & K) indicate that Greg approached the MMPI-2 in a valid manner. His L- and K-scale scores are not indicative of defensiveness. His T score of 89 on the F scale suggests that he was admitting to a large number of deviant attitudes and behavior. However, the F-scale score is not high enough to suggest random or fake-bad responding.

The high score on the F scale, two clinical scale T scores higher than 75, and the 8-6 two-point code (highest elevations) are indicative of serious psychopathology. This impression is reinforced by significantly elevated scores on six of the content scales and by the positive slope (left side of profile low, right side high) of the clinical scale profile. The absence of high scores on Scales 2 and 7 suggests that Greg is not feeling overwhelmed by emotional turmoil.

(continued)

BOX 7.2 CONTINUED

The 8-6 code type, with both scales quite high and both higher than the Scale 7 score, indicates that Greg is likely to be experiencing frankly psychotic symptoms. His thinking is likely to be autistic, fragmented, tangential, and circumstantial, and thought content is likely to be bizarre. Difficulties in concentration and attention and deficits in memory and poor judgment are likely. Delusions of persecution or grandeur and hallucinations may be present, and feeling of unreality may be reported. Greg is likely to have difficulty handling the responsibilities of daily life, and he may withdraw into fantasy and daydreaming during times of increased stress.

The MMPI-2 data are consistent with an Axis I diagnosis of schizophrenic disorder, paranoid type. No direct inferences can be made concerning Axis II diagnoses for Greg. However, the symptoms and personality characteristics suggested by the MMPI-2 scores are consistent with a diagnosis of schizoid personality disorder.

Based on Graham (1993), pp. 256–257. Adapted with permission.

of reliability with estimates ranging from .58 to .92 for the clinical scales (Butcher et al., 1992). With respect to validity, using a variety of strategies, designs, and methodologies, the accumulating evidence suggests that the MMPI-2 shows appropriate levels of validity with diverse samples and methods, and, according to some authors, validity is a real strength of the MMPI/MMPI-2 (Graham, 2000; Nichols, 2001).

Overall, the reliability and validity of the MMPI-2 appears to be adequate. Most researchers would agree, however, that still there are aspects of the MMPI-2's psychometric picture that need to be filled out and replicated.

In summary, there are numerous positive features as well as shortcomings of the MMPI-2, which are listed here:

Pros of the MMPI-2

1. It has strong and extensive empirical basis for interpretation.
2. It has a long-standing body of research.
3. It has adequate reliability and validity for clinical and research purposes.
4. The measure is familiar and popular and well-known and respected.
5. Lots of clinical information is available on the MMPI and MMPI-2.
6. It is easy to administer and can be used with a variety of populations.
7. The scoring is objective, if somewhat complicated.
8. Assessment of a broad range of symptoms, syndromes, and personality features is possible.

Cons of the MMPI-2

1. The instrument is excessively long compared to other similar measures.

2. Although the standardization sample is better than the original, it may also be problematic.

3. It is not certain if research on the MMPI can truly be generalized to the MMPI-2.

4. The labels for the subscales use antiquated terms that can produce some confusion.

5. The normative sample has a high level of education and socioeconomic status that may not be representative.

6. The interpretive process can be quite complicated.

MMPI-2 Reconstructed Form

A new version of the MMPI-2 (MMPI-2-RF) has recently been developed by Ben-Porath and Tellegen (2008) as a briefer, more comprehensive, and more sophisticated measure of the validity and clinical scales in the MMPI-2. It was developed not to supplant the MMPI-2 but to be used as an alternative. The authors developed new validity and clinical scales using the same items as the MMPI-2. This, purportedly, clarifies the validity and clinical scales, providing cleaner measures of the relevant variables. These new scales are known as the Reconstructed Scales and are reflective of current models of psychopathology and personality. The reliability and validity of these scales are currently being evaluated with new scales.

MMPI-A

Although the MMPI-2 is appropriate for adults, there is also a version that is suitable for use with adolescents, the MMPI-A (Butcher et al., 1992). This instrument is patterned after the MMPI-2 and is appropriate for ages 14 to 18. In the past, the MMPI was used with adolescents, arguably inappropriately. While the MMPI was revised into the MMPI-2, there was also an attempt to develop a version of the MMPI appropriate for adolescents (Butcher et al., 1992). The majority of original items from the MMPI, after dropping some inappropriate items, rewording some items, and including additional items that were pertinent to adolescents, comprise the MMPI-A scale. The validity and clinical scales of the MMPI-A are the same as in the MMPI-2 for the most part, although some of the clinical scales have fewer items than the adult version. In addition, the supplementary scales are similar to the MMPI-2, but there are several supplementary and content scales relevant to adolescents. Although the reliability and validity evaluation studies have not been done as extensively as with the MMPI/MMPI-2, several reports suggest that the MMPI-A is psychometrically strong and that there seems to be a good degree of confidence in its clinical utility (e.g., Arita & Baer, 1998).

◇ OTHER OMNIBUS SELF-REPORT MEASURES

Millon Clinical Multiaxial Inventories

Although the MMPI-2 has dominated the field as the omnibus inventory for clinical use, Theodore Millon and colleagues have developed several clinical measures that clinical psychologists use with adult clinical samples, adolescent clinical samples, and adult medical samples. The Millon Clinical Multiaxial Inventory (MCMI; the current version is known as the **MCMI-III**; Millon, 1997) is a 175-item measure of personality and psychopathology that is increasing in popularity. It was designed differently from the MMPI-2; it uses a different scoring system for determining whether an individual exhibits psychopathology and closely follows the *DSM* in the types of disorders assessed.

In two revisions, the MCMI-II and the MCMI-III, the original measure was revamped to directly accord with the *DSM* diagnostic criteria of the time. It has 28 subscales to measure validity of the test completion, response biases, personality patterns, and clinical syndromes.

It is important to note that the MCMI-III has been validated only on clinical samples and is appropriate for use only in clinical populations. Millon and associates have developed two other measures very similar to the MCMI-III, the Millon adolescent clinical inventory (MACI) that has subscale measures of 12 basic personality styles, 8 expressed concerns common to adolescents, and 7 clinical syndromes. Finally, there is also a measure of psychological variables relevant in the development and treatment of physical health problems that has been developed. The Millon Behavioral Medicine Diagnostic measures response patterns, coping styles, psychological symptoms, stress-related variables, treatment issues, and problem health behaviors.

The strengths and weaknesses of the MCMI, as outlined by Strack (2002), are listed here:

Pros of the MCMI-III

1. It has been developed from a comprehensive theory.
2. It reflects the current diagnostic system of the *DSM* and is especially useful with personality disorders.
3. It provides diagnostic accuracy by taking into account base rates.
4. It uses strong test construction approach.
5. It is easy to administer.
6. It contains 175 items, which is shorter than other omnibus measures.

Cons of the MCMI-III

1. There is imbalance in the number of True and False items. (Items that reflect psychopathology most often have a "true" response; therefore test is susceptible to acquiescence response set.)
2. The test is weak in assessing subclinical levels of psychopathology.
3. There are validity problems.

4. Subtypes of personality disorders are not measured.
5. The normative sample is relatively small and may not be representative of minority groups.
6. There are few validation studies.

Personality Assessment Inventory

A third objective measure that is gaining prominence in clinical settings as an omnibus measure of personality and psychopathology is the personality assessment inventory (PAI) developed by Leslie Morey (1991). The PAI is a 344-item measure that has 22 subscales that measure validity of the test responses, response biases, clinical syndromes, and personality variables. Morey also included some variables that are not available in other measures but are clinically significant such as suicide level, stress, treatment response indicators, and two variables reflecting the interpersonal style of the individual completing the test. Rather than attempting to measure the presence versus absence of a clinical disorder, the PAI was developed to measure dimensions of symptoms of disorders from mild to severe and to measure the underlying pathology. Although the test is somewhat newer than the MMPI-2 and the MCMI measures, its use seems to be increasing.

Rating Scales

At times clinical psychologists may want briefer measures of specific types of symptoms, and numerous rating scales have been developed, typically for the purpose of attempting to measure the severity of symptoms of a particular syndrome. This can be done either for screening purposes or for monitoring symptoms over the course of treatment. Although several general symptom rating scales have been developed, such as the Symptom Checklist-90 Revised (Derogatis, 1994), that have subscale measures of symptom clusters (e.g., depression, anxiety, interpersonal sensitivity), often even more specific rating scales have been used. For example, Dr. Aaron Beck has developed two rating scales that are used quite commonly in clinical assessment, the Beck Depression Inventory and the Beck Anxiety Inventory. Both of these measures are 21-item scales that list depression and anxiety symptoms, respectively, and ask the patient to rate the severity of the symptoms. With respect to these scales, it should be noted that all measures of psychological distress, such as anxiety and depression symptoms, correlate highly with each other, typically in the $r = .50$ to $.80$ range and that it is very laborious to develop a truly original scale that does not "reinvent the wheel." Our own experience with developing the Multidimensional Perfectionism Scale (Hewitt & Flett, 1991) and the Behavioral Anger Response Questionnaire (Linden et al., 2003) bear witness to this claim.

◇ PROJECTIVE TECHNIQUES

Whereas objective tests and the content of interviews provide information on aspects of patients' behavior that they have conscious awareness of, known as surface level of behavior, projective techniques attempt to assess behavior that is at a deeper level and that the person may not be aware of. Process aspects of the interview, or even the objective test administration, can inform the clinical psychologist about some of these deeper issues but only sometimes and only to a certain degree.

Projective techniques take the form of the presentation of ambiguous stimuli to the patient who is asked to interpret them into meaningful responses and report on those responses. The projective techniques sometimes provide standardized administrations, similar to objective tests, but the possible responses are not predetermined alternatives and the stimuli are ambiguous as opposed to objective. They are thought to provide information about deeper aspects of the person's personality and difficulties such as conflicts, defenses and coping strategies, interpersonal and cognitive/perceptual styles, motivations, and so forth. While there appears to be much criticism of projective techniques from some academic circles, their use remains a stable and important part of psychological assessment as indicated in the surveys of test usage in clinical assessment presented earlier.

Early on, the idea behind the projective technique was thought to be based on what is known as the **projective hypothesis**: Stimuli are perceived and organized according to an individual's motives, needs, emotions, conflicts, perceptual sets, and cognitive structures that often operate outside the individual's conscious awareness (Teglasi, 2001). In other words, responses to projective techniques reflect a projection of underlying or unconscious needs or conflicts onto the ambiguous stimuli. However, several prominent projective experts, including Hermann Rorschach who developed the Rorschach Inkblot Technique (RIT), suggested that projective techniques do not necessarily reflect the operation of the defense mechanism projection. In fact, it is thought that the responses to the stimuli are based on psychological characteristics including personality styles or traits, the current psychological state of the person, and a selection of one or more responses from a larger number of possible responses. Thus, what is seen as relevant in projective techniques is the organization of a response based on the individual's psychology rather than projection itself. This means that it is not so important that, when presented with an inkblot, the patient sees a bat. Rather, what is important is what aspects of blot were used by the patient to interpret the inkblot as a bat.

A large number of projective techniques have been developed over the years, and we will discuss some of the more commonly used.

Rorschach Inkblot Technique

The RIT (Rorschach, 1921) was developed in the 1920s by Dr. Hermann Rorschach, a Swiss physician who was interested in attempting to understand the perceptual and psychological processes involved in organizing responses to ambiguous stimuli. His belief was that responses to ambiguous inkblot stimuli reflected perceptual organizational principles and that there was a link between perception and personality (Klopfer & Davidson, 1962). Rorschach was focusing not on trying to develop a clinical instrument but on trying to develop a research paradigm to aid in understanding how different diagnostic groups differed in terms of their "psyche," and he believed that by studying individuals' cognitive and perceptually organized responses to inkblots, some important principles could be discerned. This means that what was important (and what continues to be important) is not the content of the response, but rather how the person organized or perceived the inkblot as a percept. In other words, as we stated earlier, what is important is not what the person sees, but how he sees it. Although some proponents of the RIT suggest that it provides a picture of the whole personality or the whole person, for example, coping styles, stress tolerance, psychotic disturbance, interpersonal perceptions, and personal issues, others have suggested that it is a measure of cognitive/perceptual organization (Allison, Blatt, & Zimet, 1988).

Although use of the RIT caught on quite quickly after its development, there evolved no fewer than five major scoring systems, and, often, these systems were contradictory, at odds with one another, and created confusion in terms of understanding, researching, and using the RIT clinically. As a result of this confusion, it is not surprising that, over years, the RIT came under attack from a variety of sources, and these attacks centered on the issues of:

1. Poor psychometric performance (i.e., issues of reliability and validity)
2. Nonempirical basis for scoring and interpretation
3. Methodological flaws in research
4. Lack of standardized procedure for administration, scoring, and interpretation

During the late 1960s Dr. John Exner, an American clinical psychologist, attempted to address these criticisms and provide an empirical basis for the appropriate use and interpretation of the RIT. He directed his focus on:

1. Gathering a large and broad normative sample
2. Developing a standardized procedure for administration, scoring, and interpreting the test
3. Evaluating and incorporating the most sound elements of the previous scoring systems
4. Adding special categories for a variety of components of personality including both state and trait components
5. Providing an empirical basis for the scoring and interpretation of responses

Exner's work has received a great deal of attention, and the standard now for administration, scoring, and interpretation is the system he developed known as the **Comprehensive System**. In large part because the Comprehensive System has overcome previous problems with lack of standardized administration, scoring, and inter-rater reliability, the RIT has gained further acceptance and status among many clinical psychologists.

The RIT itself involves a set of 10 black and white or color bilaterally symmetrical inkblots that are printed separately on cards that can be used for children and adults. The cards are presented one at a time to a patient who is asked to report on what she believes the inkblot image might be. The clinical psychologist administering the inkblots is to adhere to a strict protocol in terms of instructions and presentation of the inkblots. The verbatim responses of the patients are recorded as is the reaction time to the first response for each card. Following the presentation of the cards, known as the **free association stage**, each card is presented again to the patient, and she is asked to explain what features or components of the blot contributed to the perception. This latter part of the administration is known as the **inquiry stage**, and the features are used to score the responses. The responses are then coded, and the codings are used to create a structural summary of scores. Interpretation involves two stages. The first, the **proposition stage**, involves the patient's scores being compared to means and standard deviations of nonpatient and select patient groups, and hypotheses are generated based on the comparisons. The second stage, known as the **integration stage**, involves interpretation based on seven clusters of scores tapping particular domains that provide a focus of the interpretation. The domains include:

1. Information processing (i.e., effort, efficiency, and quality of information processing)
2. Cognitive mediation (i.e., reality testing, conventional versus idiosyncratic personality)
3. Ideation (i.e., conceptualization)
4. Capacity for control and tolerance for stress (i.e., person's experience of stress)
5. Affect (depression and vulnerability to depression and other similar affect states)
6. Self-perception (i.e., self-directed or self-focused)
7. Interpersonal perception and relations (i.e., cooperation, aggression, need for dependency, coping)

Some writers have suggested that the issues of reliability and validity of the RIT have created one of the greatest controversies in the history of psychology (e.g., Groth-Marnat, 1990), one that continues to rage today although it seems that issues of reliability are essentially resolved and demonstrations of validity of the RIT have also been advanced further. There are some die-hard opponents who state that there is no evidence whatsoever for the use of the RIT and die-hard proponents who state that opponents either aren't able or willing to read the literature on the efficacy and utility of the RIT.

Exner has indicated that much of the criticism of the RIT is based on one or more of the old scoring systems, poorly trained clinicians or examiners, and poor methodology of studies. In fact, when focusing only on appropriate research articles with good methodology, there is evidence of both adequate reliability and validity (Groth-Marnat, 1999). We will discuss some of this here.

Reliability and Validity

Reliability of the RIT has tended to focus on inter-rater reliability (i.e., do two independent scorers score and interpret a protocol with the same results); there are reports that when the independent scorers are properly trained and the same scoring system is used, inter-rater reliability can be very good with estimates ranging between .88 and .90 (Parker, 1983; Rose et al., 2001). In terms of validity, again, when the RIT is used appropriately by trained clinicians, there is evidence of its validity and utility in assessing various aspects of functioning

(Weiner, 1996). Parker, Hanson, and Hunsley (1988), in a meta-analysis, showed that the validity evidence for the RIT was appropriate and did not differ from validity indicators of other commonly used clinical instruments. On the other hand, looking at the construct validity of some specific scores, validity of RIT seems somewhat weaker (Rose et al., 2001). Overall, there does appear to be evidence of the validity and reliability of the RIT that commensurate with other clinical instruments in use (Parker et al., 1988; Weiner, 1996).

Pros of the RIT

1. It is easy to administer.
2. The utility of Exner's Comprehensive System.
3. It has standardized administration, scoring, and interpretation.
4. It has a large normative sample and normative data for various scores.
5. There is evidence of acceptable reliability and validity.
6. It taps information that is not tapped by objective tests.
7. It may be resistant to faking.
8. It is the second-most researched personality assessment instrument.

Cons of the RIT

1. It was not developed for purpose it is currently used for.
2. Early research with different systems has created confusion and bias.
3. There is lack of research and normative information for minorities.
4. Additional reliability and validity, especially on specific scores, is necessary.
5. There is complexity in scoring and interpretation.
6. It may be of limited use with children, especially over the long term.

Thematic Apperception Test

Another commonly used projective technique involves story telling in response to specific stimuli, and probably the best example is the Thematic Apperception Test (TAT; Murray, 1943). Although the name of this instrument includes the term "test," we refer to it as a technique. The TAT was originally developed by Dr. Henry Murray as a measure of underlying needs and motives consistent with his theory of motivation. A children's version, known as the Children's Apperception Test (CAT), is similar to the TAT.

This type of projective technique is thought to involve not just perception and organization of a perception as the RIT does, but the respondent also needs to impose meaning on the stimulus when telling a coherent story. The interpretation of the responses is completed in light of the clinician's theoretical perspective, and the assumption is that the recurring themes, interactions, and characterizations in the stories are reflective of underlying processes. The TAT is thought to measure not psychopathology or maladjustment or diagnoses per se, but rather motivational, interpersonal, and social-cognitive aspects of a person's functioning (Teglasi, 2001) that can contribute to formulation of a patient's difficulties.

The TAT itself consists of a series of 31 pictures on cards that depict a variety of ambiguous scenes, many of them involving one or more people (one card is totally blank). The stimuli themselves are generally less ambiguous than the inkblots from the RIT, and certain cards have been described as having certain "pulls" for content. The clinician selects a subset of cards (often based on the clinician's own preference), and the patient is asked to create a story about what is being depicted in the scenes. According to the administration procedure (Bellack, 1975), the patient is asked to make up as dramatic a story as he can, including a description of what is currently happening in the picture, what led up to the current scene, the thoughts and feelings of the characters, and the outcome of the story. Responses are recorded verbatim, and the story content is scored and interpreted, as indicated, based on the theoretical framework and the intent of the TAT.

Although the interpretation of the TAT has been characterized as following only impressionistic ideas and clinical intuition, several interpretive schemes have been developed. For example, early on McLelland (1961) and others developed scoring and interpretive frameworks for measuring achievement, affiliation, and power motivations, and Bellack (1993) has proposed a broader interpretive scheme that follows from a psychodynamic theoretical stance and focuses on six major categories:

1. Unconscious structures
2. Drives
3. Relationship to others
4. Conflicts
5. Defenses
6. Ego strength

As well, interpretations have been based on cognitive models such as schema theory, social cognitive theories, and object relations theory (e.g., Teglasi, 1998; Westen, Klepser, Ruffins, Silverman, & Boekamp, 1991). For example, the responses to the TAT stimuli are thought to reflect underlying cognitive or social-cognitive structures (i.e., schemas) that are internal representations of past experiences that aid in processing environmental information. It is believed that story telling responses in relation to ambiguous stimuli are illustrative of the schemas or structures that are used to organize and process information in the world and inform the clinician about the patient's self-related and interpersonal worlds.

Westen and colleagues have developed the **Social Cognitions and Object Relations Scale** (SCORS; Westen, 1991), which provides scoring and interpretation based on object relations theory. Used to understand the level of object relations in children or adults to aid in psychotherapy, four categories or domains are tapped, including:

1. Complexity of object relations (i.e., capacity to distinguish self from others, self and others are stable and multidimensional, and awareness of motives and experiences in self and others)
2. Affect tone of relationships (ranging from benevolence to malevolence)
3. Capacity for emotional investment in relationships (ranging from mutual caring to need gratification)
4. Understanding social causality (i.e., causal attributions regarding social behavior)

Reliability and Validity

Establishing reliability and validity, in the traditional sense, has been rather difficult with respect to responses to the TAT, and some have suggested that TAT is not an instrument to be scored but rather interpreted. This is likely due to the fact that there has been no agreed-upon scoring system, administration procedure, and norms, nor is there a generally agreed-upon interpretive framework. As well, there is a great deal of variability in the content of stories that are told about the cards. Having said this, there has been concern that the instrument demonstrates appropriate reliability and validity, and there is some evidence that when clear interpretive criteria are used with well-trained interpreters, or when evaluating specific motivations such as achievement, affiliation, and power motivations, the reliability of the instrument seems to be adequate (e.g., Lundy, 1985). Moreover, there is support for the reliability and validity of specific scoring and interpretive schemes (e.g., Westen's SCORS) approach and when specific scoring methods are used (Groth-Marnat, 1999; Lilienfeld, Wood, & Garb, 2000). On the other hand, there appears to be less support for the broad interpretations or descriptions of personality based on an impression or clinical intuition.

Pros of the TAT

1. It is a potentially valuable tool to assess deeper aspects of personality.
2. It focuses on global aspects of a person's interpersonal and motivational world.
3. It aids in development of rapport.
4. There is adequate reliability and validity of some scoring and interpretive schemes.

Cons of the TAT

1. There is no standardized administration or normative data.
2. General reliability and validity are difficult to establish.
3. There is subjectivity in scoring and interpretation.

Drawing Tasks

One other projective technique that is used with regularity involves drawing tasks, typically drawings of people. The idea behind the drawing process is that the drawing that is produced will access parts of the personality that either are not accessible with objective tests or will bypass the defenses or resistances that a patient might have. It is thought that the task provides information regarding the person's inner predispositions, conflicts, and dynamics as well as other aspects of the person's functioning that are not readily accessible to the patient or that can be tapped by objective tests. Drawing tasks are quite popular with many clinicians and are reported to be easy to administer, score, and interpret. They have been used as tools to interpret personality broadly and to assess interpersonal relationships and are most frequently interpreted with an intuitive approach (Kahill, 1984). The most commonly used drawing tasks are the Draw-a-Person, developed originally by Machover (1949) and revised and refined over the years, and the House-Tree-Person drawing task (Buck, 1948).

Essentially, the patient is provided with a blank piece of 8 1/2 × 11-inch paper and a pencil (sometimes colored pencils) and asked to "draw a person" or to "draw me a picture that includes a house, a tree, and a person." There can be variations in terms of also requesting drawings of a person of the opposite sex, the self, or the patient's family. No further instructions are to be given. An inquiry phase can be incorporated whereby the clinician may ask specific questions about the drawing in order to aid the clinician in interpretations. Specific instructions and scoring criteria have been developed, although it has been argued that most interpretive work is based less on the specific scorings and more on clinical intuition and clinical experience (Groth-Marnot, 1999).

The scoring and interpretive process involves several steps, including:

1. **Objective scoring:** Score the drawing based on an objective scoring system.
2. **Overall impressions:** The clinician considers the drawing as a whole in order to determine qualities such as general mood, message, or themes of the drawing.
3. **Cautious consideration of specific details:** The clinician considers, for example, size, shading, and distortions present.
4. **Integration with other assessment material**.

Reliability and Validity

Establishing the reliability and validity of these tasks has been difficult given the nature of the tasks (i.e., variation in one drawing to the next) and the subjective nature of the interpretation. When using the specific scores, reliability and validity has been reported as adequate, especially when scoring more global aspects of the drawings such as adjustment, anxiety, and maturation (Groth-Marnot, 1999). On the other hand, when the focus is on more specific components of the drawings or specific components of personality, less adequate reliability and validity is evident.

Pros of the Drawing Tasks

1. They have easy administration, scoring, and interpretation.

2. They can be used with children, adolescents, and adults.

3. They show some reliability and validity with certain components of patients' functioning.

4. They can be used with patients with poor verbal skills (e.g., intellectually disabled).

Cons of the Drawing Tasks

1. There is subjectivity in the scoring and interpretation.

2. There is no agreed-upon scoring and interpretive system.

3. It is questionable as to whether drawings accurately reflect the underlying personality features.

◇ CONCLUSION

Overall, this chapter has covered a lot ground in terms of issues pertaining to psychodiagnostic assessment. This type of assessment remains one of the most common types of psychological assessment in dealing with psychological problems. The procedures involved include clinical interviews, objective tests, and projective techniques, each of which provides different kinds and levels of information and has its own strengths and weaknesses. Each procedure also seems to have an important role in psychodiagnostic assessments as the consistency and frequency of the test usage testifies.

◇ ONGOING CONSIDERATIONS

Although there has been some global criticisms of psychodiagnostic testing as too time consuming and inefficient and conducive to managed care principles evident in the United States, it is still viewed as an important clinical activity for clinical psychologists and one that can inform, influence, and establish a successful therapeutic experience (Allison et al., 1988). Projective techniques have been the source of controversy, but most especially with respect to the RIT. It is difficult to understand why this technique in particular seems to bear brunt of so much criticism. On the one hand, many proponents of the RIT have suggested that many of the criticisms of the RIT are inappropriate and that many of the criticisms could be directed at any other clinical instrument or technique. On the other hand, the criticisms, if intended to eliminate the RIT from use, have actually resulted in more attention being paid to determine and demonstrate adequate reliability and validity as well as its utility. In any event, the data speak fairly clearly that even though some of the instruments used in psychodiagnostic assessments have been criticized, they remain important tools in the clinical psychologists' arsenal.

◇ KEY TERMS LEARNED

Closed-ended questions

Comprehensive System

Content information

Delusions

Derealization

F Scale

Free association stage

Hallucinations

Inquiry stage

Integration stage

K Scale

L Scale

MCMI-III

Mental Status Exam

Multimethod approach

Objective tests

Open-ended questions

Orientation to person

Orientation to place

Orientation to time

Process information

Process-related variables

Projective hypothesis

Proposition stage

Psychic determinism

Response sets

Self-report inventories

Social Cognitions and Object Relations Scale

Structured diagnostic interviews

Test-taking attitudes

◇ THINKING QUESTIONS

1. What are the differences between objective and projective assessment tools? What kinds of information does each provide, and why is this information important in an assessment?

2. Describe the concepts of content and process variables, and how each is useful in psychodiagnostic assessment.

3. Describe the MMPI-2 and its utility as an assessment test. What are the pros and cons of this instrument?

4. Describe the RIT and its utility as an assessment technique. What are the pros and cons of this instrument?

5. What is the importance of unstructured or semistructured interviews? How do they differ from structured diagnostic interviews? What purposes does each type of interview serve?

◇ REFERENCES

Allison, J., Blatt, S., & Zimet, C. N. (1988). *The interpretation of psychological tests.* Washington, DC: Hemisphere Publishing Corporation.

Arita, A. A., & Baer, R. A. (1998). Validity of selected MMPI-A content scales. *Psychological Assessment, 10,* 59–63.

Bekhit, N. S., Thomas, G. V., Lalonde, S., & Jolley, R. (2002). Psychological assessment in clinical practice in Britain. *Clinical Psychology & Psychotherapy, 9,* 285–291.

Bellack, L. (1975). *The T.A.T., C.A.T. and S.A.T. in clinical use* (3rd ed.). New York: Grune & Stratton.

Bellack, L. (1993). *The TAT, CAT, and SAT in clinical use* (5th ed.). New York: Grune & Stratton.

Ben-Porath, Y. S., & Tellegen, A. (2008). Empirical correlates of the MMPI-2 Restructured Clinical (RC) scales in mental health, forensic, and nonclinical settings: An introduction. *Journal of Personality Assessment, 90*, 119–121.

Buck, J. N. (1948). The H-T-P technique, a qualitative and quantitative scoring manual. *Journal of Clinical Psychology, 4*, 317–398.

Butcher, J. N. (1990). *The MMPI-2 in psychological treatment.* New York: Oxford.

Butcher, J. N., Dahlstrom, W. G., Graham, J. R., Tellegen, A., & Kaemmer, B. (1989). *MMPI-2: Manual for administration and scoring.* Minneapolis, MN: University of Minnesota Press.

Butcher, J. N., Williams, C. L., Graham, J. R., Archer, R., Tellegen, A., Ben-Porath, Y. S., et al. (1992). *MMPI-A: Manual for administration, scoring, and interpretation.* Minneapolis, MN: University of Minnesota Press.

Camara, W. J, Nathan, J. S., & Puente, A. E. (2000). Psychological test usage: Implications in professional psychology. *Professional Psychological: Research and Practice, 31*, 141–154.

Derogatis, L. R. (1994). *SCL-90-R: Administration, scoring and procedures manual.* Minneapolis, MN: National Computer Systems.

Exner, J. E., & Weiner, I. B. (1982). *The Rorschach: A comprehensive system: Vol. 3. Assessment of children and adolescents.* New York: Wiley.

First, M. B., Spitzer, R. L., Gibbon, M., & Williams, J. B. W..(1997). *Structured clinical interview for Axis I DSM-IV disorders (SCID-I)—Clinician version.* Washington, DC: American Psychiatric Press.

Graham, J. R. (2000). *MMPI-2: Assessing personality and psychopathology* (2nd ed.). New York: Oxford University Press.

Greene, R. L. (2000). *The MMPI-2: An interpretive manual.* Needham Heights, MA: Allyn & Bacon.

Groth-Marnat, G. (1990). *Handbook of psychological assessment.* New York: John Wiley & Sons.

Groth-Marnat, G. (1999). *Handbook of psychological assessment.* New York: John Wiley & Sons.

Hathaway, S. R., & McKinley, J. C. (1940). A multiphasic personality schedule (Minnesota): I. Construction of the schedule. *Journal of Psychology, 10*, 249–254.

Hewitt, P. L., & Flett, G. L. (1991). Perfectionism in the self and social contexts: Conceptualization, assessment, and association with psycho-pathology. *Journal of Personality and Social Psychology, 60*, 456–470.

Kahill, S. (1984). Human figure drawings in adults: An update of the empirical evidence, 1967–1982. *Canadian Psychology, 25*, 269–290.

Klopfer, B., & Davidson, H. (1962). *The Rorschach technique: An introductory manual.* New York: Harcourt.

Lilienfeld, S. O., Wood, J. M., & Garb, H. N. (2000). The scientific status of projective techniques. *Psychological Science in the Public Interest, 1*, 27–66.

Linden, W., Hogan, B., et al. (2003). There is more to anger than in or out. *Emotion, 3*, 12–29.

Lubin, Wallace, & Paine (1971). Patterns of psychological test usage in the United States: 1935–1982. *American Psychologist, 39*, 451–454.

Lundy, A. (1985). The reliability of the Thematic Apperception Test. *Journal of Personality Assessment, 49*, 141–149.

Machover, K. (1949). *Personality projection in the drawings of the human figure.* Springfield, IL: Charles C. Thomas.

McLelland, D. C. (1961). *The achieving society.* Princeton: Van Nostrand.

Millon, T. (1997). *The Millon clinical multiaxial inventory-III manual.* Minneapolis: National Computer Systems.

Mohr, D., & Beutler, L. E. (2003). The integrative clinical interview. In L. E. Beutler & G. Marnat (Eds.), *Integrative assessment of adult personality* (2nd ed., pp. 82–122). New York: Guilford Press.

Morey, L. C. (1991). *The personality assessment inventory professional manual.* Odessa, FL: Psychological Assessment Resources.

Murray, H. (1943). *Thematic Apperception Test manual.* Cambridge, MA: Harvard University Press.

Nichols, D. S. (2001). *Essentials of MMPI-2 assessment.* New York: Wiley.

Parker K. C. H. (1983). A meta-analysis of the reliability and validity of the Rorschach. *Journal of Personality Assessment, 47,* 227–231.

Parker, K. C. H., Hanson, R. K., & Hunsley, J. (1988). MMPI, Rorschach, and WAIS: A meta-analytic comparison of reliability, stability, and validity. *Psychological Bulletin, 103,* 367–373.

Rorschach, H. (1921). *Psychodiagnostics.* Bern, Switzerland: Bircher.

Rose, T., Kaser-Boyd, N., & Maloney, M. P. (2001). *Essentials of Rorschach assessment.* New York: Wiley.

Strack, S. (2002). *Essentials of Millon inventories assessment* (2nd ed.). New York: Wiley.

Teglasi, H. (1998). Assessment of schema and problem-solving strategies with projective techniques. In M. Hersen & A. Bellack (Eds.). *Comprehensive clinical psychology: Vol. 4, Assessment* (pp. 459–499). London, England: Elsevier Science Press.

Teglasi, H. (2001). *Essentials of TAT and other storytelling techniques assessment.* New York: Wiley.

Watkins, L. F., Jr., Campbell, V. L., Nieberding, K., & Hallmark, R. (1995). Contemporary practice of psychological assessment by clinical psychologists. *Professional Psychology: Research and Practice, 24,* 51–60.

Weiner, I. B. (1996). Some observations on the validity of the Rorschach Inkblot Method. *Psychological Assessment, 8,* 206–213.

Westen, D. (1991). Clinical assessment of object relations using the TAT. *Journal of Personality Assessment, 56,* 56–74.

Westen, D., Klepser, J., Ruffins, S. A., Silverman, M., & Boekamp, J. (1991). Object relations in childhood and adolescence: The development of working representations. *Journal of Consulting and Clinical Psychology, 9,* 400–409.

Yufit, R. I., & Lester, D. (2005). *Assessment, treatment, and prevention of suicidal behavior.* New York: Wiley.

CHAPTER EIGHT

COGNITIVE AND NEUROPSYCHOLOGICAL ASSESSMENT

CHAPTER OBJECTIVE

The previous chapter discussed one type of psychological assessment, the psychodiagnostic assessment, that assesses the individual's personality in relation to the psychological difficulties he may be experiencing. This chapter will consider two related kinds of assessments, intellectual assessment and neuropsychological assessment. The first type, intellectual assessment, is conducted in order to assess various aspects of a person's cognitive abilities, which normally entails focusing on intelligence or components of intelligence and attained levels of achievement with respect to cognitive abilities. These sorts of assessments are usually done in order to aid in making decisions regarding placements in school or employment positions, remedial training, and determination of learning and developmental problems. The second type of assessment, neuropsychological assessment, is also completed to assess intellectual and cognitive functioning, but this is done in order to determine the behavioral functioning, both deficits and strengths, of a person who has a brain injury or is suspected of having some brain damage.

◇ INTELLECTUAL ASSESSMENT

As described in chapter 5, the history of the development of clinical psychology is inextricably intertwined with the testing of intelligence and other cognitive abilities. Although testing of some mental or cognitive abilities had been developed in the 1800s (Boake, 2002), it was Dr. Alfred Binet and Theodore Simon in the early 1900s in Paris, France, who made some of the first comprehensive attempts to test children's intellectual levels and determine appropriate school placement for children (Binet & Simon, 1905). This work represents one of the first operationalizations and measures of intelligence and intellectual functioning. Binet attempted to differentiate among children who were mentally retarded, behaviorally problematic, or of normal intelligence and to make school recommendations accordingly. This was done with a series of 30 tests such as measures of language skills, reasoning, and memory, and performance on the tests formed a composite score known as mental age.

Although not particularly interested in understanding the construct of intelligence per se, Binet and Simon's work set the stage for the assessment of intellectual functioning.

The ideas and the test developed by Binet and Simon were introduced to North America by Lewis Terman at Stanford University in 1916 who translated and modified the measure somewhat to reflect experiences that American children would have had. The test was standardized on Americans, and the first Stanford-Binet Intelligence Scales were developed in 1916 (Terman et al., 1916). Intellectual assessment began in earnest in North America. Then, as today, the emphasis or focus of intellectual assessment is on intelligence and related cognitive abilities.

Purpose of Intellectual Assessment

What are the specific purposes of clinical psychologists conducting intellectual assessments? There are numerous reasons why understanding the level and efficiency of intellectual functioning can be helpful for individuals. For example, intellectual assessments can be useful to:

1. Help in the assessment of intellectual functioning to determine whether an individual meets the diagnostic criteria for mental retardation and other psychoeducational problems. For example, in the *DSM-IV-TR*, intelligence test scores are used both to make the diagnosis of mental retardation and to provide information as to the severity of the disability. Incidentally, mental retardation is the only diagnosis in the *DSM-IV-TR* that requires specific test results in making a diagnosis.

2. Aid in the grouping of individuals based on intellectual functioning and/or to aid in the provision of remedial training (e.g., remedial classes, specific occupational or training programs) and other interventions. Similarly, intellectual assessment helps in predicting academic achievement.

3. Aid in psychodiagnostic and forensic testing in terms of getting a complete picture of a person's current intellectual and cognitive functioning.

4. Determine cognitive strengths and weaknesses of an individual in comparison to peers and to evaluate outcomes of interventions, programs, or special training.

5. Provide a baseline for intellectual or cognitive functioning that can be used to track improvements or decrements in functioning.

6. Conduct research on intelligence, cognitive abilities and processes, and other issues germane to intellectual assessments.

Domains Assessed in Intellectual Assessment

Although there are some differences depending on the theoretical approach to intelligence, there are several domains that are relevant for assessment in intellectual assessment. Of course, intelligence is one of the main focuses of this kind of assessment, and, typically, both verbal and nonverbal tests of intelligence will be administered. Attention is paid to what has been termed **fluid intelligence** (which involves speed, flexibility, skill in learning, abstraction, and reasoning) and **crystallized intelligence** (which involves the knowledge that an individual has accumulated). Moreover, specific domains of cognitive abilities that comprise intelligence are assessed, although these domains vary depending on the testing instrument used. In the descriptions of two of the most commonly used intelligence tests, the Stanford-Binet Scales and the Wechsler Intelligence Scales, specific domains that are of interest will be discussed. In addition to intelligence, intellectual assessments often measure achievement, which is, essentially, the level of cognitive ability one actually attained, normally in a scholastic context.

The next section will discuss some of the definitional issues pertaining to intelligence and cognitive abilities and different conceptualizations of intelligence and describe various measures that are used to assess intelligence and related cognitive abilities.

◇ WHAT IS INTELLIGENCE?

As Neisser et al. (1996) have described, intelligence is a very difficult concept to define, and, although there is agreement on some aspects of intelligence, different experts will give somewhat different definitions (Box 8.1). Very generally, intelligence involves cognitive abilities that reflect an individual's abilities to understand complex ideas, engage in various

---

BOX 8.1

DEFINITIONS OF INTELLIGENCE

"It seems to us that in intelligence there is a fundamental faculty, the alteration or the lack of which, is of the utmost importance for practical life. This faculty is judgment, otherwise called good sense, practical sense, initiative, the faculty of adapting one's self to circumstances. A person may be a moron or an imbecile if he is lacking in judgment; but with good judgment he can never be either. Indeed the rest of the intellectual faculties seem of little importance in comparison with judgment." (Binet & Simon, 1916, pp. 42–43)

"Intelligence is the aggregate or global capacity of the individual to act purposefully, to think rationally and to deal effectively with his environment." (Wechsler, 1944, p. 3)

". . . a set of skills of problem solving—enabling the individual to resolve genuine problems or difficulties that he or she encounters, and, when appropriate, to create an effective product . . . the potential for finding or creating problems—thereby laying the groundwork for the acquisition of new knowledge." (Gardner, 1993, pp. 60–61)

"Intelligence is not a single, unitary ability, but rather a composite of several functions. The term denotes that combination of abilities required for survival and advancement within a particular culture." (Anastasi, 1992, p. 613)

forms of reasoning, effectively solve problems, adapt to environmental demands, and learn from experience (Neisser et al., 1996). Groth-Marnat (1990, p. 110) suggests that although there have been numerous and varied definitions of intelligence, all appear to include five broad domains, including:

1. Abstract thinking
2. Learning from experience
3. Solving problems through insight
4. Adjusting effectively to new situations
5. Focusing and sustaining one's abilities in order to achieve a desired goal

Although these components seem appropriate with respect to what constitutes intelligence, there are still major differences in definitions among clinical psychologists. For example, since the first meetings designed to understand the concept of intelligence in 1921 (this conference was aptly named the 1921 Conference) until today, if you ask 20 different clinical psychologists who studied in the field of intelligence, for definitions of intelligence, you would likely receive 20 different definitions. Although this might be viewed as problematic, it actually clearly illustrates and underscores the complexity of the construct of intelligence as well as its slippery nature in terms of trying to define it.

Numerous theories and models of intelligence have been presented and researched over the decades, with debates regarding whether intelligence is composed of one general factor or ability (known as "g"; Spearman, 1927) or of numerous specific factors (e.g., Thurstone, 1938).

Other theorists eventually attempted to reconcile these conceptualizations and present hierarchical models that incorporated both g and multiple specific factors. For example, Vernon (1950) suggested that intelligence had both a common or unitary component and major and minor specific factors and abilities. Furthermore, he believed that these common and specific components are arranged hierarchically. It is these kinds of hierarchical models that are reflected currently in many of the instruments used to measure intelligence. For example, one of the current models that has had a major impact on the development of contemporary tests of intelligence is known as the Cattell-Horn-Carrol (CHC) model, which actually represents a combination of three theorists' hierarchical conceptualizations of intelligence. In its most current form, the model incorporates the concept of g as well as 10 broad cognitive abilities along with over 70 narrow abilities (Alfonso, Flanagan, & Radwan, 2005).

◇ WHAT IS IQ?

The conceptualization of intelligence, as discussed earlier, has been controversial, and the concept of intelligence quotient (IQ) has also seen its share of controversy, although its definition has been relatively straightforward. What is it, and where did the idea of IQ come from?

Although Terman (Terman et al., 1916) was one of the first to use the term "intelligence quotient," his determination of an estimate of a person's intelligence was based on

Binet and Simon's work. Binet and Simon stated that an estimate of a child's intelligence could be determined by comparing the child's chronological age (CA) calculated in years with the child's mental age (MA), which is indicative of the level of mental abilities within a particular age group. When the MA is calculated and compared to the CA, the psychologist could determine the relative standing of the person's mental abilities in relation to those of individuals with the same chronological age (Groth-Marnat, 2003). This means that a child of 8 years of age with a mental age of 9 would be considered more intelligent than a child of 8 years of age with a mental age of 7. Thus, Binet and Simon used a ratio of MA/CA or what is now referred to as a **ratio IQ**. Although this approach has some initial intuitive appeal, there are some problems; for example, the difference between a 1-year lag in cognitive abilities for a 3-year-old (which is severe) versus a 1-year lag for a 15-year-old (which is less severe). Terman, in addition to revising the Stanford-Binet test, revised the representation of the relationship between mental and chronological ages with the calculation of the IQ based on work by Stern (1912). The IQ was calculated using the formula IQ = MA/CA × 100, which corrected somewhat the problem of the difference between lags at different ages. The IQ was calculated in this fashion for many years, and even though there were some issues raised with respect to difficulties with such an IQ calculation, especially with its use in adults, it was not until Dr. David Wechsler, with the development of his Wechsler-Bellevue Scale, did the use of a new form of IQ arise. Wechsler suggested using what he termed the **deviation IQ**, which was simply the degree to which a person's score deviated from the mean scores of a large group of similarly aged individuals. In order to do this, Wechsler administered his measure to large groups of individuals, grouped individuals together at different age groups, and calculated the mean and standard deviation of the distributions for the different age groups. The mean for each age group was transformed to equal a mean of 100 and the standard deviation equal to 15. The deviation IQ is now recognized as the appropriate way to calculate IQ, and most tests utilize this type of IQ score. Even though there is no quotient in the calculation of the deviation IQ, the term is maintained.

◇ INTELLIGENCE TESTS

Although there has been a great deal of controversy with respect to intelligence tests and IQ, intelligence testing and intellectual assessment, with its pragmatic goals of attempting to predict success, has developed and evolved over the decades. Test developers revised and altered intelligence tests in accordance with research, and theorizing and theoretical models reflected findings based on measures of intelligence. In many respects, this represents science and applied/clinical efforts working in concert with one another and mutually informing one another, both to increase our understanding of the concept of intelligence and to more accurately assess intellectual functioning. The next section will describe two of the major instruments used for the assessment of intelligence. Although there are numerous other intelligence tests and tests that assess various components of intellectual functioning, we will focus on the two that have the longest history and greatest popularity in terms of usage by clinical psychologists. Because Alfred Binet was the one who got the ball rolling with respect to testing intelligence, we will start with the current version of his measure.

◇ STANFORD-BINET SCALE

The original Binet-Simon measure of intelligence consisted of 30 cognitive tests that tapped into language skills, reasoning, and memory as well as other components. These tests were grouped into age levels such that items on scales that were successfully completed by a particular age group of children were grouped together to form **age tests**. A child would begin testing with items commensurate with his or her age and then complete items from progressively higher (or lower) age groups until she failed most of the items. The psychologist could then determine at what age group the child completed most items successfully and thus, determine the child's mental age (Boake, 2002).

This first test has, of course, been revised extensively and many times over the decades (revisions in 1916, 1937, 1960, and 1986, and again in 2003). The current version of the Stanford-Binet, the Stanford-Binet-5 (SB-5; Roid, 2003), is a result of building on the strengths and correcting shortcomings of the previous versions and of the massive amount of research information that accumulated over the years.

Stanford-Binet-5

The SB-5, like all the measures described in this chapter, is a test that can be administered only by trained and qualified professionals. The measure is appropriate for use in individuals 2 to 85+ years of age, and the normative sample (n = 4,800) is matched to the 2000 U.S. census. It is a 285-item scale that includes 10 subscales comprising verbal and nonverbal subtests. According to the test developer (Roid, 2003), although variable, the measure takes approximately 1 to 1.5 hours to complete. Participants complete first a routing procedure whereby verbal and nonverbal tasks are completed in order to direct or route the examination to the functional level of the participant.

The SB-5 is based on a hierarchical model of intelligence that includes global g at the apex and five factors of cognitive ability that are tapped in the measure. The factors include fluid intelligence, knowledge, quantitative processing, visual-spatial processing, and working memory. The SB-5 provides the examiner with verbal and nonverbal subtest scores, which are combined to produce factor indexes or scores on each of the five factors described earlier. Moreover, scores can be combined to form verbal (using the verbal subtests) and nonverbal (using the nonverbal tests) IQs. Finally, an overall full scale IQ is determined using all 10 subtests, and it can range between 40 and 160. All IQs and factor indexes have means of 100 and standard deviations of 15.

According to the test publishers, the SB-5 demonstrates appropriate levels of reliability and validity. Extensive reliability information is presented on the split-half, test-retest, interscorer agreement, and internal consistency in Roid (2003). For example, internal consistency estimates for the full scale, verbal, and nonverbal IQs range between .95 and .98; whereas reliability estimates for the factor indexes range between .90 and .92, and for the subtests the range is between .84 and .89.

With respect to validity, numerous and varied studies have been completed to assess construct, concurrent, and criterion validity using a variety of other measures of intelligence.

In general, the SB-5 does show appropriate evidence of validity although the validation of a measure truly takes years to firmly establish. Initial estimates are promising (Roid, 2003); for example, associations with other measures of intelligence, such as the Wechsler Scales of Intelligence, are in the expected ranges, and correlations with measures of other cognitive abilities are also appropriate.

Overall, it would appear that the current version of the Stanford-Binet is seen as a valuable and relevant test of intelligence. According to Strauss, Sherman, and Spreen (2006), the SB-5 is an excellent test with excellent reliability and appropriate levels of validity. It continues to be an important measure of intellectual functioning.

Wechsler Scales of Intelligence

Although the more recent Stanford-Binet test is for ages 2 to 85 years, another very popular set of measures of intelligence, the Wechsler Scales of Intelligence, use separate tests depending on the age range. Even though the early intelligence tests focused on children, in 1939, Wechsler published the first specifically designed intelligence test for adults called the **Wechsler-Bellevue Intelligence Scale**, which was innovative in numerous respects. First, as stated, it was designed specifically for adults and used the deviation IQ rather than the then current mental age calculation for IQ. In addition, Wechsler incorporated both verbal and performance (i.e., nonverbal) tasks in the intelligence measure, as he believed that both domains contributed to overall intelligence. Prior to this time, there was an emphasis on only verbally related items. After developing the adult measure in 1939 (later versions of the Wechsler-Bellevue were named the Wechsler Adult Intelligence Scale [WAIS]), Wechsler developed intelligence tests for children, the Wechsler Intelligence Scale for Children and Wechsler Preschool and Primary Scale for Intelligence, following the same model as used for the adult versions, and each of these has been revised over the years. These instruments became very popular measures, and in the 1960s, popularity of the Stanford-Binet was overtaken by the Wechsler Scales. The Wechsler Scales have remained the most frequently used measures of intellectual functioning, and they are considered by most to be the gold standard of intelligence measurement (Ivnik et al., 1992).

All the most current versions of the Wechsler Intelligence Scales derive from contemporary theoretical perspective that reflects four major domains of intelligence:

1. *Verbal comprehension*, which essentially measures verbal concept formation and reflects abilities to draw upon information obtained through formal and information education, reasoning, and expression of thoughts.

2. *Perceptual reasoning*, which involves nonverbal reasoning, problem solving, and visual-motor and visual-spatial skills in nonverbal tasks.

3. *Working memory*, which assesses cognitive skills necessary for high-order thinking such as ability to memorize, attention and concentration, and manipulation of mental information.

4. *Processing speed*, which entails assessing attention, scanning, and discrimination as well as planning and persistence.

The most current versions of the scales have focused on the IQ scores that reflect the four domains described earlier as well as a full scale IQ, and as a reflection of g, a **global ability index** is also calculated. Let's start with a description of the current version of the WAIS, the WAIS-IV (Wechsler, 1944).

Wechsler Adult Intelligence Scale-IV (WAIS-IV)

The newest version of the WAIS, the WAIS-IV, has 10 subtests and 5 supplemental subtests (used to either substitute for another subtest or supplement information). The subtests include tests of verbal and nonverbal intelligence and assess the four domains described earlier (i.e., verbal, perceptual reasoning, working memory, and processing speed).

Although only recently published, there are indications of the reliability and validity of the measure presented in the technical manual. For example, using both the normative sample and several special samples, internal consistency and test-retest reliabilities range from good to excellent (i.e., .70 to .94). Moreover, with respect to validity, the WAIS-IV was compared to a variety of other measures of intelligence and intellectual functioning in both clinical and nonclinical samples. This included comparing the WAIS-IV scores with WAIS-III scores. In all cases, there was evidence of appropriate levels of validity of the overall measure and the subscales. For example, correlations between the composite scores of the WAIS-IV were associated with WAIS-III scores ranged between .80 and .90.

Overall, although it is a new measure, initial indications suggest that the WAIS-IV has as good, if not better, reliability and validity as past versions of the scale and shows a great deal of promise as a well-conceptualized and well-developed measure of adult intelligence. Reliability and validity seem to be good to excellent with the measure, and future research will likely expand on this information over the next few years.

Wechsler Intelligence Scale for Children-IV (WISC-IV)

The WISC-IV was published in 2003 (PsycCorp., 2003) and represents a revision of the WISC-III, which was published in 1991. The instrument is based on the theoretical model as described earlier for the WAIS-IV and, thus, provides a full scale IQ score (range of 40 to 160) as well as four composite scores or indexes reflecting verbal comprehension, perceptual reasoning, processing speed, and working memory. The test is appropriate for children aged 6 years 0 months to 16 years 11 months (there is some overlap with the WAIS-IV), and the instrument has been translated into over 14 languages; appropriate norms have been established for each language. Some examples of similar kinds of items are presented in Figure 8.1.

FIGURE 8.1 Examples of sample items similar to those found of WISC-IV.

Similarities (23 items)
In what way are a pencil and a piece of chalk alike?
In what way are tea and coffee alike?
In what way are an inch and a mile alike?
In what way are binoculars and a microscope alike?

Vocabulary (36 items)
What is a ball?
What does running mean?
What is a poem?
What does obstreperous mean?

Comprehension (21 items)
Why do we wear shoes?
What is the thing to do if you see someone dropping a package?
In what two ways is a lamp better than a candle?
In the United States, why are we tried by a jury of our peers?

Information (33 items)
How many legs do you have?
What must you do make water freeze?
Who developed the theory of relativity?
What is the capital of France?

Word Reasoning (24 items)
The task is to identify the common concept being described with a series of clues.
Clue 1: This has a motor _____
Clue 2: _____ and it is used to cut grass.

Block Design (14 items)
The task is to reproduce stimulus designs using four or nine blocks (see below).

Picture Concepts (28 items)
The task is to choose one picture from each of two or three rows of pictures in such a way that all the pictures selected have a character in common (see below).

Coding (59 items in coding A and 119 items in coding B)
The task is to copy symbols from a key (see below).

1	2	3	4	5	6
x	o	=	L	/	V

2	4	1	5	6	3	5	2	1	6	4	3

Symbol Search (45 items in Part A and 60 items in Part B)
The task is to decide whether a stimulus figure (a symbol) appears in an array (see below).

△ ◇	☼ □ ◇ ± △ = □	YES	NO
☼ ±	◇ △ ± □ = □ △	YES	NO
= □	△ △ ☼ □ ± x ◇	YES	NO

Matrix Reasoning (35 items)
The task is to examine an incomplete matrix and select whichever of the five choices best completes the matrix (see below).

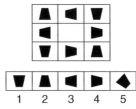

Picture Completion (38 items)
The task is to look at a picture—such as that of a car without a wheel, a scissors without handle, or telephone without numbers on the dial—and identify the essential missing part (see below).

Digit Span (16 items; 8 in Digit Span Forward, 8 in Digit Span Backward)
In the first part, the task is to repeat a string of numbers, ranging from 2 to 9 digits, in a forward direction (example: 1–8).
In the second part, the task is to repeat a string of numbers, ranging from 2 to 8 digits, in reverse order (example: 6–4–9).

Letter–Number Sequencing (10 items, each with 3 trials)
The task is to listen to a combination from 2 to 8 letters and digits (example: 1–b) and repeat the combination back with the numbers in ascending order followed by the letters in alphabetical order (example: e–6–d–9 would be repeated back as 6–9–d–e).

Arithmetic (34 items)
If I have one piece of candy and get another one, how many pieces will I have?
At 12 cents each, how much will 4 bars of soap cost?
If suits sell for 1/2 of the regular price, what is the cost of a $120 suit?

Cancellation (2 items, one Random and one Sequenced)
The task is to scan, within a specific time limit, both a random arrangement and a sequenced arrangement of pictures and mark target pictures (animals; see below).

In terms of reliability, the WISC-IV shows significant improvements over earlier versions of the measure and, with respect to validity, numerous studies attest to the WISC-IV's association with other measures of cognitive abilities (Williams, Weiss, & Rolfhus, 2003a).

Wechsler Preschool and Primary Scale of Intelligence-III (WPPSII-III)

The WPPSII-III is an intelligence measure for young children (aged 2 years 6 months to 7 years 3 months), and there are 11 core subtests that are used to determine full scale IQ as well as a performance IQ and a verbal IQ. In addition, there are composite scores as described earlier with the other Wechsler Scales and supplemental or optional subtests that can be used to determine optional scores. The measure takes approximately 30 minutes to administer for younger children and about 40 to 50 minutes for older children. Reliability estimates are seen as appropriate (Strauss et al., 2006), and evidence of validity has been demonstrated with appropriate correlations demonstrated between WPPSII-III scores and other measures of cognitive abilities (Strauss et al., 2006).

Interpreting and Using Intelligence Test Scores

What do results from intelligence tests tell the clinical psychologist? Although the full scale IQ from the measures can inform the clinical psychologist about g and the level of overall intellectual functioning, often more fine-grained analyses are conducted. For example, subtest scores can also be examined to evaluate even more specific abilities, strengths, and weaknesses in relation to intellectual functioning. In addition, there has been a long tradition of looking at patterns of subtest scores (known as **intertest scatter**) as potentially indicative of particular learning disabilities or other intellectual problems, although this approach has been viewed as likely without validity.

Because the SB-5 and any of the Wechsler Scales present items in a highly structured manner, with specific instructions on wording of questions, and so forth, **extratest behavior** can also be assessed by the clinician. The clinical psychologist can observe problem-solving strategies or behaviors that might interfere with or enhance performance on the tasks that can aid in understanding intellectual functioning.

Finally, intelligence test scores and information are usually combined with other information, including information gleaned from interviews, history taking, and other tests (e.g., tests of attained achievement in cognitive domains such as reading levels, math skill levels, and so forth) in order to address specific clinical issues.

◇ CLINICAL NEUROPSYCHOLOGY AND NEUROPSYCHOLOGICAL EVALUATIONS

Neuropsychology is a specialty area of clinical psychology and has been described as "an applied science concerned with the behavioral expression of brain dysfunction" (Lezak, 1995 p. 7). There are two main branches of neuropsychology; the first,

experimental neuropsychology, represents the scientific study of brain and behavior relationships and how brain dysfunction affects behavior. The other branch, **clinical neuropsychology**, is the applied aspect of neuropsychology that involves the assessment and treatment of brain-damaged behavior. For our purposes, we will focus on clinical neuropsychology and on the clinical work within clinical neuropsychology, neuropsychological assessments.

Overall, the concern of clinical neuropsychology tends to be the assessment and, at times, the treatment of deficits arising from damage to the central nervous system. The clinical neuropsychologist uses knowledge from research on brain-behavior relationships to assess mainly cognitive and intellectual deficits, although social, personality, physical, and other forms of behavioral functioning will also be addressed in individuals who have or are suspected to have some kind of brain damage. The general purpose is to determine the extent of impairment, location or site of lesions (particular area of damaged neural tissue), and behavioral functioning in individuals with some sort of central nervous system damage. Most typically, the damage involves the brain and can be caused by any number of conditions including head injuries; various diseases (e.g., Alzheimer's disease, Parkinson's disease) that result in progressive cognitive deterioration known as dementia; vascular diseases (e.g., coronary artery disease) that can produce cerebral vascular accidents (i.e., strokes); infectious diseases such as herpes simplex encephalitis or meningitis; toxic disorders involving, for example, chronic alcohol abuse; or brain tumors.

As a specialty area in clinical psychology, the majority of neuropsychologists have been trained as clinical psychologists. Although clinical psychology graduate programs may offer some training in neuropsychological assessment, in order to competently practice neuropsychology, more extensive and specialized training is necessary (Hannay et al., 1998). For example, in addition to training in assessment and treatment, extensive training in neuroanatomy, neuropathology, and normal and abnormal brain functioning, as well as training in specific neuropsychological assessment, is necessary (Hebben & Milberg, 2002). This is often done at the **postdoctoral level** (i.e., after the PhD) although there are more and more graduate programs dedicated specifically to training in clinical neuropsychology.

Purposes of Neuropsychological Assessment

Historically, neuropsychological assessments were conducted mainly to aid in the localization of brain lesions in order to provide information for the diagnosis of neurological problems. In other words, based on the performance results from specific psychological tests, the neuropsychological assessment provided information that could be used to determine which particular part or parts of the brain had been affected by the brain damage. By being able to localize the site of brain damage or areas of the brain affected by damage, the neuropsychological assessment provided valuable information for determining the diagnosis and prognosis of the patient. In addition, at times, neuropsychological assessments were conducted to determine whether symptoms of psychiatric disturbance were "functional or organic," meaning were the symptoms due to psychological processes (i.e., **functional** in origin) or specific structural brain damage (i.e., **organic** in origin). This would aid in determining whether the signs and symptoms exhibited by a patient were due to psychological or neurological processes.

Nowadays, the uses of neuropsychological assessments have expanded and evolved. They are used in a variety of domains to address medical, legal, educational, and rehabilitation questions and issues and, of course, research. According to Muriel Lezak (1995) there are four general purposes for neuropsychological evaluations:

1. Diagnosis: Neuropsychological assessments play an important role in helping to discriminate among neurological, psychiatric, and developmental symptoms and aid in the diagnosis of various neurological and psychiatric disorders. Although with the advent of sophisticated imaging techniques, such as positron emission tomography (PET), nuclear magnetic resonance imaging (NMRI), and computerized axial tomography (CT), some of these diagnostic uses, such as localization of lesions, have diminished; however, in particular types of brain pathology, neuropsychological examinations are crucial in determining specific sites of brain damage. In a related vein, neuropsychological assessments are also used more and more in legal situations to determine the functional impairment resulting from personal injury or in criminal cases where a defendant may have some brain damage or dysfunction that may have contributed to the commission of a crime.

The diagnostic use of neuropsychological assessment often involves careful descriptions of changes in patient's functioning (usually cognitive, emotional, and behavioral) that reflect the presence, location, and severity of brain damage.

2. Patient care and planning: Neuropsychological evaluations are often requested in order to aid in patients' adjustment to disabilities that have arisen due to brain pathology. Although the focus of neuropsychological assessment is often on the deficits that the patient experiences, there is also a concern with the strengths and capabilities as these may be very useful in determining the appropriate levels of care and rehabilitation planning and implementation. Neuropsychological assessments provide valuable information about cognitive, emotional, and personality features that influence a patient's adjustment to brain damage, educational options, as well as treatment and rehabilitation options. This information can be used to develop appropriate supports for patients and to plan for their future. For example, determining functioning in a patient with a dementing disorder (such as dementia due to Alzheimer's disease) can aid in determining how best to provide supports for the patient as well as future needs of the patient as the functioning deteriorates. An additional component of this can involve helping the patient's family understand the nature of the behavioral deficits and to help them cope with the patient's limitations.

3. Rehabilitation and treatment evaluation: As knowledge of rehabilitation and treatment of brain damage increases, the work of clinical neuropsychology increases as "careful, sensitive, broad-gauged, and accurate neuropsychological assessment is a necessary foundation on which appropriate treatment . . . can be based" (Lezak, 1995, p. 12). Information regarding cognitive strengths and weaknesses can be vital in terms of planning rehabilitation and educational programs. Moreover, neuropsychological data can be used to monitor rate of deterioration of functioning in certain patients and whether medications or other forms of treatment have any positive or negative effect on cognitive symptoms.

4. Research: Neuropsychological assessment and testing has been of importance in studying the organization of brain functioning and how brain functioning is related to behavior. Although a major goal of the field of neuropsychology is to increase knowledge regarding how the brain works and how it works in particular kinds of diseases or types of brain pathology, there is also a great deal of clinically related research that is dedicated to increasing the quality of assessments and evaluation of particular techniques (Box 8.2).

Assumptions Underlying Neuropsychological Assessment

There are several basic assumptions that underlie the process of neuropsychological assessment (Lezak, 1995). These assumptions include the following:

1. The belief that there is always some sort of behavioral deficit, usually entailing cognitive functioning, that accompanies brain damage or compromised brain functioning. The deficits, depending on the location, extent, or severity of damage, may be very subtle and detected only in highly controlled situations, or they may be gross and very obvious to anyone interacting with the person. In addition, the deficits may be extremely circumscribed (e.g., inability to recognize people by their faces) or can be very broad and, at times, very vague and difficult to describe.

BOX 8.2

WADA TESTING

One type of neuropsychological assessment concerns itself specifically with localization of language or memory functioning. One of the authors (PLH) participated as team member for WADA testing (Wada & Rasmussen, 1960), also termed "intracarotid sodium amobarbital procedure." This procedure is done to determine, for example, in which hemisphere language function tends to be localized for patients who may be undergoing neurosurgery. Localizing language functioning can allow a prediction of possible effects of the surgery. In the procedure, while the patient is awake, a catheter is inserted into one of the carotid arteries (provides blood to one hemisphere of the brain), and sodium amobarbital is administered to the patient via that artery. This, effectively, shuts down that hemisphere for a brief window of time during which the neuropsychologist administers some tasks to the patient to determine whether the functioning hemisphere can process or produce language. If so, then language is thought to be localized in the functioning hemisphere; if not, then language is thought to be localized in the hemisphere that has been deactivated.

2. The deficits or patterns of deficits can be very useful in understanding brain pathology and processes and in providing descriptive, diagnostic, and treatment information.

3. The field of psychology, with its emphasis on standardized psychological assessment, and specifically, cognitive/intellectual assessment, is the specialty that can best assess the cognitive and intellectual deficits in brain-damaged individuals. Psychological testing has developed over decades and been specifically designed to assess many of the behavioral and cognitive deficits evident in brain-damaged individuals. Moreover, there is a huge literature dealing with empirical validation of intellectual and cognitive assessment tests and techniques that lends confidence to the use of psychological testing in such circumstances.

Domains Important to Assess

Although there is some debate about particular ways to measure components of brain-behavior relationships, there is general agreement that the following areas are important to address in any neuropsychological assessment approach (Zillmer & Spiers, 2001). Some of these domains of functioning are involved in just about every form of brain damage, and others are involved more or less in specific forms of brain damage.

1. Orientation: This involves the awareness people have of themselves in their environment or surroundings. Disruptions in orientation are one of the most common symptoms of brain damage. Typically, orientation is thought of and measured in terms of awareness of time (What day [date, year, time] is it?), place (What is the name of the place we are in now?), and person (What is your full name?). Other types of orientation problems, including **orientation of personal space** such as the ability to point to particular body parts (Point to your head.) and naming one's own body parts (e.g., examiner points to person's shoulder and asks patient: "What is this?"); **spatial orientation** (ability to relate the position, direction, or movements of objects in space); and **topographical orientation** (problems in memory for familiar routes that the person travels [e.g., mailbox to home]) are also frequently assessed. The student might recognize some of these questions as coming from the mental status exam, which is used often in neuropsychological assessments.

2. Sensation and perception: Sensation is the detection of some stimulus in the environment and perception is the process of identifying or "knowing" what the stimulation is. It is these processes that keep us in touch with the external (and internal) world. In neuropsychological assessment, the neuropsychologist is especially interested in evaluating the sensation and perception processes involved in visual, auditory, and tactile levels of functioning. Specifically, problems can involve a variety of deficits; likely the most common involves the inability or compromised ability to recognize familiar objects, people, or other stimuli. This is known as **agnosia** and can have significant effects on a person's functioning. One well-known (at least in neuropsychology circles) example of a patient's visual agnosia was described by Oliver Sacks in his book entitled: *The Man Who Mistook His Wife for a Hat* (1985):

> He (the patient) appeared to have decided the examination was over and started to look around for his hat. He reached out his hand and took hold of wife's head, tried to lift it off, to put it on. He had apparently mistaken his wife for a hat! His wife looked as if she was used to such things. (p. 11)

The assessment of sensory and perceptual processes can involve specific tasks such as identifying objects only by touch or having the examiner state pairs of words that can be the same or different and having the patient identify whether the same word was repeated or whether the two words were different (Zilmer & Spiers, 2001).

3.   Attention and concentration: Because we are bombarded with a plethora of stimuli from the environment, an extremely important function of the brain is to select out and process important or relevant information and ignore irrelevant information. If you take a moment right now and try to become aware of all the stimuli around you, sounds, sights, level of light, temperature of the air, feelings in your back, and so forth, you get a sense of the amount of stimulation that bombards your senses. In order for you to read this text, your brain needs to ignore the sounds, sights, and sensations and focus your attention on the words on the page. Thus, attention and concentration reflect basic processes in terms of interacting adaptively with the environment. One particularly striking type of attentional problem, known as hemineglect, is described in Box 8.3.

A seemingly ubiquitous symptom of brain damage involves disturbances in focusing or maintaining attention or increased distractibility or shifting attention to different tasks. Because the majority of mental tasks we engage in require us to focus, attend, or concentrate, this sort of impairment underlies all manner of compromised cognitive and intellectual functioning and, of course, underlies many types of brain damage. The neuropsychological evaluation typically includes assessment of various components of attention including the ability to attend to various stimuli, sustain attention on a task, switch attention from one task to another, and pay attention to more than one thing at a time. This can be assessed by tasks such as "Recite the days of the week backward starting with Sunday" or "Count by 3's beginning with 1 and adding 3 to each number."

4.   Motor/psychomotor functioning: Control over motor skills is another domain that is important to assess as frequently control over upper and lower extremities can be affected with brain damage. Assessment involves testing gross movements of extremities such as ability to move arms as well as fine motor skills such as ability to write. Testing can involve asking patients to respond to basic commands such as "Move your left leg," "Raise your right hand," or "Touch your thumb to your forefinger as quickly as you can." It can also involve assessing grip strength or finger-tapping speed.

5.   Language and verbal functions: Of course, the ability to produce and understand language (verbal and written) is a crucial behavior that allows people to function and, perhaps most important, to establish and maintain human interactions. If you can imagine being unable to speak, write, or understand spoken or written words, you may get a sense of the devastating isolation and social disconnection a patient can feel.

Thus, evaluation of intact language skills is an important focus. Language function is assessed in terms of both **expressive functions** (i.e., speaking, writing) and **receptive functions** (i.e., understanding spoken and written words, phrases, and sentences). Although there are often signs of language difficulties that become evident in the interview and in interacting with the patient, there are many specific tests to formally assess the functioning (Strauss et al., 2006).

6. Visual-spatial organization: The ability to analyze and integrate visual information is an important function in processing information from the environment. For example, the ability to perceive and recognize visual information, store information related to visual objects, and find one's way geographically are all abilities that involve visual-spatial organization. Because these kinds of abilities are frequently compromised in individuals with brain damage, the neuropsychologist assesses various aspects of visual information processing such as spatial orientation, route finding, facial recognition, and visual reproduction. An example of a test for visual-spatial construction is the Bender Motor Gestalt, which is a projective technique, but in this case it is used for neuropsychological assessment purposes.

7. Memory: The assessment of memory can often be quite complex as not only are there various "kinds" of memory (i.e., episodic, procedural, etc.), there are numerous modalities by which memory can be stored (e.g., verbal memory, motor memory, and so forth). Moreover, memory involves numerous processes in the selection and encoding of information, storage of the information, and retrieval of that information. In the assessment, the psychologist evaluates the ability of the individual to encode or learn new information, recall new or old information, and recognize old or new information. This is usually done in verbal (i.e., learning or remembering verbal information) or visual (i.e., learning or remembering shapes, configurations, and so forth) modalities. There are many different tests developed to assess memory that contain subtests assessing various memory processes.

8. Abstract reasoning: Abstract reasoning ability underlies a person's ability to understand concepts and to process complex information, solve problems, and transfer learned information to other contexts. Abstract reasoning, such as the ability to understand abstract concepts (e.g., the concept of liberty) and abstract rules (e.g., "The apple doesn't fall far from the tree"), is known as a higher cognitive function and is often assessed in assessments.

Abstract reasoning is often assessed by asking patients to interpret abstract statements such as proverbs. For example, the patient might be asked to explain what the following statement means: "Don't judge a book by its cover." The neuropsychologist codes or rates the response on how concrete or abstract the interpretation was. For example, "You can't tell what the book is about just by looking at the outside" would be a concrete response; whereas, "*You cannot judge* the character of people by appearances" would be a more abstract response.

BOX 8.3

HEMINEGLECT

When patients have damage in a particular part of the right hemisphere, they sometimes experience a striking attention problem known as hemineglect. Patients with hemineglect fail to be aware of one side of space including objects and even their own body. Sacks (1985) described a patient with hemineglect: "She has totally lost the idea of 'left,' with regard to both the world and her own body. Sometimes she complains that her portions [of food] are too small, but this is because she eats only from the right half of the plate—it does not occur to her that it has a left half as well. Sometimes, she will put on lipstick, and make up the right half of her face, leaving the left half completely neglected" (p. 77). One neuropsychological test used to evaluate the presence of neglect is known as the "Draw a Clock" test, which involves, not surprisingly, asking the patient to draw the face of a clock. An example of the kind of response that patients with this attentional difficulty produce is below:

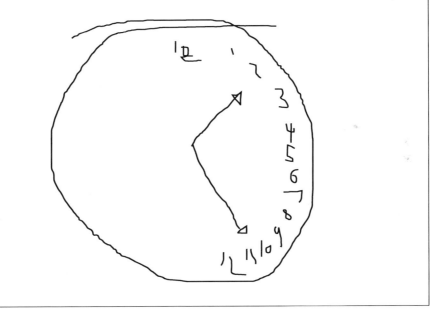

Although the above eight areas of functioning are assessed to address cognitive and intellectual functioning, other domains are often assessed to provide a comprehensive picture of the patient's functioning. For example, because of the often devastating impact of having some form of brain damage, there frequently will be evaluations of a patient's emotional and psychological distress by administering some of the instruments discussed in chapter 7, such as the MMPI-2.

◇ HOW IS A NEUROPSYCHOLOGICAL EVALUATION DONE?

There is some debate regarding specific ways to conduct a neuropsychological assessment. Some workers in the field suggest that a specific and fixed battery of tests that tap specific domains of functioning should be used, essentially, for all types of neuropsychological evaluations. It is thought that the advantage of this approach is that all relevant domains of functioning are assessed, the tests provide measurement of functioning in a standard and consistent manner, many of the tests can be administered by paraprofessionals or nonprofessionals, and the use of battery over time can be evaluated for reliability and validity and can offer reliable methods for gross screening for brain damage (Hebben & Milberg, 2002). On the other hand, others suggest that use of an unchanging battery of tests overtaxes the patient as some tests are not helpful for specific problems the person has and does not allow for additional measures to be used that reflect new knowledge and developments in the field (Lezak, 1995). The detractors of the fixed battery approach suggest that the neuropsychological assessment should instead use a flexible or a hypothesis-testing approach whereby a very basic core battery is administered and, in conjunction with information about the nature of the injury, behavioral observations of the patient, neurological reports, and so forth, hypotheses about the brain damage or function are formed, and specific instruments are chosen to administer to test the hypotheses. The advantages to this approach include that the assessment can be tailored to the individual patient's needs, can provide more of a comprehensive assessment of function, and can utilize newly developed methods and tests. On the other hand, engaging in this flexible approach requires extensive knowledge and training regarding neuroanatomy and brain function; involves observation of patients, which can be unreliable, and requires extensive knowledge regarding testing methodologies and instruments (Hebben & Milberg, 2002).

Whether it is a fixed battery or a flexible approach, comprehensive neuropsychological assessments generally involve:

1. Careful perusal of information from the referral source, medical records, and neurological reports, the nature of the injury and how it occurred (e.g., head trauma in motor vehicle accident or loss of oxygen during an operation), and other findings relevant to the patient's difficulties (e.g., injury and postinjury records).

2. An in-depth and comprehensive interview is conducted with the patient and, often, with family members of the patient. The interview is similar in some ways to clinical interview described earlier, with the addition of specific information about the nature of the brain injury or illness. The interview is especially important in order to establish the social, medical, cultural, and psychological adjustment, school and work history, and the history of the problems that led to the assessment. This is done in order to get a detailed picture of the person's functioning prior to and following the development of the brain damage. Commonly, this may involve interviewing family members regarding the patient's behavior and history. Behavioral observations of the patient (e.g., appearance, gait, speech, interpersonal skills, motivation, unusual behaviors, and so forth) are a critical part

of the interview in order to provide information about the signs and symptoms of particular types of brain damage.

3. The neuropsychologist administers neuropsychological tests. This can be a fixed battery approach or a process-oriented approach, and this component of the assessment can be lengthy and intensive. For example, it is not unusual for patients to complete neuropsychological tests in 6 or 7 hours. In addition, in some cases due to the nature of the brain damage or due to other problems the patient experiences (e.g., blindness, medications, broken bones, and so forth), the neuropsychologist may have to adapt or use variations in testing procedures in order to try to capture qualitative features of the patient's deficits, a process known as **accommodation**.

4. A patient's test responses are interpreted, and a picture of the deficits and patterns of responses that reflect damage and functioning is determined. In assessing deficits, the neuropsychologist attempts to determine whether the patient's performance on tests is consistent with the performance of normative information for brain-damaged individuals. This is done by comparing the patient's specific test performance with the normal and brain-damaged groups' performances on that same test. This provides information that can aid in inferring that brain damage is evident in the patient. If the person scores in the range of other brain-damaged individuals, the patient is assumed to have brain damage. This is known as the **statistical or normative approach** and is used in most assessments but, in particular, by those using the fixed battery approach.

In addition to using the normative approach, the psychologist, especially those using a flexible approach, will use what is termed the **differential score approach**. In this approach, the neuropsychologist needs to determine whether the functioning of a patient after developing the brain damage represents a change from her functioning prior to the brain damage. The functioning prior to the damage is known as **premorbid functioning**. Determining if the performance represents a change from premorbid functioning and determining the magnitude of the change in functioning following the damage are important to determine for a variety of reasons. First, the information can be instrumental in determining the diagnostic picture as well as treatment, educational, or rehabilitation planning. Second, it is the magnitude of cognitive changes within the individual that might be the only information that suggests the presence of brain damage. For example, it may be the case that a very intelligent person with excellent and well-above average memory functioning experiences some memory loss, but when tested, that person still scores in the normal range even though there is significant loss of memory ability. Although in using the normative approach, the person's score would be considered within the normal range and as possibility indicative of no brain damage, there can still be a significant drop in functioning that points to the presence of brain damage.

Determining premorbid functioning is not necessarily a straightforward enterprise. In fact, at times, this can entail significant detective work that can involve estimating levels of functioning. First, often in assessments using the process approach, tests that are not sensitive to brain damage (e.g., tests that measure cognitive functioning that is often not affected in brain-damaged individuals, for example, tests of vocabulary or nonverbal reasoning) can provide information on premorbid functioning. As well, the neuropsychologist can use information such as education record and level and type of employment (e.g., successful small business person, assume that person has above average intelligence), or, in the case of children, the neuropsychologist may assess whether the child had met developmental milestones in the past.

◇ NEUROPSYCHOLOGICAL TESTS: FIXED BATTERIES

For those espousing the fixed battery approach there are two main fixed batteries that exist, each based on a particular conception of brain functioning.

Halstead Reitan

The Halstead-Reitan Neuropsychological Battery (Reitan & Wolfson, 1993) is a fixed set of eight specific tests developed originally by Dr. Ward Halstead and Dr. Ralph Reitan that attempts to assess brain functioning in a comprehensive manner. The tests are invariable and are administered in a highly structured fashion, often by technicians. Based on well-developed sets of norms for test scores, the battery provides an **impairment index** that is used to predict the presence or absence of brain damage, and there are several other indexes of brain damage that are relevant for attempts to localize the damage. The tests comprising the battery tap into five general domains, listed here, that represent a hierarchical arrangement of brain-related activities.

1. Input functions (i.e., attention, concentration, and memory)
2. Verbal abilities
3. Spatial, sequential, and cognitive manipulatory abilities
4. Abstraction, reasoning, logical analysis, and concept formation
5. Output abilities (i.e., motor functions on each side of the body)

Luria Nebraska

Dr. Alexander Luria was a Russian neuropsychologist who developed a comprehensive and innovative model of brain functioning and promoted an approach to neuropsychological assessment based on his conceptualization of brain functioning (e.g., Luria, 1966). Although his model was considered remarkable and esoteric by many, it was not accepted generally until Dr. Charles Golden took some components of Luria's process approach and developed a fixed battery (the Luria-Nebraska Neuropsychological Battery [LNNB]) that was brief and that could be more easily validated empirically than the original process approach. Although the development and use of the LNNB as a battery was controversial, it did gain some popularity, due mainly to its brief nature. The LNNB contains 269 items that can be completed in about 2 to 2.5 hours. The items can be grouped into 11 scales that measure some of the domains of brain functioning described by Luria (1966). The domains include:

1. Motor functions
2. Rhythm

3. Tactile functions

4. Visual functions

5. Receptive speech

6. Expressive speech

7. Writing

8. Reading

9. Arithmetic

10. Memory

11. Intellectual processes

Five summary scores are derived that provide information regarding presence, magnitude, and general location of brain damage as well as degree of impairment.

◇ NEUROPSYCHOLOGICAL ASSESSMENT: FLEXIBLE OR PROCESS APPROACH

The process approach to neuropsychological assessment is based on the idea that each patient's functioning and deficits are different and that different cognitive processes can be involved for different people when completing the same task. This leads to the belief that testing, describing, and understanding the functioning need to be individually tailored to the patient and his difficulties.

This approach has three advantages: first, acknowledging and focusing on the unique nature of the patient; second, focusing on specific aspects of functioning that are seen as most important for the patient; and third, determining how a patient fails or succeeds on a test item. In other words, if a person fails on an item such as: "What season does it snow?" it is not necessarily clear if the person could not understand the question, cannot express the answer verbally, or does not know the answer. With a flexible approach, the neuropsychologist can determine the potential reason for the inappropriate response that can help in pinpointing the deficit.

Dr. Muriel Lezak (1995) has described the flexible approach she uses and teaches. As she states, the psychologist usually does not know what specific tests will be administered prior to the examination, with the exception of a basic battery that evaluates the major dimensions of behavior we discussed previously. Based on the responses to items and tests, behavioral observations, and so forth, the neuropsychologist then begins to formulate hypotheses regarding deficits and makes a selection of tests (and determines modifications to the tests if the person is handicapped). Based on the responses to those tests and observations of behavior, the neuropsychologist then accepts or refutes the hypotheses and continues the process until a full picture of functioning emerges. Lezak's basic battery includes individually administered tests and self-administered tests that patients can take themselves. For example, the basic battery includes most of the Wechsler Intelligence Scales, the subscales of which tap into various important domains of brain-behavior relationships. As well, a variety of other tests that tap into attention—visuospatial abilities, memory and learning, verbal and academic skills, construction skills (i.e., copying, drawing), concept formation, motor ability, and emotional status—are administered as the initial battery. The selection of specific tests following the battery is, of course, variable, and there is an accumulating number of neuropsychological testing instruments and methods that have been developed (e.g., Strauss, Sherman, & Spreen, 2006).

Other approaches to neuropsychological evaluation have been developed; for example, the Boston Process Approach was developed by Edith Kaplan. Although many neuropsychological examinations use the WAIS or components of the WAIS in order to tap various kinds of brain functioning, Kaplan developed a modification of the WAIS to be more specifically relevant for neuropsychological questions. Based on observations of brain-damaged patients' behavior, she developed the Wechsler Adult Intelligence Scale–Revised Neuropsychological Instrument (Kaplan, Fein, Morris, & Delis, 1991). This scale is again used as a part of an initial battery, and subsequent tests are added based on the performance, behavior, and individual needs of the patient.

◇ CONCLUSION

Overall, this chapter has attempted to provide the student with an overview and description of intellectual assessment and neuropsychological assessment. From its early beginnings of assessing intellectual abilities of children, this area of clinical psychology has shown tremendous growth and development in terms of research and the applied application of that research in attempting to aid those with intellectual and cognitive difficulties. A major domain of assessment has been evolving, neuropsychological assessment, that focuses on intellectual and cognitive functioning among those with suspected or confirmed brain damage. Several assessment approaches were described.

◇ ONGOING CONSIDERATIONS

The field of intellectual assessment and intelligence is always evolving. Certainly our understanding of intelligence is increasing. One direction this has taken is whether or not there are multiple intelligences and not just one general kind of intelligence. For example Dr. Robert Sternberg suggests that traditional conceptualizations of intelligence are too narrow and has proposed three different "intelligences": analytic intelligence, which is generally what we think of as intelligence and what is measured by IQ tests; creative intelligence, which involves being adept at managing novel situations and new problems; and, finally, practical intelligence, which involves abilities to adapt to environmental demands. Howard Gardner (1993) has gone even further specifying no less than seven different kinds of intelligences. These include mathematical, spatial, musical, body-kinesthetic, personal, and interpersonal intelligences. Whether these different types of intelligence will be accepted in the mainstream of psychology will be determined over the next few years.

Although the focus of much neuropsychological evaluation has been on adults, there have been attempts to develop comprehensive assessments of children. For example, a relatively new neuropsychological battery has been developed for assessing brain damage in children between the ages of 3 and 12, known as the NEPSY-II (Korkman, Kirk, & Kemp, 2007). This battery assesses six core areas including attention and executive functions, language, sensorimotor functions, visuomotor functions, visuospatial processing, memory and learning, and social perception. In addition, within each of the broad domains, it is possible to assess subcomponents of the domains. Although the battery is relatively new, there is some promise for the utility of the battery in assessing brain damage in children.

◇ KEY TERMS LEARNED

Accommodation

Age tests

Agnosia

Clinical neuropsychology

Crystallized intelligence

Deviation IQ

Differential score approach

Experimental neuropsychology

Expressive functions

Extratest behavior

Fluid intelligence

Functional

Global ability index

Impairment index

Intertest scatter

Neuropsychology

Organic

Orientation of personal space

Postdoctoral level

Premorbid functioning

Ratio IQ

Receptive functions

Spatial orientation

Statistical or normative approach

Topographical orientation

Wechsler-Bellevue Intelligence Scale

◇ THINKING QUESTIONS

1. In what ways was the early development of the Wechsler Scales innovative in comparison to other views and tests of intelligence?

2. Describe the differences and similarities between the SB-5 and the Wechsler Scales in terms of development, measure, and conceptualization of IQ and the components of intelligence measured.

3. What are the differences and similarities between flexible and fixed battery approaches to neuropsychological assessment?

4. What are the important domains to assess in neuropsychological assessment, and what are the relevant domains in an intellectual assessment?

5. How do you think the Wechsler Scales might be used in a neuropsychological assessment?

6. What features of a person's background are used to estimate premorbid cognitive functioning?

◇ REFERENCES

Alfonso, V. C., Flanagan, D. P., & Radwan, S. (2005). The impact of the Cattell-Horn-Carroll theory on test development and interpretation of cognitive and academic abilities. In D. P. Flanagan & P. L. Harrison (Eds.), *Contemporary intellectual assessment: Second edition: Theories, tests, and issues*. New York: Guildford.

Anastasi, A. (1992). What counselors should know about the use and interpretation of psychological tests. *Journal of Counseling & Development, 70*, 610–615.

Binet, A., & Simon, T. (1905/1916). New methods for the diagnosis of the intellectual level of subnormals. In H. H. Goddard (Ed.), *Development of intelligence in children* (the Binet-Simon Scale) (E.S. Kite, Trans., pp. 37–90). Baltimore: Williams & Wilkins.

Boake, C. (2002). From the Binet-Simon to the Wechsler-Bellevue: Tracing the history of intelligence testing. *Journal of Clinical and Experimental Neuropsychology, 24*, 383–405.

Gardner, H. (1993). *Multiple intelligences*. New York: Basic Books.

Groth-Marnat, G. (1990). *Handbook of psychological assessment* (2nd ed.). New York: Wiley.

Groth-Marnat, G. (2003). *Handbook of psychological assessment* (4th ed.). New York: Wiley.

Hannay, H. J. (1998). Proceedings of the Houston conference on specialty education and training in clinical neuropsychology, September 2–7, 1997, University of Houston and Conference Center. *Archives of Clinical Neuropsychology, 13*, 157–250.

Hebben, N., & Milberg, W. (2002). *Essentials of neuropsychological assessment*. New York: Wiley.

Ivnik, R. J., Malec, J. F., Smith, G. E. Tangalos, E. G., Peterson, R. C., Kokmen, E., & Kurland, L. T. (1992). Mayo's older American normative studies: WAIS-R norms for ages 56 to 97. *The Clinical Neuropsychologist, 6*(Supplement), 1–30.

Kaplan, E., Fein, D., Morris, R., & Delis, D. (1991). *WAIS-R as a neuropsychological instrument*. San Antonio, TX: The Psychological Corporation.

Korkman, M., Kirk, U., & Kemp, S. (2007). *NEPSY II: A developmental neuropsychological assessment manual*. San Antonio, TX: The Psychological Corporation.

Lezak, M. (1995). *Neuropsychological assessment* (3rd ed.). New York: Oxford University Press.

Luria, A. (1966). *Human brain and psychological processes*. New York: Harper & Row.

Neisser, U., Boodoo, G., Bouchard, T. J., Boykin, A. W., Brody, N., Ceci, S. J., Halpern, D. F., Loehlin, J. C., Perloff, R. Sternberg, R. J., & Urbina, S. (1996). Intelligence: Knowns and unknowns. *American Psychologist, 51*, 77–101.

PsycCorp. (2003). *WISC-IV Canadian manual*. Toronto, Ontario: Harcourt Assessment, Harcourt Canada Ltd.

Reitan, R. M., & Wolfson, D. (1993). *The Halstead-Reitan neuropsychological test battery: Theory and clinical interpretation*. Belmont, CA: Wadsworth.

Roid, G. (2003). *Stanford-Binet Intelligence Scales (fifth edition) technical manual*. Itasca, IL: Riverside Publishing.

Sacks, O. (1985). *The man who mistook his wife for his hat*. New York: Harper Collins.

Spearman, C. (1927). *The abilities of man: Their nature and measurement*. New York: Macmillan.

Stern, W. L. (1912). Uber die psychogischen Methoden der Intelligenzprufung. *Bericht über den V. Kongress für experimentelle Psychologie 16*, 1–160.

Strauss, E., Sherman, E. M. S., & Spreen, O. (2006). *A compendium of neuropsychological tests: Administration, norms, and commentary*. New York: Oxford.

Terman, L. M., Lyman, G., Ordahl, G., Ordahl, L, Galbreath, N., & Talbert, W. (1916). The Stanford revision of the Binet-Simon scale and some results from its application to 1000 non-selected children. *Journal of Educational Psychology, 6*, 551–562.

Thurstone, L. L. (1938). Primary mental abilities. *Psychometric monographs*, No. 1.

Vernon, P. E. (1950). *The structure of abilities*. London: Methuen.

Wada, J., & Rasmussen, T. (1960). Intracarotid injection of sodium amytal for the lateralization of cerebral speech dominance. *Journal of Neurosurgery, 17*, 266–282.

Wechsler, D. (1944). *The measurement of adult intelligence* (3rd ed.). Baltimore: Williams & Wilkins.

Williams, P. E., Weiss, L. G., & Rolfhus, E. L. (2003a). *WISC-IV technical report #2: Psychometric properties*. The Psychological Corporation.

Zillmer, E., & Spiers, M. (2001). *Principles of neuropsychology*. Belmont, CA: Wadsworth.

CHAPTER NINE

BEHAVIORAL AND BIOLOGICAL ASSESSMENT

CHAPTER OBJECTIVE

This chapter rounds out the description of the various classes of measurement tools that are available to the clinical psychologist. A particular advantage to the two methods described in this chapter is that they can provide information that is free of response biases. Nevertheless, determining when and under which conditions this is true, and for which kind of question, takes some effort to explain.

◇ BEHAVIORAL ASSESSMENT

Rationale and Basic Principles

In clinical psychology and psychiatry, the assessment of personality, psychopathology, and poor health relies heavily on self-report, either via diagnostic interview or via standardized questionnaires. As was discussed in chapter 7, this has many advantages; among them is the opportunity to also create a relationship via interviews. Furthermore, the interviewer can observe the congruence (or lack thereof) of simultaneous behavior with self-report. While the high degree of standardization and simultaneous low cost associated with the use of questionnaires has its advantages, the flexibility of behavioral assessment is also unique. Unfortunately, clients may not want to reveal problematic behaviors in self-reports and minimize reported severity, especially when the problematic behavior is socially stigmatized. Clients may not be very accurate in their recall; and this is particularly true in the very young, those with low intelligence and poor verbal skills, or individuals with certain pervasive cognitive dysfunctions like brain damage. The incipient weakness of an assessment that solely relies on self-report requires a degree of perpetual mistrust on part of clinicians and a constant need to check and understand the context in which these responses are delivered. To some degree, this problem can be remedied via the use of sophisticated tests that have built-in correction scales like the MMPI or the PAI (see chapter 7). Therefore, the trustworthiness of assessments can be greatly strengthened if an assessment package can be compiled with different approaches that are complementary to interview and questionnaires, that are difficult or impossible to fake or bias, and that don't require inference for interpretation. Behavioral and biological assessments fit these requirements (under certain circumstances) and are therefore described in this chapter.

Assessing behavior is particularly important in behavior therapy (which will be presented in detail in chapter 12) because behavioral assessment is an integral part of the whole therapy conceptualization, planning, and documentation of progress. However, this is not a reason to limit behavioral assessments to the context of purely behavioral therapies; the only requirement is that an observable behavior that is descriptive and informative about the pathology at hand is quantified.

Typical problems presented to a behavior therapist are anxiety problems and associated avoidance behaviors, substance abuse problems, or compulsive behaviors. If an individual who sought therapy for chronic nail-biting stops biting nails, then therapy was successful (unless the individual substituted the nail-biting with another problem behavior like hair pulling, of course). Or, one can think of an individual who refused to accept a desirable promotion at work because he was afraid of flying on airplanes, and the promotion would have required frequent plane travel. If after therapy he was reasonably comfortable flying and subsequently accepted the promotion, then again the therapy was successful because the target behavior (avoidance of flights) was changed. These examples readily show the great advantage of assessing overt behavior; no further complicated tests, questionnaires, or lengthy interviews are called for. Also, behavioral assessment is very suitable for individuals who cannot easily share their thoughts and feelings with a therapist, like very small children or a severely retarded adult; in fact for these individuals behavioral observation is the only usable form of assessment.

That sounds promising, right? Could it really be this simple?

Validity and Ethics in Implementation and Interpretation

It may be easier to show the strengths and potential problems with behavioral assessment using real-life examples that the reader can easily identify with. When an impatient driver runs a red light and two police officers sitting in their cruiser saw him do it, the driver has no leg to stand on in court because the judge will readily accept the validity of the officers' observations. Case closed. Behavioral assessment directly taps into what happened; no inference is required, and that gives it maximal ecological validity. This conclusion is beautifully illustrated in a court case (see Box 9.1).

By creating this hypothetical but by no means unrealistic scenario of a driver slipping through a red light, important features of behavioral assessment were opened up for discovery. First of all, somebody's behavior can be assessed and monitored by (a) the person himself or (b) somebody else. The advantage of monitoring oneself is that the observer can monitor or recall all of his behaviors over a long period of time whereas a different observer, in this case the police officers, can record only one very small window of one's behavior, namely, the singular event of running the red light. Whether or not one can trust the

BOX 9.1

This is a real-life story (we did not make it up); it happened in a Vancouver courtroom and was told to us by the presiding judge.

Mr. P. was suing his disability insurance company because he had an injury that prevented him from returning to work. If the claim was found reasonable, the insurance would have to provide him with a lifelong disability pension. The insurance company had some doubts about the truthfulness of this claim because the medical evidence was not clear. The lawyer for the insurance company was hoping that on cross-examination Mr. P. would reveal something to substantiate the insurance company's suspicion. Here is a rough recap of the dialogue:

Lawyer: "Mr. P., I have here in front of me the medical report regarding your claim, however, even after reading it twice I'm not quite clear what it is that you cannot do anymore."

Mr. P. : "Well, I have trouble moving my legs."

Lawyer (visibly more impatient now): "Yes, I can see that from the report but it still does not really tell me exactly what it is that you cannot do."

Mr. P. is now somewhat incensed by the insistence of the lawyer, and in front of the full court, he gets up and pulls his knee up to his chest with a swift and forceful action and says to the lawyer: "this is what I cannot do anymore!"

and that was the end of the court case, wrapped up quickly by the persuasiveness of observed behavior.

self-monitoring depends on the respondent's belief about the desired (or undesired) consequences of being open and honest.

Another disadvantage of a psychologist asking a patient or research participant to record her own behavior is the potential difficulty with accurate recall (especially when the events to be recorded are neither rare nor important). First of all, if one seeks to elicit information from a patient about an event that is not particularly salient (like how often did you take your pills last month?) then he may truly not be able to give a correct answer because it is not normal to pay too much attention to such details of the past. On the other hand, if asked how often he has hit his wife in the past week he will likely know the answer but will, predictably, be reluctant to honestly report such socially undesirable behavior. Similarly, there is every reason to believe that a teenager when questioned by her parents will knowingly underestimate the amount of alcohol she drank the previous night. The bottom line is that self-monitoring behavior

- Is relatively inexpensive
- Can cover a long period of time

- Can be very representative of this person's habits
- Can be of high ecological validity, but may not be an honest report if the behavior was undesirable and socially unaccepted

The context and the habits and values of observers all have an influence on what gets observed and recorded. Minimizing such biases is critical for the appropriate use of observation in clinical psychology, and a number of techniques will be described later in this chapter on how this can be achieved.

The second critical feature that was introduced in the example of the driver running a red light was that of knowing versus not knowing that one is being observed. This feature of observations is referred to as **obtrusive** versus **unobtrusive**. When we know that we are being watched, the observation is obtrusive, and we may behave in a fashion that protects our self-image or avoids punishment, and therefore this knowledge makes the measurement situation itself **reactive** (given that it may affect our subsequent behavior). For the most part, this is a serious threat to the validity of a behavioral test, but it can also have a desirable side effect. A smoker who for the first time actually records his exact number of cigarettes smoked may end up reducing his smoking behavior over time because this realization becomes a stimulus for change. Interestingly, accurate recording of behavior can be the trigger for positive change, and this point also teaches that assessment can be continuously and constructively woven into the therapy program itself. A therapist can take full advantage of this by encouraging self-monitoring and thereby hoping to achieve behavior change.

The potentially reactive nature of obtrusive measurement does not always invalidate the obtained results. For example, if an individual with a phobia of dogs shows the therapist that she will not get any closer than 10 meters to a dog without experiencing a great deal of fear, then the fact that the therapist is present and the patient is aware of his presence is not likely to invalidate the self-reported fear. The patient has already revealed that she is anxious of dogs and therefore does not need to create a different image. Similarly, if at the end of therapy she is capable of patting a dog, then this approach behavior can be seen as a success that does not require interpretation, and the obtrusiveness of the situation is not a validity threat.

Given that obtrusive observation may change the behavior itself, this does create a potential validity problem. It would be ideal if all behavioral observations were made by objective individuals without any knowledge on the part of the observed. Under the law, behavior shown in what is presumed to be a public place can be legally observed by anybody without restrictions. Insurance companies, for example, can legally use private detectives with video cameras to follow individuals around who have made questionable claims for disability benefits. If such a claimant later says in court that he is too weak to lift an office chair but is shown via unobtrusive video-recording to be helping a friend carry a piano up the third floor, the case will get quickly dismissed. On the other hand, there are ethical guidelines and laws governing unobtrusive observation of people who have reason to believe that they are in a private environment (like their own home). Therefore, a psychologist is typically prevented from making unobtrusive observations about such behaviors as whether parents were abusing their children at home or not. Doing so is unethical and probably illegal. Therefore, an inherent problem with behavioral observation is that the unobtrusive observation, that we consider most valid, is legal and ethical only if it is applied to public behavior. This raises the question whether any kind of obtrusive measurement can still be "valid and not reactive." Fortunately, that is the case. Clinical experience has shown that when couples in marital therapy are asked to discuss an issue of long-standing disagreement, experienced marital therapists know that within mere minutes these couples get angry at each other in such a way that their dispute seems utterly genuine, likely reflecting just what goes on at home. Or, if an individual is extremely anxious of giving a public speech and is asked in a treatment group to give a practice speech (also referred to as **role-play** here), the resulting anxiety is likely very real and reflective of this person's typical response. In sum, whether or not one can trust the observation of behavior depends on the context, the obtrusiveness, and any biases that observers may have, but often times the most valid form of observation (namely, unobtrusive observation) is unethical.

Maximizing the Usefulness of Observations

Key to meaningful observation and recording is a clear definition or description of the behavior to be observed. In the case of observing others, this can be achieved by creating explicit coding systems that use overt behavioral definitions for the behaviors to be recorded, and raters can be trained until they reach satisfactory concordance levels. Table 9.1 offers a lighthearted example of how such a system might be devised.

It is relatively straightforward to devise a behavioral assessment tool for individual clients and for single case use. Particularly suitable scenarios are cases with specific phobias and problematic avoidance behaviors like fears of driving over bridges or fears of deep water. The therapist may want to know how anxious the client is in the presence of the feared stimulus. Examples are the patient refusing a very desirable promotion because she has a fear of flying or has an extensive fear of water. In order to document progress in therapy, one can, together with a client, create a hierarchy of fear-arousing situations on the theme of flying or proximity to water. This can be done by placing water-related thoughts and behaviors on a scale from 0 to 100, where 100 reflects the most anxiety a client has ever experienced. Scores on such a scale are referred to as subjective units of distress (SUDs), and a client may provide a set of hierarchy steps and corresponding rankings such as those in Table 9.2.

If therapy is successful in reducing fear and minimizing avoidance behavior, then the therapy progress can be readily traced and documented by showing the client the reductions in fear ratings or the lessening of avoidance behaviors. When therapists routinely work with such clients, they can maintain a basic model or boilerplate of a **behavioral-approach avoidance test** that can be readily adjusted to the client's feared objects and the subjective anxiety level that accompanies each step in the fear hierarchy. It takes mere minutes to devise and execute such a test.

Self-Monitoring

Earlier in this chapter, it was pointed out that observations of behavior can be made by another party or by the individual himself. The principal advantages and disadvantages of each have already been discussed. In order to minimize the problem with accurate recall

TABLE 9.1 A Proposed Behavior Observation Coding System for Evaluating Candidates for Steady Boyfriend or Girlfriend

| VARIABLE | BEHAVIOR DESCRIPTION AND CODE | | | | |
	5	4	3	2	1
Generosity	Always buys thoughtful Christmas gifts for you, the mother-in-law, and the family dog	Usually buys thoughtful Christmas gifts for you	Once managed to find a decent gift	Sometimes finds a crummy gift for you at the thrift store	Borrows money from you to buy a gift for you at the thrift store
Listening skills	Guesses your thoughts before you have them	Listens carefully and understands the between-the-lines stuff	Hears half of what you say	Listens temporarily if you turn the TV sound off	Does not even notice whether you are in the room or not
Helpfulness	Gives up his or her beloved career as a brain surgeon so that you can take the hairdressing course in Alaska	Takes the bus to work in the rain and lends you his or her car when yours is in for repairs	Generously allows you to use his or her tooth paste when yours is finished	Mentions casually that your mother called three days ago, and said it was urgent	Tells you that you have a really big butt in those checkered pants you love so much
Social skills	Can convince the pope to convert to Judaism	Tells your mother with a sincere smile that the burnt cookies were delicious	Can hold a 5-minute conversation with your deaf grandfather	Pokes his or her nose only twice while your redneck cousin tells hunting stories	Keeps asking your very obese cousin when the baby is due
Sense of societal responsibility	Spends 3 months a year teaching reading to children in Antarctica and reads bedtime stories 3 times a week in a seniors home	Collects bottle caps, sorts them by size, and returns them to the factory for recycling	Drinks beer out of cans because they are easier to recycle than glass bottles	Bought only the second-largest SUV to help reduce pollution	Teaches hyperactive 10-year-olds how to have fun with fire-arms

and to facilitate quantification of recordings outside the therapist's office, it makes sense to equip patients with recording booklets that serve as diaries. More recently, researchers have moved to handheld minicomputers for diary-keeping; this eliminates expensive scoring and error-prone data entry.

TABLE 9.2   A Fear Hierarchy for a Client with Water Phobia

SUBJECTIVE UNITS OF DISTRESS	SITUATION
100	Being in deep water, unable to touch the ground or see it
80	Being in water up to one's neck, feet still touching the ground
60	Being in a shallow pool, water waist high
40	Being in a children's pool, water ankle deep
25	Standing beside large swimming pool
20	Thinking about a boat ride
10	Thinking about taking the children to a wading pool

Summary

In this section we described efforts to make the assessment of behavior standardized and structured so that change can be easily tracked over time. This facilitates comparisons between different people. Even outside the context of clinical psychology practice, observation of behavior is a standard feature of all interpersonal interactions, and this information is inevitably recorded and interpreted simply using common sense. If two spouses attend a party, they are likely to talk on their way home about conversations they had with others and may make comments to each other like this: "Did you notice that Suzy Q was very flirtatious with that new neighbor?" or "Like usual, Barry was a real pain in the butt, totally dominated the conversation and got worse as he drank more." All this is to say that informal behavioral assessment is part of everyday life and not at all reserved for clinical psychologists. The difference, of course, between everyday observation and assessment by professionals is the level of training needed for inter-rater reliability and the standardization of the assessment approach.

◇ BIOLOGICAL ASSESSMENTS

Books on psychological assessment and clinical psychology textbooks usually ignore biological assessment. Why do other clinical psychologists ignore the topic when it is considered important in this book?

Underlying this claimed "neglect" of biological assessments is an odd paradox in the development of diagnostic procedures. Clinical psychologists tend to work with the same kinds of patients as the ones who are seen by psychiatrists. The particular strength of a medical approach to psychiatry is its strong knowledge base in the biological origins of psychiatric disorder, and this knowledge is the foundation upon which psychopharmacological treatment rests, which in turn is the unique forte of psychiatrists as mental health professionals. For example, the treatment of depression with a **selective serotonin reuptake inhibitor** is the logical conclusion of research findings that the production and processing of serotonin is disturbed in depressed patients (Rausch, 1986); and similarly, the treatment of bipolar disorder with lithium is based on research showing that in these patients the internal production of lithium, a naturally occurring mineral, is insufficient (Geddes, Burgess, Hawton, Jamison, & Goodwin, 2004). Note also that psychiatric disorders placed in Axis I of the *DSM-IV-R* (American Psychiatric Association, 2000; see description in chapter 5) are characterized by emotional distress, and it is the associated suffering that brings the patient into therapy. Furthermore, the basic literature on emotion describes it as an experience that has cognitive, affective, and biological components that interact with each other to define what an emotion is (Schachter & Singer, 1962). So, why mention all this? Where does this lengthy introduction lead?

Considering these points leads up to the striking observation that "in the routine diagnosis of psychiatric disorder there is not a single biological test used to determine a diagnosis nor track change in psychiatric disease." Psychiatric diagnoses are based on the self-report of patients, the observations of (erratic or dysfunctional) behavior by others, and, of course, the observations of mental health professionals who interact with these patients. Given that psychiatrists who are biologically trained and work with the same type of patients that clinical psychologists work with do not use biological measures, it is not surprising that many clinical psychologists don't think of biological measures as being a potential "bread and butter" tool for their practice either. However, in this book, a strong case is made that the omission of biological measures also means ignoring interesting information that could otherwise be used to assist the clinical psychologist's work, both in research and in daily practice.

Coverage of this topic requires a brief review of some basic physiological principles so that it is clear what can be measured and why biological assessment is of interest. It will be shown which features of particular health problems can be inferred using biological measures. Next, it will be shown how physiological parameters can be measured, and the choice of suitable tools and measurement protocols will be described. This will include detailed descriptions of specific clinical situations where such biological measures may be of use, and demonstrations will be given of the reliability and validity of such tools for various purposes.

Physiological Systems

The purpose of this section is not to repeat what a full-fledged textbook of physiology does. The focus here is on those physiological functions that are related to the *emotions, thoughts,* and *behaviors* that clinical psychologists deal with. They include the following *negative emotions*: anger, depression, and anxiety/fear. At the *cognitive level*, prevailing attributes of psychopathology are obsessions/ruminations; poor judgment; and inability to focus, foresee consequences, and make decisions. At a *behavioral level*, degree of activation is critical in that both extreme lethargy and hyperactivity are signs of problems. Hence, clinical psychologists are interested in brain activity, central nervous system activity, endocrine functions, and control of voluntary muscles.

In this chapter we will consider only the measures that can be routinely used in a psychologist's office or research laboratory and that do not require any kind of invasive procedures like urine, saliva, or blood sampling. Measures that require sampling of specimens, transferring of samples to a biomedical laboratory, and a "few-day-wait" for test

TABLE 9.3 Classification of Physiological Measures

ELECTRICAL	ABBREVIATION	FUNCTION
Electroencephalography	EEG	Measures electrical activity in the brain; is an excellent marker of sleep stage, attention, and emotion
Electromyogram	EMG	Measures muscular tension; is responsive to voluntary muscle enervation, anger, and stress
Electrocardiogram	ECG (also EKG)	Measures cyclical activity of the heart; in psychophysiology mostly used to extract heart rate and variability in heart rate
Electrodermal activity (also Galvanic skin response)	EDA (also GSR)	Is an excellent, quick-responding marker of sympathetic nervous system activity
Pressure/volume/temperature/frequency		
Blood pressure	SBP and DBP	Marks highest (SBP) and lowest (DBP) pressure found in vasculature depending on where the cardiac cycle is at; respond moderate quickly to motor effort (SBP), emotional distress (SBP and DBP), and cognitive effort
Heart rate	HR	Is greatly affected by all motor effort but also by anger and anxiety
Heart rate variability	HRV	Changes with pain and stress
Respiration rate	RR	Increases with greater required motor effort and anxiety
Breathing volume	No particular abbreviation is popular	Reflects oxygen uptake; is reduced during anxiety
Actigraphy	No particular abbreviation is popular	Measures motor efforts and energy expenditure

results are not good candidates for routine use in clinical psychological practice. This limits the measures to be discussed to those that are electrical in nature and those that measure frequencies or changes in physical pressure or body motion. Table 9.3 summarizes measures that fit these classifications. Names and abbreviations (which will be used in the remainder of the chapter) as well as the function that is actually being measured are listed.

When using the information obtained with these measures, one needs to distinguish two classes of use for these measures.

1. The first class or type of use taps into *general levels of activation* and *inhibition* and requires some degree of inference to connect obtained data to specific psychiatric diagnoses. For example, we know that when people are angry, their blood pressure and heart rate rises, their breathing often speeds up, their muscles tense, and the increase in blood pressure is strongly affected by a narrowing of the blood vessels also referred to as vasoconstriction. Anxiety, on the other hand, is also an emotional state associated with physiological activation but is different in that the sympathetic arousal is largely driven by an increase in cardiac activity and less so by concomitant changes in the diameter of blood vessels (Watkins, Grossman, Krishnan, & Sherwood, 1998). Depressed individuals can be differentiated from nondepressed individuals by studying their heart rate patterns over at least 24 hours. A non-depressed person tends to show a prompt drop in heart rate when going to bed; it remains low and stable while sleeping and rises promptly on awakening, whereas a depressed patient shows noticeably greater variability (Gaetz et al., 2004; Iverson et al., 2005). If one were to measure physiological changes during anxiety, a recommended set of measures would be heart rate and electrodermal activity (given that anxiety is characterized by heightened sympathetic arousal which these two measures are reflective of). What the clinical psychologist needs to be aware of is the fact that these physiological functions can have multiple origins such that heart rate can change for many reasons other than anxiety. Primarily, heart rate will respond to changes in motor demand and reflect effort. Heart rate may easily rise from 60 to 100 beats per minute when a person gets anxious, but it can also increase by 40 points because the same individual carries too heavy bags of groceries up four flights of stairs (while happily whistling). This is to demonstrate that when physiological indices are used to tap into activation or inhibition, the psychologist needs to consider alternative explanations and account for them. When the context is known and reasonably well-controlled, then the interpretation and inference is easy. The psychologist working with a dog phobic may attach a heart rate monitor to the patient and record a resting heart rate of 70 beats per minute. When a helper soon thereafter brings a (hopefully harmless) dog into the office and the patient's heart rate jumps to 120 beats per minute without the patient actually physically moving about, then it is clear that the introduction of the dog, the feared stimulus, is the reason for the heart rate change.

2. The second use of biological measures is particularly easy to interpret. Here, very specific biological functions are measured because they are specific and endemic to the presenting problem, or they are the presenting problem (like high blood pressure). Table 9.4 provides a listing of various clinical problems a psychologist in a health setting may work with, and it suggests types of biological measures that index these dysfunctions.

A particularly good example may be hypertension, or high blood pressure, which not only has a strong physiological basis but is also greatly affected by psychological stress (Linden,

TABLE 9.4   Clinical Problems and Suitable Measures

CLINICAL PROBLEM	SUITABLE MEASURES
Arthritis	Finger temperature, electromyogram
Asthma	Airway resistance, frontal electromyogram
Bruxism	Frontalis, masseter, and temporalis electromyogram
Cardiac arrhythmias	Breathing activity, heart rate variability
Urinary incontinence	Bladder muscle electromyogram
Hyperactivity	EEG
Hypertension	Blood pressure, heart rate, breathing activity, finger temperature
Migraine	Frontalis electromyogram, finger temperature
Raynaud's disease	Finger temperature

2006). Psychologists can be involved in the treatment of individuals with high blood pressure. When a treatment program of biofeedback and relaxation (Yucha et al., 2001) leads to a large decrease in blood pressure levels, no inference is required. With hypertension reduced and remaining low, treatment would be called successful, and the associated risk for cardiovascular disease is also reduced (Linden, 2006).

Or, to take another example, a patient presents with stress incontinence, which is the result of a dysfunctional interplay of bladder releasing and tensing muscles. This is evident in pelvic floor muscle activity, which can be measured by attaching electrodes in the area of these muscles (Bernstein, Philips, Linden, & Fenster, 1991). The patient can be taught via EMG biofeedback to control these muscles and re-establish a synergistic function (Burgio et al., 1998). When this synergistic function is re-established and apparent on the muscular tension monitors, the therapist knows that the stress incontinence has been resolved. No further measures and no inferences are needed.

Measurement of Physiological Activity

When psychologists and other researchers began monitoring physiological functions, this was a laborious undertaking involving fairly expensive equipment, a lot of training, and time. The standard tool for data acquisition in the past was a polygraph that was rather cumbersome because it required lots of maintenance, keeping ink-fed pens going and feeding reams of chart paper into the machine. Then came the tedious extraction of data by hand, translating squiggly lines into meaningful numbers.

There is little doubt that the complexity of polygraph use has in the past prevented many psychologists from considering biological measures. However, since the 1980s, the advances in signal acquisition and processing hardware and software have been dramatic, and the result is equipment that is much easier to handle. Data can now be automatically translated into digital information that can be displayed on a computer screen and stored on desktop or laptop computers. The information that required a $20,000 to $30,000 machine for assessment in 1980 can be obtained today with equipment costing only a fraction of these amounts, and it is dramatically more user-friendly. Proper usage of a digital heart rate or automatic blood pressure monitor, for example, can be explained to a research assistant or graduate student in less than half an hour. Nevertheless, use of biological measures does require knowledge of the underlying physiology just as the use of a multifactorial personality inventories (see chapter 7) requires diligent background training.

When purchasing equipment, experience has taught that it is good to have the following characteristics in the equipment one uses:

1. The device should have the capability to display analog signal forms (like different pitches of sound, light bars that rise and go down, or waveforms) because these are often easiest to work with for clients. In addition, of course, the device should have the capability of translating the information into digital signals because these signals are easily stored for later analysis or entered into a patient's chart. Furthermore, many physiological functions are easily understood in digital form even by laypeople. Good examples are heart rate (described as beats per minute) and breathing rate (defined as breaths per minute). These functions need little explanation. Changes in muscle tension, on the other hand, are better displayed as changes in the height of light-bars, which change as tension increases or decreases. The key here is flexibility in the display modes because different clients may have different favorite display modes.

2. It is a good idea to purchase equipment that allows for multichannel recording even if the typical user will need only one or two channels at a time. The reason for this is cost savings. The basic data acquisition processing hardware is the same for a lot of different functions, and having a device that can process six or eight of these functions is hardly more expensive than one that can process only one channel. There will be additional cost, of course, in the different transducers required for each function. The clinician who works with a number of different psychophysiological disorders like pain, muscle injury, cardiovascular problems, or general stress issues might want to buy a system that can measure (a) muscle tension, (b) electrodermal activity, (c) blood pressure, (d) heart rate, (e) breathing rate, and (f) breathing depth. Any device that measures heart rate also has the basic potential to compute heart rate variability, which has become the recent focus of attention and excitement for cardiac, hypertension, asthma, and pain applications (Berntson et al., 1997).

3. Another feature to consider is the need for signal averaging that can be adjusted by the user. If, for example, the clinician wants to use a heart rate monitor to assist in the treatment of phobic patients, the device should show heart rate changes maybe every 10 or 20 seconds, but not much more often or less often. If the signals change too frequently, the user becomes confused and preoccupied and tries to desperately interpret each change as meaningful when it was just random variation. If changes in the signal, in this case heart rate, are shown only every 2 minutes or even less often, then an interesting psychological process that produced a quick heart rate change would get missed. In order to make smart choices for picking the right signal averaging length, the user needs to be aware how quickly the physiological functions they are monitoring respond to differences in environmental stimuli. Electrodermal activity, for example, can change in seconds, whereas diastolic blood pressure (the second number of the two blood pressure values that are usually given) takes considerably longer to respond and may take a minute or two before it noticeably rises or drops.

Reliability and Validity

Many issues around reliability of measurement are resolved due to the fact that biological assessment tools are carefully developed by manufacturers, tested, and then approved by the Federal Drug Administration in the United States or similar government agencies in other countries. If these tools are found unreliable, they are not approved for the market or will quickly lose out against the competition that builds better equipment. In addition, reliability during the actual assessment process is improved by taking multiple measures and then averaging them, just as a personality test is more likely reliable if it measures a construct with a number of inter-related items. Test-retest stability for many physiological functions is very high and frequently exceeds r = .8. In terms of validity, the same approval process described for tool reliability also serves to establish that the tool measures what it is supposed to measure. When it comes to measuring things like muscular tension or heart rate, there is no question about interpretation because all approved instruments measure what they are supposed to measure. Of course, there is always the risk of measurement error arising from improper application of a sensor, poor preparation of skin, or inadequate training of the individual conducting the assessment.

Some inference is required when estimating the validity of a physiological function like electrodermal activity that is being used as an index of sympathetic arousal, and the sympathetic arousal is measured because it is indicative of heightened anxiety. Can one reasonably claim that every change in electrodermal activity is indicative of a change in anxiety? No, we cannot, because there can be confounding effects like differences in room temperature, humidity levels, or preoccupations of the patient that a therapist does not know about. On the other hand, there is strong evidence of criterion validity in that changes in anxiety in a controlled setting reliably translate into changes in electrodermal activity or heart rate (Keller, Hicks, & Miller, 2000).

Applications

The listing of potential measurement and therapy applications in Table 9.4 includes a wide range of presenting problems that clinical psychologists may work with. Many of these applications are not directly reflective of psychopathology as defined in a categorization system like the *DSM-IV*, but they are often symptomatic of definable psychiatric disorders. Especially patients reporting with Axis I disorders often report sleep problems. Also, distressing affect is not always precisely described as anxiety or depression by patients, but some describe this problem as "stress." The body's response to stress activates the autonomic system, and endocrine functions can be measured to index stress (although many of these are invasive and more suited for research investigations than for clinical assessments).

There is a massive literature within the domain of health psychology and psychosomatic medicine showing the consistency with which stress is measurable via biological indices.

A large subsample of patients in general hospitals and outpatient clinics present with chronic pain problems, and they also frequently report sleep problems that can be tested via actigraphs (Wilson, Watson, & Currie, 1998). Muscular pain is reliably indexed by increased EMG activity. Individuals with post-traumatic stress disorder frequently report sleep disturbances and heightened arousal levels, which can be also be documented biologically. Phobias have concomitant sympathetic activation that can be measured. And, attention deficit and hyperactivity disorder (ADHD) in children and adults is often linked to differential brainwave activity, which has actually led to the development of EEG biofeedback protocols for the treatment of ADHD (Thompson & Thompson, 2005). In sum, there are many areas of practice for clinical psychologists where biological assessments function as complementary assessment tools, and it is a bit puzzling that these methods are not receiving more attention in other books dealing with assessment.

One particular advantage of physiological assessment is that it is minimally reactive, and it is fairly difficult for patients to fake a particular physiological response. Here is an interesting clinical case example to support this point:

> A 40-year-old woman, Ms Susan Y, with a chronic pain condition in one lower arm, was trying to settle a disability claim with the local Workers Compensation Board. When we saw her in our teaching clinic, she was angry and bitter that after 2 years there was no settlement yet. Her rather thick medical chart revealed no x-ray or other hard medical evidence that suggested a cause for the pain but her pain report was so consistent and coherent that we did not doubt her. We decided to devise a quick test to seek, if possible, an incontrovertible biological demonstration for the pain and its associated dysfunction. Ms Y could not know in advance what we were about to do because it had not been done before. We attached electrodes to both arms and assessed resting muscle tension via EMG using a structured protocol; essentially there was no difference between the two arms even when the channels on the recorder were switched. Next, we devised a quick test of actual muscle use by asking her to pick up a can of peas, grip the can firmly, hold it for 10 seconds, and put it back down on the table. During this activation test the healthy arm showed exactly the response we expected, namely a prompt increase in EMG which was stable as long as she gripped the can of peas, and then relaxed when she put the can down again. In contrast, the arm in which chronic pain and weakness was reported, showed no such muscular response doing the exact same activity. Although we never learned how the case was settled, it was still gratifying to see that Ms Y had finally seen some evidence that there was a factual difference between the two arms, and that she was not faking it as she had been given to believe [between the lines, of course, because nobody would say so directly].

This little bit of detective work was very enjoyable.

Another innovative and informative way of using physiological assessment has been applied to the identification of individually relevant stressors in a stress management approach to the treatment of high blood pressure. This methodology, referred to as hypertension individualized treatment (HIT; Linden, 2006), involves patients being continuously monitored during the assessment interview. Given that the assessor now has parallel access to very different sources of information, namely, verbal self-report and biological activity, it allows a structured, yet patient-centered approach to identifying the most promising targets for therapy and an opportunity for client and therapist to develop a strong alliance.

◇ CONCLUSION

Both behavioral and biological assessments are very distinct from interviewing methods and questionnaires discussed in chapter 7. They likely fit less into the stereotypes that outsiders have of psychological testing procedures where the Rorschach Inkblot Test may well qualify as the most intriguing and prototypical of all psychological tests. Behavioral and biological assessments are less often used than interviews and questionnaires, may be more expensive, and require additional training or efforts to tailor the observation of behavior and biology to case- and situation-specific methodologies and rating systems. These insights may seem to argue against frequent use of either behavioral or biological assessment. On the other hand, both approaches give a free hand to clinicians and researchers to create tools on short notice and maybe even for a singular use. Both methods allow (under certain circumstances that we discussed earlier) to collect unbiased data, which are then easy to trust. Therefore, both of these methods are very complementary with the assessment methods described in chapter 7, and they are very important additions to the clinical psychologist's toolbox.

◇ ONGOING CONSIDERATIONS

The use of assessment instruments is greatly driven by cost and convenience factors. As such, clinical interviews and self-report questionnaires are widely popular and are not under threat of getting replaced. Nevertheless, we urge clinical psychology students and practitioners to learn more about and use both behavioral and physiological assessment more often. Technological advances are steadily increasing the user-friendliness of biological measures, and especially when it comes to assessments involving the courts, objective assessments are urgently called for.

◇ KEY TERMS LEARNED

Arthritis
Asthma
Behavioral-approach avoidance test
Bruxism
Cardiac arrhythmias
Hyperactivity
Hypertension
Migraine

Obtrusive
Raynaud's disease
Reactive
Role-play
Selective serotonin reuptake inhibitor
Unobtrusive
Urinary incontinence

◇ THINKING QUESTIONS

1. Why is there a likely conflict between ethics and unbiased observation when it comes to behavioral assessment?

2. What types of validity apply to a Behavioral-Approach Avoidance test?

3. What are the weaknesses of role-play tests?

4. Given that psychiatry's strength is its training in the biological basis of psychopathology, which biological assessments are routinely used to make psychiatric diagnoses?

◇ REFERENCES

American Psychiatric Association. (2000). *Diagnostic and statistical manual of mental disorders* (4th ed., text revision) (DSM-IV-TR). Washington, DC: Author.

Bernstein, A. M., Philips, H. C., Linden, W., & Fenster, H. (1991). A psychophysiological evaluation of female urethral syndrome: Evidence for a muscular abnormality. *Journal of Behavioral Medicine, 15*, 299–312.

Berntson, G. G., Bigger, J. T. Jr., Eckberg, D. L., Grossman, P., Kaufmann, P. G., Malik, M., et al. (1997). Heart rate variability: Origins, methods, and interpretive caveats. *Psychophysiology, 34*, 623–648.

Burgio, K. L., Locher, J. L., Goode, P. S., Hardin, J. M., McDowell, B. J., Dombrowski, M., & Candib, D. (1998). Behavioral vs drug treatment for urge urinary incontinence in older women: A randomized controlled trial. *JAMA, 280*, 1995–2000.

Gaetz, M., Iverson, G. L., Rzempoluck, E. J., Remick, R., McLean, P. D., & Linden, W. (2004). Self-organizing neural network analyses of cardiac data in depression. *Neuropsychobiology, 49*, 30–37.

Geddes, J. R., Burgess, S., Hawton, K., Jamison, K., & Goodwin, G. M. (2004). Long-term lithium therapy for bipolar disorder: Systematic review and meta-analysis of randomized controlled trials. *American Journal of Psychiatry, 161*, 217–222.

Iverson, G. L., Gaetz, M. B., Rzempoluck, E. J., Mclean, P., Linden, W., & Remick, R. (2005). A new potential marker for abnormal cardiac physiology in depression. *Journal of Behavioral Medicine, 13*, 1–5.

Keller, J., Hicks, B. D., & Miller, G. A. (2005). Psychophysiology in the study of psychopathology. In J. T. Cacioppo, L. G. Tassinary, & G. G. Berntson (Eds.), *Handbook of psychophysiology* (2nd ed.). New York: Cambridge University Press.

Linden, W. (2006). Treating hypertension. In: A. Kuczmierczyk & A. Nicevic (Eds.), *A case formulation approach to behavioral medicine*. London, England: Routledge & Brunner.

Rausch, J. L. (1986). The neuropsychopharmacology of serotonin function in psychiatric illness. In L. L. Judd & P. M. Groves (Eds.), *Psychobiological foundations of clinical psychiatry* (Vol. 4.). New York: Basic Books.

Schachter, S., & Singer, J. E. (1962). Cognitive, social and physiological determinants of emotional state. *Psychological Review, 69*, 379–399.

Thompson, L., & Thompson, M. (2005). Neurofeedback intervention for adults with ADHD. *Journal of Adult Development, 12,* 123–130.

Watkins, L. L., Grossman, P., Krishnan, R., & Sherwood, A. (1998). Anxiety and vagal control of heart rate. *Psychosomatic Medicine, 60,* 498–502.

Wilson, K. G., Watson, S. T., & Currie, S. R. (1998). Daily diary and ambulatory activity monitoring of sleep in patients with insomnia associated with chronic musculoskeletal pain. *Pain, 75,* 75–84.

Yucha, C. B., Clark, L., Smith, M., Uris, P., LaFleur, B., & Duval, S. (2001). The effect of biofeedback in hypertension. *Applied Nursing Research (ANR), 14,* 29–35.

CHAPTER TEN

THE PROCESS OF PSYCHOTHERAPY

CHAPTER OBJECTIVE

There is something profoundly mysterious about psychotherapy. What happens in therapy sessions is not open for public inspection because clients want and deserve privacy. This is further complicated by the difficulty in describing the process of a therapy session—its accomplishments, failures, and idiosyncrasies—once it is over. It is tempting to want to learn about psychotherapies by quickly jumping into elaborate descriptions of therapy techniques and methods employed by practitioners. This attempt, however, may not allow the introductory student therapist the ability to truly understand the complexity of the therapeutic process and the emotionally intimate relationship between practitioner and client. A more comprehensive approach to learning is required. Take, for instance, the process of making furniture: You need to learn about the uses and handling of various wood-working tools, acquire an understanding of how different types of wood need to be handled, learn about glue, and so on. Applying this line of thinking to clinical psychology, the following questions are therefore tackled in this chapter:

- What is psychotherapy, and what is the necessary delivery format?
- What therapist qualities are important?
- Do some clients respond better than others?
- How much and what kind of training makes the "best" therapists?
- How long does it take before one can expect results in therapy?
- Is psychotherapy an art or just good training and experience?
- What are the typical presenting problems and themes that cut across almost all forms of therapy?
- In what ways are different sounding therapies alike?

◇ DEFINING PSYCHOTHERAPY

Therapy is much more than the application of a technique. It is a process involving the creation of an intimate relationship between two people, consisting of a sequence of inter-personal events and concurrent attempts at trying new behaviors and (hopefully) learning from these adaptations. A quick search on the web and psychology textbooks identifies an array of existing definitions, which are given here.

Psychotherapy is . . .

. . . the art and science of treating psychological, behavioral, and emotional problems by a trained and objective professional. (Cullari, 1998)

. . . the treatment of mental and emotional disorders through the use of psychological techniques designed to encourage communication of conflicts and insight into problems, with the goal being relief of symptoms, changes in behavior leading to improved social and vocational functioning, and personality growth. (from Answers.com, Health, 2007)

. . . Psychotherapy is an undefined technique applied to unspecified problems with unpredictable outcome. For this technique we recommend rigorous training. (Raimy, 1950)

. . . is not the real world. It is intimacy without friendship. Its goal is to provide you with the tools to succeed on the outside, and the caring, reassurance, and support to fail on the inside. You rehearse your life in therapy, but you live it in the world. (Jack Muskat, psychologist, *The Globe and Mail*, November 28, 1994)

Who is right? All of them? None of them? These four definitions range from curt, technical, and dry to poetic and engaging and from optimistic to cynical. The one that is the longest (the second) is likely going to appeal the most because it is very comprehensive and embraces and describes in some detail the content and the process of psychotherapy. Muskat's definition paints a rich, appealing picture of the inner qualities of therapy and touches on the dynamics of therapy. And, as the reader continues in this book, many topics will be touched on that can help understand why the cynically sounding definition (the last) has to be taken seriously, and it challenges us to be able to define ourselves and defend against such cynical stances.

◇ THE THERAPY ENVIRONMENT

Aside from content, psychotherapy, at least in its stereotypical depiction, has a distinct format that places patient and therapist together in a professional office, with comfortable chairs or a couch, with instructions to the outside world not to disrupt, and with cell phones and pagers turned off. There are many diplomas on the wall, and client and therapist see each other for one session per week, usually between 8 a.m. and 6 p.m., with the session lasting between 50 and 60 minutes.

Is that really what the visible part of psychological therapy looks like? For the most part, it is. However, there are a few needed modifications to this stereotypical portrayal.

Some therapists, for example, accommodate their patients' schedules by having evening sessions, or they open their offices to clients on Saturdays. And, of course, many psychologists work in clinics and hospitals that have their own schedules and institutional rules of practice. Nevertheless, despite the fact that most acute care hospitals provide emergency psychiatric services 24 hours a day, psychologists are not usually involved in delivering services at "off" hours.

What is the reason for one session per week, at 50 to 60 minutes a session? While this is a long-standing tradition in the field, there is terribly little evidence that any of these structured regulations are required. Of course, psychotherapists will argue that one needs a reasonable amount of time to put the patient at ease and make progress on some important issues. They will also posit that it is beneficial to have time intervals between sessions so that patients can try out new behaviors or process what they have learned in the last session. On the other hand, any therapist who has worked with an angry, sullen, resistant teenager knows that even a 30-minute session may be insufferably long (for both the young client and the psychologist) and that a crisis situation with a new patient who may be traumatized or suicidal cannot easily be brought to a satisfactory end within 50 minutes. It is not unusual that a first session with such an individual may last 2 hours; the therapist may also feel compelled to book the next appointment within the next two days rather than a week later because a whole week without support and care is simply too long for a patient in profound despair.

Psychological support offered in a refugee camp in Africa does not quite fit the standard description of the therapy environment. Permission to reprint granted by Dr. Nicole Aube (2010).

What about the decorum in therapy? Does it have to happen in an office with artfully framed diplomas on the wall? Given that clinical psychology is under ongoing pressure to define its position in a very competitive marketplace, we also need to be able to understand critiques that do not necessarily understand why we have much more to offer than lay-helpers who took a few weekend courses. Nevertheless, to clarify this critical difference, we need to understand where the criticisms come from. A number of years ago, Wiesenfeld and Weis (1979) raised the intriguing question whether or not bartenders, taxi drivers, and hairdressers provide psychotherapy even though they:

- Do not claim to do so
- Have no credentials on the wall
- Don't bill for anything but the drinks consumed, the hair curled, or the kilometers driven

One can readily see that in all three professions, the practitioners spend long periods of time with individuals in a relatively private interaction. The clients may be somewhat vulnerable, may have a loosened tongue brought on by boredom or alcohol, and are seated in a comfortable resting position. Both are captive to one another, at least for a while. If the definition of psychotherapy pivots around reduction of distress achieved by talking about one's feelings in a somewhat private environment, surely all three of these professions may indeed qualify as psychotherapists even without diplomas hanging off the visor of the taxi or the back wall of the bar. While this proposition may sound a little frivolous and superficial, it nevertheless stresses that psychotherapy is difficult to define. When it comes to legislative attempts to differentiate formal psychotherapy from a pleasant and beneficial generic human interaction, the primary differences are (a) the degree of formal education and credentialing the professional has obtained, (b) the fact that the clinical psychologist has been trained to diagnose psychological problems and build a treatment program that maps onto the diagnosis and a thorough understanding of the client's life circumstances, and (c) the jointly agreed upon role definitions and structure between therapist and client.

◇ HOMEWORK ASSIGNMENTS

For most therapies, therapists think of the time between therapy sessions as a great opportunity for patients to reflect on insights gained or practice skills learned in the therapist's office and to acquire new experiences. Even short-term psychodynamic treatments may also involve homework. These experiences can be brought back to the next session to determine what topics are worked on next. Note, however, that although techni-cally correct, the term "homework" has connotations of the client being a child, and it may be better to use the term "opportunity to practice new skills" or "time to reflect." Consistent with the learning theories that define behavioral treatments, practicing new skills is not a stigmatized activity, and behavioral therapists give home assignments just like school teachers give home assignments or piano teachers ask their students to practice between lessons. The therapist may ask a very shy client to initiate a few very simple, nonthreatening conversations with strangers or may ask a student scared to speak out in class to explicitly try out a half-dozen simple questions in class to expose himself or herself to a feared speaking situation. The benefit of homework assignments is that they can accelerate the learning that can happen in therapy, and a number of studies have explicitly evaluated the effectiveness of homework assignments over and above the benefit derived from treatment itself. In a meta-analysis of available trials evaluating the benefit of homework assignments, Kazantzis, Deane, and Roman (2000) found that the additional homework was associated with significant additional improvements and that the degree of compliance with the assigned homework also positively affected the therapy outcome. Given that homework assignment does not increase the cost of therapy itself but appears to speed up progress, there is nothing speaking against its routine use.

◇ THERAPY LENGTH

An experienced car mechanic can tell you with a fair bit of accuracy that replacing a muffler requires one hour of labor and a major transmission repair 2 days, but no clinical psychologist can give you an early and yet accurate estimate of how many therapy sessions are needed before a problem is "fixed." For starters, it is quite subjective what "fixed" means, and most clients will have more than one presenting problem; sometimes not all of these problems are even identified in the first session. Also, clients vary in their readiness for change, and it is extremely difficult to define what a natural end of therapy is, although it may be very informative and useful to ask a client in the intake interview about his or her expectations (i.e., "How will we know when you have reached your goals in therapy?"). We suggest recording this answer and documenting the client's advancement toward this goal as the sessions move forward. Also, we recommend a review of progress at a perceived midpoint of therapy.

Anecdotal evidence suggests that many psychotherapies do not end with both parties agreeing at the same time that the goal has been reached, where the client says, "Thank you, I feel much better now and can go at it alone" (occasionally such moments of victory are accompanied by a box of chocolates handed over to the therapist). Much more typical is that a client advances reasonably well, and at some point the therapist receives a phone call a few days prior to the scheduled session, where the client says, "I'm sorry but I will not be able to keep our Tuesday session because I am under a lot of pressure at work. Can I call you next week when things are lightening up a little bit to set up another session?" This promised phone call may never come, or the client will also cancel the next scheduled session. In order for the therapist himself or herself to receive some closure, he or she may be proactive and call the client and directly ask this question: "Do you really think that we should schedule another session, or do you think that this is a good point to terminate?" There is an excellent chance that the answer to this question is, "I think you're right, we don't need to meet again. Thank you for what you've done for me." Rather than having a stereotypical, textbook termination meeting, many (actually successful) therapies peter out in this rather inelegant way. It requires a confident therapist with a strong ego to interpret this scenario as a sign of success. On the other hand, some psychotherapists place importance on the termination aspect itself and see it as pivotal to treatment success.

Given his inexperience, our graduate student Vincent may find this diffuse ending rather frustrating and interpret it as a sign of failure. It takes an experienced supervisor to point out that this is a fairly typical end to a therapeutic relationship and should actually be interpreted as a good sign. Also, one should keep in mind that the purpose of therapy is not to make the therapist feel better but to help the client.

We still have not answered the question regarding how much therapy is needed. In clinical practice (as opposed to within clinical research trials), treatment lengths vary greatly, but the most studied type of therapy outcomes is for clinicians working under the umbrella of third-party payers, such as insurance companies. Here the average number of sessions is around five, and only about 20% of studied patients show notable improvement within these five sessions (Hansen, Lambert, & Forman, 2002). It is equally tempting for clients who pay out-of-pocket to keep the number of therapy sessions to a minimum due to the expenses incurred. In the controlled research environment, one large-scale review indicated that a mean observed length of 12.7 sessions equated to clinically meaningful improvements in 58–67% of patients (Hansen et al., 2002). This strongly suggests that five sessions are rarely enough, but it also tells us that there is often no need to spend years in therapy either. Therefore, it is suggested to avoid overly short exposure to treatment as is typical in third-party payer environments and instead target intervention lengths to provide about 10–20 hours of therapy, with more time being devoted to clients who bring complex, long-standing problems to the psychologist's office.

◇ MULTICLIENT THERAPY

So far, therapy has been described as an interaction between two people and that is the most likely scenario. However, sometimes therapy consists of families or couples who come together to the therapy sessions; this applies especially for cases of marital therapy. Also, a multiclient approach is most likely when the therapist has a systems orientation (discussed in much more detail in chapter 11). There are other instances when a good therapist will ask, at least occasionally, that a family member join the session. This may be needed, for example, when a caregiver who is close to burning out supports a client with long-standing troubles; in this case the therapist may want to support the caregiver as well. Or, as has been shown for behavioral weight loss programs, the intervention is much more effective when family members are brought into the intervention and are taught similar skills and are "sworn in" to work collaboratively toward healthier eating for the whole family (Pearce, LeBow, & Orchard, 1981). Sometimes the therapist simply wants to get a different perspective on the problem to better understand how a client functions in his or her natural environment.

At this point it may also be worth stressing that a psychotherapist can use a wide variety of theoretical orientations to conceptualize a given case even if the techniques ultimately chosen are derived from a more narrowly focused orientation like

Group therapy session at Hospice Michel Sarrazin, Quebec, Canada. Photographer: Henri Dupond

cognitive-behavioral or interpersonal therapy. It may be very helpful to meet for a while with the whole family to help a client with anorexia even if part of the therapy consists of working with the client alone. Occasionally, the therapist may sense that a family member subtly or openly sabotages the attempt of the client to change. This is particularly likely to happen if, for example, a client wants to quit smoking but her spouse continues to smoke or a client wants to improve his dietary habits but other family members do not want to face the fact that they are also overweight and also have very unhealthy eating habits. Ultimately, it is a combination of the therapist's choice of theoretical orientation and good training and intuition that will inform when it is best to see a client together with a spouse and/or other family members. We teach our students that every therapist needs at least some skills to work in multiclient treatment because that is often the best way to deal with relationship issues that may arise during the course of therapy, even if the initial presenting problem did not directly suggest that the involvement of a partner might be necessary somewhere down the road.

Also, there are both theoretical and economic reasons for wanting to conduct psychotherapy in groups. The more the focus is on psychoeducation, the more it makes sense to do this kind of teaching in a group format. Independent of economical factors, therapy groups have the advantage of patients learning from one another. Both critical and flattering feedback when coming from a group member may carry more weight than the same feedback coming from the therapist.

◊ ELEMENTS IN THE PROCESS OF THERAPY

Psychotherapy cannot be reduced to a technique. The ultimate therapy outcome is presumed to result from a constructive process whereby an attempt is made to maximize:

- Client variables (socioeconomic status, culture, gender, personality, readiness for change)
- Qualities of the therapist (level of education, skill, orientation, experience)
- The most suitable choice of treatment technique or theoretical orientation

The choice of technique, coupled with the interaction of therapist and patient and the type of relationship they develop, shapes the therapy process. Therefore, it makes sense to first look at the patient and client characteristics separately and then try to describe how they can be joined to maximize therapy effectiveness. First, we will discuss what the client himself or herself brings to the first therapy session.

◊ THE CLIENT

Who Goes into Therapy?

The modal client in psychotherapy is female, in her 20s or 30s, and is fairly well educated. On the whole, these client characteristics are associated with good outcomes because these clients tend to have objectively good potential for improvement, and they have been labeled **YAVIS clients** (Young, Attractive, Verbal, Intelligent, and Successful) (Brown, 1970; Schofield, 1964). Having said that, however, the literature on client characteristics and therapy outcomes suggests that stable individual differences like socioeconomic status or gender are not particularly important for predicting treatment success or failure (Garfield, 1978, Clarkin & Levy, 2004). Psychotherapists have successfully worked with clients in their 60s who have finally decided that the price they have paid for a rotten childhood, in terms of emotional and psychological impact, is too high, and they wish to enjoy their remaining years without an emotional albatross hanging around their neck. There are no known differences in therapy success for men or women, and although ethnic minorities are less likely to go into therapy, the evidence suggests that they benefit from therapy just as much as do nonminority clients (Miranda et al., 2005).

Client Readiness

More critical to the success of therapy, however, is clients' ability to understand and verbalize their own inner experience and to work successfully with the fact that psychotherapy is a verbal exchange of information. Although verbal skills are considered important in the definition of intelligence, there are many intelligent people who are not necessarily well-prepared for psychotherapy. Pivotal to the differentiation between people who benefit from traditional psychotherapy and those who do not is their ability to access, understand, and verbalize their own emotional experience. Lane and Schwartz (1987) extensively studied this ability and proposed the construct of **levels of emotional awareness** (EA), from which they developed an interview-based assessment for individual differences in EA. They have purported that the growth in the ability to be aware and manage emotions is similar to the developmental stage model proposed by Jean Piaget (see Huitt & Hummel, 2003). Becoming more sophisticated in emotional processing is to a large degree age related, in that very young children, especially those who are not yet verbal, have only the most primitive tools to express affect, namely, by either crying or smiling. Emotional expression becomes more sophisticated as people age, and this development tends to run parallel (but not always) with the growth in their language skills. Nevertheless, depending on the social environment, available role models, potentially innate differences in verbal giftedness, and the presence or absence of trauma, people develop differential abilities to process and verbalize emotion. Lane and Schwartz (1987) have summarized their model in Table 10.1,

TABLE 10.1 Psychotherapeutic Interventions Based on Five Levels of Emotional Awareness

LEVEL	PRINCIPAL REPRESENTATION MODE	NATURE OF PSYCHOPATHOLOGY	PATIENT'S GOAL	THERAPIST'S GOAL	TYPE OF INTERVENTION
5	Blends of blends	Existential crisis	Resolve major life decision	Promote comparative quantitative discrimination between patterns of emotions across context	Existential; insight oriented
4	Blends of experience	Emotional conflict (e.g., depression)	Help with work and relation-ship difficulties	Resolve intrapsychic conflicts	Insight oriented
3	Unidimensional experience	Persistent conscious distress (e.g., depression)	Relief of distress	Diminish inten-sity of distress; expand range of experience	Cognitive therapy; sup-portive psy-chotherapy
2	Actions or action tenden-cies	Impulsive or com-petitive (e.g., sub-stances abuse)	Stop prob-lematic behavior and over-come inhi-bitions	Render actions more adaptive, less self-destructive, expand behav-ioral repertoire	Behavior modification; movement therapy; physicist restraint
1	Bodily sensa-tions	Somatic distress (e.g., sanitization disorder)	Relief of physical distress	Alter physio-logical under-pinning of emotional state	Pharmacological; biofeedback; relaxation

describing five different levels of emotional experience and providing commentary for each level of experience with respect to implications for psychotherapy (Table 10.2).

In this model, clients with differential levels of emotional sophistication are predicted to present with different types of psychopathology and may also have different treatment goals. Therapists need to adjust their interactions to suit the client's presenting mode and use appropriately matched interventions. We urge the reader to study the information contained in Table 10.2, because we find that systematic integration of this knowledge greatly facilitates the selection of assessment tools and successful case conceptualization. Indeed, we posit that the therapist who pays careful attention to this individual difference and designs therapy correspondingly is more likely to be successful even though we cannot yet quote empirical research studies to support this point.

Another feature in which clients clearly differ when they enter therapy is related to the degree of distress they are experiencing. Generally, more distressed individuals are more motivated to seek help but that is true only up to a point (Garfield, 1978). Patients with complex comorbid problems and long-standing personality disorder may not respond well despite high initial distress (Mohr, 1995). Also, patients with severe depression may be so dulled and hopeless that motivation needs to be constantly challenged. An additional reason for why level of distress is a strong predictor for therapy success is that even at a statistical level, an individual scoring high on a measure of distress has a much greater potential to show improvement on this dimension (Linden & Satin, 2007).

TABLE 10.2   Sample Responses from Each Level to Scene 20 of the LEAS

You and your best friend are in the same line of work. There is a prize given annually to the best performance of the year. The two of you work hard to win the prize. One night your friend is announced the winner. How would you feel? How would your friend feel?

5. I'd feel disappointed (3) that I didn't win but ad (3) that if someone else did, that person was my friend. My friend probably deserved it! My friend would feel *happy* (3) and *proud* (3) but slightly *worried* (3) that my feelings might be hurt (3).

4. 1 would feel depressed (3)—the friend in this light is just like any other competitor. I would also begrudgingly (2) feel *happy* (3) for my friend and rationalize that the judges had erred. My friend would feel very *gratified* (3), but would take the prize in stride to save the friendship.

3. We would both feel *happy* (3). Hey, you can't win 'em all!

2. I'd probably feel bad (2) about it for a few days, and try and figure out what went wrong. I'm sure my friend would be feeling really good (2).

1. I'd feel sick (1) about it. It's hard for me to say what my friend would feel—it would all depend on what our relationship was like and what the prize meant to her.

0. I don't work hard to win "prizes." My friend would probably feel that the judges knew what they were doing.

Characteristics of the Therapist and Outcome

In chapter 1 we discussed the question of the degree to which clinical psychologists' professional activities overlap with those of other professions. There is considerable variation in the degree of training between practicing psychotherapists and counselors. Psychiatrists with their full medical training and subsequent psychiatric residency, as well as doctoral level–trained psychologists, have spent the most time preparing for the practice of psychological therapy. A counterpoint to this claim is the fact that psychiatrists, having first completed full medical training, have spent less than half of their total professional training time in psychiatry itself. Many clinical psychologists with a PhD will have graduated from a training program that is designated a scientist-practitioner program, which means that up to half of 6–7 years of graduate work was devoted to research training rather than purely to practitioner training. This observation has been a cornerstone of the rationales for the development of professional psychology programs that focus more on clinical practice and less on research and typically award their graduates a PsyD degree. If length of training and purity of focus on clinical practice was indeed a perfect predictor for therapist ability, then graduates from PsyD programs should be superior in their clinical skills to those with PhDs from scientist-practitioner programs. If this was true, it would strengthen the argument that people who want to become primarily clinicians should complete only a professional degree program. Numerous studies (Peterson, 1982, 2003) have been conducted in clinical settings comparing the skills of the PhD and PsyD practitioners and have routinely failed to find a difference in skill level. One exception is that PhD-level clinical psychologists were found to have stronger research skills, which is not surprising considering the academic rigor of their training programs; the research-trained clinical psychologists also perform better on national licensing examinations (Kupfersmid & Fiola, 1991; McGaha & Minder, 1993; Yu et al., 1997).

Expanding the question of necessary training in the other direction means testing how much (or how little) clinical training is necessary for therapists to be effective. Given the relatively high cost of highly trained professional therapists, many institutions have attempted to save money by employing individuals with minimal training or even those who are essentially laypeople. While it is easy to demonstrate the associated immediate cost savings, it is considerably more difficult to evaluate the presumed loss of quality and therapeutic effectiveness that goes with minimal training. Durlak (1979) published an influential review paper on the effectiveness of professional and paraprofessional therapists that drew on 42 studies. The core conclusions of his review paper were:

1. Paraprofessionals achieve clinical outcomes equal to or sometimes even better than those obtained by professionals.
2. Professionals may not possess superior clinical skills relative to paraprofessionals.
3. Lengthy professional training and experience may not be necessary prerequisites for an effective therapist.

Not surprisingly, the impact of this review paper was akin to a little boy stirring a hornet's nest with a big stick because it jeopardized the raison d'etre of thousands of psychotherapy training programs worldwide. The critics were quick to pounce on these challenging conclusions. There are many reasons why results from clinical trials of paraprofessionals pitched against professionals cannot be interpreted as applying to all forms of clients in all forms of therapy (Nietzel & Fisher, 1981). Among the reasons are:

1. The typical protocol for a trial comparing professional therapists with paraprofessionals involves first a careful screening of individuals that may be suitable for such a trial; this process tends to exclude patients with comorbid problems and high-risk patients.

2. Frequently, the target groups for such comparisons involve well-defined singular problems that include eating disorders, sleep problems, relationship issues, and college students' relationship problems. Some of these problems are transient and may resolve on their own even if left untreated.

3. The paraprofessionals studied in these contexts are not random individuals picked off the street, but have typically been individuals who were previously involved in university life and who were considered by students to be wise, kind, and caring adults.

4. The design quality for comparisons described in the Durlak paper was judged to be poor, and true random assignment methodologies were the exception rather than the rule.

5. Behind Durlak's overall conclusion was the habit of drawing a no-difference conclusion even though the studies may have lacked statistical power to permit the acceptance of the null hypothesis.

6. There were many inconsistencies in the definition of professional versus paraprofessional such that graduate student therapists were often called professional although they were clearly in the training stages with very limited experience.

Arguably, it may not be possible to ever fully settle the question of how much training is needed. The preponderance of current evidence suggests that training and experience do contribute to better outcomes although the evidence is not particularly strong (Alberts & Edelstein, 1990; Mohr, 1995). In a hypothetical world, one could settle the question by recruiting a very large number of individuals off the street, randomizing them into 5 years of psychotherapy training versus no training, and making sure that those in the no-training condition truly do not acquire any kind of clinical skills for many years to come. Finally, with 5 years of training completed, one could then randomly assign clients to the trained versus untrained individuals. The clients themselves should present with highly varying problems that are truly representative of clinical settings.

Of course, this suggestion is completely hypothetical, and if this perfect study cannot be done, what do we know about the question of whether or not extensively trained therapists produce better outcomes than those with minimal training? An interesting experiment in this respect was the study of treatment effectiveness of family physicians who had been offered a 3-month crash course in cognitive-behavioral therapy. Most patients with mental disorders first present to primary care physicians (PCPs), but formal counseling techniques are rarely used. When general practitioners did receive systematic (while brief) training in cognitive-behavioral therapy, unfortunately this did not translate into gains for patients (Marton, 2002).

We don't think that a conclusive study with true random assignment of potential therapists into 5-year study protocols will ever be done because it is highly doubtful that an ethics committee would approve it or that any agency would be willing to fund such a study. However, supporting data for differential outcomes as a function of provider are available (described in chapter 13 on the outcome) from thousands of people who have undergone therapy and who provided subjective post-therapy ratings of the quality of therapy they had received from differently trained professionals (Seligman, 1995).

The discussion of how much training is needed inevitably leads to the question of how therapists should be trained. It is posited that training psychotherapists should involve careful selection of suitable individuals, training in microskills that facilitate the creation of a therapeutic alliance, and lastly, training in specific techniques (like exposure treatments or Adlerian psychotherapy). The teaching of future clinicians needs to be guided by the knowledge of which treatments are most promising for what problems and should involve skillful diagnostics and case conceptualization. Detailed information on observed outcomes for all psychotherapies is presented in chapter 13 because they are easiest to compare when presented side-by-side.

People who apply for clinical psychology programs are a self-selected group, and this raises the question of who becomes a psychotherapist. The answer to this question is important for designing training programs because one wants to (a) recruit the most promising individuals (and screen out potential problem candidates), (b) determine what they already know (i.e., prior level of knowledge), and (c) add formal, complementary training to their pre-existing level of knowledge and skill. The goal is to turn out a cohort of roughly equally competent psychotherapists. Should budding therapists be barred from training if they ever suffered themselves? We argue against such expectations of perfection because we believe that having experienced some personal distress makes these therapists more empathic and able to understand their patients. These considerations have fueled the suggestion that all therapists should first go through psychotherapy themselves as part of their training. This would indeed sensitize them to the experience of their own clients and hopefully minimize the influence of their personal problems on an effective therapy process. As shown in chapter 11, for psychoanalytically oriented therapists, such self-therapy is an essential training ingredient. Ultimately, of course, the question of whether or not personal therapy for psychotherapists should be required ought to be driven by evidence, and here it appears that, to date, there is no empirical evidence that undergoing personal therapy will improve the effectiveness of therapists' working with others (Binder, 1993). Therefore, it is difficult to argue that training programs should require that all potential therapists go through personal therapy. Notwithstanding this observation, clinical supervisors are working closely with trainees, and in this intimate teaching and learning process they get to know their trainees quite well. This can lead to the recognition that a trainee may occasionally have personal problems or personality features that do interfere with successfully becoming a psychotherapist. Professors who have taught in clinical training programs will have encountered a number of students who have benefited from personal therapy even though they may have been initially reluctant to receive help. Most likely this reluctance arises from a perception that the student who agrees that he can benefit from therapy himself would be seen as tarnished. Hopefully, those training programs that suggest personal therapy for a particular student who comes to their attention also make sure that personal therapy is a positive learning and growth process to which the student willingly commits without fear of repercussions. Occasionally, clinical faculty involved in therapist training do encounter students who are intellectually gifted but not particularly suitable for clinical work; here the question is whether a program of remedy should be put into place or whether the student should be discouraged from a career of clinician altogether. There is anecdotal evidence that reference letter writers have occasionally failed to mention critical information that speaks against the suitability of the student for the role of clinician and left the training faculty hanging with the nasty job of telling a student that he or she is indeed unsuitable for the clinical career path. This is a very unfortunate situation, because at this time both the student and the university have made major commitments to each other. Nevertheless, it is generally considered wise and fair to not drag unsuitable students through a lengthy graduate program only to later see them fail during an internship, at the point of licensure application, or at earning a living because of their lack of suitability for clinical work, not to mention possible harm to clients.

What do we know about the skills needed for successful therapists? Outcome research, documented via meta-analyses, suggests that roughly half of the explainable variance in patient improvement is due to the aggregation of nonspecific factors, also referred to as "common" factors, that cut across different theoretical approaches (Lipsey & Wilson, 1993; Mohr, 1995). This raises the question of how therapists can acquire such skills. Nonspecific skills are those that all therapists should possess and that are not tied to one narrow theoretical orientation. Teachable nonspecific skills are typically subdivided into *microskills* and *macroskills* (details are found later in this chapter). Microskills received their name because they refer to moment-to-moment behaviors in therapy (listed and discussed under Therapy Process later) and are considered critical for the creation of a good client-therapist relationship. Macroskills, also summarized later, on the other hand circumscribe more complex technical and conceptual skills such as developing a therapy plan and tracking behavioral progress.

The microskills can be readily taught, although this is a time-consuming endeavor. There is a good-sized body of research on the effectiveness of skill-training programs for therapists (Albert & Edelstein, 1990; Kendjelic & Eells, 2007) which suggest that:

1. Students learn most, and particularly enjoy, training that integrates observation of experienced therapists and modeling; didactic learning of theories, skills, and techniques; as well as actual practice and corrective feedback.

2. The newly acquired skills tend to last and are generally transferable from safe training environments like classrooms to clinical practice.

3. There is insufficient knowledge whether one type of skill is more important than another for producing superior outcomes, because the training usually comprises many components whose effects cannot be evaluated individually.

4. This type of research is generally handicapped by the fact that the training is more often based on the theoretical orientation of the researchers than on actual empirical evidence that ascertains that specific skills actually have differential impacts on outcome.

◇ TECHNIQUES

One critical element in the proposed therapy process model is that of technique choice. As we have mentioned previously, the rationales and description of therapy techniques are what usually assume most of the space in psychotherapy textbooks. Correspondingly, we have also included two lengthy chapters (chapters 11 and 12) that deal with various popular theoretical orientations and their associated techniques and an additional chapter, chapter 14, not found anywhere else that tackles what we call innovative or mystical therapies. We are not shortchanging the reader with minimal coverage of therapy techniques, yet have explicitly chosen to discuss the commonalities of therapies and the importance of the client-therapist relationship first, prior to discussing specific techniques. We believe that the student is not well served with an overemphasis on mere techniques at the expense of an appreciation for the intricacies of the dynamic process of change.

Typical Presenting Problems

Psychologists are extensively trained to understand and appreciate individual differences. Why else would we develop personality and aptitude tests to evaluate the suitability of different individuals for many existing careers or to predict which offender may relapse? Yet, when it comes to psychological therapy there is a great deal of similarity in the nature of presenting problems. A large, nationwide survey (Gurin, Veroff, & Feld, 1960) established that the single most pervasive issue brought to the psychologist's office is relationship problems; other research has confirmed this to be true 40 years later; relationship problems were front and center in psychotherapy and typically focus upon the ability to create and enjoy intimacy and the management of control in relationships (Johnson, Hunsley, Greenberg, & Schindler, 1999).

These two features account for most relationship problems. Also frequent are disagreements about child-rearing, how to get along with other family members, jealousy, infidelity, and financial concerns, and these factors ultimately account for marital success or failure. Another pervasive theme is low self-esteem, which is integral to understanding anxiety and depression. In consequence, all practicing clinical psychologists irrespective of their favorite theoretical orientation need training and skills to tackle these common issues in therapy:

1. Release of emotions
2. Understanding how childhood and other earlier experiences affect daily living
3. Issues of control and emotional closeness in intimate relationships
4. Reduction of subjective distress
5. Raising self-esteem and perceived competence

Although the presenting problems of individual clients and especially the social, cultural, and economic context of the presenting problems are ultimately unique, there nevertheless exist enough commonalities that therapists can indeed acquire the skills to deal with most of these problems. As much as the range of overall problems brought into the therapist's office is fairly finite and predictable, some psychotherapy researchers similarly argue that much of what psychotherapists offer is also very similar, irrespective of the label given to the therapy approach or the theoretical orientation with which the therapist aligns. Particularly persuasive has been the work of Jerome D. Frank (1973) who has argued that there may be more similarities than differences between therapy approaches, and he has posited that all therapies have at least these four common elements that the patient can benefit from:

1. **Emotional support**
2. **Provision of hope**
3. **Offering of a rationale** for how the problem came about
4. Placement of the problem within a wider context and comparison with other people; also referred to as **normalization**.

Together, these four elements can be considered the **nonspecific benefits** that essentially all therapies have the potential to bring about. This important point will receive more attention later in the section on psychotherapy effects (chapter 13); it will help understand better the many questionable claims for superior outcomes that some therapy proponents put forth. When and where therapies do differ (elaborated throughout chapters 11–14) is often related to whether or not they mostly target problematic behavior, emotion, or thinking, and the degree of directness used by the therapist.

The skills needed to skillfully navigate through a therapy session and appropriately respond to clients on a moment-to-moment basis are referred to as **microskills** and include:

1. Showing **empathy**
2. Offering **encouragement**
3. Asking precise, well-timed, nonthreatening questions
4. Using **self-disclosure** appropriately
5. Providing clients with needed factual information

These skills have always been considered important in Carl Rogers' **client-centered treatment** approach (Rogers, 1951; chapter 11), and the *Rogerian movement* deserves special credit for offering elaborate training in these microskills.

A higher level of, and more time-consuming, training is needed to teach integrative skills and the accurate execution of theory-specific therapy; these skills are referred to as **macroskills**. Macroskills are a blend of generic skills and theory-specific skills and include:

1. **Case conceptualization**
2. Theory-specific knowledge of techniques and skill in the execution of these techniques

3. Pattern recognition with respect to resistance and control attempts on part of patients

4. Knowing "when to push" versus "holding back" with respect to client behavior change

5. Recognition of shifts within clients (toward improvement or worsening)

6. Recognition by the therapist of his or her own (inappropriate) reaction to the particular client

Acquiring a sufficient level of sophistication in these macroskills is commonly considered to take many years of formal training—including didactic teaching, modeling, and supervision—and is by no means considered complete, even after graduate school requirements have been met and a therapist has received a license to practice. Even therapists with 2 or 3 decades of experience will habitually report new insights and a growing awareness of change in their own macroskills.

The Therapeutic Relationship

Earlier on, we referred to psychotherapy as being a mysterious process. This is in good part due to the fact that clients are hoping to be able to express their innermost thoughts and feelings in a safe, confidential atmosphere, a process with which they usually have no experience, and certainly not with a stranger. Therefore, it is utterly understandable that clients are apprehensive about opening up, and trust in the therapist cannot be taken for granted. Clients need to be assured that there is confidentiality, and the therapist needs to accept responsibility for sending out clear signs that he or she can be trusted and that the therapy is safe. Consistent use of the microskills described earlier is considered integral to this process (Norcross, 2002). If therapy is to be successful, therapists need to assure clients that they will be taken care of, that the therapists are caring and competent and they understand and empathize with the client's feelings, and that some acceptance of the natural fear around opening up is necessary and ultimately beneficial. Creating this type of constructive atmosphere is also referred to as building a **therapeutic alliance**, which is characterized by three interlocking components (Bordin, 1976):

1. Bonds, referring to interpersonal attachment, trusting, and liking

2. Tasks, meaning that therapist and client share a consensus on what needs to be done in therapy

3. Goals, referring to a shared expectation of client and therapist about what the treatment outcome should be

A variety of questionnaires have been developed to assess the quality of therapeutic alliance from both the therapists' and the clients' perspective, although evidence has shown that it is the clients' perspective that is most important here (Horvath & Luborsky, 1993) (Box 10.1).

Research has consistently indicated that the quality of the therapeutic alliance is strongly predictive of a good pace of progression in therapy and a positive outcome

BOX 10.1

A number of items from the Helping Alliance Questionnaire (Luborsky et al., 1996) were paraphrased here to give a clearer sense of how this type of assessment is conducted and which types of statements are to be endorsed:
1. My therapist understood and accepted me.
2. My therapist understood my goals and helped me achieve them.
3. I was given appropriate feedback when I made progress.
4. The therapist encouraged me to express myself.
5. I felt that my therapist liked me.

(see Horvath & Symonds, 1991; Johnson & Ketring, 2006), but it is the clients' perception and subjective evaluation of this relationship that predicts good outcome, rather than the objectively measurable therapist behaviors (Horvath & Symonds, 1991).

As therapy progresses, there are bound to be moments where an important, "loaded" topic is identified for discussion or a new behavior needs to be tried out, but the client is reluctant to engage in dealing with this topic that may be quite fear arousing. Or, stopping a compulsive or addictive behavior like chain-smoking has already been tried and failed by this client, and he may be reluctant to go again through the suffering associated with withdrawal. If the material that clients deal with in therapy was easy to handle, then the client would have fixed it already and wouldn't need to go and see a professional therapist. It is for these reasons that clients will often have one or more roadblocks in therapy and need to be guided, coached, or persuaded into tackling a topic or into trying something new. Exactly how this is done is one of the major discriminating factors between different types of therapies. Some therapies are a little pushy and try to directly confront and reason through; others subtly guide the process of self-discovery. These differences in the various therapies' approaches to handling roadblocks and **resistance** largely define why some therapies take longer than others. Without giving away the details of this fascinating process right here, we will discuss only how roadblock handling must be tied in with the creation of a strong therapy alliance. In extensive studies, researchers have fully recorded therapy sessions that have later been transcribed for detailed analyses of actual therapist-patient interaction (Bedics, Henry, & Adkins, 2005; Strupp, 1993, 1996). From Hans Strupp's work we have learned that challenging the client can be effective only if the questions of timing and the strength of the alliance are carefully considered. Strupp's research has shown that the most successful therapies did have a phase of resistance and a challenge to the resistance somewhere around the middle part of the therapy. Challenging clients too early, when a solid therapeutic alliance is not yet established, likely leads to failure in therapy (Mohr, 1995). The reader will not be surprised to hear this because even in our private, nontherapy lives we are certainly not likely to listen to strangers whom we don't trust; even when we are challenged by people who love us and care for us (like spouses or parents), such challenge is not always welcome either and may require persistent nudging.

Another way of looking at the process of therapy is to see it as a set of stages to go through. Egan (1986, 1998) has done this for us and has created an easy-to-follow flowchart format proposing three stages, namely, (a) dealing with current situation, (b) a preferred or desired outcome, and (c) the actions needed to get there. During the first stage, clients need to be able to describe their current reality. Then they need to learn about the blind spots that have previously led to an overly narrow view and therefore possibly preventing solutions; finally they need to be gently coaxed into focusing on setting priorities. In the second stage, the clients will discuss various possibilities for change, without yet deciding which ones are worth going after. Next the clients need to create an agenda for change and commit to it. The third stage then involves homing in on a number of concrete action plans, selecting the one that likely works best for the client and this situation, and then of course moving forward with this plan of action.

This model describes typical therapy steps without aligning itself to one narrow theoretical approach. We posit that this view is quite descriptive of at least the great majority of therapy processes.

◇ CULTURAL COMPETENCE IN CLINICAL PSYCHOLOGY

Earlier in this chapter, we discussed how different characteristics of clients themselves might affect clinical psychology practice, and we touched on cultural differences, but we did not provide much detail. Given that people are more and more mobile, there have been many changes in the cultural composition of Western countries. Much cultural diversity has resulted from the opening of borders for international trade, from normal immigration, and from an increasing number of refugees fleeing war-torn countries. In a cosmopolitan and multicultural city like Toronto, Canada, for example, with about 5 million inhabitants, the city itself offers telephone assistance in 148 languages. Some Vancouver, Canada, suburbs have more than half of their population not speaking English at home (Bowman, 2000). Therefore, psychologists working in urban centers in the United States of America, Australia, the United Kingdom, or Canada typically deal with highly diverse client populations. Some of these areas are characterized by visible minority status, others by relative recency of immigration, and many stand out because they continue to adhere to their native cultures and values. Clinical psychologists tend to be White and of European cultural origin, and the primary approaches to understanding abnormal behavior and treating psychological problems can be traced back to Judeo-Christian traditions and philosophies. The mix of the North American population, in contrast, shows a disproportionate growth in subgroups that have come from Asia, Africa, and Latin America, and this raises the question of whether the typical, European rooted way of defining clinical psychology practice is ideally suited to their needs (Teramoto Predotti, Edwards, & Lopez, 2008).

The issue of cultural uniqueness is further complicated by the fact that some cultural subgroups are visible minorities in their country although their families have lived in this very country for many decades (this applies, e.g., to African Americans in the United States). For others, visible minority status is coupled with recent immigrant status, with English as a second language, and sometimes economic disadvantages due to language difficulties. Ethnic group membership is often associated with substantive differences in socioeconomic status, but this pattern is not universal. In the United States, Hispanic and African American subgroups have substantially lower incomes than Whites, whereas that does not apply on the other side of the border, in Canada, where earning differentials between the majority and the largest ethnic subgroups are minimal (Bowman, 2000). Apparently, the status of visible minority does not, in and of itself, tell us whether somebody may be economically disadvantaged, nor does it tell what the mother tongue is.

Elsewhere in this chapter and in chapter 4 we have presented a number of policies and rules that are supposed to guide our professional behaviors that are, however, culture-bound and not necessarily shared by all cultures (Sue, 1999). Among these are:

1. The reluctance of therapists to give outright advice even when clients directly ask for it
2. The degree to which self-disclosure of the therapists' thoughts and feelings is considered acceptable to clients
3. The therapists' negotiation of financial arrangements with patients given that we are discouraged from bartering
4. The expectation that psychotherapists resist dual-role relationships to avoid loss of objectivity
5. The acceptance of gift-giving traditions

Strict avoidance of dual relationships can be considered standoffish in some cultures, and refusal of gifts in Asian cultures, for example, is often seen as a personal offense. Also, it may be seemingly small details of human interactions that get misinterpreted as a function of culture. For example, many aboriginal cultures avoid direct eye contact, which they perceive as aggressive whereas European- or North American-raised individuals may simply interpret limited eye contact as shyness or low self-esteem.

A desire for therapist directness is one cultural feature shared by many immigrant cultures to North America. Europeans and North Americans, on the other hand, tend to emphasize independent decision-making and client self-exploration, but individuals of Asian descent and African Americans tend to favor directive, active, and structured therapies (Paniagua, 1998).

Sometimes cultural values and habits clash. A difficult-to-resolve situation centers around different habits around timeliness. In some cultures, people are frequently late, and this does not trigger ire in other members of the same cultural group. However, this tolerance is difficult to carry on work in a clinic operation, where patients are scheduled in 1-hour time slots and where a client arriving at 3:40 p.m. for a 3 p.m. appointment cannot really be offered a full hour any more, without taking away time from the individual arriving on time for his or her 4 p.m. appointment.

Earlier we provided some examples of known cultural differences, but recognize that being overly prescriptive on how to handle a situation is not necessarily a solution either and may even be counterproductive. Exposure to various cultural subgroups is uneven depending on where a therapist may work. Therefore, it is key that individuals learn to understand the cultures of the particular environment in which they work. The term **cultural competence** is applied to therapists who have made this step.

In order to assist with a definition of cultural competence, Sue, Arredondo, and McDavis (1992) have compiled a detailed list of sensible components for such a definition (see Table 10.3). They posit that cultural competence can be broken down into belief or attitude, knowledge, and skill.

TABLE 10.3 Components of Cultural Competence

BELIEF OR ATTITUDE	KNOWLEDGE	SKILL
1. Aware and sensitive to own heritage and valuing or respecting differences.	1. Knows about own racial or cultural heritage and how it affects perceptions.	1. Seeks out educational, consultative, and multicultural training experiences.
2. Aware of own background or experiences and biases and how they influence psychological processes.	2. Possesses knowledge about racial identity development. Can acknowledge own racist attitudes, beliefs, and feelings.	2. Seeks to understand self as being.
3. Recognizes limits of competencies and expertise.	3. Knows about own social impact and communication styles.	3. Familiarizes self with relevant research on racial or ethnic groups.
4. Comfortable with differences that exist between themselves and others.	4. Knows about the groups one works or interacts with.	4. Involved with minority groups work role: community events, celebrations, neighbors, and so forth.
5. In touch with negative emotional reactions toward racial or ethnic groups and can be nonjudgmental.	5. Understands how race or ethnicity affects personality formation, vocational choices, psychological disorders, and so forth.	5. Can engage in a variety of verbal or nonverbal helping styles.
6. Aware of stereotypes and preconceived notions.	6. Knows about sociopolitical influences, immigration, poverty, powerlessness, and so forth.	6. Can exercise institutional intervention skills on behalf of clients.
7. Respects religious and/or spiritual beliefs of others.	7. Understands culture-bound, class-bound, and linguistic features of psychological help.	7. Can seek consultation with traditional healers.
8. Respects indigenous helping practices and community networks.	8. Knows the effects of institutional barriers.	8. Can take responsibility to provide linguistic competence for clients.
9. Values bilingualism.	9. Knows bias of assessment.	9. Has expertise in cultural aspects of assessment.
	10. Knows about minority family structures, community, and so forth.	10. Works to eliminate bias, prejudice, and discrimination.
	11. Knows how discriminatory practices operate at a community level.	11. Educates clients in the nature of one's practice.

Adapted from D. W. Sue, Arredondo, and McDavis (1992).

This list of suggested components for cultural competence is a lengthy one and might make us wonder whether we can ever be truly competent in this respect. It is probably best to think of this long list as aspirational. Nevertheless, in order to facilitate cultural learning, Sue (1999) suggests four overarching learning strategies:

1. Individuals should experience and learn from as many sources as possible to check the validity of their assumptions and beliefs about another culture. It is not sufficient to rely on the media, but they need to be at least complemented with personal contacts.

2. Given that there are occasional beliefs about superiority of one culture over another, it is also critical that in order to obtain a balanced picture of any one cultural group we should meet and spend time with healthy and strong people of that culture.

3. Knowledge of facts about the culture is best anchored with in the experiential reality of that group.

4. Even once cultural knowledge and competence have been acquired, we need to remain constantly vigilant.

On a very pragmatic level, we suggest beginning cross-cultural learning as a leisure time activity by occasionally watching television in a language other than English or shopping and dining in ethnic neighborhoods. In a more formal fashion, students can make a systematic choice of practicum or internship experience that exposes them to particular types of cultures.

◇ CONCLUSION

The purpose of this chapter was to prepare the reader for the presentation and discussion of many different theoretical approaches and techniques that follow in chapters 11 and 12. We also wanted to raise awareness about the difficulty in defining what psychotherapy is and that, despite this difficulty, we need to be prepared to define our work and our profession. We explicitly chose to present this material first because we believe it prepares the therapist in training for the discussion of specific therapies and lays a foundation for understanding why and how therapy approaches are different from one another. Furthermore, it begins to build understanding why many therapists do not want to see themselves exclusively married to one theoretical approach, but rather choose different interventions for different targets, depending on how they conceptualize the case in front of them and what the evidence supports. As clinicians we need more than one tool at hand to solve our clients' multilayered, complex problems. Research on the degree of importance of each element of the therapy process has been quite revealing and strongly supports the value of generic therapy skills. Luborsky and his collaborators (1997) have carefully studied the contribution of each process element to the therapy success and found that therapist technical skills modestly correlated with therapy success ($r = .32$), but the quality of the alliance as judged by the patient was a much stronger predictor of the outcome ($r = .65$). In contrast, whether or not the therapist precisely executed the therapy he or she claimed to practice (based on the treatment manuals and/or judgments of "technique purity") was less important ($r = .44$) than a strong alliance. The bottom line is that building the therapeutic alliance is key to ultimate therapy success.

◇ ONGOING CONSIDERATIONS

Over the last two decades, leading thinkers in psychotherapy research have started to look for commonalities in treatment approaches (e.g., Prochaska & Norcross, 2002; Ehrenreich, Fairholme, Buzzella, Ellard, & Barlow, 2007), whereas the first 50 or so years of development of therapies had gone in the opposite direction, creating new approaches (or at least approaches that were supposed to look new and different). We welcome the trend toward integration because it will likely strengthen treatment effectiveness, benefit patients, and reduce dogmatism and in-fighting among therapy researchers and therapists. The current clinical psychology student is bound to hear much more of integrative approaches and will likely enjoy this trend toward synergy and coherence.

◇ KEY TERMS LEARNED

Bonds
Case conceptualization
Client-centered treatment
Cultural competence
Emotional support
Empathy
Encouragement
Goals
Levels of emotional awareness (EA)
Macroskills
Microskills

Nonspecific benefits
Normalization
Offering of a rationale
Pattern recognition
Provision of hope
Resistance
Self-disclosure
Tasks
Therapeutic alliance
YAVIS client

◇ THINKING QUESTIONS

1. Which therapist qualities are required for therapy to be effective?
2. Are different therapies really that different?
3. How much training is required for treatment to be effective?
4. How much treatment is needed for lasting behavior change?
5. What is psychotherapy?
6. Which topics are most likely to come up in psychotherapy?

◇ REFERENCES

Alberts, G., & Edelstein, B. (1990). Therapist training: A critical review of skill training studies. *Clinical Psychology Review, 10*, 497–511.

Bedics, J. D., Henry, W. P., & Adkins, D. C. (2005). The therapeutic process as a predictor of change in patients' important relationships during time-limited dynamic psychotherapy. *Psychotherapy: Theory/Research/Practice/Training, 42*, 279–284.

Binder, J. L. (1993). Observations on the training of therapists in time-limited dynamic psychotherapy. *Psychotherapy, 30*, 592–598.

Bordin, E. S. (1976). The generalizability of the psychoanalytic concept of the working alliance. *Psychotherapy: Theory Research and Practice, 16*, 252–260.

Bowman, M. (2000). The diversity of diversity: Canadian-American differences and their implications for clinical training and APA accreditation. *Canadian Psychology/Psychologie Canadienne, 41*, 230–243.

Brown, R. D. (1970). Experienced and inexperienced counselors' first impressions of clients and case outcomes: Are first impressions lasting? *Journal of Counseling Psychology, 17*, 550–558.

Clarkin, J. F., & Levy, K. N. (2004). The influence of client variables on psychotherapy. In: Bergin, A. E. & Garfield, S. L. (Eds). *Handbook of psychotherapy and behavior change.* New York: John Wiley & Sons.

Cullari, S. (1998). *Foundations of clinical psychology.* Boston: Allyn & Bacon.

Durlak, J. A. (1979). Comparative effectiveness of professional and paraprofessional helpers. *Psychological Bulletin, 86*, 80–92.

Egan, G. (1986). *The skilled helper* (3rd ed.). California: Brooks/Cole.

Egan, G. (1998). *The skilled helper—A problem management approach to helping* (6th ed.). Monterey: Brooks/Cole.

Ehrenreich, J. T., Fairholme, C., Buzzella, B., Ellard, K., & Barlow, D. H. (2007). The role of emotion in psychological therapy. *Clinical Psychology: Science and Practice, 14*, 423–429.

Frank, J. D. (1973). *Persuasion and healing.* Baltimore: Johns Hopkins Press.

Garfield, S. L. (1978). Research on client variables in psychotherapy. In S. L. Garfield & Bergin A. E. (Eds.), *Handbook of psychotherapy and behavior change* (pp. 191–232). New York: John Wiley & Sons.

Golden, C. A. (1997). Impact of psychotherapy. Does it affect frequency of visits to family physicians? *Canadian Family Physician, 43*, 1098–1102.

Gomez-Schwartz, B. (1978). Effective ingredients in psychotherapy: Prediction of outcome from process variables. *Journal of Consulting and Clinical Psychology, 46*, 1023–1035.

Gurin, G., Veroff, J., & Feld, S. (1960). *Americans view their mental health—A nationwide interview survey* (1st ed.). New York: Basic Books, Inc.

Hansen, N. B., Lambert, M. J., & Forman, E. M. (2002). The psychotherapy dose-response effect and its implications for treatment delivery services. *Clinical Psychology: Science and Practice, 10*, 329–337.

Horvath, A. O. (2000). The therapeutic relationship: From transference to alliance. *Journal of Clinical Psychology, 56*, 163–173.

Horvath, A. O., & Bedi, R. P. (2002). The alliance. In J. C. Norcross (Ed.), *Psychotherapy relationships that work: Therapist contributions and responsiveness to patients* (pp. 37–69). London: Oxford University Press.

Horvath, A. O., & Luborsky, L. (1993). The role of the therapeutic alliance in psychotherapy. *Journal of Consulting and Clinical Psychology, 61,* 561–573.

Horvath, A. O., & Symonds, B. D. (1991). Relation between working alliance and outcome in psychotherapy: A meta-analysis. *Journal of Counseling Psychology, 38,* 139–149.

Huitt, W., & Hummel, J. (2003). Piaget's theory of cognitive development. *Educational psychology interactive.* Valdosta, GA: Valdosta State University.

Johnson, L. N., & Ketring, S. A. (2006). The therapy alliance: A moderator in therapy outcome for families dealing with child abuse and neglect. *Journal of Marital and Family Therapy, 32,* 345–354.

Johnson, S. M., Hunsley, J., Greenberg, L., & Schindler, D. (1999). Emotionally focused couples therapy: Status and challenges. *Clinical Psychology: Science and Practice, 6,* 67–79.

Kazantzis, N., Deane, F. P., & Roman, K. R. (2000). Homework assignments in cognitive and behavioral therapy: A meta-analysis. *Clinical Psychology: Science and Practice, 7,* 189–202.

Kendjelic, E. M., & Eells, T. D. (2007). Generic psychotherapy case formulation training improves formulation quality. *Psychotherapy: Theory, Research, Practice, Training, 44,* 66–77.

Kupfersmid, J., & Fiola, M. (1991). Comparison of EPPP scores among graduates of varying psychology programs. *American Psychologist, 46,* 534–535.

Lane, R. D., Schwartz, G. E. (1987). Levels of emotional awareness—A cognitive-developmental theory and its application to psychopathology. *American Journal of Psychiatry, 144,* 133–143.

Linden, W., & Satin, J. R. (2007). Avoidable pitfalls in behavioral medicine outcome research. *Annals of Behavioral Medicine, 33,* 143–147.

Lipsey, M. W., & Wilson, D. B. (1993). The efficacy of psychological, educational, and behavioral treatment: Confirmation from meta-analysis. *American Psychologist, 48,* 1181–1209.

Luborsky, L., Barber, J. P., Siqueland, L., Johnson, S., Najavits, L. M., Frank, A., & Daley, D. (1996). The Revised Helping Alliance Questionnaire (HAq-II). *Journal of Psychotherapy Practice and Research, 5,* 260–271.

Luborsky, I., McLellan, A. T., Diguer, L., Woody, G., & Seligman, D. A. (1997). The psychotherapist matters: Comparison of outcomes across twenty-two therapists and seven patient samples. *Clinical Psychology: Science and Practice, 1,* 53–65.

Marton, K. I. (2002). Brief training in CBT for primary care physicians doesn't improve patient outcomes. *Journal Watch (General), June 4,* 2002.

McGaha, S., & Minder, C. (1993). Factors influencing performance on the examination for professional practice in psychology (EPPP). *Professional Psychology: Research and Practice, 24,* 107–109.

Miranda, J., Bernal, G., Lau, A., Kohn, L., Hwang, W. C., & LaFramboise, T. (2005). State of the science on psychological interventions for ethnic minorities. *Annual Review of Clinical Psychology, 1,* 113–142.

Mohr, D. C. (1995). Negative outcome in psychotherapy: A critical review. *Clinical Psychology: Science and Practice, 2,* 1–27.

Nietzel, M. T., & Fisher, S. G. (1981). Effectiveness of professional and paraprofessional helpers: A comment on Durlak. *Psychological Bulletin, 89,* 555–565.

Norcross, J. C. (2002). *Psychotherapy relationships that work: Therapist contributions and responsiveness to patients.* New York: Oxford University Press.

Paniagua, F. A. (1998). *Assessing and treating culturally diverse clients: A practical guide* (2nd ed). Thousand Oaks: Sage.

Pearce, J. W., LeBow, M. D., & Orchard, J. (1981). Role of spouse involvement in the behavioral treatment of overweight women. *Journal of Consulting and Clinical Psychology, 49,* 236–244.

Peterson, D. R. (1982). Origins and development of the Doctor of Psychology concept. In G. R. Caddy, Rimm, D. C., Watson, H., & Johnson, J. H. (Eds.), *Educating professional psychologists* (pp. 19–38). New Brunswick, NJ: Transaction Books.

Peterson, D. R. (2003). Unintended consequences: Ventures and misadventures in the education of professional psychologists. *American Psychologist, 58,* 791–800.

Prochaska, J. O., & Norcross, J. C. (2002). *Systems of psychotherapy: A transtheoretical analysis* (5th ed.). Belmont: Brooks/Cole.

Raimy, V. C. (1950). *Training in clinical psychology.* New York: Prentice-Hall.

Rogers, C. R. (1951). *Client-centered therapy.* Boston: Houghton Mifflin.

Schofield, W. (1964). *Psychotherapy: The purchase of friendship.* Englewood Cliffs, NJ: Prentice-Hall.

Seligman, M. E. P. (1995). The effectiveness of psychotherapy: The consumer reports study. *American Psychologist, 50,* 965–974.

Stein, D. M., & Lambert, M. J. (1995). Graduate training in psychotherapy: Are therapy outcomes enhanced? *Journal of Consulting and Clinical Psychology, 63,* 182–196.

Strupp, H. H. (1996). Lasting lessons from psychotherapy practice and research *Psychotherapeut, 41,* 84–87.

Strupp, H. H. (1993). The Vanderbilt psychotherapy studies: Synopsis. *Journal of Consulting and Clinical Psychology, 61,* 431–433.

Sue, S. (1999). Science, ethnicity, and bias: Where have we gone wrong? *American Psychologist, 54,* 1070–1077.

Sue, D. W., Arredondo, P., & McDavis, R. J. (1992). Multicultural counseling competencies and standards: A call to the profession. *Journal of Multicultural Counseling and Development, 20,* 64–89.

Teramoto, P. J., Edwards, L. M., Lopez, S. J. (2008). Working with multiracial clients in therapy: Bridging theory, research and practice. *Professional Psychology: Research and Practice, 39,* 192–201.

Wampold, B. E., & Brown, J. S. (2005). Estimating variability in outcomes attributable to therapists: A naturalist study of outcomes in managed care. *Journal of Consulting and Clinical Psychology, 73,* 914–923.

Wiesenfeld, A. R., & Weis, H. M. (1979). Hairdressers and helping: Influencing the behavior of informal caregivers. *Professional Psychology, 10,* 786–792.

Yu, L. M., Rinaldi, S. A., Templer, D. I., Colbert, L. A., Siscoe, K., & Van Patten, K. (1997). Scores on the examination for professional practice in psychology as a function of the attributes of clinical psychology graduate programs. *Psychological Science, 8,* 340–350.

CHAPTER ELEVEN

PSYCHOTHERAPIES I

CHAPTER OBJECTIVE

This chapter discusses three broad approaches to psychotherapy, which are related to one another in some ways and quite divergent in others. These approaches or domains have a historical appeal and have critically shaped the development of psychological therapies. A great deal of theorizing and research has been conducted on these approaches, and each has been acknowledged as a significant and original orientation for clinical psychologists. Their importance has resisted attempts to see them as a time-limited fashion therapy, and they continue to be the central focuses for psychological treatment. These three areas are psychoanalysis and psychoanalytic psychotherapies, client-centered psychotherapy, and systems therapies.

◇ PSYCHOANALYSIS

This section will describe a domain of psychological treatment that encompasses some of the earliest forms of talking therapy and the subsequent development and evolution of this broad domain of psychological theory and psychotherapy. This domain is known as psycho-analysis and involves **classical psychoanalysis**, as developed early in the last century by Sigmund Freud, as well as numerous **psychoanalytic psychotherapies** that have been developed over the past decades. Although we will, at times, describe components of psychoanalytic theory mainly to orient the student and clarify some often-taught incorrect assumptions, it is assumed that students will have had some coverage of psychoanalytic the-ories and thoughts in other psychology courses like personality psychology or motivation.

Terminology

There can often be some confusion that arises with respect to terms used in the broad domain of psychoanalytic theory and treatment. For example, the terms "psychodynamic" and "psychoanalytic" have come to be used almost interchangeably, and this can create some misunderstanding among those first trying to learn and understand about this broad domain of theory and treatment.

The term **"psychodynamic"** is a broad term that refers to models of normal and maladaptive human behavior as well as models of treatment. In psychodynamic models, the determinants of behavior are thought to be primarily unconscious motives, emotions, or drives that form the main characteristics of personality. These characteristics interact and, at times, conflict or are at odds with one another. That is, there is a *dynamic* interplay among the components of personality, and in order to understand the person and his or her difficulties, the clinical psychologist needs to understand that dynamic interplay. More generally, psychodynamic models and/or therapies focus on the inner motives or drives of behavior, which are usually thought to be outside of the person's awareness and result in overt and covert behavior, or in the case of psychopathology, signs and symptoms of maladjustment. **Psychoanalysis** refers to one broad and comprehensive psychodynamic theoretical perspective developed initially by Sigmund Freud that has been revised, often extensively, by many other psychoanalytic theorists. To make matters more complicated, the main treatment approach that Freud developed (and, again, that others revised) is also called psychoanalysis. We will use the term "classical psychoanalysis" in this chapter to refer to traditional psychoanalytic treatment that was developed by Freud. You will find here a brief overview of treatments that derive from psychoanalytic thought. These types of treatments will be discussed in more detail later on in this chapter.

Classical psychoanalysis is a psychodynamic treatment, focused on inborn, internal, and biological drives that are unconscious and primarily sexual in nature. Later in his career, Freud suggested that unconscious aggressive drives can also be important in influencing behavior (Sharf, 2000). It is thought that these drives influence personality development, both normal and pathological. The treatment derived from this perspective is typically long term (i.e., often several years) and intensive (i.e., several times weekly).

Psychoanalytic psychotherapies (also known as psychodynamic psychotherapies or dynamic psychotherapies, although we will use the term "psychoanalytic psychotherapies") were developed by psychoanalytic theorists who revised or refined (often extensively) many of Freud's and his followers' ideas. For example, although biological impulses characterized early models of psychoanalysis, students of Freud fairly quickly emphasized interpersonal needs and motives (e.g., Harry Stack Sullivan, John Bowlby) rather than the biological drives of sexuality or aggression (Corsini & Wedding, 2005). These interpersonal styles are thought to arise from early childhood relationships with parent(s), family, or peers, from processes involved in the development of the self and identity, or from adaptation to the environment as the driving forces for behavior. In addition to focusing on different unconscious drives, the psychoanalytic psychotherapies that arose from these models tend to be shorter in duration than psychoanalysis (i.e., perhaps a year or less), and the therapists tend to be more active and directive. Some psychoanalytic psychotherapies are time-limited, brief (e.g., 12 sessions), and very focused on a particular component of behavior. They are generally referred to as **short-term dynamic psychotherapies**.

All psychoanalytic treatments emphasize the unconscious nature of drives and generally focus on the drives as determining or influencing normal and abnormal personality development and psychopathology. Psychoanalytic treatment, whether it is classical psychoanalysis or psychoanalytic psychotherapy, involves accessing unconscious processes or information. By doing so, it allows the person to be aware of the influences on his or her behavior and to make adjustments and changes. Throughout the chapter we will use the term "psychoanalytic treatment" to refer to any treatment—classical psychoanalysis or psychoanalytic psychotherapy—that uses psychodynamic principles.

◇ HOW COMMON IS PSYCHOANALYSIS AND PSYCHODYNAMIC TREATMENT?

It has been one of the author's (PLH) experiences that in numerous academic psychology and other departments, students are taught that the psychoanalytic thought, clinical work, and research have gone the way of the dinosaur. Psychoanalytic thinking, if taught, is often taught only from a historical perspective (i.e., learn only about Freud), with many students assuming that these modes of treatment are antiquated, stagnant, and not currently utilized (see Bornstein, 1988, 2005; Hogan, 1994). In fact, one of the author's clinical psychology graduate students stated: "I was also taught in my undergraduate years that there was no empirical validation for psychoanalytic treatments, that they were basically no longer used and not appropriate choices for treatment because they were not effective or validated by research" (H. Roxborough, personal communication, 2008).

Characterizing psychoanalytic theory and treatment as antiquated and stagnant is simply not an accurate depiction of the field. In fact, Gabbard (2005) has indicated that psychoanalytic psychotherapy approaches are one of the most commonly practiced forms of psychotherapy (see also Sharf, 2000). For example, Jensen, Bergin, and Greaves (1990) found in a study of 423 clinical psychologists whose clinical orientation was endorsed as eclectic (now the term "integrative" is used) most commonly endorsed the psychodynamic perspective as making up their eclectic approach, and Norcross, Hedges, and Castle (2002) also present data suggesting that the psychodynamic perspective is the second most commonly endorsed (eclecticism is first) theoretical perspective used by clinical psychologists.

In terms of professional organizations endorsing psychoanalytic treatments, the International Psychoanalytic Association (IPA) is the world's main accrediting and regulatory body for psychoanalysis and focuses on the continued development of psychoanalysis in order to help patients. The IPA works in concert with over 70 related organizations in 33 countries (see http://www.ipa.org.uk). Moreover, the European Psychoanalytic Federation has over 4600 individual members from 22 countries, the American Psychoanalytic Association comprises 38 affiliated societies, and the national psychological associations from the United States, Canada, Australia, Britain, and numerous other countries throughout the United Kingdom and Europe have divisions dedicated to research and treatment issues in psychoanalysis and psychoanalytic therapy. Many of these divisions publish journals dedicated specifically to research and treatment from psychodynamic perspectives. In fact, searches of journal databases reveal that there are, currently, over 60 refereed journals dedicated to research from psychoanalytic and psychodynamic perspectives. Lastly, in terms of training facilities, there are hundreds of programs that train clinical psychologists and other mental health professionals in psychoanalytic and psychodynamic models in North America, the United Kingdom, and

Europe. For example, in the United States there are over 90 accredited training facilities for psychoanalytic training (see http://www.div39outreach.org/), and a large number of internship sites provide rotations in psychoanalytic treatment.

It should be clear to the reader that, far from being antiquated and stagnant, psychoanalysis and psychoanalytic psychotherapy is an active domain of research inquiry, theory development, and treatments that has been evolving over the years. There are more and more treatment efficacy studies, reviews of psychoanalytic treatment efficacy, and meta-analyses of psychoanalytic psychotherapy appearing in the literature (Gibbons, Crits-Christoph, & Hearon, 2009; Leichsenring & Rabung, 2008; Levy & Ablon, 2009; Shedler, 2010) that meet the criteria of the designation "empirically supported treatment" (APA Task Force on Evidence-Based Practice, 2006; Chambless & Hollon, 1998). Moreover, although psychoanalytic theory has often been presented as lacking empirical evidence or interest in demonstrating empirical evidence of core concepts, a great deal of research has actually been directed toward psychoanalytic concepts (e.g., Bornstein & Masling, 1998; Masling, 1986, 1990). Dr. Joseph Masling, in fact, over the years, has edited at least eight volumes of a series of books dedicated to the research addressing the empirical status of psychoanalytic theory. One well-known and much-debated example is the research of Silverman (1976, 1985) that assesses subliminal stimulation (i.e., information presented below the threshold of awareness) of unconscious wishes in participants. In this work, "The experimental stimuli consist of verbal messages and/or pictures containing content related to the kinds of unconscious wishes, anxieties, and fantasies, which according to psychoanalytic theory play a key role in motivating behavior; the control stimuli consist of relatively neutral verbal and pictorial content. In more than 60 studies . . . carried out in various laboratories, experimenters have reported that the subliminal exposure of the psychodynamic experimental stimuli has affected behavior in a way that the neutral control stimuli have not" (Silverman, 1985, p. 640). The affected behavior is in line with what would be predicted based on psychoanalytic theory.

◇ PRIMARY ASSUMPTIONS AND PRINCIPLES OF PSYCHOANALYTIC TREATMENT

Although there are some differences among the psychoanalytic perspectives and treatments, there are several basic tenets that the majority rest upon. These assumptions, listed here really form the basis of psychoanalytic thought.

1. Psychopathology and its symptoms are viewed as emanating from and a part of the person's personality and character. An important concept in the behaviors that arise from the person's personality and character is the concept of **psychic determinism** whereby psychological events (e.g., symptoms, defenses, and so forth) are causally related to one another and to the individual's past, and those psychological events are goal directed and serve some purpose for the person. Thus, in order to understand and treat the psychological difficulties that a person experiences, a rather more holistic approach is taken to

BOX 11.1

RENAMING AND REINVENTION

There are likely several reasons that psychoanalysis has been seen by some as inactive and defunct when it has actually been very active and alive (Shedler, 2006). In a paper by Bornstein (2005) there is a description of how the status of psychoanalysis and psychoanalytic treatment has been diminished in academic psychology on the one hand and how ideas, hypotheses, and models that derive specifically from psychoanalytic theorizing have been researched, supported, and infused into contemporary psychology (Silverman, 1976, 1985) on the other hand, often with little acknowledgement or referencing of the original ideas for the work. For example, he states that numerous psychoanalytic concepts have been renamed and, with the new name, are viewed as new concepts, with no or little acknowledgement of where the original ideas came from. A list he provides is reproduced here (Bornstein, 2005, p. 327):

Psychoanalytic concept[a]	Revision or reinvention
Unconscious memory (1900/1953a)	Implicit memory (Schacter, 1987)
Primary process thought (1900/1953a)	Spreading activation (Collins & Loftus, 1975)
Object representation (1905/1953b)	Person schema (Neisser, 1976)
Repression (1910/1957a)	Cognitive avoidance (Beck, 1976)
Preconscious processing (1915/1957b)	Preattentive processing (Treisman, 1969)
Parapraxis (1916/1963)	Retrieval error (Tulving, 1983)
Abreaction (1916/1963)	Reintegration (Bower & Glass, 1976)
Repetition compulsion (1920/1955)	Nuclear script (Tomkins, 1979)
Ego (1923/1961)	Central executive (Baddley, 1992)
Ego defense (1926/1959)	Defensive attribution (Lerner & Miller, 1978)

[a]Original Freudian sources are identified by year of original publication and then by date of corresponding Hogarth Press *Standard Edition* volume.

Reprinted from Bornstein (2005), with permission.

understand the person and his or her unique personality and character makeup and the influences on the development of the personality and character. There is an emphasis on trying to understand the whole patient and the patient's problems as part of an idiosyncratic and dynamic system (Magnavita, 2008). As discussed in chapter 5, there is a focus on changing the underlying issues that produce symptoms rather than focusing specifically on the symptoms themselves. Moreover, the concept of **symptom substitution** reflects the idea that underlying impulses or conflicts that are not conscious are manifested as symptoms. Thus, symptoms are viewed as representations of underlying impulses.

2. There is an importance placed on childhood and the early childhood relationships, including the relationship with the primary caregiver but also with other family members, peers, and others, in the development of normal and pathological personality. It is important to understand that parents are not to be blamed for psychological difficulties that a person experiences. It is thought that the interplay or interaction of the child's temperament and personality, parents' personalities, and environmental forces all play a role in the development of adaptive and maladaptive aspects of personality and psychological difficulties. Related to this assumption is what is termed **the Genetic Principle** (see Corsini & Wedding, 2005). This principle suggests the prevailing and enduring influence of the past on current mental activity. The past is represented in the present and influences current thoughts, behaviors, and emotions. The patterns can be seen in current relationships whereby patterns of problematic interactions are repeated with others.

As an illustration, people can often identify a person that they know who has series of intimate partners, all of whom are very similar. The person gets involved with one person, ends the relationship because it is not satisfactory, and begins a new relationship with another person who is almost a carbon copy of the last person. This, generally, is the idea regarding repetition of interpersonal scenarios that is important in psychoanalytic thought, although the patterns are often more subtle than the example given.

3. It is thought that we are not readily aware of much of our behavior nor the forces that direct our behavior. These forces, conflicts, patterns, and drives compel us to behave in certain characteristic and repetitive ways that we are not automatically aware of. The theoretical component, known as the **theory of topography**, refers to the notion that there is a layering of levels of consciousness from **unconscious** (i.e., information we are not aware of), **preconscious** (i.e., information currently not aware but can easily be made aware of), to **conscious** (i.e., what we are currently aware of). A person has varying accessibility to information contained at the various levels. A goal of treatment is to make the person more aware of unconscious influences on his or her behavior patterns. Making people aware of unconscious influences is not necessarily easy, as the patient will often evidence **resistance** because the unconscious material is often threatening or anxiety-provoking.

For example, you may have had the experience of walking away from some interaction or situation, asking yourself, "Why on earth did I just say (or do) that? That is not like me to say something like that." In that kind of situation, it is assumed from a psychoanalytic perspective that there was a reason that you said or did something that is currently incomprehensible to you. It is not readily apparent, and, potentially, with some reflection, you may be able to understand the statement or action somewhat.

4. Emotion or affect plays a major role in psychoanalytic theories and treatments. For example, early psychoanalytic writing placed great importance on different kinds of anxiety as reflecting, essentially, internal and unconscious conflict among the components of the personality. Although anxiety is still seen as a very important affect, other emotions such as shame, anger, depression, despair, guilt, and emotional numbing have also been seen to be highly relevant (Tasca, Mikail, & Hewitt, 2005). An important characteristic of emotion is that it provides a link with cognitive elements of the person's functioning including memory, forgetting, and attention or concentration (Bower, 1981). The use of affect provides a way to get access to some of the unconscious material that can be relevant for understanding and treating a person's psychological difficulties. This gives an example of the dynamics of personality or the interplay of the components and forces within the psyche or mind. Moreover, the dynamics of personality are thought to reflect psychic determinism—the idea that all behavior has meaning, a goal, and a purpose and is frequently driven by unconscious forces. For example, a person's symptoms, choice of a spouse or life partner, choice of career, or interests are all determined and fit with the characteristics and dynamics of personality.

5. The development of patterns or styles of relating to others and to the self is an integral part of psychoanalytic treatment. This has been especially emphasized in more recent psychoanalytic thought and reflects the idea that individuals develop relationship styles early in life, often with the very strong influence of the relationship with the primary caregiver. These relationship styles can be adaptive or can produce difficulties for the individual. These relationship styles are believed to be evident in current relationships that the individual has. Furthermore, individuals will respond to others they are currently interacting with in a similar manner or as if they are interacting with someone from their past. This is the concept of **transference** whereby patients will begin to interact with the therapist in a manner that is consistent with some person or people from the patient's past. Although students may typically hear about transference and transference reactions in psychotherapy, these sorts of responses also occur in other interpersonal situations for most people. In fact, the therapist himself or herself can react to patients with transference reactions (i.e., respond to the patient as if he or she is someone from the therapist's past), and this response is one type of what is termed **countertransference**.

◇ EVOLUTION OF PSYCHOANALYTIC THEORY

Psychoanalytic theories have evolved tremendously over the past century. As a quote from Arlow (2000) attests: "It is almost impossible to grasp the extent to which psychoanalysis has changed since the death of Freud in 1939 . . . there are so many differing, competing theories concerning the causes and treatment of mental illness that Wallerstein (1988) spoke of a need to recognize many psychoanalyses instead of just one" (p. 25).

As psychoanalytic theories evolved and branched out over the decades, different psychoanalytic treatments developed and sprang up as subsequent psychoanalytic theorists expanded, revised, or revamped many components of Freud's theories. Although psychoanalytic theories took many directions, depending on the theoreticians involved, we will describe some theoretical components that are representative of the major contemporary schools of treatment within psychoanalysis. These different approaches to psychoanalytic thought provide a model and rationale for the focus chosen in treatment. In other words, each of these domains views maladaptive behavior as the product of different forces or processes, and each of them focuses on these processes in treatment. We will start with classical psychoanalysis.

Classical psychoanalysis, one of the first psychodynamic treatments, was developed by Sigmund Freud, a Viennese neurologist, in the late 1800s and early 1900s, based on his psychoanalytic theory. The focus of the work was based on his treatment of hysterical neuroses (also termed conversion disorders and represent disorders that involve symptoms that appear to be neurological problems, but there are no physiological bases to explain the symptoms). Classical psychoanalysis derives specifically from Freud's theoretical perspective that places heavy emphasis on basic biological drives, mainly sexual and aggressive drives, as the unconscious motivators of behavior and, potentially, the cause of symptoms and personality difficulties. In order to understand the processes involved, Freud proposed a model of personality that involved personality structures. Essentially, the biological drives or impulses derive from the **id**, a component of personality that is entirely unconscious and houses the source and energy for the instinctual impulses. These drives or impulses seek expression and can, if expression of the impulses is inappropriate, produce an aversive state of anxiety. Both the **ego** (the functions of personality that guide the individual in the real world with emphasis on safety and survival) and the **superego** (the part of personality concerned with lawful, moral, and ideal aspirations) subdue or control both the impulses and the anxiety. This produces a state of conflict, and the impulses and attendant conflict are often channeled into neurotic symptoms or personality problems. Moreover, it was believed that the unconscious part of the mind harbored past traumas, either actual or symbolic traumas, that, because of their aversive and overwhelming nature, are banished to the unconscious.

Treatment involves attempting to make the unconscious drives or traumas conscious, and through the emotional reactions accompanying the uncovering, the symptoms or personality disturbances are released. This is done through several techniques used in classical psychoanalysis, all of which have the goal of uncovering unconscious material. These techniques include free association whereby the patient is encouraged to talk aloud about anything that comes to mind either at any point in the therapy or in specific response to cue words, dream interpretation whereby the symbolic nature of features of the dream reveal unconscious material, as well as transference responses of the patient whereby the patient interacts with the therapist in the same manner as some individual from the patient's past. An important element of the actual treatment process involves the therapist not influencing the flow of unconscious material in any way; thus, the analyst typically sits out of view of the patient, speaks little, and attempts not to direct the patient in any way.

As a simple illustration, the following description of using dream material in psychoanalytic treatment is quoted from Gabbard (2004, pp. 121–122):

> Ms. N was a 42-year-old woman who came to psychotherapy after the death of her son from muscular dystrophy. She was a stoic woman who had defended against her grief by becoming active in the local muscular dystrophy organization and by insisting that helping others kept her from feeling sad about her son. Nevertheless, she would occasionally tear up as she talked about him, only to flee her feelings when they became uncomfortable.

One day Ms. N came to therapy and said "I had a dream last night. I don't know what to make of it. It was a very short dream. I looked at my fingernails, and they were all broken." The therapist asked her what came into her mind as she thought about that image of broken fingernails. She hesitated a moment and then said that when she was changing her son's bed sheets, which was a frequent necessity during his last days alive, she would often break her fingernails. She reflected on how completely ridiculous it was to worry about such minor trivia as a broken fingernail when her son was dying. Her therapist tuned into the meaning of the dream and said: "In some ways it would be nice to have broken fingernails again, because it would mean your son was alive." The patient cried quietly.

◇ PHASES OF CLASSICAL PSYCHOANALYSIS

Classical psychoanalysis (and psychoanalytic psychotherapy) is thought to consist, generally, of four phases, although they do not necessarily occur chronologically, and often phases will overlap. Moreover, classical psychoanalysis is usually seen as long-term treatment; thus phases, especially the middle two phases, can be quite lengthy. Following are the phases as outlined by Arlow (2000):

1. The **opening phase** is characterized by determining the nature of the person's difficulties, to learn as much as possible about the person and his or her current and past life situations, history and development, as well as behaviors related to how the person relates his or her information to the therapist. The therapist attempts to detect themes that are relevant for the development of the difficulties, conflicts, or issues the person wishes to understand and change.

2. The **development of transference phase** is characterized by the patient beginning to relate current behavior to unconscious material from the past, particularly

---

BOX 11.2

INVENTION OF PSYCHOTHERAPY

It is often thought that Sigmund Freud invented psychotherapy. In reality this is not true, as there were numerous clinicians who were engaging in the treatment of psychological problems that involved talking with the patient. For example, according to Corsini and Wedding (2005), Paul Dubois (1848–1914) treated psychotic individuals by talking with them, and Pierre Janet (1859–1947) was a very well-known and respected psychotherapist before Freud began his work. Furthermore, Ellenberger (1970) lists four of the foremost psychotherapists who practiced prior to Freud between 1880 and 1910: Ambroise Liebeault (1823–1904); Hippolyte Bernheim (1840–1919); Auguste Forel (1848–1931); and, as mentioned above, Paul Dubois.

childhood, and to wishes regarding past relationships. The therapist becomes an important component of the patient's life, and the patient begins to respond to the therapist in a distorted fashion as if he or she was the same as some person from the patient's past. It is important to note that the patient does not believe that the therapist is the same person from the past, but rather the patient responds in a pattern of behavior that is similar to the behavior engaged in by the patient with that person from the past. The work of this phase involves the interpretation of the transference. The idea is to help the patient distinguish reality and fantasy, understand the unconscious influences of early experiences, and gain more control over automatic behaviors that cause or perpetuate problems.

3. The **Working Through Phase** coincides with the second phase and involves consistent interpretations of transference responses, recall of early material that relates to early relationships and development, and deepening insight into unconscious influences.

4. The final phase is known as the **Resolution of Transference Phase**, which represents the termination phase of treatment. Typically a mutually agreed-upon date of termination is set by therapist and patient, and issues pertaining to loss, dependency, and abandonment often arise. These issues are dealt with in the same manner (i.e., interpretation, insight, and so forth) and are understood in the context of ending an important relationship. Whereas many treatment orientations do not place great importance on termination of the therapeutic experience, psychoanalytic treatments view termination as a highly significant element in appropriate treatment.

Although some of the underpinnings of classical psychoanalysis have not received good support (e.g., importance of sexual and aggressive impulses in producing symptoms) and many of the concepts are difficult to operationalize, a large number of the ideas, techniques, and understanding of the therapeutic process remain in mainstream psychotherapy and have received empirical attention. Moreover, attempts to adequately operationalize these concepts have been undertaken (see Bornstein, 2005). Millon (2004) has suggested that four major contributions provided by Freud's classical psychoanalysis involved:

1. The importance of the structure and processes of the unconscious
2. The role of early childhood experiences in shaping personality development
3. The methodology for psychological treatment of mental disorders
4. The recognition that understanding the person's personality is central to understanding the person's problems

Although, as stated by Magnavita (2008), classical psychoanalysis has had its heyday as the dominant form of treatment for a variety of psychological problems, this type of treatment and training in classical psychoanalysis is still readily available, sought out, and practiced (Sharf, 2000).

◇ EGO PSYCHOLOGY

Although classical psychoanalysis was revised and refined by Freud and others, one major modality that differed substantially from the early model was known as ego psychology. We will describe this as an example of one of the earlier major revisions of psychoanalytic thought and treatment, with a focus on working directly with children. Theorists such as Anna Freud (Sigmund Freud's daughter) and Erik Erikson (you will likely have heard of Erikson as the person who developed the concept of psychosocial stages of development) extended and revised some of the original tenets of psychoanalysis. Rather than concentrating on biological drives as the primary source of psychological difficulties and the focus of treatment, ego psychology emphasized how the ego functions in the present in both adaptive and maladaptive ways. There is emphasis on the importance of current interactions and interaction patterns with others, developmental stages of the person in childhood and adulthood, as well as both conscious and unconscious processes that influence behavior. Consistent with the model, rather than focusing on past relationships, treatment tends to focus on both current relationships and the therapy itself to observe and attempt to understand psychological defenses and the anxiety underlying the defenses.

Ego psychology is based on the structural model of id, ego, superego and the conflicts that these three components exhibit. Consistent with Freud, it was believed that the three components are in constant conflict, and this conflict creates anxiety in the individual. Because the individual or the ego needs to deal with the anxiety, specific coping strategies or defense mechanisms are activated, and symptoms arise when the anxiety is not dealt with in an adaptive manner. Essentially, the anxiety and defense result in what is termed a **compromise formation**, which results in either neurotic symptoms or personality characteristics and disturbances.

Treatment focuses on the compromise formations and conflicts that make up one's character as well as developmental issues. This is done through analysis of defenses that become evident in the therapy interactions, which provides information regarding conflicts. It is the delineation of ego defenses that represents one of the major contributions that ego psychology theorists made. Although initially there were nine major defenses outlined by Anna Freud, they have been added to over the years and can be divided into three groups ranging from the most pathological (**primitive defenses**), somewhat less pathological (higher-level or **neurotic defenses**), to the most healthy or mature (**mature defenses**). A hierarchy of defenses as outlined by Gabbard (2005, p. 5) is reproduced in Table 11.1.

Ego psychology has had a significant impact on contemporary psychoanalytic treatment. For example, it has drawn attention to the importance placed on current functioning of the ego and the defenses that an individual uses to cope with the anxiety that often form the focus of treatment. Two more recent psychoanalytic models that are representative of contemporary psychoanalysis, object relations theory and self psychology, are presented here. The models share certain features such as the importance of the development of the self, self-concept, and interpersonal relationships, and, like all psychoanalytic theories, these models are concerned with how the past influences the present and how the inner world of the person distorts, colors, and influences the behavior and experience the person has (St. Clair, 2004).

TABLE 11.1 A Hierarchy of Defense Mechanisms

DEFENSE MECHANISM	DESCRIPTION
Primitive defenses	
Splitting	Compartmentalizing experiments of self and other such that integration is not possible. When the individual is confronted with the contradictions in behavior, thoughts, or affect he/she regards the differences with bland denial or indifference.
Projective identification	Both an intrapsychic defense mechanism and an interpersonal communication. This phenomenon involves behaving in such a way that subtle interpersonal pressure is placed on another person to take on characteristics of an aspect of the self or an internal object that is projected into that person. The person who is the target of the projection then begins to behave, think, and feel in keeping with what has been projected.
Projection	Perceiving and reacting to unacceptable inner impulse and their derivatives as though they were outside the self. Differs from projective identification in that the target of the projection is not changed.
Denial	Avoiding awareness of aspects of external reality that are difficult to face by disregarding sensory data.
Dissociation	Disrupting one's sense of continuity in the areas of identity, memory, consciousness, or perception as a way of retaining an illusion of psychological control in the face of helplessness and loss of control. A thought similar to splitting, dissociation may in extensive cases involve alteration of memory of events of the disconnection because of the disconnection of the self from the event.
Idealization	Attributing perfect or near-perfect qualities to others as a way of avoiding anxiety or negative feelings, such as contempt, envy, or anger.
Acting out	Enacting an unconscious wish or fantasy impulsively as a way of avoiding painful affect
Somatization	Converting emotional pain or other affect states into physical symptoms and focusing one's attention on somatic (rather than intrapsychic) concerns.
Regression	Returning to an earlier phase of development or functioning to avoid the conflicts and tensions associated with one present level of development
Schizoid fantasy	Retreating into one's private internal world to avoid anxiety about interpersonal situations.
Higher-level (neurotic defenses)	
Introjection	Internalizing aspects of a significant person as a way of dealing with the loss of that person. One may also introject a hostile or bad object as a way of giving one an illusion of control over the object. Introjection occurs in non-defensive forms as a normal part of development.

TABLE 11.1   A Hierarchy of Defense Mechanisms *(Continued)*

DEFENSE MECHANISM	DESCRIPTION
Identification	Internalizing the qualities of another person by becoming like the person. Whereas introjection leads to an internalized representation experienced as an "other," identification is experienced as part of the self. This, too, can serve a non-defensive function in normal development.
Displacement	Shifting feelings associated with one idea or object to another that resembles the original in some way.
Intellectualization	Using excessive and abstract ideation to void difficult feelings.
Isolation of affect	Separating an idea from its associated affect state to avoid emotional turmoil.
Rationalization	Justification of unacceptable attitudes, beliefs, or behavior to make them tolerable to oneself.
Sexualization	Endowing an object or behavior with sexual significance to turn a negative experience into an exciting and stimulating one or to ward off anxieties associated with the object.
Reaction formation	Transforming an unacceptable wish or impulse into its opposite.
Repression	Expelling unacceptable ideas or impulses or blocking them from entering consciousness. This defense differs from denial in that the latter is associated with external sensory data whereas repression is associated with inner states.
Undoing	Attempting to negate sexual, aggressive, or shameful implications from a previous comment or behavior by elaborating, clarifying, or doing the opposite.
Mature defenses	
Humor	Finding comic and/or ironic elements in difficult situations to reduce unpleasant affect and personal discomfort. This mechanism also allows some distance and objectivity from events so that an individual can reflect on what is happening.
Suppression	Consciously deciding not to attend to a particular feeling, state, or impulse. This defense differs from repression and denial in that it is conscious rather than unconscious.
Asceticism	Attempting to eliminate pleasurable aspects of experience because of internal conflicts produced by that pleasure. This mechanism can be in the service of transcendent or spiritual goals, as in celibacy.
Altruism	Committing oneself to the needs of others over and above one's own needs. Altruistic behavior can be used in the service of narcissistic problems but can also be the source of great achievements and constructive contributions to society.

(Continued)

TABLE 11.1 A Hierarchy of Defense Mechanisms *(Continued)*

DEFENSE MECHANISM	DESCRIPTION
Anticipation	Delaying of immediate gratification by planning and thinking about future achievements and accomplishments.
Sublimation	Transforming socially objectionable or internally unacceptable aims into socially acceptable ones.

Reprinted from Gabbard (2004) with permission.

◇ OBJECT RELATIONS THEORY

According to Gabbard et al. (2005), **object relations theory** is likely the predominant perspective in contemporary psychoanalytic theory and treatment. There are many psychoanalytic theorists associated with the development and evolution of object relations theory including Melanie Klein, D. W. Winnicott, and Otto Kernberg, and there are many others who have contributed to this psychoanalytic theory, including Harry Stack Sullivan and John Bowlby.

The term "object relations" refers to the internal and external world of interpersonal relationships, and the term "object" refers to the person to whom the individual is relating

BOX 11.3

SULLIVAN AND ADLER

Several students of Freud broke away from some fundamental aspects of psychoanalysis and focused on the interpersonal aspects of people's functioning. Two of these individuals, in particular, Harry Stack Sullivan and Alfred Adler, have had a significant impact on the field of clinical psychology, and both have emphasized the importance of the interpersonal domain on shaping personality and as focuses for treatment.

Harry Stack Sullivan was an American psychoanalyst who developed a theory of personality and psychoanalytic treatment that was based entirely on interpersonal relatedness and the critical roles that various relationships, including communal social experiences, play in an individual's life. His book entitled, *The Interpersonal Theory of Psychiatry* (Sullivan, 1953), outlines the basic premises of this theory, and he is considered the founder of interpersonal theory and therapy. Sullivan believed that personality evolved from interpersonal relationships rather than from biological or instinctual drives. He developed the concept of **self-system** whereby individuals develop a system of traits, based on their interactions with others, that constitute the self. Moreover, he described concepts related to the development of the self-system in childhood, such as the **"Good Me,"**

BOX 11.3 CONTINUED

"**Bad Me**," and "**Not Me**," based on interactions, especially with parents. Moreover, he was one of the first theorists to describe the concept of **personifications**, or the mental representations of relationships, a concept that has become pivotal in numerous personality theories. Finally, the treatment that he proposed involves the detailed explorations of the interpersonal interactions the patient has, particularly the interpersonal behaviors that become evident during psychotherapy. He described **parataxic distortions** as those whereby patients respond to therapists based on previous relationships they have had. This, of course, is very similar to Freud's notion of transference.

Sullivan's work has had a major impact not only on the development of interpersonal psychotherapy but also on theorizing and research on interpersonal behavior. His work has influenced not only other psychoanalytic theorists but also models of personality and treatment from other perspectives.

Similarly, Alfred Adler, an Austrian psychoanalyst heavily influenced by Freud and his teachings, also broke away from Freud due, mainly, to his beliefs that psychoanalysis was devoid of understanding and integration of the social influences on the self that Adler considered critical (Adler, 1956). He is considered the founder of the **Individual Psychology** school (Ellenberger, 1970), and his thinking greatly overlapped with that of other analysts of the post-Freud generation, namely, Karen Horney and Harry Stack Sullivan, both of whom also emphasized the interpersonal domain. Adler believed that early family influences, including sibling constellation and parental education style, would lead to an individual developing a life plan that guides his or her behavior without much conscious awareness of this **life plan's** details. The early family and larger social influences through school and community may create maladaptive patterns of behavior. For example, when a child does not feel equal and is either overprotected or neglected, he or she likely develops **inferiority** or **superiority complexes** and various accompanying compensation strategies, which lead to long-term maladjustment. Adler also argued for equality of the genders and a general democratic approach to family dynamics.

His therapy approach is more directive than classical psychoanalysis and is geared toward understanding one's personality in light of these early life influences. An Adlerian therapist will use Socratic questioning but also works with dreams, transference phenomena, and interpretation.

An important aspect of Adlerian thinking was that he used his theory and general developmental psychology knowledge not only to define his approach to treatment but to emphasize **prevention** as well. He has been pivotal in instituting the first parent training courses in order to ensure that parents would have the skills and understanding needed to raise healthy children. His approach to **parent training** is still apparent in many such courses taught today.

(St. Clair, 2004). This model is based, generally, on the premise that the self and the development of the self are primarily interpersonal in nature. That is, the development of the self or self-concept arises from early interactions with others (what some have termed "reflected appraisals"), and, of course, the first and predominant interactions occur with the primary caregivers. In order to understand the individual (and the difficulties that he or she is struggling with), one needs to understand the nature of the relationships that have influenced the development of the self, the personality makeup, the problems the person experiences, and how these relationship patterns are currently manifested and influence the person's behavior (Anderson, Reznik, & Glassman, 2005).

At its core, object relations theory emphasizes the development and "stamping in" of the conceptions of the self and objects and, especially, the relationship between the self and objects. That is, the nature of significant relationships (and conceptions of the self) is internalized in childhood. These relationships then color and influence personality development, past and present relationships, and psychopathology. One of the main focuses of object relations theory is on how the person, himself or herself, views significant relationships, either consciously or unconsciously (Sharf, 2000), and how these internalized relationship patterns from the past influence the development of personality.

Some of the more important concepts involve:

1. There is great importance placed on the first and predominant relationship of the infant with the infant's main caregiver (usually the mother). The nature of the unfolding of this relationship, especially as it relates to the child developing separateness and autonomy (known as **separation and individuation**), is thought to be of great importance in developing and establishing patterns of self-acceptance, autonomy and independence, interpersonal warmth, and other personality factors (Sharf, 2000).

2. The nature of this early relationship is internalized as a relational schema (i.e., a script, formula, or framework for the relationship pattern) and influences the development of the self, the personality, and related psychological difficulties. The relational internalization is not necessarily a totally accurate depiction of the relationship as there may be elements that are distorted or exaggerated.

3. The relational schema is activated in current relationships (including the therapeutic relationship) and colors and influences these relationships. It is further believed that components of the internalization can thwart development and interfere with mature relationships.

Overall, object relations theory reflects one of the major revisions to traditional psychoanalytic thinking that is currently evident, that being the focus on interpersonal aspects of adaptive and maladaptive functioning and personality development. There is less or no emphasis on biological drives, and the ideas deriving from this approach have spurred significant research not only with psychoanalytic researchers but also with social, clinical, and personality psychology researchers (e.g., Flett, 2007).

In terms of treatment, the emphasis tends to be on demonstrating and making the patient aware of how his or her characteristic relationship styles or relational schemas are problematic. It is assumed that these schemas will arise in the therapeutic relationship (i.e., transference) and that the therapist helps the patient understand the nature of these schemas. In understanding the nature and purpose of the schemas, the patient can begin to alter, shift, or change the relationship styles.

◇ SELF PSYCHOLOGY THEORY

This theory was developed by Heinz Kohut (1984) who focused on the development of the self and on how self-caring, self-esteem, and narcissism (in this case, not only the pathological level of narcissism, but the development of self-regard) precede caring for others and how development of narcissism reflects normal development. Although much of his theorizing has focused on particular types of severe personality disorders, the treatment tends to focus on the development and maintenance of self-esteem and self-regard as the most important elements. It is thought from this perspective that psychopathology is related to deficits in the development of a coherent sense of self and that individuals will develop highly vulnerable self-esteem and what are termed **self-object functions** or interpersonal strategies to elicit responses from others to correct deficits in self-esteem.

Specifically, this approach emphasizes developmental deficits rather than conflicts as important in developing psychological difficulties. Due to the lack of empathy and being taught that he or she is valued and cherished, the child goes through life with a deficit in his or her sense of self. In other words, the person comes to understand himself or herself as someone who is not a valued, cherished, or lovable person and develops what are termed **self disorders**. These self disorders or traumas derive from the child not being seen or affirmed or being regarded as an object for gratification by the caregiver, or from abuse. The child (and eventually the adult) goes through life not sure if he or she actually exists and experiences little or no self-worth. The person will attempt to correct these self-related deficits, at an unconscious level, by trying to get others to respond to him or her in a way that makes up for the deficit. For example, the person can look to others for affirming behavior or look for others to be proud of the person's accomplishments (mirroring or the **mirror transference**). Also, the person can maintain his or her self-esteem by attempting to interact with or bask in the glow of someone else's ideal or powerful position (**the idealizing transference**), and the person can imitate an idealized other as a way of being like or merging with the idealized other (**alter-ego transference**). Kohut and followers believed that these types of transferences were responsible for significant psychological difficulties known as **self disorders**.

The psychoanalytic treatment from this approach involves identifying the deficits in self-esteem or self-concept and attempting to create a therapeutic situation that allows for strong empathic responses by the therapist, mirroring of behavior (i.e., showing the patient what he or she is attempting to accomplish in his or her self-object function), and developing and fostering a cohesive sense of self in the patient.

◇ SHORT-TERM DYNAMIC PSYCHOTHERAPIES

There have been numerous psychoanalytic writers who have suggested that many of the goals of psychoanalytic treatment can be accomplished in short-term psychoanalytic psychotherapy (e.g., Alexander & French, 1946; Firenczi, 1933) rather than the years suggested by classical psychoanalysis. Over the past two decades there has been significant development in psychoanalytically oriented treatments that are very focused, intensive, and time-limited whereby treatment is expected to be of a brief duration. Due to the intensive nature of these treatments, they often use highly selected patient groups, with the understanding that several of the short-term treatments are appropriate for particular types of patients and not necessarily for others (Davanloo, 2000).

The theoretical tenets of these treatments are mostly the same as other forms of psychoanalytic treatment, essentially the ideas dealing with the unconscious, the importance of interpersonal relationships and transference responses, affect, and conflict. Also, the overarching goals of short-term treatment are similar to long-term treatment as are many of the techniques and strategies used in the treatment itself, although often the timing of interventions is different. For example, the psychotherapist attempts to help the patient uncover unconscious material and make substantial changes in his or her personality makeup and relationships. The main differences between these psychoanalytically oriented treatments and longer-term psychoanalytic psychotherapy involve the time limit of the treatment and the degree to which the therapist is directive and active.

Although many types of short-term dynamic psychotherapies (STDPs) have been developed, they share a fairly common goal and approach whereby a focal issue (e.g., central conflicts, core conflictual relationship, or central focus) is quickly determined, focused upon, and emphasized in the treatment. Depending on the particular STDP, the focus of treatment uses the therapeutic relationship and transference responses, directly confronting conflicts or issues by challenging and provoking the anxiety from the conflicts in order to restructure defenses, or by using a supportive and encouraging therapeutic stance in the treatment.

◊ GOALS OF PSYCHOANALYSIS AND PSYCHOANALYTIC PSYCHOTHERAPY

Each orientation of psychoanalytic psychotherapy emphasizes different aspects of the development of personality and psychopathology, and some of the orientations focus on different types of patients. Contemporary psychoanalytic therapists are often very eclectic in the sense that they use elements of the different modalities in the conceptualization of problems and treatment (Arlow, 2000). Having said this, there are numerous consistent goals or aims that cut across most if not all psychoanalytic treatments. The overall goal of psychoanalytic treatment, according to Magnavita (2008), is to "overcome developmental obstacles and personality patterns that interfere with the person's ability to function at the person's highest possible capacity" (p. 67). Thus, there is an attempt to view the whole person and to emphasize not just the amelioration of symptoms, but to increase the quality of the person's life. Moreover, Strupp et al. (1982) state that the essence of psychoanalytic treatment involves ". . . the utilization of an interpersonal relationship in the present to correct persistent difficulties created by an interpersonal relationship in the past" (p. 223). Specific goals include:

1. Establish strong therapeutic relationship that will provide the basis for therapeutic interventions. A component of this is to establish a collaborative relationship whereby the patient himself or herself expresses the goals of treatment and where the patient feels safe, not judged, and accepted by the therapist.
2. Bring change to the overall personality and character structure. Normal behaviors and symptoms, signs, and behaviors reflective of maladjustment result from and are caused by underlying personality structures and processes. Making changes to the underlying

structures is thought not only to eliminate symptoms and troublesome behaviors but also to prevent the reappearance of these troublesome behaviors and problems.

3. Aid in bringing unconscious conflicts, patterns, defenses, and emotions to conscious awareness. Being aware of influences on one's behavior allows one to have some potential degree of control and can give the person a focus on what to alter or change. As an example, we are likely not truly aware of how we look or sound when eating soup. Because we focus on the soup and, perhaps, on the company we are keeping while eating the soup, we are not really aware of our soup-eating behavior, and, because of this, it does not dawn on us to alter or change that behavior. If someone, perhaps a loved one, points out that our soup-eating behavior is quite repulsive and disgusting, we will become aware of it, and by doing so, it allows us to make alterations, either by trying to eat in a less repulsive manner or by exaggerating the disgusting nature of the behavior. In either case, becoming aware of the behavior makes alterations of the behavior possible.

What do the different types of psychoanalytic therapy seek to make conscious? In classical psychoanalysis, the focus is on attempting to make sexual and aggressive impulses more conscious. This has taken the form of what are termed oedipal impulses that involve sexual attraction toward the other-sex parent and aggressive impulses directed toward same-sex parent. In ego psychology, the focus is mainly on the ego and making ego defenses and the attendant anxiety more conscious. With object relations theory, the issues and concerns with separation and individuation that derive from early relationship with a primary caregiver are made more conscious. Finally, in self psychology, the focus is on having the patient understand the presence and purpose of self-object functions.

As an illustration of attempts to make the unconscious conscious through interpretations, here is an excerpt from Gabbard (2004, pp. 62–64):

> A 22-year-old man who is having difficulty establishing himself in the world tells his female therapist that his mother is upset with him because he is still living at home and can't find any productive work that he enjoys. He complains to his therapist:

P: (patient): My mother is always nagging me. I hate living under her thumb. I wish she would just leave me alone.

T: (therapist): Yet you don't apply for jobs so that you could establish yourself independently.

P: That's because I can't find anything interesting in the classified ads.

T: Sometimes you may have to work at a job that you don't really like just so you can be on your own and not be pressured by your parents.

P: Believe me, I've looked through the classifieds and there's nothing available in the current situation of high unemployment. We're in an economic crisis.

T: You, I have the impression that you actually create a nagging situation with both your mom and me by taking an oppositional stance regarding trying a new job. I wonder if being nagged makes you feel like someone cares about you.

4. Although it is often assumed that psychoanalytic treatments are used only for in-depth exploration of and making changes in the personality and the unconscious defenses,

conflicts, and interpersonal patterns of a patient (exploratory or expressive psychotherapy), this is not always the case. For example, psychoanalytic treatments are sometimes used not to effect changes in personality structure but to bolster or strengthen supports, shore up defenses and coping styles, and reduce current distress and conflict (supportive psychotherapy). The use of exploratory versus supportive approaches depends on the patient's needs or abilities. For example, in some cases, it is not necessary to make significant changes to a person's personality, but, instead, it is necessary to aid the person in dealing with distress caused by some environmental trauma.

◇ PSYCHOANALYTIC TREATMENT

Commensurate with the changes in theory, there are also significant and sometimes marked changes in the psychoanalytic treatment that has developed over time. For example, the very strong emphasis on the interpersonal aspects of functioning is evident in contemporary psychoanalytic psychotherapies. Furthermore, although it was thought that in classical psychoanalysis, the treatment had to be frequent (three to five sessions per week) and long-term (i.e., measured in years) due to the nondirective nature of uncovering unconscious material. In the 1940s there was a movement toward making psychodynamic treatments shorter in duration by encouraging therapists to become more active and directive in nature (e.g., Alexander & French, 1946). Nowadays, it is certainly possible to be trained in and to practice classical psychoanalysis; however, most of the psychoanalytic psychotherapies are quite directive, shorter in duration (e.g., measured in months, although there are still situations where long-term treatment is warranted), and, in some cases, very brief. In fact, in some forms of short-term dynamic psychotherapy, there is a specification of a finite number of sessions (e.g., 12 sessions in Sifneos' short-term anxiety provoking therapy; Sifneos, 1992).

Finally, although in the past there may have been a strict adherence to one modality, currently there is a significant integration that is reflected with psychoanalytic psychotherapy. For example, according to Magnavita (2008) the psychoanalytic psychotherapist typically chooses the psychoanalytic perspective that fits with the patient's personality, problem, and context and does not force the patient and his or her difficulty into one particular framework. Moreover, there are numerous techniques that are utilized in these orientations that are often thought to exist only in behavioral approaches. For example, most of the psychoanalytic psychotherapies utilize directive and active stances of the therapist, and in some, homework assignments are utilized (e.g., Osimo, 2003). As well, there is an emphasis on the patient determining the goals of treatment (actually this has been done for decades in psychoanalytically oriented psychotherapy), and there are numerous manuals for conducting psychoanalytic treatments that have been developed (e.g., Luborsky, 1984; Osimo, 2003). Moreover, there have been major attempts to demonstrate the effectiveness of psychoanalytic treatments. Although there are several large-scale studies that have been done (e.g., The Menninger Psychotherapy Research Project; see Blatt, 1992), more recently, and in line with concerns about empirically validated treatments, there has been good evidence of the effectiveness of several short dynamic (e.g., Anderson & Lambert, 1995; Leichsenring et al., 2004) and long-term psychotherapies (Shedler, 2010).

Vehicles for Behavior Change in Psychoanalytic Treatment

Gabbard (2005) has suggested that there are several core focuses, listed here, in psychoanalytic therapy.

1. **Observation, interpretation, and confrontation.** These techniques or strategies involve the actual work in psychoanalytic psychotherapy. **Observation** involves calling attention to behavioral displays in the therapy situation that the person may not be aware of. For example, the therapist may focus on the person's nonverbal behavior, vocal intonations, or defenses that are evident to the therapist. **Interpretation** involves linking behavior to unconscious material, childhood experiences, or relationship patterns, and **confrontation** involves helping the patient face some issue or concern that is being defended against or avoided. Confrontation is not an aggressive intervention, but normally a gentle pointing out about avoidance or difficulties in expressing ideas or emotions.

    As an illustration of some of these concepts (observation, attempt at clarification, confrontation, as well as the beginning of an example of a transference response—see if you can spot the latter, which is a bit subtle), here is an excerpt from one of the author's (PLH) treatment of a patient, with issues relating to marked distress and depression in relation to being harassed and bullied at work. The therapist and patient had discussed episodes of harassment and had been discussing some of the actual incidents of being harassed:

    P: So my boss would sneer at me . . . and . . . and make these subtle faces like . . . like . . . you know, slightly rolling his eyes back . . . tilting his head . . . so I would know that he hated me . . . thought I was stupid, worthless . . . less than a worm to him.

    T: Can you tell me what you felt like when he did that?

    P: I would just see him look around . . . I guess to see if others were watching . . . so he could share his evaluation of how stupid I was . . . share it with others who would think the same way.

    T: What did you experience inside when he would do that? Let me ask . . . in a different way . . . what are you feeling now, right this moment, as you recall the looks he would give you?

    P: I can see his face and how he thought I was just the most useless piece of garbage. There was another time when on the floor when I was working on the floor . . . when the same things happened. . . . There were too many times . . . anyway when I was working on the floor.

    T: I have noticed that we have spoken fairly often about some of the specific . . . accounts . . . instances of being subtly and not so subtly, ridiculed, humiliated by your boss . . . I know that these incidents were very painful for you . . . but each time I ask about you . . . your own feelings in response to the incidents, like I did a couple of minutes ago, . . . you seem to provide me with more elaborate descriptions or other examples. I am wondering if you find it

difficult to think about or talk about the feelings . . . what you experienced
inside . . . when your boss did this to you . . .

P: (Long pause) it is just difficult.

T: Difficult in what way?

P: (Pause and becomes tearful and moves around in chair]) It is just difficult . . . to . . . tell you . . . to just say the words out loud . . . (pause)

T: I wonder if it is difficult to tell me . . . to let me know . . . that a part of
you . . . felt almost like you agreed with your boss . . . you felt worthless . . . like
a piece of garbage . . . helpless . . . that you were not strong enough to deflect
his criticism, his ridicule.

P: [Long pause] I don't . . . I never wanted anyone to know that . . . I don't like to
even think about it . . . that I have felt that way . . . that I feel that way.

T: What is it like to feel that way . . . useless . . . like a piece of garbage.

2. **Transference.** Relating to the therapist as though the therapist was someone
from the patient's past or replaying an interaction pattern from some important
relationship in the past. Cognitive representations or schemas of past relationships
are evident in the therapeutic relationship, and there may be a desire for a corrective
experience in that relationship. Another way of thinking about transference is that
interpersonal styles, that are usually based on early relationship experiences, that
may be used excessively and inappropriately and cause difficulty for the person,
may come to the fore in the therapeutic relationship. Being able to communicate
about the interpersonal style, in the here and now, can provide an important vehicle for insight and therapeutic change.

3. **Resistance.** Difficulty expressing emotions, issues, or symptoms due to shame,
lack of awareness, or fear of being overwhelmed. Often there is ambivalence
regarding getting better, and sometimes patients will subtly interfere with the
changes. One way to think about this is that patients are dissatisfied with their
current behaviors and want to behave differently. A major component of their dissatisfaction with their own behaviors lies in the patient's inability to behave in a
manner that is adaptive, meets goals, and so forth, due to anxiety. By the patient
changing his or her behavior, the therapist is helping the patient to step into
unknown territory, which is behaving differently with no familiarity as to the consequences, other than a belief and trust that things will be better. The person can
resist changing due to the sense of security with old familiar patterns of behavior
that may not be adaptive or produce happiness but produce that sense of security.

Sometimes the concept of resistance in psychoanalytic psychotherapy is characterized by others as blaming the patient for not participating in treatment, or the
resistance is characterized by an obstinate patient and a therapist attempting to
manipulate the patient into talking. Resistance is actually viewed as the result of an
unconscious defensive process that protects the patient from anxiety. The psychoanalytic therapist views the patient not as obstinate, but as experiencing anxiety
related to dealing with or discussing certain content. The therapist attempts to help
the patient get past the resistance usually by attempting to create a safe and secure
environment in which the anxiety-producing material can be brought out.

4. **Countertransference.** This is seen as an enormously important aspect of treatment. The therapist essentially pays attention to his or her own emotional reactions to a patient and uses his or her reactions as information about the inner world of the patient. Sullivan (1953) has described how by monitoring the self, the therapist can have an understanding of how others might respond to the patient and can see how the patient may unconsciously produce the feelings in others, for example, making others angry so as to keep them at a distance.

◇ NEW ISSUES IN THE FIELD

As we stated at several points in this chapter, psychoanalytic thought and therapies have developed over time, and it is still the case that psychoanalytic treatment is evolving. For example, there has been an increasing focus on what is termed the **two-person psychology** of psychoanalytic treatment (Gabbard, 2005). That is, according to Sharf (2000), "The two-person psychology focuses on how the patient and therapist influence each other. In contrast, the one-person psychology emphasizes the psychology of the patient" (p. 67).

Within the two-person psychology perspective, there is an importance given to the idea that in attempting to understand a patient and his or her experiences and difficulties, the most appropriate stance is to acknowledge that there is not necessarily an objective reality that exists in the patient or in the therapist. Rather, the best way to understand the patient is to take a stance that both the patient and the therapist have their own conceptions of reality, and these conceptions influence one another's behavior in the therapy. In other words, the therapist must pay attention not only to the patient's psychological makeup and behavior but also to his or her own behaviors, thoughts, and feelings and how they might influence the patient and the understanding of the patient's difficulties. This conceptualization of psychotherapy arises from a broader philosophical perspective known as **postmodernism** and reflects the dynamic and evolving nature of psychoanalytic thought and treatment.

Overall, it is hoped that the student has acquired an appreciation for the important ideas that psychoanalytic theory and treatments have offered; they are the foundation and became the yardstick against which newer treatments were measured. Psychodynamic approaches have a life of their own; increasingly they are being shown to be efficacious and effective treatments and continue to be in much demand.

◇ PERSON-CENTERED THERAPY

Like the other forms of therapy described in this chapter, person-centered therapy (PCT; also known as client-centered therapy or nondirective counseling) is based on a theoretical model of human functioning; however, the theoretical model differs quite substantially from many of the other models discussed. Moreover, often the emphasis of the theory has been on therapy rather than on a model of how and why people behave as they do. With the person-centered approach, the theory is based on a phenomenological view of people, and the person known best for the development of this perspective is Carl Rogers, an

American clinical psychologist who was influenced strongly by other phenomenologists such as Abraham Maslow (1968), Otto Rank (1945), and Kurt Goldstein (1959).

According to Kirschenbaum and Jourdan (2005), the impact of PCT has been huge both in terms of the approach providing a mainstay of psychotherapist's behaviors (i.e., therapist behaviors such as empathy, warmth, unconditional positive regard, and genuineness) that cut across psychotherapy orientations and in the number of fields this approach has influenced, including clinical psychology, personality psychology, education, counseling, and many other helping professions. In fact, Rogers developed a fundamentally different approach to the treatment of psychological difficulties, with underpinnings that differed sharply from the then-current thought. For example, he viewed people as blocked rather than flawed and able to use their own resources to help themselves. He was one of the first theorists and therapists to conduct detailed research on the psychotherapy process and therapist skills and attempted empirically to determine whether and how psychotherapy worked.

There continues to be active research (even more active than when Rogers was alive) that focuses on the person-centered approach, and research articles appear in a wide number and variety of journals. Furthermore, there are many local and international professional organizations, training facilities, and journals specifically dedicated to the person-centered approach. Even though Rogers himself discouraged person-centered organizations that used his name (he was worried about fostering rigid orthodoxy), following his death in 1987, there has been an increase in the activity of person-centered theorists, researchers, and practitioners internationally.

Theory

The theory underlying the person-centered approach suggests that the focus or essence of understanding people is to acknowledge the individual experience of each human as unique and legitimate. Each person has an innate goodness and a continuous and unrelenting drive for self-improvement (Flett, 2007). The fundamental notion in the person-centered approach involves the idea that people themselves have the means and potential for growth and development and that the difficulties individuals experience are a result of blocked potential. Essentially, Rogers (1951) suggests that people have an innate tendency toward growth and self-actualization, and, left to their own devices, will grow and, possibly, realize their potential.

Several important concepts form the crux of the theory underlying the person-centered approach. First, Rogers (1951, 1961) promoted two fundamental needs people have that drive and guide their behavior. The first, the **need for self-regard**, or more explicitly, the need for unconditional positive regard, involves a positive orientation and judgment of worthiness directed toward the self that is based on learned experiences throughout a person's life. When individuals experience, through interactions with others, that they are valued or seen as worthy only when certain contingencies are met or only under certain conditions (called conditions of worth), the self-regard of the individual is compromised, leading to an incongruence between the person's behavior and his or her true nature or true self. This creates levels of dysfunction in the individual. The way to correct this dysfunction is to provide the person with consistent unconditional positive regard.

The other need that Rogers focused on was the need for self-actualization or the need to become one's best possible self. An important component of this need is what is known as the **actualizing tendency**, an innate drive that moves people toward the realization of their full potential and knowledge that people carry within themselves about what is good for them and what is bad for them. That is, people have not only an inborn drive to develop and grow, but people have an innate understanding of what is helpful to them in the pursuit of attaining one's best possible self. When the need is frustrated or thwarted, there is again incongruence.

In outlining his theoretical position, Rogers (Raskin & Rogers, 2005, pp. 139–140) developed a series of 19 basic propositions of the person-centered approach to help understanding of both the way people function and change and the role of the therapist in therapy. Some of the most central of these propositions include:

1. Every person exists in a continually changing world of experience, and he or she is the center of that experience.
2. The person reacts to the field (i.e., his or her perception of the world) as it is experienced; that is, it is the person's unique reality.
3. The person is an organized whole.
4. There is one basic tendency—to actualize, enhance, and grow.
5. Behaviors are the goal-directed attempts to satisfy needs as perceived in the field.
6. In order to understand behavior, the therapist has to understand the internal frame of reference of the individual.
7. A portion of the total perceptual field becomes differentiated and develops into the self from interactions with others and the environment.
8. Behaviors are consistent with the concept of the self; that is, experiences are incorporated if they are consistent with the self and rejected if they are not consistent with the self. These latter experiences are viewed as threatening to the self.
9. Maladjustment occurs when significant, positive, or adaptive experiences are not assimilated into the self and are experienced as threatening.
10. Positive adjustment occurs or exists when experiences are commensurate with the self and are, or may be, assimilated into the self-concept; that is, the person is open to experiences in the here and now, strives to live life to the fullest, and trusts his or her own feelings, perceptions, and intuitions.

Although not all the propositions are listed, these represent some of the core issues and are thought to provide the distinctive concepts relevant to the person-centered approach compared to other major therapeutic approaches.

Person-Centered Psychotherapy

Although some characteristics of the therapy itself have been described previously, the therapist's major role, in this type of therapy, is not to direct, advise, or change the person's behavior or personality, but to provide a setting and context that allows the blockage of growth and potential to dissipate and, ultimately, to be removed so as to allow the actualizing tendency to flourish. According to the proponents of PCT, the therapist does not engage in any techniques per se (i.e., interpretation, environmental manipulation, analysis of reinforcers, and so forth), but in a nondirective (i.e., does not direct behavior, discussions, or experiences) fashion the therapist allows the person to express his or her experiences in a nonjudgmental, warm, caring, and supportive environment. It is believed that if the psychotherapist can interact and communicate with the patient in a manner that includes three essential components, then the patient will exhibit significant change. In fact, Rogers (1961) suggested that these three components are sufficient in and of themselves to produce significant change. The three essential components are empathy, unconditional positive regard, and genuineness.

Empathy

Empathy involves the attempt of the therapist to understand the patient's experiences, feelings, or thoughts by attempting "to get under the skin of the person with whom he is communicating, he tries to get with and to live the attitudes expressed instead of observing them, to catch every nuance of [sic] their changing nature; in a word, to absorb himself completely in the attitudes of the other" (Rogers, 1951, p. 29). The therapist thus attempts to understand the patient by attempting to view the patient's world as if it was the therapist's world. The therapist attempts not to be influenced by any of his or her own views, values, or standards. Moreover, the therapist attempts to not only understand the patient's experience but also communicate this understanding back to the patient. As Rogers (1961) states:

> It (empathy) involves being sensitive, moment to moment, to the changing felt meanings which flow in this other person, to the fear or rage or tenderness or confusion or whatever, that he/she is experiencing. It means temporarily living in his/her life, moving about it delicately, without making judgments, sensing meanings of which he/she is scarcely aware, but not trying to uncover feelings of which the person is totally unaware, since this would be too threatening. It includes communicating your sensings of his/her world as you look with fresh and unfrightened eyes at elements of which the individual is fearful. (p. 4)

It is important to understand that empathic responding is not simply the repetition of the patient's utterances regarding feelings, ideas, or experiences. In fact, empathic responding often involves going beyond what the person is communicating and reflecting the intended message. This **evocative empathy** communicates not only that the therapist is closely listening and following the patient but that the therapist truly understands the patient's experience and message. The important point here is that the patient perceives the therapist's understanding and empathy.

Unconditional Positive Regard

Unconditional positive regard reflects the idea that the therapist should accept the patient as he or she is, without judgment and with no conditions of acceptance or approval. The patient is viewed as a worthwhile person no matter what, and the patient's worthiness is expressed and communicated to the patient by the therapist's behavior. The therapist needs to not only experience the patient with a positive, nonjudgmental, accepting attitude, but also express this acceptance to the patient. This does not mean that the therapist necessarily agrees with the patient and his or her utterances or ideas, but rather indicates a caring for and an acceptance of the patient as a person. Following is an example of unconditional positive regard by Rogers et al. (1967, p. 409) working with a patient named Jim who has schizophrenia:

T: I'm going to give you an appointment at that time because I'd sure like to see you then. (Pauses while writes out appointment slip.) And another thing I would say is that— if things continue to stay so rough for you, don't hesitate to have them call me. And if you should decide to take off, I would very much appreciate it if you would have them call me and—so I could see you first. I wouldn't try to dissuade you. I'd just want to see you.

P: I might go today. Where, I don't know, but I don't care.

T: Just feel that your mind is made up and that you're going to leave. You're not going to anywhere. You're just—just going to leave, hm?

P: (muttering in discouraged tone) That's why I want to go, 'cause I don't care what happens.

T: Huh?

P: That's why I want to go, 'cause I don't care what happens.

T: M-hm, M-hm. That's why you want to go, because you really don't care about yourself. You just don't care what happens. And I guess I'd just like to say—I care about you. And I care what happens.
(Silence of 30 seconds)
[Patient bursts into tears and unintelligible sobs]

T: Somehow that just—makes all the feelings pour out . . . and you just weep and weep and weep. And feel so badly . . . I do get a sense of how awful you feel inside. You just sob and sob . . . I guess all the pent-up feelings you've been feeling the last few days just—just come rolling out.

Genuineness

Genuineness or congruence is, according to Rogers and Sanford (1985), "the most basic of the attitudinal conditions that foster therapeutic growth" (p. 1379). This involves not hiding behind a mask or façade of professionalism but responding to the patient with veridical feelings and concerns and openness in communication. It is important to understand that the therapist does not burst out with any and all thoughts that enter his or her head but is open to experiencing any expressions of persistent feelings that are evident in the relationship. It is thought that by being open and honest in this fashion, the therapeutic relationship is strengthened, and the possibility of change in the patient is enhanced.

The emphasis on the relationship and the interpersonal behavior of the therapist and the exclusion of techniques contrasts with other forms of treatment that tend to place great importance on specific tasks or techniques that the therapist uses. Raskin and Rogers (2005) have detailed some of the main distinguishing characteristics of person-centered therapy, including:

1. Certain therapist attitudes (i.e., empathy, unconditional positive regard, genuineness) constitute necessary and sufficient conditions for therapeutic effectiveness.

2. Therapists need to be immediately present and accessible to patients in the treatment setting and focus on the here and now rather than the past or future.

3. There has to be a focus on the phenomenological world of the patient as he or she experiences it.

4. There is a concern with the process of personality change rather than the structure of personality, and this change is marked to the patient's ability to live more fully in the moment.

5. There is an emphasis on the need for research on psychotherapy.

6. The same principles of psychotherapy apply to all humans with all manner of problems.

7. Psychotherapy is seen as a specialized example of a constructive or positive interpersonal relationship that facilitates the patient's growth.

8. Theoretical formulations relevant for a particular person derive from the particular person's experiences, not from any preformed theory.

PCA was not developed for any particular group or type of problem, hence the term person-centered rather than problem-centered. In fact, the same approach to therapy is utilized irrespective of the person or his or her difficulty. Thus, there is no emphasis at all on diagnosis, categorization, psychological testing, history, or development of an individualized treatment plan. Each person is thought to be equal, worthy, and capable of engaging in and benefiting from the psychotherapy process.

What better therapist to present than some excerpts from Carl Rogers himself and a patient named Jill. As detailed in Raskin and Rogers (2005), a selection of the session is presented here in order to illustrate principles from the person-centered approach:

T: OK, I think I'm ready. And you . . . ready?

P: Yes.

T: I don't know what you might want to talk about, but I'm very ready to hear. We have half an hour, and I hope that in that half an hour we can get to know each other as deeply as possible, but we don't need to strive for anything. I guess that's my feeling. Do you want to tell me something that is on your mind?

P: I'm having a lot of problems dealing with my daughter. She's 20 years old; she's in college; I'm having a lot of trouble letting her go. . . . And I have a lot of guilt feelings about her; I have a real need to hang on to her.

T: A need to hang on so you can kind of make up for the things you feel guilty about—is that part of it?

P: There's a lot of that. . . . Also, she's been a real friend to me, and filled my life. . . . And it's very hard (missing part) a lot of empty places now that she's not with me.

T: The old vacuum, sort of, when she's not there.

P: Yes, yes. I also would like to be the kind of mother could be strong and say, you, "Go and have a good life," and this is really hard for me to do that.

T: It's very hard to give up something that's been so precious in your life, but also something I guess has caused you pain when you mentioned guilt.

P: Yeah, and I'm aware that I have some anger toward her that I don't always get what I want. I have needs that are not met. And, uh, I don't feel I have a right to those needs. You know. . . . She's a daughter; she's not my mother—though sometimes I feel as if I'd like her to mother me. . . . It's very difficult for me to ask for that and have a right to it.

T: So it may be unreasonable, but still, when she doesn't meet your needs, it makes you mad.

P: Yeah, I get very angry, very angry with her.

At this point in the treatment, it can be seen that Rogers is allowing the person to determine what is spoken about and to lead. At the same time, it can be seen that there are numerous empathic responses that communicate an understanding of what is being said, but also goes somewhat beyond what is being said and instead expresses the message that is being communicated. This idea is illustrated in the following exchange after a pause in the interaction:

T: You're also feeling a little tension at this point, I guess.

P: Yeah. Yeah. A lot of conflict . . .

T: Umm-hmmm

P: A lot of pain

T: A lot of pain. Can you say anything more what that's about?

P: (Sigh). I reach out for her and she moves away from me. And she steps back and pulls back . . . and then I feel like a really bad person. Like some kind of monster, that she doesn't want me to touch her and hold her like I did when she was a little girl . . .

T: It sounds like a double feeling there. Part of it is "Damn it, I want you close." The other part of it is "Oh my God, what a monster I am to not let you go."

An illustration of the focus on the here and now follows:

T: Pulling away from you

P: Yeah . . . Going away

T: . . . You feel her slipping away and you . . . it hurts . . . and

P: Yeah. I'm just sort of sitting here alone. I guess like, you know, I can feel her gone and I'm just left here.

T: Umm-hmmm. You're experiencing it right now: that she's leaving and here you are all alone

P: Yeah . . . yeah . . . Yeah . . . I feel really lonely (Cries)

In closing this section, it is also worth noting that Rogers and the PCA movement deserves much credit for having initiated and sustained research efforts on therapist skills. The topic of teachable microskills has already been discussed in chapter 10 on the therapy process, but it is only fair to highlight the origins of this important approach to therapist training.

◊ SYSTEMS THERAPIES

Introducing systems therapy is quite different from the presentation of any of the other psychological therapy approaches discussed earlier. There is no single name associated with the creation of systems therapy. Let us begin with clarification of terminology. At times, the terms **family therapy**, **couples therapy**, and **systems therapy** appear to be used interchangeably. We argue that they are not interchangeable. Although it is true that many family or couples therapists are trained in and practice a systems approach, this is not necessarily so. For example, there is a distinct *behavioral* treatment approach to couples' problems (Jacobson, Christensen, Prince, Cordova, & Elridge, 2000; Jacobson, Dobson, Truax et al., 1996) as much as there is an *emotion-focused* approach to marital problems (Johnson, Hunsley, Greenberg, & Schindler, 1999).

Systems Theory

The systems view is based on several fundamental ideas that neither began in psychology nor are they limited to psychology. Our surrounding biological and physical world is viewed as a web of relationships among elements, or a system. All systems, whether physical, biological, or social, have common patterns, behaviors, and properties that can be studied and need to be understood to develop greater insight into the behavior of complex phenomena and to move closer toward a unity of science. Many critical concepts are derived from Ludwig von Bertalanffy's **cybernetics** approach and the generation of a general systems model. The key in this model is the concept of **feedback loops** such that change in a system is recorded and may lead to resetting of certain system parameters just like the function of the thermostat in our home. The thermostat is an everyday translation of cybernetics thinking into a technology that can improve our quality of life. If the thermostat is activated to reach a room temperature of 21°C but senses that the actual room temperature is sitting at 15°C, then it turns on the heating system, which will increase the air temperature until the thermostat senses 21°C, as predetermined, and then turns off the heating. This is a feedback loop.

    Systems concepts as they relate to the systems therapies that are described here were brought into the social sciences by a group of scientists at Stanford University, most notably Gregory Bateson (Bateson, Jackson, Haley, & Weakland, 1956) and Watzlawick, Beavin, and Jackson (1967). The work of these thinkers has also been dubbed "the **Stanford communication theory**" because Stanford University is where most of the work had been done. Possibly the best-known concept emerging from these thinkers was the concept of the **double-bind** that will be described in more detail later in this chapter.

    Although we want to share our enthusiasm for systems therapy, it is not possible in the limited space available to provide more than an introduction. In order to prepare the reader for learning about the actual work of systems therapists, it is useful to know at least about some of the principal elements of the Stanford communications theory and its major propositions. Key to the link between the communications theory that is embedded in systems thinking is that Watzlawick and his collaborators see any communications structure as also reflecting the power similarity or the corresponding power differential between the individuals who communicate. In order to provide learners with tools for better understanding communication principles, Watzlawick and his collaborators have organized this knowledge around major principles or rules, which they refer to as axioms of communication. Some of the most important principles or axioms in their work are described in Box 11.4; in each case, the introduction of an axiom is initiated by providing a real-life vignette of people interacting with each other before a name is given to the underlying axiom.

BOX 11.4

AXIOMS OF COMMUNICATION

Axiom 1

VIGNETTE

A long-time married couple is at home after dinner, and given that this is a rather traditional couple, the husband is in the living room reading the newspaper with his feet up, while his wife is in the kitchen doing the dishes. At the same time, she listens to the radio where a reporter talks about relationship research showing how important it is for couples to regularly express their love to each other. She is convinced that action is needed and approaches her husband: "Do you love me?" The husband responds in a grumbling, unenthusiastic voice: "Sure, I do," while continuing to read the newspaper. The wife leaves quite unhappy with his response. This vignette describes Axiom 1, which can be summed up with the catchphrase: *You cannot not communicate.*

EXPLANATION

On the surface, the wife obtained the answer she had hoped for "Yes, I love you," but she doesn't accept this answer as meaningful because in communication there are two critical elements, namely, the verbal aspects (which in this case were clearly affirmatory) and nonverbal features (which in this case were clearly a mismatch to the content of the verbal declaration). In normal human communication, we think of an exchange as credible and unambiguous when the verbal and nonverbal elements match, which in this case would have required that the husband drops the newspaper, looks at the wife with loving eyes, and declares with enthusiasm that he loves her. This did not happen. A second question arises, namely, what the overall impression of a human interaction is when the verbal and nonverbal components are mismatched. We know from extensive research in social psychology that people

(continued)

BOX 11.4 CONTINUED

tend to believe nonverbal communication aspects more than verbal ones. In this case, it makes good sense that the wife is unhappy because the husband's lukewarm delivery of the love statement totally undermined its verbal meaning.

Even if somebody tries not to provide a verbal answer, or ignores an e-mail, or changes the topic, he or she is still communicating something, namely, that he or she is disinterested.

Axiom 2

VIGNETTE

Suzanne M. comes home from a long day at work and finds that her husband Peter has already prepared a nice dinner. Over dinner, Peter tells her that he has just finished a phone conversation with his friends, Maria and Luis, and that he has invited them for dinner and cards on Saturday. When Suzanne starts raising a variety of objections, Peter points out that only two days before Suzanne herself had suggested that they were overdue with an invitation to Maria and Luis and that they usually enjoy dinner and an evening playing cards with this couple. Nevertheless, she continues to be unhappy about this decision, and Peter cannot understand why.

This vignette depicts Axiom 2 which states, *Each communication tends to have a content and a relationship message.*

EXPLANATION

When this vignette is taken apart into the content and relationship aspects, there appears to be no problem at the content level, which consists of the overdue invitation that Peter had extended to Maria and Luis, but at the level of the relationship communication, it is likely that Suzanne reacts to the fact that Peter did not consult with her about the timing of the invitation; to her it reflects an unacceptable level of control on the part of Peter and a lack of respect for her role as a decision-maker in the process. Some experienced couples with good communication skills have learned how to recognize and separate these two components and are thereby able to avoid unnecessary fights.

Another vignette may help to further explicate this axiom. Let us imagine two men who often meet at the local pub to drink quite a bit of beer and animatedly

BOX 11.4 CONTINUED

discuss politics. They disagree on almost every political stance but continue to argue until closing hour and then repeat this scene a few days later. Why would two people who don't agree on anything spend so much time with each other? The answer is that their communication and the underlying relationship is not about agreement on political issues, but it is about the joy of debate with another person whom they respect as a debating partner. Even while disagreeing on content, they repeatedly validate the other by engaging him in the debate. If asked, they would likely refer to each other as the best of friends! On the other hand, a disagreement about political points might translate into a truly rejecting relationship, when very early in the discussion one of the men gets up and says to the other: "You are a stupid, uninformed jerk with whom I will not waste my time," and then leaves the pub. In this case, there is clear consistency between the content (disagreement on politics) and the relationship in which one of the two men rejects the other in his entirety (i.e., the message is, "we don't have a relationship"). The man left behind is understandably going to feel hurt because he was shut out at every level.

Axiom 3

VIGNETTE

Barney B is a hard worker who puts in a full day on his demanding job in a factory but spends most evenings drinking and comes home late and pretty tanked. His wife Martha gives him a hard time about his drinking and at some point threatens to leave the marriage unless they get marital counseling. During the therapy sessions, she complains about his drinking and doesn't understand why that's necessary. Barney describes the situation as his wife being so miserable and constantly complaining that he prefers to be away from home drinking so that he does not have to put up with her miserable nature. For an outsider, the unhappiness of both partners and their explanation for why they're unhappy makes some sense. If the atmosphere at home is as cantankerous as Barney describes it, then it is understandable that he wants to avoid it; his wife, of course, has cause to complain because she's constantly left alone, and Barney's drinking leaves a pretty big hole in the family's modest budget. Each accuses the other of having started or being the cause of this problem. The trouble here is that both accusations make some sense, and the vignette describes the following axiom: *Many relationship issues have no beginning or end.*

(continued)

BOX 11.4 CONTINUED

EXPLANATION

In marital therapy, couples frequently approach the therapist with a desire to have the therapist confirm that the other spouse is the source of the problem. If only this other spouse can be "fixed," the problem will go away (so they portend). The paralysis resulting from this attitude perpetuates the marital problems. Systems therapists refer to this as an **interpunction** problem because nobody can objectively determine what the beginning or the end of this problem is, nor can anybody successfully claim that he or she is completely innocent and that the other side should carry all the blame.

This axiom can be applied to the history of ongoing wars and can help us understand why after 2000 years there is still no peace in the Middle East. If a Palestinian suicide bombing kills Israelis, then the Palestinians claim that this is revenge for the violence committed against them, and the Israelis are likely to use this attack as motivation for a counterstrike. Both sides in this dispute use historical events, which did objectively happen, as a motive for their behavior and call their behavior a response, not an attack; the intent is to position oneself in a higher moral position if one is reacting rather than attacking. Of course, depending on where one stands, both are right, and thus nothing gets solved. We posit that the axiom of the interpunction problem of communications is a potent explanatory approach to understanding the history of such never-ending wars and violence. In marital therapy, this gets interpreted as a historical lack of trust in the other (often based on fact), and the therapist's task is to swear both partners in to an agreement to start with first resolutely abandoning the idea that there is one guilty party (namely, the other one) and then accept to invest in transparent little steps to rebuild this trust.

Axiom 4

VIGNETTE

Julianne and Felix have been together for 12 years and have two small children. For the most part, they seemed to get along well although after the arrival of the first child Julianne began complaining about the fact that Peter could not read and write well and was therefore stuck in a menial job with limited pay and no opportunity for promotion. However, they had not ever directly discussed this. Julianne had found Felix quite attractive when they first met and she was willing not to see his low literacy as a big problem, whereas Felix thought that she was not quite as pretty as

BOX 11.4 CONTINUED

some other girls he would have liked to go out with but that she was kind and accepted him the way he was. For a long time, the relationship appeared stable. In response to Julianne's insistence to improve his literacy, he finally caved in and began to take night classes with the goal of finally obtaining a high school graduation diploma and opening up doors for promotion and better pay at work. As it turned out, Felix was much smarter than he had thought, and he obtained his high school graduation in no time at all. He was so enthusiastic about the process of learning that he continued to take more night courses in management, and within a few years he had become a midlevel manager at his company with triple the pay. Julianne had of course noticed all these changes and was pleased with Felix's advancement at work but was totally stunned and unprepared when Felix fell in love with his very attractive, much younger secretary and told Julianne that he wanted a divorce. This vignette describes the fourth axiom: *Every action triggers a reaction.*

EXPLANATION

Systems theory sees two people in a lasting relationship as an interdependent couple that is so closely linked that any change in one of the two must have an impact on the other, who needs to make adjustments that maintain the balance between these two individuals. An analogy for the situation is that of two sailors in a small sailboat; when both sit on the opposing sides of the boat and are of equal weight, the boat is in a straight up, balanced position. If one was to move to the center or even further over to the other side, the boat must tilt and may even capsize unless the other sailor also moves to the center of the boat and counteracts this change. Along these lines, Felix's return to school and subsequent string of promotions at work has greatly changed his position in the marital relationship, and his confidence has grown. On the other hand, Julianne has not made changes that would somehow balance out Felix's gain in confidence. Even if the reader may find it difficult to accept Felix's abandonment of the marital relationship on moral grounds, systems theory would have predicted that there would be major consequences for the relationship if one partner underwent such drastic changes. Outside the world of psychotherapy there are endless further examples for such phenomena. Let's take telephone companies as an example. For many years customers had no choice in which telephone provider was available, and they were charged hefty fees for long-distance calls. Following

(continued)

BOX 11.4 CONTINUED

government deregulation laws, other businesses discovered the potential for major profit and offered competitive long-distance calling systems at lower rates; many customers jumped ship to take advantage of these low rates, and a spiraling down of long-distance telephone costs ensued to the great delight of consumers. Here, there also was initial stability in the system of provider and consumer, which lasted until deregulation kicked in; now the same provider who was used to a monopoly and high rates had no choice but to lower the rates and become competitive again.

Axiom 5

VIGNETTE

Jennifer and David are two 15-year olds with no previous dating experience; both are shy but have overcome their initial shyness and agreed to go out on a first date. Uncertain what to do on a first date, David suggests Jennifer that they go to the local museum that is currently featuring a traveling display of van Gogh paintings. Jennifer, happy to accommodate him, agrees, and the date goes sufficiently well that they arrange for another date. Not wanting to appear overly timid, Jennifer figures that David had suggested the museum visit because he likes museums and suggests to visit the local history museum on their next date. The date goes well, and David takes Jennifer's suggestion for the museum to mean that she really likes museums because she agreed to go with him in the first place and then suggested to do it again. While their relationship continues to grow more close and they visit many more museums, one day, Jennifer blurts out: "David, I like being with you but I hate museums; can't we go somewhere else?" David is floored by the sudden outburst because he has become convinced that he was making Jennifer happy with the museum visits. This vignette describes another axiom: *It is not good to act on untested assumptions.*

EXPLANATION

Due to their shyness surrounding the awkwardness of a first date, neither of the two adolescents felt comfortable to directly express personal preferences and learning from the other one what he or she most likes to do. Apparently, Jennifer overinterpreted the fact that David's first suggestion to visit a museum was simply based on his

BOX 11.4 CONTINUED

not knowing what else to do on a first date; and this scenario was made worse by David's particular interpretation of Jennifer's counterinvitation to visit another museum. Also, this type of acting on assumptions can lead to very embarrassing social situations such that somebody may ask a woman with a rather round belly when she is due to deliver the baby, whereupon she, quite embarrassed, responds with "I am not pregnant, I'm just fat." Acting on assumptions is a classic entry for "foot and mouth disease." In terms of systems therapy, understanding of this axiom strongly encourages the acquisition in practice of clear, direct, verbal communication.

In addition to capturing communication patterns in terms of axioms or rules as described in Box 11.4, there are other descriptions of how communication problems can arise. The most important concepts to be discussed in this section deal with paradoxes. A paradox by definition is an impossible situation; however, in systems theory, humans are quite able to create such situations even though a paradox is very confusing to others and may be difficult to resolve. Take, for example, the following phrase: "I am a liar." Technically, this is correct English and a complete sentence and appears at first glance to be meaningful. On close inspection, however, we are told two messages that cannot both be true. To be a habitual liar means that you do not tell the truth; therefore you would never utter such a sentence, and anybody admitting to be a liar, therefore by definition, is telling the truth. The major point to be made here is that people are able to use language to send out confusing messages that can be called **verbal paradoxes**; the listener will not know what this person is trying to say and really has only one way to resolve the situation, namely, by stating that this is confusing and contradictory and asking for clarification. Somebody who recognizes the paradox and attempts clarification uses what is called **metacommunication** (i.e., **communicating about a communication**). Metacommunication in systems theory is the equivalent to stepping back from a situation and reflecting on the situation without directly responding to the statement offered. Another interpersonal vignette can be used to describe another type of paradox. In marital therapy, the wife asks her husband to be more spontaneous. Again, it is possible to make such a request, but it is impossible to respond because spontaneity by definition is what one does without being asked. The moment we are trying to be spontaneous because we were told to do so, we are following an instruction rather than being truly spontaneous. These types of twisted and confusing communications can wreak havoc in a relationship, and this is cleverly articulated in the well-known book and subsequent film production: *Who's Afraid of Virginia Woolf?* The resolution to such an impossible request as "I want you to be more spontaneous" is to use metacommunication, where the recipient of this message says that it is impossible to do so. The ultimate most difficult scenario in the world of paradox behavior is the kind of situation where a paradox is posed but in such a context as to discourage any form of metacommunication. This scenario is what Watzlawick and his coauthors have referred to as a double-bind. A memorable display of such a scenario was actually experienced by one of the authors (W.L.), who worked as an orderly in a psychiatric hospital. Here is what happened:

> On a Sunday afternoon, it was visiting hours for patients on the locked ward. I had formed a good bond with a 16-year-old schizophrenic patient who was now moderately stable but very still emotionally fragile. He had been informed that his biological mother, little sister, and the boy's stepfather were coming to visit and he had looked forward to this visit. When the doorbell rang at 2 p.m., the beginning of visiting hours, I witnessed this interaction. The three visitors had arrived as promised and the 16-year old almost ran up to his mother, his face happy, and his arms extended for a hug. The mother accurately perceived what her son was about to do but clearly did not want him to hug her and provided very obvious nonverbal signs that she was not approving of this enthusiastic display of positive emotion. Her son accurately perceived these signs of rejection, backed off and waited for his mother to give him a sign of what she wanted him to do instead. His mother also realized that her son had backed off and said to him: "it is quite okay for a son to want to hug his mother." The effect on the 16-year old was striking as he was utterly confused and pretty much retreated into himself, obviously feeling very hurt because nothing he did or could do was going to resolve this paradoxical approach-rejection situation. The interaction, while relatively subtle, was so devastating at an emotional level that I had to spend quite a bit of time after the family visit to calm down the 16-year old patient, and we spent a lot of time discussing his complicated family dynamics.

Specific Systems Therapy Approaches

How does one move from a set of rather theoretical axioms of communication and explanatory vignettes to an actual therapy practice? The best-known therapists in the systems therapy domain have based their work on these communication principles but have done so by effectively introducing their own subtheories and concepts. Specifically, we are introducing the work of two systems therapists, namely, Dr. Virginia Satir (1964) and Dr. Salvador Minuchin (1974). Both Satir and Minuchin have made a name not only for their theorizing but also for their charismatic translation into clinical work that makes these theories come alive. To correctly execute a systematic desensitization protocol within a behavior therapy framework is quickly learned even by a novice therapist, but the development of a comfort zone for therapists in systems approaches will likely take much longer.

Satir (1964) proposes that the social systems in which we are members (especially couples and families) naturally have habits and traditions that are interconnected and interdependent, but these systems need to be open to adjust to inevitable changes, like the arrival of a new family member, children growing up and needing more space to make their own decisions, or coping with outside influences like a parent losing a job. Social systems are dysfunctional when they are rigid even if that type of stability may offer benefits in the short run.

Therapists working with immigrant families who come from very traditional backgrounds frequently encounter such a clash of rigidly held traditional values with the more liberal ones of the surrounding new culture. Especially the immigrant parents often feel that their traditional culture is an anchor, providing a feeling of safety. The more their children interact with their new surrounding culture, the more stress is placed on these traditional values.

As a therapist, Satir focuses on how family members communicate with each other, on the distribution of power, and on the styles that people use to relate to each other. She proposed the existence of five frequent interactional styles:

1. **Placating.** This describes an individual who superficially agrees with the others but may actually be ignoring or sabotaging them in the long run.

2. **Blaming.** An individual who blames seeks to defuse responsibility away from himself or herself and is not a constructively participating member of the system; he or she cannot be self-critical.

3. **Being super-reasonable.** The super-reasonable individual places so much emphasis on rationality and agreeableness that there's little room for others to have idiosyncratic emotions; also, the superreasonable may have difficulty to figure out what his or her own needs are and how they can be satisfied.

4. **Irrelevant.** The person who favors this style will not take difficult situations seriously, makes jokes where they are not called for, and does not actively participate in resolving critical issues.

5. **Congruent.** This is proposed to be the most functional style, the style that therapists aspire to nurture or create in every member of the system. The congruent individual is able to understand his own emotions as well as understands and allows those of others, will strive to allow everybody's opinions to be heard, and will do his utmost to arrive at solutions that provide the best balance of every individual's and the situation's needs.

Individuals who favor any one of the first four styles can at times be identified by the fact that his or her verbal and nonverbal communications do not jibe with each other, and they tend to make few, if any, constructive contributions to problem solving. In terms of actual therapy techniques, a systems therapist in the Satir mode can use a wide variety of techniques that can be quite directive. A therapist may be teaching good communication and negotiation skills, provide reinforcement for constructive behaviors, encourage individuals to express their emotions, and support the uniqueness of individuals. This very directive and almost prescriptive style requires a very confident, mature therapist who has developed a strong alliance with all family members, or else people will not participate.

Minuchin calls his approach structural family therapy; it addresses problems within a family by charting the relationships between family members or between subsets of family members. These charts represent communication habits and their implicit power dynamics as well as the **boundaries** between different **subsystems**. Pathology within a family is not attributed to individuals but is considered to arise when subsystems fail to do what they should. For example, parents are a subsystem that is expected to provide authority and structure when teenagers are trying to reject all authority. Teenage rebellion in and of itself is not considered pathological, but the inability to respond with flexibility to this normal developmental pattern is considered problematic. Structural family therapy is characterized by rather normative ideas about which roles a family member should play, and these are expected to be consistent with the members' typical developmental stage. Functional social systems rest on clarity and appropriateness of **subsystem boundaries**. It is normal that family subsystems are characterized by a hierarchy of *power*, typically with the parental subsystem on top, executing authority over the offspring subsystem. In healthy families, parent-children boundaries are both clear and semidiffuse, allowing the *parents* to interact and to negotiate between themselves the methods and goals of parenting. In a healthy family, the children have autonomous sibling socialization, yet the parents are not so rigid or aloof as to ignore childhood needs for support, nurturance, and guidance. Also, there may be a subsystem of males, characterized, for example, by a father and son choosing to attend a car show in town in which the family's females showed no interest. On the other hand, there should also be opportunities for a father to have occasional unique interactions with a daughter such that he might teach her how to drive a car when she gets old enough. These scenarios described clear yet permeable, and therefore appropriate, boundaries. On the other hand, parents who believe that they need to control with whom their 22-year-old daughter can date and try to enforce a 10 p.m. curfew on her would be considered to have rigid boundaries. Note that these definitions are influenced by culture and that a Minuchin-type therapist in such a case acts on his or her knowledge of developmental stages and age-typical behavior of 22-year olds but is also imposing his or her values on a family.

When these parent-child boundaries are not clear and a parent expects a child to play an adult role or is incapable of playing the role of adult herself, such a boundary is referred to as **enmeshed**. Such scenarios are unfortunately not that infrequent as psychologists who work with divorced families can tell, for example, when a mother might expect her 14-year-old son to move into the role of the adult male in the house. Of course, the ultimate extreme example of enmeshment and violation of parent-child boundaries would be the case of parent-child incest.

At the other end of the boundaries spectrum may be a family member who is emotionally aloof (not unusual for teenagers) or physically absent (like a parent who for financial reasons works in another city) on an ongoing basis; this is referred to as a **detached** family member.

In therapy, the therapist actually enters or **joins** with the family system as a catalyst for positive change. Joining with a family is a goal of the structural family therapist early on in his or her therapeutic relationship with the family. To accelerate change, Minuchin manipulates the format of the therapy sessions, structuring desired subsystems by isolating them from the remainder of the family, either by the use of space and positioning (seating) within the room or by having nonmembers of the desired substructure leave the room (but stay involved by viewing from behind a one-way mirror). The aim of such interventions is often to cause the **unbalancing** of the family system, in order to help the family members see the dysfunctional patterns and be open to **restructuring**. He believes that change must be gradual and proceed in digestible steps for it to be useful and lasting. Because structures tend to self-perpetuate, especially when there is positive feedback, Minuchin asserts that therapeutic change is therefore likely to be maintained.

Evaluating the effectiveness of systems therapies is quite difficult because by definition there is not a single symptom or a single patient. One possibility would be to evaluate marital satisfaction in both partners and then study this feature over time. Nevertheless, this does not preclude research on systems therapy outcomes as Russell and his collaborators (1987) have successfully shown in a comparison of family systems therapy with individual therapy for anorexia patients.

◇ CONCLUSION

In this chapter we have outlined the theoretical rationales and the therapeutic approaches for three major psychotherapeutic orientations used in clinical psychology: psychoanalytic psychotherapies, person-centered therapy, and systems therapy. Psychoanalytic treatments represent pioneering approaches to psychological therapies and have been around for about 100 years, they are still alive and well and evolving. Person-centered treatment was also described, and it has been praised for its emphasis on therapist training and the building of therapist microskills. Lastly, systems therapies were described with the various theoretical positions and therapy approaches described by a notable therapist working in this vein.

◇ ONGOING CONSIDERATIONS

As stated near the beginning of the chapter, many students have been taught that psychoanalysis and psychoanalytic psychotherapies are no longer utilized in the field of clinical psychology. Jonathan Shedler (2006) has written an intriguing article entitled "That was then, this is now: Psychoanalytic psychotherapy for the rest of us" that not only documents this phenomenon but also points out how this phenomenon is in error. For example, one criticism that has been promoted is that psychoanalytic treatments have been shown to be inferior to other treatments. In a recently published article that appeared in the flagship journal of the American Psychological Association, *The American Psychologist*, the same Shedler (2010) presents compelling arguments and data supporting the efficacy and effectiveness of psychoanalytic treatments. A fair criticism of classical psychoanalysis has been its length and associated cost, but that criticism has been overcome with the development of much shorter-term analytical and interpersonal therapies.

Client-centered treatment is now, as a singular treatment (i.e., not "packaged with other approaches"), mainly used in school and counseling environments where the clients usually do not need meet the criteria for a diagnosable mental illness. Although Carl Rogers was a strong proponent of research on the utility of the client-centered approach, there has been relatively little recent research suggesting its efficacy or effectiveness as a stand-alone treatment. Systems therapies are particularly dominant in the world of marital and family therapists, many of whom are not clinical psychologists by training. Nevertheless, we urge all clinical psychologists to obtain at least some basic training in systemic approaches given how much explanatory power they have for the patterns of human interaction.

◇ KEY TERMS LEARNED

Actualizing tendency

Alter-ego transference

Bad me

Blaming

Boundaries

Classical psychoanalysis

Communicating about a communication

Compromise formation

Confrontation

Congruent

Conscious

Counter-transference

Couples therapy

Cybernetics

Detached

Development of transference phase

Double-bind

Ego

Empathy

Enmeshed

Evocative empathy

Family therapy

Feedback loops

Genuineness

Good me

Id

Individual psychology

Inferiority complex

Interpretation

Interpunction

Irrelevant

Joins

Life plan

Mature defenses

Meta-communication

Mirror transference

Need for self-regard

Neurotic defenses

Not me

Object relations theory

Observation

Opening phase

Parataxic distortion

Parent training

Personification

Placating

Postmodernism

Preconscious

Primitive defenses

Psychic determinism

Psychoanalysis

Psychoanalytic psychotherapies

Psychodynamic

Resistance

Resolution of transference phase

Restructuring

Self-disorders

Self-object function

Self-system

Separation and individuation

Short-term dynamic psychotherapies

Stanford communication theory

Subsystem boundaries

Subsystems

Superego

Superiority complex

Super-reasonable

Symptom substitution

Systems therapies

Systems therapy

The genetic principle

The idealizing transference

Theory of topography

Transference

Two-person psychology

Unbalancing

Unconditional positive regard

Unconscious

Verbal paradoxes

Working through phase

◇ THINKING QUESTIONS

1. What are the main goals of psychoanalytic treatments and how are they similar to or different from the goals of other treatments?

2. What are the three main components or techniques of client-centered therapy? Do you believe these are relevant only for client-centered therapy or are useful in other forms of treatment? Why?

3. Systems treatments focus less on the individual and more on the system(s) that individuals exist in. Please explain this focus on systems as opposed to the individual.

4. Describe the axioms of communication as depicted in the chapter. Do you think these are useful in other forms of treatment? Why?

5. What are the basic components in the process of a psychoanalytic psychotherapy?

6. What are the major philosophical underpinnings of each of the three treatment modalities described in the chapter.

◇ REFERENCES

Adler, A. (1956). *The individual psychology of Alfred Adler*. H. L. Ansbacher and R. R. Ansbacher (Eds.). New York: Harper Torchbooks.

Alexander, F., & French, T. M. (1946). *Psychoanalytic therapy*. New York: Ronald Press.

American Psychological Association Task Force on Evidence-Based Practice. (2006). Evidence-based practice in psychology. *American Psychologist, 61*, 271–285.

Anderson, E. M., & Lambert, M. J. (1995). Short-term dynamically oriented psychotherapy: A review and meta-analysis, *Clinical Psychology Review, 15*, 503–514.

Anderson, S. M., Reznik, I., & Glassman, N. S. (2005). The unconscious relational self. In R. R. Hassin, J. S. Uleman, & J.A. Bargh (Eds.), *The new unconsciousness* (pp. 421–480). New York: Oxford University Press.

Arlow, J. A. (2000). Psychoanalysis. In R. J. Corsini & D. Wedding, D. (Eds.) *Current psychotherapies* (6th ed.). Itasca, IL: Peacock Publishers, Inc.

Baddley, A. (1992). Working memory. *Science, 255*, 556–559.

Bateson, G., Jackson, D. D., Haley, J., & Weakland, J. (1956). Toward a theory of schizophrenia. *Behavioral Science, 1*, 251–264.

Beck, A. T. (1976). *Cognitive therapy and the emotional disorders*. New York: International Universities Press.

Blatt, S. J. (1992). The differential effect of psychotherapy and psychoanalysis with anaclitic and introjective patients: The Menninger Psychotherapy Research Project revisited. *Journal of the American Psychoanalytic Association, 40*, 691–724.

Bornstein, R. F. (1988). Psychoanalysis in the undergraduate curriculum: The treatment of psychoanalytic theory in abnormal psychology texts. *Psychoanalytic Psychology, 5,* 83–93.

Bornstein, R. F. (2005). Reconnecting psychoanalysis to mainstream psychology: Challenges and opportunities. *Psychoanalytic Psychology, 22,* 323–340.

Bornstein, R. F., & Masling, J. M. (1998). *Empirical perspectives on the psychoanalytic unconscious.* Washington, DC: APA.

Bower, G., & Glass, A. L. (1976). Structural units and the reintegrative power of picture fragments. *Journal of Experimental Psychology: Human Learning and Memory, 2,* 456–466.

Bower, G. H. (1981). Mood and memory, *American Psychologist, 36,* 129–148. http://www.ncbi.nlm.nih.gov/pubmed/7224324

Chambless, D. L., & Hollon, S. (1998). Defining empirically supported therapies. *Journal of Consulting and Clinical Psychology, 66,* 7–18.

Collins, A. M., & Loftus, E. F. (1975). A spreading activation theory of semantic processing. *Psychological Review, 82,* 407–428.

Corsini, R. J., & Wedding, D. (2005). *Current psychotherapies* (8th ed.). Itasca, IL: Peacock Publishers, Inc.

Davanloo, H. (2000). *Intensive short term dynamic psychotherapy.* New York: Wiley.

Ellenberger, H. F. (1970). *The discovery of the unconscious: The history and evolution of dynamic psychiatry.* New York: Basic Books.

Firenczi, S. (1993). Confusion of tongues between adults and child. In M. Balint (Ed.) & E. Mosbacher (Trans.), *Final contributions to the problem and methods of psycho-analysis* (pp. 156–167). (First published in English in 1949 in *International Journal of Psycho-analysis, 30*(255).)

Flett, G. L. (2007). *Personality theory and research.* New York: Wiley.

Gabbard, G. (2004). *Long-term psychodynamic psychotherapy: A basic text.* Arlington, VA: American Psychiatric Association.

Gabbard, G., Beck, J. S., & Holmes, J. (2005). *Oxford textbook of psychotherapy.* Oxford: Oxford University Press.

Gabbard, G. O. (2005). *Psychodynamic psychiatry in clinical practice: Fourth edition.* New York: American Psychiatric Publishing.

Gibbons, M. B., Crits-Christoph, P., & Hearon, B. (2009). The empirical status of psychodynamic therapies. *Annual Review of Clinical Psychology, 4,* 93–108.

Goldstein, K. (1934/1959). *The organism: A holistic approach to biology derived from psychological data in man.* New York: American Book.

Hogan, R. (1994). Heritage has value. *Dialogue, 9,* 8.

Jacobson, N. S., Christensen, A., Prince, S. E., Cordova, J., & Elridge, K. (2000). Integrative behavioral couple therapy: An acceptance-based, promising new treatment for couple discord. *Journal of Consulting and Clinical Psychology, 68,* 351–355.

Jacobson, N. S., Dobson, D. S., Truax, P. A., Addis, M. E., Koerner, K., et al. (1996). A component analysis of cognitive-behavioral treatment for depression. *Journal of Consulting and Clinical Psychology, 64,* 295–301.

Jensen, J. P., Bergin, A. E., & Greaves, D. W. (1990). The meaning of eclecticism: New survey and analysis of components. *Professional Psychology: Research and Practice, 21*, 124–130.

Johnson, S. M., Hunsley, J., Greenberg, L., & Schindler, D. (1999). Emotionally focused couples therapy: Status and challenges. *Clinical Psychology: Science and Practice, 6*, 67–79.

Kirschenbaum, H., & Jourdan, A. (2005). The current status of Carl Rogers and the person-centred approach. *Psychotherapy: Theory, research, and practice, 42*, 37–51.

Kohut, H. (1984). *How does analysis cure?* Chicago: University of Chicago Press.

Leichsenring, F., & Rabung, S. (2008). Effectiveness of long-term psychodynamic psychotherapy: A meta-analysis. *Journal of the American Medical Association, 300*, 1551–1565.

Leichsenring, F., Rabung, S., & Leibing, E. (2004). The efficacy of short-term psychodynamic psychotherapy in specific psychiatric disorders: A meta-analysis. *Archives General Psychiatry, 61*, 1208–1216.

Lerner, M. J., & Miller, D. T. (1978). Just world research and attribution process: Looking back and ahead. *Psychological Bulletin, 85*, 1030–1051.

Levy, R. A., & Ablon, J. S. (2009). *Handbook of evidence-based psychodynamic psychotherapy.* New York: Humana Press.

Luborsky, L. (1984). *Principles of psychoanalytic psychotherapy: A manual for supportive-expressive treatment.* New York: Basic Books.

Magnavita, J. J. (2008). Psychoanalytic psychotherapy. In J. Lebow (Ed.), *Twenty-first century psychotherapies: Contemporary approaches to theory and practice.* Hoboken, NJ: Wiley.

Masling, J. (1986). *Empirical studies of psychoanalytic concepts: Volume 2.* Hillsdale, NJ: Analytic Press.

Masling, J. (1990). *Empirical studies of psychoanalytic concepts: Volume 3.* Hillsdale, NJ: Analytic Press.

Maslow, A. (1968). *Toward a psychology of being.* Princeton: Van Nostrand

Millon, T. (2004). *Masters of the mind: Exploring the story of mental illness from ancient times to the new millennium.* Hoboken, NJ: Wiley.

Minuchin, S. (1974). *Families and family therapy.* Harvard University Press, 1974.

Neisser, U. (1976). *Cognition and reality.* San Francisco: Freeman.

Norcross, J. C., Hedges, M., & Castle, P. H. (2002). Psychologists conducting psychotherapy in 2001: A study of the Division 29 membership. *Psychotherapy: Theory, Research, Practice, and Training, 39*, 97–102.

Osimo, F. (2003). *Experiential short-term dynamic psychotherapy: A manual.* Bloomington: 1st Books.

Rank, O. (1945). *Will therapy, truth, and reality.* New York: Knopf.

Raskin, N. J., & Rogers, C. R. (2005). Person-centered therapy. In R. J. Corsini & D. Wedding, D. (Eds.) *Current psychotherapies* (6th ed.). Itasca, IL: Peacock Publishers, Inc.

Rogers, C., & Sanford, R. (1985).Client-centered psychotherapy. In H. I. Kaplan, B. J. Sadock, & A. M. Friedman (Eds.), *Comprehensive textbook of psychiatry* (4th ed.) (pp. 1374–1388). Baltimore: William & Wilkins.

Rogers, C. R. (1951). *Client-centered therapy.* Boston: Houghton Mifflin.

Rogers, C. R. (1961). *On becoming a person.* Boston: Houghton Mifflin.

Rogers, C. R., Gendlin, E. T., Kiesler, D. J., & Truax, C. (1967). *The therapeutic relationship and its impact: A study of psychotherapy with schizophrenics.* Madison, WI: University of Wisconsin Press.

Russell, G. F. M., Szmukler, G. I., Dare, C., & Eisler, I. (1987). An evaluation of family therapy in anorexia nervosa and bulimia nervosa. *Archives of General Psychiatry, 44,* 1047–1056.

Satir, V. (1964). *Conjoint family therapy: A guide to theory and technique.* Palo Alto, CA: Science and Behavior Books.

Sharf, R. S. (2000). *Theories of psychotherapy and counseling: Concepts and cases.* Belmont, CA: Wadsworth.

Shedler, J. (2006). That was then, this is now: Psychoanalytic psychotherapy for the rest of us. Retrieved from *http://psychsystems.net/shedler.html*

Shedler, J. (2010). The efficacy of psychodynamic psychotherapy. *American Psychologist, 65,* 98–109.

Sifneos, P. (1992). *Short-term anxiety-provoking psychotherapy: A treatment manual.* New York: Basic Books.

Silverman, L. H. (1976). Psychoanalytic theory: The reports of my death are greatly exaggerated. *American Psychologist, 31,* 621–637.

Silverman, L. H. (1985). Comments on three recent subliminal psychodynamic activation investigations. *Journal of Abnormal Psychology, 94,* 640–643.

St. Clair, M. (2004). *Object relations and self psychology.* New York: Brooks Cole.

Strupp, H. H., Sandell, J. A., Waterhouse, G. F., O'Malley, S. S., & Anderson, J. L. (1982). Psychodynamic therapy: Theory and research. In A. J. Rush (Ed.). *Short term psychotherapies for depression.* New York: The Guildford Press.

Sullivan, H. S. (1953). *The interpersonal theory of psychiatry.* New York: Norton.

Tasca, G., Mikail, S., & Hewitt, P. L. (2005). Group psychodynamic interpersonal psychotherapy: Summary of a treatment model and outcomes for depressive symptoms. In M. E. Abelian (Ed.), *Focus on psychotherapy research.* New York: Nova Science Publishers.

Tomkins, S. S. (1979). Script theory. In H. E. Howe & R. A. Diensbeir (Eds.), *Nebraska symposium on motivation* (Vol. 26, pp. 306–329). Lincoln, NE: University of Nebraska Press.

Treisman, A. M. (1969). Strategies and models of selective attention. *Psychological Review, 76,* 282–299.

Tulving, E. (1983). *Elements of episodic memory.* Oxford, England: Clarendon Press.

Wallerstein, R. S. (1988). One psychoanalysis or many? *Psychoanalytic Quarterly, 55,* 414.

Watzlawick, P., Beavin, J. H., & Jackson, D. D. (1967). Pragmatics of human communication. *A study of interactional patterns, pathologies and paradoxes.* New York: W.W. Norton & Company.

CHAPTER TWELVE

PSYCHOTHERAPIES II

CHAPTER OBJECTIVE

Chapter 11 and this chapter have the same principal objectives, namely, to introduce mainstream therapies, their history, underlying theory, and the treatment process and technique. To some degree they are presented as two separate but neighboring chapters simply to avoid an overly long single chapter. Aside from this minor, organizational reason, a second and more substantive reason for the breakdown is to cluster together those therapies that can be crudely subordinated under the broad title of "cognitive-behavioral therapies," where the intention is to change behavior using learning and cognitive theories of behavior control. Another key feature shared by the treatment approaches described here is that they are particularly suitable for empirical testing regarding their effectiveness.

⬧ BEHAVIOR THERAPY

Roots and Underlying Theory

As the name suggests, in behavior therapy the focus is on changing observable behavior, and this is achieved by systematic applications of learning theory–based principles. In order to understand why and how behavior therapy became so rapidly popular, its rise and development needs to be placed in a historical context. Learning theories have been gradually refined ever since the concept of classical conditioning was first described and experimentally shown by Ivan Pavlov in the early 20th century. Later, when clinical researchers like Joseph Wolpe and Andrew Salter described the learning principles behind anxiety conditioning (Wolpe, 1958), they provided the groundwork for behavioral therapies to control anxiety. Given that learning theories are eminently testable and have been subjected to thousands of animal studies, this also opened the door to various forms of learning-based psychotherapies that were objectively testable and hence laid the groundwork for evidence-based approaches to mental health). This was in stark contrast to the psychoanalytic tradition where key terms like "psychological defenses," "the unconscious," "ego strength," and "projection" were pivotal to the psychodynamic view of psychopathology, yet defied easy quantification and testability. The only other form of intervention available at the time of behavioral therapy's rise was client-centered therapy, which, given its roots in humanistic existential theory and the belief in human growth, was imbued with a positivistic attitude that de-emphasized psychopathology and any quantification of disturbance.

The limited amount of hard empirical testing that could be done by (or that was of interest to) the early psychoanalysts and the followers of Carl Rogers (for a detailed discussion, see chapter 11) had often created major chasms in psychology departments where academics of various theoretical camps at times didn't even talk to each other, or if they did, it was hostile and divisive. This division made it especially difficult for Rogerians and Freudians to thrive, or even survive, in a university department of psychology that had strong empirical traditions, namely, the exploration of psychology via animal models. We posit here that the success of behavior therapy was largely due to the fact that clinical psychologists now had tools at their disposal that were based on theories and that used a language that many experimentally working, academic psychologists were familiar with; these were approaches that could be subjected to objective evaluations. It was dramatically easier for a behavior therapist, to find acceptance among peers who conducted experimental research than it was for a psychoanalyst. To fully appreciate the progress of science, one needs to remember that such progress is inextricably linked to the career advancement and inherent opportunities of the scientist herself. Research and teaching that is not understood or appreciated by academic colleagues cannot facilitate the scientist in his aspirations of career advancement. Thus, with a lack of momentum and growth in one's academic and professional abilities, it is impossible to move forward, resulting in the possible displacement of an entire track of work in psychology.

Another very important feature of behavior therapy that further strengthened its popularity is the fact that the underlying models of pathological behaviors emphasize learning, rather than an inherent fault of oneself. As such, people are less likely to feel stigmatized or reproached by society. If a client is told that he has simply not yet learned to do something the right way or has been taught wrong, then the client is much more likely to accept that change is possible; the client is able to faithfully commit to alter such behavior without feeling dejected or as though he is harboring undesirable character flaws. Experienced clinicians have seen much relief in their clients when they were able to provide a learning theory explanation for why the clients had acquired, for example, a dog phobia or unusual shyness.

The basic terminology of learning theories will still be familiar from the Introduction to Psychology course that clinical psychology students will have taken a few years prior. Nevertheless, the concepts may have become a little rusty, and, given their importance for this section, a summary of terms and their definitions is provided in Box 12.1.

Behavior therapists have developed quite a catalog of interventions, and the corresponding terminology can look a little overwhelming at first. These methods of intervention can be organized in a number of ways. First of all, they can be clustered into two large groups depending on whether or not their target is to:

- *Increase the number of desirable behaviors* (i.e., compliments made by spouses to one another), or

- *Decrease the number of undesirable behaviors* (i.e., chronic nail-biting)

BOX 12.1

A REFRESHER OF LEARNING THEORY TERMS AND DEFINITIONS

Term	Definition
Classical conditioning	Classical conditioning is a powerful form of learning and can prepare us to respond rapidly to future situations. It associates a neutral stimulus (being awoken by a violent thunderstorm) with an **unconditioned stimulus** (a sudden rise in heart rate). Through repeated pairing, the neutral stimulus becomes a conditioned stimulus that elicits a **conditioned response** (fear).
Extinction	Failure of an unconditioned stimulus to follow the neutral stimulus extinguishes (weakens) a conditioned response. Due to extinction, the frequency of behavior (a fear response) declines in a situation where the anticipated response (rapid and shallow breathing) does not follow.
Operant conditioning	Operant conditioning leads to change in future behavior as a function of its previously experienced consequences. Behavior may increase or decrease in frequency depending on whether it was previously reinforced or punished.
Positive reinforcement	In positive reinforcement, behavior (preparing extensively for an exam) is followed by a positive consequence (good grade) that increases its future likelihood in situations with similar **discriminative stimuli** (the next upcoming exam).
Negative reinforcement	In negative reinforcement, a particular behavior (practicing breathing exercises) allows the person to escape from or avoid an aversive state (anxiety induced by a dental procedure), thereby increasing its future likelihood in situations with similar discriminative stimuli (the dentist's office). It is easy to get thrown off by the term "negative" and to think of this term as being a form of punishment; it is not! Negative reinforcement is reinforcement and increases the probability of behavior.
Relational or associative learning	Relational or associative learning is conscious and allows us to connect stimuli and behavior that occur at the same time. This learning process provides us with **autobiographical knowledge** (information about our experiences). In a clinical context, it provides conscious memories a patient can retrieve and use to guide behavior.
Punishment	A situation where an undesirable behavior followed by an aversive consequence (like an expensive traffic ticket for tailgating) reduces its probability of reoccurring in the future.

A second major organizing principle is to link the treatment method to the presumed type of learning that may represent the etiology of the presenting problem. Many anxiety-reducing treatments are based on a model that describes the beginning of the problem as having been induced by **classical conditioning**. A good example would be a dog phobic client who was subject to a surprise attack by a ferocious dog who bit him in the leg, causing pain and distress. Alternatively, a lack of social skills may be interpreted as due to **poor modeling** (i.e., observing and learning from parents who are very shy or possibly very aggressive), and **social avoidance** may result from subsequent failure to obtain positive reinforcement from others with whom the person regularly interacts, such as teachers, friends, and/or parents.

In consequence, **modeling** and positive reinforcement strategies are considered ideal tools with which to teach new behaviors like public speaking or building friendship skills in preschool children. On the other hand, the need to reduce undesirable behaviors is more challenging. In an individual with severe developmental and intellectual disability who engages in repetitive, self-injurious head banging, for example, some form of punishment would seem to be most appropriate, as punishment has been shown to reduce undesirable behaviors. In applying any of these methods, the therapist needs to consider two core features:

- The ethical acceptability of the treatment approach
- The availability of effective punishing methods and/or reinforcers

Ethical Considerations

Our ethical codes as clinicians and researchers make it abundantly clear that we are not allowed to harm our patients—nor would we wish to do so. For punishment to work, it must be aversive; yet doing something aversive to another person means possibly evoking harm, even if it is mild in effect. Does that mean that a clinician can never use a form of punishment to reduce undesirable behaviors? No, it does not, but it *does* imply that a lot of thinking and planning needs to go into a therapy plan in order to assure that the most effective and least harmful means of changing behavior are attempted first. Aside from the question of ethics, there are other important considerations for using punishment, namely:

1. Even at best, punishment teaches a person only what not to do. In the real world, it is important to teach somebody the right thing to do, so as to improve her quality of life and evoke approval by others. A parent who attempts to teach a hyperactive child to stop wiggling his chair during dinner through punishment techniques alone (i.e., persistent scolding) has not solved the problem at all. The same boy will find another way to act out his need for impulsive behavior. Instead, he may repetitively bang his fork against the plate; once that is punished and eliminated, he is likely to move on to relentlessly teasing his sister, and so forth. In such a scenario, there are a number of possible strategies. The parents could reduce the expected quiet time at the dinner table to no more than 10 minutes instead of 30, or, alternatively they might try to keep this hyperactive child occupied by a lively conversation or a little question-and-answer game.

2. Any individual who attempts to control others by reinforcement or punishment affects not only the specific behavior but also the pre-existing relationship with this individual. This relationship aspect is critical because the person whose behavior is supposed to change will (a) increase his liking of the individual who provides reinforcements and also respond favorably to the individual's future interactions or (b) learn to dislike or even despise the person who readily dishes out punishment.

Punishment

The existing ethical limitations for constructive use of punishment leave relatively few opportunities for the appropriate use of punishment in psychotherapy. In fact, when psychotherapy is provided one-on-one in the clinician's office, the concept of punishment imparted by the therapist is essentially unheard of. However, punishment may be suitable when the patient in question is not able to comprehend, consent, or participate in choosing a therapy, has failed to respond to reinforcement procedures, and shows problematic behaviors that are dangerous and self-injurious in nature. A striking example of such a scenario has been reported by Lang and Melamed (1969). The patient in question was a 3-month old baby who had developed a vomiting reflex that prevented food from being forwarded from the mouth to the stomach. No positive reinforcement approach had produced beneficial results, and the child was emaciated and had to be fed via intravenous tubes. Both the parents and the child's physician believed that the situation was untenable and was putting the child at risk for serious health consequences; thus, they agreed that something potentially aversive, while not harmful, ought to be tried. The ultimately chosen method was to give mild electroshocks to the baby the very instant that she was about to clamp down her throat musculature. It was considered well-established that a mild shock was unpleasant but could not produce any harm. The child's reaction clearly demonstrated that she found it aversive, and repeated use of this method let to a gradual decline in the child's reflex cramping of throat muscles, ultimately allowing for normal eating and swallowing habits to develop.

A second opportunity for using punishment procedures that are ethical and useful lies in the fact that clients can apply punishment to themselves. Two examples demonstrate this methodology. One such method is using an aversive drug (i.e., disulfiram, typically called Antabuse) in the treatment of alcohol dependency. When this drug is taken, it produces no adverse consequences whatsoever, as long as the user does not drink alcohol. If alcohol is ingested, however, the alcohol interacts with the Antabuse such that the patient will feel an urge to vomit. This urge is (not surprisingly) perceived as highly unpleasant and has been found to be somewhat effective in the treatment of alcoholism (for review see, Hughes & Cook, 1997). The key to making this procedure ethical and acceptable is that the patient fully agrees to undergo this treatment and has the consequences explained to him. Only when he judges that the risk of continuing drinking is greater than the unpleasantness of the Antabuse-alcohol interaction is it considered acceptable to use this method.

A second, much less drastic, scenario implies the use of a little rubber band placed around the wrist of an individual with compulsive tendencies, like hair pulling (trichotillomania), skin picking, or nail chewing. The client is taught that every time the client realizes that she is about to perform the compulsive behavior of choice, she is to flip the rubber band and inflict a minute, harmless pain to her wrist (Mavissakalian, Turner, & Michelson, 1985).

In sum, punishment as a therapy method:

1. Is usually not a first-choice treatment
2. Must avoid risk for long-term harm
3. Is preferably conducted with the permission of the client, or even better, is executed by the client himself

Reinforcement

Working with reinforcement to change behavior is a much more pleasant process for all parties involved. Extensive animal research has shown that very effective reinforcers are food, drink, sex, and chemically induced pleasure (like that produced by illicit substances such as cocaine); they are also categorized as **primary reinforcers**. For routine use in therapy all primary reinforcers have tremendous limitations. The therapist cannot offer any form of sexual pleasure to clients in exchange for desired behaviors; this is harmful to the client, undermines a privileged relationship, and is plain unethical. It also is almost guaranteed to be violation of law. Food and drink are essential for survival and cannot be ethically withheld. An exception might be to offer dessert or other treats as reinforcers after basic survival needs have been met. Even then, this cannot be repeated very often. Although one or two portions of dessert may be very desirable, consuming an excessive number may become aversive and would probably not be recommended to achieve long-term treatment goals.

The limitations associated with the use of primary reinforcers have generated an elaborate array of choices for **secondary reinforcers**, which are not confined to the limits of psychotherapy; rather, they govern much of our daily lives. Employees receive paychecks as a "thank you" for their work, and this money can be traded in for a variety of necessities and pleasures. Parents may use allowances to reinforce children's participation in household chores, with the intention of teaching them responsibility at the same time. In a psychiatric hospital, where patients may not be free to leave, and cash is of limited value, the concept of a token economy has been used to facilitate the learning of desirable behaviors in exchange for tokens, that in turn can be traded again for other reinforcers like a chocolate bar at the canteen or a weekend pass to go visit family. Another readily available reinforcer is verbal praise, which can principally be used without limitations and has the added benefit of strengthening positive interpersonal relationships. If, however, many desirable behaviors need to be reinforced in short order, as is the case trying to teach an autistic child, the therapist either will run out of verbal reinforcers in a relatively short time frame or will have to accept much repetition. In such a case, it is a good idea to sit down and create a list of possible words of praise, which can help the therapist remember the possible variety. Also, the therapist can give out symbols of good performance that serve as reinforcers, like gold stars. When a planned weight loss of 5 kg has been attained, clients can reinforce themselves by earmarking the purchase of a new pair of pants, one size smaller than the previous one. Lastly, people who want to change their behavior can engage in contracts with others, such as therapists or friends. Two friends might agree that both will stop smoking beginning January 1st of a new year and offer each other a fishing trip to the lake 6 months later as reinforcement for successfully quitting.

So far, rationales and techniques have been described for many methods that the behavior therapist has in his arsenal. A summary of the many techniques is laid out in Box 12.2.

BOX 12.2

BEHAVIOR THERAPY TECHNIQUES

Term	Goal	Definition or Description
Flooding	Provoke extinction and encourage approach behavior	A method used for anxiety reduction where a phobic client is exposed to a highly fear-arousing situation and where the therapist provides ongoing encouragement to assure that the client remains in the situation until noticeable anxiety habituation has set in.
Systematic desensitization	Provoke extinction and encourage approach behavior	A method used to treat phobias. Step one is to learn relaxation and uses a hierarchy of fear-producing situations. An exposure procedure is used, either in imagination or in the real world, to the feared stimuli. Begins with the least fear-producing situation and gradually works up to the more fear-producing situation.
Graduated exposure	Provoke extinction and encourage approach behavior	A method based on the rationale that the avoidance of the feared stimulus needs to be stopped; very much like systematic desensitization, it exposes the client to more and more fear-arousing stimuli in a previously established hierarchy.
Contingency contracting	Help eliminate an undesirable behavior	An agreement, preferably a written one, between client and patient or possibly two parties outside the therapy context that spells out what the consequence is for not completing a contract.
Token economy	Provide a systematic reinforcement for desirable behaviors	A reinforcement system that has explicitly developed tokens to be present for certain types of reinforcers, like an extra dessert or a weekend pass.
Satiation or overcorrection	Help eliminate an undesirable behavior	A relatively mild aversive punishment procedure in which somebody is required to engage in an activity that may be initially pleasant (like smoking a cigar) but that needs to continue until the subjective quality becomes unpleasant.

(continued)

BOX 12.2 CONTINUED

Term	Goal	Definition or Description
Response cost	Reduce undesirable behaviors	A punishment procedure where, contingent on the production of an undesirable behavior, a corresponding specified amount of reinforcement is removed (a good example is a $200 fine for speeding).
Time-out	Stop an undesirable behavior	A method where an individual is removed from the environment after he shows an undesirable behavior and is asked to spend time in a less pleasant environment (e.g., a child who disturbed the learning in class is sent out into the hallway for 5 minutes).
Shaping	Learn a complex behavior	A sequential learning process where individuals learn through reinforcement procedures to acquire all the skills needed for a relatively complex behavior (like giving a public speech).
Chaining	Learn a complex behavior	Also a sequential learning process where, however, the ultimate target behavior can be broken down into steps that one can learn with reinforcement, one after the other (like beginning how to drive a car with automatic transmission in a safe school yard, then move to a regular street, and later learn how to do the same thing with manual transmission).
Rehearsal	Practice a new behavior	The practice of a new behavior in an initially safe environment like a role-play in order to prepare for later performance.
Modeling—mastery model	Provide a sample for a desirable behavior	A method of helping an individual acquire a new behavior by showing how it is done very well.
Modeling—coping model	Provide a sample for a desirable behavior	A method of helping an individual acquire a new behavior by showing her how it can be done by most people.
Aversion therapy	Help eliminate an undesired behavior	A method that provides an unpleasant consequence after an undesirable behavior was shown (e.g., a self-applied flip of a rubber band attached to the wrist after a client noticed that he was starting to compulsively ruminate).

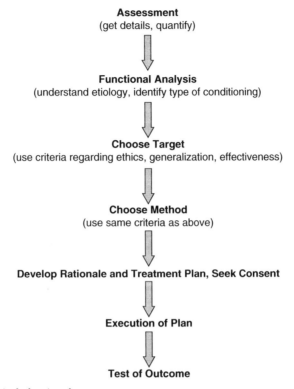

FIGURE 12.1 Steps in behavior therapy.

However, well-executed behavioral therapy is a process with a number of systematic steps involved.

As is apparent from Figure 12.1, the behavioral therapist strives to quantify the problem behavior and collect sufficient information so that he can build an etiological model that can then form the foundation for developing a therapy program (referred to as a **functional analysis**). Provided that the client is reasonably intelligent, the entire reasoning of the program can and should be explained to the client, and prior to initiating treatment the client should understand and consent to the treatment program (i.e., provide informed consent). Given that the target for change is usually overt behavior, it is relatively easy to monitor ongoing changes; the use of diagrams to mark improvements can, in and of themselves, be used not only to document positive change but to serve as reinforcement. How such functional analyses are conducted goes beyond detailed description in an undergraduate textbook and becomes the content of a graduate course in behavior therapy. Nevertheless, the interested reader can read up on this way of conceptualizing a behavior therapy case (Woody, Detweiler, Teachman, & O'Hearn, 2003).

Given that the description of the many techniques in behavior therapy can be dry, two case scenarios are offered in Boxes 12.3 and 12.4 that show how these techniques can actually be applied to clinical problems. One is a brief description of a case where flooding was used, while the second is a multicomponent case scenario, reprinted from the *Journal of Behavior Therapy and Experimental Psychiatry* (1980). This paper was written by one of the authors of this textbook when he was still a graduate student. In the mid-seventies he saw his first young patient presenting with bulimia before the term "bulimia" had even entered the clinical psychology literature. This case report is considered informative because at the time there was no established treatment for this newly coined behavioral problem, and the author had no choice but to construct, from the ground up, an etiological model for this presenting problem, devise a treatment program consistent with this conceptualization, and then apply it while carefully tracking progress. Without knowing it at the time, this paper turned out to be the first published behavioral therapy case study of bulimia.

BOX 12.3

CASE REPORT OF A FLOODING TREATMENT (SIMPLIFIED DESCRIPTION)

Carl P, a 34-year old, midlevel executive presented to the clinic with a phobia of public washrooms. He was in a good, supportive long-term relationship and had a promising career ahead of him; the only presenting problem was his phobia. His avoidance of public washrooms had become so pervasive that any work-related travel had become impossible and he even started skipping work to avoid having to use the bathroom in the office. He knew that his avoidance was a problem that had to be stopped, but remembered a critical incident (permitting interpretation as being a classically conditioned fear) and understood very well the reinforcing properties of his subsequent avoidance behavior.

Approximately 1 year before coming to our clinic, he had used the bathroom in a restaurant, felt generally rushed to get back to work, but found that he could not open the door from the inside. As it turned out later, there was a broken piece in the lock itself that made it indeed impossible to unlock the door from the inside. After numerous frustrating and futile attempts to open the door from the inside, he became understandably and increasingly anxious and began calling for help. Unfortunately, it took many calls to be heard through the thick door; his anxiety mounted before he was noticed, and restaurant staff started responding to the problem. It took a professional locksmith and another hour to free him of his involuntary prison. For a brief while after that he had used public washrooms but did not dare lock the door from the inside to avoid a recurrence of the previous incident, but found that this led to embarrassing situations and was not an acceptable alternative either.

Given the absence of comorbid problems, the exceptionally clear causal explanation, and his willingness to tolerate some anxiety, a flooding protocol was executed. After having explained the full details of the therapy plan, assuring him that the therapist would be on the other side of the door, and after a demonstration that the door could be opened from outside

BOX 12.3 CONTINUED

if Carl needed to call for help, he agreed to the exposure protocol. He was taught breathing techniques and was given an explanation that his anxiety would initially increase but then decrease. An absolute assurance was given that this was exactly what was going to happen. Further, he was taught how to provide anxiety ratings on a 0 to 100 scale, and it was tested that the therapist asking for anxiety ratings could actually hear him through the closed door. In addition, he was given a digital heart rate monitor to serve as a second and objective source of information about anxiety levels. A bathroom in the psychology building was chosen that was in a remote corner with very rare traffic to minimize possible embarrassment.

Once Carl had entered the bathroom and closed the door, there was continuous verbal interaction through the closed door, with the therapist repeatedly reinforcing him for his courage and intermittently asking for subjective ratings of anxiety and readouts from the heart rate monitor. Even more quickly than predicted, namely, within 5 minutes, his anxiety peaked and began decreasing to the point where he was clearly able to recognize that the therapist's prediction of an increase and decrease had materialized and that he was able to tolerate the situation. After 15 minutes of this exposure and a clear demonstration of decreasing anxiety levels, this flooding session was terminated, and the success and the reasons for the success were further discussed in the therapy office. During the next therapy session, flooding was repeated in the same manner and declined not only to lower anxiety levels at the beginning but also to a more gradual and less dramatic rise in fear and an even quicker habituation. After only two such sessions he was able to tolerate public washrooms with a reasonable level of comfort, and this rapid success was a pleasant surprise to the client.

Concluding Observations

Behavior therapy stands out among psychological treatment approaches because it shows exceptionally clear links with experimentally derived principles and translation of these principles into treatment methods. Given that behavior therapy is eminently testable, researchers have, from its inception, provided quantitative case studies and group comparisons to document the effectiveness of behavioral methods (Linden, 1981; Smith & Glass, 1977; and see chapter 13). Furthermore the techniques used in behavior therapy are particularly easy to standardize and write up in manual format and are therefore good tools with which to teach relatively junior therapists. Given that reinforcement and punishment can be used with individuals who have limited verbal skills, such as young children or the intellectually challenged, it offers a uniquely broad range of applications and is suitable to more populations than any other type of psychological intervention.

Behavioral or learning theory principles are not limited to applications in psychotherapy, but can govern many of our overt behaviors, for example, as drivers on the road, as students who seek feedback on their performance, or citizens at large who are expected to be respectful and caring in their behavior and be protective of their environment. Students are given grades to encourage learning (or punish poor effort); Nobel prizes are awarded for a lifetime worth of important research contributions; tailgating drivers are given tickets to discourage this behavior; and the use of individual water meters is meant to be a direct

BOX 12.4

BULIMIA TREATMENT

MULTI-COMPONENT BEHAVIOR THERAPY IN A CASE OF COMPULSIVE BINGE-EATING FOLLOWED BY VOMITING

WOLFGANG LINDEN
McGill University

Summary—A 20-yr old female university student was treated for compulsive binge-eating with subsequent vomiting that occurred nearly every day. A variety of behavioral procedures including construction of alternative response, stimulus control, response delay and individualized assertiveness training resulted in a rapid decrease of compulsive behaviors. Recovery was nearly complete over a 6-month follow-up.

Several behavioral techniques are available for the treatment of over-eating in obese persons (Stuart, 1967; Stuart and Davis, 1972; Leon, 1976). Similarly, with compulsive disorders behavioral strategies have been favored (Marks, 1978). It appears however, that the treatment of compulsive binge-eating followed regularly by vomiting in patients of normal weight is presently not covered in the literature. Hence a treatment package for this behavior problem had to be specifically designed for this case. Some components of behavioral procedures used to institute self-control in obesity and compulsion disorders seem to be applicable.

The assessment of a single case, the subsequent development of a treatment plan, and the course of therapy are presented in this article.

Background and Problem

A 20-yr old female university student sought therapy at a university counseling service for her frequent compulsive binge-eating followed regularly by severe vomiting. During the day she followed a strict dietary regimen limiting the calorie intake to what she thought would correspond to her actual energy expenditure. Subsequent to her third dietary controlled meal around 5 or 6 p.m. she felt a compulsive urge to eat between 7 and 11 p.m. On these occasions, she would eat excessively large amounts of "forbidden" high-calorie food. These could be, for example, 6–8, 3 oz bars of chocolate, or up to 20 slices of peanut-butter and jelly toasts. During this process of excessive eating the compulsive feeling used to decrease quickly to a point where she stopped eating, went to the bathroom and vomited. These episodes had occurred nearly every day for the last 4 yrs.

The patient had sought therapy because she feared a break-up with her boyfriend. He was previously unaware of her problem. Her parents, with whom she lived, knew of the problematic behaviors, but underestimated their frequency.

At the age of 14 the patient had felt that she was too obese to be attractive to boys. Although, according to her own report, she was only about 10–15% overweight, she was the "fattest" girl in her class, a fact that had made her extremely preoccupied with her eating behavior. She had started strict dieting and lost so much weight that she was only "skin and bones," became extremely weak and experienced frequent fainting spells. According to her self-report all main criteria for a diagnosis of anorexia nervosa (Feighner et al., 1972) were present at that time. She then became frightened and allowed herself

BOX 12.4 CONTINUED

to eat more, but limited the nutrition to low-caloric and low-carbohydrate foods. The client regained a weight of about: 115 lb which can be considered normal according to her height of 5 ft 5 in. This weight was maintained until the present day. Shortly after reaching normal weight she began the compulsive episodes which had increased in frequency to six times per week at the time she sought therapy.

The client had a good relationship with her parents and no essential problems at school. With her boyfriend there were, however, two problem areas. She found sex pleasurable but was not able to reach orgasm and felt unable to communicate openly about this. A second problem was her boyfriend's rigid habit of spending the whole weekend with his family. The client was extremely annoyed about being left alone for the weekends and about her failure to change her friend's attitude towards this issue.

Before deciding on specific treatment objectives it was further necessary to eliminate the possibility of an organic and/or an affective disorder. A recent physical check-up suggested excellent physical health and no somatic involvement in the compulsive behaviors. There was no evidence of severe emotional pathology as no unusual mood swings, recent weight loss, suicidal thinking or hallucinations were reported.

Treatment

The client did not want her parents or her boyfriend to be involved in the treatment. This prevented a potential conjoint assessment and necessitated individual consultations. Two major objectives were defined for therapy: decrease in the frequency or, possibly, total elimination of the binge-eating/vomiting episodes while maintaining her present weight; strengthening of assertive behaviors with her boyfriend and widening the range of her social activities. Between the first and the second assessment session client was asked to self-monitor her thoughts in the binge-eating situations, to record in detail her food intake, physical exercise, and count the compulsive episodes over a period of 1 week.

The self-monitoring revealed the following baseline data:

- a daily calorie intake of dietary food of about 800–1200 calories;
- a total differentiation between the food for regular eating vs the food for overeating (i.e. whole grain bread, crackers, cottage cheese, lean meat, salads vs greasy food, chocolate, toast, cakes, sausages, pizza);
- overeating meant a calculated intake of 3000–5000 calories daily (though a high proportion was lost by vomiting);
- a frequency of six "binging" episodes per week;
- intensive physical activity during daily commuting to university and sporting exercises;
- a feeling of loneliness and total inability to resist when the compulsion to eat would arise;
- a feeling of strong relief after vomiting.

Therapeutic Plan and Procedures

As a first step in intervention the therapist provided a description of the operant mechanisms that contribute to the maintenance of the problematic eating behavior. It appeared that the overeating and subsequent vomiting—although in itself problematic—had in the past led permanently to an important benefit: the

(continued)

BOX 12.4 CONTINUED

maintenance of her ideal weight. The self-reinforcing properties of the behavior pattern were explained; this behavior cycle permitted the client to "sin" (eat forbidden food), and to do "penance" (vomit) without the negative consequences of weight gain. Therefore, the therapeutic goal had to modify the problem behavior without losing the objective of weight maintenance.

Further important information regarding therapeutic planning was derived from the relationship between food intake and actual energy expenditure. The fact that, although clearly under-nourished by the dietary meals, the client had maintained a constant weight over a 4-yr period could only be explained by the supposition that despite the severe vomiting the body retained some of the "forbidden" food to meet its actual energy need.

On the basis of this rationale, behavior change of the binge-eating/vomiting was to be instituted via three main strategies (cf. Bandura, 1969; Kanfer and Philips, 1970):

   a. construction of an alternative response;
   b. stimulus control;
   c. response delay.

These strategies were put into effect in the following ways:

a. *Construction of an alternative response*

   1. Food choice was changed while maintaining the total amount of intake by: continuing her three diet meals a day, adding a late evening snack exactly planned with 600–800 calories chosen from the "forbidden" item list of high-caloric food. Ten different 800-caloric snacks were to be written on index cards to make her aware of the choices available. Rationale: according to her body weight and activity level it was calculated that she had an energy expenditure of about 2000 calories daily (cf. Stuart and Davis, 1973). The extra planned snacks would permit formerly forbidden food to fill the gap in her insufficient diet, and probably allow her to maintain the present "ideal" weight.
   2. Food intake was self-monitored and constantly recorded.

Daily weight was controlled and diagrammed. A reinforcing effect was expected by her realizing that with the new regimen she would be able to maintain her present weight.

b. *Stimulus control*

   1. Her parents were informed about the problem and her mother asked to buy less high calorie food.
   2. One section of the refrigerator was reserved for the client's planned meals.
   3. Somebody was asked to bring the extra snacks to her room instead of her going to the kitchen.

Rationale for 1, 2 and 3: structuring of stimulus situation, removal of unnecessary cues to inappropriate eating.

c. *Response delays*

   1. Her interest and joy in yoga was used by making her do an exercise when she felt the urge to eat.

The second objective for treatment was the improvement of assertiveness. The client described being lonely before the compulsive episodes. In order to prevent these

BOX 12.4 CONTINUED

experiences of loneliness it was planned to support and strengthen more assertive behaviors in her relationship with the boyfriend and other peers. Behavioral analysis, instruction and some role-playing were to be used for assertion training.

Outcome and Follow-up

During the baseline period binge-eating/vomiting behaviors occurred six times within 1 week. After the first week of treatment the frequency dropped to four per week; from the second to the fourth week of treatment the rate remained stable at one episode per week. The decrease of overeating/vomiting behaviors over the total observation period is illustrated in Fig. 1 below.

After 4 weeks of treatment the client reported that she had given up counting calories because she knew by that time how much she could eat without gaining weight.

During sessions 3–6 problems with the boyfriend were focused upon and the client showed improvement in her assertiveness.

After session 6 the client left for a 4-week vacation. Upon her return she reported that the frequency of compulsive episodes had been constant at about once per week. She was communicating better about sex and enjoying it more.

In the 7th therapy session the client stated happily that the overeating/vomiting behavior had not recurred and insisted on terminating therapy. She expected the relationship with her boyfriend to improve further as the start had already been promising.

A follow-up session 3 months later revealed that during this period the compulsive episode had recurred twice. The client felt able to control this on her own. Her boyfriend had changed his mind about spending weekends with his family only, and she was able to reach an orgasm in their sexual relations. Besides this, she had made some new friends at the university with whom she socialized, alone or with her boyfriend. A 6-month follow-up by telephone indicated maintenance of these improvements.

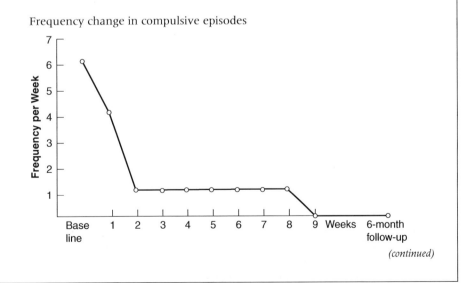

Frequency change in compulsive episodes

(continued)

BOX 12.4   CONTINUED

Discussion

The rapidity of decrease in the frequency of the problematic eating behaviors, and the strengthening of assertion in social situations were most gratifying. Although the effective therapeutic ingredients must remain hypothetical in the absence of an experimental design, the therapeutic approach described allowed the patient to modify the problem behavior without losing the benefit of weight maintenance—a major reinforcing consequence of her maladaptive behavior. Her increased assertiveness with her boyfriend and others effectively eliminated her feelings of loneliness and thus removed an important emotional antecedent to the same maladaptive behavior.

References

Bandura A. (1969). *Principle of Behavior Modification*. New York.

Feighner J. P. *et al.* (1972). Diagnostic criteria for use in psychiatric research, *Archs Gen. Psychiat.* 26, 57–63.

Kanfer F. H. and Philips J. S. (1970). *Learning Foundations of Behavior Therapy*. New York.

Leon G. (1976). Current directions in the treatment of obesity, *Psych. Bull.* 83. 557–578.

Marks I. (1978). Behavioral psychotherapy of adult neurosis. In *Handbook of Psychotherapy and Behavior Change* (Ed. by Garfield S. L. and Bergin A. E.). 2nd Edn., John Wiley, New York.

Stuart R. H. (1967). Behavioral control of overeating, *Behav. Res. & Ther.* 5, 357–365.

Stuart R. B. and Davis B. (1972). *Slim Chance in a Fat World*. Research Press.

response cost that can minimize the waste of drinking water, a scarce resource. None of these activities can be construed as psychotherapy, but all are examples of effective behavior control based on learning and conditioning methods.

The ability of a behavior therapist to manipulate an individual's behaviors, without his consent or understanding of what is being done, is also referred to as a **black box principle**. The "black box" notion of behavior therapy has, not surprisingly, earned it an image of being mechanistic and inhumane. The use of punishment strategies can be seen as a good example where irresponsible use of punishment (e.g., a parent physically beating a child for not finishing her dinner) would indeed be inhumane. Judicious use of mild punishment (like self-punishment for nail-biting via snapping of a rubber band on the wrist) can be simultaneously effective and humane. The differences between these scenarios are the intensity and potential harmfulness of the punishment, the spirit behind the act, and the degree of consent by the receiving individual.

◇ COGNITIVE THERAPY

In the previous section, we stressed that the critics of behavior therapy considered it a symptom cure with an inhuman flavor that treats people like black boxes. In part, cognitive therapy was developed to counter this criticism. Cognitive therapy is a natural outgrowth of extensive experimental research on the regulation of mood and emotions that is associated with healthy adjustment and various types of psychopathology (Zaretsky, Segal, & Fefergrad, 2007).

Before going into details about the theoretical underpinnings and the major thinkers in this area, it may be worthwhile to portray some typical thought patterns that might be presented to a cognitive therapist by patients with depression or anxiety disorder.

Everybody wants me to go for job interviews because I complain all the time about being broke, living on welfare. But I have no experience, I don't know how to write a resume, and nobody will ever give me a job.

My boss always picks on me, I'm certainly not getting a promotion, and I might even get fired if I cannot get my sales record up. All the other guys in sales are doing much better, and I can see that the boss likes them more.

Giving close attention to each of these statements demonstrates what cognitive therapists want to focus on. Both individuals express pessimism and low self-esteem. They are speculating about a fixed outcome without factual evidence, or they take a single situation that can be interpreted in many different ways and draw one very narrow conclusion. In both cases, the way they think about the situation ends up discouraging them from trying to break out of their misery, making it difficult to consider alternative explanations that would be less upsetting. Based on having listened to many depressed and distressed patients over the years, cognitive therapists have tried to identify the nature of the presumably underlining types of thinking errors and have classified them in order to aid identification. A list of the corresponding terms is found in Box 12.5.

BOX 12.5

LIST OF DYSFUNCTIONAL THINKING PATTERNS

1. Labeling: using a negatively toned word or label that you reflexively attach to certain problematic behaviors (I am such an idiot because I forgot to update my virus software).
2. Discounting or disqualifying positive features: refers to selective attention such that you attend only to the problematic parts of a situation ("How horrible that my girlfriend broke up with me" when you had actually planned a break-up yourself).
3. Catastrophizing: anticipating the worst outcome despite lack of evidence to support it (If one jet on my airplane fails, it will crash).
4. Black-and-white thinking: being overly categorical in one's thinking "if I don't get a test score over 90% on this test I will never be admitted to any law school" or "as long as I get 90% or more I'm guaranteed to get into any law school I want."
5. Fortune-telling: making unjustified and untested forecasts; "given that my last boyfriend dumped me, I will never be able to attract a boyfriend again."
6. "Must" or "should" statements: these reflect very rigid rules about how other people are expected to behave and how terrible it is if these expectations are not met (We must arrive at the party on time, or the host will never forgive us).
7. Emotional reasoning: convincing yourself that just because you feel or believe something, it is a fact.
8. Mind reading: you firmly believe that you know what others are thinking although this person has not actually said anything. This in turn leads to nonconsideration of other possibilities and can paralyze people.

The concept of errors in thinking is a unique feature of cognitive therapy and may be interpreted by some individuals as patronizing, because it carries the strong connotation of right and wrong while appearing at once both categorical and dogmatic. The intention, of course, is not to distress the client but to direct the client to think in more functional terms and to teach him to create thought patterns that are empowering and that open up new opportunities. The application of cognitive therapy to treating depression is a good example of this kind of discourse about the notion of right and wrong in cognitive therapy.

There is intense discussion in the field of abnormal psychology about whether or not the depressed person is more realistic than a nondepressed person or whether the nondepressed individual has a more accurate view of the world (for review see, Dobson & Franche, 1989), although there is no dispute that depressed individuals see the world in relatively more negative terms (Beck, 1987). Raising the topic of "whose view is more accurate" is not trivial to the cognitive therapist; the accuracy or truthfulness of the patient's thought pattern has great impact on what a therapist can and needs to do for treatment efficacy. Let us imagine two types of depressed individuals. One is an attractive 21-year-old college student, who is performing reasonably well academically and is physically healthy, but who is also depressed and socially isolated. It would make sense to contrast this person's self-perception with how others see the same individual. Most people would think of this 21-year-old as somebody with a potentially great life ahead of her and see little objective reason for being depressed. We have already described such clients as YAVIS (**Y**oung, **A**ttractive, **V**erbal, **I**ntelligent, **S**tudent or **S**uccessful; see chapter 10). The expectation for therapy is that this type of patient can relatively quickly improve because her negative self-view can be tested against the many positive characteristics that she possesses, and it is likely that an overgeneralizing and irrational thought pattern may lie underneath this depression. One can see that a therapist may be able to relatively quickly point out to her the many untested opportunities ahead of her; there is reason for optimism.

Now let us compare that scenario with that of an 82-year-old woman who is in hospital after quadruple coronary bypass surgery. She is a widow, lives on a limited pension, and has two children who live far away and who are not close to her. In addition, most of her friends have died, she is diabetic, she has frequent painful arthritis episodes, and her eyesight is failing her. She's also very depressed. How would a cognitive therapist approach this individual? Would Dr. Melissa A, our hospital-based psychologist, try to point out to the 82-year-old that depressive thoughts are unreasonable and irrational and that she should ignore these thoughts? Clearly, this scenario is a very different type of challenge for a therapist although both clients presented with depression. The point of comparing these two types of clients with each other is to stress that the cognitive therapist should not approach each patient with the same simplistic attitude about rationality or irrationality of having depressed or anxious thought patterns and feelings. In each instance, the therapist needs to make an effort to learn about the patient's habitual thinking patterns, to look for recurring themes that may be dysfunctional or that are open to change, and to try to look for alternatives.

Two Major Proponents: Ellis and Beck

Having had a chance to discuss cognitive therapy in general terms, the reader is now prepared to take a look at the more historical origins of cognitive therapy and to learn about the work of its two major proponents, namely, Albert Ellis and Aaron Beck.

Albert Ellis

Ellis can be credited with having created rational emotive therapy (RET; Ellis, 1962, 1977), which is really the first form of cognitive therapy. While originally trained in psychoanalytic therapy, Ellis experienced a great deal of frustration with its slow and passive process and therefore sought a more direct and aggressive approach. Much of the underpinnings of cognitive therapy in general, and especially RET, dates back to Greek philosophers (quoted in Ellis, 1962): Epictetus can be quoted as having said that "men are disturbed not by things, but by the views which they take of them." Ellis also gives credit to Shakespeare, who expressed a similar concept in *Hamlet*: "there is nothing either good or bad but thinking makes it so." Ellis was a charismatic therapist, and, in an attempt to make his approach easily understood, he simplified this thinking by describing an "ABC" concept where:

- A stands for Antecedent
- B stands for Belief
- C stands for Consequence

He argues that it is not the fact that a man's girlfriend left him that makes him miserable, but rather the man's belief that he cannot find another suitable girlfriend actually accounts for his misery. Also built into this line of thinking is that the beginning of this course of action, namely, the antecedent (that his girlfriend left him) cannot be changed, whereas the belief about his inability to find another girlfriend can be modified, and will then change corresponding feelings. In order to drive home his point about irrational thinking, Albert Ellis has created a list of colorfully worded principles (Table 12.1) that he considers to be the typical ways in which people set their own mental traps.

In addition to his groundbreaking book *Reason and Emotion in Psychotherapy*, published in 1962, Ellis built a freestanding training institute in New York that is active to this date. He has also written a string of popular psychology books, which all advance the cause for RET, using tongue-in-cheek titles such as: *How to Stubbornly Refuse to Make Yourself Miserable About Anything*, *How to Live with a Neurotic*, *The Civilized Couple's Guide to Extramarital Adventure*, and

TABLE 12.1 Irrational Ideas Typical for the Albert Ellis Approach

1. It is necessary that everybody loves me and approves of me.

2. I am a worthwhile human being only if I'm highly competent and consistently achieving in everything I try.

3. I need to be preoccupied with other people's wrongdoing and find ways to judge and punish them.

4. It is horrible when the world does not turn out to be as nice as I would like it to be.

5. Unhappiness comes from the outside, and I cannot control it.

6. When something scares me, I need to really preoccupy myself with it and constantly scan the environment for signs that it will happen.

7. It is easier to avoid difficult decisions and responsibilities than to face and live up to them.

8. It is necessary that I can always lean on somebody else because I myself am weak.

9. My personal history powerfully determines my current life, and because of this I'm not really free to make needed changes.

10. I should be greatly preoccupied with other people's problems.

11. Life's problems always have a perfect solution, and it is horrible if I cannot find that perfect solution.

Adapted from Ellis (1962).

Sex Without Guilt. RET itself largely progresses by the therapist engaging in a Socratian dialogue with the client where the therapist (a) identifies the types of thinking errors the client engages in, (b) points out the irrationality and dysfunction of such thoughts, and (c) assists the client in rewriting his inner dialogue or script.

Interestingly, Aaron Beck, while being a psychiatrist by profession, was also initially trained in psychoanalytic approaches. His development of a cognitive treatment approach for depression was similarly fueled by his dissatisfaction with the limited usefulness of analytical therapy. Beck's work is strongly anchored in extensive research on the nature of depression and the typical thought patterns observed in depressed patients. A cornerstone to Beck's work is the formulation of typical, biased thought patterns of depressed patients that fit into a **cognitive triad**, which describes the patient's overly pessimistic view of the self, her environment, and the future (Figure 12.2).

In terms of the therapeutic approach designed to change these pessimistic thought patterns, Beck developed a layer model depicting the varying degrees of awareness about one's own thinking. Closest to the surface are the thoughts that accompany everyday activity, and this layer is often described as the *inner script* that accompanies what individuals see, what they're planning to do, how they feel, or why they may want to engage in a particular behavior. If all such thoughts were written out in full, each of us could fill a book a day—a fact which precludes us from keeping systematic records of all our thoughts. This layer is described as "**automatic thoughts.**" The next layer, according to Beck, connects these seemingly accidental patterns in our own thinking, referred to as "**underlying assumptions.**" It is at this level where a cognitive therapist starts to recognize the idiosyncratic,

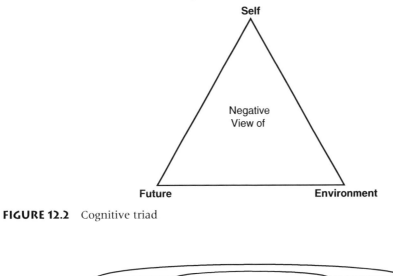

FIGURE 12.2 Cognitive triad

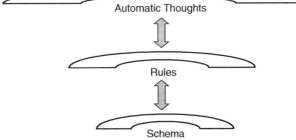

FIGURE 12.3 Beck's cognitive schema model

rule-driven, and often dysfunctional thought patterns of depressed patients (Figure 12.3). Lastly, the deepest and most long-standing level of influence is likely to have been created during childhood years and is referred to as "**schemas**" or "**core beliefs**." (The reader may also find the term "**schemata**" in the literature, which is the technically correct way of forming a plural for this word of Greek origin.)

A classic core belief found among depressed patients is a profound experience of the world as one in which people feel easily rejected, unsafe, and/or incompetent. In terms of therapy process, it is pivotal that patients first learn how to become aware of their own thought habits. Therapists are likely to use diaries or thought records in order to raise awareness of people's thoughts and feelings and then begin looking for systematic patterns in these inner scripts. At the beginning of therapy, the thought record tends to use a simple three-column method, where the first column describes salient events occurring during a given day that may have a bearing on the client's presenting problem. For example, a client may report with poor anger control that is most pronounced while driving his sports car. In this case, an anger-arousing driving scenario would be the stimulus to report in the left column. In the middle column, clients are asked to record what they were feeling at the time and how strong these feelings were. Notably, cognitive therapists recognize that clients rarely feel only one emotion at a time, but rather they may experience a bit of sadness at the same time that they are quite angry. The cognitive therapist seeks to encourage the client to write down what he was thinking at the time when he was really angry at the other driver and when he was honking and yelling. By having a chance to read over many thoughts thus recorded, the therapist hopes to recognize particularly frequent, recurring thought patterns. When that happens, the theme is referred to as a "hot thought," which means that they are the ones receiving the most attention. The very fact that Beck describes core beliefs as being deep-seated and long-standing reveals his original training in psychoanalytic therapy and shows the evolution of analytical, interpretive psychotherapy into a more cognitive therapy (Table 12.2).

The client is a very anxious breast cancer patient who has been told that her first chemotherapy was successful but that the chance of malignant tumor recurrence is very high.

The use of thought records as an attempt to uncover dysfunctional thinking habits is an excellent first step in cognitive therapy. Nevertheless, just recognizing that a particular thought pattern exists is not very helpful and is not likely sufficient to produce rapid therapeutic change. The negative anticipations that are typical of depressed (and also anxious or angry) clients often serve as a major handicap in attempting change. It does not make sense to initiate a behavior if one expects the outcome to be unpleasant or ineffective. A highly socially anxious individual is not likely to start casual conversations with a stranger because she anticipates that the person will not want to talk to her, or even worse, will say something dismissive and hurtful. However, when such generalized negative expectations are predominant, the client also cannot find out that she may be wrong. Hence, a critical part of cognitive therapy is to test the truthfulness of such negative expectations by conducting *behavioral experiments*. First, one formulates the expectation in the form of a hypothesis and then tests it through actual behavior and observation. An example of behavioral experiment is described in Box 12.6.

TABLE 12.2 Sample of Thought Record

EVENT	MOOD	THOUGHT
Daughter sends first-birthday photos of my grand daughter	Happy 70% Anxious 30%	This is so exciting. She looks a bit like me. Next month I will visit them and look forward to holding my granddaughter. I hope to live long enough to see her complete school and get married
Noticed an odd tingling feeling in my breasts	Anxious 60% Angry 30%	What if this means a recurrence? This cannot happen to me; I did everything my oncologist told me to. Will I ever be able to stop worrying?

BOX 12.6

EXPERIMENTS IN COGNITIVE-BEHAVIORAL THERAPY; AN EXAMPLE
FOR JOE'S BELIEF THAT HE WAS NOT LIKABLE

Experiment	Prediction Arising from Core Belief	Actual Consequence
Tell 10 cashiers in a store, "Must be hard to stand on your feet all day."	All of them ignore me or give a flippant return comment.	Two said nothing in return. Four started a little conversation. Four said, "You got that right" and smiled.
Approach up to six classmates to try to get a study group of you and three others together.	All of them turn me down.	Two said, "Thanks for asking but I already have a group." Two just said, "No, not interested" or "I live too far away." Two agreed, and they formed a study group of three.

Through a progression of challenges to irrational thought patterns and behavioral experiments, a client learns how to create his own successful experiences and how to gradually shape them into more adaptive thought patterns.

◇ COGNITIVE-BEHAVIORAL THERAPY

So far, we have presented **behavior therapy** and **cognitive therapy** as distinct therapies, and given their unique origins, this is appropriate and informative. However, throughout much of the literature in clinical psychology, one finds the use of the term **cognitive-behavioral therapy (CBT)** as if the cognitive and behavioral therapies were so overlapping that they always needed to be mentioned in the same breath.

The position taken here is that pure cognitive therapy is not actually practiced. As much as cognitive therapy focuses on cognition, it does not deal with cognitions in isolation, but rather ties them to mood and behavior. What makes certain cognitions dysfunctional and problematic is that they create or maintain avoidance behaviors and prevent people from doing things that are enjoyable, could widen their range of function, and may potentially reduce disability. If a young man believes that no female will ever be interested in him, he may never approach any prospective partners. As such, he may also never find out that he is indeed well liked by some young women and that simply changing cognitions is not enough for success. As was mentioned earlier in this chapter, an essential ingredient of cognitive therapy is to get clients to test some of their cognitive sets or expectations by actually trying out new behaviors and checking the accuracy of their assumptions. This is considered pivotal to the success of cognitive therapy. If it turns out that these new behaviors become reinforced (e.g., a depressed and lonely person finding out that joining a club was very pleasant and led to the development of new friendships), then a behavior therapy principle has become integrated into cognitive therapy and has complemented the tool kit of the cognitive therapist. What was initially intended to be just cognitive therapy really is CBT; it integrates attempts at changing thought patterns *and* corresponding behaviors through experiments. Although these two therapeutic modalities are derived from two different bodies of theory defined by distinct terminology and techniques, ultimately it is a combination of these techniques that makes the best use of cognitive therapy principles. Therefore, it makes sense to package these two descriptors together into the term "CBT."

While cognitive therapy usually ends up packaged together with behavioral techniques, the reverse does not need to be true. Behavior therapy can actually stick to its black box principle and achieve positive outcomes without directly targeting patient cognitions. This is apparent when, for example, reinforcement and punishment principles are used to help a self-mutilating, individual with severe intellectual disabilities or an autistic child with whom one cannot reason. In everyday clinical practice, behavior therapy can be, and is often, applied in a relatively pure fashion, without direct focus on cognitions.

Given its popularity—based to a large degree on its overall positive effects (see chapter 13)—it may be worthwhile to stress what makes CBT unique and effective:

1. Use of homework and out-of-session activities
2. A high level of direction of session activity by the therapist
3. Teaching of skills used by patients to cope with symptoms
4. Emphasis on patients' future experiences
5. Providing patients with information about their treatment, disorder, or symptoms
6. An intrapersonal or cognitive focus

◇ BIOFEEDBACK, RELAXATION, AND STRESS MANAGEMENT

Throughout this book we have shown how the work of clinical psychologists applies to mental and physical health problems and is executed in both inpatient and outpatient settings. In a larger sense, interventions described in this forthcoming section are also behavior therapy (or CBT) techniques because they are largely based on learning principles.

Some clinical psychologists work primarily in organizational settings and attempt to increase the efficiency of such environments, by improving the quality of life for employees, and/or providing primary prevention services. In all these nonclinical environments, clinical psychologists may deal with people who see themselves as stressed, burned-out, or having **trouble adjusting**. It can be difficult to draw the line between an anxiety disorder that meets the criteria listed in the *DSM-IV*, the feeling of exhaustion that goes with clinical depression, and the terribly generic term "**stress.**" Obviously, tools are needed to deal with all these problems or, even better, to prevent them from becoming problems.

Furthermore, as we have shown, clinical psychologists are frequently involved in caring for individuals who present with medical disorders that have strong psychological components. Broadly, these disorders include chronic pain conditions, sleep problems, high blood pressure, chronic fatigue, autoimmune diseases, or irritable bowel syndrome, and this list is by no means complete. For these clinical applications there is the possibility (a) that psychopathology and poor emotional adjustment can play contributing, causal roles (Kop, 1999) or (b) that low or worried mood states are a frequent (and understandable) consequence of certain medical conditions. The latter has certainly been true in the case of cancer, cardiac conditions, or HIV-AIDS diagnoses (Poole, Hunt Matheson, & Cox, 2008; see also chapter 17).

There is a widespread consensus that the majority of conditions presented in family physicians' offices are primarily psychological in nature (Rosen & Wiens, 1980). When patients who presented themselves with psychosomatic complaints to a family physician were randomized into receiving as little as 2 hours of psychologically supportive therapy versus no psychological treatment, the subsequent number of physician visits and overall health care costs went down considerably (Rosen & Wiens, 1980), saving valuable health care dollars. Clearly, there is a place for clinical psychologists in general health care settings.

The connection between emotion, cognition, behavior, and physical health is explicitly captured by the fields of psychosomatic medicine and health psychology, each of which has huge bodies of (largely overlapping) literature associated with it (see also chapter 17). Also, there are fraternal associations for these types of psychology providers (i.e., American Psychosomatic Association, Society of Behavioral Medicine, etc.) that organize annual meetings and publish specialty journals and position papers; the resulting publications are readily accessible on numerous websites. One pathway between emotion and physical disease is of particular interest to clinical psychologists, namely, the path that connects emotion to changes in the nervous system. There is ample evidence that:

- Pain is a complex psychosomatic process with intertwined emotional and sensory processes (Melzack & Wall, 1989).
- Depression has cognitive, biological, and behavioral components (Craig & Dobson, 1995).
- Anxiety is often tied to excessive sympathetic nervous system arousal (Hoehn-Saric, & McLeod, 2000).
- High blood pressure is characterized by an imbalance of the sympathetic and parasympathetic components of the central nervous system (Linden, 1988).

Another pathway for linking behavior, emotion, and cognition to health is more indirect via health behaviors like smoking cessation, exercise patterns, maintaining good nutrition, and adhering to medical prescriptions. These health behaviors, and attempts to modify them, are described in chapter 17; however, methods used for arousal reduction and the establishment of good autonomic self-regulation are described here because they are bread-and-butter methods for clinical psychologists who work in physical health care environments.

These methods will be described in three sections:

1. First, methods for **biofeedback** will be elucidated, because this is a unique area of practice given the involvement of specific equipment.
2. Next, descriptions are provided for a variety of **autonomic self-regulation** tools that clinical psychologists can offer to a wide range of patients.
3. Lastly, how all these methods fit together into the world of **stress management** will be discussed more broadly.

Biofeedback

Biofeedback is a form of CBT because it involves learning principles, tying sensory perception processes to feedback, and reinforcement techniques. It also involves models of skill development. In chapter 9, where the assessment of physiological functions had been described, the reader already became familiar with the process of acquisition and the measurement and display of human physiological functions of interest to clinical psychologists, in particular those reflecting arousal, blood flow, as well as a variety of muscular activity indices. A therapist can share with her client what particular physiological signals mean and encourage her to use this

Photographer: Henri Dupond

information to change the signal itself; this process would be described as **biofeedback therapy**. In the sections of assessment the concept of reactivity of measurement was discussed; our position, as presented throughout this book, is that reactivity of measurement is generally undesirable because it changes the information one wants to objectively measure, and as such it is a major threat to validity. Nevertheless, we have pointed out that reactivity can be used constructively in that a man using a diary to record the frequency of smoking behavior is likely going to decrease the amount of cigarettes smoked simply because now, after record-keeping, he realizes exactly how much he smokes. The same applies to biofeedback where clients can be made acutely aware of physiological functions that they may otherwise have difficulty sensing. There are a number of physiological functions that humans are typically aware of, especially when they change measurably and rapidly; this is particularly true for respiration rate and depth, heart rate, and to a lesser degree muscular tension or blood sugar levels. Despite frequent claims to the contrary, clients are actually not very good at sensing change in their blood pressure, and humans are essentially unable to sense changes in body functions like blood lipids or increased output of stress hormones. Therefore, the basic principle of biofeedback is to encourage learning by showing clients acute changes in biological functions especially when they are not usually open to awareness; this process is referred to as **proprioception**. A schematic display may help to understand the sequence of steps involved in biofeedback (Figure 12.4).

In terms of applications, biofeedback is frequently used for one of these two different functions:

1. To help individuals achieve a generalized **relaxation response**, for example, reduce heightened arousal in a patient with an anxiety disorder.

2. To help a client improve control or relearn biological functions that are site-specific autonomic self-regulatory processes. This applies to the teaching of pelvic muscular floor muscle control in a case of stress enuresis (problems with urinary flow control) or chronically cold hand and feet due to inadequate blood circulation (Raynaud's disease).

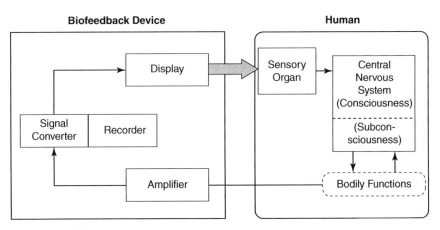

FIGURE 12.4 Biofeedback schematic display

The Training Process

The effect of biofeedback information depends on how it is used. When biofeedback is combined with physical therapy, it becomes biofeedback-assisted rehabilitation. When combined with relaxation training, it becomes biofeedback-assisted relaxation. In its most elementary form, biofeedback does not have to require expensive equipment. The beginning runner can learn about peak heart rates and heart rate recovery by using pulse sensing and counting on his wrist together with the use of a watch, to determine acute heart rate and heart rate changes. Also, part of biofeedback training is to strengthen an individual's ability to become more aware of his own body changes, referred to as natural proprioception. This principle has been used very effectively to teach patients with frequent epilepsy attacks to sense changes in their electrical brain activity and then use this information to adopt relaxation or other compensatory strategies to prevent a pending seizure (Lubar & Bahler, 1976).

Relaxation or Self-Regulation Methods

Describing the rationales and benefits of different arousal-reduction strategies at great length may not be needed here because differences and similarities between various methods have been extensively discussed elsewhere (Lehrer, Woolfolk, & Sime, 2007; Linden, 1990; Vaitl & Petermann, 2000). Furthermore, as the reader will see later in this chapter, the outcomes are much more similar than they are different (Benson, 1975), although proponents of specific techniques predictably stress the uniqueness and differences of their favored methods. The primary purpose of arousal-reduction methods is to help people recognize sympathetic hyperarousal and provide them with techniques to reduce such arousal and achieve balance between sympathetic and parasympathetic activation (Linden et al., 2007; Lehrer, Woolfolk, & Sime, 2007). In addition to teaching a technique, most proponents of relaxation methods (in particular those of meditation and autogenic training, a form of self-hypnosis) stress that experienced relaxation practitioners adopt a more distanced, reflective view of potentially stressful situations in their natural environment (Linden, 1990; see Box 12.7).

When studying multiple self-regulation strategies, the reader quickly learns that aside from differences in rationales and techniques, there are many similarities (Benson, 1975). Benson (1975) argues that the shared features of arousal-reduction strategies (i.e., a vehicle for focus, removal of external stimuli, a comfortable body position, perceived permission to focus on oneself) may be accounting for most of the benefit.

Even though arousal-reduction strategies achieve more than mere physical inactivity does, it is considerably more challenging to show differential benefits and/or ideal matches of particular strategies to specific applications. Benson's (1975) position is that all arousal-reduction interventions share critical features that account for a significant proportion of the benefits. These features include provision of a rationale, permission to focus on oneself, spending time in a stimulus-reduced environment, and the use of a vehicle to facilitate focus of one's attention. Where methods differ most is in the type of vehicle used for attention focusing; in meditation it is the mantra, in progressive muscular relaxation it is the clearly structured and sequenced following of tensing-relaxing steps for various muscle groups, in biofeedback it is the availability of a physiological monitor and displays of one's functions, and in autogenic training it is the structured sequence of attending to formulas that suggest particular physiological changes. The shared target of these relaxation techniques is the production of a relaxation response that includes shifts in the pattern of the electroencephalogram (i.e., increase dominance of alpha activity); reduced muscle tone and blood pressure; and reduced breathing rate with simultaneously greater inspiration and expiration depths. Aside from physiological arousal reduction, these techniques are likely to lead to accompanying changes in subjective arousal, and it is worthwhile for researchers to measure and report biological and psychological changes separately, given that they may not always occur in synchrony. One arousal-reduction technique that is somewhat distinct and rapidly growing in popularity is that of mindfulness-based stress reduction (Grossman, Niemann, Schmidt, & Walach, 2004; Kabat-Zinn, 2003). Although mindfulness stress reduction has some of its origins in meditation as practiced on the South-Asian subcontinent, it is not to be confused with traditional meditation. As opposed to the passive acceptance that defines transcendental meditation, mindfulness meditation focuses on achieving an astute awareness and the ability to see and accept without judgment one's own behavior and interactions with the environment (Kabat-Zinn, 2003). A potential problem with discussing mindfulness meditation in a comparative sense with other arousal-reduction methods is that mindfulness meditation is considered more of a multicomponent approach. It is more of an intervention *program* rather than just a unitary, single technique intervention. More details about mindfulness meditation are provided in chapter 14 (Table 12.3).

Summary

Biofeedback and other forms of self-regulation training have many advantages. They can be easily standardized and are therefore particularly accessible to therapy outcome research. The self-regulation methods that do not require equipment can also be taught very economically in groups. The range of applications as described earlier is quite wide because arousal reduction is the goal of many different psychological therapies. Self-regulation techniques are also excellent adjuncts or components of the multidisciplinary or multicomponent treatment

TABLE 12.3 Comparison of Relaxation Methods

TECHNIQUES	ROLE OF THERAPIST	VEHICLE OF CHANGE
Autogenic training	Therapist instructs and guides, and encourages self-control.	Imagery of organ-specific changes
Biofeedback	Therapist provides instrumentation, instruction, and guidance. Client partially controls the process.	Biological feedback and systematic behavioral or cognitive activity to acquire control
Hypnosis	Therapist controls the process. Client is recipient.	Therapist suggestions
Meditation	Therapist instructs and guides. Client controls the process.	Repetition of meaningless syllable in imagery
Progressive muscular	Therapist instructs and guides. Client follows the instructions.	Systematic tensing and relaxing of specific muscle groups

BOX 12.7

SELF-HYPNOSIS EFFECTS

A number of years ago, One of the authors (WL) needed some very minor surgery that required only a local anesthetic. After the surgeon had administered this anesthetic, he said to WL: "I need to look after another patient and will be back in 10 minutes to do the procedure. It takes a bit of time for the anesthetic to be effective anyway, so just relax." Given that WL was alone in the room, not supposed to get up, and with nothing else to do, he decided to go through a well-practiced autogenic training routine. Fortunately, he was not too apprehensive about the procedure itself and was able to focus on the formulas fairly quickly. He vaguely recalled that the surgeon returned and completed the procedure (which took at most 5 minutes). When he was all done, he gently touched WL and told him it was over. WL gradually got up and when he seemed reasonably alert, the surgeon looked at him curiously and said: "Where were you? You seemed far away and did not respond the way patients usually do; you were very passive, kind of detached." WL told him what he had done, and the surgeon listened with interest. WL was quite surprised that his autogenic exercises had been distinctly perceivable by another person who had no idea what he had been doing. To him, this was a subtle yet powerful demonstration of the effect of self-hypnosis.

packages that are typically used in anxiety clinics, in pain clinics, with cancer populations, in sleep clinics, and in cardiac rehabilitation (Lehrer, Woolfolk, & Sime, 2007; VanDixhoorn & White, 2005). A potential drawback, especially for self-regulation interventions that require equipment, is that patients can learn quite well how to use the equipment and improve functions in the therapist's office, but then have difficulties in transferring the learning to their everyday lives.

Stress Management

The term "stress management" is so frequently used that everybody seems to intuitively know what it is. Unfortunately, different researchers have assigned highly variable meanings, thus opening the door for much confusion (Linden, 2005; Ong, Linden, & Young, 2004). Stress management as typically practiced is a mélange of techniques, most of which are taught in a superficial manner. Researchers often disagree on operational definitions of what stress management is, thus making it very difficult to compare efficacy studies with each other (Ong, Linden, & Young, 2004). Ong and her collaborators conducted a review of stress management and reported that stress management applications were most often studied for health problems (40% of the sample of studies), workplace interventions (22%), problems with students (16%), sports applications (3%), psychiatric problems (3%), and other (16%). The "other" category included studies of spouses of older people, patients undergoing acute medical procedures, and individuals with low social support and/or poor problem-solving skills. Despite much variation in treatment protocols, the authors noted that a modal type of stress management program existed, characterized by:

1. A preferred group treatment format (59% of studies were group only; 18% paired group and individual sessions)
2. The teaching of a modal number of different techniques (between six and eight)
3. A typical treatment length of six sessions, with a mean session duration of 1.5 hours

Attempts to classify stress management studies by their theoretical orientation indicated that 77% used an approach that broadly qualifies as a "cognitive-behavioral approach," 85% taught some form of relaxation, 15% used at least one form of biofeedback, 10% were classified as being based on a systems model, and 6% could not be readily classified. Similarities notwithstanding, Ong and colleagues (2004) reported that intervention descriptions were frequently cryptic and would be difficult to replicate by another researcher. Especially confusing was the use of certain technique descriptions and labels such that (a) techniques may appear to vary across studies although they were actually comparable upon close inspection, (b) some technique descriptors were so vague as to be meaningless, and (c) levels of categorization were often confusing. These observations are further elaborated below.

A Model of the Stress Process: Major Components and Moderating Variables

Aggregation of knowledge from the basic research on the physiology and psychology of stress and coping leads to a model that describes a multistep, sequenced approach with three basic components: (a) stressor, (b) initial response (or coping) and failing successful initial coping, and (c) a lasting physiological stress response (see Figure 12.5). All steps in the process are influenced by known predispositions and coexisting buffers. The term

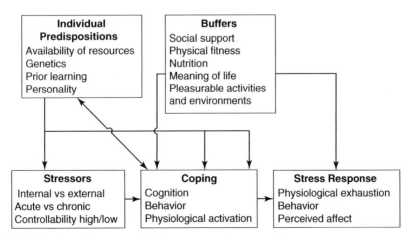

FIGURE 12.5 A stress process model

"**buffer**" is used to describe environmental or personal characteristics that, when present, have been shown to protect an individual against exaggerated acute arousal and to facilitate recovery. While some of these features (e.g., physical fitness) may serve as mediators in a stress-disease pathway, the term "buffer" is used and preferred here because its use does not require the more stringent proof needed for claims of true mediation; on the other hand, calling a characteristic a buffer does not prevent it from serving a mediational function.

The model tries to clarify the sequential process of stress, differentiating stressors from initial responses (coping efforts) and from a (possibly, but not necessarily) ensuing stress response. Individual predispositions are seen as correlated with, contributing to, and/or even shaping stressors themselves. For example, people with high incomes have more control over stressors, possess a wider range of coping options, and potentially have a lower risk of developing stress responses (Gallo & Matthews, 2003). The negative effect of limited resources that accompanies low socioeconomic status is worsened with a pattern of psychological adversity that is characterized by high job strain and low support (Steptoe & Marmot, 2003).

The techniques themselves can be meaningfully organized into four categories: (a) systems or environment interventions (i.e., stressor manipulations), (b) coping skills training, (c) creation of stress buffers (like social support), and (d) arousal-reduction techniques. Most of the typically used techniques have a sound rationale and are grounded in basic research; there is generally supportive evidence for clinical utility from numerous controlled, clinical trials. Stimulus recognition and manipulation are logical first activities in a stress management program, and they represent a primary prevention objective that is germane to stress management. To facilitate communication, researchers and practitioners should distinguish these four classes of stress management techniques and clearly describe which ones are built into an intervention protocol.

On the whole, controlled stressor manipulations and systemic change research have been the "orphans" of this literature—the neglected children, who have received minimal and not well-structured attention. It is noteworthy that European stress researchers see the topic as a societal issue much more than North Americans who tend to see the need to manage stress as an individual responsibility. Best developed is the area of workplace stress that is more likely to deal with organizational issues (i.e., the stressor environment) than are other applications; yet, even here, systemic changes are often asked for and rarely researched and practiced. Also underdeveloped is the area of social skill building that is meant to understand and minimize interpersonal strain, and this vacuum is particularly noteworthy because research described by Linden (2005) has identified interpersonal stress as particularly insidious, persistent, and difficult to recover from.

As a result of this discourse on stress management and its theoretical and practical roots, Linden (2005) has offered the following definition:

> Stress management is both a set of relatively concrete techniques for distress reduction and skill building, as well as an attempt to view, organize, and shape our world to maximize quality of life even at times of adversity. These two core features do not readily form a coherent, simple definition of stress management; instead, to be meaningful, the definition embraces a broad view of stress that reflects how people interact with each other and how they construct their environment, and that accepts that stress management is both preventive and reactive in nature.

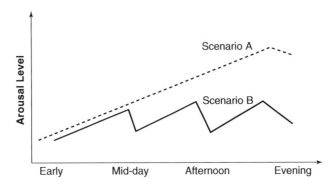

FIGURE 12.6 Schema of 2 days: one with nonstop stress and one with the effect of recovery breaks

Lifestyles with built-in recovery phases (like evenings off and weekends) are disturbed for the case of shift workers, and many self-employed people take few holidays, if any. During such recovery phases, people may seek out restorative environments like a weekend cabin or a comfortable living room or may read, listen to music, spend time with friends, or walk their dog. A schematic display of how recovery strategies can be systematically used in planning a day is shown in Figure 12.6, where a typical day with continuously rising stress and arousal is displayed as one line and a better-planned day (the goal of good stress management and time planning) is represented in the zigzag pattern of the second line.

The dotted line represents a day with steady demands, no recovery breaks, and correspondingly rising stress or arousal (scenario A); the solid line represents the same amount of demand (i.e., total additive incline in arousal). However, because of recovery breaks the arousal level at the end of the day is much lower (scenario B). This figure is clearly a simplistic way of making a point for the importance of recovery, but showing it to participants in stress management programs can help convince them of the benefits of recovery breaks (Linden, 2005).

Summary

On the whole, the rationales for various stress management techniques map well onto models of how stress can lead to disease. The simplest designs and most closely matched rationales of technique to known pathophysiology are found in the category of arousal-reduction strategies. The area of coping, although recognized as very important for stress management, is vast and yet inconclusive, due at least in good part to ill-defined terminology (Skinner, Edge, Altman, & Sherwood, 2003). Adaptive coping is recognized as requiring a "behavior by situation" match that requires individually tailored strategies and thus does not readily lend itself to group formats and standardized stress management approaches. Although rationales for systemic interventions are sometimes well developed, especially in the organizational behavior literature, the intended systemic interventions still tend to place too much emphasis on individual responsibility rather than needed social policy or system change (Newton, 1995).

In order to increase the comparability of different approaches to stress management, Linden (2005) has proposed a new taxonomy of stress management approaches. The resulting categories and their inherent qualities (and flaws) are given here:

1.   **Primary Systemic Stress Prevention:** This label is applied to a truly primary prevention type of stress management that achieves its goals via system and policy changes. These changes are possibly triggered by empowered individuals but are generally implemented by politicians, administrators, or managers, and they affect workplaces and society at large. Examples would be government programs or policies to reduce poverty; to increase public safety; to minimize harassment due to gender, race, religion, or sexual preference; or to support job stability. While this approach is not the type of work that clinical psychologists typically undertake on a daily basis, the aspirational aspect of such systemic preventive activities is actually mandated in the Ethics Code of Psychologists in many jurisdictions, with the intent of raising the social conscience and the level of emancipation of health professionals.

2.   **Preventive, Skill-learning Stress Management:** This term refers to a preventive, skill-learning-based approach that is not necessarily reactive to a preceding diagnosis of acute distress; it can be offered as a manual-driven, standardized program because it needs to prepare individuals for a variety of future demands with stress potential that are only partly predictable. It provides individuals with a flexible tool kit and is meant to be the psychological analogy to a "beginner's home repair tool kit" that one can buy in a hardware store. Some narrowing of objectives can be achieved by recruiting intervention participants who share a similar environment; examples would be all employees of a company or all first-year students attending a particular university. On the other hand, if participants come from all walks of life and represent varying age groups, then a broad, multitechnique approach may be best.

Intervention protocols that embrace multiple techniques have earned such loaded and pejorative descriptors as "shotgun" or "gardenhose" approaches; however, the intended use for a preventive purpose justifies the teaching of multiple techniques. If learners do not present with a specific problem to solve (i.e., a trigger to react to), then the acquisition of a wide arsenal of tools for undetermined future use is highly desirable. An analogy to this approach is the vaccination against multiple strains of flu when public health experts cannot foretell which of six possible strains may become the most dominant one in an upcoming flu season. Similarly, not all future psychological or emotional challenges can be forecast, and we can benefit from possessing many different tools in order to be ready for such pending challenges.

3.   **Reactive, Problem-Solving Stress Management:** The third type of approach is reactive to a known, existing problem; it is applied to situations that are predictably and commonly stressful like massive layoffs in a company, dealing with a positive diagnosis of breast cancer and its pending lengthy and frightening treatment protocol, survival in a hostile workplace, or handling the challenges faced by the caregivers of Alzheimer's patients. This approach requires tailoring of interventions to the situational triggers that brought the need for coping to light, and it is probably most efficacious when matched to participant preferences and individual context. A heart disease or cancer patient with a

supportive spouse may not need or even benefit from additional support, but may seek to quell her disease-specific fears with accurate information about symptoms and warning signals as well as tips for risk reduction. Nevertheless, the combination of clinical experience and both qualitative and quantitative research can be drawn on to identify frequent and typical stressors and stressor qualities, and this knowledge can be built into treatment rationales and technique selections (Linden, 2005).

◇ EMOTION-FOCUSED THERAPY

As has often been the case in the development of new forms of psychotherapy, a perceived need for a new form of treatment is driven by dissatisfaction with existing therapies. Greenberg's (2002) decision to focus on emotions in therapy can be considered a reaction to the observation that other popular therapies like behavioral or analytical approaches pay relatively little attention to emotions, although emotions are critical for defining our well-being and are very instrumental in defining daily decisions (Greenberg & Johnson, 1988). Emotion-focused therapy has its roots in research in attachment theories, basic research on emotion processing, and the study of interactional patterns in distressed relationships. It should therefore not come as a surprise that the focus and primary application of emotion-focused therapy has been for the resolution of marital problems using a conjoint couples therapy format. By helping couples understand how emotions develop and follow each other, and how the two partners in a relationship mutually influence one another, it is presumed that distress can be reduced or prevented. In order to achieve this end, emotionally focused couples therapy follows a sequence of nine steps, which comprise three phases (Johnson, Hunsley, Greenberg, & Schindler, 1999):

1. Cycle de-escalation
2. Changing interactional positions
3. Consolidation or integration

A more detailed description of the model including all nine steps is presented in Box 12.8.

A fairly typical scenario in emotionally focused couples therapy is that one partner is withdrawn and guarded, which is often interpreted by the other partner as a personal rejection. The more one partner rejects, the more the other one calls for more openness and intimacy, and the more threatened the first one feels, causing further withdrawal (Gottman & Notarius, 2000). The therapist will therefore attempt to uncover the reasons for one partner's sense of threat and tries to gradually get her to express her feelings and contribute to a more active emotional engagement. At the same time, it is necessary that the therapist also develops a deeper understanding of the attachment needs of the other spouse to make it easier for both partners to meet each other's emotional needs. The first step in the change process is to raise the client's awareness and get the client to accept his feelings. In the regulation stage, the client must learn to tolerate these emotions and control any self-destructive behaviors that seriously interfere with his daily life. The point is not to let emotions spin out of control, but rather to

BOX 12.8

STEPS IN EMOTIONALLY FOCUSED COUPLES THERAPY

Phase A: Cycle De-Escalation

Step 1. Assessment; Creating an alliance and explicating the core issues in the couple's conflict using an attachment perspective.

Step 2. Identifying the problem interactional cycle that maintains attachment insecurity and relationship to stress.

Step 3. Accessing the unacknowledged emotions underlying interactional positions.

Step 4. Reframing the problem in terms of the cycle, the underlying emotions, and attachment needs.

Phase B: Changing Interactional Positions

Step 5. Promoting identification with disowned needs and aspects of self, and integrating these into relationship interactions.

Step 6. Promoting acceptance of the partner's new construction of experience in the relationship of new responses.

Step 7. Facilitating the expression of specific needs and wants and creating emotional engagement.

Phase C: Consolidation/integration

Step 8. Facilitating the emergence of new solutions to old problematic relationship issues.

Step 9. Consolidating new positions and new cycles of attachment behavior.
Reprinted from Johnson et al. (1999) with permission.

---

learn healthy methods of coping with one's feelings before the final processes—**transformation** and **reflection**—can occur.

◇ MOTIVATIONAL INTERVIEWING

Motivational interviewing (MI) was born out of therapists' frustrations associated with the very frequent relapses that occur in the treatment of substance abuse disorders. It is a relatively new mode of client-centered therapy, with a moderately directive therapeutic style. Furthermore, MI is designed to enhance readiness for behavior change as well as support

Leslie Greenberg

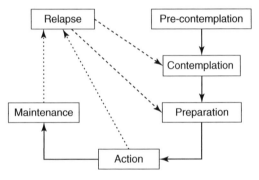

FIGURE 12.7 Stages of change

change once the motivation is strong enough. Developed initially for work with alcoholics, it was first described by Miller (1983) in an article published in *Behavioural Psychotherapy*. Given that it leaves responsibility in the hands of the client, many see it as an evolution of Rogers's person-centered counseling approach, although it can also be blended with cognitive-behavioral methods. MI is theoretically compatible and comfortable with both of these related theoretical approaches; its uniqueness lies mostly in the explicit identification of how ready a client is for change and the matching of interventions to this degree of readiness (Quilan & McCaul, 2000).

The underlying **stages of change model** has been proposed by Prochaska, DiClemente, and Norcross (1992) and are displayed in Figure 12.7.

In a number of ways, the stages of change model and its embedding into the MI approach are similar to mainstream CBT. However, the largest difference between the two treatment methods is that there is an implicit belief in CBT that clients are ready to change when they walk through the therapist's door. Recall that MI has largely been developed for

TABLE 12.4 Motivational Interviewing: Technique Stage Match: Stages of Change and Therapist Tasks

CLIENT STAGE	THERAPIST'S MOTIVATIONAL TASKS
Precontemplation	Raise doubt and increase the client's perception of the risks and problems with current behavior
Contemplation	Tip the balance and evoke the reasons to change; risks of not changing strengthen the client's self-efficacy for the change of current behavior
Determination	Help the client determine the best course of action to take in seeking change
Action	Help the client take steps toward change
Maintenance	Help the client identify and use strategies to prevent relapse
Relapse	Help the client renew the processes of contemplation, determination, and action, without becoming stuck or demoralized because of relapse

substance abuse disorders, which have previously been treated with some success with CBT. CBT on the other hand is seen as a method that presumes that the client is ready for change and is no longer hesitant to change his maladaptive behaviors. The MI therapist is explicit in his willingness and patience to ride it out with a client, who may be flip-flopping in his willingness to abstain from smoking or alcohol.

The focus in MI tends to be around a client's ambivalence of quitting and the dynamic nature of resistance. The therapist expects a cycle of attempt and failure and makes no fuss when it happens. In fact, clients are told ahead of time that relapse can happen and that the patient will not be labeled a failure when relapse happens. The therapeutic relationship more resembles a friendly partnership rather than an expert-client interaction. The therapist respects the client's autonomy and freedom of choice (and consequences) regarding her own behavior. The therapist, using MI techniques, carefully assesses the prevailing stage of change and then uses this knowledge to implement a matching technique. For instance, a client who is not at all motivated to quit smoking (i.e., precontemplation stage) is at best responsive to receiving health information rather than concrete suggestions for how to quit (Table 12.4). Much of the process focuses on strengthening the patient's motive for change and on weakening the arguments for maintenance of the problem behavior. Only when a strong motivation for change has been achieved will there be any suggestion of specific behavioral strategies. There are crucial and trainable therapist skills that characterize an MI style. Most important among these are listed here:

- The ability to understand the person's frame of reference, particularly via reflective listening
- Expressing acceptance and affirmation

- Eliciting and selectively reinforcing the client's own self-motivational statements, expressions of problem recognition, concern, desire and intention to change, and ability to change

- Monitoring the client's degree of readiness to change and ensuring that resistance is not generated by jumping ahead of the client

- Affirming the client's freedom of choice and self-direction

- Accurate knowledge about the prevalence, pathophysiology, and cost of the problematic behavior under scrutiny

◇ DIALECTICAL BEHAVIOR THERAPY

Rationale

This chapter so far introduced therapy methods that could be applied to many target problems. However, we think it can also be very informative to show how a therapy approach based in good part on existing methods gets specifically modified and expanded for one particular population of patients. In this case we are talking about **dialectical behavior therapy** (DBT) developed for notoriously difficult-to-treat patients with **borderline personality disorder** (Linehan, 1993a). These patients generally don't think they have problems and tend not to seek therapy on their own. However, when they do, they make huge demands on therapists because they are volatile, histrionic, hypersensitive, seen as manipulative, and at times suicidal. These qualities also imply that they frequently challenge authority (including their therapist), and they are the type of client who is most likely to complain about professionals to their licensing bodies. Marsha Linehan at the University of Washington devised DBT and initiated clinical trials of this distinct approach that has become the gold standard for the treatment of this clinical problem. DBT is based on the premise that the disorder is a consequence of growing up within an environment where children are frequently invalidated, meaning they have been frequently rejected or outright abused, and parental responses to the child behavior are inconsistent, making it difficult for the child to know how to secure love. The child becomes hypersensitive to stressors especially those involving social acceptance and inclusion and develops chronic problems with emotion control. A pattern of self-mutilation often develops as a means of coping with the intense and painful feelings experienced by these patients; suicide attempts may be seen as an expression of the fact that life is simply not seen as worth living. Patients with profound borderline features reveal histories of frequent episodes of admission to psychiatric hospitals.

Method

DBT is nondogmatic and open, placing much emphasis on the interaction with the therapist. What makes the treatment dialectical is the alternating focus on acceptance on the one hand and change on the other. Thus DBT includes specific techniques of acceptance and validation designed to counter the **self-invalidation** of the patient. Further added is problem-solving and emotion-regulation skill training to help the client learn more adaptive ways of dealing with her difficulties and acquire these skills to do so. Dialectical strategies underlie all aspects of treatment to counter the extreme and rigid thinking encountered in these patients, but the treatment is also behavioral in that, without ignoring the past, it focuses on present behavior and the current factors that are controlling that behavior. The therapist is encouraged to be:

1. Accepting of the patient as he is, which encourages change
2. Centered and firm, yet flexible when the circumstances require it
3. Nurturing, but benevolently demanding

Effective therapy requires clear and consistent contingencies, and clients need to learn the limits of behavior acceptable to the therapist; an unconditional relationship between therapist and patient is not seen as possible, and it is possible for the patient to cause the therapist to reject her if the patient only tries hard enough. It is in the patient's interests to learn to treat her therapist in a way that encourages the therapist to want to continue helping her. Unlike most forms of therapy, DBT routinely uses:

1. Individual therapy
2. Group skills training
3. Telephone contact
4. Therapist consultation

This multimodal approach reflects the patient's neediness and is very demanding on the therapist but is seen as necessary to offer the patient a sense of safety. The training aspect itself can be broken down into four modules of skills training that are described in more detail in the therapist training manual (Linehan, 1993b):

1. Core mindfulness skills
2. Interpersonal effectiveness skills
3. Emotion modulation skills
4. Distress tolerance skills

Borderline personality disordered patients tend to present with a string of problem behaviors that need to be targeted in a structured format to avoid flip-flopping among different therapy focuses. The course of therapy is organized into stages and structured in terms of hierarchies of targets at each stage.

The *pretreatment stage* focuses on assessment, commitment, and orientation to therapy.

Stage 1 focuses on suicidal behaviors, therapy-interfering behaviors, and behaviors that interfere with the quality of life, together with developing the necessary skills to resolve these problems.

Stage 2 deals with post-traumatic stress disorders (PTSD).

Stage 3 focuses on self-esteem and individual treatment goals.

The targeted behaviors are each brought under control before moving on to the next. In particular post-traumatic stress-related problems like childhood sexual abuse are not dealt with directly until stage 1 has been successfully completed. How well psychotherapy works is presented in chapter 13, and special reference is made to the outcome of dialectical behavior therapy.

◇ CONCLUSION

In this chapter we described what are probably the most often used forms of treatment used by clinical psychologists today. They are backed by strong evidence for their effectiveness (detailed in chapter 13), and they tend to be short-term and cost-efficient. A particular strength to these approaches is that their underlying theories are not in conflict with each other, and a single therapist may be using a blend or sequence of many of these techniques for a single patient.

◇ ONGOING CONSIDERATIONS

Every time a textbook like this is written, the authors make decisions about which therapies should be discussed. To some degree therapies are fads like fashion, although, predictably, we encourage decisions about which therapies to include to be based on strong rationales and demonstrated positive outcomes. All the therapies in chapters 11 and 12 have long histories, high visibility, good rationales, and generally strong backing by data. Having said that, we also want to entice the reader to go through chapter 14 where we introduce therapies that are a little more mysterious, more recent, and less well researched. You decide how much evidence is enough before you are getting interested in a particular approach.

◇ KEY TERMS LEARNED

Autobiographical knowledge

Automatic thoughts

Autonomic self-regulation

Aversion therapy

Behavior therapy

Biofeedback

Biofeedback therapy

Black box principle

Borderline personality disorder

Buffer

Chaining

Classical conditioning

Cognitive therapy

Cognitive triad

Cognitive-behavioral therapy (CBT)

conditioned response

Contingency contracting
Core beliefs
Dialectical behavior therapy
Discriminative stimulus
Extinction
Flooding
Functional analysis
Graduated exposure
Modeling
Modeling—coping model
Modeling—mastery model
Negative reinforcement
Operant conditioning
Operant conditioning model
Poor modeling
Positive reinforcement
Primary reinforcers
Proprioception
Punishment
Reflection
Rehearsal

Relational or associative learning
Relaxation response
Response cost
Satiation or overcorrection
Schemas
Schemata
Secondary reinforcers
Self-invalidation
Shaping
Social avoidance
Stages of change model
Stress
Stress management
Systematic desensitization
Time-out
Token economy
Transformation
Trouble adjusting
Unconditioned stimulus
Underlying assumptions

◇ THINKING QUESTIONS

1. Can one do cognitive therapy without introducing behavioral elements?

2. How many different self-regulation treatments do we need? Are they not all very similar?

3. What clients are likely going to benefit most from which type of treatment?

4. Can I mix different types of therapy when working with one client who has multiple presenting problems?

5. Does behavior therapy have to be mechanical? How important is the therapist in behavior therapy?

◇ REFERENCES

Beck. A. T. (1987). Cognitive models of depression. *Journal of Cognitive Psychotherapy, An International Quarterly, 1*, 5–37.

Benson, H. (1975). *The relaxation response.* New York: Morrow.

Craig, K. C., & Dobson, K. S. (Eds.). (1995). *Anxiety and depression in adults and children.* Thousand Oaks, CA: Sage.

Dobson, K., & Franche, R. (1989). A conceptual and empirical review of the depressive realism hypothesis. *Canadian Journal of Behavioural Science, 21*(4), 419–433.

Ellis, A. (1962). *Reason and emotion in psychotherapy.* Secaucus, NJ: Lyle Stuart.

Ellis's Irrational Thoughts: *http://www.psychotherapynetworker.org/index.php? category= magazine&sub_cat=articles&page=1&type=article&id=The%20Top%2010*

Ellis, A. (1977). *Handbook of rational–emotive therapy.* New York: Springer.

Gallo, L. C., & Matthews, K. A. (2003). Understanding the association between socioeconomic status and physical health: Do negative emotions play a role? *Psychological Bulletin, 129,* 10–51.

Gottman, J. M., & Notarius, C. I. (2000). Decade review: Observing marital interaction. *Journal of Marriage and the Family, 62,* 927–947.

Greenberg, L. S. (2002). Integrating an emotion-focused approach to treatment into psychotherapy integration. *Journal of Psychotherapy Integration, 12,* 154–189.

Greenberg, L. S., & Johnson, S. M. (1988). *Emotionally focused couples therapy.* New York: Guilford.

Grossman, P., Niemann, L., Schmidt, S., & Walach, H. (2004). Mindfulness-based stress reduction and health benefits: A meta-analysis. *Journal of Psychosomatic Research, 57,* 35–43.

Hoehn-Saric, R., & McLeod, D. R. (2000). Anxiety and arousal: Physiological changes and their perception. *Journal of Affective Disorders, 61,* 217–224.

Hughes, J. C., & Cook, C. H. C. (1997). The efficacy of disulfiram: A review of outcome studies. *Addiction, 92,* 381–396.

Johnson, S. M., Hunsley, J., Greenberg, L., & Schindler, D. (1999). Emotionally focused couples therapy: Status and challenges. *Clinical Psychology: Science & Practice, 6,* 67–79.

Kabat-Zinn. J. (2003). Mindfulness-based interventions in context: Past, present, and future. *Clinical Psychology: Science and Practice,* 144–156.

Kop, W. J. (1999). Chronic and acute psychological risk factors for clinical manifestations of coronary artery disease. *Psychosomatic Medicine, 61,* 476–487.

Lang, P. J., & Melamed, B. G. (1969). Avoidance conditioning therapy of an infant with chronic ruminative vomiting. *Journal of Abnormal Psychology, 74,* 1–8.

Lehrer, P. M., Woolfolk, R. L., & Sime, W. E. (2007). *Principles and practice of stress management* (3rd ed.). New York: Guilford Press.

Linden, W. (1981). Exposure treatments for focal phobias: A review. *Archives of General Psychiatry, 38,* 769–775.

Linden, W. (1988). Biopsychological barriers to the behavioral treatment of essential hypertension. In Linden, W. (Ed.), *Biological barriers in behavioral medicine.* New York: Plenum.

Linden, W. (1990). *Autogenic training: A practitioner's guide.* New York: Guilford Press.

Linden, W. (2005). *Stress management: From basic research to better practice.* Thousand Oaks, CA: Sage.

Linehan, M. M. (1993a). *Cognitive behavioural treatment of borderline personality disorder.* New York and London: The Guilford Press.

Linehan, M. M. (1993b). *Skills training manual for treating borderline personality disorder.* New York and London: The Guilford Press.

Lubar, J. F., & Bahler, W. W. (1976). Behavioral management of epileptic seizures following EEG biofeedback training of the sensorimotor rhythm. *Applied Psychophysiology and Biofeedback, 1,* 77–104.

Mavissakalian, M., Turner, S. M., & Michelson, L. (Eds.) (1985). *Obsessive-compulsive disorder: Psychological and pharmacological treatment.* New York: Plenum.

Melzack, R., & Wall, P. D. (1989). *Textbook of pain.* New York: Churchill Livingstone.

Newton, T. (1995). *Managing stress: Emotions and power at work.* Thousand Oaks, CA: Sage.

Ong, L., Linden, W., & Young, S. B. (2004). Stress management: What is it? *Journal of Psychosomatic Research, 56,* 133–137.

Poole, G., Hunt Matheson, D., & Cox, D. N. (2008). *The psychology of health and health care* (3rd ed.). Englewood Cliffs, NJ: Prentice-Hall.

Prochaska, J. O., DiClemente, C. C., & Norcross, J. C. (1992). Stages of change in the modification of problem behaviors. In M. Hersen, R. M. Eisler, & P. M. Miller (Eds.), *Progress in behavior modification* (pp. 184–218). Newbury Park, CA: Sage.

Quilan, K. B., & McCaul, K. D. (2000). Matched and mismatched interventions with young adult smokers: Testing a stage theory. *Health Psychology, 19,* 165–171.

Rosen, J. C., & Wiens, A. N. (1980). On psychological intervention and medical services utilization. *American Psychologist, 35,* 761–762.

Skinner, E. A., Edge, K., Altman, J., & Sherwood, H. (2003). Searching for the structure of coping: A review and critique of category systems for classifying ways of coping. *Psychological Bulletin, 129,* 216–269.

Smith, J. C. (2004). Alterations in brain and immune function produced by mindfulness meditation: Three caveats. *Psychosomatic Medicine, 66,* 148–149.

Smith, M. L., & Glass, G. V. (1977). Meta-analysis of psychotherapy outcome studies. *American Psychologist, 32,* 752–777.

Steptoe, A., & Marmot, M. (2003). Burden of psychosocial adversity and vulnerability in middle age: Associations with biobehavioral risk factors and quality of life. *Psychosomatic Medicine, 65,* 1029–1037.

Vaitl, D., & Petermann, F. (2000). *Handbuch der Entspannungsverfahren.* Volumen I: Grundlagen und Methoden (2nd ed). Weinheim/Germany: Betz Verlag.

van Dixhoorn J., & White, A. (2005). Relaxation therapy for rehabilitation and prevention in ischaemic heart disease: A systematic review and meta-analysis. *European Journal of Cardiovascular Prevention and Rehabilitation, 12,* 193–202.

Wolpe, J. (1958). *Psychotherapy by reciprocal psychotherapy.* Stanford, CA: Stanford University Press.

Woody, S. R., Detweiler, B. J., Teachman, B. A., & O'Hearn, T. (2003). *Treatment planning in psychotherapy: Taking the guesswork out of clinical care.* New York: Guilford Press.

Zaretsky, A., Segal, Z., & Fefergrad, M. (2007). New developments in cognitive-behavioural therapy for mood disorders. *The Canadian Journal of Psychiatry, 52,* 3–4.

CHAPTER THIRTEEN

PSYCHOTHERAPY OUTCOME

CHAPTER OBJECTIVE

At first glance, the question of whether or not psychotherapy works does not seem overly difficult. Yet, considering that psychotherapy, as described in chapter 10, is a dynamic, multicomponent process in which client and therapist influence one another in order to achieve a lasting therapy benefit, one can see that this global question harbors a potential myriad of subquestions. In order to do this complexity justice, this chapter will begin with a brief rereview of the methods that are available for answering questions about therapy effects. Once equipped with tools to understand the pertinent research literature, this chapter begins with a historical review of major developments in psychotherapy outcome research. We will show how outcome research has become much more sophisticated in terms of the questions it asks and also the techniques it uses to obtain responses. Next, actual research findings will be summarized while highlighting the remaining gaps in our knowledge.

◇ METHODS

Chapter 3 placed special emphasis on research methods that can help determine how well psychotherapy works. Methods range from single case observations to randomized clinical trials with multiple control groups and large samples. There is a logical progression in moving from observations of single cases to large clinical trials. In terms of observed outcomes, this is reflected in the degree of trust readers can place in the results. As research evidence accumulates, it can become rapidly overwhelming in volume and potentially confusing because sometimes contradictory findings emerge. It is therefore necessary to regularly take stock, summarize the available evidence, and make practice recommendations.

Even within the options available for conducting reviews, there is a natural progression from qualitative to quantitative methods, from sharing case observations to measuring many process and outcome variables in multiple treatment groups that had been carefully screened for a clinical trial.

Historically, the first type of review was one where a researcher provided detailed descriptions of the existing studies and finally summed up the results in a conclusion section that reflected the author's judgment of that literature. It was always considered important that for a good review the author clearly indicated how he conducted the literature search so that another research team could go ahead and replicate the results. This type of review is referred to as a **narrative review** because the reader is following the writer as a story is being told. Here is what a paragraph in such a review might look like:

> . . . in the Miller and Jones study (2006, *fictitious reference*) 42 first-year college students were treated with psychoanalysis for their separation anxiety and received an average treatment of 40 sessions; the treatment was considered a success because the great majority reported subjective improvement. In a similar study, also using psychoanalysis to treat separation anxiety, Horvath, Schmidt & Lee (2005, *also fictitious reference*) treated 25 young patients with documented personality disorder, for a typical treatment length of 24 sessions, and failed to notice substantial improvement in their sample. Given the differential findings of the two studies, differences between the protocols need to be considered in order to understand the seemingly contradictory outcomes. It is possible that in the Miller and Jones study a significant effect was observed because the sample was larger, or because the treatment was longer, or because the patients were reasonably well-adjusted college students relative to the sample of Horvath et al. (2005) whose patients presented with a higher level of pathology. It is also possible that a combination, or interaction, of differences between the studies' varying methods, accounted for the different outcomes. To clarify this issue we recommend that in future studies the researchers keep treatment length and sample size similar in order to facilitate comparison across studies.

This narrative review methodology is particularly suitable to accommodate the many differences that exist between therapy outcome studies, in that studies vary in terms of the presenting problems; their severity; the types and levels of therapist experience; the differences in clients themselves, including considerations of age or gender or socioeconomic status, and how (and how much) therapy was delivered, and so on. While flexible, this type of review has been considered potentially biased because it is not always transparent how a reviewer arrived at a particular conclusion and there is anecdotal evidence that different reviewers evaluating essentially the same topic still end up drawing different conclusions (mind you, in the previous example the reviewer played it pretty safe and did not finish off with a provocative conclusion). Of course, the public is not very impressed with contradictory findings and is likely to dismiss all research where the outcome does not lead to consensual and useful practice recommendations.

In an attempt to make reviews more objective and easier to replicate, a second generation of reviews used quantitative methods to make decisions about what works and what does not. Consistent with widespread habits in psychological research, therapy outcome researchers have used inferential tests to determine whether a given null hypothesis, namely, that a given therapy "XX" is not useful, can be safely rejected. A decision to reject this null hypothesis is typically based on the determination of a statistical significance value

TABLE 13.1 Hypothetical Results Derived from a Box-Score Review

NUMBER OF STUDIES (K) AVAILABLE	NUMBER OF STUDIES SUGGESTING SUPERIOR OUTCOME	NUMBER OF STUDIES SUGGESTING EQUIVALENT OUTCOME	NUMBER OF STUDIES SUGGESTING INFERIOR OUTCOME
BBD is better than no treatment k = 24	22	2	0
BBD is better than client-centered therapy k = 15	3	11	1

This table assesses whether the new bye-bye-depression (BBD) treatment is effective.

that reveals a probability value of less than .05; if the result $p < .05$ is found, the treatment is called successful. The practical meaning of this cutoff value of $p = .05$ is that if the study was repeated over and over again, 19 times out of 20 the same results would be obtained. The use of this statistical decision-making method categorizes studies as either success or failure; it dichotomizes outcomes. The resulting information can then be entered into a simple table with **box scores** (Table 13.1).

As Table 13.1 reveals, two questions of interest were addressed, namely, (a) whether or not the treatment called bye-bye-depression (BBD) is better than no treatment and (b) whether or not it is more effective than a pre-existing active treatment. Twenty-four clinical trials were available that met the stated inclusion criteria and that tested whether the hypothetical treatment BBD was superior to a wait-list control group; 15 clinical trials were available to compare this same new treatment with client-centered therapy. As the box scores show, BBD was statistically superior to no treatment in 22 out of 24 tests, and was superior to client-centered therapy in 3 out of 15 clinical trials. Organizing outcome data into a table with multiple cells or boxes is what has led to the name **box score reviews**. If one accepts the usefulness of categorical success or failure decisions, then the conclusion is that BBD is overwhelmingly superior to no treatment but essentially similar in impact to another active treatment, namely, client-centered therapy.

Box score reviews were considered major advances relative to narrative reviews given their objectivity, transparency, and replicability, but they were soon criticized for their inherent logical and statistical weaknesses and were replaced by a more sophisticated approach. As much of the entire field of psychology has gradually become critical of a dichotomous approach, which considers all research findings with statistical probabilities greater than $p = .05$ as null results, so has psychotherapy outcome research (Rosenthal, 1983; Rosenthal & DiMatteo, 2001).

There are numerous valid arguments for why the dichotomy of a less than or greater than $p = .05$ approach is a weak method:

1. **The meaning of cutoffs.** Consider this example: A student who achieved a course performance of 81% is given a letter grade of "A," whereas his friend who

achieved a percent performance of 79% received a letter grade of "B." Nobody is seriously going to argue that student A is a much better student than student B just because one is on the other side of the threshold of the A/B distinction; the 2% spread on a scale from 0 to 100 is considered trivial. The same argument can be made for psychotherapy outcome. If 20 clinical trials had been conducted in different cities and varying samples, and every single one of them showed a pre-post treatment effect that was accompanied by a statistical probability of p < .06 or p < .08 (but failed to reach the typical significance cutoffs of p = .05), then a rigid application of the logic of a box score method would lead to the conclusion that this treatment is not effective at all—all 20 were "failures." True, it would have been more impressive if at least the majority of the trials had reached the magical p = .05 cutoff, but it is still considered highly meaningful that all 20 trials replicated this small treatment effect.

2. **Variation in sample size.** A second, inter-related criticism of box score approaches is that they tend to ignore differences in the sample size, such that a study involving 400 patients would make the same contribution to a final judgment as a study that had involved only 15 patients. Even unsophisticated readers will argue that a study that showed important results in 400 patients must be more meaningful than one that showed the same results in 15 patients.

3. **Consideration of statistical power.** Especially in the last few decades, psychology students have learned about the importance of statistical power when they are taught how to conduct experiments. They are taught that an underpowered study does not allow the researcher to either accept or reject the null hypothesis. In this context, it is rather striking that some psychology researchers have shown that the typical effect sizes observed in psychology experiments (published in peer-reviewed journals) are remarkably small (typically around $d = 0.3$; Sedlmeier & Gigerenzer, 1989). Therefore, there is good reason to believe that many clinical trials of psychotherapy that failed to show significant treatment effects were underpowered to begin with; they never allowed for meaningful conclusions in the first place (Linden & Satin, 2007). This lack of power translates into overly negativistic conclusions, suggesting that psychotherapy does not work. While grant review panels for clinical trials routinely refuse funding for underpowered trials, providing a well-justified estimate of the needed sample size is not necessarily sufficient to eliminate the problem because (a) researchers may estimate quite correctly how many participants are needed for a properly powered trial but then fail to obtain the needed numbers because they run out of time or money, or both; or (b) researchers make a solid educated guess of the anticipated effect size but may still overestimate the attainable effect at the time of trial planning, or, conversely, may underestimate how much better the untreated control group patients would get on their own.

The solution to the weaknesses of box score analysis has been (a) to obtain a single statistic for each available and comparable clinical trial that captures group mean scores and their variability and (b) to assure that the contribution of this statistic to the final conclusion is weighed by the differences in sample size for each study. Studies with large samples should have a greater impact than those with very small samples. This method has become known as **meta-analysis** and is now a very frequently used tool not only in psychotherapy research but also in other areas of research. The full statistical intricacies of meta-analysis have become a booming area of theory and research, and we will not attempt here to delve deeply into these aspects (Rosnow & Rosenthal, 1996). Nevertheless, the basic logic and method of meta-analysis is not complicated, and the reader who understands it can easily draw his or her own conclusions from the many meta-analyses available in the therapy outcome literature that is summarized later in this chapter. In fact, we consider basic knowledge of how meta-analysis works and what effect sizes mean crucial information for any budding clinical psychologist. It is pivotal that the reader not proceed to the results tables shown later in this chapter if he or she does not understand the meaning of an effect size.

Depending on the nature of the data set and the scaling levels of the tools used for data acquisition, there are many different types of **effect sizes** that can be used in meta-analysis. The most frequently reported effect statistics are the correlation coefficient r and the so-called Cohen's d effect, where d = 1.0 for psychotherapy means that the average patient after treatment is one standard deviation better off than he or she was prior to treatment. How to calculate an effect size is best demonstrated with a concrete example (see Box 13.1).

There is no need to be scared away from meta-analysis because the underlying arithmetic requires no more than grade 8 math skills and can be done by hand or with the help of a $3 pocket calculator.

BOX 13.1

EXAMPLE

A new treatment, bye-bye-depression (BBD), is tested, and the scores on a self-report questionnaire (high score = high depression) taken before and after therapy look like this:

Pretreatment mean score (M1) = 24 (SD = 12)
Post-treatment mean score (M2) = 16 (SD = 8)

Computation of effect size d is based on this simple formula:

$$\frac{\text{Mean at post-treatment (M2)} - \text{mean at pretreatment (M1)}}{\dfrac{(SD1 + SD2)/2}{(12 + 8)/2}} = d$$

It is considered best to average the standard deviations accompanying these two means.

In our case: Step 1 (nominator)   M2 − M1 = 24 − 16 = 8
                 Step 2 (denominator) 12 + 8/2 = 10
                 Step 3 (solution)   8/10 = .8

EFFECT SIZE (d) = 0.8

For the remainder of this chapter, we are reporting tables and outcomes reflecting only effect size d to avoid any confusion. Psychologists tend to favor Cohen's d, whereas in medical journals the preferred effect size is r. Unless it is made obvious by authors, the astute reader of meta-analyses should seek clarification each time which effect-size statistic was used. This is important because the resulting numbers have very different meanings. On the other hand, one type of effect size can readily be converted into another using tables or formulas (Rosnow & Rosenthal, 1996). Note that the relationship of the effects r relative to d is not linear. We also explain whether reported effect sizes describe change within a sample (pre-post treatment effect) or are based on comparisons across treatments. It is common practice to call an effect of approximately d = .2 a small effect, d = .5 a moderate-size effect, and d = .8 a large effect.

◇ A BRIEF HISTORY OF THERAPY OUTCOME RESEARCH

Researchers and clinicians have asked for a long time how effective psychotherapy is; however, the British psychologist Hans Eysenck (1952) is considered the author of the first major review paper on psychotherapy effects. Review of existing medical charts of 7000 patients led to the conclusion that the rate of "improved" patients who received psychotherapy was no better than those who didn't receive therapy; more specifically, those who received no particular treatment showed 72% remission of their problems after 2 years, whereas those who had received psychoanalysis showed improvement in only 44% of the cases, and others who received (ill-defined) eclective therapy reported improvement rates of 64%. This was definitely not what anybody considered to be a promising beginning.

Critics quickly came alive, criticized the methods, and challenged the conclusions of the review. First and foremost, Eysenck's data were not derived from controlled trials, and the groups were unlikely to be actually comparable at the point of hospitalization, in terms of social class, illness severity, or illness type. Also, this conclusion required that the reader would trust that all hospitals and health care providers kept records the same way and made their clinical decisions in a fully standardized way. Eysenck's very pessimistic conclusion was soon undone with more and better reviews (Luborsky, Singer, & Luborsky, 1975; Smith & Glass, 1977; Shapiro & Shapiro, 1982), but Eysenck nevertheless deserves credit for having challenged people into critically thinking about these questions and to come up with better methods leading to results that consumers can actually trust.

The methods described in chapter 3 and earlier in this chapter for evaluating and describing the effects of psychotherapy are the standard tools of researchers trained in psychology; however, the potential value of psychotherapy can also be assessed using surveys of the type that commercial polling companies use to evaluate voter preferences in election campaigns or to assess whether consumers prefer bacon *A, B*, or *C*, or soft drink *P* versus *C*. A particularly influential survey of this nature was published in *Consumer Reports* (1995), a magazine that routinely describes comparisons of a variety of consumer goods but also occasionally compares services like cell-phone providers or insurance companies. In this survey, 4100 respondents who had seen a mental health professional during the past three years were asked to describe their experiences (Seligman, 1995). A potential criticism of this survey is that the respondents tended to be more educated than is true for the general U.S. population. Respondents were to provide commentary on these aspects:

- The degree to which professional treatment had helped alleviate the presenting problem
- How satisfied they were with the treatment they had received
- How they judged their overall emotional state as a result of the professional intervention

Of these 4100 responses, about 90% reported that they felt better after having received professional treatment; there was no reported difference in the effect of psychotherapy alone versus psychotherapy plus medication, and these consumers did not indicate any particular preference for one approach over another. Across the different professional groups who had provided such treatment, essentially all were perceived as helpful, and psychologists, psychiatrists, and social workers were described as having been more effective than family physicians or marriage counselors. There is little debate that such surveys suffer from the usual weaknesses of self-report; however, it is these very subjective experiences that determine whether these respondents would return for psychotherapy if needed and also whether or not these individuals would provide word-of-mouth advertising for psychotherapy. Positive word-of-mouth advertising, in turn, is the best marketing psychologists can obtain and cannot be bought even with lots of money. Therefore, it makes sense to add the information that can be obtained from such consumer satisfaction surveys to the conclusions that are available from controlled research.

As described earlier, quantitative reviews can be clustered into two groups, namely, box score reviews and meta-analyses. The results from a series of box score reviews have quite consistently indicated that active psychotherapies are largely similar in their effect and that the majority of treated patients do get better. What does stand out as more effective than other active treatments is the use of behavioral exposure techniques for phobias (Feske & Chambless, 1995; Linden, 1981). The truly remarkable similarity of magnitudes of change has received the commentary that "everybody has won and everybody should win a prize" (Luborsky et al., 1975). This expression stems from the book *Alice Adventures in Wonderland*, where a number of animals engaged in a race but took off in different directions such that the speed of their running couldn't be directly compared with each other; there actually was no race. This "everybody-has-won" conclusion had been drawn by the dodo bird in the novel, and Luborsky's comment has subsequently been called the "**dodo bird verdict**."

◇ WHAT QUESTIONS ARE META-ANALYTIC REVIEWS TRYING TO ANSWER?

Given the dissatisfaction with box score reviews (Table 13.1 was a hypothetical demonstration of a results table), the addition of meta-analyses has dramatically changed the world of psychotherapy outcome research because much more sophisticated questions could be asked and more differentiated conclusions were possible. The obvious overall questions asked in meta-analyses are whether a given treatment XX alleviates a particular disorder and whether or not treatment XX is superior to other available treatments. The first question can be answered by computing effect sizes for within-person changes following therapy (pre-post or within effect sizes), and the second question is answered by showing that treatment XX is associated with a statistically significantly greater effect size than a comparison treatment (between-group comparison). This type of comparison requires controlled clinical trials that have comparison groups built in. All comparisons of this nature are commonly referred to as "horserace comparisons," where each therapy of interest is directly pitched against one another, just like horses at a race starting simultaneously at the same starter line to determine who the fastest racer is.

Before dousing the reader with actual outcome data, a little injection of critical thinking, providing a set of reading glasses, may be beneficial. Many critics of meta-analysis have justifiably argued that the results, however clear they may look, are worth nothing if the study selection process was disorganized or illogical and if the data extraction process was faulty. This type of criticism has been given the catchy descriptor of "garbage in = garbage out." It is therefore necessary to show that truly comparable methods have been pitched against one another (like "all psychological treatments for major depression"); that the literature was sampled in a comprehensive, transparent, and replicable fashion; and that the data extraction process was also transparent, well-explained, and meeting the basic statistical principles (Rosenthal & DiMatteo, 2001).

As was described in considerable detail in chapter 10, the outcome of psychological therapy is affected by many demographic and process features that can and should be considered in meta-analysis. Therapy outcome may be affected by:

- Experience and training of the therapist
- Ethnicity
- Gender of the client
- Gender of the therapist
- Age of the patient
- Level of distress prior to treatment
- Quality of the alliance between therapist and patient
- Adherence by the therapist to the required treatment protocol
- Length of therapy
- Delivery form (single client or multiclient)

These types of factors are considered moderator or mediating factors depending on the role they play (Baron & Kenny, 1986). Meta-analysis not only provides an overall effect size for a given treatment but also permits further exploration of mediating factors that explain how the good outcome came about. Study of these moderators may be particularly useful for clinical practice because the moderators not only help decide which treatment technique is suitable but also reveal how this treatment should be delivered and which type of client is most likely to benefit from it. Linden, Phillips, and Leclerc (2007), for example, found that psychological cardiac rehabilitation was effective for men but not for women, and that distressed patients treated early after a heart attack did not benefit from this treatment whereas those who were recruited many months later benefited greatly. The explanation given was that many patients have good natural supports and personal resilience and may rebound quickly even without professional help; on the other hand, those who are coping poorly even 4–6 months after the event may be the ones most in need of help.

Another important consideration is what type of outcome the effect size refers to. The underlying question here is whether the result is statistically significant or clinically meaningful or both. Ideally, a strong result meets both criteria, but there are examples where the result may be very clinically meaningful while based on a rather small effect size and vice versa. Aside from mere statistics, what needs to be considered is the **value of particular outcomes**. A good example is that of the well-known Aspirin trial, where it had been shown that the active treatment group taking Aspirin rather than placebo had a roughly 50% reduction in mortality, which was reflected in a very small effect size of a mere $r = .034$ (roughly $d = .10$; The Steering Committee, 1989). The higher mortality rate in the control group, however, was considered so problematic that the trial was stopped at this point, and the conclusion was that Aspirin should be routinely given in clinical practice to minimize the risk of developing cardiovascular disease.

The Golden Fleece of the applications of psychological interventions for health problems has been the attempt to extend life with psychological treatment. However, even this seemingly worthy goal has been subjected to much discussion (Coyne, Stefanek, & Palmer, 2007) because overemphasis on extending life may push aside treatments that alleviate distress and improve quality of life as being trite although patients themselves may consider these changes extremely meaningful. Also, as is discussed in chapter 17, patients themselves, especially when they are older and already have many health problems, do not necessarily think of a longer life as a highly desirable outcome if it simply means more suffering.

With respect to the marketability of psychological services, outcomes are particularly important when they affect costs and benefits. Later in this chapter, a section is devoted to show whether or not the implementation of psychological therapy can be offset by financial gains, like reduced medication costs. Third parties, like employers and insurance companies, are particularly excited by psychological therapy outcomes that get their patients back to work more quickly; reduce the duration of disability pensions; or reduce the number of times that patients come to the emergency room, visit their family physician, or require hospitalization or repeated surgeries. A few quick examples can powerfully back this point. Let us consider an individual who earns $80,000 a year, and including benefits, costs the company $100,000 per year. This individual might receive a disability pension of $60,000 a year if he is unable to work due to injury, provided of course he had a good insurance plan. If such an individual returns to work within 6 months when provided with excellent psychological rehabilitation, instead of 2 years without such help, $90,000 would be saved. Even if the therapy consisted of 20 sessions that had cost $150 each, the total therapy cost of $3,000 would still leave an absolute saving of $87,000. No wonder disability insurance companies are interested in psychological therapies.

Alternatively, a clinical psychologist might be particularly interested in a psychodynamic therapy approach where the desired result is a gain in ego strength, which is assessed via self-report. If the result of this therapy was a mean group gain of an effect size of $d = 1.2$, then statistically this is a very large effect and compares favorably with other outcomes of psychotherapy. However, it would be pretty difficult to convince an insurance company that it should spend thousands of dollars for such an outcome. This type of reasoning has led many researchers who have published meta-analyses to cluster the outcomes they are studying into variables like:

- Mortality rates
- Reoccurrence of a critical event (like another heart attack)
- Reduced use of medications or fewer physician visits
- Biological markers of a disease (like reduced cholesterol levels)
- Important behavioral outcomes (like reduced recidivism in a violent offender)
- Self-report measures of distress

Each of these outcomes may be associated with the same statistical effect size, but the implication for real-life applications (also referred to as **ecological validity**) depends on who is involved and what the objective of the treatment was. If the benefits of psychotherapy can be shown to be similarly true for a variety of different classes of outcomes, then it is much easier to sell this form of therapy to nonpsychologists and to convince hospital administrators of the need for psychologists on staff and insurance companies of the need to pay for psychological services.

The primary focus in publications of treatment outcome studies is on **group means** and on the variability of change within the group; this approach makes the study very suitable for statistical analysis. What this type of data reporting does not tell us is what happened to *individual patients*, although the answer to this question is pivotal for clinical practice. If you were a patient with an anxiety disorder approaching a psychologist, you will want to know what the probability is that you will get better and how many sessions are needed to achieve this. You're not likely to care very much about what happened to a group of people receiving similar treatment elsewhere (although that may be all the psychologist can tell you). Therefore, in order to fully understand what happens to people in treatment groups and in control groups, researchers need to pay attention to the numbers of patients who actually improved, to determine how many did not change, and consider the possibility that somebody might actually get worse. How the reported mean changes in a therapy study may have come about is elegantly described in Figure 13.1.

The layout of this display looks like a butterfly (with slightly different-sized wings, though) such that the two columns on the far outsides are comparable to each of the columns on the inside; each butterfly wing represents the process of change in one group. This graph illustrates how a psychotherapy where the group means of the treatment group (M4) were significantly superior to the group means of a control group (M2) harbors considerable variability in outcomes. Oftentimes, significant improvement occurred in only a small group of patients, but that may suffice to produce statistically significant differences

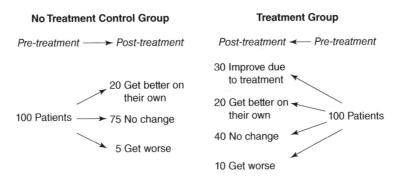

FIGURE 13.1 Butterfly diagram of treatment effects

between the group means. This is then called a successful therapy, but anybody trying to sell this new therapy to the real world is not going to be very convincing if the reported superior outcome was derived from only 30% of the patients in the trial. The feature that is often forgotten is that patients can also get worse, and treatment should not be automatically considered to be benign for everybody. For obvious ethical reasons it is important to look at all individual outcomes and determine whether there is a subgroup of patients for whom treatment led to deterioration. If such a group exists, it is then mandatory to investigate whether this poor outcome can be predicted and prevented in future trials.

Similarly relevant is the question of duration of treatment effects. Ideally, of course we seek a cure for the presenting problem, meaning that the benefits observed at the end of treatment last a lifetime. This assumption about psychotherapy effects requires testing via extended follow-ups, which reveal the degree to which treatment benefits are maintained. Conducting follow-up investigations can be a costly and frustrating experience because patients themselves, even if they had benefited greatly from therapy, may not want to return for follow-up tests because in their heads the study has been completed. As a consequence, many published clinical trials report no follow-up data, and even when follow-up data are collected, the follow-up lengths rarely exceed 6 months beyond the end of treatment.

An additional potential frustration is that the kinds of processes that make psychotherapy work may also exist outside of the therapy environment, and patients may coincidentally learn new things that either account for relapse or facilitate maintenance of gains. This may occur via:

- Media reports about the outcome of other trials
- Information or advice received from a family physician or family members or friends
- Information that patients read about on the web

One good example for demonstration purposes may be that of a weight-loss program. Once an individual has completed a weight-loss program (hopefully a successful one), he will be continuously hammered with new information offered by the media about new trends in weight-loss programs. It is likely that this type of information has a **confounding effect**, and that weight maintenance at 1 year is not necessarily attributable to the structured weight-loss program that the patient had participated in. Another interesting twist in the study of maintenance of treatment gains is that some patients who may not have improved from pre- to post-test show significant improvement during the follow-up period; these people are sometimes described as "**sleepers**," and the phenomenon is probably best explained with psychotherapy being the equivalent of a planted seed that did not begin to grow until therapy itself was over. Linden et al. (2001) have observed such a phenomenon in the treatment of high blood pressure with a stress management approach. A researcher not conducting extended follow-up will miss this interesting phenomenon and may underestimate the potential of his treatment approach.

The same logic can also be applied to test the question of whether a treatment that is suitable for multiple applications will be equally good in affecting all outcomes; it is possible that the same treatment may produce good short-term benefits that don't last for one application, but may trigger the opposite pattern of responses for other targets. Such effects have been carefully evaluated and elegantly displayed in a meta-analysis of the effects of motivational interviewing (Hettema, Steel, & Miller, 2005; Figure 13.2).

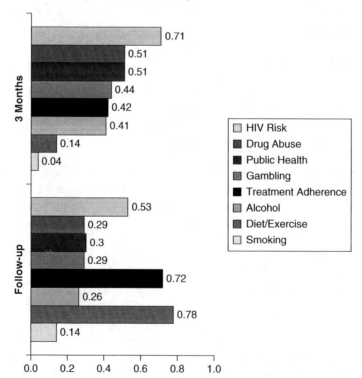

FIGURE 13.2   Mean combined effect size by problem area (N = 72 clinical trials)

◇ WHAT HAS BEEN LEARNED FROM EXISTING META-ANALYSES?

Meta-analysis quickly became popular, and its application spread like a wildfire. There were two, early, major meta-analyses that have set the tone and been very influential. A number of tables from these analyses are reprinted here, and we have extracted tables that:

- Describe outcomes as a function of technique (reflecting what we have previously called a "horserace comparison"; Table 13.2)
- Show the effectiveness of psychotherapy in general (clustered together across different types of therapy) for a large number of different applications (Table 13.3)

For this textbook we have newly created Table 13.4 that lists effect sizes for newer psychotherapies that are not covered in the earlier meta-analyses and that also includes outcomes of psychotherapy applications for physical health problems.

Table 13.2 is taken from the meta-analysis of Smith and Glass, 1977) and provides two statistics for each type of therapy mentioned, namely, the effect size d as well as a percent equivalent, which refers to the number of treated patients who are better off after therapy than those who did not receive the treatment in question. The overall effect size for active treatment (comparing pre- with post-tests) is d = 0.85 and is therefore classified (using the standard language) as a **large effect**. However, there is a lot of variation in the effects, and these require some thought and discussion. Most therapies fall in the range of 0.60 to 1.1,

TABLE 13.2 Average Effect Size (ES) and Percentile Equivalent for Select Forms of Psychological Intervention

TYPE OF THERAPY	ES	PERCENTILE EQUIVALENT (%)
Psychodynamic therapy	0.69	75
Client-centered therapy	0.62	73
Gestalt therapy	0.64	74
Rational-emotive therapy (RET)	0.68	75
Non-RET cognitive therapies	2.38	99
Systematic desensitization therapy	1.05	85
Behavior modification therapy	0.73	77
Cognitive-behavioral therapy	1.13	87
Undifferentiated counseling	0.28	61
All forms of psychological intervention	0.85	80

Note: Percentile equivalent indicates the percentage of those not receiving treatment whose outcome is exceeded by those receiving the treatment in question.

Source: Adapted from Smith and Glass (1977).

TABLE 13.3 Effect Sizes (ES) for Different Treatment Targets: Breakdown of ES by Treatment Type and Target Class

TARGET CLASS	TREATMENT TYPE				
	Behavioral	*Cognitive*	*Dynamic/ Humanistic*	*Minimal*	*Total*
Anxiety and depression					
ES	.74	1.34	.40	.38	.67
x	21	1	5	3	30
Phobia					
ES	1.46	.92		.66	1.28
x	56	9		11	76
Physical/habit problems					
ES	1.19	.37	.37	1.07	1.10
x	80	5	5	14	104
Social or sexual problems					
ES	1.08	1.19	.36	.55	.97
x	51	9	8	6	74
Performance anxieties					
ES	.81	.97	.65	.36	.80
x	102	15	2	7	126
Total					
ES	1.06	.94	40	.71	.98
x	310	39	20	41	410

Note: x = number of groups.

but there are two notable exceptions. One is the relatively small effect for undifferentiated counseling. The other is the reported effect of 2.38 for cognitive therapies, which looks rather stunning. It should be noted, however, that this number is based on a relatively small number of clinical trials that were indeed very successful, whereas the addition of further clinical trials has led to a **regression to the mean** effect. Together, these data also demonstrate what Luborsky et al. (1975) meant when he said "everybody has won and all deserve prizes" in that most active treatment appears to produce very similar effect sizes.

The data shown in Table 13.3 reflect a more sophisticated approach to assessing therapy outcome because it integrates the two dimensions of different treatment types and different target problems to which treatment is applied. This table was reprinted with permission from the meta-analysis by Shapiro and Shapiro (1982), and we begin the discussion by citing typically observed effect sizes. The average effect size for active treatments (pre-post test) ranges from d = 0.93 to 0.85, hence telling us that even different review strategies and different reviewers end up with largely comparable conclusions, namely, that psychological therapy typically produces a large pre-post effect. Shapiro and Shapiro (1982) clustered different treatments into fewer categories (reflecting more studies in each) and

TABLE 13.4 A Selection of Reported Psychological Effects for Various Types of Interventions and Also Different Target Problems

TREATMENT OR APPLICATION (AUTHOR)	NUMBER OF STUDIES FROM WHICH EFFECT SIZE WAS CALCULATED	EFFECT SIZE FOR PRE-POST COMPARISON	EFFECT SIZE (D) FOR TREATMENT EFFECT RELATIVE TO NO TREATMENT CONTROL
Type of treatment			
Motivational Interviewing (Hettema et al., 2005)	72	.77 Shrinking to .30 at follow-up	
Cognitive-behavioral therapy for eating disorders (Lewandoswski, Gebing, Anthony, & O'Brien, 1997)	26	Behavioral measures 2.2 Cognitive-attitudinal 1.9 measures	Behavioral measures 1.7 Cognitive-attitudinal 1.7 measures
Psychodynamic treatment (Leichsenring, Rabung, & Leibing, 2004)	17	Target problem 1.39 Social function .80 Tendency to improve scores at follow-up	n/a
Emotion-focused therapy for couples (Johnson et al., 1999)	7	n/a	1.34
Varying applications			
Hypertension (Linden & Chambers, 1994)	12	Blood pressure 1.16	n/a
Distress reduction in cancer patients (Osborn, Demoncada, & Feuerstein, 2006)	5 4	Depression 1.20 Anxiety 1.99	
Chronic pain (Flor et al., 1992)	104	Psychophysiological measures 2.04 Mood 3.11 Somatic .94	Psychophysiological measures 0.84 Mood 0.63 Somatic n/a
Autogenic training (Stetter & Kupper, 2002)	60	Biological measures .68 Subjective measures .75	n/a

also found a more narrow range of effect size. Cognitive-behavioral approaches revealed notably larger effects than dynamic and humanistic approaches and minimal treatment. Although the relatively strongest treatment effect is seen for behavioral treatments, it is noteworthy that in the area of achievement motivation and personality change both are substantially weaker than is observed for other treatment orientations, such that dynamic and humanistic therapies led to stronger outcomes for these applications.

In Table 13.3, the objective was to show the differential effects that psychotherapy can bring about for a wide variety of treatment targets without considering differential effects for different techniques. There we see major categories of treatment targets like "anxiety and depression" or "performance anxieties," and each of these categories is further broken down into more narrowly defined targets within this category. While not wanting to comment on every number in this fairly comprehensive table, it may be worthwhile to pay attention to outliers, namely, the very large effects ($d > 2.0$) for the treatment of fear of flying and rat phobia as well the lack of effects for generalized anxiety disorders and public speaking anxiety and stuttering. Together, the information provided in various meta-analyses clearly indicates that the clinical psychologist has access to an impressively large repertory of effective treatment approaches. The typical effect size observed for psychological therapy for pre-post changes is roughly in the neighborhood of $d = .08$ to 1.0.

The amount of information given earlier about the effect of psychotherapy outcome was fairly detailed (hopefully not overkill), and still it is only an overview of the vibrant literature on psychotherapy outcome research. Given that such an explosive growth of information can easily lead to confusion, two researchers have conducted what is best called a meta-analysis of meta-analyses, where they culled the results from hundreds of meta-analyses that had measured change within psychological interventions (Lipsey & Wilson, 1993). A number of intriguing observations from this review will be summarized here. The more "traditional" therapies listed earlier typically have large effects with averaged d scores for within patient change: pre-post effects ranging usually around .8 to 1.0 (Lipsey & Wilson, 1993). Minimal treatments (which tap the nonspecific effects) usually have a pre-post effect ranging from $d = .3$ to $.5$, thus backing the earlier statement (see chapter 10) that about half of all treatment outcomes is accounted for by nonspecific factors like quality of the therapeutic alliance, support, and normalization.

Methodology leaders in psychotherapy research have urged researchers to adhere to quality standards so that the findings can be trusted. The prediction was that poor quality studies will produce highly varying and nontrustworthy results. The Lipsey and Wilson (1991) review has explicitly addressed many of these questions and has provided us with some surprising answers, namely, that methodology variation had less impact than was anticipated. Here are the conclusions that, at least in some instances, came as a surprise:

- Published studies overestimate the effects of treatment relative to unpublished studies by about 20%, suggesting that it may be harder to publish papers with weak results.
- Studies with high methodology quality ratings led to neither stronger nor weaker outcomes ($d = .40$ versus $d = .37$).

- Studies with very large samples (n > 100) produced weaker effects than those with small samples (n < 50; d = 0.35 versus d = 0.58).

- Studies with randomized assignments to treatment conditions lead to effects of similar magnitude than did studies without random assignment (d = 0.46 high and d = 0.41 low).

◇ COST-EFFECTIVENESS OF PSYCHOLOGICAL THERAPIES

When one considers the fact that medicine has been around for thousands of years whereas psychotherapy has existed for only about 100 years and that real variety in psychological treatment approaches has existed only for the last 50 or so years, it is no wonder that clinical psychology is still a newbie in health care. This newbie needs to raise its visibility and market itself. Although 10 sessions of psychotherapy cost only a fraction of what surgery or a lengthy hospital stay cost, there is no debate about the need for certain surgeries and hospitalizations. On the other hand, patients themselves as well as insurance companies want to know how effective and cost-effective psychological services are if they are to pay for them. Given the cost explosions in healthcare worldwide, clinical psychology has no choice but to both document how effective services are and show what the cost implications are. The strongest possible case is, of course, that the systematic use of psychological therapies will reduce the cost of health care overall and ideally also have an impact on other costs; for example, those related to workplace accidents, absenteeism, or low productivity that all may have been the result of poor mental health. What do the data tell us? Can we actually show how psychotherapy costs are offset with savings in other areas of our economy?

Fortunately, there has been a great deal of interesting and useful research on the topic, and clinical psychology is in an excellent position to market itself. Hunsley (2003) provided a thorough review of existing literature on the cost offset of psychotherapy services. He reported that 90% of all studies on cost offset have shown that the gains in terms of reduced overall health care costs are greater than the cost of psychotherapy itself, typically leading to cost offsets of 20% to 30%. Note that these analyses have looked only at how much is saved in terms of direct health care costs rather than the economy as a whole.

Cost benefit or cost offset analyses can be done in the various levels of depth and detail. To be truly comprehensive, such an analysis should not only describe how much money treatment has cost relative to other health care expenses but also include an evaluation of the benefits to the economy (e.g., by calculating the economic gain of an earlier return to work, reduced absenteeism, or higher work productivity; Zhang, Rost, & Fortney, 1999). This would be a truly comprehensive evaluation; however, an analysis of such depth is extremely difficult to execute and likely beyond the means of the typical clinical trial researcher.

A good compromise, demonstrating Hunsley's (2003) conclusion, would be an evaluation that tracks in reasonable detail changes and other health-related behaviors to which a dollar amount can be attached. In some medical systems it is possible to extract information on the average cost of a physician visit or a day spent in an acute-care hospital bed. A good example of such an evaluation has been provided by Linehan and Heard (1999) in a relatively small-scale study of dialectical behavior therapy (DBT; a type of cognitive therapy well suited for the treatment of personality disorders), which not only computed the effectiveness of the

TABLE 13.5   Example of Cost-Effectiveness Demonstration

HEALTH CARE COST VARIABLE	DIALECTICAL-BEHAVIORAL THERAPY (N = 22) IN DOLLARS	CONTROL GROUP (N = 22) IN DOLLARS
Outpatient treatment cost (including individual and group treatment)	5410	3938
Psychiatric treatment cost		
Emergency room visits	216	543
Medical hospital days	342	1094
Physician days	712	621
Total medical cost	1270	2258
Grand total cost	**9291**	**18275**

Source: Extracted from Linehan and Heard (1999).

treatment but provided a nicely laid-out and informative comparison of costs for the active treatment and the control group. These data are provided in Table 13.5.

The group treated with DBT required a greater initial cost for the active treatment than the control group, but when the subsequent costs, related to additionally needed health care for both groups, were computed in detail, the DBT group had cost only half as much to the health care system as the control group and thus came out a clear winner in terms of cost benefits.

◇ CONTROVERSIES AROUND KNOWLEDGE TRANSLATION FROM THERAPY OUTCOME RESEARCH

Showing that psychotherapy is effective and marketing this knowledge is broadly supported by the clinical psychology community; however, how this information is used to determine which types of treatment will be paid for by insurance companies, which ones are taught to students, and recommending specific choices to individual practitioners are enormously controversial topics (Herbert, 2003). Let us begin with the evidence itself before we discuss thorny issues around the appropriate use of this information.

A constructive tradition of the field is that psychotherapy outcome researchers routinely write review papers of both qualitative and quantitative nature to document the effectiveness of therapy. There is widespread agreement that taking stock is useful for the advancement of the profession and can serve as a roadmap for future research activities on the topic (DeLeon, VandenBos, & Cummings, 1983). Also, it can inform health care administrators and insurance companies on where to best invest their money. Given that reviews by individual researchers are occasionally tainted with the brush of suspicion of bias, larger professional organizations or foundations interested in best patient care also call together on a regular basis groups of researchers to form consensus committees who will publish their findings to serve as guides for decision-making. The rationale for forming such consensus committees is that a group of maybe 10 experts working together will even out the biases an individual researcher may hold and will better represent the full spectrum of available knowledge. Wherever possible, individual reviewers and consensus committees use meta-analyses to assist their conclusions or alternatively use the best other available evidence (see also chapter 3 for research methods and quality ratings of therapy outcome designs). They fill gaps in knowledge and create agendas for future research.

Earlier in this chapter we provided evidence from the therapy outcome research literature about what works and what does not work and pointed out that the so-called horserace comparisons, where one technique is pitched against another, do not provide very interesting conclusions, because other important therapy features like patient or therapist qualities and therapy process variables are ignored. The good news is that the literature is remarkably consistent (Lipsey & Wilson, 1993); the great majority of meta-analyses confirmed over and over again that the typical effect size for psychological therapies for pre-post change is in the range of d = 0.8 to 1.0. Although individual studies occasionally show noticeably larger effects when similar studies get bundled together into meta-analyses, these exciting large effects tend to regress to the same mean of roughly d = 1.0. There are a few, and we argue surprisingly few, incidents where specific therapy techniques are particularly good matches for particular clinical problems and effect sizes may exceed d = 1.0. Primary examples of such incidents are exposure-based, cognitive-behavioral therapies for phobias and PTSD (Smith & Glass, 1977; Van Etten & Taylor, 1998). Also, there is a tendency that client-centered therapies produce weaker overall effects than cognitive-behavioral or interpersonal therapies (Robinson, Berman, & Neimeyer, 1990). Certain therapy approaches have very little, if any, outcome literature attached to them because their creators and propagators saw them more as methods of growth and empowerment than as treatments suitable for a medical model, and they discouraged therapy outcome research altogether. This was particularly true for Gestalt therapy (Perls, Hefferline, & Goodman, 1951). There also is very little empirical evidence available (as can be derived from randomized clinical trials) for systemic approaches. In this case, sparseness of evidence is, however, most likely due to the fact that systemic therapy is more of an outlook on life and social interactions or a philosophy than a coherent package of manual-driven treatments with typical techniques. In fact, there is no published how-to manual for systemic therapy that lends itself to standardized therapy.

By now, there is a solid body of literature supporting the clinical benefit of psychodynamically oriented treatments (Crits-Christoph, 1992), and these recent additions to the literature draw more strongly supportive conclusions about the efficacy of these approaches than did the classic meta-analyses of Shapiro and Shapiro (1982) and Smith and Glass (1977). It should be noted, however, that these reviews describe the effects of relatively short-term treatments, and we still have no conclusive evidence about the comparative benefits of long-term, traditional psychoanalysis.

We have also learned in this chapter that nonspecific effects in psychotherapy (like creating a good alliance, allowing venting, and establishing hope) account for up to half of the effect of psychotherapy outcomes (Luborsky et al., 2002; Strupp & Hadley, 1979). This means that creators of new therapies will have a relatively easy time showing that small to moderate treatment benefits can be shown even with peculiar sounding interventions that have poorly justified rationales as long as the therapists are nice and caring. On the other hand, it is quite difficult to show that a new treatment can lead to benefits that significantly exceed those derived from nonspecific effects. In consequence, a considerable burden is faced by therapy outcome researchers who need to show that they have sufficient statistical power and a correspondingly large sample size, to assure that the difference between their innovative treatment outcome and the nonspecific element still reaches statistical significance.

Given the consistency of therapy outcome findings showing that the great majority of people who receive psychotherapy also benefit from it, researchers have largely lost interest in conducting more horserace comparisons. Researchers are now much more interested in understanding which factors maximize therapy process and which matches of treatment to specific application work best. In the area of psychotherapy, the Division 12, Clinical Psychology, of the American Psychological Association, has created a standing committee on what is referred to as empirically validated therapies (APA Task Force, 2006). Using rating systems like the one described in chapter 3, interventions and outcomes are entered into a list of empirically validated therapies. The explicit purpose of such a list is to guide practitioners in choosing the right therapy for their clients and to assist clinical psychologists to get funding from insurance companies or obtain support from hospital administrators to use these therapies. Tables 13.6 and 13.7, respectively,

TABLE 13.6 APA List of Supported Treatments

EXAMPLES OF WELL-ESTABLISHED EMPIRICALLY VALIDATED TREATMENTS (EVTS)

Anxiety and stress problems
Cognitive-behavior therapy for panic disorder (with and without agoraphobia)
Cognitive-behavior therapy for generalized anxiety disorder
Exposure treatment for agoraphobia
Exposure or guided mastery for specific phobia
Exposure and response prevention for obsessive-compulsive disorder
Stress inoculation training for coping with stressors

Depression
Behavior therapy for depression
Cognitive therapy for depression
Interpersonal therapy for depression

Health problems
Behavior therapy for headache
Multicomponent cognitive-behavior therapy for pain associated with rheumatic disease
Multicomponent cognitive-behavior therapy with relapse prevention for smoking cessation
Cognitive-behavior therapy for bulimia

Childhood problems
Behavior modification for enuresis
Parent training programs for those having children with oppositional behavior

Marital problems
Behavioral marital therapy

Source: Adapted from Chambless et al. (1998). Update on empirically validated therapies, II. *The Clinical Psychologist*, 53–16 with permission of the Division of Clinical Psychology, American Psychological Association.

TABLE 13.7   Efficacy Ratings for Biofeedback-Based Treatments

Efficacious and specific (fifth level):
1. Urinary incontinence in women

Efficacious (fourth level):
1. Anxiety
2. Attention Deficit Disorder
3. Headache—Adult
4. Hypertension
5. Temporomandibular disorders
6. Urinary incontinence in men

Probably efficacious (third level):
1. Alcoholism or substance abuse
2. Arthritis
3. Chronic pain
4. Epilepsy
5. Fecal elimination disorders
6. Headache—pediatric migraines
7. Insomnia
8. Traumatic brain injury
9. Vulvar Vestibulitis

Possibly efficacious (second level):
1. Asthma
2. Cancer and HIV, effect on immune function
3. Cerebral palsy
4. Chronic obstructive pulmonary disease
5. Depressive disorders
6. Diabetes mellitus
7. Fibromyalgia
8. Foot ulcers
9. Hand dystonia
10. Irritable bowel syndrome
11. Mechanical ventilation
12. Motion sickness
13. Myocardial infarction
14. Post-traumatic stress disorder
15. Raynaud's disease
16. Repetitive strain injury
17. Stroke
18. Tinnitus
19. Urinary incontinence in children

Not empirically supported (first level of evidence):
1. Autism
2. Eating disorders
3. Multiple sclerosis
4. Spinal cord injury

present the most recently compiled lists of empirically validated therapies generated by the American Psychological Association (for mental health applications) as well as the equivalent list from the Association for Applied Psychophysiology and Biofeedback (Yucha & Gilbert, 2004).

Contrary to what many outsiders and critics believe, these lists are impressively long, indicating that clinical psychology has a large amount of valuable expertise to offer to the health care system and to patients. It is also interesting and noteworthy that certain types of therapies are considered empirically validated for only one specific application, and that for some disorders (e.g., depression) there often is more than one validated therapy to choose from. These lists are very useful in guiding training programs for clinical psychologists because they are understandably interested in equipping their students with therapy skills and methodologies that are known to be effective and allow graduates to market themselves.

◇ CONCLUSION

There is a massive and still steadily growing literature on the effects of psychotherapy and very consistent evidence that treatment is better than no treatment, that the treatment effect on average is large (using the language of meta-analysis). This knowledge has been around for about 3 decades, and the core conclusions since then have been remarkably stable, getting replicated again and again. Very few active treatments (or specific applications of a treatment to a target problem) have been shown to be superior to other active treatments, and in the real, clinical world many treatments are too short to offer patients the maximum benefit.

◇ ONGOING CONSIDERATIONS

Without a doubt, clinical psychology benefits from strong and consistent evidence that our clients benefit from our efforts. Recall, however, that we described the profession as one that is both science and art because not every problem we encounter has been resolved with research efforts, and published literature is not always available to guide our practice. A decision to call some therapies effective also means that other existing therapies are thereby implicitly labeled less effective and their practitioners feel pushed aside and perhaps see themselves as the second-class citizens in clinical psychology. Being on the list of empirically validated therapies usually translates into an insurance company's willingness to pay for the treatment of phobias with cognitive-behavioral therapy, for example, but not pay for treatment if a psychoanalytic approach is proposed. Such decisions directly impact how practitioners with varying theoretical orientations will run their practices (and so they should, argue the supporters of these classification systems). In order to prevent premature stoppage of developing new psychotherapies, it is therefore necessary that the advantages and disadvantages of having and maintaining lists of empirically validated therapies are considered living documents, which need to be reviewed and updated on a regular basis. Also, awareness needs to be raised about the potential problems arising from their existence. Here are key arguments speaking against the lists (or at least rigid and dogmatic use thereof):

1. The existence of the list reduces the momentum in the field for creating promising and innovative therapies.

2. There is always the possibility that a given patient is not likely to respond well to the supposedly most efficacious approach or has a subjective dislike for it that can lead to poor adherence.

3. Graduate training programs have to carefully balance the need to teach the skills required for the application of empirically validated treatments but at the same time should encourage future clinical psychologists to be open-minded and consider more than just a mere technical match of a client's presenting problem with the suitable treatment extricated from the list. In fact, much of the training in graduate school is about preparing clinical psychologists for a practice in which individual context variables are skillfully considered in developing an appropriate,

individualized treatment plan. A cookbook-like matching of treatment to problem makes psychologists look like mere technicians and denigrates the profession and its lengthy training requirements.

4. It will be difficult to convince grant review committees to fund a new treatment research project when there are already two (or more) effective treatments for a given problem. Thus, innovative research may be harder to get funded.

Given the current economic realities, it is highly unlikely that the dogmatic opponents of all empirical validation and publishing of lists will win the argument. In a world, where accountability is called for and where there is competition for every health care dollar, one cannot justify spending health care dollars while ignoring evidence. Also, in a free-market world an informed client is more likely to pay good money to a therapist who advertises the practice of empirically validated therapies rather than some method that is considered highly controversial and for which no real evidence exists.

◇ KEY TERMS LEARNED

Box score reviews
Box scores
Confounding effect
Dodo bird verdict
Ecological validity
Effect sizes
Group means

Large effect
Meta-analysis
Narrative review
Regression to the mean
Sleepers
Value of particular outcomes

◇ THINKING QUESTIONS

1. Why do most active treatments tend to produce similar benefits?

2. Which criteria are the most important for determining whether or not therapy worked?

3. Who should define therapy success: patients, insurance companies, or therapists?

4. What are the most urgent, unresolved questions in psychotherapy research?

5. Which therapist produces the best treatment outcomes?

◇ REFERENCES

APA Task Force on Evidence-Based Practice. (2006). Evidence-based practice in psychology. *American Psychologist, 61*, 271–285.

Baron, R. M., & Kenny, D. A. (1986). The moderator-mediator variable distinction in social psychological research: Conceptual, strategic, and statistical considerations. *Journal of Personality and Social Psychology, 51*, 1173–1182.

Bradley, R., Greene, J., Russ, E., Dutra, L., & Westen, D. (2005). A multidimensional meta-analysis of psychotherapy for PTSD. *American Journal of Psychiatry, 162*, 214–227.

Christensen, B. (2005). Motivational interviewing: A systematic review and meta-analysis. *The British Journal of General Practice, 55*(513), 305–312.

Crits-Christoph, P. (1992). The efficacy of brief dynamic psychotherapy: A meta-analysis. *American Journal of Psychiatry, 149*, 151–158.

Coyne, J. C., Stefanek, M., & Palmer, S. C. (2007). Psychotherapy and survival in cancer: The conflict between hope and evidence. *Psychological Bulletin, 133*, 367–394.

DeLeon, P. H., VandenBos, G. R., & Cummings, N. A. (1983). Psychotherapy—Is it safe, effective, and appropriate? The beginning of an evolutionary dialogue. *American Psychologist, 38*, 907–911.

Eysenck, H. J. (1952). The effects of psychotherapy: An evaluation. *Journal of Consulting Psychology, 16*, 319–321.

Feske, U., & Chambless, D. L. (1995). Cognitive behavioral versus exposure only treatment for social phobia: A meta-analysis. *Behavior Therapy, 26*, 695–720.

Flor, H., Fydrich, T., & Turk, D. C. (1992). Efficacy of multidisciplinary pain centers: A meta-analysis. *Pain, 49*, 221–230.

Fonagy, P., Target, M., Cottrell, D., Phillips, J., & Kurtz, Z. (2002). *What works for whom? A critical review of treatments for children and adolescents*. New York: Guilford.

Herbert, J. D. (2003). The science and practice of empirically supported treatments. *Behavior Modification, 27*, 3.

Hilgard, E. R., Crawford, H. J., & Wert, A. (1979). The Stanford Hypnotic Arm Levitation Induction and Test (SHALIT): A six-minute hypnotic induction and measurement scale. *International Journal of Clinical and Experimental Hypnosis, 27*, 111–124.

Hettema, J., Steele, J., & Miller, W. R. (2005). Motivational interviewing. *Annual Review of Clinical Psychology, 1*, 91–111.

Hunsley, J. (2003). Cost-effectiveness and cost offset considerations in psychological service provision. *Canadian Psychology, 44*, 61–73.

Johnson, S. M., Hunsley, J., Greenberg, L., & Schindler, D. (1999). Emotionally focused couples therapy: Status and challenges. *Clinical Psychology: Science and practice, 6*, 67–79.

Leichsenring, F., Rabung, S., & Leibing, E. (2004). The efficacy of short-term psychodynamic psychotherapy in specific psychiatric disorders. *Archives of General Psychiatry, 61*, 1208–1216.

Lewandoswski, L. M., Gebing, T. A., Anthony, J. L., & O'Brien, W. H. (1997). Meta-analysis of cognitive-behavioral treatment studies for bulimia. *Clinical Psychology Review, 17*, 703–718.

Linden, W. (1981). Exposure treatments for focal phobias: A review. *Archives of General Psychiatry, 38*, 769–775.

Linden, W., & Chambers, L. (1994). Clinical effectiveness of non-drug treatment for hypertension: A meta-analysis. *Annals of Behavioral Medicine, 16*, 35–45.

Linden, W., Phillips, M. J., & Leclerc, J. (2007). Psychological treatment of cardiac patients: A meta-analysis. *European Heart Journal, 28*, 2972–2984.

Linden, W., Len, J. W., & Con, A. (2001). Individualized stress management for essential hypertension: A randomized trial. *Archives of Internal Medicine, 161*, 1072–1080.

Linden, W., & Satin, J. R. (2007). Avoidable pitfalls in behavioural medicine outcome research. *Annals of Behavioral Medicine, 33*, 143–147.

Linehan, M. M., & Heard, H. (1999). Borderline personality disorder: Costs, course, and treatment outcomes. In N. Miller & K. Magruder (Eds.), *The cost-effectiveness of psychotherapy: A guide for practitioners, researchers and policy-makers* (pp. 291–305). New York: Oxford Press.

Lipsey, M. W., & Wilson, D. B. (1993). The efficacy of psychological, educational, and behavioral treatment. *American Psychologist, 48*, 1181–1209.

Luborsky, L., Rosenthal, R., Diguer, L., Andrusyna, T. P., Berman, J. S., Levitt, J. T., et al. (2002). The dodo bird verdict is alive and well—Mostly. *Clinical Psychology: Science and Practice, 9*, 2–12.

Luborsky, L., Singer, B., & Luborsky, L. (1975). Comparative studies of psychotherapies: Is it true that "Everyone has won and all must have prizes"? *Archives of General Psychiatry, 32*, 995–1008.

Osborn, R. L., Demoncada, A. C., & Feuerstein, M. (2006). Psychosocial interventions for depression, anxiety, and quality of life in cancer survivors: Meta-analyses. *The International Journal of Psychiatry in Medicine, 36*, 13–34.

Perls, F. S., Hefferline, R. F., & Goodman, P. (1951). *Gestalt therapy*. New York: Julian Press.

Robinson, L. A., Berman, J. S., & Neimeyer, R. A. (1990). Psychotherapy for the treatment of depression: A comprehensive review of controlled outcome research. *Psychological Bulletin, 108*, 30–49.

Rosenthal, R. (1983). Assessing the statistical and social importance of the effects of psychotherapy. *Journal of Consulting and Clinical Psychology, 51*, 4–13.

Rosenthal, R., & DiMatteo, M. R. (2001). Meta-analysis: Recent developments in quantitative methods for literature reviews. *Annual Review of Psychology, 52*, 59–82.

Rosnow, R. L., & Rosenthal, R. (1996). Computing contrasts, effect sizes, and counternulls on other people's published data: General procedures for research consumers.*Psychological Methods, 1*, 331–340.

Sedlmeier, P., & Gigerenzer, G. (1989). Do studies of statistical power have an effect on the power of studies? *Psychological Bulletin, 105*, 309–316.

Seligman, M. (1995). The effectiveness of psychotherapy: The Consumer Reports study. *American Psychologist, 50*, 965–974.

Shapiro, D. A., & Shapiro, D. (1982). Meta-analysis of comparative therapy outcome studies: A replication and refinement. *Psychological Bulletin, 92*, 581–604.

Smith, M. L., & Glass, G. V. (1977). Meta-analysis of psychotherapy outcome studies. *American Psychologist, 32*, 752–777.

Steering Committee of the Physicians' Health Study Research Group. (1989). Final report on the aspirin component of the ongoing Physicians' Health Study. *New England Journal of Medicine, 321*, 129–135.

Stetter, F., & Kupper, S. (2002). Autogenic training. A meta-analysis of clinical outcome studies: A replication and refinement. *Applied Psychophysiology and Biofeedback, 27*, 45–98.

Strupp, H. H., & Hadley, S. W. (1979). Specific vs. nonspecific factors in psychotherapy: A controlled study of outcome. *Archives of General Psychiatry, 36,* 1125–1136.

Van Etten, M. L., & Taylor, S. (1998). Comparative efficacy of treatments for posttraumatic stress disorder: A meta-analysis. *Clinical Psychology and Psychotherapy, 5,* 126–144.

Yucha, C., & Gilbert, C. (2004). *Evidence-based practice in biofeedback and neurofeedback. Association for applied psychophysiology and biofeedback.* Colorado Springs, CO: Association for Applied Psychophysiology and Biofeedback.

Zhang, M., Rost, K. M., & Fortney, J. C. (1999). Earnings changes for depressed individuals treated by mental health specialists. *American Journal of Psychiatry, 156,* 108–114.

CHAPTER FOURTEEN

INNOVATIVE/MYSTICAL THERAPIES

In chapters 11 and 12, psychological treatment methods were introduced that are considered mainstream—the bread-and-butter techniques of the great majority of practicing psychotherapists. The mainstream therapies have been introduced in this book largely in the order in which they were developed, beginning with Freud's seminal work on psychoanalysis. The last major additions to this body of literature and therapy practice (as described in chapter 12) were cognitive therapy, the continuing developments in the interpersonal therapies (chapter 11), motivational interviewing, and emotion-focused psychotherapy.

The objective of this additional chapter on treatment approaches is threefold:

1. Introduce the reader to treatment approaches that have remained somewhat mysterious and/or have been developed fairly recently but are rapidly gaining popularity.

2. Present these treatment approaches with a critical eye toward definition, rationale, and techniques and highlight their potential and known limits; identify whether the claimed mechanisms of action have been demonstrated

3. Sensitize the reader to the generic issues that arise when any new treatment is brought to market and provide the tools needed to critically analyze innovative treatments

◇ DEFINING TREATMENT SPECIFICITY AND UNIQUENESS

Clinical psychology is not a static field; new evidence is introduced, which requires rethinking; and creative new approaches (or seemingly new approaches) to change behavior and reduce human suffering are continuously being proposed. Whenever such innovation and its associated techniques are presented, it makes sense to also ask the critical question whether or not a pre-existing method is just given a new name (with the objective being the enhancement of the career or the earnings of the innovator) or whether something truly new is being added to the clinical psychologist's toolbox. To witness, many large cities have newspapers that serve the local cultural scene and alternative lifestyles, and advertisements in these papers serve as a mirror of what innovative approaches are being offered in a given community. A number of such ads from a Vancouver newspaper were reworded to avoid copyright violations and are presented in Box 14.1. The inherent claims and method descriptions are being offered as illustrations.

These ads promise a wide range of services; make at times surprising (and often unbelievable) claims; and are characterized by frequently vague, esoteric language. In addition,

---

BOX 14.1

MODIFIED SAMPLE TEXTS FROM ADVERTISEMENTS OF ALTERNATIVE THERAPIES AND TRAINING WORKSHOPS IN A COMMUNITY NEWSPAPER (PHOTOS, GRAPHICS, AND IDENTIFYING INFORMATION WERE REMOVED TO AVOID COPYRIGHT VIOLATIONS)

Advertisement 1

Deep Belief Engineering, Founder *Albert F* (PPSEC Registered)
Professional Certification Program: This gentle, powerful approach leads to lasting, definitive, and meaningful change; it has an excellent reputation across North America since 1986. We offer 4-day basic course.

Advertisement 2

Love Heals, *Anna P*, PhD, Reiki Master
I offer healing sessions blending Reiki, crystals & gemstones, channeling, sacrocranial massage, aromatherapy and color healing. Past life regressions and deep trance are also available. Ongoing workshops offered for Reiki I, II, III, and IV as well as crystal and gemstone therapy.

Advertisement 3

Intuition:
Learn an energy technique and deep intuition to assess and balance the energy body that will lead to optimum well-being for yourself and those around you.

Offered by Dr. *Maria O*, who is a doctoral graduate of Dr. *Norm M* and Dr. *Karla H*'s Energy Medicine Program. Prerequisite for *College of Medical Intuition Sept* 2010 Intake 2-evening workshop: Call yyy–xxxx.

potential clients are enticed to purchase services from practitioners who offer strings of creative professional titles, and evidence of professional competence is claimed that may be unconventional, to say the least. In Box 14.1, you can see numerous colorful self-descriptors of the healers themselves as well as descriptions of their vast areas of practice.

In this occasionally flaky marketplace, licensed psychologists still need to market themselves, put their best foot forward, and convince their clients to see a licensed clinical psychologist rather than the spiritual-cleansing therapist next door. On one hand it is necessary for professional psychology to be open to change, but it also needs to avoid fraudulent claims about effectiveness on the other (APA Presidential Task Force, 2005; Hunsley, 2003). The code of ethics also makes it clear that psychologists are not allowed to make claims that they cannot back with evidence so as to prevent deception of clients; that aside, we believe that truthful claims maintain credibility and market share in the long run.

A key question that needs resolution is how many truly different therapies there are. There is little debate that Rogerian client-centered therapy is different from Freudian psychoanalysis (as discussed in chapter 11), but it is already difficult to draw a line between cognitive therapy a la Beck (1995) and rational-emotive therapy a la Ellis (1962) described in chapter 12. They are similar in that they target irrational and hence dysfunctional thought patterns that in turn are characterized by rigidity, by overly negative tones and often are derived from untested assumptions. They use treatment methods of Socratian dialogue and are very directive. Still, they use somewhat different language and techniques to achieve their ends, and it is therefore arguable whether or not they should count as distinct psychotherapy approaches. As much as the existence of many different therapies makes the field richer and more interesting, in the extreme such variety confuses the public and makes it exceedingly difficult for researchers to demonstrate differential effectiveness of different approaches. Such variety challenges clinical psychology to take a stance on how many truly different therapy approaches there are.

Anecdotal evidence holds that the Yellow Pages of the San Francisco phone book list no less than 135 different types of psychotherapy, and the corresponding figure for Los Angeles is 220. Are there really that many truly different psychotherapies? Can a trained observer reliably hold them apart by watching videotaped sessions? Arguably, a more realistic number is maybe in the 10 to 20 range, and even that might consist of an even smaller number of distinguishable major approaches. That aside, the field would be totally overwhelmed by a requirement of showing differential efficacy of over 200 different forms of psychotherapy. For the last few decades, the traditionally taught and best-known approaches (as documented via coverage in various clinical psychology textbooks) are psychodynamic, interpersonal, client-centered, behavioral, cognitive-behavioral, biofeedback, and systems therapies. These therapies were described in chapters 11 and 12 in this book, and their effectiveness was illustrated in chapter 13.

Here, we describe approaches that are sometimes newer, are less well developed, do not fit this category system, and/or have seen limited testing to date. New approaches spring up frequently and at times find enthusiastic receptions because (a) they fill an identified need, (b) they appear particularly efficient, or (c) the propagator of the method is particularly charismatic. The latter point should not be underestimated because progress in the sciences is not linear, and major changes can at times be triggered by single individuals

(Gladwell, 2000). When a new treatment emerges, there is an obligation to be aware of its potential and limitations and to be ready for its comparison with other psychotherapies (Barlow, 2004). The majority of clinical psychologists likely agree that solutions sometimes need to be found for problems that are unique and that had not been covered in their training program. After all, clinical psychology is a science and an art, and it is appropriate to use methods that are essentially based on clinical judgment and experience even if they have not undergone controlled evaluations, provided that (a) no harm is likely to come to patients and (b) that no other effective approach already exists for a given target problem. Furthermore, for any given new approach, there cannot be empirical evidence right from the beginning; somebody has to begin with case studies, then conduct controlled research, and somebody has to publicly document the accumulation of findings and comparisons of new approaches with other treatments.

There are many questions that need answers when new approaches come on stream (Kazdin & Bass, 1989):

- Is there measurable benefit from pre- to post-treatment?
- Is the treatment approach as equally good as, better than, or weaker than other available treatments?
- What percentage of patients are likely getting better?
- Why does a treatment work?
- Is the claimed rationale testable? And if so, does the research on the claimed rationale or pathway of effects show specificity?
- How much and what therapist training is needed?

These questions are answered not only in this chapter. The concepts of therapy rationales and specificity issues are at focus here, but data on therapy outcome were already presented in chapter 13 so that the reader can readily compare the innovative/mystical therapies with the effects of mainstream therapies.

◇ HYPNOSIS

Description and Rationale

Hypnosis is probably the most mysterious, maybe even scary, yet alluring, of all therapy approaches because it seems to place a great deal of power in the hypnotist's hands and is sometimes seen as a frightening loss of control by patients. A review of existing beliefs and actual known facts on hypnosis (based on a scan of the printed literature and the Internet) has revealed an interesting discourse on myths and truths about hypnosis (see Box 14.2).

The observations in Box 14.2 remove some of the mystery, but even once the myths are stripped away, we still have not explained what hypnosis actually is. Hypnosis is defined as a heightened state of suggestibility that likely arises from a trusting therapeutic relationship, a state of relaxation, and a reduced level of environmental stimulation. These elements

BOX 14.2

HYPNOSIS MYTHS (BY WILLIAM HEWITT), RETRIEVED FROM HTTP://WWW.LLEWELLYNENCYCLOPEDIA.COM/ARTICLE/222

There are probably more myths, misconceptions, and misinformation about hypnosis than any other subject. This is due in large part to movies, television, and novels that make no attempt to be truthful in dealing with hypnosis. They are more interested in creating dramatic effect than in presenting truth. Drama sells! Truth doesn't sell. As a result, the public gets fed tons of drama, half-truths, and tons of false information about hypnosis.

MYTH: The hypnotist can make you do things against your will.

Absolutely false. The hypnotist has no power over you at all and cannot make you do anything against your will. Hypnosis is really just self-hypnosis. All the hypnotist does is guide you into a hypnotic state, which you can easily learn to do for yourself, if you wish. The hypnotist is not a master, but a guide, and does not have any special power or magic.

MYTH: You can get stuck in hypnosis and never come out.

False again. If you are hypnotized and the hypnotist left the room and never returned, your own mind would pull you safely out of the hypnosis in one of two ways. You would either realize the hypnotist was no longer talking to you, and you would open your eyes and be wide awake and feeling fine, or you would drift into a normal sleep for a few minutes and then wake up normally, feeling fine.

MYTH: When hypnotized, you are in a trance and have no control.

Not true. First, hypnosis does not put you into a trance. You are always awake and aware of what is happening. Hypnosis is like a daydream state. You are awake and aware but are very relaxed with your attention focused on a specific thought or image. Second, you always have control. If the hypnotist told you to rob a bank you would just say, "No," and open your eyes. You would not rob the bank. Of course, if you really wanted to rob a bank anyway, then you would follow the suggestion to do so. The point is that it is you, not the hypnotist, who makes hypnosis work or not work.

MYTH: Everyone can be hypnotized.

False. No one can be hypnotized against his will. In addition, people with certain mental or neurological conditions cannot be hypnotized. And about one percent of the population cannot be hypnotized for reasons that are not known. However, most people can be hypnotized if they want to be.

MYTH: Hypnosis can cure anything or solve any personal problem.

No, hypnosis is not a cure-all. Hypnosis is very powerful and can cure, or aid in the cure, of a great many ailments. Hypnosis can also solve a great many personal problems. At times hypnosis can produce what seems to be miracles. But it is not the answer for everything. Hypnosis is a powerful, natural tool we all have available to us to help improve our lives in a great many ways.

(continued)

BOX 14.2 CONTINUED

MYTH: **Hypnosis is dangerous.**

> Untrue. It is quite the opposite. Hypnosis is safe and natural.

MYTH: **Only weak-minded people can be hypnotized.**

> Again, false. The contrary is true. It is easier to hypnotize people who are intelligent.

MYTH: **Deep hypnosis is necessary for good results.**

> Not true. Any level of hypnosis from light to deep can bring good results.
>
> Forget the Hollywood-type hype that depicts people walking around like zombies under the control of some madman who merely has to look into a person's eyes in order to put them into an alleged hypnotic trance. This is pure myth that has absolutely no basis in fact.

---

are held to be critical ingredients in achieving therapeutic trance, which in turn is considered pivotal in defining hypnosis, and there has been extensive research grappling with a better understanding of hypnosis. The research on hypnosis and its mechanism of action has distinguished two key questions: (a) Who is hypnotizable? Is hypnotizability a stable individual characteristic? and (b) How can hypnotic trance be defined and measured?

Hypnotic Susceptibility

Hypnotic susceptibility (the degree to which people can be hypnotized) is generally thought to be a trait that remains stable over time. High levels of test-retest reliability have been observed over periods of 10 to 25 years (Hilgard, 1965). Not all researchers agree that **hypnotizability** is stable, and there is disagreement about the magnitude to which hypnotizability can be affected (e.g., Lynn & Rhue, 1988). Nevertheless, the degree of hypnotic susceptibility varies between people and is also affected by the relationship that the hypnotist has to the hypnotizee. For stage hypnotists, this means that quick and effective tests are required to identify those who are susceptible because the stage hypnotist wants to appear in control. Hypnotists carefully screen audiences for their degree of susceptibility. Even after people came forward, they likely screen again by asking participants to allow themselves to fall backward with eyes closed, trusting that the hypnotist will catch them. Note that none of this is necessary when hypnosis is embedded in a therapeutic relationship with a strong alliance. A psychotherapist using hypnosis typically explains to patients what hypnosis is all about and provides them with a description of the process that minimizes fears and removes myths.

When researchers are trying to identify research participants and the participants vary in degrees of hypnotizability, they often use self-report questionnaires to measure individual differences in susceptibility. The gold standard of hypnosis scales is currently considered to be the Stanford Hypnotic Susceptibility Scale, Form C (Weitzenhoffer & Hilgard, 1962; Hilgard et al., 1979). As part of the validation process of hypnotizability scales, researchers have conducted studies on the construct validity of this concept (Barnier, Wright, & McConkey, 2004) and have learned that certain constructs, that are also measurable via self-report, correlate well with the hypnotizability, and these include self-absorption, fantasy proneness, and reaction time (Tellegen & Atkinson, 1974; Lynn & Rhue, 1988).

Understanding and Measuring Hypnotic Trance

The reader of this book will have seen demonstrations of trance in movies and television shows and has an intuitive sense of what trance might feel like. There are a number of different hypnotic induction methods, ranging from relatively indirect instructions to gradually relax to more direct methods that may involve tools like a rhythmically moving pendulum. However, the demonstration that a distinct trance state has been achieved is difficult. In principle, there are at least three ways of determining that a trance is present: (a) using quantifiable physiological activity to document a unique event, (b) seeking self-reports of the experience as being different from normal levels of awareness and relaxation, and (c) observing motor behavior.

Unfortunately, the results of such studies have not fully removed the ambiguities in judgment about whether a true trance had occurred or not, and in consequence it is still debated whether a trance is a unique experience or whether this experience occurs on a continuous scale, where one end of the continuum is fully alert and not very suggestible and very relaxed and highly suggestible at the other end (Hadley & Staudacher, 1985).

Clinicians do use observed minimal motor behavior and low irritability as well as posttrance subjective reporting by the patient himself as criteria to determine whether or not a trance was achieved. However, at a physiological level, hypnosis has not been reliably distinguished from deep relaxation (Spanos, 1991).

The Method

The techniques for hypnosis induction are widely published and quite structured, and this fact alone removes some of the mystery surrounding hypnosis.

Common hypnosis phases are:

1. **Preparation**. This involves having the subject sit or lie down and get comfortable. The key is achieving a body position of physical comfort that encourages letting go.
2. **Induction**. Induction takes the subject from normal awareness to a state of enhanced relaxation. The methods can vary from subtle relaxation instructions to rather provocative, stereotypical hypnosis induction with a swinging pendulum, for example.
3. **Deepening**. The deepening phase takes the subject from a very relaxed state to a fully hypnotized state, where conscious thinking is minimized. Having such a phase over and above mere relaxation instructions is to suggest to the client that hypnosis is somehow distinct.
4. **Purpose**. As a clinical psychologist, the use of hypnosis is purposeful, to assist with healing. Here the subject is encouraged to see himself as what he wants to become,

such as a nonsmoker or somebody who constructively manipulates her pain experience through imagery.

5. **Awakening**. The awakening phase is when the subject is taken out of the hypnotic state. If the session is to try to alleviate insomnia, then the subject is encouraged to sleep; otherwise the subject is brought back to a state of awareness with the conscious mind fully re-engaged.

Hypnosis has a very wide range of potential applications (see also outcome data in chapter 13), and the interested reader can go to a website that lists no less than 315 hypnosis scripts for various applications (see the references to this chapter). A particularly popular application of hypnosis is for chronic pain conditions (Jensen & Patterson, 2006; Spanos, 1991). The probably best-known and validated method for evaluating the existence of hypnotizability is via the Stanford hypnotic arm levitation and induction test (SHALIT; Hilgard, Crawford, & Wert, 1979). In SHALIT the hypnotist makes suggestions for imagery that is expected to lead to lowering or raising of arms that are stretched out in front. The degree to which the arms follow these diverging instructions is then measured as a function of distance. The degree of this response is literally measured in centimeters and then used as a numerical score.

Treatment Outcome

Evidence for Positive Treatment Outcome

There are a number of review papers on the effectiveness of hypnosis (Kirsch, 1996; Montgomery, DuHamel, & Redd, 2000), and on the whole, they suggest that hypnosis is effective with a variety of clinical problems, including chronic pain conditions, preparation for surgery, warts, anxiety reduction, and weight loss. Effect sizes vary greatly for different targets, but overall they are large.

Is It Possible to Test for the Specificity of the Rationale?

Given that the existence of a hypnotic trance is at best indirectly testable, claims about the specificity of a hypnotic trance (and corresponding claims that reaching a trance is needed for a positive treatment effect) are very difficult to test.

Is There Evidence for Specificity?

Consistent with the existing doubt about the unequivocal testability of a trance state, there is no convincing evidence that hypnosis is a unique method which produces treatment outcomes that are not otherwise possible with deep relaxation and suggestion.

Summary of Hypnosis

Hypnosis becomes much less mysterious when commercialism and hype is removed from its description and use. Nevertheless, given the remaining ambiguity about whether or not trance is a unique experience, clearly distinct from deep relaxation, it is almost impossible to empirically verify that specificity claims are justifiable. Also, researchers do not really know what an appropriate attention control condition would be. On the other hand, clinicians enjoy having in their possession a highly original tool that is often liked by patients and that is associated with good clinical outcomes (see chapter 13 and Table 14.1), even when the mechanism remains a little nebulous.

◇ EYE MOVEMENT DESENSITIZATION AND REPROCESSING

Description, Rationale, and Method

Eye movement desensitization and reprocessing (EMDR) is a relatively new method that, however, has a lot of very enthusiastic followers. Prior to discussing the procedure, the reader needs to realize that the approach has changed since the first presentation of the method, and that these differences in the original versus the more recent procedure may have correspondingly distinct impacts. The original claim was that even relatively brief exposure to rhythmic, forward-backward, semicircular finger movements that patients visually focus on would quickly reduce the negative effect associated with post-traumatic events. During the procedure, patients imagine these events while their eyes follow the rhythmic movements of the therapist's finger. Initially, it was believed that stimulation of the visual sensory channel would be particularly effective. This belief has changed over time as clinical researchers found that a similar effect could be achieved by rhythmic tapping as well. This latter observation contradicts the pivotal claim of the unique importance of visual stimulation. Much of the excitement about EMDR has arisen from the observation that acute anxiety during treatment sessions rapidly subsided and that patients quickly felt relief within a session (Shapiro, 2002; Sharpley, Montgomery, & Scalzo, 1996).

The website of the EMDR Institute, www.emdr.com, provides this definition:

> EMDR integrates elements of many effective psychotherapies in structured protocols that are designed to maximize treatment effects. These include psychodynamic, cognitive behavioral, interpersonal, experiential, and body-centered therapies. EMDR is an information processing therapy and uses an eight phase approach.

The proposed eight phases of treatment are:

1. **History taking:** The therapist wants to learn recent distressing events, current situations that elicit emotional disturbance, related historical incidents, and the development of specific skills and behaviors that will be needed by the client in future situations.

2. Stress-reduction techniques (relaxation training)

3–6. **Eye movement desensitization:** A target is identified and processed using EMDR procedures. These procedures involve the client identifying the most vivid visual image related to the memory (if available), a negative belief about self, related emotions, and body sensations. Changes in beliefs and emotions are tracked. For the actual exposure, the client is instructed to focus on the image, negative thought, and body sensations while simultaneously moving his eyes back and forth following the therapist's fingers as they move across his field of vision for 20 to 30 seconds or more, depending upon the need of the client. Other than eye movement, similar repetitive, rhythmic sensory stimulation may also be used. Key is the presence of dual stimulation (trauma image and rhythmic stimulation). After several sets, the therapist checks with the client regarding body sensations. If there are continuing negative sensations, additional exposure sets are provided.

7. Clients keep a journal of trauma and coping-related events during the week.
8. The therapist re-evaluates previous work and progress made.

The EMDR approach was initially referred to as just eye movement desensitization and was believed to be very effective even with very short treatments. However, as more clinical trials were conducted, it appeared that the quick improvements noted within session would not similarly generalize and lead to lasting outcomes. Based on these observations, the reprocessing component was added to the methodology. Reprocessing refers to essentially cognitive methods that are used to identify and change thought and behavior patterns.

Treatment Outcome

Evidence for Positive Outcome

A string of randomized controlled trials and a published meta-analysis consistently indicate that overall EMDR is an efficacious method for reducing trauma-related distress. The effect sizes usually observed are large and suggest considerable clinical benefit for patients (Davidson & Parker, 2001; Bradley, Green, Russ et al., 2005; Rubin, 2004).

Is Specificity Testing Possible?

Given that the current protocol of EMDR delivery is composed of the eye movement desensitization component itself, the imaginal exposure to the distressing traumatic memory, as well as the reprocessing component (which essentially is cognitive therapy), this method could be, and has been, subjected to treatment dismantling procedures where one or the other component is removed from the full protocol, and effects could then be compared with and without this feature.

Is There Evidence for Specificity?

Aggregation of results from these dismantling approaches has consistently shown that EMDR with eye movement desensitization is no more effective than treatment with only the other two components, that is, when the eye movement desensitization component was not present (Lohr, Lilienfeld, Tolin, & Herbert, 1999; Taylor et al., 2003). Hence, claims for a specificity effect of the eye movement desensitization component are not supported, and the observed benefit of EMDR is apparently attributable to the exposure and reprocessing components. These two components, however, are not innovative and overlap with standard cognitive-behavioral therapy for post-traumatic stress disorder, which has been shown to be equally or even more effective than EMDR (Davidson & Parker, 2001; Lohr et al., 1999; Taylor et al., 2003). Exposure to the feared stimulus appears to be the single most potent treatment ingredient, which, in turn, has been well-established knowledge for a number of decades (Linden, 1981).

Summary of EMDR

Given that the definition and actual treatment methodology of eye movement desensitization has changed over time, readers need to be very cautious and clear about which exact version they are dealing with. The research literature provides clear support that the package of methods that is clustered together in the recent version of EMDR is efficacious, although it is at best comparable in effect size with competing methods like cognitive-behavioral therapy. Research has also clarified that the eye movement component is not pivotal to treatment success and that a claim for uniqueness and specificity is not supported.

◇ ACCEPTANCE AND COMMITMENT THERAPY

Description, Rationale, and Method

Acceptance and commitment therapy (ACT) is considered to have its roots in cognitive and behavioral therapies (Hayes & Smith, 2005). What makes it different is the very specific cognition theory that the method's creator, Steven Hayes, has developed and tested over two decades. Hayes argues that many individuals use language and associated learning to maintain their own suffering by repeating behaviors that are not productive. He posits that making new experiences is the most promising avenue for improving quality of life and reduction of suffering. People are trapped in repetitive thoughts and belief systems; this therapy centers on the belief that suffering can be avoided or removed. In ACT, there is an initial treatment phase that can be very frustrating for patients because the therapist attempts to convince the patient to accept the fact that to some degree human suffering is normal and inevitable and that desperate attempts to avoid painful experiences create suffering or make it worse (this is the **acceptance** component). Another critical component in the rationale is that individuals avoid making new experiences that would help them move forward because they are afraid to try new solutions with unknown outcomes. However, if

BOX 14.3:

Insanity: doing the same thing over and over again and expecting different results

ALBERT EINSTEIN

old attempts at solution routinely fail, then the only avenue of promise is to risk trying new ones even if positive outcome cannot be guaranteed. The latter phase consists of a **commitment** to try risky new behaviors.

Treatment Outcome

Treatment Effectiveness

Meta-analysis supports the efficacy of ACT with typically large effects in pre-post comparisons and at times superior effects when compared with other active treatments (Hayes, Luoma, Bond, Masua, & Lillis, 2006).

Is Specificity Testing Possible?

Given that the procedure is mostly cognitive in nature, critical cognitive concepts have to be operationalized and then tested. Hayes has shown that emotional suffering is associated with experiential avoidance (i.e., the unwillingness to try new solutions), and his team has developed a standardized assessment tool that can be used to test patient progress in ACT (the acceptance and action questionnaire [AAQ]; Hayes et al., 2004). Specificity would be apparent if progress in therapy is linked to corresponding changes in experiential avoidance as assessed by the AAQ. Hence, it is principally testable.

Is There Evidence for Specificity?

Testing of this mediational hypothesis around change in experiential avoidance has revealed moderately good support for a specificity claim. Hayes and colleagues (2004) have shown that change in experiential avoidance correlated r = . 40 to .54, with other signs of improvement achieved via implementation of ACT.

Summary of ACT

ACT has quickly gained in popularity because outcome research supports its effectiveness; Hayes has very effectively propagated the method by generously sharing treatment protocols, and users see the approach as original and a logical extension of cognitive-behavioral therapy. Specificity can be tested, and early research supports that the claimed treatment rationale indeed accounts for therapeutic change.

◇ MINDFULNESS MEDITATION

Roots, Rationale, and Procedure

Mindfulness meditation (MM) has its roots in ancient Buddhist practices and beliefs. A number of forms of MM are used today (Linden, 1993). The most common MM approach used in health care settings is based on the westernized mindfulness-based stress reduction

(MBSR) approach developed and evaluated by Kabat-Zinn (1990) at the University of Massachusetts in the late 1970s. He was the first to apply MM in a behavioral medicine setting for populations with a wide range of chronic pain and stress-related disorders.

MM is based on the premise that many people go through life on "auto-pilot," without paying attention to what is going on in and around them. MM training enables individuals to attend to the moment and to explore the full range of physical experiences inherent in posture; bodily sensations; and pleasant, neutral, and unpleasant feelings and thoughts. This dispassionate state of self-observation is thought to introduce a space between one's perception and the subsequent response such that reactions to life stressors will become reflective rather than merely reflex-like (Bishop et al., 2004; Kabat-Zinn, 1990). MM and other self-regulation techniques already presented in chapter 12 are not only treatments for diagnosable disorders but are conceived to be useful skills for healthy individuals as well and are considered tools for disease prevention. MM has been taught in medical schools, law schools, and prisons.

Recent research by Davidson (with support from the Dalai Lama) using brain scanning technology that was applied to experienced meditators (Tibetan monks with over 20 years of daily practice) provided evidence that meditation changes blood-flow patterns in the brain (Davidson et al., 2003). These meditation patterns resemble and intensify the left brain blood-flow patterns found in people who are experiencing joy and happiness. This suggests that happiness might be a skill rather than a trait—something that can be practiced and even trained for.

The Method

MM teaches its students to allow full awareness (mindfulness) of their thoughts, feelings, and sensations. They are not to be pushed away but to be accepted. One of the most attractive aspects of MM is that once the skills are learned, individuals can regulate their attention to evoke mindfulness in many situations, for example, while stuck in waiting situations like red traffic lights. The same feature, of course, applies to other self-regulation methods like autogenic training (Linden, 1990). A typical 4 to 10 week course in mindfulness training includes instruction in sitting and walking meditation (20 to 60 minutes a day) as well as how to be mindful during all daily life activities to the extent possible. The most frequently cited method of mindfulness training in clinical populations is the structured MBSR program developed by Kabat-Zinn and colleagues. See Box 14.4 for a prototypical description of MM training.

Treatment Outcome

MM has been applied to numerous medical conditions, including chronic pain, fibromyalgia, anxiety and panic disorders, psoriasis, depression, substance abuse, binge eating disorders, burnout, personality disorders, cancer, and heterogeneous patient populations. Meta-analysis has revealed overall medium effect sizes (slightly exceeding $d = .5$ for all reported analyses), and this implies that these improvements are likely to be clinically

BOX 14.4

TYPICAL MINDFULNESS SITTING INSTRUCTION

As you begin your meditation, simply let go of your thoughts about the past and future, pay attention to the present, and focus on your body's posture and silently note "sitting." Feel the uprightness of the body and try to maintain a balance between letting go and still keeping a somewhat upright posture. Keep it this way from here on without paying too much attention to it. Note the vibration, pressure, firmness or softness, or temperature where the body touches the chair. Breathe normally without trying to actively control your breath. Follow the changing sensations as you breathe in and out. Feel the air flow, the change in air temperature, and lightness. Imagine the notion of rising during the in-breath and falling during the out-breath. You can also use sounds as a vehicle of meditation. Allow awareness and seek and embrace sounds and silent intervals. Feel the vibration at the entrance of your ears without seeking to figure out what sounds they are (not thinking about them). If you find yourself lost in thoughts, rather than judging yourself (e.g., "I should not be thinking about that"), simply acknowledge those thoughts as "thinking" or "wandering," allow them to happen, and don't push them away. Gently bring your attention back to your breath. Patiently begin again and again in the present moment by returning to the primary object regardless how many times the mind wanders. Try to stay with the primary object until you become concentrated rather than keep changing objects. When your mind becomes more and more quiet, you are able to pay attention to the object that is most predominant, or obvious, at each moment. The object that you are attending to at this point does not reflect the result of an effort. Instead, it comes from a mindset that is choiceless (without preferences and preconceptions) and nonjudgmental and open to all physical and mental objects that are happening at that particular moment in time. It is often described as "bare attention."

You can apply mindfulness during daily activities. Try to be aware of one of the following activities, and add one more each week: feel the sensations that accompany change in posture; feel what steps while walking are like; and be mindful of the arm or hand bending, stretching, or reaching for an object or the pressure or temperature while holding it. An experienced practitioner will also notice mental impulses before such movements. Extend this mindful attitude to all routine activities such as putting on clothes, driving, working in the garden, and so on. A traffic light, a chirping bird, or a computer's preprogrammed sounds can become reminders of mindfulness. Pause and relax for a few seconds, and/or take a couple of mindful breaths, or simply (come back to the present moment and) be mindful of what you are doing at each reminder. Remind yourself periodically to be mindful by asking if you are present (aware) or lost. Check your attitude to see if you are relaxed, having no expectation. It is also helpful to be aware of likes and dislikes in the mind while interacting with people or doing chores. With time, the mindfulness will include thoughts (such as judging) and emotions and their corresponding physical sensations within the body.

meaningful (Grossmann, Niemann, Schmidt, & Walach, 2004; Ospina et al., 2007). MM has gained particular popularity for chronic disease conditions, which have to be endured rather than allowing patients to respond with active coping efforts.

Several studies of cancer patients, led by Carlson and colleagues, illustrate the kind of research that has been reported (Carlson, Speca, Patel, & Goodey, 2003; Carlson, Speca, Faris, & Patel, 2007; Speca, Carlson, Goodey, & Angen, 2000). For example, in a study with patients who had breast or prostate cancers, significant improvements were seen in overall quality of life and reduced stress following MM training; at 1-year follow up (Carlson et al., 2007) there were continued enhanced quality of life, decreased stress symptoms, and cortisol and immune patterns consistent with less stress and mood disturbance, and decreased blood pressure.

Is Specificity Testing Possible?

Specificity could be shown if experienced meditators are physiologically different from non-meditators; they may show physiological recovery more quickly or have lower resting values of various biological indices of health. Also, physiological change from pre-post treatment can be shown, and specificity would be apparent if meditators made physiological changes not apparent in treatment control groups using alternative active self-regulation methods.

Has Specificity Been Demonstrated?

There is ample research support for physiological changes in experienced meditators, and the same has been observed in pre-post treatment evaluations (e.g., Davidson et al., 2003; Kristeller, 2007). However, there is no convincing research to date that mindfulness meditation triggers physiological or cognitive changes that differ from those obtained with other forms of meditation or self-hypnosis (Grossman et al., 2004; Linden, 2005).

Summary of MM

Mindfulness meditation has readily grown in popularity and is readily accepted by clients. The data support clinical utility for a variety of health conditions, especially illnesses that require acceptance and emotional coping. There is no evidence to date that the physiological pathways or outcomes for MM differ from those of other self-regulation methods described in chapter 12.

◇ REVISITING CLAIMS OF UNIQUENESS AND SPECIFICITY FOR ALL FOUR TREATMENTS DESCRIBED

Applying the critical analysis tools that were offered throughout this book makes it a very interesting and revealing task to subject these four treatment methods to an analysis about overall effects but also to review claims for uniqueness and specificity regarding mechanisms and effects.

The nature of the proposed mechanisms inherently places limits on the degree of their testability. A major stumbling block in creating such innovative therapies can be the inability to measure what is proposed as the mechanism for change. When no acceptable tools are available to track change and isolate the unique benefit of these techniques, clinicians can use only the evidence for pre-post effects to justify the use of these techniques, but they cannot credibly claim that the treatment works for the very reason that the creators claimed. As is always the case, reviewers and critics need to carefully separate what is a demonstrated absence of an effect versus the absence of research that sought to show effects. Oftentimes, research simply has not been conducted, and, in consequence, not having answers to critical questions does not imply that those answers would be negative. As such, we are still somewhat in the fog regarding the specificity of hypnosis. On the other hand, there has been convincing demonstration that the eye movement desensitization component in EMDR is not critical to the treatment outcome. Given the fact that continuous advances and measurement technologies are likely, some of the conclusions drawn here may change over the next decade or so. Meanwhile, scrutiny of these innovative and mystical treatment approaches serves as a good training tool for critical thinking regarding therapy outcome innovation and research.

Distinguishing technique-specific effects from overall effectiveness of therapy is possible, but it requires high-quality and complex treatment outcome study designs. Unteasing the components and their effects is achieved via choice of control group as well as research on the mediating role of specific treatment rationales and mechanisms (see also chapter 3 for basic research methodologies). For example, showing that change in irrational cognitions accounts for the lifting of depression would count as a demonstration that specific claims of cognitive therapy are justified. Similarly, a comparison of accurate electromyographic feedback for pelvic floor muscle training with noncontingent feedback (unbeknownst to the trainee) also reveals specificity. It is well established that the nonspecific features of therapy, like a supportive relationship, establishment of hope, provision of a rational explanation for the existence of a problem, and the systematic building of a therapeutic alliance are, in and of themselves, predictors of good outcome (see chapter 10) and that these particular features are not uniquely tied to any one theoretical approach (Horvath & Luborsky, 1993). In fact, outcome research, documented via meta-analyses, suggests that roughly half of the explainable variance in patient improvement is due to the aggregation of nonspecific factors (Lipsey & Wilson, 1993; for more detail see chapter 13). Interestingly, much of the terminology and strategizing in psychotherapy outcome research is derived from pharmacological research that tries very hard to isolate and remove nonspecific effects via placebo controls. Psychotherapists, on the other hand, argue that nonspecific effects are good and should be maximized in psychotherapy. If and when the addition of well-defined techniques for specific targets further enhances the outcome, all the better!

The fact that a good portion of the positive outcome of psychotherapy is due to nonspecific factors benefits the patient but makes life difficult for psychotherapy researchers who are trying to identify component effects, and it provides an opportunity for the inventors of psychotherapy to claim uniqueness and specificity when it actually does not exist. The critical clinical psychologist needs to be on the perpetual lookout for unjustified claims of the specific effects of new treatments. For this chapter, four treatments that either are

TABLE 14.1 Summary of Findings

	HYPNOSIS	EMDR	ACT	MINDFULNESS MEDITATION
Pre-post effects	Large	Large	Large	Moderate
Effect relative to no treatment control	Small	Moderate	Large	Moderate
Effect relative to active control	Equivalent	Moderately weaker	Moderately stronger	Equivalent
Can specificity be tested?	Questionable	Yes	Yes	Yes
Has specificity been shown?	No, due to question-able testability	No	Yes	No

innovative or hold certain mystical qualities (or both) have been subjected to scrutiny. Choosing to discuss these four treatments was in part due to their popularity, but also because meta-analytic results were available for all four. To prevent drowning the reader in numbers, the extracted numerical effect sizes are not used in Table 14.1 but are given as verbal descriptors as follows:

Effect Size	**Descriptor**
$d < .10$	no effect
$d > .10$ and $< .30$	small effect
$d > .30$ and $< .70$	medium effect
$d > .70$	large effect

Here are the questions that were asked of the data for a comparison:

- Is there a pre-post (within patient) effect associated with the treatment?
- Is the effect for the new experimental treatment larger than the observed change in a wait-list, minimal treatment control condition?
- How does the observed effect compare with other active treatments for the same target?
- Can the claimed rationale or mechanisms actually be tested empirically?
- If the answer to the previous question is "yes," has the claimed rationale actually been subjected to empirical tests and what has been learned?

As is rather apparent from this summary of results, all four treatments consistently lead to significant clinical improvements, with effect sizes being in the moderate to large range. When compared to active treatment controls, none sticks out as clearly superior. Where treatment mechanism could be readily tested, the findings support these claims, except for EMDR where the most innovative component does not appear to add unique benefit.

◇ CONCLUSION

The arguments and data presented earlier served a dual purpose. On the one hand, it was shown which clinical trial methodologies are needed to reveal overall benefits, and how, with additional effort, specificity of effects can be determined once clinical researchers are trying to bring a new psychotherapy on board. As such, this chapter provided a magnifying glass and a tool kit for creating critical readers of a rich literature on therapy outcome that ranges from flaky to serious science. There are often vigorous debates about whether or not a given treatment works, and this is usually the result of limited knowledge on how to properly interpret the results from clinical trials. Many people do not appreciate how difficult it is to show specificity of effects and to properly document the mechanism of action in psychotherapy. We have tried to provide the reader with tools to make his own decisions. The publication of consensus committee reports that judge the available levels of evidence for a particular psychotherapy (see chapters 3 and 13) greatly helped in clarifying this tricky issue. The underlying logic for this system of levels of evidence was applied here in this chapter to four intriguing and innovative interventions. On the plus side, there is good evidence that all these methods can benefit our patients to some degree (as shown in effect size calculations for pre-post effects). However, that alone does not tell *why improvements happen*, nor does it tell what the best available treatment options are. We posit that our patients have a right to get the best available treatment rather than the one to which the therapist has the strongest theoretical allegiance.

It is difficult and laborious to test claims for specificity of methods. In that respect, neither EMDR, nor hypnosis, nor MM lives up to claims of specific effects. To some degree that is attributable to the inherent nontestability of assumptions (e.g., there is no clear operational definition of hypnotic trance). In other instances, specificity was testable, and for the case of ACT research findings are beginning to provide support for method specificity.

An important point to consider after reviewing therapy outcome research is the implication for therapy training. On the whole, there is a wide variety of methods to choose from for generating nonspecific improvements and distress reduction in our patients; these tend to produce moderately sized benefits. Such nonspecific benefits can likely be generated by individuals with varying degrees of training in psychotherapy, provided that they have certain caring, sensitive personality predispositions, and some basic therapy training (see also chapter 10). However, maximizing the utility of psychological treatments that possess generic and specific qualities and teaching therapists how to properly tailor treatments to individual needs require considerably more training (Woody, Detweiler-Bedell, Teachman, & O'Hearn, 2003) in order to achieve some of the especially large effects shown in the literature.

◇ ONGOING CONSIDERATIONS

In chapter 10 we tried to stress how difficult it is to define psychotherapy, and we alerted the reader that we need to be ready to deal with this challenge. Unfortunately, this also means that the door is at least partly open for self-proclaimed healers and for unsubstantiated claims about what a new miracle treatment can achieve. Charismatic healers are unfortunately often successful in defrauding needy individuals with over-reaching promises. Clinical psychologists need to be perpetually on the alert for such claims and challenge these individuals to provide the evidence.

◇ KEY TERMS LEARNED

Acceptance	Hypnotizability
Awakening	Induction
Commitment	Preparation
Deepening	Purpose

◇ THINKING QUESTIONS

1. How does hypnosis work?

2. Is acceptance and commitment therapy essentially a cognitive therapy, or is it distinct?

3. Why is EMDR so popular when there is so little support for its specificity of effect?

4. How much and what kind of evidence is needed before a new treatment approach should be declared effective?

◇ REFERENCES

APA Presidential Task Force on Evidence-Based Practice. (2005). *Draft policy statement on evidence-based practice in psychology.* Retrieved from http://forms.apa.org/members/ebp/

Barlow, D. H. (2004). Psychological treatments. *American Psychologist, 59,* 869–878.

Barnier, A. J., Wright, J., & McConkey, K. M. (2004). Posthypnotic amnesia for autobiographical episodes: Influencing memory accessibility and quality. *International Journal of Clinical and Experimental Hypnosis, 52,* 260–279.

Beck, J. S. (1995). *Cognitive therapy: Basics and beyond.* New York: Guilford Press.

Bishop, S. R., Lau, M., Shapiro, S., Carlson, L. E., Anderson, N. D., Carmody, J., et al. (2004). Mindfulness: A proposed operational definition. *Clinical Psychology: Science and Practice, 11,* 230–241.

Carlson, L. E., Speca, M., Faris, P., & Patel, K. D. (2007). One year pre-post intervention follow-up of psychological, immune, endocrine and blood pressure outcomes of mindfulness-based stress reduction (MBSR) in breast and prostate cancer outpatients. *Brain Behavior and Immunity, 21*(8), 1038–1049.

Carlson, L. E., Speca, M., Patel, K. D., & Goodey, E. (2003). Mindfulness-based stress reduction in relation to quality of life, mood, symptoms of stress, and immune parameters in breast and prostate cancer outpatients. *Psychosomatic Medicine, 65,* 571–581.

Davidson, R. J., Kabat-Zinn, J., Schumacher, J., Rosenkranz, M., Muller, D., Santorelli, S. F., et al. (2003). Alterations in brain and immune function produced by mindfulness meditation. *Psychosomatic Medicine, 65*, 564–570.

Davidson, P. R., & Parker, K. C. H. (2001). Eye movement desensitization and reprocessing (EMDR): A meta-analysis. *Journal of Consulting and Clinical Psychology, 69*, 305–316.

Ellis, A. (1962). *Reason and emotion in psychotherapy*. New York: Lyle Stuart.

EMDR Institute homepage: http://www.emdr.com/briefdes.htm

Gladwell, M. (2000). *The tipping point*. New York: Little, Brown.

Grossmann, P., Niemann, L., Schmidt, S., & Walach, H. (2004). Mindfulness-based stress reduction and health benefits: A meta-analysis. *Journal of Psychosomatic Research, 57*(1), 35–43.

Hadley, J., & Staudacher, C. (1985). *Hypnosis for change. A practical manual of proven hypnotic techniques*. Oakland, CA: New Harbinger Press.

Hayes, S. C., Luoma, J. B., Bond, F. W., Masua, A., & Lillis, J. (2006). Acceptance and commitment therapy: Model, processes and outcomes. *Behaviour Research and Therapy, 44*, 1–25.

Hayes, S. C., & Smith, S. (2005). *Get out of your mind and into your life. The new acceptance and commitment therapy*. Oakland, CA: New Harbinger Press.

Hayes, S. C., Strosahl, K., Wilson, K. G., Bissett, R. T., Pistorello, J., Toarmino, D., et al. (2004). Measuring experiential avoidance: A preliminary test of a working model. *The Psychological Record, 54*, 553–578.

Hilgard, E. R. (1965). *Hypnotic susceptibility*. New York: Harcourt, Brace & World.

Hilgard, E. R., Crawford, H. J., & Wert, A. (1979). The Stanford hypnotic arm levitation induction and test (SHALIT): A six-minute hypnotic induction and measurement scale. *International Journal of Clinical and Experimental Hypnosis, 27*, 111–124. http://www.informaworld.com/smpp/462288414-42084546/title~content=t713657963~db=all~tab=issueslist~branches=27-v27

Horvath, A., & Luborsky, L. (1993). The role of the therapeutic alliance in psychotherapy. *Journal of Consulting and Clinical Psychology, 61*, 561–573.

Hunsley, J. (2003). Cost-effectiveness and cost offset considerations in psychological service provision. *Canadian Psychology, 44*, 61–73.

Huynh, T. V. (retrieved Aug 2010). Introduction to mindfulness meditation. Retrieved from http://vipassanahawaii.org/?q=node/19.

Jensen, M., & Patterson, D. R. (2006). Hypnotic treatment of chronic pain. *Journal of Behavioral Medicine, 29*, 95–124.

Kabat-Zinn, J. (1990). *Full catastrophe living: Using the wisdom of your body to face stress, pain and illness*. New York: Delacorte.

Kazdin, A. E., & Bass, D. (1989). Power to detect differences between alternative treatments in comparative psychotherapy outcome research. *Journal of Consulting and Clinical Psychology, 57*, 138–147.

Kirsch, I. (1996). Hypnotic enhancement of cognitive-behavioral weight loss treatments—Another re-analysis. *Journal of Consulting and Clinical Psychology, 64*, 517–519.

Kristeller, J. L. (2007). Mindfulness meditation. In P. Lehrer & R. L. Woolfolk (Eds.), *Principles and practice of stress management* (3rd ed.) (pp. 393–427). New York: Guilford Press.

Linden, W. (1981). Exposure treatment for focal phobias. *Archives of General Psychiatry, 38,* 769–775.

Linden, W. (1990). *Autogenic training: A practitioner's guide.* New York: Guilford Press.

Linden, W. (1993). Meditation. In D. Vaitl & F. Petermann (Eds.), *Handbuch der Entspannungsverfahren. Psychologie Verlags Union* (pp. 207–216). Weinheim, Germany: Muenchen.

Linden, W. (2005). *Stress management: From basic research to better practice.* Thousand Oaks, CA: Sage.

Lipsey, M. W., & Wilson, D. B. (1993). The efficacy of psychological, educational, and behavioral treatment. *American Psychologist, 48,* 1181–1209.

Lohr, J. M., Lilienfeld, S. O., Tolin, D. F., & Herbert, J. D. (1999). Eye movement desensitization and reprocessing (EMDR): An analysis of specific and non-specific treatment factors. *Journal of Anxiety Research, 13,* 185–207.

Montgomery, G. H., DuHamel, K. N., & Redd, W. H. (2000). A meta-analysis of hypnotically induced analgesia: How effective is hypnosis? *International Journal of Clinical and Experimental Hypnosis, 48,* 138–153.

Ospina, M. B., Bond, T. K., Karkhaneh, M., Tjosvold, L., Vandermeer, B., Liang, Y., et al. (2007). Meditation practices for health: State of the research. Evidence Report/Technology Assessment No. 155 (Prepared by the University of Alberta Evidence-Based Practice Center under Contract No. 290-02-0023.) AHRQ Publication No. 07-E010. Rockville, MD: Agency for Healthcare Research and Quality.

Rubin, A. (2003). Unanswered questions about the empirical support for EMDR in the treatment of PTSD: A review of research. *Traumatology, 9,* 4–10.

Rubin, A. (2004). Fallacies and deflections in debating the empirical support for EMDR in the treatment of PTSD: A reply to Maxfield, Lake, & Hyer. *Traumatology, 10,* 91–105.

Shapiro, F. (2001). *Eye movement desensitization and reprocessing: Basic principles, protocols and procedures* (2nd ed.). New York: Guilford Press.

Shapiro, F. (2002). *EMDR as an integrative psychotherapy approach: Experts of diverse orientations explore the paradigm prism.* Washington, DC: American Psychological Association Books.

Sharpley, C. F., Montgomery, I. M., & Scalzo, L. A. (1996). Comparative efficacy of EMDR and alternative procedures in reducing the vividness of mental images. *Scandinavian Journal of Behaviour Therapy, 25,* 37–42.

Spanos, N. P. (1991). Hypnosis, hypnotizability, and hypnotherapy. In C. R. Snyder & D. R. Forsyth (Eds.), *Handbook of social and clinical psychology* (pp. 644–663). Elmsford, NY: Pergamon.

Speca, M., Carlson, L. E., Goodey, E., & Angen, M. (2000). A randomized, wait-list controlled clinical trial: The effect of a mindfulness meditation-based stress reduction program on mood and symptoms of stress in cancer outpatients. *Psychosomatic Medicine, 62,* 613–622.

Taylor, S., Thordarson, D. S., Maxfield, L., Fedoroff, I., Lovell, K., & Ogrodniczuk, J. (2003). Comparative efficacy, speed, and adverse effects of three PTSD treatments: Exposure therapy, EMDR, and relaxation training. *Journal of Consulting and Clinical Psychology, 71,* 330–338.

Weitzenhoffer, A., & Hilgard, E. (1962). *Stanford Hypnotic Susceptibility Scale, Form C.* Palo Alto, CA: Consulting Psychologists Press.

Woody, S. R., Detweiler-Bedell, J., Teachman, B. A., & O'Hearn, T. (2003). *Treatment planning in psychotherapy: Taking the guesswork out of clinical care.* New York: Guilford Press.

A useful resource: 315 hypnosis scripts for different applications: http://www.hypnosisdownloads.com/

CHAPTER FIFTEEN

CHILD CLINICAL PSYCHOLOGY

This chapter differs from the previous chapters in that it focuses on a particular population and age group. Up to this point we left the reader with the impression that the ethical problems and diagnostic and treatment procedures that clinical psychologists have in their arsenal are universally applicable. True, much of what has been said applies to people of different cultures, genders, and age groups; however, there would be many missed chances and ignored responsibilities if we did not acknowledge that different age groups have different needs. In fact, when it comes to licensure as a psychologist, practitioners are usually asked to spell out which age groups they have confidence in working with, and this is documented via academic transcripts and practical experiences with particular populations. Many clinical training programs have specifically designated child clinical program tracks, and there are numerous journals and books that focus on the uniqueness of clinical psychology applications for children. The organization of this chapter will largely mimic (on a smaller scale, of course) the basic organization of this book in that we will talk about some unique ethical challenges (in particular issues around consent), then discuss how normal child development and child psychopathology can be seen on a continuum, discuss unique features of the assessment of children, and survey how interventions can be offered effectively and how well they work.

What are the important issues that make work with children so different? Here is a list of unique features of child clinical psychology that also imply particular responsibilities as well as great opportunities to make a difference:

1. Even more problems go untreated in children than in adults, possibly because children have less of a sense of what is abnormal and what is normal. Also, they have limited verbal ability to express problems and have few means of their own to access the health care system. Furthermore, many assessment methods are based on ratings or observations made by parents who may be quite biased in judging their own child.

2. Unresolved childhood problems powerfully mediate adaptation to the demands of adult life regarding ability to learn, job performance, and ability to maintain

relationships and to carry responsibility (Middlebrooks & Audage, 2008). Attending to childhood problems early is critical to minimize long-term damage.

3. Children are legally minors and depend on their parents for emotional, instrumental, and economic support. Under the law they can make few decisions on their own. Parental permission is required to treat or assess younger children.

4. Unique to child clinical work is the need to differentiate normal development from delayed development and from actual pathology. Given that children change rapidly and are a product of their environment, it is not obvious what is an incipient pathology, a passing phase, or a consequence of changes in the immediate environment.

5. Some problems are predominant in childhood but can be outgrown (like shyness and egocentrism); others last a lifetime (e.g., severe attention deficit/hyperactivity disorder). Many child problems or developmental abnormalities call for a lifelong perspective because they are not open to outright cure; these problems include autism, Asperger's syndrome, fetal alcohol spectrum disorders, and mental retardation. Some exceptional children will grow into exceptional adults with needs different from that of the general population.

For example, the population prevalence of fetal alcohol syndrome (FAS) is estimated at 0.3% to 1% (Burd, Selfridge, Klug, & Juelson, 2003), but in a juvenile prison sample the rate was reported as 23% (Fast, Conry, & Loock, 1999). Nevertheless, inability to cure certain problems should not justify lethargy or ignorance. Early recognition and support can make a difference to the affected families' quality of life. For example, there is no known curative treatment for FAS, but the likelihood of a child with FAS ending up in prison is greatly reduced when this child can be raised in a stable, nurturing environment and is diagnosed early (Burd et al., 2003).

Photo by Henri Dupond

◇ DEVELOPMENTAL STAGES AND CHILDHOOD PSYCHOPATHOLOGY

In adults certain behaviors like extreme dependence on others, rash decision-making, or stubbornness are considered maladjustment and are often a criterion for a diagnosable mental disorder. In children, on the other hand, such behaviors are quite normal for certain developmental stages and are usually outgrown. A good delineation of what is age-specific normal achievement, what are potential problems of behavior arising within a specific developmental phase, and what are actually clinical disorders (typically arising within a particular age range) can be found in Table 15.1.

In terms of formal diagnostic classifications, it is noteworthy that versions I and II of the *Diagnostic and Statistical Manual* saw childhood pathology as being a junior version of adult psychopathology, whereas the more recent versions, III and IV (*DSM-IV-TR*, American Psychiatric

TABLE 15.1 An Overview of Development Stages and Examples of Associated Problems (adapted from Mash & Wolfe, 1999)

APPROXIMATE AGE	NORMAL ACHIEVEMENTS	AREAS OF COMMON BEHAVIOR PROBLEMS	CLINICAL DISORDERS
0–2	Eating, sleeping, attachment	Stubbornness, temper, toileting	Mental retardation, feeding disorders, autistic disorder
2–5	Language, toileting, self-care skills, self-control, peer relationships	Arguing, demanding attention, disobedience, fears, overactivity, resisting bedtime	Speech and language disorders; problems stemming from child abuse and neglect; some anxiety disorders, such as phobias
6–11	Academic skills and rules, rule-governed games, simple responsibilities	Arguing, inability to concentrate, self-consciousness, showing off	ADHD, learning disorders, school phobia, conduct problems
12–20	Relations with opposite sex, personal identity, separation from family, increased responsibilities	Arguing, bragging	Anorexia, bulimia, delinquency, suicide attempts, drug and alcohol abuse, schizophrenia, depression

Source: Mash, E. J., & Wolfe, D. A. (1999). *Abnormal child psychology*. Pacific Grove, CA: Brooks/Cole/Wadsworth, p. 33.

"You're spending the best years of your life doing a job
that you hate so you can buy stuff you don't need to
support a lifestyle you don't enjoy. Sounds crazy to me!"

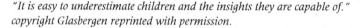

"It is easy to underestimate children and the insights they are capable of."
copyright Glasbergen reprinted with permission.

Association, 2000), have explicitly defined some disorders as being childhood disorders (see Table 15.2) for a listing. Note that, in the next few years, we can anticipate the release of the *DSM-V*, which may also include changes of diagnostic categories for childhood problems.

In addition to the disorders described in Table 15.2, that are particularly applicable to children and adolescents, relevant additional diagnoses for adolescents include substance-related problems, schizophrenia, mood disorders, anxiety disorders, and eating disorders. For these latter disorders it makes particularly good sense to see continuity from adolescence to adulthood.

If some disorders are indeed unique to childhood, then there also needs to be a distinct body of research directed at understanding the underlying pathology, and we need research on effective interventions. An urgent question to deal with is whether or not treatments that work with adults will work with children with the same (or similar) problems, whether the components of a successful therapy are similar, and whether or not it is necessary to modify treatments to make them suitable for children. Alternatively, some treatments have to be developed that are particularly suitable for children and for childhood disorders. How researchers have responded to these challenges will be discussed in this chapter.

◇ ETHICAL CHALLENGES

The fact that children are minors under the law in all Western nations creates considerable complications and calls for caution and extra alertness for those clinical psychologists working with minors. It is critical that practicing child clinical psychologists are fully aware of the legal situation regarding **age of consent** in their particular country, state, or province. While there are many commonalities, important differences across jurisdictions are also found. For example, in the home province of the authors of this textbook, British

TABLE 15.2   Diagnostic Categories Found in the *DSM-IV* That Are Particularly Relevant for Children and Adolescents

Mental retardation (which is coded as an Axis II disorder); it allows for five levels of diagnosis depending on how well the individual functions

Learning disorders

Reading disorder

Mathematics disorder

Disorder of written expression

Elimination disorders

Encopresis

Enuresis

Pervasive developmental disorders

Autistic disorder

Asperger's disorder

Attention deficit and disruptive behavior disorders

Attention deficit and hyperactivity disorder (subdivided into three types)

Conduct disorder (subdivided into two types)

Oppositional defiant disorder

Feeding and eating disorders of infancy or early childhood

Pica

Rumination disorder

Feeding disorder of infancy or early childhood

Other disorders of infancy childhood or adolescence

Separation anxiety disorder

Selective mutism

Reactive attachment disorder (subdivided into two types)

Columbia, Canada, children below the age of 12 years cannot be held legally responsible for their actions. At the age of 19 years, they become full adults who can vote, purchase liquor, and sign legally binding major contracts. The period between the ages of 12 and 19 years is a gray zone where young people can make their own decisions only on certain issues. This is an example for the legal situation in one specific jurisdiction, but the same issues principally apply in all Western nations, and clinical psychologists have to familiarize themselves with the laws affecting children in every new jurisdiction that they move to.

Especially tricky are the grey zones for decision-making. For example, first-year university students are most likely 18 years old and could normally not independently participate in research studies given that they are legally under age. Nevertheless, there is a widely accepted understanding, backed by local ethics committees, that they can indeed participate in a research study that uses example questionnaires to assess their personality traits, without having to seek permission from their parents. Also, young people in this age group have a right to seek medical care as needed, and the law assures them confidentiality for such issues as a 16-year-old seeking a prescription for contraceptives from her physician. Although this may not be popular with some parents, the law is quite clear about it and the physician's hands are bound. Similarly, a 15-year-old with normal intelligence can legally seek the help of a psychologist without formal parental consent.

Parents have legal responsibilities for children and don't require their **consent** for assessments or treatment, but it is a good practice and recommended by professional bodies in psychology to inform the child as much as possible and seek an agreement from the child to participate. This process differentiates the notions of consent, which is legally binding, from **assent**, which is not required but a good practice that increases the probability of good collaboration and the formation of an effective alliance in treatment when working with young children.

Given that children have few, if any, liberties in making their own choices about the parental home and are deeply embedded in family and school systems, this also means that particular problems and stressors can arise from this environment. These problems need not necessarily be seen as a problem of the individual child but may require a systems perspective (see also chapter 11, on systems treatment). For example, it makes little sense to provide intensive therapy for an anxious, school-avoidant child who is repeatedly bullied by another child in school. There's a good chance that the bully does the same thing to other children, and a good approach may be to involve teachers and the school principal. The parents of the bully may also need to be called on to solve the underlying problem. Also, an eating disorder like anorexia nervosa is most likely to begin during adolescence and cannot be understood or treated outside the context of the family in which the youth lives. Furthermore, without a full understanding of the child's home, community, and school context, it is easy to misinterpret the source and implication of other problem behaviors. Children who are defiant and act out in school may do so because of problems at home, or they may be showing early signs of sociopathic tendencies (or, of course, both). All of this is meant to stress that effective interventions for children require a broad systems perspective and often call for the collaboration of the many people who already play important roles in a child's life.

◇ IMPACT OF DEVELOPMENT ON ASSESSMENT

Developmental stage greatly affects the suitability of typical psychological assessment tools for children. Some tools are uniquely developed for children, and other tools originally developed for adults may still be suitable for older children and adolescents who have developed high levels of language and reading skills as well as abstract thinking abilities. Note that intelligence tests set an age threshold for the distinction of child versus adult IQ tests at age 16 (see chapter 7), given the knowledge that IQ is quite stable after age 16. For interviews, the practicing psychologist can relatively easily adjust the level of questioning to the age-specific readiness of the child. Many of the frequently used psychological testing

Pain Faces Scale

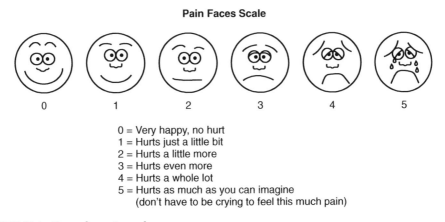

0	1	2	3	4	5

0 = Very happy, no hurt
1 = Hurts just a little bit
2 = Hurts a little more
3 = Hurts even more
4 = Hurts a whole lot
5 = Hurts as much as you can imagine
    (don't have to be crying to feel this much pain)

FIGURE 15.1 Faces for pain scale

procedures involve standardized scales with rating systems, like 1 to 10 Likert-type scales, where an individual may be asked to state "how often do you think about suicide?" or "how likely are you to use little white lies to avoid hurting other people?" The use of such scales implies that the user is able to translate self-perception, intention, or sensation into meaningful numbers. While this can be a challenge for adults, it is even more difficult for children and worse for those who have not yet received any training in mathematics. An interesting and useful approach to handling such a challenge has been to develop tools that do not require quantification via numbers. A good example is that of an assessment tool for acute pain that use faces to express different degrees of distress. Research has shown that children can quite readily handle assessments using the pain faces scale, whereas they might not be able to make good use of a Likert-type scale with 1 to 9 ratings (Wong, Hockenberry-Eaton, Wilson, Windelstein, & Schwartz, 2001). For illustrative purposes, a copy of the faces for pain scale is provided in Figure 15.1.

Typically from the age of five forward, children spend much of their time in school, and school performance is carefully tracked as children progress toward high school and possibly toward postgraduate training. Throughout this time period, it is critical for educators to follow children's performance and identify children who are falling behind, with the hope of intervening with remedial programs before such children develop a pervasive, ingrained self-perception of failure. Hence, psychologists working in schools need to have carefully validated tools that allow age-appropriate cognitive assessments and identification of specific weaknesses.

In chapter 7, the reader was introduced to the most frequently used intelligence tests and has already learned that the beginning of intelligence testing was very much tied to and originated in the need for assessing cognitive abilities of children. When it comes to the assessment of cognitive abilities of children via the most frequently used tools, namely, the **Wechsler Intelligence Scale for Children** and the **Stanford-Binet Scale**, we already noted in chapter 8 that the same test is suitable for individuals from 16 years old to old age. Below this age, however, assessment tools are carefully chosen and normed to be suitable for very particular age groups, given that children's knowledge and skill grow at an amazingly rapid rate. The same popular intelligence tests for adults also usually have corresponding versions for younger age groups. The Wechsler Intelligence Scale for Children (WISC-R, Wechsler, 2003) is appropriate for 6- to 16-year-olds but also has age-adjusted norms for each single year within that range. Test takers who are 12 years old, for example, start at a higher level of difficulty than 6-year-olds to avoid wasting time answering many test items that almost 100% of 12-year-old test takers would know correctly. Here are examples of typical beginning questions (slightly modified by the authors from the original to avoid violating test security) for a vocabulary information test for a 6-year-old relative to that for a 12-year-old.

6 years: "What is a hammer?" or "What is a ship?"

12 years: "What is a telephone?" or "What is a law?"

The WISC-R (and also the one for adults, of course) is based on the premise that individuals have learned some math and reading, which means that children less than 6 years old are inherently incapable of using this test. For the age range of 4 to 6 years, tests have been developed that are much less reliant on school learning. Best known for use in this age group is the Wechsler Preschool and Primary Scale of Intelligence (WPPSI; Wechsler, 2004) that primarily differs from the WISC-R (Wechsler, 2003) by having fewer tests where verbal skills are needed and fewer that have timed performance pressures. Also, of the 14 available subtests, only 4 are used for the youngest respondents given that their attention span is much shorter. As the respondent gets older, more subscales are used for IQ determinations, for example, those 4 to 7 years old are evaluated on six subtests.

Any attempt to determine an overall IQ score, or even more specific subabilities of cognitive function, for children less than 3 years old is seriously handicapped by the limited and uneven acquisition of language and cognitive processing ability of young children. Furthermore, children in this age group simply don't have the patience to sit for 1 hour or more and focus on lengthy tests. For them, cognitive function is typically judged by comparing the child's developmental stage to that of age-matched norms, without actually expecting the child to sit down and respond to formal test questions.

Most tests of personality and psychopathology suitable for adults are not appropriate for children, and there is no version of the MMPI for first graders. However, once children approach high school level, personality tests and structured interviews start to be usable. In the meantime, child behavior is usually evaluated by parents and teachers using interviews or structured observation.

One particularly innovative example of adapting structured interviews to children is the Dominic Interview (Valla, Bergeron, & Smolla, 2000). Here children are shown drawings of other children and are asked to indicate whether or not they would behave similarly in the situations covered by the drawings. Test-retest reliability and criterion validity have been established, but construct validity is unclear.

Projective tests like the House-Tree-Person test (already described in chapter 7) are also used by clinicians. Given that psychometrics for a projective test like the House-Tree-Person test are extremely difficult to establish even for adults, there is even less information available for children, and the clinician can really form only a subjective interpretation of the information inherent in the House-Tree-Person test. This could be elaborated on by actually engaging the child's inner conversation about who the people are in a drawing or what particular drawings mean to the child.

◇ INTERVENTION

The targets of interventions for children are frequently subdivided into three categories:

1. Developmental disorders. An example is learning disabilities.
2. **Externalizing problem behaviors** (behaviors that may be disruptive to others and/or risky). An externalizing problem would be an attention deficit and hyperactivity disorder (ADHD) or oppositional defiant behavior.
3. **Internalizing problems**. Examples of internalizing problems are elective mutism, depression, and shyness.

There has been extensive research on the suitability of various treatment approaches for children's problems. Before reviewing evidence on what works for whom and for what problem, the most frequently used treatments for children are described next.

Behavior Therapy

Behavior therapy has been described in considerable detail in chapter 12. One noted distinct advantage of behavior therapy is that many conditioning and modeling techniques do not require language abilities on part of the person whose behavior is to change, and behavior therapy applications have no age limits. As you may recall, in chapter 10 we gave an example of a behavior therapy application for a child less than 1-year old. It would be redundant to rediscuss the elementary principles and techniques of behavior therapy here.

Play Therapy

Below 12 year old, children lack capacity for abstract thinking which, in turn, largely prevents them from benefiting from insight-oriented or talking therapies (Weisz, 2001). As described earlier, behavior therapy principles can be applied to people of all ages, whereas therapeutic use of play is unique for children and has not been discussed previously in this book. Play is in and of itself considered essential to a child's healthy development and can be used as a tool of communication and catharsis with children. Through play, children may spontaneously act out feelings, thoughts, and experiences that they cannot otherwise express due to their lack of vocabulary or inhibition. Play and toys become vehicles for indirect communication, and this indirect nature of play therapy is less threatening to children than direct interaction with a therapist. Although play therapy has been described as early as half a century ago (Bratton, Ray, Rhine, & Jones, 2005, for a review), its efficacy was in dispute until two recent meta-analyses. Leblanc and Ritchie (2001) reported an average treatment effect of 0.66 standard deviations. The duration of therapy was related to treatment outcomes, with maximum effects occurring after approximately 30 treatment sessions. Very similar results were reported by Bratton et al. (2005). In a review of 93 clinical trials an average pre-post effect size of $d = .80$ was observed, and play therapy appeared to be as effective as nonplay therapies in treating children experiencing emotional difficulties. Recommendations for future researchers focused on explaining therapeutic or participant characteristics that are related to treatment effectiveness. Bratton and her colleagues also noticed particularly positive outcome for forms of play therapy with a humanistic orientation and equally noted that involving parents in play therapy further magnified effects. Neither the child's gender, nor the presenting issue, nor age was associated with differential outcomes.

Systems Therapy

Given the high degree to which children are embedded in their families and immediate social environment, it often makes little sense to pathologize and blame the child for his own misfortune. Systems therapy is particularly suitable for child clinical work even if it is not easily suited for clinical trials of its effectiveness (see also chapters 11 and 13). As we presented in chapter 11, in the section on systems therapy, frequently a child or adolescent is identified as the patient. Nevertheless, careful assessment by a trained systems therapist often reveals that the child lives in a family with problematic dynamics such that the whole family context and the interactions of all family members with one another need to be considered if positive, lasting change is to come about (Minuchin, 1974). Therefore, a systems approach to treating children is particularly suitable in that the therapist has a chance to study direct interactions between the child, her siblings, and parents. When equipped with observational data of the family's dynamics, the therapist can suggest changes that remove the child from the role of black sheep and target ways how the entire family can benefit from the intervention. A great advantage arising from this approach is that nobody is singled out for blame and therefore likely to become defensive, thus blocking the process of change. Even if a child clinical psychologist is not particularly well-trained in systems therapy, attention to immediate environment factors that may maintain problem behaviors is critical, and successful behavioral change requires that others in the child's social network support these changes.

Overview of Treatment Outcome

Fortunately there is an abundance of research on the effectiveness of psychological therapies for children and adolescents, at least for some treatment approaches. Most often tested are cognitive-behavioral approaches because (a) they are eminently testable given their focus on observable behavior, and (b) there is striking evidence that talking therapies for children simply don't work. Weisz (2001) reported that talking therapies had an effect size of $d = 0.0$.

On the whole, the observed effect sizes are very similar to those noted for the treatments of adults (see also chapter 13) and typically qualify for the designation of large effect. Also, there are many interventions that meet the criteria for evidence-based treatment using the same evaluation criteria that were used to derive this designation for adult treatments, described in chapter 13. Table 15.3 provides a listing of treatment applications that are shown to be efficacious, and Figure 15.2 provides an overview of observed effect sizes from meta-analyses (Brestan & Eyberg, 1999; McQuaid & Nassau, 1999; Ollendick & King, 2004).

TABLE 15.3 Empirically Validated Treatments for Specific Applications

APPLICATION	TREATMENT
Recurrent pain	CBT
Medical procedure–related pain	CBT
Chemotherapy side effects	Imagery, distraction, relaxation
ADHD	Behavioral parent training
	Behavior modification in the classroom
Anxiety	CBT
Depression	CBT
Phobias	Behavior therapy
Conduct disorder	Cognitive therapy
	Parent training
	Problem-solving skills
	Behavior modification
	Stress inoculation/anger control training (also CBT in nature)

Redrawn from Hunsley and Lee (2005).

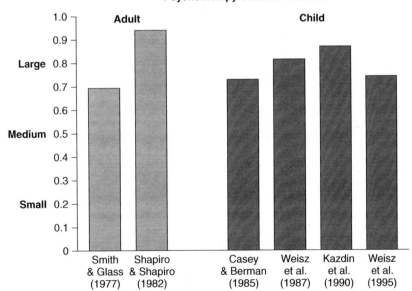

FIGURE 15.2 Meta-analytic comparisons of outcomes for child/adolescent treatments

◇ THE EXAMPLE OF ATTENTION DEFICIT AND HYPERACTIVITY DISORDER

We have intentionally chosen to discuss this one treatment area in more detail because it demonstrates not only how different health professionals can work with each other but also how their work is colored by societal trends. ADHD is a pervasive problem that appears to be growing in importance (Rey & Sawyer, 2003); it invites illustration of how psychological and pharmacological agents can be used together for effective interventions and makes for great discussion material, given the extensive controversy over the diagnosis itself and the ensuing treatment process. Drug prescription patterns are usually well informed and guided by science, but they are also shaped by societal trends.

One clue backing the argument of trendiness is apparent in different frequencies with which psychostimulant drugs are being used to treat ADHD in different environments. Approximately 5% of children in the United States and Canada are currently treated with psychostimulants; the corresponding figures are 2% in Australia and 0.03% in Britain (Rey & Sawyer, 2003). These numbers partly reflect differences in population prevalence of diagnosed impulse control disorders, which are highest in North America (approx. 6–7%) and notably lower in Europe (approx 1–2%), but especially the prescription rates in Britain do not correspond with the population prevalence of impulse control disorders in other countries. Therefore, the numbers speak at least in part to a certain culture of diagnostic and treatment patterns. The question then is whether North Americans are overprescribing or whether Britons are underprescribing. Depending on one's stance, suitable references can be found in support of either argument. Undertreatment appears to be the problem in a study by Jensen and colleagues (1998), who reported that among children meeting ADHD diagnostic criteria, only 12.5% had received treatment with psychostimulants within the last year. On the other hand, the prescription rate is roughly 5% in all children in Canada and the United States. Some critics urge parents of ADHD children to be more patient, to learn behavioral management techniques, and to stay away from medication unless absolutely necessary. Others advocate first of all for a proper diagnosis (nobody disagrees on this one) but also support prompt writing of prescriptions for psychostimulants. While there does not appear to be any major disagreement that psychostimulants are effective in helping children with ADHD to focus and improve their academic performance, the reservations are partly justified by the fact that severe ADHD treated with drugs would need to extend to drug treatment for the entire childhood and adolescence in order to be effective (Barkley et al., 1990). There is documentation that adults with ADHD can also benefit from such stimulants, and this might mean that individuals might spend their entire lives on medication. This prospect carries very limited appeal to many who are worried about side effects, cost, and the associated self-image as being dependent on the drug to function. The bottom line is that the ultimate extent of psychostimulant use is a blend of scientifically based recommendations and social trends, and the inherent controversy is not going to go away quickly. Still, the predominant opinion among experts is that in severe cases of ADHD a combination of parent and child training and psychostimulant drug use is best, whereas for mild cases parents might want to begin with behavioral training programs (Barkley, 1998; Johnston, Hommersen, & Seipp, 2008).

Another treatment option that can be brought into play is that of biofeedback, which again is both promising and controversial. The use of electroencephalogram (EEG) biofeedback for ADHD (Monastra et al., 2005) is based on studies showing that about 90% of ADHD children have an underaroused frontal lobe—the region of the brain that is involved in sustained attention, focus, concentration, and problem solving (Monastra et al., 2005). Biofeedback of electrical brain activity (via display of the EEG teaches self-regulation of brain activity. How well does it work? In a treatment study, 51 young patients received biofeedback and medication. In the added biofeedback condition they played a video game that continued only when they exercised the portion of their brain that is deficient in the ability to focus and stay attentive. The other group received only a stimulant medication. Researchers could show a reduced need for medication and better maintenance of self-control than with drug treatment (Monastra, Monastra, & George, 2002). Forty percent were able to discontinue their medication. The bad news is that the training is lengthy and expensive; in the Monastra study, for example, the children received weekly treatment for one full year. Notwithstanding these positive findings, medication is still considered a necessity for most children with ADHD although biofeedback may be a useful adjunct or possibly alternative treatment for those who don't tolerate stimulant medication.

◇ CONCLUSION

This chapter was designed to show how, on the one hand, clinical work with children is similar to that with older individuals but also how it is a very distinct field requiring additional training, awareness, and distinct skills:

- There are unique ethical constraints in working with children.
- Psychopathological labels are more difficult to justify because the child's identity is very much tied up with that of its family and immediate environment, which may have been disturbed and pathological even before the child arrived.
- Ignoring early signs of trouble in children can become very expensive in that the sequelae are harder and more expensive to treat, whereas early recognition and handling could be cost-effective prevention.
- Assessment tools need to be developed and validated for specific age groups.
- Some treatments are suitable only for children, others not at all, and some may work equally well with adults and children.

◇ ONGOING CONSIDERATIONS

We encourage all readers to remain alert to the fact that research findings based on samples of adults may not generalize to children (and vice versa). Many tests will continue to require development or adaptation for child test takers. There is a growing literature recognizing the importance of following childhood problems into adulthood. Oftentimes, health care systems are designed as distinctly for children or adults, whereas continuity of understanding and care is vital for effective care. Also, a thorough understanding of how childhood problems (especially when left untreated) will affect an entire life can inform us how important and cost effective early intervention or primary prevention can be.

◇ KEY TERMS LEARNED

Age of consent

Assent

Attention deficit and disruptive behavior disorders

Consent

Elimination problem behaviors

Externalizing disorders

Feeding and eating disorders of infancy or early childhood

Internalizing problems

Learning disorders

Mental retardation

Pervasive developmental disorders

Stanford-Binet Scale

Wechsler Intelligence Scale for Children

◇ THINKING QUESTIONS

1. Are children just small adults?

2. Which problems that occupy much of a child clinical psychologist's work have no adult equivalent?

3. Why is social environment so much stronger as an influence on children (affecting etiology of disorders as well as treatment options) than it is for adults?

4. Is there an adult equivalent to play therapy?

◇ REFERENCES

American Psychiatric Association. (2000). *Diagnostic and statistical manual of mental disorders* (4th ed., revised). Washington, DC: Author.

Barkley, R. A. (1998). *Attention deficit-hyperactivity disorder*. New York: Guilford.

Barkley, R. A., Fischer, M., Edelbrock, C. S., & Smallish, M. A. (1990). The adolescent outcome of hyperactive children diagnosed by research criteria: I: An 8-year prospective follow-up study. *Journal of the American Academy of Child and Adolescent Psychiatry, 29,* 546–587.

Bratton, S. C., Ray, D., Rhine, T., & Jones, L. (2005). The efficacy of play therapy with children: A meta-analytic review of treatment outcomes. *Professional Psychology: Research and Practice, 36,* 376–390.

Brestan, E. V., & Eyberg, S. M. (1999). Effective psychosocial treatment of conduct disordered children and adolescents: 29 years, 82 studies, and 5257 kids. *Journal of Clinical Child Psychology, 27,* 180–189.

Burd, L., Selfridge, R. S., Klug, M. G., & Juelson, T. (2003). Fetal alcohol syndrome in the Canadian corrections system. *Journal of Fetal Alcohol Syndrome International, 1,* 14.

Fast, D., Conry, J., & Loock, C. A. (1999). Identifying fetal alcohol syndrome among youth in the criminal justice system. *Journal of Behavioral and Developmental Pediatrics, 20,* 370–372.

Hunsley, J., & Lee, C. M. (2005). *Introduction to clinical psychology: An evidence-based approach.* Mississauga, Ont.: John Wiley & Sons.

Jensen, P. S., Kettle, L., Roper, M. T., Sloan, M. T., Dulcan, M. K., Hoven, C., et al. (1998). Are stimulants overprescribed? Treatment of ADHD in four U.S. communities. *Journal of the American Academy of Child and Adolescent Psychiatry, 38,* 797–804.

Johnston, C., Hommersen, P., & Seipp, C. (2008). Acceptability of behavioral and pharmacological treatments for attention-deficit/hyperactivity disorder: Relations to child and parent characteristics. *Behavior Therapy, 39,* 22–32.

Leblanc, M., & Ritchie, M. (2001). A meta-analysis of play therapy outcomes. *Counselling Psychology Quarterly, 14,* 149–163. http://www.informaworld.com/smpp/title~content=t713411705~db=all~tab=issueslist~branches=14-v14

Middlebrooks, J. S., & Audage, N. C. (2008). *The effects of childhood stress on health across the lifespan.* Atlanta, GA: Centers for Disease Control and Prevention, National Center for Injury Prevention and Control.

Minuchin, S. (1974). *Families and family therapy.* London, England: Tavistock Publications.

Monastra, V. J., Lynn, S., Linden, M., Lubar, J. F., Gruzelier, J., & LaVaque, T. J. (2005). Electroencephalographic biofeedback in the treatment of attention-deficit/hyperactivity disorder. *Applied Psychophysiology and Biofeedback, 30,* 95–114.

Monastra, V. J., Monastra, D., & George, S. (2002). The effects of stimulant therapy, EEG biofeedback, and parenting style on the primary symptoms on attention deficit/hyperactivity disorder. *Applied Psychophysiology and Biofeedback, 27,* 231–249.

McQuaid, L., & Nassau, J. H. (1999). Empirically-supported treatments of disease related symptoms in pediatric psychology: Asthma, diabetes, and cancer. *Journal of Pediatric Psychology, 24,* 305–328.

Ollendick, T. H., & King, N. J. (2004). Empirically supported treatments in children and adolescents: Advances toward evidence-based practice. In P. M. Barnett & T. H. Ollendick (Eds.), *Interventions that work with children and adolescents: Prevention and treatment* (pp. 3–25). New York: Wiley & Sons.

Rey, J. M., & Sawyer, M. G. (2003). Are psychostimulant drugs being used appropriately to treat child and adolescent disorders? *The British Journal of Psychiatry, 182,* 284–286.

Valla, J. -P, Bergeron, L., & Smolla, N. (2000). The Dominic-R: A pictorial for 6–11 year-old children. *Journal of the American Academy of Child and Adolescent Psychiatry, 39,* 85–93.

Wechsler, D. (2004). *Wechsler preschool and primary scale of intelligence* (3rd ed.). *Canadian manual.* Toronto, Ont.: The Psychological Corporation.

Wechsler, V. (2003). *Wechsler intelligence scale for children* (4th ed.). San Antonio, TX: The Psychological Corporation.

Weisz, J. R. (2001). *Two traditions in psychotherapy with children and adolescents: The state of the evidence.* Paper presented at the 2nd Annual Niagara Conference on Evidence-based treatments for childhood and adolescent mental health problems. Niagara-on-the-Lake. http://www.who.int/whr/2001/en/whr01_ch2_en.pdf

Wong, D. L., Hockenberry-Eaton, M., Wilson, D., Windelstein, M. L., & Schwartz, P. (2001). *Wong's essentials of pediatric nursing* (6th ed.). St. Louis, MO: Mosby Inc.

CHAPTER SIXTEEN

FORENSIC PSYCHOLOGY

CHAPTER OBJECTIVE

This chapter deals with the areas of practice where clinical psychology interconnects with the law. There are many facets of the law and legal processes where clinical psychologists can be of immense use. Clinical psychologists are not the only psychologists interested in this topic. Biopsychologists, for example, may take an interest in explaining violence, or social psychologists could contribute to the study of jury selection processes. Therefore, this chapter describes the field at large and attempts to clarify where and how clinical psychologists can fit into and contribute to this domain.

◇ WHAT IS FORENSIC PSYCHOLOGY?

Although many have seen forensic psychology as a specialization within clinical psychology (Craig, 2005), the general area, also referred to as **psychology and the law**, **law and psychology**, or **legal psychology** (Wrightsman & Porter, 2006), encompasses many different domains of psychology including clinical, social, developmental, cognitive, and community psychology (American Psychology-Law Society). Moreover, there are other professional groups that provide clinical services in forensic contexts, including social workers, psychiatric nurses, and psychiatrists.

Even though there is some disagreement on the specific definitions of this area, forensic psychology can be defined, generally, as the intersection or the confluence of psychology and legal issues, and it involves the application of knowledge and principles derived from the field of psychology to issues pertaining to law and legal processes. Clinical psychology has played and continues to play a major role in many of the tasks that forensic psychologists engage in, although the area of forensic psychology has broadened considerably and draws on many other areas within the field. Although we will be describing the domain of forensic psychology, we will try to focus much of our discussion to issues that pertain to the research and applied work of clinical psychologists.

According to Bartol and Bartol (2006), forensic psychology ". . . is both (1) the research endeavor that examines aspects of human behavior directly related to the legal process (e.g., research on eyewitness memory and testimony, jury decision making, and criminal behavior) and (2) the professional practice of psychology within or in consultation with a legal system that encompasses both criminal and civil law and the numerous areas they intersect" (pp. 3–4). According to these authors, there are two general views of forensic psychology. The first, known as the broad view, encompasses a large number of potential activities that fall under titles such as police psychology, expert witness and testimony, assessment and treatment of offenders, child custody evaluations, research and theory building, and development of interventions and prevention programs for at-risk individuals. The second view, known as the narrow view, involves a definition of forensic psychology that entails simply the application of clinical practice within the legal system that would involve assessment, treatment, and consultation.

In this chapter, we will describe forensic psychology as a branch (and one of the newest branches) of applied psychology that involves many of the roles and activities that clinical psychologists engage in. For broader discussions of the field of forensic psychology, the student is directed to several excellent resources such as Wrightsman and Porter (2006) and Weiner and Hess (2006).

It was not until the 1970s that the field of forensic psychology truly emerged when, according to Bartol and Bartol (2006), there was an explosion of research and writing on all aspects of forensic psychology. There were numerous professional journals dedicated solely to the area of forensic psychology emerging in North America and the United Kingdom, and training facilities specializing in forensic psychology began to spring up as did the certification of practitioners (Ogloff, Tomkins, & Bersoff, 1996). The field of forensic psychology began to flourish during this time, not only in the United States but also in the United Kingdom, Europe, Australia, and Canada (see Blackburn, 1996). Forensic psychology is seen as an exciting and growing area of applied psychology, with expanding roles for the psychologists who practice and research in this area.

Although the field truly found its legs in the 1970s, psychology's involvement in legal activities actually has a lengthy history (see Bartol & Bartol, 2006, for a historical review). For example, Alfred Binet (1905), in France, was one of the first to look at psychological issues in legal testimony and actually suggested the creation of a "science psycho-judiciere." Moreover, two researchers in Germany, William Stern and Franz von Liszt, in 1901 became quite active in the research of court-related testimony (Stern, 1939). It was in Germany, as early as 1904, where research into the development of psychological instruments to detect lying in legal situations began. Early on, the involvement of psychologists in legal processes was not extensive but was more common in Europe than in North America, and the involvement extended not only to providing testimony regarding eyewitness accounts and credibility of witnesses' statements, but also to serving as expert witnesses in criminal cases. In North America, Hugo Munsterberg, a particularly colorful, if not a particularly scientifically minded German psychologist, was instrumental in the development of forensic psychology. He was director of the Psychology Laboratory at Harvard University in the early 1900s and argued vehemently for the inclusion of psychological knowledge and psychologists within legal proceedings and processes (e.g., Munsterberg, 1908). He was generally disliked (in fact, he has been described by Benjamin [2003, p. 734] as "one of the most despised individuals in America") within the legal and psychological communities for his brash and despicable demeanor as well as his rather cavalier attitude toward scientific rigor. Despite all this, however, his work provided an impetus for the inclusion of psychological knowledge into the legal arena, and he is considered by some to be the founder of forensic psychology (Bartol & Bartol, 1999; Wrightsman & Porter, 2006). Thus, just as the field of clinical psychology developed, with its beginnings in testing and research, so too did its connection with the law and legal matters evolve and develop.

◇ FORENSIC PSYCHOLOGY TODAY

Nowadays, forensic psychology is viewed as a vibrant and respected domain of psychology. For example, the American Psychological Association, in 2001, established forensic psychology as a specialty area within psychology. Training opportunities in forensic psychology have been on the increase in North America, Europe, the United Kingdom, and Australia, including the master's doctoral, postdoctoral, and continuing education levels (Ogloff et al., 1996), and various kinds of programs are also available. For example, there are a large number of clinical psychology programs that offer forensic streams or forensic training as a part of the program. As well, there are programs that have been specifically developed to train forensic psychologists, such as the psychology and law program at Simon Fraser University in Canada, the combined law psychology PhD degrees offered at the University of Nebraska-Lincoln, and various investigative psychology programs in the United Kingdom. Moreover, there are several organizations that provide certification and grant credentials for forensic psychologists and the development of specific **specialty guidelines** (i.e., guidelines that determine specific credentials and training necessary), and **practice standards** (i.e., specific guidelines for tasks and practice areas) are being called for and developed (Otto & Heilbrun, 2002). Finally, research within forensic psychology is also an indication of the vibrancy of the area, with thousands of books and over 25 peer-review journals dedicated solely to forensic psychology (Bartol & Bartol, 2006).

◇ THE CLINICAL FORENSIC PSYCHOLOGIST

The clinical psychologist who has been trained to practice in forensic contexts is often known as a **clinical forensic psychologist**. This is a psychologist who is involved in the delivery of assessment, treatment, or consultation services, is often involved in the training or supervision of students or other professionals, and may be involved in research-related pursuits. Clinical forensic psychologists typically have a PhD in applied areas of psychology, such as clinical psychology, and have specific training in the delivery of forensic services as well as the law and legal processes. In addition, they require a license to practice (although if the work is solely research, then licensure is not necessarily needed) and often have certification to practice forensic psychology. They can work in a variety of settings including prisons, secure forensic units in hospitals, various court-related agencies, private practice, or universities. They have been trained, as described earlier, in traditional clinical skills and research as well as in delivery of forensic services, and will be licensed with specialization in clinical forensic work.

There are numerous domains wherein clinical forensic psychologists play a variety of roles and engage in applied or research-related work. Several authors in the field have delineated these domains, which are presented here:

Police Psychology

Although the involvement of psychologists within law enforcement is relatively new, psychologist involvement in police-related activities has been increasing, and now the role of psychologists has a significant impact on law enforcement services (Scrivner, 2006). The roles of clinical forensic psychologists in this context can vary from evaluating, identifying, and selecting appropriate applicants for law enforcement work, providing psychological services for police officers and families (stress management, treatment of trauma, critical incident stress debriefings, and also treatment for other psychological problems such as depression, substance abuse, post-traumatic stress disorder (PTSD), family problems, and so on), conducting fitness-for-duty evaluations on police officers, and aiding in police work such as providing training to police officers for dealing with the mentally ill.

Some police departments use psychologists in activities such as **criminal profiling** to aid in investigations. Criminal profiling involves examining evidence obtained from a crime scene, witnesses, or victim in order to construct an accurate description of the criminal. Although television shows and Hollywood movies may give the impression that this is a common activity of clinical forensic psychologists, in reality this is often not true (Wrightman & Porter, 2006). In fact, criminal profiling is most likely done not by psychologists but by law enforcement officers, and the training for this activity is not done in forensic psychology programs; thus, there are many who do not consider profiling as within the purview of forensic psychology.

Crime and Delinquency

This domain is concerned with the research on criminal behavior and how it develops, is maintained, is evoked, and is changed (Bartol, 2002). For example, there has been a great deal of research on the development and manifestation of **psychopathy**—a personality style that is characterized by lack of emotions such as guilt, empathy, or remorse; impulsivity; and consistent violation of societal norms, rules, and laws. Psychopathy is very common among prison populations (e.g., between 15% and 25% in comparison to about 1% in the general population) and accounts for significant amounts of crime, violence, and social distress (Hare, 1996). In terms of more clinically related activities, work in this area could involve the development of strategies and tools to identify the at-risk or potentially dangerous individuals and designing and evaluating the effectiveness of intervention strategies to deal with violent or criminal behavior.

Victimology

Very often the effects of criminal behavior on victims or witnesses can be distressing in some cases and absolutely devastating in others. Psychologists can play an important role in assessing and treating persons who are victims. For example, although the necessity of treatment of individuals who are victims of major crimes (such as rape, assault, and so forth) is obvious, individuals who are victims of harassment, discrimination, and negligence are also often in need of and can benefit greatly from appropriate treatment. Individuals who have been victimized in such a manner can also experience profound distress and symptomatology not just from the initial experience but also from the bureaucracy of attempting to secure clinical services and compensation, work absences, or inefficiency (Campbell, 2008).

Correctional Psychology

Psychologists working in this area typically deal with individuals in correctional facilities. The major goals of psychologists working in correctional psychology activities include developing and providing treatments that focus on the rehabilitation and reintegration of inmates as well as provision of treatment for a variety of psychological disorders and problems. Not infrequently, individual and group psychotherapy as well as specific treatment modules, such as stress management, social skills training, or crisis intervention, are offered. In addition, psychologists are often involved in testing and assessment, and they provide information and opinions regarding security levels of prisoners, information pertaining to parole, and suitability for various programs. As well, research efforts can be directed at the effectiveness of various interventions, at the effects of imprisonment on behavior, or on special populations such as sex offenders, psychopaths, or juveniles.

Psychology and Law or Legal Psychology

This is a broad domain that encompasses a variety of activities that involve the relationship between psychology and the court (Bartol & Bartol, 2006)—research, consultation, and assessment as well as some of the activities described earlier. Psychologists working within this domain might be involved in such activities as research on or acting as expert witnesses in a particular area of expertise, aiding in jury selection, assessing competency (i.e., does the person have the capacity to understand the nature of the proceedings), criminal responsibility (i.e., was or is the person not responsible for crime because he had had a mental disorder at the time of the crime), or appropriate child custody and access, conflict resolution, or child abuse allegations. This domain can, of course, involve all types of activities by clinical forensic psychologists in terms of knowing and/or contributing to relevant research domains in order to establish one's expertise, assessment techniques and strategies, and knowledge of interventions.

This list is not meant to be exhaustive, but rather to illustrate, in a broad fashion, areas that clinical forensic psychologists work in.

◊ DIFFERENCES BETWEEN TRADITIONAL CLINICAL PSYCHOLOGY AND FORENSIC PSYCHOLOGY PRACTICE

Differences between the usual clinical psychology practice and forensic practice have been detailed by Craig (2005) and are useful in order to illustrate that to practice clinical psychology within a forensic context, there are often different assumptions and specific tasks that need to be done differently. These are detailed here:

1. The clinical psychologist's goal is to help his patient, whereas the forensic psychologist's goal is to help the court. This is a fundamental difference in terms of who the psychologist is working for, and this affects the nature of the interactions between the psychologist and the person being interviewed, observed, or tested as well as the specific responsibilities of the psychologist. Although the psychologist may be working with only one individual, depending on whether the individual is the psychologist's client or the court is the psychologist's client, the behaviors and responsibilities of the psychologist will differ.

2. Clinical psychologists often see patients for multiple sessions over a period of time that is often extended and not highly structured. Forensic clinical psychologists, however, may see a client for only a couple of sessions in a highly structured and evaluative context. Additionally, whereas the clinical psychologist in a nonforensic setting may deal with broad issues pertaining to the clinical question, in a forensic setting the psychologist is likely to focus narrowly on issues germane to the court.

3. Confidentiality is the mainstay of the clinical psychologist and allows freedom of exploration of issues that are extremely personal. In the forensic context this is not so, and, in fact, patients or clients are informed that information gleaned from an evaluation can be used against them in court. Whereas maintaining confidentiality is strictly adhered to in clinical contexts, it is not a requirement in the forensic context. In fact, it is incumbent upon the forensic psychologist to inform the person being interviewed or tested that his responses can and likely will be discussed openly in proceedings and that findings can be used against the person.

4. Clinical psychologists normally need to know about laws and how they pertain to their practice, whereas forensic psychologists need to know about laws and legal processes as they pertain to their practice and to particular cases the psychologists are involved with. Moreover, the forensic psychologist needs to understand the various rules and regulations regarding testimony as well as proceedings that bear directly on the data and evidence that may be presented.

5. Consequences of the involvement of the psychologist differ in the two contexts. In the traditional clinical situation, the outcome of the work of the psychologist will hopefully improve the person's functioning, alleviate suffering or turmoil, and deter future relapses or recurrences of problems, in effect, increase the person's quality of life. In the forensic situation, the outcome of the work of the psychologist can influence whether the person loses or gains custody of a child, is denied or

awarded compensation (sometimes worth millions of dollars), or is found guilty of crimes with attendant punishment.

6. With respect to treatment, the traditional clinical context involves a psychologist who is supportive, caring, and empathic (i.e., Rogerian) in dealing with patients and assumes that the patient wants help and will be forthcoming in discussing the personal issues. The patient, in this case, is normally seeing the psychologist voluntarily and wants help from the psychologist. In forensic psychology contexts, the psychologist takes more of an investigative stance and may act neutral and detached and, importantly, make the assumption that malingering or biased responding or withholding and misrepresenting the truth can be a distinct possibility in the client's responses. Moreover, the client is normally not seeing the psychologist voluntarily and may be quite resistant to the psychologist's investigation.

7. In research in psychology, there are strict guidelines with respect to determining probability, and psychologists use empirical methods and results to trust in findings and to determine whether particular findings are close to being established truths. This differs from trust in findings or evidence in forensic settings. According to Wrightsman and Porter (2006), whereas psychologists are trained to answer questions about behavior by gathering reliable data and obtaining valid and replicable findings, lawyers, judges, and other legal professionals tend to use past experience, intuition, and other sources of information that have been shown, often, to be less than accurate. Thus, assumptions regarding trust in research findings or evidence can differ depending on the context.

It should be obvious from the earlier list that the clinical psychologist who is doing forensic-related work must think and act differently in different contexts and when performing forensic duties. Many of the parameters, assumptions, and practices in clinical work shift and change when clinical issues are conducted in a forensic context.

◇ TASKS OF THE CLINICAL FORENSIC PSYCHOLOGIST

In this section, we will discuss some of the issues relevant to the major tasks and foci of clinical psychologists and how they are conducted and performed in a forensic context. We will focus on the types of tasks we have discussed in the text thus far, including assessment, treatment, consultation, and research.

Assessment

As described in previous chapters, assessment is a frequent and specific task engaged in by clinical psychologists and is commonly a major part of the clinical forensic psychologist's work. Assessment in a clinical context normally involves a clinical interview, behavioral observation, objective and projective personality testing, intellectual and/or neuropsychological testing, and, at times, collateral information from others. In forensic settings these sorts of activities are also engaged in with acknowledgement that, as described earlier, some of the assumptions, responsibilities, and tasks of the clinical psychologist differ when conducting forensic assessments. Also, perhaps more important, the kinds of questions being addressed are fundamentally different. In clinical contexts, questions revolve around issues of diagnosis, formulation, and treatment recommendations, whereas in forensic assessments questions revolve around attempting to answer or provide information on specific legal questions such as whether the person is competent to be involved in court proceedings.

Later in this chapter we delineate several areas within forensic psychology in which assessments, broadly defined, are used. These are not exhaustive but should be considered illustrative of the kinds of work conducted. Although many of the tests and assessment methods described already in this text (e.g., intellectual and neuropsychological assessment instruments) are used in forensic contexts, they are, of course, used for different purposes. The results of these tests and methods must not only demonstrate reliability and validity but must also withstand scrutiny in court and during cross-examination by defense or prosecution lawyers.

With respect to testing in forensic assessments, it is useful to describe a typology developed by Grisso (1986), who delineates three broad kinds of instruments used in forensic psychology:

Forensic Assessment Tools

The types of instruments in this category of forensic tests were developed to assess specific legal standards or legal constructs rather than personality or psychological variables more generally. For example, tests that assess competence or a person's ability to manage his own finances would fall in this category. These tests can be quite challenging to develop because definitions of validity and reliability are tied in with the definitions of the legal constructs, and these definitions may vary quite markedly from jurisdiction to jurisdiction. Moreover, it is challenging to conduct the necessary research to firmly establish the validity and reliability of the measures, and there tends to be less than ideal empirical support for many of the instruments (Ogloff, 2002).

For example, measures such as the Competency Screening Test (Lippsitt, Lelos, & McGarry, 1971) or the MacArthur Competence Assessment Tool–Criminal Adjudication (MacCAT–CA; Hoge et al., 1997) and the MacArthur Competence Assessment Tool–Clinical Research (MacCAT–CR; Applebaum & Grisso, 2001) assess a person's ability to understand proceedings, knowingly make a plea, and to proceed to trial.

Forensically Relevant Assessment Tools

These instruments do not focus on legal standards or clear legally defined constructs but assess clinical issues that are pertinent to the evaluation of a person in a legal situation, for example, the assessment of malingering (i.e., voluntarily and consciously presenting a negative picture of one's functioning or lying to appear as if one has a disorder or disability), other response sets, or personality variables germane to criminal activity. For example, the Structured Interview of Reported Symptoms (Rogers, 2010) is a measure specifically designed to assess malingering.

One very commonly used forensically relevant instrument is the **Hare Psychopathy Checklist** (PCL; Hare, 2003) that is used in the assessment of psychopathy. This measure is an extremely popular instrument among psychologists; in fact, according to Otto and Heilbrun (2002) this instrument is administered between 60,000 and 80,000 times per year in North America. This measure is a 20-item scale that is administered as an interview and assesses the behavioral, affective, and interpersonal characteristics of the pathological personality style. It also includes a review of written records and documents. Although developed initially as a research instrument (Hare, 1991), the PCL has become one of the most commonly used measures of psychopathy in forensic assessments.

Clinical Measures and Assessment Techniques

These are instruments that have been developed for clinical purposes (i.e., assessment, diagnosis, formulation, treatment issues) that can also be used in forensic assessments. Often these instruments are very well developed and have demonstrated the levels of appropriate reliability and validity but do not directly assess legally defined constructs or standards.

There are a variety of objective intellectual and personality tests that are utilized very commonly in various forensic assessments. One of them is the MMPI/MMPI-2. Although the MMPI/MMPI-2 can be used generally as measure of personality and psychopathology, various subscales have been developed within the MMPI-2 specifically for forensic issues. For example, Megargee (1977) developed an MMPI-based classification system of offenders and in 1994 (Megargee, 1994, 1997) evaluated and revised the classification system scoring for the MMPI-2 for males and females. The system was based on different elevations of various clinical scales. Megargee's classification system includes 10 types of offender MMPI-2 profiles. For example, high elevations on clinical scales 4, 8, and 9 constituted the "Foxtrot" profile that was characterized by individuals who were streetwise, tough, cynical, and antisocial with extensive criminal histories. As well, the MCMI-III (Millon & Davis, 1996) is also used in forensic settings as an alternative to the MMPI-2 and can be used to detect malingering although it is not used as frequently as the MMPI-2, nor is it uniformly considered to be appropriate for forensic purposes (Dyer & McCann, 2000). In addition to the objective tests, projective tests are also used in forensic assessments (Craig, 2005). For example, the Rorschach Inkblot Test, with scoring based on the Comprehensive System meets the appropriate criteria for test usage in American courts and has been used for several decades in court proceedings (Craig, 2005) as well as in personality testing of police recruits. The Thematic Apperception Test has also been used in U.S. courts, custody evaluations, and matters related to sexual abuse (Craig, 2005).

◇TREATMENT

In contrast to forensic assessment, psychological treatment–related issues germane to forensic psychology have received less attention, although clinical psychologists engage in and evaluate treatments to some degree. Some psychologists have argued that, for the most part, treatment is treatment irrespective of whether there are forensic issues or not; whereas others suggest that although generally specific forensic treatment emphasis within forensic psychology has been minimal, some domains of forensic psychology, for example, corrections psychology, have been focused upon. We will briefly discuss three such areas.

Treatment of Perpetrators of Crime

Typically, treatment of the perpetrators of crime occurs in correctional settings, although this can occur in a variety of other outpatient or private practice settings. The primary goal of treatment of offenders is to reduce criminal behavior. According to Gendreau, Goggin, French, and Smith (2006) such treatment programs:

1. Target characteristics, such as personality characteristics, appraisals of events, and life circumstances that are seen to have a close connection to the criminal behavior of interest.

2. Use psychotherapy techniques to help develop appropriate attitudes, skills, and behaviors.

3. Use recidivism (i.e., reoffending) as the final criterion of success.

The most common treatment approaches used in correctional settings include person-centered, cognitive, behavioral, and group therapies, although mainly individual treatment modalities seem to be focused on by psychologists. These forms of treatment can be useful for general groups of individuals and for a variety of difficulties. There are also treatments that have been developed for specific populations within many correctional settings. Although treatments for specific groups may be seen by some as an appropriate strategy for treating large numbers of patients, developing a generic treatment based on criminal behavior (e.g., treatment for sex offenders) results in extremely heterogeneous groups that are not necessarily amenable to effective treatment (Otto & Heilbrun, 2002).

   As an example of treatment of special populations within corrections, violent offender treatment programs are not uncommon in prisons and are seen as very important, likely due to the seriousness of the behavior and because reduction or elimination of these behaviors is an important goal for those incarcerated. Most violent offender treatment approaches have two foci: the first of which is to help patients develop self-regulatory behaviors for aggression and anger and the second, addressing cognitive deficits or irrational beliefs in order to change thinking. Thus a focus on both emotional and cognitive processes is thought to be appropriate in reducing violent behavior (Weiner & Hess, 2006).

   Another example of a fairly common treatment for special populations involves the treatment of psychopathy, which has utilized treatments from a variety of perspectives (Hare, 1996). In a strong statement regarding the treatment of psychopathy, Hare (1996, p. 41) made the following observation: "There is no known treatment for psychopathy . . . the justice system and public routinely, are fooled into believing otherwise." Not only is there a lack of evidence that treatment of psychopathy is effective. Incredibly, there is an indication that treatment of psychopathy can result in *increases* in violent and criminal behavior because the treatment may actually help the psychopath develop better ways to manipulate and control others (Rice, Harris, & Cormier, 1992). Recently, on the other hand, there is some suggestion that if the treatment of psychopaths is intensive, frequent, and long term, it may show some promise (Bonta, 2002).

Does treatment of offenders, in general, work? This has been an incredibly contentious issue. Over the past 100 years there has been what is called the **rehabilitation ideal**, which generally refers to the idea that prisons and correctional settings should not focus so much on punishment but rather on rehabilitation of offenders in order to eradicate reoffending. Early accounts suggested that there was no evidence that rehabilitation or good treatment outcome was achieved in any way (e.g., Martinson, 1974). On the other hand, Gendreau et al. (2006) have summarized some recent meta-analyses of studies of correctional treatment programs and, generally, concluded that the most effective types of treatment are highly structured, cognitive-based interventions that are delivered outside of a correctional facility.

Treatment of Victims of Crime

The emotional and psychological impact on victims of criminal acts can be massive. This can derive both from the criminal act itself and from the processes that the victim goes through in terms of reporting and accessing services following the victimization (Campbell, 2008). Victims of crimes can experience a variety of psychological problems and disorders, for example, depression, substance abuse, dissociative states, and so on (Kilpatrick et al., 2003), although the majority of attention with respect to treatment in forensic situations tends to be on PTSD and related symptoms (Amstadter, McCart, & Ruggerio, 2007).

Although there is sometimes a perception that more clinical and research attention is paid to the perpetrators of crime than the victims, there is work that has been done with respect to treatment of those on the receiving end of criminal or illegal activities. For example, although the development of treatment for disorders such as acute stress disorder or PTSD arose from work with military personnel, it is clear that there is much work being done on trauma associated with crime. For example, treatments for sexual abuse (these have actually been around for a long time) among children and adults and for the victims of sex crimes, assaults, and all manner of trauma have been developed over the past several decades (Rizzo, Stover, Berkowitz, & Kagan, 2008).

With respect to trauma, there is some evidence of the effectiveness of both early interventions and interventions that commence after PTSD has developed. For example, Foa, Zoellner, and Feeny (2006) found that a brief CBT-based treatment was effective in reducing trauma-related symptoms. The treatment itself included psychoeducational components to teach individuals about symptoms, the process of responses to trauma, relaxation training, cognitive restructuring, and exposure-based elements. These elements have also been shown to be effective in other approaches to treatment of PTSD, although, most typically, the techniques are used in combination in treatment programs. As an example, exposure-based treatments expose the patients to fear-related cues either in their imagination or in actual situations, and patients work with the therapist to reduce fear responses and symptoms in a supportive and trusted therapeutic relationship (Amstadter et al., 2007). Similarly, other behavioral or cognitive-behavioral approaches are used, including anxiety management (i.e., focusing on reducing anxiety through breathing and relaxation techniques) and cognitive therapy that involves focusing on irrational beliefs, unrealistic appraisals, and responses to cues.

Further to the point regarding early interventions, Campbell (2008) has called attention to an important role that psychologists can take in what is termed **psychological first aid**, which involves working with patients in the midst of or in the immediate aftermath of disasters, violence, or other traumas (e.g., Ruzek, Bryner, Jacobs, Layne, & Vernberg, 2007). According to Campbell, there are eight goals and actions in providing psychological first aid to distraught survivors:

1. Initiate contact in a nonintrusive, compassionate manner
2. Enhance safety and provide comfort
3. Calm and help to orient the person
4. Identify immediate needs and concerns
5. Offer practical help to address immediate needs and concerns
6. Reduce distress by connecting to primary-support persons
7. Provide individuals with information about stress reactions and coping
8. Link individuals to services and information

Although Vernberg et al. (2008) indicate that research on the effectiveness of this approach needs to be demonstrated, there is some promise that the approach may be an effective and useful intervention.

Treatment of Workers in the Field

Although treatment can be directed at perpetrators of illegal activity and victims of those perpetrators, there is another group that is focused on by forensic clinical psychologists. These are the police officers, correction officers, or other frontline workers who are dealing with various levels of the legal system. For example, many agencies connected with police forces or corrections will have periodic critical incident stress debriefings following traumatic events such as motor vehicle accidents, shootings, murders, or any event that is viewed as potentially traumatic to the workers. The debriefings can be viewed as early interventions designed to help with coping with traumatic events in order to mitigate the development of PTSD or symptoms of PTSD. In these debriefings, participants are asked, usually in a group format that is supportive and confidential, to describe their role in the traumatic event and to express their thoughts and feelings in relation to the event. In addition, there is usually a psychoeducational component that teaches participants about stress reactions, symptoms and signs of PTSD, and coping strategies (e.g., talking to others about the event) as well as professional resources. Debriefings following distressing events have become very common in a variety of organizations. The evidence as to the efficacy or utility of the debriefings is controversial (e.g., Devilly, Gist, & Cotton, 2006), although these sorts of interventions remain a part of policing and corrections.

In addition to debriefings that are used to protect workers and others from trauma-related symptoms, some do develop PTSD and other disorders as a result of their work. In these situations, clinical forensic psychologists will provide treatment in much the same way as described earlier. Moreover, because policing in particular has stressful events that are uncommon in other workplaces, a variety of disorders and psychological problems can develop. Clinical forensic psychologists can play a major role in the treatment of such difficulties.

◇ CONSULTATION AND OPINIONS

Several areas of consultation have been touched on to some degree in other sections of this chapter. Clinical forensic psychologists may be called upon or asked for consultations or opinions by lawyers or judges or other legal agencies. These consultations are requested either due to the unique expertise that psychologists have generally as psychologists, or idiosyncratically, depending on the particular interests and expertise of the individual psychologist. Clinical forensic psychologists may testify in courts or other legal situations and/or provide written reports or briefs. In both cases, the psychologist needs to defend her opinions and conclusions. Sometimes when psychologists are acting as consultants they may meet with individuals, couples, or families depending on the question to be addressed, and at other times they will be asked to provide opinions on research or other domains of interest to the courts. Although the possibilities are seemingly endless with respect to potential consultations, some fairly common areas that psychologists provide consultation include expert testimony (whereby the psychologist will be deemed an expert in a particular domain and be asked to provide information and/or express an opinion to the court on that particular domain; see Table 16.1), assessment of competence (e.g., as described in the forensic assessment section), child custody and/or access issues (i.e., opinions, often based on the assessment of parents and children), or jury selection for trials. As well, although not common, a psychologist may provide consultation on criminal profiling, which involves crime scene investigations and attempting to determine a profile or detailed description of the perpetrator.

◇ LIE DETECTION

As an example, one domain that clinical forensic psychologists have been involved in as consultants (and researchers) deals with lie detection. We will describe lie detection in detail because it is both fascinating and highly controversial, given that the consequences of imperfect measurement and subsequent errors in decision-making can be grave because of the fact that this method may affect judicial proceedings.

The application we are referring to is the use of **polygraphs** (a multichannel recording device for physiological functions) for the **detection of lying**. The ability to detect liars using the polygraph has not only attracted police forces but holds enough interest to make it into Hollywood movies. However, a big problem with such popular knowledge is that

TABLE 16.1   Examples of Topics for Psychologists as Expert Witnesses

1. Criminal responsibility	What is the relationship between the defendant's mental condition at the time of the alleged offence and the defendant's responsibility for the crime with which the defendant is charged?
2. Competence to stand trial	Does the defendant have an adequate understanding of the legal proceedings?
3. Sentencing	What are the prospects for the defendant's rehabilitation? What deterrent effects do certain sentences have? What is the defendant's level of risk for reoffence?
4. Eyewitness identification	What are the factors that affect the accuracy of eyewitness identification? How is witness confidence related to witness accuracy?
5. Trial procedure	What effects are associated with variations in pretrial and/or trial procedures?
6. Civil commitment	Does a mentally ill person present an immediate danger or threat of danger to self or others that require treatment no less restrictive than hospitalization?
7. Psychological damages in civil cases	What psychological consequences has an individual suffered as a result of tortuous conduct? How treatable are these consequences? To what extent are the psychological problems attributable to a pre-existing condition? Is post-traumatic symptomatology related to another person's behavior?
8. Trademark litigation	Is a certain product name or trademark confusingly similar to a competitor's? Are advising claims likely to mislead consumers?
9. Class action suits	What psychological evidence is there that effective treatment is being denied or that certain testing procedures are discriminatory against minorities in the schools or in the workplace?
10. Guardianship and conservatorship	Does an individual possess the necessary mental ability to make decisions concerning living conditions, financial matters, health, etc.?
11. Child custody	What psychological factors will affect the best interests of the child whose custody is in dispute? What consequences are these factors likely to have on the family?
12. Adoption and termination of parental rights	What psychological factors will affect the child whose parents' disabilities may render them unable to raise and care for the child?
13. Professional malpractice	Did defendant's professional conduct fail to meet the standard of care owed to plaintiffs?
14. Social issues in litigation	What are the effects of pornography, violence, spouse abuse, etc., on the behavior of a defendant who claims that his misconduct was caused by one of these influences?

Reproduced from Nietzel (1986). With permission of Pearson Education, Inc.

people tend to think of the machine itself as a lie detector. It is not. It can, however, provide information that can be used by a trained assessor to assess responses.

The scientific background to this type of lie detection is the core observation that it takes less effort to tell the truth than to lie. When we lie we need to go through a complex cognitive process because we are trying to figure out how to deliver the lie in a credible fashion, while appearing relaxed. Also, the lie needs to be coherently embedded in surrounding truthful information that is public knowledge or easily tested. This is quite a challenge, and the fear of getting caught accentuates the overall effort and apprehensiveness. In contrast, the truth is inherently consistent with other surrounding truths, and concerns about a particular delivery are unwarranted. The additional required effort associated with lying triggers sympathetic nervous system activation, and as the validation research for lie detection has shown, lying is typically associated with more arousal than truth-telling (Iacono, 2000).

The methodology for lie detection is to collect physiological change data from multiple channels with the typical choices being respiration, continuous blood pressure, electrodermal activity, and/or heart rate. Alone, and even better in combination, these variables reflect changes in the sympathetic nervous system. To maximize reliability and validity, more than one index of sympathetic function is chosen, and many questions are asked. A full polygraph examination can last hours. The questions themselves are usually subdivided into three categories, and many questions are asked within each of three types of categories of questions:

1. The first category is that of the **neutral control question**, which consists of questions about factual knowledge that the test taker knows is public knowledge and is not in any way problematic. For example, both the polygrapher and the test taker know where the test taker lives, how old he is, what day of the week it is, and where he is. Raising any of these questions is not likely to trigger much arousal because it makes no sense to even attempt to lie. Having these types of control questions allows the assessor/polygrapher to establish what is considered to be a resting baseline for the level of arousal that is typical while an individual speaks about neutral material. However, the very moment that questions and topics become personalized and potentially threatening, they trigger an arousal response, and additional control questions are needed to learn about a typical response.

2. Given that lie detection tests may be given in the context of criminal investigations or other kinds of probing with legal consequences, the outcome of the test is also linked to potentially aversive consequences for a test taker. An individual who is accused of having stolen something from her employer is probably very anxious about the entire test situation because the individual may well lose her job if the lie detection test makes her look guilty. Therefore, the entire test situation is considered emotionally charged even for people who are innocent but who cannot be certain that the test will actually reveal them to be innocent. In order to prevent false positives, meaning innocent people looking guilty, a second type of control question is used, namely, a **high affect control question**. For the scenario of an employee being suspected of theft from a company, the key issue is one of honesty

and whether or not the person has a habit of stealing. Therefore, good high affect control questions are like the following: "Have you ever stolen something in your life?" or "Have you at some point in the past lied to get out of trouble?" Both questions are clearly unrelated to the crime at hand, and even if the answer to both was "yes," that does not mean that the employee has stolen something this time. However, the employee does know (because these questions have intentionally high face validity) that the question is trying to provoke affect and tap into the individual's general honesty. It is therefore expected that during question and answer of this type, the test taker will be more aroused and show more of a physiological response than doing the neutral test situation.

3. Now, in order to round out this approach, a third type of question is asked, namely, ones that are truly focused on the current situation—the crime under investigation. Together, comparison of the responses to these three types of questions is called the **control question technique**. For the relevant question, the employee may be asked: "Have you, during the last month, taken any DVD players from the store without paying for them?" or "Do you know another employee involved in these thefts?" The answers to these questions are the key because, if the individual is anxious given the importance of this assessment scenario but is innocent regarding this specific accusation, then there will be no difference between a physiological response to the high affect control question and the one that is specific to the crime. If, however, the individual is lying in response to specific questions, then the physiological response to the actual crime question will be even greater than the ones to the high affect control questions.

In the past, the responses were recorded in analog fashion by a polygraph on chart paper and later analyzed by an expert interpreter. Today, this type of data acquisition and processing is undertaken by computer, which provides digitized information and has built-in interpretation algorithms that directly compare specific versus control questions, thus simplifying the task and reducing interpreter error.

There is extensive research that the reasoning behind polygraph-based lie detection is sound and that lying is indeed associated with greater physiological arousal than telling the truth. Well-trained interpreters reach inter-rater reliability of $r = .90$ (Horvath, 1977; Patrick & Iacono, 1991). This is impressive by the usual standards of psychometrics we presented in chapter 3. On the other hand, almost nothing is known about the test-retest reliability of polygraph testing largely because the nature of this test prevents a repeat without being influenced by the previous exposure to the test (Iacono, 2000).

Especially tricky, however, is the question of validity. In order to decide on innocence or guilt, there has to be proof of some sort. If lie detection was used in a criminal trial, somebody who appeared to have lied on the polygraph test is also more likely to get convicted in court. Can one therefore conclude that all people who were convicted were also guilty? The answer is "no" because it is well-established that some of the guilty go free for lack of evidence, and some innocent people are falsely convicted, especially when the evidence is circumstantial. There are even documented cases of individuals being so confused or pressured during police investigations that they admit to things they never did. Therefore, resulting convictions in court can be partially used to support validity of lie detection, but it will remain a flawed method of validation.

Another possibility of testing lie detection is by using a contrived, but well-controlled experiment in the laboratory (Iacono, 2000). A fairly typical design involves an experimenter placing a $20 bill inside a book that is placed on top of a table in a research room that has no other person in it. Research participants are then told to enter the room and either take or not take the $20 bill, and another researcher, who does not know what the subject had been instructed to do, will subsequently conduct a polygraph test and determine on the basis of the differential physiological responses to various types of questions, whether or not this research participant has told the truth. In order to evaluate the meaning of such research findings, one needs to remember that the decision options are "lied" or "told the truth"; one out of two, 50%, will be correct just by chance. Ideal, of course, would be a 100% accuracy rate. The real question is how much better can lie detection do than 50% chance? Such well-controlled, contrived test conditions are not actually implying a risk that the participant suffers grave consequences when lying (like a typical college student who participated in the earlier experiment does not get punished); in this case, accuracy rates of detection have been reported to average 88% (Kircher, Horowitz, & Raskin, 1988). At the other end of the scale, however, when real-world tests are conducted where the test taker actually is suspected of a crime and is likely to suffer the consequences, the accuracy rate is more like 60% (Lykken, 1981). Interestingly, when a similar scenario involves data interpretation by the same polygrapher who also asked the questions, the accuracy rate is more like 70% (Iacono, 2000).

What does this all mean? The most likely explanation for the difference is that an experienced polygrapher noticed additional verbal and nonverbal clues of lying emitted from the person who had been tested, and she integrated the information based on behavioral observation during the interview with the physiological information collected at the same time. Hence, it is the blending of the two forms of assessment (a multimethod approach) that accounts for a somewhat greater accuracy rate. In an attempt to better explicate the large discrepancy between 90% accuracy possible in laboratory-based experiments and 60% accuracy typical of real-world situations, Patrick and Iacono (1991) have devised a clever protocol, where a controlled experiment was conducted in a prison with inmates who actually did have something to gain or lose by lying. This methodology blended the advantages of a controlled study with the advantage of conducting an experiment that has personal, meaningful consequences for the study participant. Maybe not surprisingly, the observed accuracy under these conditions was 79% and therefore higher than the one reported by Lykken in real-world situations but still substantially lower than the one reported by Kircher et al. (1988) for experiments with students. Irrespective of whether one concludes that the error rate is 10% or 30%, this is less important than understanding what the consequences of an error are.

Whether or not polygraph evidence can be used in criminal proceedings varies across different countries. In the United States polygraph evidence can, under certain circumstances, be used in court, whereas in Canada this is considered illegal given the concerns about imperfect validity of the test. Nevertheless, Canadians do allow police to use polygraph evidence to assist in their criminal investigations, such that they might rule out a suspect on the basis of a negative lie detection test result.

Let us get back to the consequences of wrong decisions resulting from inherently flawed lie detection procedures. Recall that even in the most optimistic scenario—where a roughly 10% error rate is apparent—some of the guilty will go free and some innocent will get convicted. There is no argument that being found guilty for a murder one did not commit is very grave, and a 10% error rate is unacceptably high. In fact, in criminal law the definition of "beyond reasonable doubt" is described as reflecting greater than 99% probability. The good news is that very few people ever get accused of murder.

Let us consider a different, ultimately more insidious scenario, though. There are now commercial testing firms who are employed by private companies in personnel recruitment procedures and internal investigations of theft (Sackett & Decker, 1979). If an employee was accused or suspected of theft of goods and refused to participate in a lie detection test, she is very likely to get fired because this refusal will be interpreted as suspicious. If she did participate, there is a 10% probability that she will be found guilty although she didn't do anything wrong. Unfortunately, theft of goods from companies by employees is very frequent, and it would not be unusual that a long-term employee might be asked to undergo lie detection tests as often as four or five times over a 10-year period. This also means that the employee's chance of being found guilty for one of these incidents while being innocent has now reached about a 50–50 probability, and the employee has a 50% chance of getting fired for theft although she has not committed a single one. Given that these are not criminal court proceedings but internal matters, the innocent employee does not have full protection of the law the way an accused murderer has in the criminal system. Therefore, the problems with an imperfect test in criminal court are bad enough, but when such tests are used repeatedly in an environment where individuals have few protections, the probability of injustice rises quickly.

The bottom line regarding validity is that with inaccurate tests there are always problems, but when the consequence is that an innocent person serves a lifetime prison term, this imperfection becomes unacceptable. The researcher or clinician conducting assessments needs to be aware of not only what the probability of error is, but what the cost of an error is when using psychological tests to make important decisions. These issues were already discussed earlier in this book when diagnostic assessments and decision-making processes were described.

Fortunately, there is a method to protect the innocent better. Here, the assessor, typically the police, holds back critical information on crime details, like the exact choice of weapon, the location where a body was found, or the number of times a victim was stabbed. This information is then embedded in a series of answer options that looks like a multiple-choice test students take; for example: "Did you dump the body (a) behind the tool shed, (b) beside the garage, (c) down by the creek, or (d) in the ditch beside the gas station? A truly innocent person will show the same physiological responses to all options because none of these options has a unique value, whereas a guilty person is likely to respond more strongly to the correct option because he indeed knows the difference. The method is therefore called the **Guilty Knowledge Test** and has been shown to be much better able at protecting innocent people from getting falsely accused (Iacono, 2000).

◇ SUMMARY

Overall, clinical forensic psychology is a specialty area that has been increasing in popularity, scope, and credibility. There are numerous areas with the law that clinical forensic psychologists can work in, both in conducting research and in providing clinically related services. We want to stress that the rigorous training in critical, analytical thinking and multilayered assessment that is typical for clinical psychologists is also ideal preparation for forensic work. We posit that no other profession offers the same balance of depth and breadth in how their training prepares for forensic work. Consequently, psychologists doing forensic work do not need to compete with nurses, counselors, or social workers with whom, in other contexts, they may sometimes have "turf wars." Provided you have the thick skin needed to defend your opinion in court and stand up to often hostile cross-examination, clinical psychologists willing to do court work can earn a very good living.

◇ONGOING CONSIDERATIONS

Otto and Heilbrun (2002) present several areas or strategies, listed here, that need to be focused on in order to further develop the field and move forward.

1. Updating, clarifying, and broadening the scope of specialty guidelines and practice standards for forensic psychology. Although some areas within the field of forensic psychology have well-developed practice standards and regulations, other areas fall short.

2. Enhancing and delineating different training levels for those involved in the field. Three levels of training and specialization are proposed, each one differing in breadth and depth of training:
   a. **Legally informed clinician**, who has a basic education in law and psychology and knows the distinction between clinical psychology and clinical forensic psychology
   b. **Proficient clinician**, who has midlevel training and received some formal training in forensic psychology
   c. **Specialist clinician**, who has the highest level of expertise and certification and has formal and both intensive and extensive training in forensic psychology

3. Educating the consumers of forensic psychology in order to delineate and demonstrate not only the skill and ability of psychologists working within the broad parameters of legal processes but also the efficacy and utility of the work that clinical forensic psychologists perform.

4. Evaluating empirically these three strategies in order to determine whether they are effective in promoting the field.

◇ KEY TERMS LEARNED

Clinical forensic psychologist
Control question technique
Criminal profiling
Detection of lying
Guilty knowledge test
Hare psychopathy checklist
High affect control question
Law and psychology
Legal psychology
Legally informed clinician

Neutral control question
Polygraphs
Practice standards
Proficient clinician
Psychological first aid
Psychology and the law
Psychopathy
Rehabilitation ideal
Specialist clinician
Specialty guidelines

◇ THINKING QUESTIONS

1. What are the differences between clinical psychologists and forensic psychologists in terms of their practices?

2. How does assessment differ between a forensic clinical psychologist and a clinical psychologist?

3. What are the rationale for and the evidence of the effectiveness of lie detection?

4. What are the different domains of practice in forensic clinical psychology?

5. What are the differences between forensic assessment tools and forensically relevant tools, and what are some examples of each?

6. Do the ethical principles that guide clinical psychologists' work change as a result of working as a forensic psychologist? If so, how?

◇ REFERENCES

Amstadter, A. B., McCart, M. R., & Ruggerio, K. J. (2007). Psychosocial interventions for adults with crime-related PTSD. *Professional Psychology: Research and Practice, 38*, 640–651.

Applebaum, P. S., & Grisso, T. (2001). *MacCAT-CR: MacArthur Competency Assessment Tool: Clinical research*. Sarasota, FL: Professional Resource Press.

Bartol, C. R., & Bartol, A. M. (1999). *Introduction to forensic psychology: Research and applications*. Thousand Oaks, CA: Sage.

Bartol, C. R., & Bartol, A. M. (2006). History of forensic psychology. In I. B. Weiner & A. K. Hess (Eds.), *The handbook of forensic psychology* (pp. 3–27). New York: Wiley.

Benjamin, L. T. (2003). Behavioral science and the Nobel Prize: A history. *American Psychologist, 58*, 731–741.

Binet, A. (1905). La science du termoignage (The science of testimony). *L'Annee Psychologique, 11*, 128–137.

Blackburn, R. (1996). What is forensic psychology? *Legal and Criminological Psychology, 1*, 3–16.

Bonta, J. (2002). Offender risk assessment. Guidelines for selection and use. *Criminal Justice and Behavior, 29,* 355–379.

Campbell, R. (2008). The psychological impact of rape victims' experiences with the legal, medical, and mental health systems. *American Psychologist, 63,* 702–717.

Craig, R. J. (2005). *Personality-guided forensic psychology.* Washington, DC: American Psychological Association.

Devilly, G. J., Gist, R., & Cotton, P. (2006). Ready! Fire! Aim! The status of psychological debriefing and therapeutic interventions: In the work place and after disasters. *Review of General Psychology, 10,* 318–345.

Dyer, F., & McCann, J. T. (2000). The Millon clinical inventories, research critical of their forensic application, and Daubert criteria. *Law and Human Behavior, 24,* 487–497.

Foa, E. B., Zoellner, L. A., & Feeny, N. C. (2006). An evaluation of three brief programs for facilitating recovery after assault. *Journal of Trauma Stress, 19,* 29–43.

Gendreau, P., Goggin, C., French, S., & Smith, P. (2006). Practicing psychology in correctional settings. In I. B. Weiner & A. K. Hess (Eds.). *The handbook of forensic psychology* (pp. 721–750). New York: Wiley.

Grisso, T. (1986). *Evaluating competencies.* New York: Plenum.

Hare, R. D. (1991). *Manual for the revised psychopathy checklist.* Toronto, Ont.: Multihealth Systems.

Hare, R. D. (1996). Psychopathy: A clinical construct whose time has come. *Criminal Justice and Behavior, 23*(1), 25–54.

Hare, R. D. (2003). *The Hare psychopathy checklist—Revised manual* (2nd ed.). Toronto, Ont.: Multihealth Systems.

Hoge, S., Poythress, N., Bonnie, R., Monahan, J., Eisenberg, M., & Feucht-Haviar, T. (1997). The MacArthur Adjudication Competence Study: Diagnosis, psychopathology, and adjudicative competence-related abilities. *Behavioral Sciences & the Law, 15,* 329–345.

Horvath, F. S. (1977). The effect of selected variables on interpretation of polygraph records. *Journal of Applied Psychology, 62,* 127–136.

Iacono, W. G. (2000). The detection of deception. In J. T. Cacioppo, L. G. Tassinary, & G. G. Berntsen (Eds.), *Handbook of psychophysiology* (2nd ed.). New York: Cambridge University Press.

Kilpatrick, D. G., Ruggeiro, K. J., Acierno, R., Saunders, B. E., Resnick, H. S., & Best, C. L. (2003). Violence and risk of PTSD, major depression, substance abuse/dependence, and comorbidity: Results from the National Survey of Adolescents. *Journal of Consulting and Clinical Psychology, 71,* 692–700.

Kircher, J. C., Horowitz, S. W., & Raskin, D. C. (1988). Meta-analyses of mock crime studies of the control question polygraph technique. *Law and Human Behavior, 12,* 79–90.

Lippsitt, P. D., Lelos, D., & McGarry, A. L. (1971). Competency for trial: A screening instrument. *American Journal of Psychiatry, 128,* 105–109.

Lykken, D. T. (1981). A tremor in the blood: Uses and abuses of the lie detector (2nd ed.). New York: Plenum.

Martinson, R. (1974). What works? Questions and answers about prison reform. *The Public Interest, 35,* 22–54.

Megargee, E. I. (1977). Development and validation of an MMPI-based system for classifying criminal offenders. In J. N. Butcher (Ed.), *New developments in the use of the MMPI* (pp. 303–324). Minneapolis: University of Minnesota Press.

Megargee, E. I. (1994). Using the Megargee MMPI-based classification system with MMPI-2s of male prison inmates. *Psychological Assessment, 6,* 337–344.

Millon, T., & Davis, R. D. (1996). The Millon Multiaxial Clinical Inventory-III (MCMI-III). In C. S. Newmark (Ed.). *Major psychological assessment instruments* (2nd ed.). Boston: Allyn & Bacon.

Munsterberg, H. (1908). *On the witness stand.* New York: Doubleday.

Nietzel, M. T. (1986). *Psychological consultation.* New York: Pearson Education Inc.

Ogloff, J. R. P. (2002). *Taking psychology and law into the twenty-first century.* New York: Springer.

Ogloff, J. R. P., Tomkins, A. J., & Bersoff, D. N. (1996). Education and training in psychology and law/criminal justice. *Criminal Justice and Behavior, 23,* 200–235.

Otto, R. K., & Heilbrun, K. (2002). The practice of forensic psychology: A look toward the future in light of the past. *American Psychologist, 57,* 5–18.

Patrick, C. J., & Iacono, W. G. (1991). A comparison of field and laboratory polygraphs in the detection of deception. *Psychophysiology, 28,* 632–638.

Rice, M. E., Harris, G. T., & Cormier, C. A. (1992). An evaluation of a maximum security therapeutic community for psychopaths and other mentally disordered offenders. *Law and Human Behavior, 16,* 399–412.

Rizzo, A., Stover, C., Berkowitz, S., & Kagan, R. (2008). *Traumatic stress: New treatments for children and war veterans.* American Psychological Association Media Advisory.

Rogers, R. (2010). *Structured interview of reported symptoms, 2nd edition (SIRS-2).* Lutz, FL: PAR.

Ruzek, J. L., Bryner, M. J., Jacobs, A. K., Layne, C. M., Vernberg, E. M., & Watson, P. J. (2007). Psychological first aid. *Journal of Mental Health Counseling, 29,* 17–49.

Sackett, P. R., & Decker, P. J. (1979). Detection of deception in the employment context: A review and critical analysis. *Personnel Psychology, 32*(3), 487–506.

Scrivner, E. (2006). Psychology and law enforcement. In I. B. Weiner, & A. K. Hess (Eds.). *The handbook of forensic psychology* (3rd ed.). pp. 534–551.

Stern, L. W. (1939). The psychology of testimony. *Journal of Abnormal and Social Psychology, 40,* 3–20.

Vernberg, E. M., Steinberg, A. M., Jacobs, A. K., Brymer, M. J., Watson, P. J., Osofsky, J. D., Layne, C. M., Pynoos, R. S., & Ruzek, J. I. (2008). Innovations in disaster mental health: Psychological first aid. *Professional Psychology: Research and Practice, 39,* 381–388.

Weiner, I. B., & Hess, A. K. (2006). *The handbook of forensic psychology.* New York: Wiley.

Wrightsman, L. S., & Porter, S. (2006). *Forensic psychology.* Toronto, Ont.: Thomson Canada Ltd.

CHAPTER SEVENTEEN

HEALTH PSYCHOLOGY AND BEHAVIORAL MEDICINE

CHAPTER OBJECTIVE

To frame this chapter, the reader is reminded of this book's title: *Clinical Psychology: A Modern Health Profession*. Clinical psychologists assess and treat people with psychological disorders and also play a role in the treatment of a variety of physical diseases. In recognition of this fact, numerous psychological interventions and their content and outcomes, when applied to medical populations, have been described throughout chapters 10 and 13. For example, stress management approaches are useful for anxiety disorders but also for high blood pressure (Linden, 2006), and biofeedback can be used for anxiety reduction, as well as for neuromuscular rehabilitation or chronic pain conditions (Moss, 2007). The title contains both "health psychology" and "behavioral medicine" because the relevant literature is covered in a variety of journals with one or the other term in the title. In everyday reality, the research and clinical content covered by these areas is largely overlapping; many of the same researchers serve on the journals' editorial boards and also contribute articles. Where these areas differ is that health psychology embraces research on healthy functioning more so than does the domain of behavioral medicine, which is somewhat more likely to cover clinical application issues.

The majority of presenting problems in family physician offices are in good part psychological in nature even though they may present as physical health problems (Steven, 1999). This strongly suggests that a separation of health issues into physical versus mental problems is arbitrary and belies what health professionals encounter in everyday practice (Cummings, 2005). A family physician needs to understand the interaction of physical disease with a patient's emotional well-being and with social context factors, and the same applies for clinical psychologists. Therefore, in chapters 8 and 9 and 12–14 there have been descriptions of physical health problems where psychologists are either the primary therapists or important players on multidisciplinary health care teams. Integrating this knowledge into a clinical psychology textbook is meant to prepare the student of clinical psychology for the practice of health care in the broadest sense (Linden, Moseley, & Erskine, 2005; Talen, Fraser, & Cauley, 2005). Clinical psychologists may, for example, be called on to:

- Consult on psychological suitability of patients waiting for organ transplantation (Rodrigue, 1996)
- Treat post-traumatic stress disorder in victims of violence whose immediate physical problems have been effectively treated by the medical team (http://www.helpguide .org/mental/post_traumatic_stress_disorder_symptoms_treatment.htm)
- Help educate other health professionals on how to maximize adherence in patients who need to follow strict regimens of medication, diet, or blood sugar monitoring (Kripalani, Yao, & Haynes, 2007)
- Accept referrals for psychological treatment of patients with high blood pressure who also have anger problems or are stressed out (Linden, 2006)
- Work in a multidisciplinary clinic to help people with chronic pain conditions
- Teach pelvic floor muscle biofeedback for women with urinary incontinence (Burgio et al., 2002)
- Assist governments and insurance companies in devising cost-efficient health care delivery (Hunsley, 2003)

Having a separate chapter on health psychology provides an opportunity to highlight the similarities and differences between clinical psychology as a traditional *mental health profession* and clinical psychology as a broadly defined *health profession*. This chapter's objective is to provide the conceptual and research background to better understand the work of clinical psychologists in primary care and rehabilitation settings. The chapter is organized around specific areas of practice where clinical psychologists are making contributions to health care. We also stress that knowledge accumulated by psychology researchers who are not clinical psychologists can still be applied to improve patient care (Brody, 2003). For example, our colleagues with expertise in social psychology offer knowledge on how to understand and use social support systems (Sarason, Sarason, Potter, & Antoni, 1985) or frame health behavior messages. Developmental psychology teaches us to understand psychopathology as age-related and encourages adjustment in our treatment selections and methods as a function of patient age. Physiological psychologists have offered in-depth knowledge of pain processes (Melzack & Wall, 1965) and the reinforcing properties of drugs (Pinel, 2000) and help us develop treatment and prevention approaches that have a solid biological foundation.

As much as we can learn from our nonclinical colleagues, the question is what clinical psychologists can do in primary health care settings. This chapter discusses the most important clinical problems that are encountered in family practice, in medical specialties, and in general hospital care, namely:

- Chronic pain
- Cardiovascular diseases
- Cancer

Aside from directly managing specific diseases, clinical psychology knowledge can advance more generic objectives in health care. Therefore, a second objective of this chapter is to delineate the tasks and skills needed for:

- Prevention of disease
- Maximizing adherence
- Teaching of skills to better tolerate adverse medical procedures and actively participate in self-care of chronic diseases (Clark, Becker, Janz, Lorig, & William, 1991)
- Rehabilitation from illness

◇UNDERSTANDING HEALTH AND THE CAUSATION OF DISEASE

To be effective as a player in health care, the clinical psychologist needs to understand at least the basics about the medical etiology of common diseases. In Western countries, the two major causes of death are cardiovascular disease and cancer. These diseases have no single known cause but are multicausal in origin and still not fully understood. On the plus side, there is overwhelming evidence that both are in good part due to behavioral factors, which may be controllable (Yusuf et al., 2004).

When a demographic, behavioral, or psychological factor has been demonstrated to predict the development of disease and there is a plausible biological pathway, such a factor is referred to as a **risk factor**, and the intensity of the relationship between the risk factor and an outcome is referred to as the **risk ratio** or the **odds ratio**. Smoking behavior is a good example to demonstrate odds ratios. Smokers who smoke one pack of cigarettes a day for many years are roughly three times as likely to die of cardiovascular disease as nonsmokers; this can also be described as an odds ratio of 3:1 (Yusuf et al., 2004). The reader will see the terms odds ratio, risk ratio, and **hazards ratio** in the literature; all three terms describe the intensity of the relationship between a risk and an outcome, but they are computed using different formulas. Odds ratios by definition are slightly larger than risk ratios although they do tell, in essence, the same story. Hazards ratios are extracted from studies with multiple repeated measurements. In order to demonstrate the importance of behavioral and psychological factors in predicting disease outcomes, we include Table 17.1, which represents summarized results from a large review describing the inter-relationship between risk factors and cardiovascular disease across 52 countries (Yusuf et al., 2004).

We consider this table to be informative for many reasons. First of all, it reveals that modifiable behavioral risk factors like smoking and lack of physical fitness are important predictors, as are certain personality traits and mood (i.e., psychosocial factors). The strength of the relationship between psychological risk factors and heart disease as an outcome is as large as the risk associated with many traditional, medical risk factors. Finally, although none of the individual risk factors carry a risk ratio greater than 4:1, their joint presence dramatically increases somebody's risk of developing heart disease. A person who carries all risk factors is 129 times more likely to die from heart disease than an individual

TABLE 17.1 Odds Ratios (OR) for Risk Factors from the INTERHEART Study

RANK	RISK FACTOR	OR (AND CI)
1	Lipids (top versus lowest quintile)	3.87 (3.4–4.4)
2	Diabetes	3.08 (2.8–3.4)
3	Current smoking	2.95 (2.7–3.2)
4	All psychosocial	2.51 (2.2–2.9)
5	Hypertension	2.48 (2.3–2.7)
6	Abdominal obesity	1.36 (1.2–1.5)
7	Diet (protective effect)	0.70 (0.64–0.77)
8	Exercise (protective effect)	0.72 (0.65–0.79)
9	Alcohol intake (higher intake, lower risk)	0.79 (0.73–0.86)
	All risk factors together	129.2 (90.2–185.0)

"Don't tell me to improve my diet. I ate
a carrot once and nothing happened!"

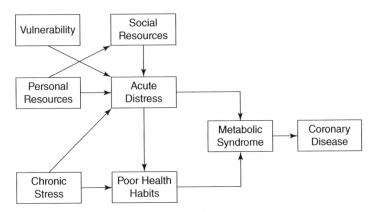

FIGURE 17.1   A model of pathways for stress leading to disease

Redrawn from Vialiano et al., 2003.

without any of these risk factors. This statistically cumulative risk, however, does not reveal that psychological, biological, and behavioral risk factors actually do tend to occur in clusters, such that anxious individuals are also more likely to reveal depression (Friedman, Tucker, & Reise, 1995), depressed individuals are less physically active (Strawbridge, Deleger, Roberts, & Kaplan, 2002), and people with diabetes are also more likely to have problems with their blood lipids and their weight (Ford, Giles, & Dietz, 2002). These are just a few examples of risk factor inter-relationships. In a related vein, one can pool information of known risk factors and display the presumed etiological model in a path diagram such as the one proposed by Vitaliano (Figure 17.1, Vitaliano, Zhang, & Scanlan, 2003).

The advantage of proposing and testing this type of model is that it represents a sequential approach which blends genetic effects and early-life influences as well as presents risk behaviors. The model is complex and requires expensive longitudinal studies for full testing, but it supports and guides effective interventions with multiple benefits as has been elegantly demonstrated, for example, in a clinical trial conducted by Kostis et al. (1992). In this study, hypertensive patients had been recruited and randomized into three treatment groups:

1. Treatment with a so-called beta-blocker, a drug that dampens sympathetic nervous system arousal and is considered to be a first-line, effective pharmacological treatment for hypertension

2. Treatment with a drug placebo, designed to test whether people would've gotten better on their own

3. A multicomponent, nondrug treatment consisting of relaxation training, exercise, and nutrition support

Both active treatments were associated with substantial and clinically meaningful reductions in blood pressure, whereas the wait-list control group did not improve on their own. As mentioned, the drug treatment reduced blood pressure but had no discernible impact on other risk factors that were present in this sample. The nondrug treatment, however, was as effective in reducing blood pressure as the drug (but not the placebo), and it also improved other health risks. This study was chosen for discussion here because it indicates how behavioral and psychological treatments may have positive effects for multiple, inter-related health outcomes, thereby improving the entire risk factor profile for patients, whereas no such generalized benefits appeared for the drug treatment.

◇ EARLY-LIFE INFLUENCES ON HEALTH

The model shown in Figure 17.1 begins with recognizing the possibility of critical genetic and early-life influences on long-term health. This view is consistent with current thinking in the behavioral medicine literature, which looks upon the field as dealing with potential chal-lenges and opportunities across an entire lifespan (Hayman, 2007; Hawkley et al., 2005). In this vein, we will briefly review some discoveries regarding early-life influences on health and prepare the reader for a discussion of how clinical psychologists working in a physical health domain can make valuable contributions to the management of chronic diseases.

Even in wealthy Western countries, children grow up in many different environ-ments, some poor, some wealthy, and in varying subcultures as a function of their race, ethnicity, and maybe recency of immigration. Some of these environments are detrimental to psychological well-being and negatively affect long-term resilience. Studies have shown that exposure to short-term acute stressors poses no particular risk for long-term health, while chronic stress weakens the immune system (Segerstrom & Miller, 2004). Along this line, a rapidly growing body of literature reveals that exposure to chronic stress in the child's early years can impair the development of brain circuitry and can lower thresholds for stress and physical pain resulting from the release of high levels of stress hormones. In consequence, this child is more vulnerable to a variety of infections, more susceptible to substance abuse, and less able to learn and remember (Middlebrooks & Audage, 2008). For such children life is not "equal opportunity." On the other hand, a supportive and caring environment can buffer the impact of events such as parental separation, a frightening acci-dent, or a natural disaster (Middlebrooks & Audage, 2008).

Particularly damaging are emotional, physical, and sexual abuse and neglect during childhood (Chen, 2004; Middlebrooks & Audage, 2008; see also chapter 15 on this issue). Such neglect is even more frequent in environments that are laced with violence and where chronic mental illness and substance abuse among caregivers are found (Anda, Brown, Felitti et al., 2007). Unfortunately, toxic environments are fairly prevalent. Middlebrooks and Audage (2008) report the results from a large representative U.S. survey (n = 17,337) of adverse childhood experiences: There was a roughly 10% frequency of neglect, 13% physical violence in the family, 23% parental separation or divorce, and 5% with an incar-cerated household member. When children who grow up in toxic environments reach adulthood, their greater vulnerability to disease becomes apparent, and we cannot, of course, turn the clock back. However, the knowledge about childhood stress can sensitize us as to how to formulate the problems of such individuals, remind us of the need for empathic help and avoiding blame, and possibly trigger efforts at prevention of toxic envi-ronments for future generations of children by sharing our knowledge with the media and politicians.

◇ PREVENTION AND MANAGEMENT OF CHRONIC DISEASES

In the previous section, we demonstrated that emotional and behavioral factors are inter-woven, and we explained their role in the development of chronic and life-threatening diseases. We have also shown that when it comes to the development of chronic diseases, not all individuals are equal, given their differential early-life stress exposure. Equipped with this understanding, the clinical psychologist can now use knowledge acquired by all branches of psychology to play a role in the prevention and management of disease. It may be easiest to understand what can be done, and how, by introducing the major concepts of the literature on disease prevention. In this area of practice, one distinguishes three types of prevention, namely, *primary*, *secondary*, and *tertiary*.

The term **primary prevention** is applied to any attempt to stem disease development in healthy individuals; that is, people who do not have any sign of disease. These attempts may include advertising campaigns that discourage teenagers from starting to smoke, encouraging seat belt use, routine vaccinations for children and adults, or providing tips on how to handle stress. This can, in part, be implemented via the popular media, such as via newscasts or documentaries. Also, any government attempt to reduce poverty and violence via policy changes and income redistribution can be perceived as primary prevention. There is limited opportunity for clinical psychologists to participate in primary prevention, although effective advertising can be guided by research findings on attitude change and per-suasive communication that our colleagues in social psychology have contributed.

Secondary prevention is specifically directed at individuals who are known to be at risk for disease development, and it moves the prevention effort from the indirect, sprinkler-like nature of primary prevention to direct action with individuals. Such persons may have a predisposition for disease through genetics or early-life stress exposure (e.g., stunted growth and learning capability due to malnutrition or young adults with difficulty attaching to long-term partners when as children they had early rejection experiences). Secondary prevention similarly applies to screening and early intervention for risk factors like smoking, stress, high cholesterol, or elevated blood pressure.

Given that the presence of risk factors like blood pressure or high cholesterol is generally not noticeable by the afflicted, the health care system occasionally undertakes mass screenings in the community. Many secondary prevention efforts are built into routine medical care deliv-ered by family physicians, who use office visits to assess heart function and blood pressure level and conduct Pap smear tests for women and rectal examinations for the detection of prostate cancer in men. More directly related to clinical psychology are community-wide screenings for the presence of depression or anxiety disorders that are offered by mental health volunteer associations. You may recall that psychologist Dr. A, in chapter 1, was in the process of devel-oping a suitable screening tool for psychological distress in cancer patients.

Last but not least, **tertiary prevention** includes efforts to maximize rehabilitation and adjustment in diseases like cancer or coronary heart disease and also includes recom-mendations for behavior change that may prevent recurrence or at least help to prevent the disease from worsening. Given the unfortunate high prevalence and incidence of diseases like diabetes, arthritis, heart disease, or cancer, there is a huge patient population out there that can benefit from tertiary prevention efforts.

Given these many opportunities for action, the clinical psychologist is most likely involved in tertiary prevention via rehabilitation and disease management. To prevent or minimize the impact of chronic diseases we can contribute to change in health behaviors by:

- Raising physical fitness

- Encouraging healthy eating

- Assisting with attempts to quit smoking

- Keeping stress levels at bay (Linden, 2005)

- Increasing adherence to the numerous health recommendations that patients receive from their physicians

Ultimately, this means that a major role of the clinical psychologist in primary health care is to teach and support self-management behaviors for chronic diseases (Clark et al., 1991). Despite the fact that people in Western countries are barraged with media reports and advertising about healthy behaviors, adherence to many health recommendations is remarkably poor, even when nonadherence is acutely dangerous with possibly deadly outcomes, such as with major dietary deviations in diabetics. Table 17.2 offers some frightening data on the extent of noncompliance with physician recommendations for managing chronic diseases.

TABLE 17.2 Degree of Noncompliance

	% COMPLIANCE RATE
Treatments	
Hypertension treatment	53
Tuberculosis drugs	55
Antiasthma drugs	46
Antibiotic treatment	33
Insulin injection for diabetes	48
Physician's advice	
Quitting smoking	29
Weight-reducing diet	20
Kidney disease diet	28
Hemodialysis diet	70
Appointment keeping	
Dental checkup	72
Psychiatrist visit	60
Pap test	52
Hearing and eyesight, follow-up with doctor	35
Hypertension, follow-up after diagnosis	58
Hypertension treatment, annual check	30

Redrawn from Burrell & Levy (1985).

Given the intensive investment of money into public health, it is informative to review which investments have paid off and where health messages still fall on deaf ears. We can readily find examples of major worsening of risks as well as some successes with respect to population-wide risk reduction. Since the mid-1970s, for example, the prevalence of obesity has increased sharply for both adults and children. Data from two NHANES surveys (http://www.cdc.gov/nchs/nhanes) show that among U.S. adults 20–74 years old the prevalence of obesity increased from 15.0% (in the 1976–1980 survey) to 34% (in the 2005–2006 survey). The prevalence of overweight children 2–5 years old increased from 5.0% during 1976–1980 to 13.9% during 2003–2004, and for young people 6–11 years old, the prevalence during the same time period increased from 6.5% to 18.8% and from 5.0% to 17.4% among those 12–19 years old.

On the other hand, as much as there are trends of growing health problems (like obesity or diabetes), there also is a truly "good news story," namely, that of changes in smoking behavior. Research has shown the remarkable success of antismoking campaigns: in 1965, 49% of the adult Canadian population smoked, whereas by the year 2002 this figure had dropped to 24% and has continued to decrease (http://www.ncic.cancer.ca/ncic/internet/standard/0,3621,84658243_85787780_399354909_langId-en,00.html). The same trend has been observed in the United States (http://www.jointogether.org/news/research/summaries/2005/us-smoking-rates-continue.html). This success is widely attributed to high taxation of cigarettes, legislation that prohibits smoking at the workplace and in public buildings, antismoking ads, and prominent warning labels printed on cigarette packages themselves. This success has been furthered by the aggressive pursuit of tobacco companies in civil court for their insidious efforts to encourage smoking and to intentionally foster nicotine dependence.

Researchers have taken the inherent health threats of unhealthy lifestyles very seriously and have built an impressive knowledge base about the factors that foster or interfere with good **adherence**. Surprising to many, this literature has consistently shown that many suspected demographic and individual difference variables do not actually play a consistent role in supporting adherence: neither age, nor gender, nor education nor intelligence are associated with differential adherence. On the other hand, the variables found critical for adherence are specific to the disease, the treatments themselves, the cost and efforts of prevention, and characteristics of the health care environment (Poole, Hunt Matheson, & Cox, 2008). A summary of these variables is offered in Table 17.3.

Later in this chapter we will describe how clinical psychologists help specific patient groups. Prior to that, however, we feel that it is useful to first delineate in what ways diseases themselves represent both similar and dissimilar challenges to patients, and we highlight which of the many common self-management tasks are, in turn, useful for a multitude of diseases.

Key issues for patients are:

- Disease-induced interference or loss of function with important life roles (like caregiver or doing one's job)
- Fear of death and disability associated with varying diseases

TABLE 17.3 Predictors of Adherence

NO CONSISTENT EFFECT ON ADHERENCE	CLEARLY AFFECTING ADHERENCE
Age	Belief about threat
Gender	Belief about the efficacy of intervention
Education/income/intelligence	Supportive environment
General knowledge about illnesses	Symptom strength
	Complexity of treatment (length, inconvenience, interference with other actions, effort, actual cost)
	A caring, stable health provider

- Unpredictability of the course of the disease
- Knowing to what degree treatment and adherence to self-management tasks will actually help them live longer and maintain a high quality of life (QOL)

Key features of the most frequently seen diseases in general medical practice have been aggregated into a single table that compares diseases along these key variables (Table 17.4).

As much as Table 17.4 is designed to stress differences between diseases and their implications for patients, it also reveals many shared features that can then be translated into a variety of common tasks that patients can learn to regularly engage in to minimize the impact of their disease. This has been summarized in Table 17.5, reprinted from an article by Clark and her collaborators (1991) who presented an excellent review of the issues in dealing with chronic health care not only for clinical psychologists but for all health care providers.

Routine adoption of these tasks can benefit from input by clinical psychologists who are trained in research on disease etiology and in behavior change principles.

◇ADHERENCE

In the previous section we already gave many examples of how frequent and potentially deleterious poor adherence is. This section will provide brief descriptions of programs designed to enhance adherence and provide some data on the effectiveness of adherence interventions. The basic principles that can be used for developing adherence enhancement strategies are described in Table 17.6.

One example for the study of adherence is cardiac rehabilitation. In cardiac rehabilitation, patients who have had a heart attack or cardiac surgery participate in systematic exercise programs, receive nutrition counseling, and learn more about problem recognition and healthy lifestyles. Although it is well established that multidisciplinary cardiac

TABLE 17.4 Chronic Diseases: A Comparison

DISEASE	RISK OF EARLY DEATH	PREDICTA-BILITY OF THE COURSE OF THE DISEASE	CHANCE OF SUCCESS OF TREATMENT/ REHABILITATION	CONTROLLA-BILITY WITH ADHERENCE TO BEHAVIOR CHANGE RECOMMEN-DATIONS	IMPACT ON DAILY LIFE
Cancer	Extremely variable	Low	Highly variable	Limited impact of adherence on disease outcome	Highly variable; function of type and stage
Diabetes, Insulin dependent	Moderate	Fairly high	Good	Good	Fairly high
Diabetes, non–insulin dependent	Low	High	High	Very good	Modest
Asthma	Low	Fairly high	Good	Very good	Modest
Irritable bowel syndrome	Low	Fairly high	Poor	Modest	Moderate
Rheumatoid arthritis	Very low	Fairly high	Limited	Modest at best	Variable
Heart disease	Variable	Fairly high	Often very good	Good in most cases	Mostly low
Hypertension	Low (if no other risk factors are present)	High	Potentially excellent	Excellent	For the most part, none
HIV+/AIDS	Moderately high	Fairly high	Very low	Moderate	Initially little, severe in very late stage

rehabilitation programs save lives, only about a quarter of eligible patients participate, and the participation rate of women is only half that of men (about 30% versus 15%; Abbey & Stewart; 2000). In a review of the many factors that determine adherence to cardiac rehabilitation, the single most important predictor was the strong endorsement of cardiac rehabilitation programs by the treating physician (Jackson, Leclerc, & Erskine, 2005); also important was automatic referral from a cardiac in-patient unit to cardiac rehabil-itation. Interestingly, these two key predictors of adherence have to do with physician

TABLE 17.5 Common Self-Management Tasks for Five Chronic Diseases

TASKS	HEART DISEASE	ASTHMA	ARTHRITIS	COPD	DIABETES
Recognizing and responding to symptoms, monitoring physical indicators, controlling triggers to symptoms	X	X		X	X
Using medicine	X	X	X	X	X
Managing acute episodes and emergencies	X	X	X		X
Maintaining nutrition and diet	X		X	X	X
Maintaining adequate exercise and activity	X	X	X	X	X
Giving up smoking	X	X	X	X	X
Using relaxation and stress-reducing techniques	X	X	X		
Interacting with health care providers	X	X			X
Seeking information and using community services		X	X		X
Adapting to work	X	X	X		
Managing relations with significant others	X	X	X	X	
Managing emotions and psychological responses to illness	X	X	X		X

COPD, chronic obstructive pulmonary disease; X, reported in a study of self-management.
Source: Clark et al. (1991).

attitude and system organization; no long-term financial investment is required to use this knowledge to improve adherence.

A very simple and highly effective way of increasing adherence to taking medication is that of using little plastic boxes with compartments for every day, or even four subcompartments for every day. Although this may not look very psychological, these boxes greatly increase convenience and clarity (about what pills to take and when) and are especially welcomed by older patients who often have very complex medication regimens. Kripalani and colleagues analyzed 37 randomized controlled trials on interventions designed to increase adherence. These authors noted that the most predictable and (consistent with the information on pill boxes just described) large effects were observed for behavioral interventions that simplified complex medication regimes. Provision of feedback to clients and those offering information were also quite effective but resulted in more variable outcomes depending on the specific intervention and population. The diseases that had been targets for such interventions were hypertension, asthma, diabetes, chronic obstructive pulmonary disease, and HIV/AIDS.

TABLE 17.6 Strategies to Increase Adherence: the Four C's

For easier memorization, the suggested strategies for maximizing adherence to recommended health behaviors can be organized into four categories, each of which carries a name beginning with a "C."

Conviction

1. Explain the importance of adherence by showing how it affects outcomes that the patient himself is interested in.
2. Anticipate resistance, prepare for it, and encourage questions.

Convenience

3. Make a few suggestions that are prioritized and easy to remember, consider barriers, and look for ways to minimize the complexity of treatment regimens.
4. Tailor the regimen to coincide with existing habits.
5. Make adherence aids available (special packaging, diaries, or calendars).

Clarity

6. Provide written instructions and diaries to facilitate record-keeping.
7. Ask whether the instructions are clear, and have the patient repeat instructions.

Control

8. Consider entering a contract with patients.
9. Make follow-up calls, and/or book follow-up meetings.

◇ PAIN

Understanding Pain

This chapter can provide only an overview of pain research and practice and mostly focuses on the role of clinical psychologists in managing pain. Understanding and managing pain is a fascinating topic for psychologists because it brings together the biological, social, and behavioral roots of their profession. Ever since Melzack and Wall (1965) proposed that pain is a complex process where pain signal processing is modulated by cognitive and emotional activity, pain has moved from being a purely medical topic to being a bio-psycho-social topic, where the expertise of health and clinical psychology joins in order to better understand and manage pain. It is pivotal to consider acute pain as distinct from chronic pain.

Acute Pain

Pain is obviously unpleasant but useful; it has a valuable evolutionary function in that it tells us that there is something wrong in our body, alerting us to take action. In the case of acute pain (like that experienced after a surgical procedure) there is generally no reason to endure pain when we know that the problem leading to pain has been managed and that the pain sensations are likely temporary. It has become common practice that patients who have undergone some kind of invasive surgery are immediately treated for pain and are encouraged to take painkillers (also called analgesics) for the next few days. Modern post-surgery pain management actually begins as soon as the surgery is complete and the patient is still under the influence of an anesthetic. Unfortunately, there are surgical interventions where patients cannot receive general anesthesia, such as when a surgeon must be able to communicate with the patient about critical functions during the surgery. This applies, for example, to some joint surgeries where an orthopedic surgeon will ask a patient to engage in certain kinds of movements during the surgery to make sure that the nerves, tendons, and muscles do not lose their functions. Certain medical tests like spinal taps can also be painful and should not be done under full anesthesia. In these cases, psychologists can help patients prepare for potentially painful procedures by explicitly alerting the patient to the emotions and physical sensations that he is likely to experience (Poole et al., 2008).

Chronic Pain

Experiencing pain is a normal human experience; we all suffer from minor injuries such as an occasional minor burn by accidentally touching a hot frying pan or falling off a bicycle. These are usually short-lived pain experiences, and a combination of analgesic use and distraction strategies is usually sufficient to tolerate them. Some pain experiences, however, become chronic; typically these are the result of workplace accidents, or other accidents that may result in extensive skin burns, broken bones, or severe muscle damage. In these instances the degree of damage is usually obvious and easy to document. Other pain triggers are based on soft tissue or nerve damage that is not obvious and not easy to treat. These latter conditions in particular also lead to litigation for damages and pension claims because patients may be debilitated for a long time. Insurance companies are very familiar with disability claims such as those arising from whiplash due to rear-end car accidents or repetitive strain at the workplace that may result in soft tissue injury of neck or lower back musculature; clinical psychologists are often brought in to assess the causes and functional losses of these chronic pain conditions. At the medical level it is important to swiftly apply extensive and multimodal treatments to traumatic injuries in order to speed up healing and prevent long-term damage. Some injuries do not respond well to these treatments, and patients begin a dangerous spiral of trying a variety of medical treatments that do not always work; they may become discouraged and passive, trying even more medications and giving up hobbies; and they may ultimately stop engaging in interpersonal activities they used to enjoy. They may also become unresponsive to medications, and then depression and chronic pain frequently co-occur. The most common types of pain that clinical psychologists deal with are **headache pains** (either migraine or tension headaches), **arthritis**, and **lower back pain**.

The treatment of chronic pain conditions is ideally achieved by smooth collaboration of a number of different health professionals. Multidisciplinary pain clinics were the first kind of patient care where clinical psychologists worked hand-in-hand with other health professionals in order to assist patients. Since then, many such pain clinics have been set up and are used by individual patients, insurance companies, and worker safety and compensation organizations to help workers with chronic pain problems. Physiotherapists work with pain patients to restore function and minimize strain on muscles and joints, physicians prescribe and oversee treatments with various levels of analgesics, and psychologists typically work with patients on depression and anxiety. Psychologists may also involve family members in treatment to ensure that patients remain active and plan for the future. The content of psychologists' work is largely derived from the work of Melzack and Wall (1965), whose groundbreaking **Gate Control Theory** of pain has helped to define what psychologists can do for pain patients. Melzack and Wall proposed (and then extensively tested) that pain varies as a function of the extent of the damage, but also by how it is interpreted and experienced. Under some conditions pain will worsen (i.e., the "gate" is open to allow easy flow of pain sensations); in others the pain experience is alleviated by engaging in activities that close the pain gate. The typical conditions that either open or close the pain gate are described in Table 17.7.

A major challenge for psychologists working with pain patients (like Dr. Ann C) is the accurate assessment of pain. There is a very high correspondence of self-reported pain with actual extent of injury in cases of burn injury, where pain is proportional to the amount of skin actually damaged. However, pain is an inherently idiosyncratic experience impacted by the patient's history, the meaning of the event, the pain coping models he has developed, and acute emotional and behavioral responses and the intensity and quality of

TABLE 17.7 Conditions that Open and Close the Pain Gate

Conditions that close the pain gate

Physical
• Medication
• Counterstimulation (e.g., massage, heat)

Emotional
• Positive emotions like happiness and gratefulness
• Relaxation
• Rest

Mental
• Pleasant diversions like listening to calm music
• Involvement in social activities

Conditions that open the pain gate

Physical
• Extent of an injury
• Inappropriate activity level (too little or too much)

Emotional
• Anxiety, worry, tension
• Depression
• Anger

Mental
• Focusing on the pain
• Boredom; lack of involvement in hobbies or social activities

the experience. The subjective nature of pain provides considerable challenges when attempting to assess it in animals or children. Neither animals nor young children have the ability to effectively communicate their pain experience, and there has been a growing recognition that they may have been undermedicated in the past and that careful attention should be given to nonverbal pain behaviors in order to minimize suffering (Craig, Lilley, & Gilbert, 1996). Particularly challenging is the assessment of pain in litigation situations, where the outcome of the assessment may have an impact on whether or not damages are paid or whether disability pensions are offered. In these scenarios it is important that the psychologist who conducts the assessment and provides testimony in court uses multiple modalities of assessment in order to assure that a comprehensive picture of the patient's pain can be drawn. Insurance companies will, unfortunately, encounter occasional cases of fraud or exaggeration of an individual's pain experience and therefore do not trust all self-reports. Do you remember the illustration of one such court case that was provided in chapter 9? While this was, of course, meant to be entertaining, that anecdote, a true story, addressed the very problem described here.

Psychological treatment of chronic pain, and especially the work of multidisciplinary pain clinics, not only has been shown to be effective but represents a model case for cost-offset studies where the cost of therapy itself is compared with money saved on other medical procedures and income loss due to extended dysfunction (see chapter 13 for a discussion of this topic; Flor, 2002).

◇WORKING WITH CARDIOVASCULAR DISEASE PATIENTS

Clustered together, cardiovascular diseases (atherosclerosis, myocardial infarction, heart failure, stroke, and thrombotic disease) remain the number one cause of death in Canada and in Western countries, in general (Heart & Stroke Foundation of Canada, http://www .heartandstroke.com/site/c.ikIQLcMWJtE/b.3483919/). Given the prominence of cardiovascular diseases, it comes as no surprise that there is a massive body of research trying to understand the pathogenesis of cardiovascular diseases as well as learn about the modifiability of the risk factors involved in disease development and the diseases themselves. Fortunately, there now is widespread consensus about what constitutes major cardiovascular disease risk factors. When using such knowledge to develop government and health insurance policies, one needs to distinguish between known but currently **unchangeable risk factors** and those that are open to change, with the obvious implication that the latter deserves special attention. Furthermore, it is extremely helpful for the development of cost-efficient health care policies to know how much impact these various risk factors currently have for the development of disease and to be able to forecast to what degree the same risk factor may predispose patients to multiple disease outcomes. Similarly, identification and modification of the most important risk factors in the order of their relative impact promises to maximize the cost-effectiveness of health care and prevention.

In order to provide a foundation for the psychologists' work described later, a listing of the agreed-upon risk factors, broken down into two categories of "changeable" versus "not changeable," is available on the website of the Canadian Heart and Stroke Foundation:

Risk Factors that Can Be Modified

- High blood pressure (**hypertension**)
- High blood cholesterol
- Diabetes
- Being overweight
- Excessive alcohol consumption
- Physical inactivity
- Smoking
- Stress

Risk Factors Cannot Be Modified

- Age
- Gender
- Family history
- Ethnicity
- History of stroke or transient ischemic accident

In psychosomatic medicine, the earliest hypothesized links between emotion and a disease outcome are those between anxiety, depression, and cardiovascular disease (Kubzansky & Kawachi, 2000; Rozanski, Blumenthal, & Kaplan, 1999). During the last few decades, researchers have moved from what was once clinical lore with little evidence to back it up to an impressive body of literature with fairly consistent findings (Rozanski et al., 1999; Kubzansky & Kawachi, 2000). We now have strong prospective evidence that anxiety, depression, and trait anger predict the development of coronary heart disease over and above risk factors like poor diet, sedentary lifestyle, genetics, or smoking (Linden, 2008). Depression, in particular, has been associated with a high risk of disease recurrence in patients who already had one heart attack, with documented risk ratios ranging from 2:1 to 4:1 (Lesperance & Frasure-Smith, 2000). Given the prevalence of at least some depression symptoms in 30% of cardiac patients and the high costs associated with psychological distress in cardiac patients (Lesperance & Frasure-Smith, 2000), psychology researchers have developed treatment programs for cardiac patients that focus on reduction of stress and arousal via relaxation, breathing (van Dixhoorn & White, 2005), and other cognitive-behavioral methods for stress reduction and treatment of depression (Langosch, Budde, & Linden, 2007). The outcome literature on how well these treatments work has created some confusion because reports have alternated between positive reports indicating that the distress and mortality rates can be reduced and negative reports arising from large clinical trials that have failed to show unique benefits of psychological treatments (Writing Committee for the ENRICHD investigators, 2003). Fine-grained meta-analyses have looked at which patients, under which conditions, benefit from psychological intervention and have helped to establish the current state of knowledge, which is notably more clear now (Dusseldorp, Van Elderen, Maes, Meulman, & Kraail, 1999; Linden, Phillips, & Leclerc, 2007). The Dutch research group of Dusseldorp and colleagues has clearly shown that psychological treatment of cardiac patients reduces subsequent mortality as long as the treatment actually reduces psychological distress. Curiously, some clinical trials have offered psychological treatments to all patients even though some were not distressed to begin with and then failed to find that the treatment was effective (see the reviews of Dusseldorp et al., 1999; Linden et al., 2007). Further clarifications have been offered by Linden and his colleagues (2007) in the most comprehensive meta-analysis to date. Psychosocial interventions when added to other active rehabilitation conditions reduced the odds of mortality and the recurrence of nonfatal cardiac events, but this applied only to male participants. Those patients with little emotional distress did not benefit, and patients who received treatment very soon after their cardiac event also did not derive a lot of benefit. On the other hand, patients recruited many months after their surgery or hospitalization who were still in distress showed, by far, the greatest mortality reduction when distress was treated. The current challenge for the field is to develop interventions that meet the unique needs of female cardiac patients who appear to respond quite differently to cardiac disease (Abbey & Stewart, 2000).

◇ HYPERTENSION

High blood pressure (or hypertension) is one of the most significant risk factors for coronary heart disease and a highly prevalent disease in and of itself. Genetic factors play a major role in the development of hypertension, but the current view is that genetics need to interact with behavioral and psychological factors to fully account for the disease. Personality factors like trait hostility may play a critical role in understanding why people over-respond to stress and thereby maintain arousal levels longer than necessary (Schwartz et al., 2003; Linden et al., 1997). Consistent with research findings that link stress to hypertension via disturbed self-regulation of the autonomic nervous system (Sakakibara, Takeuchi, & Takeuchi, 1994; Sakakibara & Hayano, 1996), psychological treatments are designed to reduce blood pressure by reducing stress and arousal. This is attempted via two different strategies. One approach is to emphasize physiological arousal reduction and autonomic balance through relaxation training, meditation, and/or biofeedback, all of which are designed to improve a person's autonomic, self-regulatory skills. Such methods can be taught in a standardized, manual-driven fashion, and one can package two or more methods together (e.g., relaxation and temperature biofeedback are often taught together; Linden, 2005).

A second approach is to view stress as a multistep process involving triggers, coping behaviors, cognitions, and physiological stress responses (Linden, 2005). Thus, treatment or intervention may require the teaching of a broad array of problem-solving skills. Treatments using this second, less narrowly focused approach target deficient cognitive and behavioral stress coping skills and require more individually tailored, multicomponent interventions because the presumed critical skills deficits are not likely the same across all hypertensive patients nor are the patients' stimulus environments presumed to be the same. The second approach also requires a higher level of skill and more training in psychological therapies for the therapist.

Extensive evidence from over 100 randomized controlled trials indicates that behavioral treatments reduce blood pressure to a modest degree, and this change is greater than what is seen in wait-list or other inactive controls; however, the effect sizes are quite variable. Observed blood pressure reductions are highly positively related to blood pressure levels at pretest, and behavioral studies tend to underestimate possible benefits because they usually work with patients whose blood pressure is not greatly elevated and who, therefore, can also not improve as much. Multicomponent, individualized psychological treatments lead to greater blood pressure changes than do single-component treatments like relaxation training (Linden & Moseley, 2006).

◇ CHRONIC HEART FAILURE

Improved surgical techniques and new, more potent medications allow cardiac patients to live longer. However, given that better management of heart disease is not equivalent to a cure, a growing number of patients survive their first myocardial infarction or respond well to revascularization (a surgical clean-out of blood vessels) or bypass surgery, but they may ultimately move into a condition of **chronic heart failure (CHF)** that cannot be cured. Correspondingly, this provides new challenges for psychological support staff trying to manage symptoms and maximize QOL. Once diagnosed, CHF patients have an average life expectancy of 5 years (Mckelvie et al., 1995), and QOL is generally poor because of chronic symptoms and the sufferer's awareness of the poor prognosis. These patients account for a large portion of expensive emergency hospitalizations, often due to poor compliance with the treatment regimen (e.g., irregular use or complete refusal of medications and excess salt and fluid intake; Wagdi, Vuilliomonet, Kaufmann, Richter, & Bertel, 1993). With noncompliance being the most frequent reason for medical crises, Wagdi and colleagues further investigated patient knowledge and found that a prime reason for nonadherence was a lack of knowledge about the purpose and procedure for the medication regimen; there also was insufficient follow-up by local physicians. The conclusion was that thorough patient education and close follow-up was considered a highly cost-efficient means of managing these patients and of preventing repeated emergency hospitalizations. Adding a psychoeducational component to standard medical care of heart failure patients improved functional status and led to an 85% decrease in the hospital readmission rate for the 6-month follow-up; at that time the estimated savings for the health care organization or hospital were US$9800/patient (Fonarow et al., 1997).

Not only do CHF patients show low adherence to treatment regimens, but many suffer from depression, which has serious implications for disease prognosis. In a meta-analysis of 36 published studies on depression and heart failure (Rutledge, Reis, Linke, Greenberg, & Mills, 2006), clinically significant depression was present in 21.5% of heart failure patients; these figures varied, however, as a function of questionnaire use versus diagnostic interview (33.6% and 19.3%, respectively) and disease severity. Combined results suggested higher rates of death and secondary cardiac events like myocardial infarction (risk ratio = 2.1:1), trends toward increased health care use, and higher rates of hospitalization and emergency room visits among depressed patients. Treatment studies thus far have generally relied on small samples, but do suggest consistent reductions in depression symptoms. Furthermore, researchers have studied how depression affects adherence in heart failure patients. In a prospective study of 492 patients, persistently depressed patients were less likely to adhere to behaviors that reduce the risk of recurrent acute symptoms (Kronish et al., 2006). Differences in adherence to these behaviors may explain in part why depression predicts mortality in cardiac patients. Compared with persistently nondepressed individuals, persistently depressed patients reported much lower rates of adherence to quitting smoking (OR = 0.23), taking medications (OR = 0.50), exercising (OR = 0.57), and attending cardiac rehabilitation (OR = 0.50). These findings reinforce the importance of psychosocial research in heart failure populations and identify a number of areas for future study.

◇ HEART TRANSPLANTATION

A subgroup of heart failure patients may have the opportunity to undergo heart transplantation, and, due to more experience with the transplantation surgery itself and the necessary subsequent rejection management, success rates for heart transplantation today are quite good, with 10-year survival of about 60% (Davies et al., 1996). Nevertheless, transplantation is a medically complex and emotionally difficult process, and it poses particular challenges in the area of adherence. A group of 108 transplant recipients were followed for an average of 970 days (Owen, Bonds, & Wellish, 2006), and pretransplant evaluations were retrospectively coded for psychiatric risk factors. Previous suicide attempts, poor adherence to medical recommendations, previous drug or alcohol rehabilitation, and depression significantly predicted attenuated survival times.

An additional, largely unavoidable stressor is the fact that transplantation surgery is done only in major hospitals, typically university teaching hospitals, and patients living in rural areas may have to relocate at least for a few months, often isolated from their families and at considerable expense. After transplantation, patients need to follow a complex medication regimen consisting of immune suppressants and cardiac and often other medications. Considerable pressure has to be put on transplant patients to maintain an extremely healthy lifestyle: Weight control and a healthy diet are crucial to prevent rejection of the new heart, as is a reasonable exercise program, and avoidance of sun exposure. Return to work is a viable prospect for some but certainly not all patients, and the transplantation often triggers deep existential questions like:

- How is the donor family affected?
- Why do I deserve this heart?
- What is important in my next years of life?

Heart transplantation is a very good demonstration of a primary health problem that is not psychological to begin with but where the burden of treatment and required behavior changes call for the input of a multidisciplinary health care team where a clinical psychologist can make valuable contributions.

◇ RESTENOSIS

A surgical procedure called angioplasty (clearing out clogged blood vessels) has become a frequently used intervention largely because it is less invasive than bypass surgery. Unfortunately, 30–40% of vessels reocclude following angioplasty (this process is called **restenosis**), mostly within 6 months following surgery. Although severity of initial blockage and location of the vessel predict restenosis to some degree, much of the medically unexplained variance has been linked to psychological and behavioral factors. The single strongest predictor for restenosis is continued smoking, and many surgeons don't want to do angioplasties on people who continue to smoke. From a psychological perspective, the constructs of **vital exhaustion** and **cognitive adaptation theory** have been used to show the predictive power of psychological factors for explaining restenosis (Appels, Baer, Lasker, Flamm, & Kop, 1997; Helgeson & Fritz, 1999). Cognitive adaptation theory captures a sense of optimism, high self-esteem, and mastery and predicts lower likelihood of restenosis (Helgeson & Fritz, 1999), whereas vital exhaustion refers to a lack of perceived energy, demoralization, and irritability and predicts greater rates of restenosis (Appels et al., 1997). Appels and his colleagues have developed a brief cognitive-behavioral intervention to increase self-efficacy and psychological adjustment; this treatment program has potential for reducing restenosis rates (Appels et al., 1997).

◇ WORKING WITH CANCER PATIENTS

There has been excellent progress in the quality of cancer care, and the average survival rates have risen steadily over the last 3 decades. For example, in British Columbia, the 5-year survival rate for patients with prostate cancer is now 96% (http://www.bccancer.ca). Unfortunately, however, cancer incidence (i.e., the number of new cases being diagnosed) has continued to rise. Cancer remains the second most frequent cause of death after cardiovascular diseases, and the gap between the two in terms of cause-of-death prevalence is closing. A diagnosis of cancer is very emotionally threatening, can provoke anxiety and depression, and is difficult to live with because of the prognostic uncertainty (Ganz et al., 1996; Ganz & Hahn, 2008). It usually takes many months, if not years, before cancer patients know whether or not their first wave of treatment has been really effective. Emotional distress can be reduced with psychological support, whether delivered by professionals or through social support networks (Helgeson et al., 2000). Psychologists working in the area of cancer refer to their field as "psycho-oncology," which is concerned with etiological factors as well as adjustment to the disease. Research on psychological contributions to the etiology of cancer has been vigorous and has brought about interesting theoretical concepts like the type C personality (a tendency to be introverted, respectful, eager to please, conforming, and compliant; Temoshok & Dreher, 1992) or that of **traumatic loss** (Gurevich, Devins, & Rodin, 2002) and **search for meaning** (Brennan, 2001), but there is unfortunately little evidence to date that any particular psychological factor serves as a reliable predictor for cancer development or cancer remission (DeBoer et al., 1999). The most researched predictive factor is depression; a meta-analysis of prospective studies of the effect of depression on mortality in recently diagnosed cancer patients revealed that depressed cancer patients have a small, but still significantly elevated, risk for cancer mortality, with risk increments of 20–60% depending on how risk was calculated and whether depressive symptoms or clinical depression was used as the predictor (Satin, Linden, & Phillips, 2008).

To better understand the challenges of dealing with a cancer diagnosis and treatment, it may be useful to compare cancer and cardiovascular disease. In the previous section on cardiovascular diseases, we described how heart disease often reveals itself suddenly (the classic example is heart attack) and the patient is understandably distressed and confused by the suddenness of this arising threat. However, within a few weeks or months, patients have a pretty clear idea about what behavior changes they can and need to make for their own benefit as well as what their functional limitations are, if any. Some patients with heart disease who commit to cardiac rehabilitation are healthier afterward than they had been prior to their disease (Ornish, 1990). Very much in contrast to this kind of predictable trajectory in heart disease, with relatively quick and often good outcomes, is the entire process

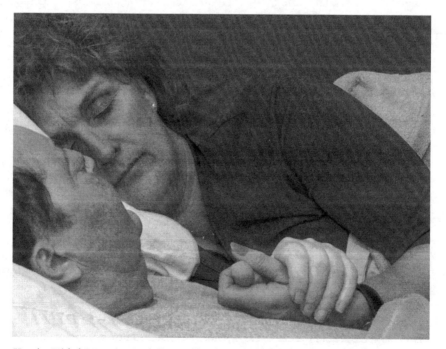

Hospice Michel Sarrazin, Quebec, Canada Photographer: Henri Dupond

of dealing with the diagnosis and treatment of cancer. There are two subgroups of cancer patients for whom the future is relatively clear: one is unfortunately the palliative group which is told that they have a very limited time to live and that the disease itself is no longer controllable. The second group of patients is at the other end of this spectrum; their treatment can be effective, and they may find out over a period of relatively few months that they are probably disease-free (this hopeful scenario can, for example, be seen in some melanoma patients with very clearly localized lesions). The majority of patients, however, undergo lengthy and very aversive treatments, at the end of which they still don't know for sure whether the disease has been beaten and how high the probability of a return is. In fact, they never feel totally safe (Ganz & Hahn, 2008). It is this uncertainty, with its inbuilt fear of recurrence, that represents a major challenge for the patient's QOL. Researchers are learning about the process of seeing oneself as a survivor (Ganz et al., 1996; Ganz & Hahn, 2008), and clinicians are trying to help patients adapt to this self-perception. However fear arousing cancer typically is, many patients respond well, and typically show gradual improvement in physical and psychological function (Helgeson, Snyder, & Seltman, 2004). Nevertheless, there are subgroups for whom the trajectory of change is marked by deterioration, fear, depression, overwhelming fear of recurrence, and helplessness. It is therefore necessary to determine on repeated occasions how well patients are adjusting so as to identify the ones who may need professional support at some stage (Helgeson et al., 2004).

How well do psychological treatments work, and what areas of psychological function benefit? An important target for treatment is patient's QOL (Coyne, Stefanek, & Palmer, 2007). Zimmermann, Heinrichs, and Baucom (2007) published results from a meta-analysis of psychological treatment outcomes revealing a small overall treatment effect $(d = -.26)$ for distress reduction and also provided many additional details for the most effective delivery of psychosocial treatment for cancer patients. Interventions led by nonpsychologists produced notably smaller effects; and psychoeducation was more effective than supportive therapy. One-on-one treatment was more effective than group interventions.

Even the application of a single, relatively nonspecific treatment, namely, relaxation training, was beneficial (Luebbert et al., 2001). Fifteen studies were identified in this review, and they revealed significant beneficial effects on affective distress for patients undergoing chemotherapy, radiotherapy, bone marrow transplantation, and hyperthermia. Outcomes were clustered into biological indices (blood pressure, heart rate, nausea, pain), and the corresponding aggregate effect size was $d = -.49$ (weighted for sample size) for the pre-post comparison. Outcome for subjective distress (depression, tension, anxiety, mood) was also $d = -.49$.

While psychological interventions for cancer patients can have a positive effect on patient's QOL, there is no convincing evidence to date that it prolongs life and directly affects the disease process (Chow, Tsao, & Harth, 2004). In a meta-analysis on survival enhancement in psychologically treated cancer patients, 1- and 4-year overall survival rates were obtained from eight and six trials, respectively. There was no statistically significant difference in the overall survival rates at 1 and 4 years (risk ratios = .94 and .95; note that neither was significantly different from chance). Four trials had examined 511 metastatic breast cancer patients. Again, there was no statistically significant difference in the overall survival rates at 1 and 4 years (risk ratios were .87 and .91, respectively). It would be

BOX 17.1

CANCER AND THE FIGHTING SPIRIT

We suspect that few university students follow the obituaries in their local newspaper. If, however, they did, they would notice that when patients have died of cancer, they are frequently described as having engaged in a "heroic battle" (or some other description of a struggle is often given) that was ultimately lost. This kind of image has developed because of initial reports that breast cancer patients with a fighting spirit seemed to fare better than those who had given up (Pettingale et al., 1985). Many professionals working with cancer patients have at best mixed feelings about this image of a heroic battle, and even more rather dislike it (Coyne, Stefanek, & Palmer, 2007). Why is that you may wonder? First of all, nobody quite knows *how* a patient can actually fight such a battle against tiny little tumor cells nor is there continuing evidence that a heroic battle will extend life for cancer patients (although adherence to recommendations from health professionals may help). Given the lack of evidence that engaging in a "battle" actually helps, patients may unnecessarily get their hopes up and then spend a lot of energy fighting something they can't win. Even worse is the hidden message that those who do not engage in a battle are somehow responsible for their own ill fortunes when the tumor continues to grow. Blaming victims of a potentially deadly illness for having contributed to their own death by not fighting hard enough is not justified by the facts, nor is such imposed blame appreciated by patients themselves.

premature, however, to abandon research on mortality effects of psychological treatments because not all types of patients, at all possible stages of disease, have been evaluated in clinical trials, and the types of treatments offered have been restricted to supportive therapy (Classen et al., 2001), mindfulness meditation (Speca et al., 2000), and cognitive-behavioral interventions (Antoni et al., 1991).

◇CONCLUSION

This chapter had two objectives. On the one hand it was meant to provide an introduction to the growing fields of health psychology and behavioral medicine as specialty areas of psychology but also as subspecialties within clinical psychology. The second objective was to clarify the place of the clinical psychologist within primary care using research findings from the applied health psychology field. It should be noted that health psychology has been taught as a distinct course in North American universities for less than 3 decades. Many psychologists who taught health psychology courses during this time never had the advantage of having been able to take a health psychology course themselves simply because this course did not exist when they went to graduate school. This includes one author of this textbook (W.L.), who introduced the first health psychology course at his university in the 1980s. The health psychology and behavioral medicine fields of today have largely grown out of the practice of clinical psychology in physical health care settings. The contribution of clinical psychology to health psychology is especially apparent in the application of cognitive-behavioral principles to understand problem behavior and for behavior modification in medical settings. It is for these reasons that we view clinical psychology as a health profession in the broadest sense, a profession that integrates physical and mental health in order to understand human beings as a whole. Even though this is a fairly lengthy chapter, we could scratch only the surface of what is a rapidly growing domain of psychology, and we could provide only samples of the role of clinical psychologists within this domain.

◇ ONGOING CONSIDERATIONS

One of the areas of practice for clinical psychologists that has grown in importance is that of primary health care and rehabilitation (Humbke et al., 2004). We predict that there will be additional growth in years to come, and these may be good areas to specialize in. A potential problem with this trend is that clinical psychologists may join multidisciplinary health care, thus allowing patients one-stop shopping for complex health care, but this also usually means that the clinical psychologists will be the only member of their profession on this team. Operating in such relative isolation from colleagues makes it hard to maintain a professional identity and requires a seasoned, assertive psychologist to begin with. Unfortunately, the training of young psychologists becomes very difficult when there is no psychology department within which to work, and we have yet to resolve the question of how one becomes a specialized, seasoned psychologist under these circumstances. There is a risk of fragmentation that we need to find ways to counteract.

◇ KEY TERMS LEARNED

Adherence	Primary prevention
Arthritis	Restenosis
Chronic heart failure (CHF)	Risk factor
Cognitive adaptation theory	Risk ratio
Gate Control Theory	Search for meaning
Hazards ratio	Secondary prevention
Headache pains	Tertiary prevention
Hypertension	Traumatic loss
Lower back pain	Unchangeable risk factors
Odds ratio	Vital exhaustion

◇ THINKING QUESTIONS

1. How well do traditional clinical psychology programs prepare their graduates for work in primary health care?

2. Which aspects of professional clinical psychology developed in psychiatric contexts are similarly suitable and/or transferable to work with physical health problems?

3. When an older patient has a major, chronic health problem like heart failure with its poor prognosis and depression, is that comparable to depression in a psychiatric environment with a 20-year-old patient? Should these two be treated the same?

4. Given that many patients with physical illnesses adjust relatively well on their own, is there a risk that we overtreat as psychologists?

◇ REFERENCES

Abbey, S. E., & Stewart, D. E. (2000). Gender and psychosomatic aspects of ischemic heart disease. *Journal of Psychosomatic Research, 48,* 417–424.

Antoni, M. H., Baggett, L., Ironson, G., LaPerriere, A., August, S., Klimas, N., et al. (1991). Cognitive-behavioral stress management intervention buffers distress responses and immunological changes following notification of HIV-1 seropositivity. *Journal of Consulting and Clinical Psychology, 59,* 906–915.

Appels, A., Baer, F., Lasker, J., Flamm, U., & Kop, W. (1997). The effect of a psychological intervention program on the risk of a new coronary event after angioplasty: A feasibility study. *Journal of Psychosomatic Research, 43,* 209–217.

Boyes, A. W., Girgis, A., Zucca, A. C., Lecathelinais, C. (2009). Anxiety and depression among long-term survivors of cancer in Australia: Results of a population-based survey. *Medical Journal of Australia, 190,* S94–S98.

Brennan, J. (2001). Adjustment to cancer—Coping or personal transition? *Psycho-Oncology, 10,* 1–18.

Brody, D. S. (2003). Improving the management of depression in primary care: Recent accomplishments and ongoing challenges. *Disease Management Health Outcomes, 11,* 21–31.

Burrell, C. D., and Levy, R. A. (1985). Therapeutic consequences of noncompliance. In *Improving Medication Compliance: Proceedings of a Symposium.* Reston, VA: National Pharmaceutical Council.

Burgio, K. L., Goode, P. S., Locher, J. L., Umlauf, M. G., Roth, D. L., Richter, H. E., et al. (2002). Behavioral training with and without biofeedback in the treatment of urge incontinence in older women. A randomized controlled trial. *JAMA, 288,* 2293–2299.

Chen, E. (2004). Why socioeconomic status affects the health of children: A psychosocial perspective. *Current Directions in Psychological Science, 13,* 112–115.

Clark, N. M., Becker, M. H., Janz, N. K., Lorig, K., & William, J. (1991). Self-management of chronic disease by older adults: A review and questions for research. *Journal of Aging and Health, 3,* 3–27.

Classen, C., Butler, L. D., Koopman, C., Miller, E., DiMiceli, S., Giese-Davis, J., et al. (2001). Supportive-expressive group therapy and distress in patients with metastatic breast cancer: A randomized clinical intervention trial. *Archives of General Psychiatry, 58,* 494–501.

Chow, E., Tsao, M. N., & Harth, T. (2004). Does psychosocial intervention improve survival in cancer? A meta-analysis. *Palliative Medicine, 18,* 25–31.

Coyne, J. C., Stefanek, M., & Palmer, S. C. (2007). Psychotherapy and survival in cancer: The conflict between hope and evidence. *Psychological Bulletin, 133,* 367–394.

Craig, K. D., Lilley, C. M., & Gilbert, C. A. (1996). Barriers to optimal pain management in infants, children and adolescents. *Clinical Journal of Pain, 12*, 232–242.

Cummings, N. A. (2005). Delivering the nuts without the bolts: The plight of clinical psychology practice. *Journal of Clinical Psychology, 61*, 1071–1107.

Davies, R. A., Rivard, M., Pflugfelder, P., Teo, K., Jlain, B., Champagne, F. et al. (1996). *Heart transplantation in Canada and determinants of survival.* Paper presented at the Annual Meeting of the Canadian Cardiovascular Society, Montreal.

DeBoer, M. F., Ryckman, R. M., Pruyn, J. F. A., & Van den Borne, H. W. (1999). Psychosocial correlates of cancer relapse and survival: A literature review. *Patient Education and Counseling, 37*, 215–230.

Dusseldorp, E., Van Elderen, T., Maes, S., Meulman, J., & Kraail, V. (1999). A meta-analysis of psycho-educational programs for coronary heart disease patients. *Health Psychology, 18*, 506–519.

Feuerstein, M., Labbe, E. E., & Kuczmierczyk, A. R. (1986). *Health psychology: A psychobiological perspective.* New York: Plenum.

Flor, T. (2002). Clinical effectiveness and cost-effectiveness of treatments for patients with chronic pain. *Clinical Journal of Pain, 18*, 355–365.

Fonarow, G. C., Stevenson, L. W., Walden, J. A., Livingston, N. A., Steimle, A. E., Hamilton, M. A., et al. (1997). Impact of a comprehensive heart failure management program on hospital readmission and functional of patients with advanced heart failure. *Journal of the American College of Cardiology, 30*, 725–732.

Ford, E. S., Giles, W. H., & Dietz, W. H. (2002). Prevalence of the metabolic syndrome among US adults: Findings from the third National Health and Nutrition Examination Survey. *JAMA, 287*, 356–359.

Friedman, H. S., Tucker, J. S., Reise, S. P. (1995). Personality dimensions and measures potnetially relevant to health: A focus on hostility. *Annals of Behavioral Medicine, 17*, 245–253.

Ganz, P. A., Coscarelli, A., Fred, C., Kahn, B., Polinsky, M. L., & Petersen, L. (1996). Breast cancer survivors: Psychosocial concerns and quality of life. *Breast Cancer Research and Treatment, 38*, 183–199.

Ganz, P. A., & Hahn, E. E. (2008). Implementing a survivorship care plan for patients with breast cancer. *Journal of Clinical Oncology, 26*, 759–767.

Gurevich, M., Devins, G., & Rodin, G. (2002). Post-traumatic stress disorder and cancer: Conceptual and assessment issues. *Psychosomatics, 43*, 259–281.

Hawkley, L. C., Berntson, G. G., Engeland, C. G., Marucha, P. T., Masi, C. M., & Cacioppo, J. T. (2005). Stress, aging, and resilience: Can accrued wear and tear be slowed? *Canadian Psychology, 46*, 115–125.

Hayman, L. L. (2007). Behavioral medicine across the life course: Challenges and opportunities for interdisciplinary science. *Annals of Behavioral Medicine, 33*(3), 236–241.

Helgeson, V., & Fritz, H. (1999). Cognitive adaptation as a predictor of new coronary events after percutaneous transluminal angioplasty. *Psychosomatic Medicine, 61*, 488–495.

Helgeson, V. S., Cohen, S., Schulz, R., & Yasko, J. (2000). Group support interventions for women with breast cancer: Who benefits from what? *Health Psychology, 19*, 107–114.

Helgeson, V. S., Snyder, P., & Seltman, H. (2004). Psychological and physical adjustment to breast cancer over 4 years: Identifying distinct trajectories of change. *Health Psychology, 23*, 3–15.

Humbke, K. L., Brown, D. L., Welder, A. N., Fillion, D. T., Dobson, K. S., & Arnett, J. L. (2004). A survey of hospital psychology in Canada. *Canadian Psychology, 45*(1), 31–41.

Hunsley, J. (2003). Cost-effectiveness and medical cost-offset considerations in psychological service provision. *Canadian Psychology, 44*, 61–73.

Jackson, L., Leclerc, J., & Erskine, Y. (2005). Getting the most out of cardiac rehabilitation: A review of referral and adherence predictors. *Heart, 91*, 14–19.

Kostis, J. B., Rosen, R. C., Brondolo, E., Taska, L., Smith, D. E., & Wilson, A. C. (1992). Superiority of nonpharmacologic therapy compared to propranolol and placebo in men with mild hypertension: A randomized, prospective trial. *American Heart Journal, 123*, 466–474.

Kripalani, S., Yao, X., & Haynes, R. B. (2007). Interventions to enhance medication adherence in chronic medical conditions. *Archives of Internal Medicine, 167*, 540–550.

Kronish, I. M., Rieckmann, N., Halm, E. A., Shimbo, D., Vorchheimer, D., Haas, D. C., & Davidson, K. W. (2006). Persistent depression affects adherence to secondary prevention behaviors after acute coronary syndromes. *Journal of General Internal Medicine, 21*, 1178–1183.

Kubzansky, L., & Kawachi, I. (2000). Going to the heart of matter: Do negative emotions cause coronary heart disease? *Journal of Psychosomatic Research, 48*, 323–337.

Langosch, W., Budde, H. G., & Linden, W. (2007). Psychological interventions for coronary heart disease: Stress management, relaxation, and Ornish groups. In J. Jordan, B. Barde, & A. M. Zeiher (Eds.), *Contributions toward evidence-based psychocardiology: A systematic review of the literature* (pp. 231–254). Washington, DC: APA Books.

Lesperance, F., & Frasure-Smith, N. (2000). Depression in patients with cardiac disease: A practical review. *Journal of Psychosomatic Research, 48*, 379–392.

Linden, W. (2005). *Stress management: From basic science to better practice.* Thousand Oaks, CA: Sage.

Linden, W. (2006). Treating hypertension. In A. Kuczmierczyk & A. Nicevic (Eds.), *Formulation and treatment in clinical health psychology.* London, England: Routledge.

Linden, W. (2008). *Psychological and behavioral risk factors for cardiovascular diseases, technical report.* Ottawa, ON: Public Health Agency of Canada.

Linden, W., Moseley, J. V., & Erskine, Y. (2005). Psychology as a health care profession: Implications for training. *Canadian Psychology, 46*, 179–188.

Linden, W., & Moseley, J. V. (2006). The efficacy of behavioral treatments for hypertension. *Applied Psychophysiology and Biofeedback, 31*, 51–63.

Linden, W., Phillips, M. J., & Leclerc, J. (2007). Psychological treatment of cardiac patients: A meta-analysis. *European Heart Journal, 28*, 2972–2984.

Luebbert, K., Dahme, B., & Hasenbring, M. (2001). The effectiveness of relaxation training in reducing treatment-related symptoms and improving emotional adjustment in acute non-surgical cancer treatment: A meta-analytic review. *Psycho-Oncology, 10*, 490–502.

McKelvie, R. S., Koon, K. T., McCartney, N., Humen, D., Montague, T., & Yusuf, S. (1995). Effects of exercise training in patients with congestive heart failure: A critical review. *Journal of the American College of Cardiology, 25*, 789–796.

Melzack, R., & Wall, P. D. (1965). Pain mechanisms: A new theory. *Science, 150*, 971–979.

Middlebrooks, J. S., & Audage, N. C. (2008). *The effects of childhood stress on health across the lifespan.* Atlanta, GA: Centers for Disease Control and Prevention, National Center for Injury Prevention and Control.

Moss, D. (2007). Advances in neuromuscular rehabilitation. *Biofeedback, 35*, 1–2.

Ornish, D. (1990). *Dr. Dean Ornish's Program for Reversing Heart Disease.* New York: Random House.

Owen, J. E., Bonds, C. L., & Wellisch, D. K. (2006). Psychiatric evaluations of heart transplant candidates: Predicting post-transplant hospitalizations, rejection episodes, and survival. *Psychosomatics, 47*, 213–222.

Pinel, J. (2000). *Biopsychology* (4th ed.). Boston, MA: Allyn & Bacon.

Poole, G., Hunt Matheson, D., & Cox, D. N. (2008). *The psychology of health and health care: A Canadian perspective* (3rd ed.). Toronto, ON: Pearson Prentice-Hall.

Rodrigue, J. R. (1996). Introduction to the Special Issue on "Psychological research and practice in organ transplantation." *Journal of Clinical Psychology in Medical Settings, 3*, 299–302.

Rozanski, A., Blumenthal, J. A., & Kaplan, J. (1999). Impact of psychological factors on the pathogenesis of cardiovascular disease and implications for therapy. *Circulation, 99*, 2192–2217.

Rugulies, R. (2002). Depression as a predictor for coronary heart disease. A review and meta-analysis. *American Journal of Preventive Medicine, 23*, 51–61.

Rutledge, T., Reis, V. A., Linke, S. A., Greenberg, B. H., & Mills, P. J. (2006). Depression in heart failure: A meta-analytic review of prevalence, intervention effects, and associations with clinical outcomes. *Journal of the American College of Cardiology, 48*, 1527–1537.

Sakakibara, M., & Hayano, J. (1996). Effect of slowed respiration on cardiac parasympathetic response to threat. *Psychosomatic Medicine, 58*, 32–37.

Sakakibara, M., Takeuchi, S., & Hayano, J. (1994). Effect of relaxation training on cardiac sympathetic tone. *Psychophysiology, 31*, 223–228.

Sarason, I. G., Sarason, B. R., Potter, E. H. 3rd, & Antoni, M. H. (1985). Life events, social support, and illness. *Psychosomatic Medicine, 47*, 156–163.

Satin, J., Linden, W., Phillips, M. J. (2009). Depression as a predictor of disease progression and mortality in cancer patients: A meta-analysis. *Cancer, 115*, 5349–5361.

Schwartz, A., Gerin, W., Davidson, K., Brosschot, J., Thayer, J., Pickering, T. G., & Linden, W. (2003). In search of a coherent model of stressor effects on short-term cardiovascular adjustments and the development of cardiovascular disease. *Psychosomatic Medicine, 65*, 22–35.

Segerstrom, S. C., & Miller, G. E. (2004). Psychological stress and the human immune system: A meta-analytic study of 30 years of inquiry. *Psychological Bulletin, 130*, 601–630.

Speca, M., Carlson, L. E., Goodey, E., & Angen, M. (2000). A randomized, wait-list controlled clinical trial: The effect of a mindfulness meditation-based stress reduction program on mood and symptoms of stress in cancer outpatients. *Psychosomatic Medicine, 62*, 613–622.

Steven, I. D. (1999). *Patient presentations in general practice: A comprehensive guide to diagnosis and management.* Sydney, Australia: McGraw-Hill.

Strawbridge, W. J., Deleger, S., Roberts, R. E., & Kaplan, G. A. (2002). Physical activity reduces the risk of subsequent depression for older adults. *American Journal of Epidemiology, 156*, 328–334.

Talen, M. R., Fraser, J. S., & Cauley, K. (2005). Training primary care psychologists: A model for pre-doctoral programs. *Professional Psychology: Research and Practice, 36,* 136–143.

Temoshok, H., & Dreher, H. (1992). *The type C connection: Behavioral links to cancer and your health.* New York: Random House.

van Dixhoorn, J., & White, A. (2005). Relaxation therapy for rehabilitation and prevention in ischemic heart disease: A systematic review and meta-analysis. *European Journal of Cardiovascular Prevention and Rehabilitation, 12,* 193–202.

Vitaliano, P. P., Zhang, J, & Scanlan, J. (2003). Is care-giving hazardous to one's physical health? A meta-analysis. *Psychological Bulletin, 129,* 946–972.

Wagdi, P., Vuilliomonet, A., Kaufmann, U., Richter, M., & Bertel, O. (1993). Ungenuegende Behandlungsdisziplin, Patienteninformation und Medikamentenverschreibung als Ursachen fuer die Notfallhospitalisation bei chronisch herzinsuffizienten Patienten. *Schweizer Medizinische Wochenschrift, 123,* 108–112.

Writing Committee for the ENRICHD investigators. (2003). Effects of treating depression and low perceived social support on clinical events after myocardial infarction: The enhancing recovery in coronary heart disease patients (ENRICHD) trial. *JAMA, 289,* 3106–3116.

Yusuf, S., Hawken, S., Ounpuu, S., Dan, T., Avezum, A., Lanas, F., et al. on behalf of the INTER-HEART Study Investigators. (2004). Effect of modifiable risk factors associated with myocardial infarction in 52 countries (the INTERHEART study): Case control study. *The Lancet, 364,* 937–952.

Zimmermann, T., Heinrichs, N., & Baucom, D. H. (2007). "Does one size fit all"? Moderators in psychosocial intervention for breast cancer patients: A meta-analysis. *Annals of Behavioral Medicine, 34,* 225–239.

CHAPTER EIGHTEEN

PSYCHOPHARMACOLOGY

CHAPTER OBJECTIVES

You may wonder why a clinical psychology textbook addresses the topic of pharmacological treatments when psychologists are not typically allowed to prescribe medications. Does that not fall exclusively into the domain of licensed physicians?

There are many good reasons to provide at least an overview of **psychopharmacology** here. We want to alert the reader and budding clinical psychologist to these advantages of having basic knowledge in psychopharmacology:

- Effective professional interactions between psychologists and prescribing physicians treating the same patient

- The possibility of being proactive in collaborating with a physician to compose an ideal treatment package for patients that may consist of drug treatment and parallel psychological supports

- Better understanding of the patient's full medical status in order to complete meaningful assessments (see the discussion of Axis 3 information from the *DSM-IV* in chapter 6)

- Better understanding of potential somatic and psychological symptoms that can arise from medication effects and medication side effects

The first two reasons for why clinical psychologists want to have knowledge in psychopharmacology arise from the fact that the great majority (87%) of **psychoactive drugs** are prescribed by family physicians and other specialists but not by psychiatrists (DeLeon & Wiggins, 1996). Family physicians typically receive only 4–12 weeks of training in psychoactive drugs and are not routinely trained in psychotherapy (Tucker, 1992; Zimmerman & Wienckowski, 1991). Together, the latter two facts greatly increase the likelihood that a clinical psychologist will work jointly with a general practitioner in the care of a patient, whereas it is highly unlikely that a clinical psychologist and a psychiatrist will treat the same patient. Having a shared language with and respect for the other professional in turn enhances the chances of getting the patient the best treatment.

◇ A CLINICAL CASE SCENARIO

An example from clinical practice may help to demonstrate the value of knowing at least the basics of psychopharmacology:

Our graduate student Vincent has made excellent progress in graduate school and managed to defend his thesis before going on the 1-year full-time internship required by his accredited training program. One of his rotations in the internship is in a geriatrics unit, and Vincent gets involved in the process of evaluating patients to determine whether or not they should be hospitalized or moved to a long-term care facility, or whether they can continue to live safely on their own. He is asked by his supervisor to conduct an assessment of the cognitive abilities of Joseph M, who is a slight, 69-year-old widowed man living on his own. Joseph M's children live too far away to look after him on a daily basis, and he has refused an offer from his oldest son to move in with him. On the other hand, the children are worried about him, noting that he has deteriorated. Vincent is meeting Joseph M. for the first time today and plans to complete a mental status exam and a full IQ test, using the Wechsler IV intelligence test. Also, in preparation for this test day, Mr. M. was asked to bring all his medications with him. Vincent was not initially planning to look into Mr. M.'s pharmacological regimen because that is not the psychologist's usual domain of expertise. When, however, Vincent begins his interaction with Mr. M., he finds him very slow and disoriented. Although Mr. M. provides mostly correct answers during the mental status exam, he does so with long breaks between answers, he hesitates a lot, and he displays slightly slurred speech. He appears so subdued that Vincent doubts Mr. M.'s ability to complete a full IQ test, and even if he did, wonders whether or not the test would be valid for the current assessment objective. Given his age, and Vincent's knowledge that Mr. M. has had psychotic episodes earlier in life (and still takes antipsychotic medication), Vincent directly asks Joseph M. which drugs he takes. Mr. M. tells Vincent that he doesn't know the names but shows the pills to Vincent. He says that he takes four round blue-grey ones "for the nerves" every day and another blue cylindric one "for the heart." Vincent pulls out a reference manual for pharmaceuticals (the *Compendium of Pharmaceuticals and Specialties*; published annually by the Canadian Pharmaceutical Association) that is readily available in his hospital department (and also on the Internet) and learns that the round blue-grey ones are Stelazine (an antipsychotic agent) that has the pill strength engraved into the pill itself. In Mr. M's case, there is a number 10 on the tablet. The other medication is a so-called beta-blocker with the trade name Inderal. Comparing this knowledge with the pill boxes that Mr. M. fortunately brought along, Vincent learns that the blue, cylinder-shaped pill is the 80 mg pill and this is consistent with the instruction on the pill container. But, he also discovers a worrisome discrepancy: Mr. M. has been taking 40 mg of Stelazine/day (4×10 mg) although according to the pillbox he should be taking 20 mg/day (in the form of 4×5 mg). Mr. M. tells Vincent that he has recently been taking four little round blue-grey pills per day (as he should) except he did not notice that he actually had the 10 mg pills instead of the prescribed 5 mg pills, thus unintentionally ending up doubling the dosage. The second medication, the Inderal, is a beta-blocker, which is meant to reduce arousal and strain on the heart, and is often prescribed for patients who have had a heart attack (as Mr. M did 2 years prior). The dosage of 80 mg/day is at the high end of the recommended dosage range for adults. Noteworthy is the fact that beta-blockers reduce sympathetic nervous system arousal and may therefore synergistically act with the Stelazine to reduce Mr. M.'s alertness and activity level. Stelazine is an antipsychotic medication that has a very strong sedation effect, and typical dosages for adults are 15–20 mg/day (*CPS*, 1994; Simacola & Peters-Strickland, 2006). Vincent wonders whether Mr. M. may be overly sedated and thinks that conducting a full IQ test is probably not a good idea at this time. Vincent knows from a class he took in psychopharmacology that geriatric patients have a slower metabolism, and even a standard adult dosage can more quickly become toxic. He consults the resident psychiatrist and asks for a review of Mr. M's prescription to ensure that Mr. M. is indeed properly medicated. If Vincent had not made the effort to fully understand Mr. M.'s medication regimen and its implications, he might have wasted time completing a cognitive evaluation with the patient's very slow and spotty performance, increasing the likelihood that Mr. M. would not be considered capable of living on his own.

In summary, Vincent clearly recognized that it was not his role to be the ultimate judge on the appropriateness of Mr. M.'s medication regimen, but his recognition of Mr. M's possible oversedation and its effect on the validity of his test performance was a valuable step. A medication review preceding the cognitive assessment may ultimately lead to a different conclusion from the one derived from a cognitive evaluation that would have ignored medication status.

◇THE LANGUAGE OF PHARMACOLOGY: IMPORTANT CONCEPTS

Medical and pharmacological terminology has been around for thousands of years, and that explains the Greek and Latin roots of many medical terms. It also creates what seems to be a secret code that only members of a privileged club know how to speak. As with many profession-specific lingos, this one is also learnable with a bit of effort. The plan here is not to make the reader an expert but at least provide a few explanations that make this world less mysterious.

When it comes to prescription drugs there is considerable opportunity for confusion because each drug company creates **trade names** for its drugs. In order to provide a standard or shared language, the science of pharmacology uses a terminology of its own that associates one specific name with one specific drug type; we refer to these terms as generic names. For example, a frequently prescribed and effective prescription drug for use with attention deficit and hyperactivity disorder in children is the generic drug methylphenodate (classified as a psychostimulant drug) that is sold under the trade names Ritalin, Meta date, Methylin, and Concerta, depending on who the drug manufacturer is (Simacola & Peters-Strickland, 2006). It becomes quickly apparent that the use of generic terms also allows a systematic approach to the development of names that can help recognize which type of drug we are talking about. For example, generic drug names ending in ". . . ine" are usually tranquilizers. Drug companies, for reasons of competition, are not particularly interested in having similar sounding trade names for the same generic drug type because they want their trade name to stick just like people tend to refer to Kleenex when they mean paper tissue.

To retain transparency and assure patient safety, the medical-pharmaceutical world has created a reference book, referred to as the ***Compendium of Pharmaceuticals and Specialties (CPS)***, that is updated annually. The *CPS* provides a listing of trade names that can then be matched with generic names and also allows the reverse, namely, to look up a generic drug name and identify which company offers this product under what trade name. For each drug listed in the *CPS*, there is also information about the chemical itself, typical dosages, the intended effect, and known side effects. Another helpful feature, especially in emergency situations, is the beginning section of the *CPS*, where a very large number of prescription drugs are displayed visually so that the reader can take a given medication and, judging simply by its size, color, shape, and whatever is inscribed on a pill, can determine which drug and dosage it is without having to ask the patient or the prescribing physician. We think it is a highly commendable habit for a clinical psychologist to have either a relatively recent *CPS* sitting within reach on the bookshelf or corresponding websites bookmarked on her office computer so that she can quickly determine the intended purpose of her patient's medications.

In addition to the thousands of drug names that are in use (have no fear, we will not try to teach these here), there is a much smaller list of concepts that we do, however, want to introduce to help understand basic principles of drug action, and also clarify what written prescriptions mean.

Frequently Used Terms and Abbreviations

Frequently used terms and abbreviations are listed and explained in Tables 18.1 and 18.2.

◇ TYPES OF PSYCHOPHARMACOLOGICAL MEDICATION AND AREAS OF APPLICATION

A crude, but useful, approach to classifying psychoactive street drugs is to block them into (a) uppers (drugs that increase arousal and alertness) and (b) downers (drugs that decrease excessive arousal and produce calm). Prescription drugs, however, have more complex mechanisms and do not fit well into this simple classification scheme. In terms of drug actions, there is some overlap between street drugs and prescription drugs. For example, both amphetamines and cocaine have stimulant effects, whereas anxiolytics and heroin have numbing effects. What does apply to all drugs (illicit and prescription) is that increasing dosage also increases toxicity and ultimately the probability of death. Some uppers (like amphetamines) and many hypnotic sedatives (e.g., morphine or strong painkillers like

TABLE 18.1   Concepts and Definitions

Toxicity	This term refers to the fact that prescription drugs often are powerful in order to have their intended impact but that taking too much of a drug becomes actually harmful.
Side effects	Because prescription and illicit drugs have potentially strong effects, they may also produce uncomfortable and undesirable symptoms that are not intended but are often unavoidable. To complicate things, not every drug produces the same side effects in every patient. Relatively frequent and predictable side effects should be mentioned to patients early on so that they are not scared when side effects do occur.
Adverse effects	While side effects are often surprising and may be unpleasant, they tend to be predictable and often harmless. However, with some drugs the unintended effects can become truly dangerous and lead to such dangerous conditions as liver failure, pulmonary hypotension, or damage to an unborn baby if the medication is taken by a pregnant woman.
Tolerance	This term describes the fact that with many medications patients will need higher dosages to attain the same effect if the medication is taken over an extended period of time.
Half-life	Whether medication is taken orally or injected, it usually takes a while before a therapeutic effect is reached, and this effect has a limited life span. It is therefore useful to know what the length of the likely effect is by describing at what point the medication has roughly reached the midpoint of the time interval for which it is effective.
Withdrawal	Stopping of medications or illicit drugs often leads to unpleasant symptoms because the patient's body has adjusted to the medication; when this chemical is no longer in the system, the body will have to readjust. It is therefore common practice to gradually fade out medication to minimize withdrawal effects.
Potentiation and synergism	Many patients take more than one kind of medication, and some individuals even mix prescription drugs and illicit chemicals without being aware that these chemicals may interact with each other. For example, both may have the same basic drug action, such as uppers, that is, drugs that increase arousal and alertness. In such a case, the taking of two or more medications will produce a much stronger outcome. The use of two or more downers like alcohol and a drowsy-making type of antihistamine can be dangerous.
Dependence	Medications and illicit drugs taken over a long period of time lead to adjustments of the patient's physiological functions such that he will become used to, and even rely on, the presence of such chemicals in his body. In some cases, medications or street drugs replace chemical compounds that the body naturally produces on its own. A classic example for this is that the extended consumption of heroin, morphine, or methadone leads to cessation of production of enkephalin, which is a natural painkiller. When this happens, dependence is at its worst because an attempt at withdrawing the drug produces highly aversive withdrawal symptoms.

TABLE 18.2 Abbreviations

Rx	Prescription (recipere)
qd	Every day (quaque 1 diem)
b.i.d.	2×/day (bis in idem)
t.i.d.	3×/day (ter in diem)
q.i.d.	4×/day (quater in diem)
p.r.n.	As needed (pro re nata)
p.o.	Per mouth (per os)
stat	Immediately (statim)

Demerol) have very high addiction potential and should be taken only for well-defined, short periods of time, prescribed by a physician who closely follows the patient (Schatzberg & Nemeroff, 2004).

The relevant main areas of psychological, psychiatric, and general medical practice applications and the corresponding use of drugs that can be broadly called psychopharmacological agents are:

- Pain (analgesics)
- Anxiety (anxiolytics)
- Depression (antidepressants)
- Bipolar disorder (lithium derivatives)
- Schizophrenia (major tranquilizers or antipsychotics)
- Post-traumatic stress disorder (various affect-modulating drugs)
- Smoking cessation (affect-modulating drugs like Bupropion)
- Weight loss (stimulants like amphetamines)

The nature of possible relationships between pharmacological medication and psychological interventions can be seen as fitting into one of these four categories:

1. Pharmacological medication is recognized as a highly effective and necessary first-line treatment. A widespread consensus is that this is currently true for the treatment of schizophrenia, schizoaffective disorder, bipolar disorder, acute pain, and attention deficit hyperactivity disorder (ADHD; Baethge, 2002; Goodwin, 2002; Sachs, 2004; Schatzberg & Nemeroff, 2004). However, despite the fact that medication is needed and effective for these conditions, there also is consistent evidence that the addition of psychological support and behavioral training can further

enhance the benefits of many first-line drug treatments (see, e.g., Barkley, 2002; Huxley, Rendall, & Sederer, 2000).

2. Both psychological and drug treatments are recognized as effective, and either one can be an appropriate first-line treatment. Typically, it is true that the medication takes effect more quickly than psychological treatment, whereas the psychological treatment is often associated with lower relapse rates and better follow-up outcomes (Rupke, Blecke, & Renfrow, 2006). Areas where this second principle applies are depression, generalized anxiety disorders, and smoking cessation. Also, to maximize treatment outcomes for patients, one could begin with a psychological treatment and, if it fails, or is not sufficient, switch to medication or follow the reverse order.

3. There is evidence that psychological treatment is a superior choice to medication (where "superior" is defined by high efficacy, lack of side effects, and durability of outcomes) and should be considered as a first option, even though this may not necessarily rule out that medication can also produce some benefit or be added later. Currently, this applies to the treatment of phobias, post-traumatic stress disorder, and bulimia with cognitive-behavioral interventions and to the treatment of urinary incontinence with biofeedback (e.g., Burgio et al., 2002; see also chapter 13).

4. A fourth possible option is to plan from the outset to integrate medication and psychological therapy. For example, this could involve a severely depressed patient with suicidal tendencies, where the quicker initial response of the drug appears desirable to swiftly tackle suicide risk but where long-term maintenance with added psychological treatment appears more promising. Similarly, multidisciplinary pain clinics (as described in chapter 17) systematically plan integrated approaches of pharmacological and behavioral treatments to act synergistically for the benefit of the patient. Another example for this category would be the treatment of ADHD, where the use of a stimulant medication is best paired with a behavioral intervention involving the parents, the child, and possibly teachers (Barkley, 2002, and see related coverage in chapter 14).

When clinical psychologists enter the world of clinical practice, they will quickly discover that there are varied views about which disorder is best treated by what method. As described in chapter 13, clinical psychologists don't necessarily agree with each other, and neither do physicians. And, predictably, clinical psychologists often take a profession-specific stance that physicians do not necessarily share. Of course, treatment decisions should be based on empirical evidence and consensus committee reports, which, if properly conducted, avoid fruitless boundary disputes arising from mere personal opinions or false beliefs in the superiority of one's own clinical experience (Meehl, 1960).

Another important area where clinical psychology is connected to pharmacological treatment is frequently via the problem of poor adherence. In chapter 17, we discussed the frequency and severity of the problem and provided some strategies and tips for how to handle this issue.

◇ HOW THE ARRIVAL OF THE INTERNET HAS CHANGED CLINICAL PRACTICE

With the advent of the Internet, patients themselves have developed a great deal of savvy about medical conditions, diagnoses, and possible interventions. It is therefore more and more frequent that patients approach either their physician or clinical psychologist with very specific ideas on what disease they have and what treatment they should be getting for it. More and more patients know of effective psychological treatments and will try to sway their physicians to try a psychological intervention over a drug treatment. Not surprisingly, the patient's physician will not always agree with the patient, and good communication and bedside manner on part of the professional is needed to resolve a possible impasse. The authors of this book have encountered a number of patients over the years who were unhappy with the medications they took, either because of side effects or lack of desired effects, and they were planning to stop or had already stopped taking some medications. Sometimes, they would do so without informing their prescribing physician. While it may be tempting for a clinical psychologist to side with the patient and prefer psychotherapy over a drug, it is not only a major lack of professional courtesy but actually a safety requirement that the psychologist communicates with the patient's physician so that a proper flow of communication between all three parties can occur and that a coherent treatment plan can be implemented (Vos, Corry, Haby, Carter, & Andrews, 2005).

Given that patients have grown more cognizant of treatment options, they often try to reduce their medication intake because they

- Dislike medication dependence and don't accept the implicit role of "chronic patient."
- Notice unpleasant side effects.
- Are aware that long-term drug use can negatively affect their liver or lead to dependency.
- Learn from reports of scientific advances in the popular press that particular drugs are not as effective as initially believed. For example, most recently, it was learned that a frequently prescribed antidepressant drug, referred to as selective serotonin reuptake inhibitor (SSRI), is ineffective for a substantial number of patients, may lose its effect over time, and is less effective overall than was initially claimed (Kirsch et al., 2008).

◇ SHOULD PSYCHOLOGISTS HAVE DRUG PRESCRIPTION PRIVILEGES?

The practice of medicine is tightly regulated by law and is relatively easy to define, namely, diagnosis, prescription of medications, surgery, or direct injection of drugs. In almost all jurisdictions, clinical psychologists are not allowed to prescribe medications although (in recognition of their good training) they often do have protected diagnostic privileges.

Interestingly, and unknown to many people, senior nurse practitioners in geographically remote areas are permitted to prescribe medications under certain conditions (Lavoie & Fleet, 2002).

What started the debate about prescription privileges for psychologists? Clinical psychologists in the United States had noted that there are many counties that have no psychiatrist services, meaning that patients needing psychiatric medications can obtain them only through family physicians. Clinical psychologists in the United States have argued that this is a violation of antitrust legislation and a poor service to patients who may not have access to a psychiatrist. In order to meet these demands, but also to expand their own range of practice, clinical psychologists have challenged authorities to consider opening up the question of prescription of psychotropic medications to professionals other than physicians. The first arena in which this type of practice has been evaluated was via a demonstration project in the U.S. military. In 1989, the U.S. Congress directed the Department of Defense (DoD) to create a Psychopharmacology Demonstration Project (PDP) to train military clinical psychologists to issue appropriate psychotropic medications to beneficiaries of the Military Health Services System. This program was put into place in 1991 (Lavoie & Fleet, 2002). Between 1991 and 1997, 10 military psychologists completed a thorough training program and were subsequently granted the right to prescribe medications. Predictably, medical associations spoke out against the program and raised concerns about effectiveness and safety. Although many of the supervising clinical psychiatrists had reservations about the appropriateness of affording psychologists prescribing privileges, in the end they unanimously rated the quality of care provided by these psychologists as good to excellent. Some supervisors reported that graduates brought a unique combination of psychopharmacology and behavioral expertise to their programs that many of the psychiatrists in these programs lacked. Clinical supervisors reported no adverse patient outcomes resulting from treatment provided by psychologists who completed the PDP program (Lavoie & Fleet, 2002). Following these positive outcomes of the DoD demonstration project, some groups of clinical psychologists in New Mexico and Louisiana have battled for psychopharmacology privileges and have won this (lengthy and expensive) battle. Predictably, the medical profession provided vigorous opposition because they considered prescribing medications to be their unique turf and argued that patient safety would be at risk if psychologists were given psychopharmacology privileges. To this date, there is no evidence that clinical psychologists exercising prescription privileges (following appropriate training, of course), produce outcomes that are in any way dangerous to patients and different in quality from the prescription habits of physicians. Although psychologists in New Mexico and Louisiana ultimately did persist after great efforts, a similar push in Hawaii looked initially promising but was finally killed in the Hawaiian legislature in 2007, again with the unproven claim that patient safety would be a problem.

Irrespective of the major implementation problems and well-organized vocal opposition by physicians against psychologists obtaining prescription privileges, the profession itself is split over the issue, with one group arguing that a combination treatment of medication and psychological support is often best and that patients are not well served by having two different practitioners providing these two forms of treatment in parallel. This is a reasonable argument. The other side takes a more philosophical stance and posits that the very values and beliefs that characterize the practice of clinical psychology are the emphasis on emotion, thought, and behavior and an attempt to gradually empower patients to look after themselves. Many psychologists see medications as a quick fix that just manages, instead of cures, symptoms. At the current time, it appears that most clinical psychologists are not interested in prescription privileges, and in most jurisdictions no substantive efforts are under way to obtain such prescription privileges (Lavoie & Fleet, 2002). Nevertheless, the prescription privilege debate highlights an existing moral obligation to provide patients with the best possible care. Also, this discussion challenges the field of clinical psychology to define itself, and we posit that this discussion in and of itself can be seen as constructive and progressive.

◇CONCLUSION

Psychopharmacological agents are a reality and a necessity in psychiatric care. In fact, the prescription rates for psychopharmaceuticals have risen greatly over the last few decades (Cavalucci, 2007). Medication can be a blessing for many psychopathological conditions, most notably psychoses and bipolar disorders where treatment without medication is unthinkable today. In many other instances, psychopharmacological agents compete with psychological treatment (e.g., sleep problems, anxiety, depression, PTSD), and there also are good examples where drugs and psychotherapy can enhance each other's effects (depression, ADHD).

We believe the closing quotation is well placed here because it poignantly describes how most clinical psychologists see themselves and their role when it comes to the treatment of psychopathological conditions:

"Pills don't give skills" (anonymous)

Some (Sobering) Additional Considerations

Another important issue for the question of psychological versus drug treatment is simply affordability. Certain drugs no longer have patent protection, and long-term use can therefore be quite inexpensive. On the other hand, the cost of drugs varies extraordinarily even within the same class of treatment like antipsychotic medications where unfortunately the most-easy-to-tolerate antipsychotics also tend to be most expensive. In most Western countries, medications are fully or partly paid for by health insurance companies whereas only a fraction of people, even in rich Western countries, have full third-party coverage for professional psychological services. Therefore, affordability alone sometimes determines the choice of the first-line psychiatric treatment that is offered and received, with psychoactive drugs often winning this decision. We do anticipate that in the long run psychologists and physicians will collaborate in designing clinical treatment paths where pharmacological agents and psychological therapies will work together for maximal patient benefit. For example, prescription drugs may be used to kick-start treatment and the pharmacological agent will be weaned as nondrug treatments start being effective.

◊ KEY TERMS LEARNED

Adverse effects

Compendium of Pharmaceuticals and Specialties (*CPS*)

Dependence

Half-life

Potentiation and synergism

Psychoactive drugs

Psychopharmacology

Side effects

Tolerance

Toxicity

Trade names

Withdrawal

◊ THINKING QUESTIONS

1. How do you feel about prescription privileges for psychologists?

2. Is pharmacotherapy the enemy of or the competition for psychological therapies?

3. How much should clinical psychologists know about psychopharmacology?

◊ REFERENCES

Baethge, C. (2002). Long-term treatment of schizo-affective disorder: Review and recommendations. *Pharmacopsychiatry, 36*, 45–56.

Barkley, R. (2002). Psychosocial treatments for attention-deficit/hyperactivity disorder in children. *Journal of Clinical Psychiatry, 63*(Suppl 12), 36–43.

Burgio, K. L., Goode, P. S., Locher, J. L., Umlauf, M. G., Roth, D. L., Richter, H. E., et al. (2002). Behavioral training with and without biofeedback in the treatment of urge incontinence in older women: A randomized controlled trial. *JAMA, 288*, 2293–2299.

Cavalucci, S. (2007). What's topping the charts in prescription drugs this year? *Pharmacy Practice*, 25–32.

Compendium of pharmaceutical and specialties (29th Ed.). Ottawa, Canada: Canadian Pharmaceutical Association, 1994

DeLeon, P. H., & Wiggins, J. G. (1996). Prescription privileges for psychologists. *American Psychologist, 51*, 225–229.

Lavoie, K. L., & Fleet, R. (2002). Should psychologists be granted prescription privileges? A view of the prescription privilege debate for psychiatrists. *Canadian Journal of Psychiatry, 47*, 443–449.

Goodwin, F. (2002). Rationale for long-term treatment of bipolar disorder and evidence for long-term lithium treatment. *Journal of Clinical Psychiatry, 63*(Suppl 10), 5–12.

Huxley, N., Rendall, M., & Sederer, L. (2000). Psychosocial treatments in schizophrenia. *The Journal of Nervous and Mental Disease, 188*, 187–201.

Kirsch, I., Deacon, B. J., Huedo-Medina, T. B., Scoboria, A., Moore, T. J., & Johnson, B. T. (2008). Initial severity and antidepressant benefits: A meta-analysis of data submitted to the food and drug administration. *PLoS Medicine, 5*(2), e45–53.

Meehl, P. E. (1960). The cognitive activity of the clinician. *American Psychologist, 15*, 19–27.

Rupke, S. J., Blecke, D., & Renfrow, M. (2006). Cognitive therapy for depression. *American Family Physician, 73*, 83–66.

Sachs, G. S. (2004). Strategies for improving treatment of bipolar disorder: Integration of measurement and management. *Acta Psychiatrica Scandinavica, 11*(Suppl 422), 7–17.

Schatzberg, A., & Nemeroff, C. (2004). *Textbook of psychopharmacology* (3rd ed.). Washington, DC: American Psychiatric Press.

Simacola, R. S., & Peters-Strickland, T. (2006). *Basic psychopharmacology for counselors and psychotherapists*. Boston, MA: Allyn & Bacon.

Tucker, M. E. (1992). Psychologists crusade for Rx privileges not likely to abate. *Clinical Psychiatry News, 1*, 15.

Vos, T., Corry, J., Haby, M. M., Carter, R., & Andrews, G. (2005). Cost-effectiveness of cognitive-behavioural therapy and drug interventions for major depression. *Australian and New Zealand Journal of Psychiatry, 39*, 683–692.

Zimmerman, M. A., & Wienckoswki, L. A. (1991). Revisiting health and mental health linkages: A policy's whose time has come . . . again. *Journal of Public Health Policy, 12*, 510–524.

CHAPTER NINETEEN

CURRENT TRENDS AND THE FUTURE OF CLINICAL PSYCHOLOGY

CHAPTER OBJECTIVE

Closing this book with a chapter on the future of clinical psychology is like forecasting the weather or predicting how the economy will perform. In each case, experts have learned from changes that have occurred over time, try to see the patterns driving such changes, and then complement these efforts with plenty of guesswork and subjective opinion. This chapter will be no different, and we encourage the reader to take it with a grain of salt.

The topics we raise are definitely in current debate (and may have a long history), or they are brewing. The wide range of topics and the vigor of the debate speak to the creativity, drive, and willingness of clinical psychologists to renew the profession. Given that this book is meant to help educate and create sparks in future clinical psychologists like our graduate student Vincent, it is opportune to alert them to the issues and problems that will stare them in the face when they start practicing. Not only is it good to be prepared to *react* to these pending changes, but *alerting* future clinical psychologists now underlines that they are going to benefit more by being *proactive* and getting involved in shaping trends rather than merely reacting to them.

Our observations can be organized into four theme groups:

1. The implications of global changes in demographics and health care delivery systems
2. Ongoing issues around training and the place of psychologists in the health care system (i.e., issues of turf), which includes discussion of the hot topic of prescription privileges for psychologists
3. Challenges and opportunities arising from the increasing role the Internet plays regarding the practice of clinical psychology
4. The growth of the positive psychology movement

◇CHANGES IN HEALTH CARE

The last century has seen dramatic improvements in health care, and the pace of change appears to have accelerated over the last few decades. A number of important trends are converging that together place massive strain on existing health care systems. On the one hand, this includes good news: Life expectancy continues to increase and is now in the range of 80–85 years in Western countries. These improvements in longevity are largely attributable to the almost complete eradication of many previously mortal childhood diseases like the measles, effective treatment of infectious diseases at all ages, and improvements in the quality of care for many other prevalent diseases, in particular, cardiovascular disease and cancer. The latter two cause roughly two-thirds of the deaths in the United States (http://www.benbest.com/lifeext/causes.html). Nevertheless, although annual mortality due to heart disease and cancer has decreased, the frequency remains high, and for cancer, the incidence is unfortunately increasing (http://www.bccancer.bc.ca/NR/rdonlyres/95E7EFA1-57A4-4BA6-A3B4-4A1C661A9E1F/25076/IncidenceAllCancers1.pdf).

One result of the improvements in medical care is also a mixed blessing, namely, that patients stay alive today even when afflicted with diseases that might have led to certain death just a few decades ago. Unfortunately, this also means that there is a growing segment of the population with chronic, often debilitating diseases; their quality of life is frequently poor, and they need a great deal of expensive medical care to manage their symptoms (Emanuel & Emanuel, 1994). In fact, the practice of family medicine is dominated by symptom management in older patients with chronic diseases. Considering the large number of deaths due to controllable behavior, clinical psychologists have much to offer to the health care system (see Table 19.1, and Johnson & Radcliffe, 2008; see also chapter 17).

In chapter 13 we have challenged the wisdom and desirability of a narrow focus on lowering mortality as the endpoint for medical and psychological interventions in older people. Patients themselves have indicated that they do not want to have their lives extended at all cost but seek quality of life and dignity instead. For example, it has been

TABLE 19.1   Frequency of Behavioral Causes of Death: U.S. Data, 2008

CAUSE OF DEATH	PER YEAR
Tobacco	400,000
Diet/physical inactivity	300,000
Alcohol consumption	100,000
Microbial agents	90,000
Toxic agents	60,000
Firearms	35,000
Unsafe sexual behavior	30,000
Motor vehicle accidents	25,000
Use of illicit drugs	20,000

shown that over 90% of gravely ill older patients who are sufficiently lucid to make their own decisions will refuse to participate in any dramatic (and likely expensive) medical treatment that simply maintains an incurable and painful disease for just a few months more (Malloy, Urbanyi, Horsman, Guyatt, & Bédard, 1992). This realization has led to the burgeoning area of research on **living wills** and **advanced directives**, where older patients are increasingly permitted, and even encouraged, to clearly express their personal wishes for the palliative stage of a degenerative disease. Often it is patients themselves who trigger and define this process. It is estimated that more than half of all the dollars spent on a person's health care in a lifetime is spent during his last year of life. The growing expenditures in health care mostly serve to support older people, and routine use of advanced directives may save as much as 10% to the entire health care system (Rachlis & Kushner, 1994). Given the cost of high-tech medical care and aging patients' general lack of interest in it, we predict that much more attention will be paid in the future to personalized, emotional support in palliative care that is delivered in the dignity of patients' own homes. Supported home care reflects a true win-win scenario because it reduces the financial burden on the health care system while actually giving patients what they ask for, namely, more dignity rather than more technology.

Arguably, Western countries have reached the point where technical advances in medical care allow for improved patient care but the ability of these countries to actually pay for these expensive services has not followed suit. There is a widening gap between what can be done and what is actually accessible to the average citizen. Together, these health care trends lead to the realization that a growing portion of health care dollars will need to be spent on an aging population that makes up a steadily growing segment of the population. In 2008 there were four times as many Canadians over 65 years of age than there were in 1956 (http://www12.statcan.ca/english/census06/analysis/agesex/NatlPortrait1 .cfmref). Gerontology is the science and professional specialty of the future.

Partly driven by aging populations, all Western countries have seen frightening increases in needed health care expenditures to the point where they represent a major economic threat. At the top of the list of big spenders in health care is the United States of America where health care expenditures make up over 15% of the country's gross national product (http://www.southsearepublic.org/story/2005/8/29/05538/332315). At least 18% of U.S. citizens have no health insurance at all primarily because they cannot afford to pay the premiums (http://www.nchc.org/facts/coverage.shtml). Other countries with a similar style of life and high prosperity have succeeded in keeping their percentages of health care expenses at or below 10% of gross national product (http://www.southsearepublic.org/ story/2005/8/29/05538/3323).

However, even in these countries, health care expenditures are heavily scrutinized and are threatening to choke the economy. All Western countries are continuously looking for ways to provide better health care at the same cost, or preferably, at lower cost. Given that such a large proportion of health care expenditure is related to behavioral factors, psychologists are well placed to play pivotal roles in the future of health care, and psychologists' skills, if widely applied, may impact the economics of health care. Consistent with this reasoning, clinical psychologists need to consider whether or not current training models are properly preparing them for this future. Linden, Moseley, and Erskine (2005) have called for review and revision of training models to prepare the profession for the future. In particular, it is recommended that clinical psychologists are trained to apply their skills outside their usual offices and to provide services not only in a one-on-one fashion. The section Clinical Psychology, Computers, and the Web (later in this chapter) provides numerous examples of where and how clinical psychologists can "step outside their offices" to provide innovative and cost-effective services. Given the long and comprehensive training of clinical psychologists, they are well prepared to serve as consultants to many aspects of the health care system, ranging from prevention to treatment and rehabilitation, embracing mental health and physical applications (see Table 19.1 and chapter 17).

◇ CLINICAL TRAINING

For well over half a century the predominant training model in clinical psychology has been the scientist-practitioner model that was first defined in a conference in the city of Boulder (Raimy, 1950) and has since then been dubbed the **Boulder model**. As the title suggests, clinical psychologists are seen as wearing two hats or carrying dual aspirations that are meant to be closely integrated with each other. The emphasis on science was brought in because the attendees at the Boulder conference had recognized that clinical psychology was so young that it had a limited research base to draw from. It was deemed necessary to train practitioners in science, so that they can understand and apply the available empirical evidence as well as use all of their learning experiences to expand the scientific basis itself. Both the scientist and the practitioner roles were meant to nurture each other, and it is difficult to find a principal flaw in this thinking. Nevertheless, it is expensive to train students in both skill sets, and the Boulder model has therefore been considered an idealistic view of the profession. Since the Boulder conference, the knowledge base available to clinical psychologists has dramatically changed as, for example, the long lists of empirically validated therapies presented and discussed in chapters 11–14 have shown. Along with this growth of scientific knowledge supporting the practice of clinical psychology has been the ongoing debate about the best training models. These changes have fueled the creation of practitioner-oriented training programs, most of which operate on a cost-recovery basis and provide their graduates with PsyD degrees. Now, some 60 years later, it may be time to raise the question of whether all practitioners still need to be trained as potential creators of scientific evidence. If we were following the model of medical school training, then the typical practitioner would no longer be extensively trained in creating more scientific knowledge. A counterposition would be to see the scientist-practitioner orientation as so pivotal to our professional identity that major changes would be disorienting and maybe even self-destructive. The authors of this textbook encourage this debate but do not hold strong views for either stance themselves because they see the validity of the pro and the con arguments as being similar in weight.

Another trend that has fueled major changes in training models has been the economics of training and the issue of supply and demand. Academic programs that follow the Boulder model train very small numbers of students, usually fewer than 10 per year, and are therefore expensive to operate. Given these small numbers, academic training programs may not be able to supply the market with enough needed practitioners. Furthermore it is routine that clinical psychology programs in academic departments of psychology receive more applications for each available training spot than any other program in their department. In consequence, large numbers of students are refused admission and find themselves thwarted in their desire to receive training as a clinical psychologist. This has also spurred the growth of freestanding PsyD programs and has encouraged nonclinical psychology graduates with somewhat of a patchwork of training experiences to still go out there and market themselves as practitioners (Linden et al., 2005). In order to do justice to future patient populations and assure patient safety, licensing and other regulatory bodies in psychology have moved to defining core competencies that applicants need to possess before they can be licensed to practice. Ultimately, the regulation of training and licensing ought to be driven by the supply and demand of the job market and should include dialogue and collaboration of governments, the universities that train clinical psychologists, and the colleges of psychologists that regulate their practice. Unfortunately, many governments do not do human resource forecasting and subsequently fail to integrate this knowledge into the funding of training programs.

A highly innovative approach to training and licensing has recently been undertaken in Québec, Canada. Here, the licensing body, L'Ordre des psychologues du Québec (OPQ), has joined forces with the universities and government to move toward a minimum standard of doctoral level training (http://www.ordrepsy.qc.ca/fr/psychologue/devenir.html). This licensing body no longer trains individuals or licenses psychologists to begin their practices with only master's-level training. These dialogues have been critically influenced by a government assessment of the future need for psychologists, which had projected a large need for psychologists that was not met by the universities.

Another major trend in clinical psychology, already described in chapters 1 and 2, has been the massive shift from practicing clinical psychology in employed positions to private practice models (Cantor & Fuentes, 2008). Henceforth, graduate students in clinical psychology need training in how to set up a private practice and how to run their profession as a business. This represents a challenge to the university faculty who train psychologists because faculty are employees and are unlikely trained to run a business. Similarly, there is widespread agreement that the typical 1-year internship is critical in preparing for independent practice, yet almost all such internships occur in hospital-type environments although this environment no longer represents the setting where the majority of clinical psychologists will end up practicing. To prepare students for such careers as independent business operators, the best training model might be internship training programs that are integrated with clinical psychology practices and that are operating outside of hospitals. At the current time, such training is rare, and those attempting to implement it will encounter challenges. In private practice most patients pay directly for services, and they may not want to be seen by students or residents. Also, there is lots of variety in how private practices are run; some are very narrow in focus, and in order to function as internship training programs, these practices would have to become broader in focus and operate on agreed-upon models of cost-efficient practice. Whether or not that is logistically possible or desirable remains to be seen.

◇ PRESCRIPTION PRIVILEGES

The practice of medicine is protected by law, and it is relatively easy to define medicine as the prescription of medications and any form of surgery or injection of needles into people. In almost all jurisdictions, clinical psychologists are not allowed to prescribe medications. Interestingly, and unknown to many people, senior nursing practitioners in outlying areas are permitted to prescribe medications under certain conditions (http://www.ordrepsy.qc .ca/fr/psychologue/devenir.html). Clinical psychologists have challenged authorities to consider opening up the question of psychotropic medication prescription privileges to professionals other than physicians. Details on the history and outcome of this process as well as underlying issues regarding our professional self-definition have already been provided in chapter 18.

◇ CLINICAL PSYCHOLOGY, COMPUTERS, AND THE WEB

The advent of computers and the Internet has revolutionized the world. Although this is strong language, we posit that there is no disagreement anywhere about such a claim. Inevitably, this new technology spills over to the practice of clinical psychology as well. But, is it a constructive development?

Our graduate student Vincent and three practicing psychologists no longer go to the library to search for hours and hours in the library stacks. An extraordinary amount of information is literally at their fingertips while sitting in their offices in front of a computer hooked to the Internet, and especially to the local electronic library system. Both authors of this book began their careers spending endless hours in the library tracking journal articles, making expensive photocopies, and returned home with heavily smudged hands from ink that did not stick to the paper. Now, we don't need to leave our offices to conduct massive searches that will return 2000 relevant references in 5 minutes or less. Mind you, this search strategy is great for speed and comprehensiveness in that it gives masses of information, but the paring-down process to the maybe 50 articles that we actually need still requires time and analytical skill.

This section will touch on the advantages and disadvantages of this electronic revolution. Undisputed is the tremendous time saving inherent in Internet access for data searches. Both clients and psychologists now have similar access to web-based information, and patients are likely to come to psychologists' offices having some idea of what's wrong with them.

Complex personality tests like the Minnesota Multiphasic Personality Inventory 2 (MMPI-2) or Personality Assessment Inventory (PAI) that were presented in chapter 7 can now be scored on the computer, and there are even computer programs that provide a narrative interpretation of the findings. Patients can sign on to support groups that meet only on the Internet and can download programs for self-help treatments.

A review of usage patterns of online support groups revealed that patients with debilitating diseases (that present physical mobility challenges like chronic fatigue or multiple sclerosis) and patients with illnesses that are stigmatized (like HIV/AIDS status) are the

**"I already diagnosed myself on the Internet.
I'm only here for a second opinion."**

most likely users (Davison, Pennebaker, & Dickerson, 2000). Of course, people in outlying areas may be able to access services via the Internet that are otherwise not available to them (Stambor, 2006). The physical distance inherent in treatment that is not direct, one-on-one, does come at a cost. Rees and Stone (2005), for example, observed that therapist empathy ratings obtained in a videoconference format were almost a full standard deviation lower than those obtained when one-on-one therapy was delivered in an office.

The difficulty with making standardized self-help programs useful to individuals in varying circumstances can be countered with program tailoring. Using decision trees, computer programs can identify readiness and stage of change as well as focus on specific targets that are in need of intervention for one given individual. Tailored treatment increases the efficacy of an intervention and the satisfaction with and completion rates of a treatment program (Ryan & Lauver, 2002; Kaufmann, 2007).

Table 19.2 summarizes the advantages and disadvantages of computers and Internet applications and uses within clinical psychology.

A remaining key question, of course, is whether or not web-based interventions work. In evaluating this question, we may need to distinguish between professionally led and self-help efforts, and allow for the fact that web-based interventions are not equally strong for the wide range of possible treatment targets (Danaher & Seeley, 2009). A diligent meta-analysis of computer-delivered interventions for changing unhealthy behaviors can answer a number of these critical questions. Portnoy, Scott-Sheldon, Johnson, and Carey (2008) studied the results of 75 trials on computer-delivered interventions on a wide range of targets, namely, obesity, nutrition, exercise, tobacco use, safe sex, health maintenance, and eating disorders. The observed effect sizes for pre-post changes were comparatively small, ranging from $d = .05$ to $d = .36$. Interestingly the effects on knowledge and attitude were as strong as were the effects seen for actual behavior change. The strongest benefits were seen for safe sex behaviors, tobacco use, and knowledge acquisition, whereas physical activity and weight

TABLE 19.2 Advantages and Disadvantages of Using the Web

DOMAIN	ADVANTAGES	DISADVANTAGES
Literature search for scientific facts about disease etiologies, diagnoses, and treatments	Tremendous time savings and greater transparency in available information	User must be sophisticated in differentiating possibly biased commercial websites from web information that is more objective/free of commercial interests
Diagnoses	Time and cost savings	Overstandardization may lead to laziness and loss of context information
Treatment	Access to self-help information not otherwise available due to financial and/or geographic reasons	Internet information is not sufficient for individual case formulation
		Maintenance of confidentiality is difficult and may require sophisticated users and encryption technologies

loss saw essentially no impact. Also, there was a dose-response relationship in that the more sophisticated, tailored programs tended to produce larger effects. One may be disappointed with these observed effect sizes, but we posit that a replicable small effect of $d = .2$ or $.3$ for relevant behavior change obtained with a very inexpensive treatment is a major cost-efficient addition to the tools needed for population-wide health behavior changes.

◇ RESEARCH IN CLINICAL PSYCHOLOGY

Although there are almost an infinite number of directions for research in this field, recently, Illardi and Roberts (2006) have described several directions that they believe are particularly relevant, and we share their views. They suggest:

1. Research on the formulation and dissemination of the development of novel interventions and assessment strategies as well as demonstration of the reliability and validity of these clinical endeavors. There are always new or renewed treatments and treatment elements that are developed or offered in the literature. For example, we have described various newer treatment approaches in chapters 11–14 that need to be shown to be effective. Moreover, numerous traditional treatments that have been used for many years need to be evaluated appropriately. Future research needs to focus on these treatments to demonstrate their efficacy, efficiency, utility, and assessment procedures.

2. Establishment of the specific and nonspecific active ingredients in the treatment approaches. Questions as to what it is that facilitates change still have not been

answered. It is important to understand and demonstrate what it is about psychotherapeutic experiences that is helpful to people. For example, after decades of psychotherapy research it is still the case that nonspecific factors, rather than specific techniques, often account more for good outcome in treatments.

3. **Advantages and disadvantages of pharmacological and psychological interventions.** As there is an ease with which medications can be dispatched to reduce symptoms and a rather warm reception by much of the public for what is viewed as a quick treatment for various psychological difficulties, it is important to delineate and understand the differences between drug and psychotherapy approaches to treatment. This knowledge is particularly relevant as the number of clinical psychologists prescribing medication increases. It is imperative to have a good empirical basis for the choice of medication versus psychotherapy or for a combined medication and psychotherapy approach.

4. **Integration of neuroscience methods and theories to aid in understanding psychological disorders.** With this last point, we would suggest that all human behavior is represented in the central nervous system, and, as technology increases, the ability to use newer forms of technology to understand psychological processes in clinical psychology also increases. One domain where this is evident is neuroimaging, and there is much literature that identifies brain differences among individuals with or without certain types of psychopathology. There seem to be incredible possibilities for understanding many psychological processes that have been traditionally assigned to "the mind" and often thought to be inaccessible via imaging techniques. For example, Howard Shevron (2006) has described procedures from neuroscience to help understand unconscious processes germane to clinical issues. Certainly, the technological advances that have occurred and advances that we can anticipate in the future will influence the kinds of psychological constructs available for research.

Lastly, we will leave you with what we believe to be an essential issue for future research in clinical psychology and psychology more generally. This issue deals with the scientific method and psychology's approach to using research to understand psychological processes, including, of course, psychological processes that are relevant to clinical psychology. Machado and Silva (2007) describe the three overarching principles that were first described by Galileo (yes, that Galileo), which comprise the scientific method and guide research and activities in psychological research. They are:

1. **Observation/experimentation**, which essentially reflects the activities, such as methodology, that are used to generate theories and test hypotheses

2. **Quantification/mathematization**, which reflects the use of statistical procedures and mathematics to obtain and test data to determine relationships

3. **Theoretical/conceptual analysis**, which reflects the clear explication and detailed specification of concepts, constructs, and ideas that derive from or are the focus of research.

All three of these components are important to truly understanding the nature of relationships among psychological constructs; however, Machado and Silva (2007) argue that only the first two tend to be used in psychology research or taught in psychology training programs. For example, although there are courses and emphases in the field on methodological and statistical issues, the issues germane to conceptual analysis tend to be ignored (also see Machado, Lourenco, & Silva, 2000). Although you, as a student of psychology, know, already, a great deal about methodology and statistics from courses you have taken and even from sections of this book, you have likely not been taught about the importance or conduct of conceptual analysis. This means that the clarity and specification of concepts within the field is wanting, which creates incredible confusion. One of the better examples of this is the use of the term "stress," which in the literature has referred to nonspecific responses to events, the events themselves, or negative responses to events. Both authors of this text have experienced the problems with the lack of focus on conceptual analysis in their own respective research areas of perfectionism (e.g., Hewitt et al., 2003; Hewitt, Habke, Lee-Baggley, Sherry, & Flett, 2008) and stress management (Ong, Linden, & Young, 2004). It is hoped that emphases on clear explications of theoretical concepts will be incorporated in both the training and the research in the field.

◇ POSITIVE PSYCHOLOGY AND SPIRITUALITY

Clinical psychology has at times been accused of being too closely allied with medicine and as having adopted a "deficit model." This value then leads to treatments that stop when the disease has been removed and the patient is back to neutral. To counterbalance this slanted view of the world, a number of psychologists, especially those with social psychological and personality expertise, have been advancing the **positive psychology** movement. The challenge for clinical psychology is to expand its self-definition and move away from the mere alleviation of distress and misery (Duckworth, Steen, & Seligman, 2004). Treatment models in the stress-management domain were among the first to adopt this more balanced approach and suggest that the use of humor, systematic building of social support networks, forgiveness, and gratefulness are good ways to expand stress-management packages (Linden, 2005). All these treatment elements are meant to create a counterbalance such that many stressors may be unfixable whereas the addition of pleasure is under the patient's control and may weaken the salience of the stressor. A particularly good use of such an approach has already been suggested for pain control in patients with chronic pain conditions (see chapter 17).

At a theoretical level, it has been proposed that happiness results from three core subconstructs: pleasure, engagement, and meaning (Duckworth et al., 2004), and there is now vigorous research activity around the development and evaluation of interventions geared toward increasing happiness and meaning. At the current time, the field is too new to allow strong conclusions about the degree of effectiveness of positive psychology interventions, but we anticipate explosive growth in this area. A caveat is that medical insurance companies may not want to pay for making people happy; for them it might be expensive enough to alleviate signs of disease.

◇ CONCLUSION

This chapter contained a mix of facts and opinions, and the authors' opinions about trends in the field may not be ideally suited for rote-memorization and repetition on a test. On the other hand, they accurately reflect overarching and very important questions in the clinical psychology field that are hotly debated at professional conferences, in journals, and at after-hours meetings of psychologists over a drink or at dinner. Especially with regard to the topics discussed in this chapter, we challenge you to write to us a few years down the road and tell us that we were out to lunch or maybe dead-on. In either case, we want to know.

◇ KEY TERMS LEARNED

Advanced directives
Boulder model
Living wills
Observation/experimentation

Positive psychology
Quantification/mathematization
Theoretical/conceptual analysis

◇ REFERENCES

Cantor, D. W., & Fuentes, M. A. (2008). Psychology's response to managed care. *Professional Psychology: Research & Practice. 39*, 638–645.

Danaher, B. G., & Seeley, J. R. (2009). Methodological issues in research on web-based behavioral interventions. *Annals of Behavioral Medicine, 38*, 28–39.

Davison, K. P., Pennebaker, J. W., & Dickerson, S. S. (2000). Who talks? The social psychology of illness support groups. *American Psychologist, 55*, 205–217.

Duckworth, A. L., Steen, T. A., & Seligman, M. E. P. (2004). Positive psychology in clinical practice. *Annual Review of Psychology, 1*, 629–651.

Emanuel, E. J., & Emanuel, L. L. (1994). The economics of dying: The illusions of cost savings at the end of life. *New England Journal of Medicine, 330*, 540–544.

Hewitt, P. L., Flett, G. L., Sherry, S. B., Habke, M., Parkin, M., Lam, R. W., et al. (2003). The interpersonal expression of perfectionism: Perfectionistic self-presentation and psychological distress. *Journal of Personality and Social Psychology, 84*, 1303–1325.

Hewitt, P. L., Habke, A. M., Lee-Baggley, D. L., Sherry, S. B., & Flett, G. L. (2008). The impact of perfectionistic self-presentation on the cognitive, affective, and physiological experience of a clinical interview. *Psychiatry: Interpersonal and Biological Processes, 71,* 93–122.

Illardi, S. S., & Roberts, M. C. (2006). *Handbook of research methods in clinical psychology.* New York: Blackwell Publishing.

Johnson, N. G., & Radcliffe, A. M. (2008). The increasing role of psychology health research and interventions and a vision for the future. *Professional Psychology: Research & Practice, 39*, 652–657.

Kaufmann, P. G. (2007). Debate: What type of evidence will advance behavioral medicine? From basic science to population health. *Proceedings of the 2007 Annual Meeting of the Society of Behavioral Medicine, Washington, DC 21–24 March 2007.*

Linden, W. (2005). *Stress management: From basic research to better practice.* Thousand Oaks, CA: Sage.

Linden, W., Moseley, J. V., & Erskine, Y. (2005). Psychology as a health care profession: Implications for training. *Canadian Psychology, 46,* 179–188.

Machado, A., Lourenco, O., & Silva, F. J. (2000). Facts, concepts, and theories: The shape of psychology's epistemic triangle. *Behavior and Philosophy, 28,* 1–40.

Machado, A., & Silva, F. J. (2007). Toward a richer view of the scientific method: Role of conceptual analysis. *American Psychologist, 62,* 671–681.

Malloy, D. W., Urbanyi, M., Horsman, J. R., Guyatt, G. H., & Bédard, M. (1992). Two years experience with a comprehensive health care directive in a home for the aged. *Annals of the Royal College of Physicians and Surgeons of Canada, 25,* 433–436.

Ong, L., Linden, W., & Young, S. (2004). Stress management: What is it? *Journal of Psychosomatic Research, 56,* 133–137.

Portnoy, D. B., Scott-Sheldon, L. A. J., Johnson, B. T., & Carey, M. P. (2008). Computer-delivered interventions for health promotion and behavioral risk factor reduction: A meta-analysis of 75 randomized controlled trials, 1998–2007. *Preventive Medicine, 47,* 3–16.

Rachlis, M., & Kushner, C. (1994). *Strong medicine: How to save Canada's health care system.* Toronto, ON: Harper Collins.

Raimy, V. C. (1950). *Training in clinical psychology.* New York: Prentice-Hall.

Rees, C. S., & Stone, S. (2005). Therapeutic alliance in face-to-face versus video-conferenced psychotherapy. *Professional Psychology: Research and Practice, 36,* 649–653.

Ryan, P., & Lauver, R. D. (2002). The efficacy of tailored interventions, *Journal of Nursing Scholarship, 34,* 331–337.

Shevron, H. (2006). The contribution of cognitive behavioral and nueorphysiological frames of reference to a psychodynamic nosology of mental illness. In PDM Task Force. *Psychodynamic diagnostic manual.* Silver Spring, MD: Alliance of Psychoanalytic Organizations.

Stambor, Z. (2006). The forgotten population. *APA Monitor, 37*(10), 52–53.

NAME INDEX

Abbey, S. E., 39, 236, 413, 420, 447
Ablon, J. S., 230
Achenbach, T. M., 105
Adams, H. E., 109
Adkins, D. C., 224
Adler, Alfred, 240b, 241b
Alberts, G., 212, 214, 224
Alden, L. E., 85
Alexander, F., 243, 246
Alfonso, V. C., 162
Allison, J., 149
Altman, J., 305
Amstadter, A. B., 391
Anastasi, A., 161
Anderson, S. M., 242, 246
Andrews, G., 440
Angen, M., 357
Antoni, M. H., 404, 426
Appels, A., 423
Applebaum, P. S., 388
Arita, A. A., 145
Arlow, J. A., 233, 235, 244
Audage, N. C., 408
Auerbach, J. S., 108

Baer, F., 423
Baer, R. A., 145
Baethge, C., 438
Bahler, W. W., 300
Bandura, A., 286
Barkley, R. A., 377, 439
Barlow, D. H., 223, 346
Barnier, A. J., 348
Baron, R. M., 324
Bartol, A.M., 381, 383, 384
Bartol, C. R., 381, 383, 384
Bass, D., 346
Bateson, G., 256
Baucom, D. H., 425
Beavin, J. H., 256
Beck, A. T., 84, 103, 110, 147,
        290–292, 403, 404, 410, 419
Bédard, M., 447
Bedics, J. D., 224
Beernheim, Hippolyte, 235b
Bekhit, N. S., 131

Bellack, L., 152
Ben-Porath, Y. S., 145
Benjamin, L. T., 90, 383
Benson, H., 300
Bergeron, L., 372
Bergin, A. E., 80, 112, 229
Berkowitz, S., 391
Berman, J. S., 335
Bernstein, A. M., 194
Bernston, G. G., 195
Bersoff, D. N., 382
Bertel, O., 421
Beutler, L. E., 137
Binet, A., 159, 161, 163, 382
Bishop, S. R., 355
Blackburn, R., 382
Blatt, S. J., 108, 109, 149, 246
Blumenthal, J. A., 419
Boake, C., 159
Boekamp, J., 152
Bond, C. L., 354
Bonds, C. L., 422
Bonta, J., 391
Bordin, E. S., 217
Bornstein, R. F., 229, 230,
        231, 236
Bower, G., 233
Bowman, M., 219
Bradburn, N., 39
Bradley, R., 352
Bratton, S. C., 373
Brennan, J., 424
Brestan, E. V., 374
Brody, D. S., 404
Brown, R. D., 408
Bryner, M. J., 392
Budde, H. G., 419
Burd, L., 366
Burgess, S., 191
Burgio, K. L., 404, 439
Burrell, C. D., 410t
Butcher, J., 103, 105, 139, 145
Buzzella, B., 223

Calhoun, K. S., 109
Callender, J. C., 105

Camara, W. J., 131
Campbell, R., 131, 385, 391
Cantor, D. W., 449
Carey, M. P., 451
Carey, R., 52
Carlson, L. E., 357
Carter, R., 440
Castle, P. H., 229
Cauley, K., 403–404
Cavalucci, S., 442
Chambless, D. L., 230, 323, 336t
Chen, E., 408
Childs, R. A., 104
Chow, E., 425
Christensen, A., 256
Clark, L. A., 84
Clark, N. M., 38, 410, 412t, 414t
Clarkin, J. F., 208
Classen, C., 426
Cohen, J., 47, 102
Comrey, A., 38
Conry, J., 366
Cook, C. H. C., 277
Cordova, J., 256
Cormier, C. A., 391
Corry, J., 440
Corsini, R. J., 232, 235b
Cotton, P., 392
Cox, D. N., 297
Coyne, J. C., 325, 425, 426b
Craig, K. D., 297
Craig, R. J., 386–387, 389, 418
Crawford, H. J., 350
Crits-Christoph, P., 230, 335
Cromer, T. D., 113
Cullari, S., 202
Cummings, N. A., 334, 403
Currie, S. R., 197

Dahlstrom, W. G., 139
Danaher, B. G., 451
Davanloo, H., 244
Davidson, K., 148, 352, 353, 355
Davies, R. A., 422
Davis, R. D., 284, 286, 389
Davison, K. P., 451

Deane, F. P., 205
DeBoer, M. F., 424
Decker, P. J., 398
Deleger, S., 407
DeLeon, P. H., 334, 433
Delis, D., 180
Derogatis, L. R., 147
Detweiler, B. J., 281
Detweiler-Bedell, J., 360
Devilly, G. J., 392
Devins, G., 424
Dickerson, S. S., 451
DiClemente, C. C., 309
Dietz, W. H., 407
DiMatteo, 324
DiMatteo, M. R., 319
Dobson, K., 256, 290, 297
Dougherty, T. W., 105
Dreher, H., 424
Dror, O., 60
Duckworth, A. L., 454
DuHamel, K. N., 350
Durlak, J. A., 211
Dusseldorp, E., 420
Dyer, F., 389

Eddy, W. A., 64
Edelbrock, C. E., 105, 212
Edelstein, B., 214
Edge, K., 305
Edwards, L. M., 219
Egan, G., 218
Ehrenreich, J. T., 223
Elbert, R. J., 105
Ellard, K., 223
Ellenberger, H. F., 85, 235b
Ellis, A., 290
Elridge, K., 256
Emanuel, E. J., 446
Emanuel, L. L., 446
Emery, G., 84, 103
Epictetus, 291
Erikson, E., 237
Erskine, Y., 2, 51, 403, 413, 447
Exner, J., 149
Eyberg, S. M., 374
Eyde, I. D., 104
Eysenck, H., 322

Fairholme, C., 223
Faris, P., 357
Fast, D., 366
Feeny, N. C., 391
Fefergrad, M., 288
Fein, D., 180

Feld, S., 215
Fenster, H., 194
Feske, U., 323
Fiola, M., 211
Firenczi, S., 243
First, M. B., 137
Fisher, S. G., 212
Flamm, U., 423
Flanagan, D. P., 162
Fleet, R., 441
Flett, G. L., 147, 242, 250, 454
Flor, T., 418
Floyd, F., 38
Foa, E. B., 391
Folkman, S., 85
Fonarow, G. C., 421
Ford, E. S., 407
Forel, Aguste, 235b
Forman, E. M., 206
Forsyth, J. P., 25
Fortney, J., 333
Franche, R., 290
Frank, Jerome D., 215
Frankl, V., 44, 113
Fraser, J. S., 403
Frasure-Smith, N., 419
Freedman, A., 46
French, S., 243, 246, 390
Freud, A., 85, 237
Freud, S., 44, 88, 227, 228, 234
Friedman, H. S., 407
Fritz, H., 423
Fuentes, M. A., 449

Gabbard, G., 229, 234, 237, 240,
    245, 247
Gaetz, M., 193
Gallo, L. C., 304
Ganz, P. A., 423, 425
Garb, H. N., 110, 153
Gardner, H., 161
Garfield, S. L., 208, 224
Geddes, J. R., 191
Gendreau, P., 390, 391
Gibbon, M., 137
Gibbons, M. B., 230
Gigerenzer, G., 320
Gilbert, C. A., 337, 418
Giles, W. H., 407
Gill, M. M., 106
Gist, R., 392
Gladwell, M., 346
Glass, D. R., 283, 322, 329t, 335
Glassman, N. S., 242
Goggin, C., 390

Golden, C., 178
Goldstein, K., 250
Goodey, E., 357
Goodman, P., 335
Goodwin, F., 191, 438
Gorenstein, E. E., 79
Gottman, J. M., 307
Graham, J. R., 139, 141, 144
Greaves, D. W., 229
Greenberg, B. H., 256, 307, 421
Greenberg, L. S., 215, 309
Greene, R. L., 140
Greenway, P., 121
Gregory, R. J., 99
Grisso, T., 388
Grossman, P., 193, 301, 357
Groth-Marnat, G., 102, 112, 150,
    153, 154, 162
Grove, W. M., 124, 125
Gurevich, M., 424
Gurin, G., 215
Guyatt, G. H., 447

Habke, A. M., 454
Haby, M. M., 440
Hadley, S. W., 335, 349
Hahn, E. E., 423, 425
Haley, J., 256
Hall, J. E., 60, 103
Hallmark, R., 131
Halstead, W., 178
Hannay, H. J., 169
Hansen, N. B., 206
Hanson, R. K., 151
Hare, R. D., 390
Hare-Mustin, R. T., 60
Harris, G. T., 391
Harth, T., 425
Hathaway, S. R., 139, 140
Hawkley, L. C., 408
Hawton, K., 191
Hayano, J., 420
Hayes, S. C., 354
Hayman, L. L., 408
Haynes, R. B., 404
Heard, H., 333, 334t
Hearon, B., 230
Hebben, N., 169, 175
Hedges, M., 229
Hefferline, R. F., 335
Heilbrun, K., 383, 390, 399
Heinrichs, N., 425
Helgeson, V. S., 423, 425
Henry, W. P., 224
Herbert, J. D., 334

Herbert, J. D., 352
Hess, A. K., 382, 390
Hettema, J., 328
Hewitt, P. L., 84, 108, 147, 232, 454
Hewitt, W., 347b
Hicks, B. D., 196
Hilgard, E. R., 348, 350
Hilsenroth, M. J., 113
Hockenberry-Eaton, M., 371
Hogan, R., 229
Hoge, S., 388
Hollon, S., 230
Hommersen, P., 377
Horsman, J. R., 447
Horvath, A. O., 217, 218
Horvath, F. S., 358, 396
Horwitz, S. W., 397
Housman, L. M., 57
Hughes, J. C., 277
Humbke, K. L., 426b
Hunsley, J., 151, 215, 256, 307,
    333, 344b, 345, 375t, 404
Hunter, J., 41
Hunter, R., 41
Huxley, N., 439

Iacono, W. G., 395, 396
Illardi, S. S., 452
Iverson, G. L., 193

Jackson, L., 256, 413
Jacobs, A. K., 392
Jacobson, N. S., 256
Jamison, K., 191
Janet, P., 235b
Jensen, J. P., 229
Johnson, 256, 307
Johnson, B. T., 446, 451
Johnson, S. M., 215, 218, 307
Johnston, C., 377
Johnston, J. R., 64
Jolley, R., 131
Jones, L., 373
Jourard, S., 81b
Jourdan, 250
Juelson, T., 366

Kabat-Zinn, J., 301, 355
Kaemmer, B., 139
Kagan, R., 391
Kahill, S., 154
Kahneman, D., 124
Kanfer, F. H., 286
Kaplan, Edith, 180
Kaplan, J., 407, 419

Karpiak, C. P., 13t, 103
Kaser-Boyd, N., 105
Kaufmann, P. G., 451
Kaufmann, U., 421
Kawachi, I., 419
Kazantzis, N., 205
Kazdin, 346
Keith-Spiegel, P., 56
Keller, 196
Kemp, S., 181
Kendjelic, E. M., 214
Kenny, D. A., 324
Kerns, L. L., 124
Ketring, S. A., 218
Kilpatrick, D. G., 391
King, N. J., 374
Kircher, J. C., 397
Kirk, U., 181
Kirsch, I., 350, 440
Klepser, J., 152
Klinger, E., 82
Klopfer, B., 148
Klug, M. G., 366
Kohut, Heinz, 243
Koocher, G. P., 56
Kop, W., 297, 423
Korkman, M., 181
Kostis, J. B., 407
Kraail, V., 420
Kraepelin, Emil, 88
Kripalani, S., 404, 414
Krishnamurthy, R., 103
Krishnan, R., 193
Kristeller, J. R., 357
Kronish, I. M., 422
Kubzansky, L., 419
Kupfersmid, J., 211
Kushner, C., 447
Kuther, T. L., 17

Lalonde, S., 131
Lambert, M. J., 80, 112, 206, 246
Lane, R. D., 208
Lang, P. J., 277
Langosch, W., 419
Lasker, J., 423
Lauver, R. D., 451
LaVaque, T., 49
Lavoie, K. L., 441
Layne, C. M., 392
Lazarus, R. S., 85
Leblanc, M., 373
LeBow, B. S., 124
LeBow, M. D., 206
Leclerc, 325, 413, 420

Lee-Baggley, D. L., 454
Lehrer, P. M., 300, 302
Leichsenring, F., 230, 246
Lelos, D., 388
Lesperance, F., 419
Levy, R. A., 208, 230, 410t
Lezak, M., 169, 170, 175, 179
Liebeault, Ambroise, 235b
Lilienfeld, S. O., 153, 352
Lilley, C. M., 418
Lillis, J., 354
Linden, I., 54
Linden, W., 2, 3, 51, 52, 105, 147,
    193, 194, 197, 198, 210, 283,
    297, 300, 302, 304, 305, 306,
    307, 320, 323, 325, 328,
    331t, 353, 354, 355, 357,
    403, 404, 410, 419, 420, 421,
    424, 447, 449, 454
Linehan, M. M., 333, 334t
Linke, S. A., 421
Lippsitt, P. D., 388
Lipsey, M. W., 214, 332, 335, 358
Liszt, Franz von, 382
Lohr, J. M., 352, 353
Loock, C. A., 366
Lopez, S. J., 219
Lourenco, O., 454
Lubar, J. F., 300
Luborsky, L., 217, 246, 322, 323,
    330, 335, 358
Lucock, M. P., 103
Luebbert, K., 425
Lundy, A., 153
Luoma, J. B., 354
Luria, A., 178
Lykken, D. T., 397
Lynn, S., 348

Machado, A., 453, 454
Maes, S., 420
Magnavita, J. J., 231, 236, 244, 246
Malloy, D. W., 447
Maloney, M. P., 102, 105
Marks, I., 284
Marmot, M., 304
Marsh, E. J., 367t
Martinson, R., 391
Marton, K. I., 213
Masling, J., 230
Maslow, Abraham, 250
Masua, A., 354
Matthews, K. A., 304
Mavissakalian, M., 277
Mayne, T. J., 18

Mays, N., 51
McCann, J. T., 389
McCart, M. R., 391
McCaul, K. D., 309
McConkey, K. M., 348
McDavis, R. J., 220
McGaha, S., 211
McGarry, A. L., 388
Mckelvie, R. S., 421
McKinley, J. C., 139, 140
McLelland, D. C., 152
McLeod, D. R., 297
McQuaid, L., 374
McWilliams, N., 110
Meehl, P. E., 123, 124, 439
Megargee, E. I., 389
Melamed, B. G., 277
Melton, G. B., 64
Melzack, R., 297, 404, 415, 417
Meulman, J., 420
Meyer, G. J., 103
Michelson, L., 277
Middlebrooks, J. S., 408
Mikail, S., 232
Milberg, W., 169, 175
Miller, E., 196, 318, 328, 408
Millon, T., 236, 389
Mills, D. H., 56
Mills, P. J., 421
Minder, C., 211
Minuchin, S., 264, 266, 374
Miranda, J., 208
Mnookin, R. H., 63
Mohr, D., 137, 212, 214, 218
Monastra, V. J., 377
Montgomery, G. H., 350
Morey, L., 147
Morris, R., 180
Mors, O., 92
Moseley, J. V., 2, 51, 404, 421,
    447–448
Moss, D., 403
Munsterberg, H., 382–383
Murray, H., 151

Nassau, J. H., 374
Nathan, J. S., 131
Neimeyer, R. A., 335
Neisser, U., 41, 161
Nelson, C., 124
Nemeroff, C., 438
Newman, M., 121
Newton, T., 305
Nichols, D. S., 139, 140, 144
Nieberding, K., 131
Niemann, L., 301, 357

Nietzel, M. T., 212, 394t
Noble, R., 103
Norcross, J. C., 13t, 18, 103, 217,
    223, 229, 309
Notarius, C. I., 307

Ogloff, J. R. P., 382, 383
O'Hearn, 281, 360
Ollendick, T. H., 374
Ong, L., 302, 303, 454
Orchard, J., 206
Ornish, D., 424
Osimo, F., 246
Ospina, M. B., 357
Otto, R. K., 383, 390, 399
Owen, J. E., 422

Palmer, S. C., 325, 425, 426b
Paniagua, F. A., 220
Parker, K. C. H., 150, 151, 352, 353
Patel, K. D., 357
Patrick, C. J., 396
Pavlov, Ivan, 273
Pennebaker, J. W., 451
Perls, F. S., 335
Persons, J., 110
Petermann, F., 300
Petrila, J., 64
Pettifor, J. L., 67
Philips, H. C., 194, 286
Phillips, S. M., 102, 325, 420, 424
Piaget, J., 209
Poddar, Prosenjit, 62b
Poole, G., 297, 416
Pope, C., 51
Porter, S., 381, 383, 384
Portnoy, D. B., 451
Posavac, E., 52
Potter, E. H., 404
Poythress, N. G., 64
Prince, S. E., 256
Prochaska, J. O., 223, 309
PsycCorp., 167
Puente, A. E., 131

Quilan, K. B., 309

Rachlis, M., 447
Radcliffe, A. M., 446
Radwan, S., 162
Raimy, V. C., 202, 448
Rank, O., 250
Rappaport, D., 106
Raskin, D. C., 397
Raskin, N. J., 251, 253, 254
Rausch, J. L., 191

Ray, D., 373, 376
Redd, W. H., 350
Rees, C. S., 451
Reis, V. A., 421
Reise, S. P., 38, 407
Reitan, R. M., 178
Rendall, M., 439
Reznik, I., 242
Rhine, T., 373
Rice, M. E., 391
Richter, H. E., 421
Ritchie, M., 373
Rizzo, A., 391
Roberts, M. C., 452
Roberts, R. E., 407
Robiner, W. N., 15
Robinson, L. A., 335
Rodin, G., 424
Rodrigue, J. R., 404
Rogers, C. R., 112, 215, 250, 251,
    253, 254
Roid, G., 164
Rolfhus, E. L., 167
Roman, K. R., 205
Rorschach, H., 105
Rose, T., 105, 150, 151
Rosen, J. C., 297
Rosenthal, R., 50, 319, 321,
    322, 324
Rosnow, R., 321, 322
Rost, K. M., 333
Rozanski, A., 419
Rubin, S. S., 60, 352
Ruffins, S. A., 152
Ruggerio, K. J., 391
Rush, A. J., 84, 103
Russ, E., 352
Rutledge, T., 421
Ruzek, J. L., 392
Ryan, P., 451
Ryff, C., 81b

Sachs, G. S., 438
Sackett, P. R., 398
Sakakibara, M., 420
Salovey, P., 125
Sanford, R., 253
Santoro, S. O., 13t, 103
Sarason, B. R., 404
Sarason, I. G., 404
Saric, R., 297
Satin, J., 424
Sawyer, M. G., 376
Sayette, M. A., 18
Scanlan, J., 407
Schachter, S., 191

Schafer, R., 106
Schatzberg, A., 438
Schindler, D., 215, 256, 307
Schmidt, S., 301, 318, 357
Schwartz, P., 208, 371, 420
Schwarz, N., 39
Scott-Sheldon, L. A. J., 451
Scrivner, E., 384
Sederer, L., 439
Sedlmeier, P., 320
Segal, Z., 288
Segerstrom, S. C., 408
Seipp, C., 377
Selfridge, R. S., 366
Seligman, M. E. P., 213,
     322, 454
Seltman, H., 425
Shahar, G., 108
Shapiro, D., 322, 330, 335
Sharf, R. S., 228, 236, 242, 247
Shaw, B. F., 84, 103
Shedler, J., 246
Sherman, E. M. S., 180
Sherry, S. B., 454
Sherwood, A., 193, 305
Sifneos, P., 246
Silva, F. J., 453, 454
Silverman, L. H., 152, 230
Sime, W. E., 300, 302
Simon, T., 159, 161, 163
Sinclair, C., 67
Singer, J. E., 191, 322
Skinner, E. A., 305
Slobogin, C., 64
Smith, M., 283
Smith, P., 322, 329t,
     335, 390
Smolla, N., 372
Snitz, B. E., 124
Snyder, D. R., 425
Sorensen, M. J., 92
Spanos, N. P., 349
Spearman, C., 162
Speca, M., 357, 426
Sperry, L., 103
Spiers, M., 172, 173
Spitzer, R. L., 137
Spreen, O., 180
St. Clair, M., 85, 237, 241
Stake, J. E., 57
Stambor, Z., 451
Staudacher, C., 349
Steeley, 451
Steen, T. A., 454
Stefanek, M., 325, 425, 426b

Steptoe, A., 304
Stern, W. L., 162, 382
Steven, I. D., 403
Stewart, D. E., 413, 420
Stone, S., 451
Stover, C., 391
Strack, S., 146
Strauss, E., 174, 180
Strawbridge, W. J., 407
Strupp, H. H., 218, 244, 335
Sudman, S., 39
Sue, S., 220
Sullivan, H. S., 85, 240b, 241b, 247
Swerdlik, M. E., 102
Symonds, B. D., 218
Szasz, T., 80

Takeuchi, S., 420
Talen, M. R., 404
Tasca, G., 232
Taylor, C. T., 85
Taylor, S., 335, 352
Teachman, B. A., 281, 360
Teglasi, H., 148
Tellegen, A., 139, 145
Temoshok, L., 424
Teramoto, P. J., 219
Terman, L. M., 160, 162
Thomas, G. V., 131
Thomsen, P. H., 92
Thurstone, L. L., 162
Tolin, 352
Tomkins, S. S., 382
Truax, 256
Tsao, M. N., 425
Tucker, J. S., 407, 433
Turk, D. C., 125
Turner, S. M., 277
Tversky, A., 124

Urbanyi, M., 447

Vaillant, G. E., 85
Vaitl, D., 300
Valla, J., 372
van Dixhoorn, J., 419
Van Elderen, T., 420
Van Etten, M. L., 335
VandenBos, G. R., 334
Vernberg, E. M., 392
Vernon, P. E., 162
Veroff, J., 215
Vitaliano, P. P., 407
Vos, T., 440
Vuilliomonet, A., 421

Wagdi, P., 421
Walach, H., 301, 357
Wall, P. D., 297, 404, 415, 417
Waller, N., 38
Wallerstein, R. S., 233
Ward, M. P., 102
Watkins, L. F., Jr., 131, 193
Watson, D., 38, 84, 197
Watzlawick, P., 256
Weakland, j., 256
Wechsler, D., 105, 163
Wedding, D., 232, 235b
Weiner, I. B., 382, 390
Weis, H. M., 204
Weiss, L. G., 167
Weisz, J. R., 373, 374
Weithorn, L. A., 63
Weitzenhoffer, A., 348
Wellish, D. K., 422
Wert, A., 350
Westen, D., 152
White, A., 302, 419
Widaman, K., 38
Wienckowski, L. A., 433
Wiens, A. N., 297
Wiesenfeld, A. R., 204
Wiggins, J. G., 433
Williams, J. B. W., 137, 167
Wilson, D., 197, 214, 332, 335, 358
Windelstein, M. L., 371
Wolfe, D.A., 367t
Wolfson, D., 178
Wong, D. L., 371
Wood, J. M., 153
Woody, S. R., 281, 360
Woolfolk, R. L., 300, 302
Wright, J., 348
Wrightsman, L. S., 381, 383, 384

Yao, X., 404
Young, S., 302, 454
Yu, L. M., 211
Yucha, C. B., 194, 337
Yusuf, S., 405

Zald, D. H., 124
Zaretsky, A., 288
Zhang, J., 333, 407
Zillmer, 172, 173
Zimet, C. N., 149
Zimmermann, M. A., 433
Zimmermann, T., 425
Zoellner, L. A., 391
Zuckerman, M., 88
Zuroff, D. C., 108

SUBJECT INDEX

Pages including tables, figures, and information in boxes are indicated t, f, and b.

a-test, 47
ABAB design, 44
"ABC" concept, 291
Abnormal Child Psychology (Marsh and Wolfe), 367t
abstract reasoning, 174
abuse and neglect during childhood, 408
academic preparation, 21–30
acceptance and commitment therapy (ACT), 353–354
accommodation, 177
accredited training facilities, 230
accredited training programs, 2
Achenbach Child Behavior Checklist, 36t, 95b
ACT (acceptance and commitment therapy), 353–354
acting out, 238t
action, 310t
action and reaction, 261b
activation, general levels of, 193
actualizing tendency, 251
actuarial approach, 123
acute pain, 415–416
adaptive coping, 305
ADHD (attention deficit hyperactivity disorder), 197, 376–378, 435–436
adherence, 411, 412t, 413–415, 415t
Adlerian thinking, 240–241b
adolescent diagnostic categories, 369t
adoption, 394t
advance directives, 447
adverse effects, 437t
affect, 232, 233
age of consent, 367t
age tests, 164
aging populations, 447
agnosia, 172, 173
alcohol dependency, 277
alter-ego transference, 243

altruism, 239t
Alzheimer's disease, 170
American Psychoanalytic Association, 229
American Psychological Association, 49, 64, 65, 66b, 383
analytical section (GRE), 24
anger control, 293–294
Antabuse, 277
antecedent, 291
anticipation, 240t
antitrust legislation, 441
anxiety, 185, 193, 232, 297, 330t, 332
anxiety conditioning, 273
APA-accredited PsyD programs, 19t
APA list of supported treatments, 336t
arousal, sympathetic, 193, 196
arousal reduction, 298, 300–302
arthritis, 414t, 416–418
asceticism, 239t
aspirational behavior, 57
Aspirin trial, 325
assent, 370
assessment, 281f
    and diagnoses, 108–109
    and forensic psychology, 387–388
    and formulation, 109–110
    idiographic approach to, 104
    importance of context, 122
    interpretation, decision-making, and prediction, 122–123
    nomothetic approach to, 104
    overview, 99, 100
    procedures, 60
    purpose of, 104
    and research, 122
    and therapeutic context, 112–113
    vignettes, 100, 101

assessment of needs, 52
assessment tools, forensic, 388
Association for Biofeedback and Applied Psychophysiology, 49
associative learning, 275b
asthma, self-management tasks for, 414t
attention and concentration, 173
attention deficit and hyperactivity disorder (ADHD), 197, 376–378, 435–436
autobiographical knowledge, 275b
autoimmune diseases, 297
automatic self-regulation, 298
automatic thoughts, 292, 293f
autonomic balance, 420
availability heuristic, 125
average effect size (ES), 329t, 330t
aversion therapy, 280b
aversive drugs, 277
avoidance behaviors, 185, 276, 282
Axis 1 diagnosis, 108

"Bad Me," 241b
Barnum effect, 124
base rate issue, 124
baseline recordings, 44
basic principles of ethics, 63
BBD (bye-bye-depression), 319, 321b
Beck Anxiety Inventory, 147
Beck Depression Inventory, 147
Beernheim, Hippolyte, 235b
behavior change, vehicles for, 247–249
behavior observation coding system, 189t
behavior therapy, 273–288
    case study, 282b, 284b
    children and, 373
    concluding observations, 283–288

ethical considerations, 276–277
learning theory terms, 275b
punishment, 276, 277–278
reinforcement, 278–283
roots and underlying theory, 273–276
steps in, 281f
techniques, 279b
Behavioral Anger Response Questionnaire, 105, 147
behavioral-approach avoidance test, 188
behavioral assessment, 106
implementation and interpretation, 185–186, 185–188
rationale and basic principles, 184–185
self-monitoring, 188–189
usefulness of observations, 188
validity and ethics, 185–186
behavioral medicine and health psychology, 403–427
belief, 291
Bender Motor Gestalt, 174
Beneficence and Nonmaleficence, 66b
Benjamin, Lorna, 90
Binet, Alfred, 99, 159, 163, 382
binge-eating, 284b
biofeedback, 298–300, 377
biofeedback-based treatments, efficacy ratings for, 337t
biofeedback research, 46
biofeedback schematic display, 299f
biofeedback therapy, 299
biological assessments, neglect of, 190–191
biological impulses, 228
biological psychology, 1
bipolar disorder, 191
black-and-white thinking, 289b
black box principle, 288
blaming, 265
blaming the patient, 248
"blending into the woodwork," 81–82
bonds, 217
borderline personality disorder, 311, 312
Boston Process Approach, 180
Boulder model, 448
boundaries between subsystems, 265–266
boundaries of competence, 63

boundary violations, 60
box score reviews, 319, 319t
buffer, 304
bulimia, 282, 284b
bullying, 370
burnout, 31
butterfly diagram, 326, 327f
bye-bye-depression (BBD), 319, 321b

Canada
age of consent, 369t
innovative approach to training, 449
and polygraph evidence, 397
Canadian Code of Ethics, 67–68
cancer patients, 423–426, 426b
cancers, 446
cardiac rehabilitation
and adherence, 413–415
gender issues, 325, 420
cardiovascular disease patients, 418–420
case conceptualization, 216
case formulation, 109–111
case study methodologies, 34, 43–44
catastrophizing, 289b
Cattel-Horn-Carrol (CHC) model, 162
causes of death, behavioral, 446t
CBT (cognitive-behavioral therapy), 295–296
chaining, 280b
change in therapy, measuring, 42–43
changeable risk factors, 418–419
changing interactional positions, 308b
charisma of practitioners, 345–346
CHF (chronic heart failure), 421–422
Child Behavior Checklist, 105
child clinical psychology
assessment, 370–373
attention deficit and hyperactivity disorder, 376–377
developmental stages, 367–368
ethical challenges, 368–370
intervention, 373–375
unique features of, 365–366
child custody, 394t
childhood diseases, 446
childhood pathology, 366

childhood relationships, 232
children
aggressive behaviors in, 35
behavior checklist, 36t
behavior therapy, 373
and chronic pain, 418
cognitive abilities, 371–372
custody evaluation guidelines, 65b
diagnosis of disorders in, 95b
diagnostic categories, 369t
and obesity, 411
psychological assessment of, 99
psychological therapies for, 374
systems therapy, 256, 264–267
Wechsler Intelligence Scales, 165
Children's Apperception Test (CAT), 151
Chinese Classification of Mental Disorders (CCMD-3, 90
choice of method, 281f
choice of target, 281f
chronic disease
comparison of, 413t
longevity and, 446
prevention and management of, 409–412
chronic fatigue, 297
chronic heart failure (CHF), 421–422
chronic pain, 197, 297, 416–418, 417t
chronological age (CA), 163
civil commitment, 394t
The Civilized Couple's Guide to Extramarital Adventure (Ellis), 291
clarity, adherence and, 415t
class action suits, 394t
classical conditioning, 273, 275b, 276
classical psychoanalysis, 227, 228, 235–237
Classification of Mental and Behavioural Disorders, 92
classification of physiological measures, 192t
classification systems, 90–95
client-centered therapy, 274
client-centered treatment, 216
client confidentiality, 61
client readiness, 208–210
client relationships, 60
clinical decision-making, 124–125

clinical experience, 27
clinical forensic psychologist, 383–384
clinical interviews, 132–136
clinical judgment approach, 123
clinical neuropsychology, 169
clinical problems, 10–11, 194t
clinical psychologists
  academic setting, 9–11, 10b
  complaints against, 60
  cultural competence, 219–220
  defined, 3b
  earning potential, 13–15
  as expert witnesses, 394t
  and forensic psychology, 383–384
  in general health care settings, 297
  in general hospital settings, 5–7, 6b
  job satisfaction, 15
  as neuropsychologists, 169
  in private practice, 7–9, 8b
  professional activities, 13t
  skills needed, 213–214
  students, 2–5, 4b
  typical day, 4b, 6b, 8b, 10b, 13t
clinical psychology
  academic preparation, 21–30
  accredited training programs, 2
  career planning, 17–20
  claim for "distinctness," 1–2
  computers and the Internet, 450–451
  creative approaches to, 343–346
  cultural competence in, 219–220, 221t
  employment opportunities, 11–15
  ethical standards of practice, 59
  and forensic psychology practice, 386–387
  ongoing considerations, 15
  personality fit, 18–20
  practice realities, 11–15
  primary employment sites, 12t
  profession described, 1–2
  program comparisons, 19t
  programs, 213
  research in, 452–453
clinical psychology, future of
  changes in health care., 446–448
  clinical training., 448–450
  computers and the web, 450–452
  prescription privileges., 450

  research, 452–454
  spirituality, 454
clinical scales, 141–142
clinical training, 448
clinically significant depression, 421–422
clinically significant effect, 47
codes of conduct, 61, 63
codes of ethics, 6b, 64, 65
coding systems, behavioral, 35, 37
coefficient "kappa," 35
coefficient r, 35
cognitions, 84, 420–421
cognitive adaptation theory, 423
cognitive and neuropsychological assessment
  intellectual assessment, 159–160
  intelligence, 161–162
  intelligence tests, 163
  neuropsychological evaluation, 176–178
  neuropsychological tests, 178–180
  neuropsychology, 164
  Stanford-Binet Scale, 164
cognitive-behavioral therapy (CBT), 295–296, 295b
cognitive therapy, 288–296
cognitive triad, 292, 293f
Cohen's d effect, 321, 322
communication, axioms of, 257b–263b
Compendium of Pharmaceuticals and Specialties (CPS), 436
competence to stand trial, 394t
Competency Screening Test, 388
Comprehensive System, 149
comprehensive trials, 47
compromise formation, 237
compulsive behaviors, 185, 287f
computerized axial tomography (CT), 170
conceptualizations of psychopathology, 86–87
Concerta, 435–436
concurrent validity, 40
conditioned response, 275b
conditions of worth, 250
confidential psychological evaluation, 113–121b
confidentiality, 60
confounding effect, 327–328
confounding treatment, 45
confrontation, 247
congruence, 253, 265

conscious, 232
conscious awareness, 245
consent, 370
consequence, 291
conservatorship, 394t
consolidation/integration, 308b
construct validity, 40
contemplation, 310t
content information, 133
content validity, 40
contingency contracting, 279b
continuing education, 30
control, adherence and, 415t
control groups, 45
control question technique, 396
convenience, adherence and, 415t
conviction, adherence and, 415t
COPD, self-management tasks for, 414t
coping behaviors, 85, 392, 420–421
coping model 4, 280b
core beliefs, 293
core competencies, 103
correctional psychology, 385
corrections officers and forensic psychology, 392
correlation coefficient r, 35
cost benefit/offset analyses, 333
cost effectiveness, 334t
counseling psychologists, 3b
countertransference, 233, 249
couples therapy, 206–207, 256, 307–308, 308b
CPA code of ethics, 6b
CPS (Compendium of Pharmaceuticals and Specialties), 436
crime and delinquency, 384
criminal activity, personality variables germane to, 388
criminal profiling, 384
criminal responsibility, 394t
criterion validity, 40
CT (computerized axial tomography), 170
Cuban Glossary of Psychiatry, 90
cultural competence in psychology, 219–220, 221t, 376, 408
custody and access assessments, 63, 64
cutoffs, meaning of, 319–320
cybernetics, 256
cycle de-escalation, 308b

data acquisition and processing, 194–195

DBT (dialectical behavior therapy), 311

death, behavioral causes of, 446t

decision-making, children and, 369–370

defense mechanisms, hierarchy of, 238t

dementing disorder, 170

denial, 238t

dependence, 437t, 440

depression, 193, 290, 297, 330t, 332

depression scales, 141

derealization, 133–134

descriptive classification system, 88

descriptive psychopathology, 85–86

desensitization, systemic, 279b

detached family members, 266

detection of lying, 393–394

determination, 310t

development issues, 85

development of the self, 241

development of transference phase, 235–236

developmental psychology, 1

developmental stages, children and, 366, 367t, 370–371

deviation IQ, 163

diabetes, self-management tasks for, 414t

Diagnostic and Statistical Manual of Mental Disorders, 83, 88, 92–93

diagnostic classification systems, 90–91

diagnostic privileges, 440–441

dialectical behavior therapy (DBT), 311–313

dialogues, 133

differential score approach, 177

dimensions of psychological well-being, 81b

direct observation form (DOF), 35

disability insurance, 325

discounting positive features, 289b

discriminative stimuli, 275b

disease causation, 405–408

diseases, international classification of, 92

disgruntled patients, 64

disorders, trends in descriptions of, 88–89

displacement, 239t

dissociation, 238t

distress screening tool, 6

divorce proceedings, guidelines, 65b

"dodo bird verdict," 323

DOF (direct observation form), 35

domains of functioning, 172–173

Dominic Interview, 372

double-bind concept, 256

double-blind study, 46

downers, 436

Draw a Clock test, 175b

Draw-a-Person drawing task, 154

drawing tasks, 154–155

DSM-IV diagnosis, 109b

DSM-IV-TR, 89

DSM-IV-TR Axis 1 disorders, 111

dual relationships, 220

Dubois, Paul, 235b

duty to inform, 61

dynamic psychotherapies, 228, 243–244

dysfunctional thinking patterns, 289b

EA (emotional awareness), 209, 209t, 210t

eating disorders, 370

ecological validity, 326

effect sizes, 321

efficacy, 46

ego, 234, 237

ego psychology, 237–239

ego strength, 112, 273, 326

EMDR (eye movement desensitization and reprocessing), 350–353

emotion, 232

emotion-focused therapy, 307–308

emotion-regulation skill training, 312

emotional awareness (EA), 209, 209t, 210t

emotional distress, 191

emotional reasoning, 289b

emotional regulation, 84

empathy, 216, 252

empirically validated treatments for children, 375t

employment, lie detection and, 398

encouragement, 216

English as a second language, 25, 41, 219

enmeshed boundaries, 266

epilepsy attacks, 300

episodic memory, 174

equal-emphasis PHD programs, 19t

equipment, for testing physiological functions, 194–196

equipoise principle, 46

errors in judgment, 124–125

errors in thinking, 290

ES (average effect size), 329t, 330t

ethical behavior, 57–59

ethical considerations of behavior therapy, 276–277

ethical decision-making process of, 56 ten steps to, 70–72b

ethical dilemmas, 58b

ethical principles, 6b, 56

ethical standards of practice, 59–60, 67

Ethics Code of Psychologists, 306

ethnic group membership, 219–220

etiological classification system, 95

etiological model, 407

European Psychoanalytic Federation, 229

evaluation guidelines, child custody, 65b

"everybody-has-won" conclusion, 323

evidence, quality of, 49–50

evocative empathy, 252

execution of plan, 281f

existential questions, heart transplant patients and, 422–423

experimental neuropsychology, 169

experiments, 43–44

expert witnesses, 394t

exposure-based treatments, 391

expression of values, 81b

expressive functions, 174

externalizing problem behaviors, 373

extinction, 275b

extratest behavior, 167

eye contact, 220

eye movement desensitization and reprocessing (EMDR), 350–353

eyewitness identification, 394t

F Scale, 141

F-test, 47

face validity, 39
faces pain scale, 371f
factual information, 216
family medicine, 297, 403,
    441, 446
family therapy, 256
FAS (fetal alcohol syndrome), 366
fear hierarchy, 190t
feedback loops, 256
fetal alcohol syndrome (FAS), 366
Fidelity and Responsibility, 66b
fighting spirit, cancer patients
    and, 426b
findings, communication of,
    113, 121
fixed battery approach, 176,
    178–179
flooding, 279b, 282b
forensic assessment, 107
forensic psychology
    clinical practitioner, 383–384
    consultation and opinions, 393
    contemporary, 383
    defined, 381–383
    lie detection, 393–398
    tasks of, 387–389
    and traditional practice,
        386–387
    treatment, 389–393
    two general views of, 382
formative evaluation, 52
formulation, 109–110
fortune-telling, 289b
four ethical principles, 6b
four-phase protocol, 44
"Foxtrot" profile, 389
fragmentation, risk of
    professional, 427
free association stage, 150
functional analysis, 281, 281f
functional symptoms, 170

"g" (intelligence factor), 162, 167
Galen (Roman physician), 57
Gate Control Theory, 417
general levels of activation, 193
General Principles (APA), 66b
generic therapy skills, value
    of, 222
Genetic Principle, 232
genuineness, 252, 253–255
Gestalt therapy, 335
global ability index, 166
goals, 217, 244–245
"Good Me," 240b

grade-point averages, 21–22
graduate record exam (GRE),
    23–30
graduate school, tips for, 28–29
graduated exposure, 279b
GRE (graduate record exam),
    23–30
group means, 326
group therapy, 206–207
guardianship, 394t
guilty knowledge test, 398

habits, 330t
half-life, 437t
Halstead Reitan Neuropsychological
    Battery, 178
hand scoring, 37
Hare Psychopathy Checklist
    (PCL), 389
hazards ratio, 405
headache pains, 416–418
health, early-life influences on,
    408–409
health assessment, 106
health behaviors, 297–298, 409
health care, 446–448
health psychology, 297, 403–427
healthy personality, characteristics
    of, 81b
heart disease, self-management
    tasks for, 414t
heart rate, 193
heart rate monitors, 195
heart transplantation, 422–423
Helping Alliance
    Questionnaire, 218b
hemineglect, 173, 175b
heuristics, 125
heuristics, inappropriate use of, 125
hierarchical model of intelligence,
    164–165, 165f
hierarchy of power, 266
high affect control question,
    395–396
high blood pressure, 420–421
history effect, 45
homosexuality, 87b
Horney, Karen, 241b
horse race comparisons, 335
Hospice Michel Sarrazin, 207, 424
"hot thoughts," 294
House-Tree-Person drawing task,
    154, 372
How to Live with a Neurotic
    (Ellis), 291

How to Stubbornly Refuse to Make
    Yourself Miserable About
    Anything (Ellis), 291
humor, 239t
Hunt Matheson, 297
hyperarousal, sympathetic, 300
hypertension, 193–194, 297, 419,
    420–421
hypertension individualized
    treatment (HIT), 197–198
hypnosis, 346–351, 347b
hypochondriasis scales, 141, 142
hypomania scales, 141
hypothesis-testing approach, 176
hysterical neuroses scales, 141

ICD-10, 89, 92
ICD-11, 96
id, 234, 237
idealization, 238t
idealizing transference, 243
identification, 239t
illusory correlations, 125
impairment index, 178
impulse control disorders, 376
Individual Psychology
    school, 241b
inferential tests, 318–319
inferiority complexes, 241b
information processing, 84
informed consent, 63
inhibition, 193
innovative/mystical therapies,
    343–346, 344b
inquiry stage, 150
insanity, Einstein's definition
    of, 353
insurance companies, 418, 454
integration stage, 150
Integrity, 66b
intellectual assessment, 159–161
intellectual/cognitive
    assessment, 106
intellectual functioning, 84
intellectualization, 239t
intelligence, 161–162, 161b
intelligence tests, 41, 163,
    167–169, 168f
inter-rater reliability, 35, 37
intereset scatter, 167
Interheart study, 406t
internal consistency, 38
internalizing problems, 373
International Psychoanalytic
    Association (IPA), 229

Internet, clinical practice and the, 440–441, 450–451
interpersonal processes, 85
The Interpersonal Theory of Psychiatry (Sullivan), 240b
interpretation, 122–123, 247
interpunction, 260b
interventions, behavioral, 274–275
interviews, 133
"intracarotid sodium amobarbital procedure," 171b
introjection, 238t
IQ, 41, 162–163
irrational cognitions, 358
irrational ideas (Ellis approach), 292t
irrelevance, 265
irritable bowel syndrome, 297
isolation of affect, 239t

Journal of Behavior Therapy and Experimental Psychiatry, 44
judgments of abnormality, 82
jurisprudence exam, 30
Justice, 67b

K Scale, 141
kappa, 35, 37

L Scale, 141
labeling, 289b
language and verbal functions, 173–174
large effect, 329
Latin American Guide for Psychiatric Diagnosis, 90
law and psychology, 381
learning-based psychotherapies, 273
learning strategies, 222
learning theory, 274, 275b
legal facts, ethics and, 60–61
legal psychology, 381
letters of reference, 26–27
levels of emotional awareness (EA), 209, 209t, 210t
licensing, 30–31, 61, 211
lie detection, 393–394, 395, 397–398
life expectancy, 446
life plan's details, 241b
Likert-type scale, 371
limitations on confidentiality, 61
List of Causes of Death, 92

lithium, 191
living wills, 447
LNNB (Luria-Nebraska Neuropsychogical Battery), 178
long-term resilience, 408
L'Ordre des psychologues du Québec (OPQ), 449
low self-esteem, 289
lower back pain, 416
Luria-Nebraska Neuropsychogical Battery (LNNB), 178

MA/CA ratio, 163
MacArthur Competence Assessment Tool–Clinical Research (MacCAT–CR), 388
MacArthur Competence Assessment Tool–Criminal Adjudication (MacCAT–CA), 388
macroskills, 214, 216–217
magnitude of change, 177
maintenance, 310t
maladaptive functioning, 79–80
malingering, 388
The Man Who Mistook His Wife for a Hat (Sacks), 173
mandatory reporting requirements, 61
manifest symptoms and concerns (S-axis), 95
marital problems, 256
mastery model, 280b
mature defenses, 237, 239t
MBSR (mindfulness-based stress reduction), 354–355
medication
    abbreviations, 438t
    affordability, 442
    dependence, 440
    regimens, 414
meditation, 301
Meehl, Paul, 123
memory, 174
Menninger Psychotherapy Research Project, 246
mental age (MA), 163
mental disorder, 83
mental functioning (M-axis), 94
mental status exam (MSE), 135–136
meta-analysis, 49–50, 321
meta-analytic reviews, 323–329
Meta date, 435–436

metacommunication, 263
method, choice of, 281f
Methylin, 435–436
methylphenodate, 435–436
MI (motivational interviewing), 308–311
microskills, 214, 216
Millon Clinical Multiaxial Inventory (MCMI), 146–147
mind reading, 289b
mindfulness-based stress reduction (MBSR) approach, 301, 354–355
mindfulness meditation (MM), 354–355
mindfulness sitting instruction, 356b
minimal treatments, 332
Minnesota Multiphasic Personality Inventory, 139–140
    clinical scales, 141–142
    interpretation, 142
    pros and cons, 144–145
    reliability and validity, 142–143
    scores and interpretation, 143b
    validity scales, 141
Minnesota Multiphasic Personality Inventory 2, 105, 140t, 145, 450–451
minority status, 219
mirror transference, 243
MM (mindfulness meditation), 354–355
MMPI-A, 145
modeling, 276, 280b
moral behavior, 57
motivational interviewing (MI), 308–311, 310t
motor memory, 174
motor/psychomotor functioning, 173
MSE (mental status exam), 135–136
multiclient therapy, 206–207
Multidimensional Perfectionism Scale, 147
multidisciplinary health care teams, 403–404, 416–418
muscular pain, 197
"must" statements, 289b

narcissism, 243
narrative review, 318
natural proprioception, 300

needs and motives, interpersonal, 228
negative anticipations, 294
negative emotions, 191
negative reinforcement, 275b
neologisms, 82
NEPSY-II, 181
neuropsychological assessment
  assumptions underlying, 171–172
  performance of, 176–178
  purposes of, 169–171
neuropsychological evaluations, 170–172
neuropsychological testing, 178–180
neuropsychology, 169
neuroscience methods and theories, integration of, 453
neurotic defenses, 237, 238–239t
new issues, 249
The 1921 Conference, 162
"noisy" tests, 38
nomothetic approach to assessment, 104
non threatening questions, 216
noncompliance, degree of, 410t
nonpayment, withholding records for, 64
nonspecific factors, 358
nonspecific treatment approaches, 452–453
nonverbal communication, 257b
normal behavior, 81b
normality, 81b
normative approach, 79, 177
nosologies, 90–91
"Not Me," 241b
nuclear magnetic resonance imaging (NMRI), 170
null hypothesis, 318–319
nurse practitioners, 440–441

obesity, 411
object relations, 85
object relations theory, 237, 240–242
objective tests, 138–139
observation, 247
observation/experimentation, 453
observational methods, 34
observed effect sizes, 374
odds ratios (OR), 405, 406t
omnibus self-report measures, 146–147

online support groups, 450–451
OPD (Operationalized Psychodynamic Diagnostics), 90
open-ended questions, 135
opening phase, 235
operant conditioning, 275b
Operationalized Psychodynamic Diagnostics (OPD), 88, 90
OR (odds ratios), 405, 406t
organic symptoms, 170
orientation of personal space, 172
outcome, test of, 281f
outcome research, 214
outcomes, meta-analytic comparisons of, 375t
overcorrection, 279b

PAI (personality assessment inventory), 147, 450–451
pain, 297, 415
pain scale faces, 371f
palliative care, 447
palm pilots, 37
paradoxes, 263
paranoia scales, 141
parataxic distortions, 241b
parent training, 241b
pathological personality traits, 84
pattern recognition, 216
patterns or styles, development of, 233
PCL (Hare Psychopathy Checklist), 389
PDM (Psychodynamic Diagnostic Manual), 94
PDP (Psychopharmacology Demonstration Project), 441
percentile equivalents, 329t
perceptions, 85
perceptual reasoning, 166
performance anxieties, 330t, 332
perpetrators of crime, treatment for, 390
person-centered therapy (PCT), 249–255
personal therapy, value of, 213–214
personality assessment inventory (PAI), 147, 450–451
personality development, 242
personality factors, 420
personality patterns and disorders (P-axis), 94

personifications, 241b
pessimism, 289
pharmacological interventions, 453
pharmacological medication and psychological interventions, 438
pharmacology, language of, 435–436
PhD programs, 19t, 211
phobias, 197, 282, 330t
physiological activity, measurement of, 194–198
physiological arousal reduction, 420
physiological measures, classification of, 192t
physiological stress responses, 420–421
physiological systems, 191–194
physiotherapists, 416–418
Piaget, Jean, 209
pill boxes, 414
placating, 265
placebo effect, 45, 46
plan, execution of, 281f
play therapy, 373
police officers and forensic psychology, 392
police psychology, 384
polygraphs, 194, 393–394
poor modeling, 276
positive psychology, spirituality and, 454–455
positive reinforcement, 275b, 276
positron emission tomography (PET), 170
post-traumatic stress disorder (PTSD), 197, 353, 384, 391, 392
postdoctoral training, 29–30, 169
postmodernism, 249
postsurgery pain management, 416
potentiation, 437t
practice guidelines, 61, 63–64
practice of medicine, regulation of, 440–441
practice-oriented PHD programs, 19t
preconceived ideas and confirmatory bias, 125
preconscious, 232
precontemplation, 310t
predictive validity, 40
predictors of good outcome, 358
premorbid functioning, 177

prescribing privileges,
440–441, 450
prescription drugs, 436
prevention, 241b
preventive stress management, 306
primary prevention, 409
primary reinforcers, 278
primary systemic stress
prevention, 306
primitive defenses, 237, 238t
private practice models, 449
problem explication, 107–108
problem-solving skills
training, 312
problems in living, 80–82
procedural memory, 174
process information, 133
process-related variables, 132
processing speed, 166
professional competence, 60
professional malpractice, 394t
professional psychology
programs, 211
professional social workers, 3b
prognosis, 111
program planning and evaluation,
51–53
projection, 238t, 273
projective hypothesis, 148
projective identification, 238t
projective techniques, 147–148
proposition stage, 150
proprioception, 299
proverbs, 174
psychasthenia scales, 141
psychiatric diagnoses, 191
psychiatrists, 3b
psychic determinism, 134, 230
"psycho-oncology," 423
psychoactive drugs, 433
psychoactive street drugs, 436
psychoanalysis, 227–236
accredited training
facilities, 230
common use of, 229
defined, 228
goals of, 244–246
historical perspectives,
229–230
terminology, 227–229
psychoanalytic concepts, renaming
of, 231b
psychoanalytic psychotherapies,
227, 228
goals of, 244–246

meta-analyses appearing in
literature, 230
resistance, 248
psychoanalytic theory, evolution of,
233–235
psychoanalytic thinking, historical
perspective on, 229
psychoanalytic treatment, 230–233,
246–249
psychodiagnosis, 106
psychodiagnostic assessment, 106
and clinical interviews, 132–136
multimethod approach to, 131
overview, 130–131
tests and tools used in, 131, 132t
psychodynamic case formulation,
110, 111b
Psychodynamic Diagnostic Manual,
81b, 94
psychodynamic
psychotherapies, 228
psychodynamic treatment, 228, 229
psychoeducational
components, 391
psychological assessment
defined, 102
goals of, 107–108
overview, 99, 100
in practice and training, 103–104
versus testing, 102–103
tools of, 104–105
and treatment recommendations,
111–113
types of, 106–107
psychological assessment,
techniques in, 105
psychological damages, 394t
"psychological defenses," 273
psychological first aid, 392
psychological intervention,
329t, 453
and cancer patients, 425
and pharmacological
medication, 438
psychological mindedness, 112
psychological pain, 79
psychological problems,
defining, 79
psychological reports, 113–121b
psychological research, principles
of, 453
psychological services,
marketability of, 325
psychological testing, 34–41,
102–103

psychological therapies
for children, 374
cost-effectiveness of,
333–334
psychological well-being, 81b
psychologists defined, 3b
psychology
and the law, 381, 385
specialty areas within, 1–2
Psychopathic Deviation scales, 141
psychopathology, 76
current conceptualizations of,
89–90
orientations to, 87–88
vignettes, 76–78
psychopathy, 384
psychopharmacological
agents, 438
psychopharmacology
clinical case scenario, 434–435
drug prescription privileges,
440–441
and the Internet, 439
language of, 435–436
medications and areas of
application, 436–439
Psychopharmacology
Demonstration Project
(PDP), 441
psychophysiological
assessment, 106
psychophysiological disorders, 195
psychosomatic complaints, 297
psychosomatic medicine, 297
psychostimulant drugs, 376,
435–436
psychotherapies
behavior therapy, 273–288
biofeedback, 298–300
cognitive-behavioral therapy,
295–296
cognitive therapy, 288–296
dialectical behavior therapy,
311–313
ego psychology, 237–239
emotion-focused therapy,
307–308
goals, 244–245
motivational interviewing,
308–310
new issues, 249
object relations theory,
240–242
person-centered therapy,
249–255

psychotherapies (*Continued*)
psychoanalysis, 227–236
psychoanalytic treatment, 246–249
relaxation, 300–301
self psychology, 243
self-regulation, 300–301
short-term dynamic psychotherapies, 243–244
systems therapies, 256, 263–267
psychotherapy
clients, 208–215
defined, 202
homework assignments, 204–205
invention of, 235b
multiclient therapy, 206–207
process elements, 208
roadblocks, 218
techniques, 215–219
termination, 205
therapeutic relationship, 217–219
therapist and outcomes, 211–215
therapy length, 205–206
psychotherapy outcome
cost-effectiveness of, 333–334
existing meta-analyses, 329–333
history of research, 322–323
knowledge translation controversies, 334–337
meta-analytic reviews, 323–328
methods, 317–322
psychotherapy research, innovation in, 44
psychotherapy techniques, 215–219
PsyD programs, 19t, 211, 449
PTSD (post-traumatic stress disorder), 391, 392
punishment, 275b, 276, 277–278

qualitative research, 50–51
quality studies, 332
quantification/mathematization, 453
quantitative approach, 123
questionnaires, 34
questions, for lie detection, 395–396

randomized, controlled trial, 45
rating scales, 147

ratio IQ, 163
rational emotive therapy (RET), 291
rationale, development of, 281f
rationalization, 239t
Raynaud's disease, 299
reaction formation, 239t
reactive stress management, 306–307
reactivity measurement, 299
Reason and Emotion in Psychotherapy (Ellis), 291
receptive functions, 174
recovery strategies, stress, 305
referral source, communication of findings to, 113, 121
"reflected appraisals," 241
regression, 238t
regression to the mean, 330
regulatory behavior, 85
rehabilitation, biofeedback-assisted, 300
rehabilitation ideal, 391
rehabilitative assessment, 107
rehersal, 280b
reinforcement, 277–278
relapse, 310t
relational internalization, 242
relational learning, 275b
relational schema, 242
relationship communication, 258b
relationship problems, 215
relaxation, biofeedback-assisted, 300
relaxation methods, 300–302, 301t
relaxation response, 299
relaxation training, cancer and, 425
reliability, 34–41, 35–39
reliability and validity, 42t
representativeness heuristic, 125
repression, 239t
research experience, 27
research-oriented PhD programs, 19t
research trends, 452–453
resistance, 218, 232, 248, 310
Resolution of Transference Phase, 236
Respect for People's Rights and Dignity, 67b
response cost, 280b

response sets, types of, 139
restenosis, 423
restructured family systems, 266
RET (rational emotive therapy), 291, 292
risk factors, 405, 407, 418
risk ratio, 405
RIT (Rorschach Inkblot Technique), 148–151
Ritalin, 435–436
Rorschach, Hermann, 148
Rorschach Inkblot Technique (RIT), 148–151
rubber bands, 277
rules (cognitive triad), 293f
Ryff, Carol, 81b

Sacks, Oliver
The Man Who Mistook His Wife for a Hat, 173
Salter, Andrew, 273
sample size, variation in, 320
satiation, 279b
schemas, 293
schemata, 293
schizoid fantasy, 238t
Schizophrenia scales, 141
"science psycho-judiciere," 382
"scientist-practitioner," 2
SCORS, 152
second-generation narrative reviews, 318–319
secondary cardiac events, 422
secondary prevention, 409
secondary reinforcers, 278
selective serotonin reuptake inhibitor, 190–191
self-actualization, 251
self-assessment, trustworthiness of, 184–185
self concept, development of, 241–242
self-disclosure, 216
self disorders, 243
self-esteem, 243, 289
self-evaluation of behavior, 37
self-hypnosis, 302b, 347b
self-invalidation, 312
self-management tasks for chronic diseases, 414t
self-monitoring, 188–189
self-mutilation, 311
self-object functions, 243
self psychology, 237
self psychology theory, 243

self-regard, 250
self-regulation methods, 300–302
self-report inventories, 138, 184
self-report measures, 146–147
self-report tests of behaviors, 37–38
self-system, 240b
self-therapy, 213
semi-structured clinical interviews, 105, 108
sense and perception, 172
sentencing, 394t
separation and individuation, 242
serotonin, 190–191
Sex Without Guilt (Ellis), 292
sexual misconduct, 31
sexual problems, 330t
sexualization, 239t
Shakespeare, 291
SHALIT (Stanford hypnotic arm levitation and induction test), 350
shaping, 280b
short-term acute stressors, 408
short-term dynamic psychotherapies (STDP), 228, 243–244
"should" statements, 289b
side effects, 437t, 440
Sifneos' short-term anxiety provoking therapy, 246
signal acquisition and processing, 194–195
signal averaging, 195
significance test, 47
signs, 82
single-blind study, 46
single case design, 44
sleep problems, 197, 297
"sleepers," 328
smoking behavior, 405, 411
social avoidance, 276
Social Cognitions and Object Relations Scale (SCORS), 151–152
social contract, 68
social issues in litigation, 394t
social problems, 330t
Socratian dialogue, 292
somatization, 238t
spatial orientation, 172
specialty guidelines, forensic psychology and, 383
specific treatment approaches, 452–453

spirituality, positive psychology and, 454–455
split-half reliability, 38
splitting, 238t
spontaneity, 263
stages of change model, 309f
Stanford-Binet-5, 164–165
Stanford-Binet Scale, 160, 164–165, 166, 371–372
Stanford communication theory, 256
Stanford hypnotic arm levitation and induction test (SHALIT), 350
Stanford Hypnotic Susceptibility Scale, Form C, 348
statement of interest, 25–26
statistical approach, 79, 177
statistical power, consideration of, 320
statistically significant effect, 47
stigmatized illnesses, 450–451
stimulus recognition and manipulation, 304
street drugs, psychoactive, 436
stress, 297
stress, pathways for, 407f
stress enuresis, 299
stress incontinence, 194
stress management, 302–307
stress process model, 303f
stress schema, 305f
structured clinical interview, 108
structured diagnostic interview, 137–138
Structured Interview of Reported Symptoms, 388
subabilities of cognitive function, 372
subject test, 23
subjective approach, 123
subjective interpretation, 79
subjective units of distress (SUDs), 188, 190t
sublimation, 240t
substance abuse problems, 185
subsystem boundaries, 265–266
suicide risk, assessment of, 136b
summative evaluation, 52
superego, 234, 237
superiority complexes, 241b
suppression, 239t
surveys, 34
sympathetic arousal, 193, 196
sympathetic hyperarousal, 300

symptom as focus, 89
Symptom Checklist-90 Revised, 147
symptom management, 446
symptom substitution, 231
symptoms, 82
syndromes, 83
synergism, 437t
systemic desensitization, 279b
systems therapies, 256, 263–267, 374

tablet computers, 37
talk therapy, 227
Tarasoff v. Regents of the University of California, 61, 62b
target, choice of, 281f
tasks, 217
TAT (Thematic Apperception Test), 151–153
ten ethical standards, 67
termination of parental rights, 394t
tertiary prevention, 409
test descriptions, reliability and validity of, 41
test of English as a foreign language (TOEFL), 25–26
test-retest reliability, 38
test taking, 39
test-taking attitudes, 139
testimonials, 63
tests, 104–105
Thematic Apperception Test (TAT), 151–153, 389
theoretical/conceptual analysis, 453
theory of topography, 232
therapeutic alliance, 133, 217
therapeutic context, assessment and, 112–113
therapies, evaluating, 43
therapies, innovative/mystical, 343–346
therapist directness, 220
therapy, nonspecific benefits of, 216
therapy approaches, nonspecific benefits of, 216
therapy environment, 202–204
therapy outcomes, 324
  case studies, 43–44
  controversies, 334
  research, 45–50, 322
  research protocols, 49t
  studies, 34, 48t, 49

therapists and, 211–212
thought patterns, 290
thought record, 294b
thoughts, 84
Tibetan monks, 355
time-out, 280b
TOEFL (test of English as a foreign
    language), 25–26
token economy, 278, 279b
tolerance, 437t
topographical orientation, 172
toxic environments, 408
toxicity, 437t
trademark litigation, 394t
traditional therapies compared, 345
trait hostility, 420
trance, hypnotic, 348–349
transcendental meditation, 301
transference, 233, 235–236, 248
trauma, 391
treatment decisions, 439
treatment effect, 45
treatment effect specificity, 47
treatment outcomes
    prognosis and, 111
    publication of, 326
treatment phases, 44
treatment plan, development
    of, 281f
trial procedure, 394t
trichotillomania, 277
triggers, 420
trouble adjusting, 297
tuition costs, 18
two-person psychology, 249
type C personality, 424

unbalanced family systems, 266
unchangeable risk factors, 418–419

unconditional positive regard, 250,
    252–253
unconditioned stimulus, 275b
the unconscious, 232, 273
unconscious drives or
    traumas, 234
underlying assumptions, 292
underlying cause as focus, 89
undoing, 239t
unstructured clinical interviews,
    105, 108, 136–137
unstructured discussion
    groups, 46
untested assumptions, 262b
uppers, 436

validity, 39–41
validity and lie detection, 396–397
validity scales, 141
value of particular outcomes, 325
verbal communication, 257b
verbal comprehension, 166
verbal memory, 174
verbal paradoxes, 263
verbal praise, 278
victimology, 385
victims of crime, treatment for,
    391–392
videotape, use of, 37
visual agnosia, 173
visual-spatial organization, 174
vital exhaustion, 423
vocabulary, 24
vomiting reflex, 277

WADA testing, 171b
wait-list control group, 45
web-based interventions,
    451, 452t

Wechsler Adult Intelligence
    Scale-IV (WAIS-IV), 166
Wechsler Adult Intelligence
    Scale–Revised
    europsychological
    Instrument, 180
Wechsler-Bellevue Scale, 163
Wechsler Intelligence Scale for
    Children-IV (WISC-IV), 167,
    371–372
Wechsler Intelligence
    Scales, 179
Wechsler Intelligence
    Tests, 105
Wechsler Preschool and Primary
    Scale of Intelligence
    (WPPSI), 372
Wechsler Preschool and Primary
    Scale of Intelligence-III
    (WPPSII-III), 167
Wechsler Scales of Intelligence,
    165–166, 165–169
weight-loss programs,
    327–328
WHO, 83
"whose view is more
    accurate," 290
withdrawal, 437t
withholding records for
    nonpayment, 64
working memory, 166
Working Through Phase, 236
workplace stress, 304
Writing Committee for the
    ENRICHD investigators, 419

YAVIS clients (Young, Attractive,
    Verbal, Intelligent, and
    Successful), 208, 290